MW00564564

JOHN G. ALDEN
and His Yacht Designs

Robert W. Carrick · Richard Henderson

JOHN G. ALDEN
and His Yacht Designs

Foreword by Donald G. Parrot
Introduction by Olin J. Stephens II

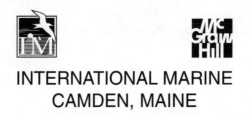

INTERNATIONAL MARINE
CAMDEN, MAINE

First McGraw-Hill paperback edition, 1995.

Published by International Marine®
10   9   8   7   6   5   4   3   2   1

Copyright © 1983, 1995 International Marine®, a division of McGraw-Hill, Inc.

All rights reserved. The publisher takes no responsibility for the use of any of the materials or methods described in this book, nor for the products thereof. The name "International Marine" and the International Marine logo are trademarks of McGraw-Hill, Inc. Printed in the United States of America.

Library of Congress Cataloging-in-Publication Data

Carrick, Robert W.
    John G. Alden and his yacht designs.
    Includes index.
    1. Yacht-building—History—20th century. 2. Alden,
John Gale, 1884–1962. 3. Naval architects—United
States—Biography. I. Henderson, Richard, 1924–
II. Title
    VM331.C297   1983   623.8'1223'0924 [B]   77-85407
    ISBN 0-07-028254-4

Questions regarding the content of this book should be addressed to:

International Marine
P.O. Box 220
Camden, ME 04843
207-236-4837

Questions regarding the ordering of this book should be addressed to:

McGraw-Hill, Inc.
Customer Service Department
P.O. Box 547
Blacklick, OH 43004
Retail customers: 1-800-822-8158
Bookstores: 1-800-722-4726

John G. Alden and His Yacht Designs is printed on acid-free paper.

This book is dedicated to Robert Carrick, captain of the other watch, who got the book underway; Roger Taylor, who navigated it around many a shoal; and Jonathan Eaton, expert sail trimmer and relief helmsman on my watch.

Contents

Foreword
by Donald G. Parrot

I feel honored to have been asked to write a foreword to this book about John Alden and his yacht designs.

I first met John in the 1930s, when my father bought one of the 34-foot yawls that had been designed by John and built by N. Blaisdell and Son in Woolwich, Maine. In the late 1940s I went to John and asked him to design a 55-foot coaster-type schooner, which I built in Newfoundland. Because this design was a throwback in some ways to what he had designed in his early days, I think he had more than the usual interest in her. I will never forget his roughing out the lines with a stubby, dull pencil and turning them over to Carl Alberg to develop. I am sure Carl did not enjoy the task, as the boat was a far cry from what Carl believed in. I might also add that the pencil did double duty as a toothpick.

My recollection of dates is poor, but as I remember, I went to work for John as a broker about 1950. At that time, Fred Wakelin and John Leavitt headed up the brokerage department. Dwight Simpson, Cliff Swaine, Bill Harris, and Fenwick Williams headed the design department. While John's main interest was always in the design of new yachts, he was a most effective salesman. He had a low-key approach and would never pressure anyone into buying or, for that matter, building a boat. For that reason and because of his reputation, his customers — most of whom either were

already or later became his friends — had complete confidence in him. He advised people not to puy a particular boat as often as he suggested that they should. I only wish this approach were prevalent today.

With the advent of the Korean War, the yacht business declined and the office suggested that I try to develop government design contracts, as had been done in World War II. We were reasonably successful in this, building up a design staff of more than 100 people. I don't think John had a great deal of interest in what the office was doing, but I do remember the U.S. Coast Guard asking him to take a look at the lines of a 95-foot patrol craft we had been commissioned to design. He suggested that she be given a bit more fullness forward, which was done.

After the Korean War, the yacht business took some time to recover. John, at 70, didn't have as much enthusiasm as in the past, and he sold the firm to my associates and me, all of us people who knew John and had owned Alden boats.

John retained his own office at 131 State Street, Boston, where the firm had been located for years, and he used to come in for at least part of the day for some time. He was interested in what we were doing, but I am sure it was difficult for him to adjust to the fact that he no longer controlled John G. Alden. For a while he came in less frequently, and then not at all, spending his time at Sakonnet, Rhode Island, in the summer and Florida in the winter.

We tried to carry on the business in a manner we thought John would have approved of, and I think we did, designing wholesome cruising boats. In retrospect, we may have made the same mistake John did in that it took us longer than it should have to realize that design concepts change and some of the changes may be improvements. In 1967, my partner and I sold John G. Alden to the present owner, Tillotson Corporation. Neil Tillotson, the owner of Tillotson Corporation, has always loved boats, and in spite of the limited potential a business such as this offers, he has provided the capital necessary today to run a yacht business successfully. With this infusion of capital we have managed, even today, to remain in the black. Perhaps because we have what I believe to be an extremely competent design staff, we have kept up with the changes in design concepts. As a result, the office is busy — busier than anytime I can remember except for the Korean War.

We have designed and are designing principally cruising-racing auxiliaries, which range in size from 38 feet to 127 feet. In general, they have a modern underbody and rig, and frankly, they perform much better than the boats of John's day. I think John would approve of them, although I question whether or not he would approve of the gadgets most of the owners insist on. In John's day, yacht owners built or bought a boat for the fun of sailing her and the challenges offered. Today, most owners want to take with them to sea the creature comforts they are used to at home. They require navigational aids that I believe (and I think John would agree) detract from the challenge an owner used to be faced with in getting the maximum performance out of his vessel just from her feel and in determining where he was at a given moment with simple instruments and his own skills. Many an owner today has become a captive of the equipment he insists on having, and I can't help but wonder if he gets as much pleasure out of sailing as John Alden did sailing his *Malabars*.

Preface

America has been blessed with a multitude of talented yacht designers, but standing out among these are a few giants who have created the trends and written permanent chapters in the history of yacht design. Some of these leaders who come immediately to mind are Nathanael G. Herreshoff, Olin J. Stephens II, Philip L. Rhodes, and certainly John G. Alden. During his lengthy career from the early 1900s to 1955, Alden and his stable of gifted designers supplied the American yachtsman with thousands of excellent boats, varying in size from dinghies to large, offshore, cruising yachts. He had the ability to create smart-performing, attractive-looking craft that could be built soundly at a price affordable for sailors of modest means. His oceangoing sailing yachts were first and foremost able, seakindly, stable, and comfortable cruisers, yet the *Malabars* and many others proved that boats designed to this healthy concept need not be slow.

Robert W. Carrick began this book 11 years ago. He was familiar with the work of John Alden and had sailed in a number of Alden boats. Harriet and Chester M. Sawtelle — John Alden's daughter and son-in-law — and Alden associates and shipmates such as Henry T. Meneely made themselves available as sources of photographs, tapes, information, and memories, and the book began to take shape. Mr. Carrick completed the biographical section and began work on the design section, but somehow he got becalmed, and the project lost headway. When Roger C. Taylor of International Marine Publishing Company asked me if I'd be interested in taking up where Mr. Carrick had left off, it didn't take me long to say yes. Being a longtime Alden fan, and having been raised in an Alden yawl, I was excited at the prospect of writing Part Two, the descriptions of a hundred Alden yachts. We all wish Bob Carrick could have lived to see this book in print.

Most of these boats were selected because their voyages or racing careers are known to many; or they were popular class boats; or they were simply typical of the designer's work. There is also a sprinkling of atypical boats, however, to show Alden's versatility and to add variety. As the selections were made, it became obvious that a hundred designs could not adequately represent the scope of a half-century of work. I added an album of plans and photographs of another hundred or so Alden boats, and a complete yacht design appendix condensed from the Alden office records.

This book required the help of many. My special thanks go to Donald G. Parrot and Niels C. Helleberg of John G. Alden, Inc., and to former Alden friends and associates Clifford P. Swaine, Henry T. Meneely, Carl A. Alberg, Fenwick C. Williams, K. Aage Nielsen,

Philip L. Ross, George C. Welch, and Charles W. Wittholz. Chester M. Sawtelle was most helpful to the publisher during the gestation period and birthing of the book. Also helpful with general information or details about specific boats were: Langford T. Alden; John G. Bacon; George E. Bahen; Humphrey Barnum; Howard Benedict; Carl J. Berg; David J. Bohaska; Kathleen M. Brandes; Mrs. Mervin C. Briggs; W.J. Broughton; Kenneth Brown; Robert Buffum; Tyler M. Burton, Jr.; Deborah Carmen; John Carter; Elsie Chiperfield; Dr. Walter S. Clark, Jr.; Thomas H. Closs; Judy S. Clough; Mrs. Stephen Connelly; Ed Coogan; Charles E. Cotting; Joseph Crampes; James W. Crawford; Elizabeth Dawson; George C. Devol; Peter Dion; Bartlett S. Dunbar; Franklin W. Eaton; Jonathan F. Eaton; Noel Field, Jr.; Julian D. Fischer; Gerald W. Ford; Edward B. Freeman; Horace W. Fuller; U.E. Gallanos; Eleanor Scott Guckes; Franklin M. Haines; Anne M. Hays; Robert Henstenberg; Robert Hinckley; Dr. Charles E. Iliff; Dr. Nicholas T. Iliff; Jan Iserbyt; Paul James; Mrs. Richard N. Johnson; Virginia Jones; A. Preston Kelly; A. Preston Kelly, Jr.; William W. Kelly; Mayotta S. Kendrick; Gustav Koven; Nan Kulikauskas; Charles A. Langlais; Commodore George Lauder; James Lobdell; Caleb Loring, Jr.; John McCalley; Ray E. McGowan; William McMillan; Harold C. McNulty; William McRae; Ralph H. Magoon; Linda Massey; Robert Rulon Miller; Allen P. Mills; Carleton Mitchell, Jr.; Roger Morse; Henry A. Morss, Jr.; Ralph J. Naranjo; F.E. Newbold, Jr.; Nick Nicholson; Paul C. Nicholson, Jr.; Bradley Noyes; William C. Page; Capt. W.J.L. Parker, U.S.C.G. (Retired); Kenneth M. Parsley, Jr.; Lydia C. Perkins; Alice R. Pope; Cecilia deMille Presley; William Lee Pryor; W. Douglas Richmond; Mrs. John Robinson; Paul Rollins; Ernest Sanders; Arthur Santry; Joseph R. Santry; Harriet Sawtelle; Esther B. Schrot; Frank Thomas Sheehy; Carl Sherman; Philip C.F. Smith; Phineas and Joanna Sprague; Olin J. Stephens II; Jim Stevens; Robert K. Stryker; Donald L. Tate; Roger C. Taylor; Mrs. Richard Thayer; Mrs. Winfield Tice; Mrs. Wallace E. Tobin; Allan H. Vaitses; Margery H. Van Sciver; Charles Vilas; Ronald L. Ward; Mrs. Clarence A. Warden; Carlisle V. Watson; Edward B. Watson, Jr.; William Wertenbaker; Bruce W. White; Harold R. White; William F. Whitmarsh; C.T. Williams; Mike Williams; Clifford W. Wolfe; and Woodson K. Woods.

At the Mystic Seaport Museum, assistance was given by Carole Bowker, Amy D. German, and Alicia G. Crossman. Invaluable assistance was given by *WoodenBoat* magazine and its staff members Anne Bray, Maynard Bray, and Cynthia Curtis. Assistance was also given by the following organizations: The American Yacht Club; Camden Yacht Club; General Dynamics, Electric Boat Division (L.E. Holt); Landmark School for Dyslexic Children (Charles Harris); The Mariners' Museum (Roger T. Crew and Ray Foster); Museum of Yachting (Dawne J. Pinheiro); National Maritime Museum (John Maounis); Peabody Museum (Paul Winfisky); and the U.S. Naval Academy.

Some of the old Alden office plans have been ravaged by time and repeated handling. I wish to thank John W. Sims for tracing many of these for inclusion in the book. If any plans have reproduced imperfectly, it is through no fault of his; rather, it is because I believe it better to see an imperfect drawing than none at all.

Last but not least, I want to thank my wife, Sally, and especially my daughter, Sarah, for typing the manuscript and formidable appendix.

I never had the privilege of knowing Robert Carrick, but I know we would have agreed completely about the capability and genius of John Alden.

Richard Henderson
Gibson Island, Maryland

Introduction
by Olin J. Stephens II

From the time when I looked up to him from a dinghy in Edgartown Harbor until I was well along on my own career as a yacht designer, John Alden was to me, by turns, hero, teacher, friend, and competitor.

It must have been in 1923, some time after he had won the Bermuda Race in *Malabar IV,* that he brought her into Edgartown in a fresh afternoon southerly and anchored in the inner harbor. My admiration for *Malabar* and her designer and skipper could not be exaggerated. I tried to tell him how beautiful I thought she was, and I can see him now, smiling his thanks and waving by moving his palm from side to side. About three years later, my father and I visited John Alden in his Boston office after he agreed to talk with us about yacht design as a profession. My mind was set in concrete, so that whatever he said made no lasting impression. He was polite, but I think he knew, too, that my mind was completely made up.

Our paths crossed over the years. We both went to dinners of the Cruising Club of America, which were held then at the Yale Club in New York. My brother, Rod, and I attended most of these with our father, and John came down from Boston quite regularly. We became a little better acquainted, and my own admiration was stirred by the sketches he drew on napkins and tablecloths. To me, as to others, they were real works of art. His eye and sketching ability were outstanding.

I owe to John my first clear understanding of the process of building a wooden yacht. It happened at the New York Boat Show, then held at the Grand Central Palace. One year in his booth, he had an album of photographs illustrating the sequence of steps in the construction of one of his schooners in a Maine shipyard. The photographs started with patterns in the mold loft and went on to the setting up of the backbone and the sawn frames, the planking, the rigging — all the work up to the launching. I learned only recently that a partner in this particular schooner was the father of Lynn Williams of Chicago, whose *Dora IV* I had the pleasure of designing, and with whom I have worked closely on rating rules, including the CCA, IOR, and MHS rules. The world of sailing is happily not very large.

By another coincidence, the offices of *Yachting* magazine and of Harry J. Gielow were in the same New York building when I went to work for Gielow in the autumn of 1927. The lucky part of this was that I could visit frequently with Sam Wetherill, the magazine's assistant editor, who was mate on John Alden's racing crew. One way or another, I pressed Sam to get me a berth on the new *Malabar IX* for the Bermuda Race of 1928, and one way or another it worked, so I was invited. John Alden, Sam Wetherill, and their crew were certainly the most successful offshore racing sailors of their day. My excitement can only be imagined.

Although we didn't win, the race was in no sense a disappointment. John managed the boat so well that the race was virtually without incident. The sails and all the equipment were good, and the crew was ready for whatever might come. I recall particularly the good food on board. The paid cook did well at sea, although he fell completely apart in Bermuda, where there was too much liquor.

Until recently, when I read the text of this new book, I knew little of Alden's earliest days and of his experience with the fishing schooner *Fame*. His great confidence at sea and his skill as a deep-water helmsman and ocean-racing tactician were notable and were clearly grounded in experience. Combined with his eye for balance and shape, his experience gave him a unique ability to find the geometry that worked with the sea.

If there is such a thing as typical Bermuda Race weather, we had it on that 1928 race in the form of moderate-to-fresh southwesterly winds. Until we crossed the Gulf Stream and the wind went light, we had a good race with *Rugosa II,* the boat we considered most dangerous, but as the wind lightened, she drove off, footing out from under our lee bow until, on the evening before our landfall, she was some miles to the south and east of our position. The next morning on a high barometer, a light easterly filled in, putting her well to weather on the port tack. That was the boat race.

I was about to say that our navigator flew home, but the flying came later. Anyway, I was navigator on the return, and, being short on experience, I was glad to have a large target.

After returning either to New London or Newport, we went on to Marblehead, where John asked me to sail with him on his new Q boat *Hope*. There were a number of new boats in the class that year, and a series of races was being held in Marblehead. John's boat seemed quite good, but the combination of designer and skipper was not as effective around the buoys as it was in deep water.

I had been able to do well enough as a designer that John suggested I might join him in his office, but during the spring of 1928, Drake Sparkman and I had agreed to form our partnership. I would have given my eye teeth to join John's firm if the offer had come sooner. But I had none of John's skill as a draftsman, so I think things worked out for the best.

After 1928, John and I were competitors rather than members of the same crew, but I respected him greatly even though I preferred a rather different type of boat than his. My last experience aboard one of John's designs was in the Mackinac Race of 1932. A friend had bought *Malabar X* and taken her to Lake Michigan, and he asked me to take charge of her. I was impressed by the ability that had been built into this gaff-headed schooner. Her windward performance was truly surprising, and it was only in light weather near the finish of the race that this *Malabar* lost out, much as her predecessor had lost in 1928 on the way to Bermuda.

As a yacht designer, I naturally think of John in terms of his work, through which he set his followers such a fine example. He loved going to sea and he loved to race. Further, winning was good for his business, but he never let the urge to win overcome his judgment as to the nature of a proper seagoing yacht. I say this as one who has faced the same problem, and I feel sure that it was John's nature to think first of the sea. With his eye and his feeling for shape, he had the tools to apply his seagoing experience.

It has been a pleasure to be reminded of those days and to have the opportunity to think again of the part John played in the development of offshore sailing and racing. He provided a great boost to a great sport.

JOHN G. ALDEN
and His Yacht Designs

Part One

John Alden: A Biography
by Robert W. Carrick

1

The Great Bermuda Race Sweep

The 27 boats entered in the 1932 Bermuda Race were making ready to sail from New London, Connecticut, on Saturday, June 25. On board, last-minute stores were packed into galley lockers, a few boats sent new wind pennants aloft, and here and there halyard blocks were given an extra squirt of oil. Watch captains took an appraising squint at the morning weather. Under overcast skies the breeze was moderate-to-fresh out of the west.

Fourteen boats were sailing in Class A, 12 in Class B, and one, the 78-foot schooner *Adriana,* because of her large size, was racing alone but against the fleet on corrected time. The Depression had reduced the number of starters; 42 boats had sailed in the 1930 race. The Cruising Club of America race committee had shifted the starting location from Sarah's Ledge, off New London, used in previous races, to a line out near Montauk Point, where it was figured that the fleet could get away in open water without having to cope with the strong currents of The Race, at the entrance to Long Island Sound.

By the time the yachts converged on the starting area, the wind had shifted to southwest-by-west and had slacked off a bit. The rhumb line to Bermuda was southeast-by-south, and the boats could lay this course with cracked sheets. The starting gun for Class A went at 3:10 p.m. Frank Paine had the powerful cutter *Highland Light* on the line and to windward. He was followed by the schooner *Grenadier,* designed by John Alden and sailed by the Morss brothers, and by P.S. duPont in the schooner *Barlovento.* The *Jolie Brise,* the cutter Robert Somerset sailed over from England for the race, also got away in the van, with a big jib topsail pulling beautifully. The *Malabar X,* designed and being sailed by Alden, and George Mixter's *Teragram* (Margaret spelled backward), another Alden schooner, were several minutes behind the leaders. George Roosevelt got away late in the schooner *Mistress* but quickly worked up to the front-running group.

Class B started at 3:15, and the yawl *Dorade,* designed by Olin Stephens, immediately surged into the lead, with the *Viking,* sailed by Philip le Boutillier, and Jay Wells in his new cutter, *Cyclone,* moving up astern. With only five minutes between starts, the top Class B boats soon began to overhaul the slower yachts of the big-boat division.

As the afternoon wore on, the boats, all on the starboard tack, spread out like a line of ducks in flight. The *Malabar X* had full sail on, including a main topsail and a genoa jib that overlapped the staysail and stretched aft of the foremast. John Alden sat astride the wheelbox, gently fingering the spokes and translating what he felt in his hands into orders for changes in sail trim. This was one of his great skills, and he continually made slight adjustments until he sensed that the *Malabar* had hit her stride.

To Alden, however, the *Malabar X* was much more than a boat trying to win a race. She was the culmination of a line of schooners designed to be ideal for off-shore cruising and fast enough to have a good chance at winning hardware in the less-than-all-out competition of the ocean races of the day. Besides sailing her at her very best on this close reach, Alden would be enjoying the feel and look of his latest schooner creation. He'd glance aloft and sense the strong parallelism of her rig, with masts and gaffs making slow, steady arcs together in response to the heave of the sea. He'd particularly ad-mire the big, flat-cut, gaff mainsail and sense its power-ful drive. As she rolled to leeward, he'd admire the sweep of her deck and house closed in by the stout, lift-ing bulwarks of the weather rail and the lee bulwarks dipping toward the sea. He'd watch with satisfaction the way her bow lifted to the seas and spit them cleanly off to leeward. And all this complex fabric of a vessel was controlled easily, sailing in these conditions, with a spoke or two this way or that of the big, varnished wheel in his hands.

The *Malabar X* had been designed and built for Alden's own use, but before the Bermuda Race, Alden had sold her to Robert I. Gale of Cleveland, Ohio, with the proviso that Alden could race the boat to Bermuda with his own crew. Gale and his son, Robert Jr., were on board as guests. Henry T. Meneely, longtime ship-mate and associate of Alden, was second in command. Wolcott Fuller was the navigator, and the professional captain's name was Cunningham. Much of the cockpit chatter centered on the *Dorade,* which had won the Transatlantic and Fastnet races the year before and was considered the schooner's most serious competition for the fleet prize.

At dusk, the *Highland Light* held the lead, moving easily through the short seas in the moderate breeze. Not far astern were the four schooners: *Barlovento, Grenadier, Teragram,* and *Malabar X.* The *Dorade,* with a big jib topsail filling most of her fore-triangle, continued to make ground on the trailing boats in Class A.

About 10 p.m., the breeze began to freshen. Short bursts of rain forewarned of the weather to come, and, an hour later, a vicious squall struck the line of boats. Everyone scrambled to shorten sail. The stinging down-pour penetrated foul weather gear and reduced visibility to a few boat lengths. As the disturbance passed, the breeze hauled slightly to the west and continued to blow moderate-to-fresh, which kept the fleet footing fast through the darkness.

A short while later, the wind swung back to the southwest and began to breeze up. Soon it was blowing a solid 20 knots and jumping to 30 and more in the puffs and short, intermittent squalls. The seas built up rapid-ly, and most boats, especially the smaller ones, cut down to working sail. The Class A boats, sailing on a close reach, were smoking along at something over eight knots, a speed that they managed to maintain or even exceed all the way to Bermuda.

At three o'clock Sunday morning, the off-duty watch below in J.H. Ottley's *Adriana* was awakened by the smell of smoke. They quickly discovered a growing blaze in a locker for oilskins and rope. Apparently, the heat from the stove in the cabin had cooked the contents of the locker to the point of spontaneous combustion, and the whole locker was suddenly a mass of flames. Distress flares were fired from a Very pistol. They were short-lived in the blustery night but were spotted by someone in the *Jolie Brise* who happened to look astern. The British cutter, some three miles ahead of the *Adriana,* quickly reversed course and headed for the burning vessel, lighting flares to acknowledge the distress signal.

The oft-recounted rescue was a classic, though the *Adriana*'s helmsman, Clarence Kozlay, was lost in the leap to the deck of the *Jolie Brise.* The cutter abandoned the race she had crossed the Atlantic to sail in and headed back for Montauk, 80 miles away, where the rescued crew of the *Adriana* was put ashore.

Meanwhile, the big yachts were slogging it out on the rhumb line, their crews unaware of the tragedy. The wind was still fresh, and the great sheets of spray thoroughly drenched the night watches in most of the boats. The lee rail of the *Malabar X* was out of sight in a torrential stream, and moving about on deck called for much care. Nor was there hot food available for the watch below.

In preparing for this race, Alden, always fastidious about his galley, had interviewed 33 applicants for the cook's billet and had tested many of them at sea. In every case, either the man couldn't stand the motion of an average day on Block Island Sound or John couldn't tolerate the food he served. Two days before the start of the race, one of Alden's crew discovered an unemployed Norwegian who had been relief cook in the Brenton Reef Lightship. He sounded like a great find and was promptly signed on board the *Malabar X.* However, the "find" proved to be worse than useless and took to his bunk the first night out.

As Hank Meneely recalled:

The tenth and probably most famous of the Malabars *making good use of a nice sou'wester soon after the start of the 1932 Bermuda Race. This photograph, as much as any, conveys the sense of power and grace of an Alden schooner. (Morris Rosenfeld photo)*

This was a blow to all of us. I remember we had gotten a little fed up with snacks. Finally, the Captain and I took some meat that was about to go bad and we trimmed that up and cut it into hunks and threw it into a pot with potatoes and everything else we could get our hands on. We came up with a stew that had to be skimmed but was the most delectable thing you can imagine. And rough as it was, we all dug in for fair. I shall never forget that meal. I suppose it was dirty but it was good. The only cooking facility we had was a Shipmate stove fired with wood and coal. Fortunately it dried things out below pretty well, which is a blessing when you're battened down and everybody's clothes are wet and the air is beginning to get on the grungy side.

At daylight Sunday morning, the *Highland Light* was still out in front, with the *Mistress* next in line. The wind, still from the southwest, was whipping the froth from the breaking waves, and the fleet continued its fast — and exhausting — pace. Noon position plots on that day showed that many of the racers had averaged 8½ miles per hour since the start the day before. Visibility remained poor, and the fleet had broken up, so many boats had the horizon to themselves.

Sometime Sunday night the toilet in the *Malabar X* started leaking. There was a bit of confusion and nobody noticed that it was only a sticky foot pedal. Alden finally got down on his hands and knees and took some paper and bailed the thing out, with Hank Meneely holding him from nosediving into it. Alden lost his supper and was put to bed saying, "Call me when it moderates," one of his favorite instructions. Meneely was on watch that night, and he later recalled what followed.

One thing John told me was, "Drop the mainsail if it blows any harder, Hank. I don't think we can do much else." As he gave me that order, the rail was pretty well down and I won't say the boat was laboring, because I don't suppose she was, but we had all the wind we wanted. Well, my watch that night was the twelve 'til four, and it did blow harder, in fact, quite noticeably so. And the boat was heeled over to a point where she would normally more or less stick. However, she went down farther and began to labor a bit. Our lee deck was tending to bury. We were sucking up water from the lee side. The boat took a couple of lurches and we sort of thought we'd consider taking in the mainsail. It would have made things a lot more comfortable. But it was cold and wet. The spray was flying and it was awfully easy to stay huddled in the cockpit hanging on, and I asked the boys whether they would agree that we might sort of lug it. So, out of laziness more than anything else — not good sense certainly — we lugged it. And toward morning as the sky began to brighten, the wind let up enough so that we realized our decision was acceptable.

But there's more to this. After we finished the race, we went into St. George's Harbour and anchored with almost no wind whatsoever, a very delightful day. Everything had been secured except the mainsail, and we decided to drop it and furl it. So we cast off the halyards and nothing happened. The halyards, of high-grade manila, had swollen so they absolutely would not budge in the blocks, and it was impossible to move the lines by any normal means. In fact, it took all hands and we had to unreeve the rope bit by bit to get the sail down. Had we decided to take the sail down at sea, we could not have done so except with a knife, which would have been quite a piece of nonsense. So I guess we were pretty lucky we decided to leave it up.

Lucky or not, the *Malabar X* was up there with the leaders who reeled off the knots Sunday night. Noon positions on Monday showed such remarkable performances as the 222 nautical miles logged by the schooner *Brilliant* in the 24-hour period. The hard weather persisted with no letup in the wind and an endless expanse of jagged seas. Paine was still out in front with the *Highland Light,* but the *Mistress* was close enough astern to make it interesting.

Alden had no idea of how he stood in the fleet, but he kept on pushing his *Malabar* to the utmost. He had the kind of enthusiasm for racing — in any kind of weather — that caught on with his shipmates. Despite the motion and spray and the shambles below of wet clothes and dislodged crockery, the crew of the "Ten" were eager to keep her lunging along. At dusk Monday evening, the watch captain in the *Malabar* ordered the main topsail lowered. Somehow the topsail sheet came out of its block at the end of the gaff. Early next morning, when they wanted to reset the sail, a lightweight member of the crew managed to claw his way out along the gaff and re-reeve the sheet through the block. This made it possible to reset the topsail without the loss of speed that would have resulted from lowering the mainsail so the block could have been reached from the deck. It was just one of the little things that made a great difference in a close finish.

On Tuesday, the wind moderated slightly and the seas lost some of their punch. Around noon, the *Highland Light* made her landfall and strapped down for the windward haul to the finish at St. David's Head. She got the gun at 3:45:43 p.m. (Bermuda time) with a record-breaking elapsed time of 71 hours, 36 minutes, a performance that was to stand unbeaten for 24 years. The *Mistress* was the next boat in at 7:20:51 p.m. With her time allowance of 3:00:27, she had lost to *Highland Light* by just over half an hour, but there were still six schooners within striking distance of the overall prize for the best corrected time.

After more than 600 miles of racing, the *Barlovento* and *Malabar X* converged on the Kitchen Shoals buoy simultaneously. They were close enough for the *Barlovento* to take the *Malabar*'s wind and close enough, too, to bring loud cries for "buoy room." Alden, with his magic touch, worked the *Malabar* to windward. She gained slowly but steadily on the larger boat and beat the *Barlovento* over the finish line by more than five minutes boat for boat.

The *Malabar X*, the third boat to finish, crossed the line at 7:52:29 p.m., but the *Grenadier, Teragram, Brilliant,* and *Water Gypsy* (designed by Alden and owned by Bill McMillan) were strong contenders on the horizon. The *Malabar* had to give the *Grenadier* about an hour's time allowance, and it was hard to tell whether or not she had saved her time. Alden's crew did some quick calculating; it appeared that the *Teragram,* the *Brilliant,* and the *Water Gypsy* couldn't quite catch them, but with the *Grenadier* it was very close. When the Morss brothers brought their schooner in just before 9 p.m., no one could be sure who had won. There was no way of contacting the race committee on shore, so the *Malabar X* and the *Grenadier* swung on their hooks in St. George's Harbour while their crews speculated on the outcome over a round of grog.

It was not until the boats made Hamilton Harbour the next morning that they got the word that the *Malabar X* had beaten the *Grenadier* by three minutes and 16 seconds, a scary-enough margin to excite even the imperturbable John Alden. But there was more icing to the Alden cake. Not only had two Alden schooners placed first and second, but when the committee finished their arithmetic, two more Alden schooners, the

Water Gypsy and the *Teragram,* were found to have finished third and fourth on corrected time. All four schooners finished within one hour and 15 minutes of each other.

The great pacemaker, *Highland Light,* was fifth in fleet, with *Mistress* seventh. *Dorade* and the Stephens family (Olin as her designer and Rod as her skipper) cleaned up in Class B, but the 1932 Bermuda Race belonged to John Alden.

The Bermuda Race has been the World Series of ocean racing in North America since the beginning of the century. John Alden won the race with the *Malabar IV* in 1923 and with the *Malabar VII* in 1926. The triumph of the *Malabar X* in 1932 made him the first skipper to win the Bermuda Race three times. No one but Alden has sailed three boats of his own design to victory in this race. That is a performance that could only be achieved by a man who had devoted his life to the design and handling of small sailing vessels.

2

Alden's Sakonnet

Nine generations after Priscilla Mullens married that shy Puritan, John Alden, John Gale Alden was born in Troy, New York. It was January 24, 1884. He was born into a family of some means and some misfortune. His father, Charles L. Alden, was a lawyer, 20 years older than his mother, Mary Langford Taylor Alden. Of their eight children, four survived: Antoinette, John, Langford, and Charles. An earlier John G. had died.

The Aldens were wealthy enough to have New England summers of boating, yet there was little salt in Charles's and Mary's blood. Their summer home was at Sakonnet, Rhode Island. When he had grown up and become famous in the world of boats, John Alden recalled those early summers.

My first recollection of any kind of a boat was a flat-bottomed row boat that we had on Long Pond. It was called the Antoinette Boat, named after my older sister, as I suppose she owned it, but even if she did not, she certainly managed it. I was the oldest of three brothers, and at first there were no others interested in boating. I can vaguely remember going on the pond with my sister when I was about six years old, and shortly after, being punished for "stealing" the boat because I went out without her.

At first, we used to sail down the pond with an umbrella for a sail, and then a little later we made a squaresail, but we had to row home against the wind, as the boat had no centerboard. This was about 1890.

Then the Withington family built on Warren's Point. Their three boys, Sydney, Robert, and Paul, along with another family, the Lloyds, arrived, and at once the newcomers started their own boating. We soon got to know each other, and before long we had three catboats with jibs, the Lloyds' *Kea,* the Withingtons' *Swan,* and my boat, the *Wasp,* a nice little cat 10 feet long that was given to me when I was 10 years old. With several others, we raced the boats hard on Long Pond for four or five years and part of the time used them on Round Pond. One afternoon, however, after completing a race, we became very ambitious and carried the boats over the bank from Round Pond to the ocean and raced them around West Island to the breakwater, arriving there after dark. Anxious parents were in carriages awaiting our return, and I remember there were several girls among us, a Miss Isabel Lynde being my crew with Sydney Withington. After that, we never got back on the ponds again, but I really think we enjoyed them more than the salt water.

As a youngster, John spent a great deal of time making toy boats. Most of them followed the lines of some famous yacht, such as the *America.* He would find a piece of 6 by 6 or 8 by 8 about two feet long and painstakingly whittle it to the shape he wanted. Then he

John Alden, age 1½.

John (right) and his
brother Langford, about 1890.

The house on Warren's Point,
Sakonnet, Rhode Island.

At the reins of the buckboard,
Sakonnet, circa 1930.

John Alden and Helen Cooke in
a Dorchester Bay dory,
circa 1903.

All photos courtesy Chester M. and Harriet Sawtelle.

The designer as a young man.

gouged out the hull until only a thin shell remained. He added the keel and rudder. A cigar box provided material for the decking. Finally spars and sails were rigged. He seldom used any paint or varnish, but his boats sailed circles around some of the fancy store models.

No one knows just how John Alden became so skilled at handling boats, whether models or full-size ones, at such an early age. His brother Langford said he probably picked up some ideas from the hunchbacked Portuguese fisherman who took care of the Aldens' horses and cows. The man had been shipwrecked on the beach near the family home, and Mrs. Alden had taken him in and cared for him over the winter. He remained with the family until he died.

At the age of 11 or 12, John had a remarkable statistical knowledge of sailing yachts. There is one story about six or eight men who had gathered to watch America's Cup contenders turn a buoy about two miles directly south of the Aldens' house on Warren's Point. The men formed a circle around John, who proceeded to give them complete details, such as length overall, waterline length, beam, draft, and sail area of each of the yachts in the trial race. He also knew the particular qualities of each boat, how she performed on or off the wind, and the special talents of each skipper.

The young Sakonnet sailors eventually outgrew their 10-foot catboats and decided to form a yacht club and start a class of knockabouts. The boats, 21 feet long, were decked over and planked lapstrake. They were built from the same plans as the dories designed for Dorchester Bay. The Dorchester boats, however, had wooden centerboards and were rather tender. So the Sakonnet boats were equipped with galvanized metal centerboards and carried additional inside ballast. They were built in Neponset, Massachusetts, for about $65 each.

One of the young sailors in the group was a girl named Helen Cooke, and Langford recalls that Helen, who was very fond of sailing, wanted one of the knockabouts but was forbidden by her father to have one. John urged him to relent, claiming the boat was very steady and was unsinkable, but the father was adamant.

One day there was a 40-knot southeaster blowing, and a big, four-masted schooner was sheltering under the lee of the point, riding out the blow at anchor. On the porch of the Cooke house a small group gathered, and Helen's father, as was his custom, scanned the sea through his big telescope. Mr. Cooke remarked that the four-master had to stay at anchor and that a knockabout would be destroyed in the seas.

"I can take a dory around that ship and back," John said.

Mr. Cooke replied that he would bet $100 that John's dory couldn't last in those conditions.

John and three boys slipped away. "We'll get a couple of sandbags," John said, "and double-reef the sail." They picked up an extra pump and started out. The boat went well until they got out of the lee of the lighthouse and West Island, and even then they made it close-hauled to the four-master with hardly any pumping.

After they rounded the ship, however, Mr. Cooke's money looked safer. It was a broad reach now, and the waves started breaking over the stern. Everyone took a hand at the pumps. They lost a washer off one pump, and with only the other pump and a two-quart tin lard pail going, they almost swamped. But the boys finally made it in to relatively calm water.

John and his crew headed for the Cooke house, where they found that Mr. Cooke had watched the whole performance, skipping dinner and almost suffering a stroke. John apologized for causing so much worry and said he just wanted Helen to get her boat. About two weeks later, Mr. Cooke said Helen could have her knockabout on the condition that John would crew for her and teach her more about sailing. It appears, however, that Mr. Cooke did not pay the hundred dollars.

This was not the first bit of hard sailing John had done in his knockabout, the *Little Rhody*. It would have been a simple matter to transport the *Little Rhody* from the builder in Neponset to Sakonnet, but John managed to have the boat delivered to Troy so he could sail her down the Hudson, through the Harlem and East rivers, into Long Island Sound, and down the coast to Sakonnet.

He had planned to take a friend from Troy with him, but after the boat was delivered, the boy's father wouldn't let him go. So Alden put his provisions aboard the *Little Rhody* and set out alone. He made it to Albany beating down the river against a head wind. He went over some rapids near Troy with the centerboard down, and the strain started a leak that made bailing a necessity for the rest of the trip.

Next morning he was hailed by a youth on the river bank and ended up taking him aboard as crew. They headed downstream and ran into vicious weather for several days, with head winds and thundersqualls for the next 100 miles. The ebb tide running against a fresh southerly created a nasty chop on the river, and Alden recalled, "My crew always wanted to catch on to a tow of barges, but I did not want to do that as I had brought the boat on to sail, not to be towed."

After minor mishaps, the *Little Rhody* got as far as Haverstraw Bay, near Yonkers, where the river was wide for quite a stretch. Here, John saw a bad-looking squall making up and ran the boat in close to shore. No sooner had he anchored and furled the sails than the squall struck with torrents of rain. A bolt of lightning hit alongside and the boat capsized. When John came to the surface, he could hear his crew yelling for help but couldn't see him. Luckily, a tug was coming up to a nearby dock and picked up the crew on one side as John clawed his way up the other side of the vessel. The wind continued to blow with intense puffs, uprooting trees along the shore.

After the storm, the boat was righted and bailed out. The crew had had it and headed back for Albany, but John took on some supplies and pushed on single-handed.

The rest of the trip was less strenuous, save for John's diet. With only a dollar in his pocket, he lived for 10 days on canned frankfurters, tomato sauce, and bread. He made his way down the Sound and one day just at sunset turned into a small harbor with a private breakwater near Noroton, Connecticut. He later found that the owner of the property was John Sherman Hoyt.

His butler came down to order me out, but after talking with him he told me to come up to the house and have a square meal and spend the night, only I had to be back on board by 6:30 in the morning, when the master took his swim.

At that hour [next morning], it was beginning to rain a little, and when Mr. Hoyt came down, he exclaimed, "Hullo, what are you doing here?" I told him I was cruising and he said I was not cruising that day as it was blowing east and he told me to come up to the house. So I had breakfast (my second) as his guest, and my previous hosts waited on table. I told him I expected to become a yacht designer, and 25 years later he wrote me saying: "The boy grows up to be a man and his fondest ambition is realized. I am thinking of building a schooner, so please drop in to see me the next time you are in New York." I designed him a schooner in 1926.

John sailed on for Sakonnet, where he arrived just three weeks after leaving Troy. It was anything but a glamorous cruise, but it was what John Alden liked — just being alone in a boat.

3

Alden Becomes a Designer

In 1900, the Aldens moved from Troy to Dorchester, Massachusetts. It wasn't a happy move. John's father had had a stroke, and Mrs. Alden did not want his friends of 50 years to see him in his failing condition. John and Langford spent their first months in the new surroundings nosing about the Boston shipyards and docks — especially T Wharf, where the Gloucester fishermen tied up. John talked with the skippers and made countless sketches of the boats, quickly and accurately reproducing the lines of the graceful schooners. He was a compulsive doodler on or off the docks, but instead of geometric patterns, he produced profiles and details of boats on scraps of paper, napkins, envelopes, or whatever was handy. This habit remained with him throughout his life.

In Troy, John had had a run-of-the-mill high school education, but when the family moved to Boston his mother wanted him to go to Massachusetts Institute of Technology. His father died in 1902, leaving no huge estate, but enough funds for a college education for his children. John, however, decided he had had enough formal education (he later took some technical courses at M.I.T.) and set out to train himself in naval architecture.

He wormed his way into the design office of Edward Burgess, who had designed the America's Cup Defenders in 1885, 1886, and 1887. His son, W. Starling Burgess (who himself designed three Defenders in the 1930s), was running the office when Alden arrived to do odd jobs and run errands for the draftsmen. When he found a free drawing board, he sketched design ideas of his own. Apparently, the precocious young man began to get in the way, and Burgess asked him to leave.

So Alden turned to B.B. Crowninshield, another leading designer of the period, whose office turned out, among other designs, plans of prominent Gloucester schooners. For a year, John worked without pay as an apprentice, and then in 1903 got on the payroll as a draftsman. He worked on the lines and other plans for the 130-foot sistership schooners *Tartar* and *Fame*. The *Tartar* later was acknowledged as the fastest schooner in the fishing fleet and was "highliner" for several years. (Some 25 years later, John designed himself a Q boat and named her *Tartar*.) Crowninshield designed some six-masted schooners for the Coastwise Transportation Company, and Alden had a hand in developing their sail plans.

Even in these early, impecunious years, John Alden managed to own one or another small cruising boat

The Tartar, *a 130-foot fishing schooner designed by B.B. Crowninshield. Alden drew the lines, traced the sail plan, and constructed the table of offsets.* (Transactions of the Society of Naval Architects and Marine Engineers, *1907. Courtesy Captain W.J.L. Parker, U.S.C.G. (Retired))*

most of the time. He recounted how he got the best of these small vessels many years later, in a letter to the editor of *Yachting* magazine.

When I was a young draftsman in the office of B.B. Crowninshield, I spent most of my spare daylight hours wandering from one yacht yard to another in the vicinity of greater Boston, looking with longing and somewhat critical eyes at the large number of cruising sailing craft then in existence. With a weekly salary of not over $15.00, my yachting was necessarily restricted to the simplest and smallest of sailing craft and, after owning several small cruising yawls, I ran across the *Sea Fox* laid up at Borden's Yard, Cow Pasture, South Boston. At one glance I completely lost my heart to this lovely little craft, which proved to be for sale at the modest figure of $250.00. I was told by her owner, a man named Briggs, of Winthrop, that she was quite smart. By working nights and by borrowing from my friends, I managed to scrape up the necessary funds.

The *Sea Fox* was designed and built by E.L. Williams of South Boston in about 1892, and her model and general design are a credit to any designer at any time. She was about 28'11" overall, 22' waterline, 8'6" extreme beam, 7'3" waterline beam, 5'3" draft. She had a very easy bilge, a rather light displacement, and a high ratio of ballast to displacement, which I believe was over fifty percent. She was strongly but lightly built and had very little below, except two full-length berths on each side and about 5'4" headroom.

Her rig was large but it seemed very effective, and her hull form was a delight to the eye. I had no money to run the boat after I acquired her, and when placing her in commission was only able to paint one-half of her deck with conventional buff, the other half being green.

Her great speed was at once evident and I sailed her in the races at Marblehead under the Universal Rule. In the first race, by the Eastern Yacht Club, there were over forty entries, yet *Sea Fox* won in a light air with a borrowed spinnaker, vertical cut sails, and little or no racing gear. The next two days *Sea Fox* won both her races and, as cash prizes were then given by all the Marblehead clubs, the writer was the proud possessor of $87.50, which was promptly spent at the various clubhouses.

Sea Fox was astonishingly fast, especially to windward in light and moderate weather. She could point with the best of the racing classes and the helmsmen of such boats would look at this craft with surprise and disdain. Her one fault was running free, when she had a tendency to roll.

I consider this boat the most remarkable small craft of her time (or almost any time), and I have always wanted to design and build another boat of this waterline length, but possibly changing the hull a little and modernizing the rig. For this overall length, with a modern rig, I doubt if any faster cruising boat has ever been built. Mr. R.C. Simpson and myself took the lines off the hull and I believe they are quite accurate. When I turned out the 53-foot-overall yawl *Tioga Too* I had the memory of this boat very much in mind.

In 1905, Mrs. Alden, Langford, and Charles moved back to Troy, and Antoinette left with her husband, leaving John on his own and reveling in his work with Crowninshield. He was a part of the process that produced tall vessels with great seagoing ability, and this is what he had been reaching for as his main objective in life. Gradually, he took on more responsibility and, reportedly, turned out many designs that bore the firm's name with no individual credit to John Alden.

While working with Crowninshield, he had an experience that probably had more influence on his future design ideas than any other single factor. There are several accounts of John's trip in the *Fame*. He gave his version to the Boston station of the Cruising Club of America in 1954:

It was in 1907 when I worked for B.B. Crowninshield, the yacht designer, that he announced that smallpox had broken out on the schooner *Fame* which was owned by the Eastern Fishing Company and controlled by Mr. Crowninshield. The *Fame* was about 125 feet overall, about 96 feet waterline, 25 feet beam and drew about 16 feet. She was a gaff-rigged schooner which the fishermen seemed to prefer, and had no motor though auxiliary engines were beginning to appear in the fishing fleet. She carried a normal crew of 23. Look at them now! Not a single sailboat left, and the cost of a diesel-driven fisherman is about 15 to 20 times the cost of a good sailing vessel of the offshore type. As a result, the bulk of the fishing is done in Canada.

The *Fame* had a 51-foot main gaff (as I recall it) and about a 78-foot main boom and was a very smart sailer. She was afterwards run down by the Yarmouth boat, all but one of her crew of 23 being lost. At the time of this story, the Captain, named Doggett, and crew were in quarantine at Halifax with smallpox and the authorities of that place had a good deal of trouble in getting them to leave the boat at all. They finally did, however, and the next problem was to get the *Fame* back to Boston.

I was 23 years old at the time and I volunteered to get a crew together and bring the boat back, and I supposed I was in charge. We got old Captain "Josh" Nickerson of South Orleans, who was over 60 at the time, and I got hold of four other boys all younger than I was, one of whom had never been on a sailboat before, and we also took along Raymond Brackett of Marblehead, though he was not one of those I asked. However, he appointed himself cook and also mate, not recognizing me at all.

We left Boston by steamer in December, and for a starter, I was almost pushed overboard about sunset by a drunk who was swinging far out over the side of the steamer but he never seemed to let go and ended up by swinging into me, almost sending me over the side of the boat and badly bruising my face and neck. We arrived in Yarmouth the next day and at Halifax that evening. Captain Nickerson had gone down 24 hours ahead to arrange the papers and see that the boat was fumigated, which it was, and that morning we warped *Fame* to the

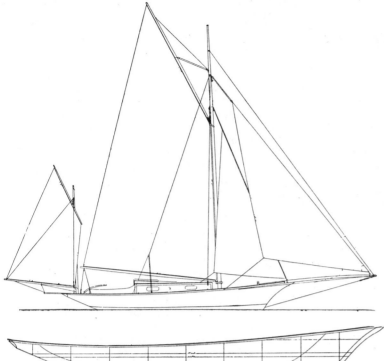

The Sea Fox, *a fast little yawl owned by Alden when he was a young draftsman in the Crowninshield office. Years later, Alden recalled her ballast-displacement ratio as being over 50 percent. Her sail plan shows a high-peaked main and a lug mizzen.* (Yachting, *May 1944*)

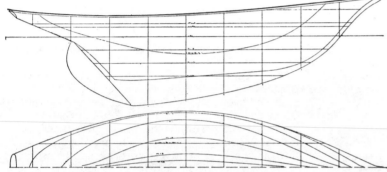

end of the dock. The anchors weighed 700 pounds apiece, and the ballast was all inside as was universal with those boats . . . .

On our arrival at Halifax, we were joined by a young sailor from Newfoundland who wanted to come to this country, and by a man named Slade who was assistant manager of the boat under Mr. Crowninshield. Slade didn't last long, as I suspected he wouldn't, and he suddenly disappeared. He was a bad actor and later left Crowninshield's office in disgrace. The Newfoundlander was a good sailor, and we were very sorry to lose him, as I will describe later.

We got underway from the dock the morning after we arrived in Halifax, and it took us several hours to hoist the main. We ran into a head wind outside and we turned back after a long consultation, anchoring with the 700-pound anchor and about 300 feet of heavy chain in Halifax harbor. We again got underway several days later, eventually getting up the anchor and setting the main, using up most of the day in doing this. The trouble was not so much the weight of the anchor but the weight of the chain which made it very hard to raise. There was a big ground swell outside and a south wind with every sign of a winter blow coming. On top of this the peak halyard on the main carried away with a bang, so we decided to again return to Halifax, coming into that port in a heavy southeaster and heavy rain at night. We again anchored letting out all our chain, but as we

dragged, we lowered our mainsail, after which we stopped dragging.

After a long consultation we then decided to wait until after Christmas and then sail back with several of the old crew, but our hopes dimmed when they came by us in a steamer from quarantine, shaking their fists at us and threatening us in no uncertain terms. We had Christmas dinner in rubber boots at the principal hotel in Halifax, and saw a headline in the local paper which said, "Young American Millionaires Come to Take the *Fame* Home." Right after Christmas we decided to leave for Boston without any of the old crew, and Captain Nickerson went ashore to buy some food. He didn't return and about five o'clock Brackett went ashore to see where he was. We were about half a mile from shore, and about eleven o'clock that night they returned. The old Captain told us that the American Consul told him that we should be outside the three-mile limit by sunrise the next day, and that the Halifax authorities had made plans to seize the boat at the request of the former skipper, Captain Doggett, who had reported that the boat had bought bait without a license (as they all did at that time) and that the Canadian authorities had telegraphed Ottawa for instructions. [At the time of the story, according to the version given by Alden's brother Langford to the *Cruising Club News* in 1970, the Canadian government was entitled under terms of a treaty to seize any Gloucester vessel attempting to buy bait or ice in a Canadian port without a license. The resentment borne by the *Fame*'s former crew and skipper was apparently deep.]

The harbor was partly filled with American fishermen who were not sympathetic with us, and we figured it would take five or six hours to get up the anchor and hoist the sails, so we decided to slip our chain, taking careful compass bearings as to its location. I might add that just before Christmas both Slade and the Newfoundlander disappeared, the latter not even getting some clothes that he had, and Captain Nickerson nonchalantly said, "He was killed." At any rate we liked him very much, and I have often wondered what happened to him. The working crew consisted of only four men plus Brackett who was a good cook but of little use on deck. The old Captain talked all the time of his former glories, but as far as I know he did not do a stroke of work. He occupied the one stateroom on the boat, and kept the temperature of the after cabin up to at least 80 degrees. The galley was forward of the fish hold and the deck leaked very badly forward but not aft. There was no plumbing — a typical layout of the fishermen of that time.

About 2 a.m. we crawled out on deck, taking care to have no lights burning, and crawled forward, overhauling the chain and taking the stops off the sails. At a given signal, overboard went the chain and up went the sails except the mainsail, and *Fame* filled away on starboard tack before a northwest wind. The former crew rushed up on deck of the schooner *Squanto* which they had noisily boarded earlier in the evening, and we were a little afraid they would come over and throw us overboard, which they were perfectly capable of doing. By dawn, with a fair northwest wind, we were well clear of land and under all four lower sails. The wind shifted to southeast and we were able to sail along the south coast of Nova Scotia on the port tack, clearing all buoys and headlands. It gradually breezed up and we then decided to lower the jib and main, jogging, as the fishermen call it, under foresail and jumbo. We were in the Bay of Fundy that night and it was blowing hard southwest. We could see white water on the reefs to leeward of us off Yarmouth and we had visions of piling up on them. We were set closer and closer by a head current, when to our relief, the wind hauled northwest and freshened. It was very clear, and we were able to lay a course very nearly to Cape Ann. We had visions of a short trip to Boston, but it was not to be.

We double-reefed the main, putting in a miserable reef, and then the jib broke loose and split into atoms. Soon the main split at the reefpoints and we lowered it. The wind hauled southeast and it started to rain and became very rough. Suddenly, through the rain, I spotted a lobster pot buoy and when we sounded, got 35 fathoms. I soon spotted another and got 28 fathoms. To our great surprise, the *Fame* tacked easily and we headed offshore on starboard tack, heading about east and gradually heading southwest as the wind continued to shift. As I see it now, we were on Cashes Ledge, but in the rain we thought we might be approaching the New England coast and perhaps we were.

It blew very hard and we saw a Nova Scotia four-master running south with only a jib up. We lay hove-to for three days on the starboard tack and I figured we were somewhere off Cape Cod. Our food supply began to run out as the food which was ordered in Halifax never came aboard, and it was a case of every man for himself. Those who worked at all were Dwight Foster, a fellow named Babcock, who has left these parts, my brother Langford and the speaker, the others being worse than useless and little attention was paid to them. Towards the end, I took a bath on deck, and we figured we were bound to hit the coast if we headed northwest, which we did, sailing for about three days that way. We set the main although it had bad rips in it, and I guess we averaged 5 or 6 knots.

Later the wind hauled from northwest to southwest and we sighted a three-master, the *William E. Litchfield,* reefed and heading southeast. We asked him where we were and we thought he said "Nauset Light, 6¼ miles northwest." The Captain and I were in the fore rigging and I soon saw land. I said to Captain Nickerson, "That doesn't look like Nauset, more like Chatham." The Captain yelled at the top of his lungs, "By God, put her about boys. We are way down off the Jersey coast."

We tacked with the wet, torn mainsail and she came around and we headed east. On the way out we passed a black can buoy that made us very uncomfortable with our 16 feet of draft. However, we didn't hit and it got very rough and started to rain. We completely split the main and dropped it, running up the Jersey coast under fore and jumbo. We were very weak and dizzy from lack of food and we couldn't lift the mainsail off the stove pipe and as a result a bad hole was burned in it. The old Captain quite distinguished himself by recognizing Absecon lighthouse when he saw it. He hadn't been down that way for 20 years, so he said.

When we were nearer the land, right after tacking, a sea broke over the stern and Raymond Brackett, who was standing near the helmsman, was carried up by it over the top of the house to between the two masts on the lee side, hopelessly tangled up in the sounding lead line. The high rail kept him from being washed overboard. A good deal of water came below and the two men at the wheel were soaked.

On our long starboard tack, we set the trysail which was intact, but the boat seemed to sail better to windward without it. We also found that the side lights had been filled with water which we replaced with kerosene. We ran up the Jersey shore by memory, making at least 7 knots under foresail and jumbo, and after dark we could see the reflections of the Navesink lighthouse. We had visions of being anchored back of Sandy Hook before the expected northwester broke but we were unable to get there in time. It was then early in January and the thermometer dropped on shore to nearly zero and it was well below freezing on the *Fame.*

When we were headed by the nor'wester after dark, we kept over to the Long Island shore and then back to the Jersey shore. It was necessary to jibe each time we altered our course, and we fully expected the foresail to blow out each time we jibed, but while it started, it seemed to hold. As it blew harder and harder and we were not making much progress, we decided to anchor well offshore. We were icing up badly, and the dories which had been new when we left Halifax, were badly smashed by seas coming aboard.

We had one 700-pound anchor left and some 300 fathoms of 3½-inch-diameter brand new manila cable in the hold. We rigged the end of the cable to the anchor, the cable leading directly from the hawsepipe to the hold. We should first have taken a turn around the bitts, which we did not do, but we were afraid of the anchor which we had on the rail. It was blowing around 60 miles an hour and very cold. My rubber boots had worn through, but nevertheless I was quite warm as I guess we all were due to the hard work. It was nearly 3 a.m. when the anchor got away from us and the boat started to go astern at a high rate of speed. It was before the days of electric lights on fishermen, but we had flares. We did not have a turn around the bitts and we were unable to overhaul enough of the new cable to get one.

We dropped the sails but the boat continued to go astern very fast and we had visions of losing our one remaining cable and anchor. There were kinks in the new cable and we tried jamming the cable in the kinks by inserting some large beams which we found in the hold, but they were snapped at once and it seemed as if we would surely lose our cable. However, Dwight Foster, who was one of the best sailors I have ever seen, had more brains than the rest of us and he jammed the hawsepipe with some canvas so we were able to get a turn around the bitts, and to our great relief, *Fame* did not drag.

By that time we were utterly fagged out. The boat was covered with ice and we had been up most of the night with next to nothing to eat. I recall turning in in my wet clothes after we had hung out a riding light and then rushing up on deck to find our light had gone out and we were nearly cut down by a liner. We were cursed out from the liner as she rushed by. It is lucky we were not hit, as if we had been, we would have had little chance for survival.

The next day it blew very hard and no one paid any attention to us. We had nothing to eat and the ensign was set upside down in the rigging. About 4 a.m. the second morning, the wind had moderated and we heard a tooting alongside of us. It was a Revenue Cutter who asked us various questions and said they would rather wait until daybreak before sending a crew aboard. As we were not dragging we consented and about 7 a.m. they sent 11 men and a big load of food aboard. They got up the anchor and towed us to quarantine. We ate until we went to sleep. We were then towed to Fulton Market for $6.00 and most of us left the ship.

On this trip my brother Langford lost 22 pounds and all of us lost from 10 to 12 pounds. We had been given up for lost and we were about 10 days out from Halifax. I don't see just what else we could have done in our crippled shape. We were very shorthanded and sailing a big schooner in the middle of winter is no easy job.

The boat had made magnificent weather of it at all times and from then on I was very much in love with this type of boat, a vessel that sails on her bottom, not on her beam ends. While she seemed very large at first, she

seemed to get smaller and smaller as we became used to her, and toward the end, we always had her under control. Of course, we were fresh from offices which was quite a handicap.

Most of us left the boat in New York except Raymond Brackett and Captain Joshua Nickerson who stayed aboard. Brackett furnished the press with an entirely wrong account of the trip in which he was quite a hero, which was not the case. The trip was highly educational, but we all wished it was over except Leslie Babcock who seemed to enjoy it all. The man who should get the greatest credit is Dwight Foster, whom I have lost all track of. He kept his head about him and was always willing to do more than his share.

The *Fame* was towed to Boston, refitted at great expense and that spring was run down and sunk, which ended her career.

Alden's account of this almost disastrous trip is more than just a sea story. It explains a lot of things about the man and the kinds of vessels he designed. It was his sense of inner security that led him to take *Fame* offshore in the dead of winter with a handful of young men and an old captain. Instead of shaking his confidence, the exhausting ordeal strengthened his self-assurance. That's why the first schooners he later designed for himself were planned so they could be sailed singlehanded. That's also why every Alden cruising boat was primarily a rugged seagoing vessel with speed subordinated to seaworthiness. His design ideas crystallized while he was still quite young, and, although they were modified as time went on, the basic principles never changed.

In 1908, while he was still with Crowninshield, Alden married Helene Harvey, a singer at the Boston Conservatory of Music. The following year, their daughter Harriette was born, and John left Crowninshield to start his own business. There are several accounts of why he made this move. One was that friends urged him to open his own office so that he could take credit for much of the work he was doing at Crowninshield's. Another story is that he had saved $250 and had bought a secondhand boat (perhaps the *Sea Fox*). The craft was damaged and he had to sell her to pay the repair bill. At this juncture, he hit Crowninshield for a raise, and, when he didn't get it, he left.

Alden's first office was a dingy room at 27 Kirby, a Boston side street. Later, at his mother's suggestion, he moved to 131 State Street, then he went to 148 State Street, and finally back to 131 State Street, which was his main office until he retired. The money that had been set aside for his college education was transferred to him in installments as he started out on his own.

The next few years were bleak. Design commissions

were scarce, and the family was beset by financial problems. His marriage ended in 1911, and his daughter, Harriette, went to live with her mother but spent summers with her father at Sakonnet. Alden lived a frugal life, saving money by scrimping on food to the point that he got dyspepsia. He worked long hours with grim determination. Nothing was going to thwart his implacable desire to become a successful boat designer.

There was some relief from the austerity in sailing. In 1910, Alden sailed aboard Demarest Lloyd's schooner *Shiyessa* in the Bermuda Race, but, while he enjoyed being at sea, the pleasures of the voyage were somewhat tempered by the outcome of the race. They were racing mainly against the *Vagrant,* a Herreshoff schooner owned by Harold S. Vanderbilt. Alden later recalled:

> We didn't see each other all the way down at all, but on the morning of the finish, there was the *Vagrant,* which we had thought safely under our lee.
>
> We had made the mistake of thinking we had won the race, especially as we had a time allowance of an hour and a half, as I remember it. To our great surprise and disappointment, the *Vagrant* sailed around us, and while we [were so close to the finish that we] could see bottom plainly, we didn't have a breath of wind.
>
> The *Vagrant* crossed the finish line safely ahead and when the wind finally struck in, it was dead ahead and we had a long slow beat up to the finish. Lloyd was disgusted and didn't even want to continue on, but I said we had to.

The sea tonic was refreshing but didn't do much for the company books. In 1914, after five years in business, John had one draftsman, John Pinaud, in his employ and some 50 designs to his credit, but Alden & Company was just about in irons financially. There were more bills than cash and Alden was faced with closing shop. At this point, the postman arrived with a letter from shaving-soap tycoon George B. Williams, authorizing Alden to go ahead with a 51-foot-waterline schooner. Then came an order for a 124-foot-overall commercial schooner for F.S. Grubey and, subsequently, a commission for a 102-foot motor yacht. Alden's ascension had begun, but his new success, along with yacht designing in general, was soon to be dampened by World War I.

In the beginning, Alden did some war-related commercial work, designing first a 135-foot patrol boat, which was never built. In 1917, he turned out the lines for a 150-foot, three-masted cargo schooner. For several years, this vessel was John's greatest advertisement, for she was christened *Priscilla Alden* by the owner's daughter, Priscilla Alden Dennett. As the big sailing schooners left the sea lanes to more efficient craft, the *Priscilla Alden* was converted to a yacht. Later she was sold to the Russian government.

When the United States entered the war in 1917, Alden virtually closed his office. Since he had mate's papers, he applied to the Merchant Marine, but apparently the documents weren't impressive enough to get him a commission unless he took six to nine months of training. So he joined the Army as an enlisted man, not deigning to call on friends in Washington for an officer's commission. He spent the war in North Carolina, first being trained, then training others, and, when the Armistice was signed, was one of the first to be demobilized — this time with some help from his friends.

As we look back on John Alden's early struggles to get into the yacht design business, it is interesting to assess his abilities and his approach to designing. He lacked the technical educational training that even self-taught naval architects acquire nowadays. He had never worked in a shipyard. John was a natural-born sailor, however, with the gift of being able to translate his intuitive ideas into three-dimensional form. He was much like George Steers, the designer of the schooner yacht *America,* who could take what he saw in his mind's eye and carve a perfect model of it.

Neither Alden nor Steers created his designs from scratch. Each had an existing prototype in the back of his mind. Steers took the fast pilot boat of the mid-19th century as his basic frame of reference, while Alden used the Gloucester fishing schooner of the early 20th century as his point of departure.

With the design of the *America* in 1853, Steers refined the pilot schooner model and began a design trend in yachting that lasted several decades. Sixty-five years later Alden modified another type of commercial vessel to create another long-lasting trend in yacht design. The fishing schooner had been designed to carry a load in the fish hold. Since a yacht would not carry this kind of a load, it would be necessary to give her more ballast. If all the ballast were stowed inside, the yacht could require full sections that could produce a slow hull. So Alden began balancing his ballast, putting some inside and some outside. The fishing schooner rig, easily handled by a large, professional crew, was reduced to a size that could be worked with a small group of amateurs. Beam was cut down to add to speed. Alden gave his boats more freeboard to provide additional living space below.

In the January 1913 issue of *Yachting* magazine — years before he drew the boats that would make him famous — Alden spelled out some of his design prin-

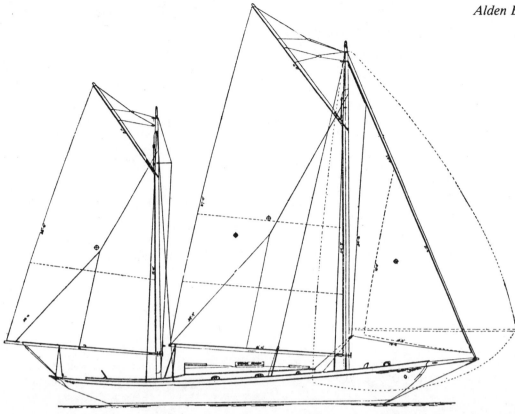

The sail plan of the ideal two-man cruiser as Alden envisioned it in 1913. He liked the ketch rig because sail can be shortened without undue sacrifice to drive or balance simply by dropping the mainsail. The jib was hanked to an inner stay (just abaft the headstay), which could be slacked off enough to allow the jib to be hauled down from the foredeck. (Yachting, *January 1913*)

ciples. Although he was writing about "The Ideal Two-Man Cruiser," a 41½-foot ketch he had designed especially to illustrate the article, his comments in that article are representative of the thinking behind many of his designs.

While it is desirable to have an able boat and one in which the owner can go to sea for long runs without causing undue anxiety to those left on shore, an effort has been made to avoid freak types of the extreme "chunkiness" of a vessel designed primarily for long deep-sea voyages.

What I have attempted to turn out is not an exploring ship or a Nova Scotia pilot vessel, but a comfortable, able little cruiser which will appeal to the average yachtsman who wants the most for his money in the form of an all-around boat which will be equally in her element going to Bermuda or Newfoundland, or cruising in Long Island Sound.

She should not, however, be confused with many of the so-called "cruising yawls," with long overhangs and all-outside ballast, which sail "on their ear" in anything over a 15-knot breeze and would pound themselves open in a summer gale on Georges. Such boats are merely racers in disguise, and bring speedy disillusionment to the trusting smooth-water sailor who attempts to take them to sea. On the contrary, the present design is that of a good, able, little sea boat, and yet one which, owing to her easy lines, will prove a good sailer in anything but very light airs, when the engine will drive her faster than the addition of bothersome light sails could do.

The principal dimensions are as follows: length overall, 41 feet 6 inches; length, waterline, 28 feet 10 inches; beam (extreme), 10 feet 6 inches; draft, 6 feet; freeboard (bow), 4 feet 6 inches; freeboard (least), 2 feet 6 inches; sail area, 900 square feet; ballast, 7,000 pounds outside, 800 pounds inside. A study of these figures in connection with the lines and sections brings out some interesting features. In the first place, note that, while the underbody is finely molded, with easy entrance and smooth run, it has not been found necessary to carry the hull out in excessive overhangs. Moreover, the midship section shows a generous submerged area, with bilges sufficiently hard to insure the boat's sailing on her bottom instead of on her side, a very important consideration for comfort, as all who have attempted to cruise in a racing machine know to their sorrow.

Then the generous freeboard and easy sheer, combined with good buoyancy and easy entrance forward, will produce the type of vessel which alone is fit to go to sea — that is, one which will ride the seas easily and be relatively dry, and, at the same time, will be able to go to windward through a head sea and wind . . . .

It is difficult to say which is the most dangerous proposition for such work — the boat which is so fine forward that she dives bows under into a head sea (like the old English cutters) and takes everything on deck, or the high-sided, tubby-bowed affair which will heave-to beautifully and not take a drop of water on deck, but which no amount of sail or power could force to make any progress against a head sea. Obviously the ideal type of hull is one which will, so far as possible, combine the two very desirable features of seaworthiness and ability

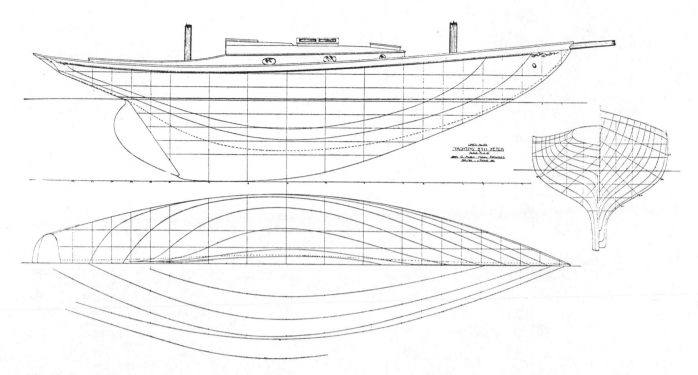

The ideal two-man cruiser is listed as design number 36 in the Alden company's design index. Her lines show a well-balanced, graceful hull. Her waterlines are more symmetrical than those of many Alden hulls designed early in his career. (Yachting, January 1913)

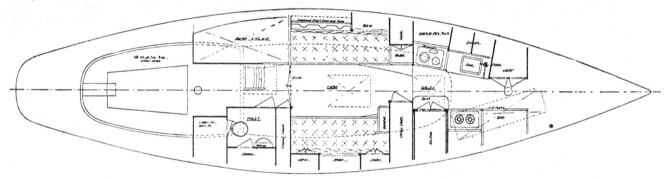

In anticipation of wet-weather or night sailing, Alden designed a vestibule around the companionway ladder of Number 36. The toilet room and oilskin locker are immediately to starboard, and the main cabin is entered through doors forward. The galley has both an alcohol and a coal stove, "as both have advantages." (Yachting, January 1913)

to go to windward: herein lies the most important criterion of any seagoing cruiser. An inspection of the accompanying lines . . . will show how I have attempted to secure these qualities by keeping the forward sections buoyant and the lines of entrance easy — both at the same time . . . .

Looking at the other end of the vessel, we see a stern which is fairly enough molded to leave the water cleanly without dragging, and which, at the same time, has a sufficiently sharp upward rake to prevent slapping and to give it strength. At the same time, it has buoyancy enough when partly submerged to lift the after part of the vessel nicely above a following sea and make her behave well in running free.

After the hull, the most important thing about any sailing vessel is her rig. The ketch rig has been selected in this case on account of its simplicity, moderate area and

ease of handling. The sail plan is so arranged that the boat will handle equally well under full sail; jib and mizzen; jib, mizzen and reefed mainsail; or reefed mizzen and storm jib. Under the last-named combination the boat would lie practically hove-to in anything but a hurricane.

With his apprenticeship in sailing many kinds of boats behind him, particularly his hard trip in the *Fame*, with his sound ideas about boat design well formed, with his early business trials and the war past history, John Alden was now ready to put his ability and knowledge to work to bring to the yachting world a fleet of able vessels that would carry him to the forefront among designers.

VETSMART 395
4379 GUIDE MERIDIAN ST
BELLINGHAM   WA 98226

DATE: 04/25/98
MERN: 000000826974   TER#: 0001

S-A-L-E-S D-R-A-F-T

REF: 2816   BCH# 364
CD TYPE: VI
TR TYPE: PR
AMOUNT: $25.90

ACCT: 4024004669206400   EXP: 0699
AP: 063145
NAME: BRIGER F LARSSEN

I AGREE TO PAY ABOVE TOTAL AMOUNT
ACCORDING TO CARD ISSUER AGREEMENT
(MERCHANT AGREEMENT IF CREDIT VOUCHER)

THANK YOU FOR USING VISA

TOP COPY-MERCHANT BOTTOM COPY-CUSTOMER

4

The Golden Age of John Alden

... early success ... comes from William H. Taylor, longtime editor ... of *Yachting* ... article on Alden ... appeared in the January and February 1962 issues ... Taylor wrote:

He was back designing yachts immediately after the Armistice of 1918, and began building up what became a great organization, primarily in design but also in brokerage and insurance. John Robinson, who became a member of this organization in 1919, recalls that at that time the rest of the staff consisted of S.S. [Sam] Crocker and an efficient stenographer. Others who joined within the next few years were Clifford Swaine, William McNary, Charles MacGregor and Dwight L. Simpson.

The strength of the Alden organization over the years was no doubt due in part to the caliber of assistants John was able to attract and hold for greater or lesser periods. Some stayed with the firm for many years, others broke off and went into designing on their own. In addition to those mentioned above, some names that come to mind as onetime Alden associates are Winthrop L. Warner, Howard I. Chapelle, K. Aage Nielsen, Carl Alberg, Ralph Winslow, Fenwick Williams, Murray Peterson, Al Mason, Charles W. Wittholz, Charles Schock and others — an impressive cross-section of the profession.

All of these men, some self-taught and some with highly technical training, came to Alden because he was building a successful business and could provide work. They performed as draftsmen and subsequently designers, but always under the supervision of Alden, who knew what his boats should look like and saw to it that they were designed to his satisfaction.

John evidently treated the designers and draftsmen working for him with restraint. Aage Nielsen recalls: "One night when everyone had been working late, John came into the drafting room, twirling his No. 2 yellow pencil, as he always did, and spent about ten minutes looking over everybody's shoulder. Then he walked off without a word, but paused at the door of his office and said, 'And furthermore, please do not talk too much to Miss Craven in the outer office. It bothers somebody, I don't know who.' That was his way of giving somebody hell, and that's as tame as you can get it."

Most of the early designs from the Alden office were drawn by John himself, but after 1920 he did little work on the drawing board. He was the idea man, and his draftsmen and designers took it from there. His usual procedure was to sit down in his office with a client. The prospective boat buyer would describe what he had in mind. He'd say, "John, I like the lines of the *Minerva,*

21

but I want my boat maybe a bit longer. The schooner rig is fine, but I don't want to bother with topsails, and maybe you could lengthen the cabin house a bit." While the client was talking, John would quickly translate his words into a fairly accurate sketch. Almost inevitably the client would say, "That's just what I had in mind." After the satisfied customer departed, John would call in one of his draftsmen. "Bill, get out Number 145. It's pretty close to this sketch. Draw the ends out a foot and a half, bow and stern, and give her a little more sheer. Without topsails, you won't need quite so much weight below. Maybe use the same keel as you did on Number 126." So the design process was started. The draftsman laid down the lines, and from time to time John would come by and grunt approval or make changes with several quick strokes of his soft pencil. The draftsman did the computations and specifications but the lines always had to be pleasing to John's eye.

That was the way the design office operated. The team created many new boats, but a great number of the designs were refinements of some existing plan. John could always find ways to improve lines. In fact, he was a kind of compulsive "improver" who would take yachting magazines as they came into his office and at once start in with his pencil altering the published lines of other designers.

William H. Taylor continues:

> To an unusual degree, John Alden combined the talents of a sailor, yacht designer, and business man. A yachtsman once wrote Alden that he considered John's operations an important contribution to maritime interests, for he was designing safe, able and comfortable craft and getting them built within the means of many who otherwise could not afford to go cruising.
>
> Prices at the better yacht yards 40 years ago sound like a bargain basement today, but they kept many men with 1920 dollars from building new boats. John knew a number of yards in Maine building fishing boats. They had little experience with the niceties of yacht finish and joinerwork, but they turned out good, able, solid craft in which fishermen made a living offshore, fair weather and foul, and turned them out at prices the fishermen could pay. So Alden went to Maine, lined up a few of the best qualified yards, and began feeding them work, some for design clients and a few — more as time went on — for the Alden account, on speculation.
>
> In time the business originating from the Alden office got to be the main support of quite a few Down East builders. It pulled them through some hard times . . . . Dwight Simpson, from the Boston office, spent most of his time for many winters in Maine, looking in on the yards and supervising construction of Alden-designed yachts of all kinds and sizes.

In 1924, Alden hired a secretary named Ethel Bacon, who, in time, was virtually to take over the administra-

A rough sketch John Alden made on a restaurant place mat not long before he retired. Hank Meneely rescued the drawing and had John sign it. Note the concession to the fin keel and aft-hung rudder, and also the lower profile, which resembles that of the Sea Fox. *(Courtesy Henry T. Meneely)*

tion of Alden and Company. Ethel, trained at Boston University, had a sharp business sense and a boundless capacity for hard work. She quickly developed an understanding of the design business and more importantly an intuitive understanding of John Alden. She became aware of his distaste for business detail. She also recognized John's great ability to sell boats. Ethel made up for John's weaknesses and facilitated his use of his own strengths.

The man Ethel Bacon came to understand gave the impression of being hewn out of oak. His features were sharp. He was of medium height with powerful arms and legs and a barrellike chest, and his eyes were keen. In shoreside clothes and with his crew cut and graying hair he had a statesmanlike look, but he dressed more to his liking in faded khaki shorts and salt-encrusted sneakers.

Alden was shy at times and was embarrassed by large crowds. His sociability was marred by the fact that he was hard of hearing but hated to admit it. He avoided office parties and launchings, but on a boat he was anything but aloof.

One of John's trademarks was his absentmindedness, which might be explained as an intense preoccupation with boats. How else could a man of his intelligence carry forgetfulness so far? It is said that driving by an anchorage he would run right off the road while studying an interesting boat. He was known to land in a dinghy, throw the painter on the dock, and walk off without making it fast. On one occasion, he drove his car from Boston to Sakonnet, left it running all night, and boiled all the water out of the radiator. Next morning, he tried to correct the deficiency by pouring tea kettles of water into the oil fill. Another time, he was towing a dinghy on a trailer from Larchmont to Boston and arrived at his destination without the trailer. He retraced his route the next day and found the rig in a gas station.

The best Alden stories, though, were surely the ones he told himself. He had a couple of versions of his infamous trips to the supermarket. He would return with his groceries to the apartment he rented for a time on Beacon Hill, and he might store the toilet paper in the refrigerator and the tomato juice in the bathroom. Once, by John's account, he felt that he had suddenly become unusually hard of hearing. In distress, he went immediately to the Massachusetts Eye and Ear Infirmary, where the doctor pulled a cotton plug out of each of John's ears. John had put them in when he was working around a noisy engine, and he had forgotten to take them out. Such were the stories John told. Some who knew him well believe that his absentmindedness — at least to some extent — was more pretended than actual, but it really didn't matter. The stories were entertaining, and they became part of the man.

Ethel Bacon gradually assumed more and more administrative control in the Alden office, and, by the late 1930s, she was acting as general manager and comptroller. Ethel's rapid climb up the executive ladder gave her no delusions of grandeur. She made no attempt to run the business singlehanded. She was wise enough to know the decisions she could make and those that should be made by members of the technical staff or by Alden himself.

Alden built the first *Malabar* schooner for himself in 1921 and then built one a year, ending with *Malabar X* in 1930. There were three additional *Malabars: Malabar XI,* built in 1937, was a yawl; *Malabar XII,* a ketch, was designed in 1939; and *Malabar XIII,* another ketch, was built in 1945. These vessels are treated in detail in Chapter 5, but it is important to note here that the

Malabar name and look became synonymous with Alden and the kind of boats he designed, and this had considerable impact on the success of the whole Alden operation. The *Malabars* made headlines, and John's reputation grew.

In the late 1920s and the 1930s, business surged in the Alden office. Alden designs were in great demand, and the crew worked overtime turning them out. (John hung a sign in the office that described the state of affairs with his characteristic droll sense of humor: "The work may be hard, but the hours are long.") As mentioned, John's boats became popular at least partly because the price of the Maine-built hulls was within the reach of many cruising sailors who could not afford goldplaters from yards such as Herreshoff (Bristol, Rhode Island) or Nevins (City Island, New York). So Alden not only influenced design by producing the most important type of offshore boat for a period of years, but also he had the right product at a time when yachtsmen were turning their eyes seaward to deeper water and broader horizons. Some people theorized that Navy veterans of World War I had come home with a newfound love of the sea and the confidence to get afloat on their own. It has also been argued that Alden himself generated much of the new interest in going offshore in well-found cruising boats with his own exploits at sea and his boundless enthusiasm and dedication to sailing. Whatever the reason, there was a marked upsurge in offshore cruising and long-distance racing, and Alden supplied the kind of boats that were wanted. The drafting room ground out the seagoing sailers in all sizes, including six schooners over 100 feet long and two three-masters about 150 feet long.

Alden was very fussy about rigging and worked hard to improve it. He introduced wire halyards with tackles and later winches to keep the luffs of sails taut, and he developed a method of getting a flat trim on a fisherman staysail so it would be efficient on the wind. He accomplished this by using wire halyards and rigging jackstays on the foremast on which the luff of the sail was set.

John gave his boats a trial run, whenever possible, before delivery. He checked out every detail of hull and rigging until he was satisfied the vessel was his kind of boat.

Clifford Swaine described one of these inspection runs, and, while it was on John's own boat, it was typical of the way he operated:

When *Malabar VIII* was finished, John, Tunk Stevens and Frank Cummins of Goudy and Stevens, and I went on a shakedown cruise for three days. On two of the days, John tried her out in every way possible. On the

The Alden company staff, probably circa 1940. Front row (left to right): Fred Wakelin (broker); Emmons Alexander (broker); Alden; Dwight Simpson; Sam Wetherill. Middle row: Jack Curtiss (broker); not identified; not identified; Ethel Bacon; not identified; Helen Craven; Emmy Curtiss; George Colley (inspector of commercial craft). Back row: not identified; Frank Mather (draftsman); Carl Alberg; Bill McNary; Cliff Swaine; Fenwick Williams. (Courtesy Carl Alberg)

third day, a miserable one, John spent all the time below to see how a timid guest or wife would fare. When we looked in on him, he had the floorboards up and was cleaning shavings out of the bilge.

Evidently arrangements below in the *Malabar VIII* were satisfactory, especially in the galley. Hank Meneely sailed in her with John in a Gibson Island Race and recalls:

We had a cook who was the most fantastic artist in the galley I have ever been shipmates with. Nothing stopped him from producing gourmet meals on that trip. The first night out I don't remember the main course except that it was something you would not expect to get on a sailing vessel in a race at sea. But for dessert, we had nothing less than baked Alaska, which was prepared up forward on that schooner. In fact, I remember hearing the cook grinding the hand freezer when he made his own ice cream for that delectable dish.

Well, after the meal, John said to the rest of us, "This absolutely cannot go on. It's going to kill me and not do you fellows any good either. There's only one way to

cope with a situation like this and that is go on a hunger strike. So tomorrow night when he comes in with his dessert, don't touch it." We all harkened to these words and agreed that we would strike against the cook.

So, the following night, I remember, our main course was one of the most beautifully cooked roasts of beef you ever saw and with all the fixings. After we virtually demolished everything, the cook cleared the table. Shortly thereafter he came in with a large platter and set it down in the middle of the cabin table. It turned out to be a strawberry shortcake such as had never been cooked before. With thick cream the cook had written across the top, "Malabar VIII." It was a beautiful thing to behold. John Alden had two helpings and we knocked off the rest of it. I don't think we saved any for the cook. That's how we had our hunger strike. Eventually, we fired the cook down in the Chesapeake because John just couldn't live that way.

Throughout the 1920s and into the 1930s, Alden schooners dominated the burgeoning sport of ocean racing. It was the golden age of "John O'Boston," as he came to be known. In his personal life, though, success was interrupted by another unworkable marriage. In

Three Alden schooners hauled for the winter in the early 1930s. Left to right: Mattakeeset *(Number 449);* Rogue *(Number 390-C); and* Malabar X *(Number 453). (Courtesy Mrs. John Robinson)*

1927, Alden married Evelyn Dinan. They were divorced, then they remarried and had a son, John Taylor Alden, in 1935. Again they were divorced, and Alden remained single, and at times lonely, until 1946, when he married Virginia Harris. She was with him the rest of his life. John Taylor Alden never took to sailing and eventually gravitated to Vermont, where he became a state representative.

When Alden achieved his great sweep of the 1932 Bermuda Race, the winds of change in ocean racing yacht design were already making up. Olin Stephens's yawl *Dorade,* which had won the Transatlantic and Fastnet races in 1931, was the winner in Class B. In the next thrash to the Onion Patch in 1934, Rudolph Schaefer's sloop *Edlu,* a new Stephens creation, led the fleet, followed by *Water Gypsy* and *Grenadier,* the still-competitive Alden schooners. The storm-wracked passage to Bermuda in 1936 produced a winner for designer Philip Rhodes, who had turned out the sloop *Kirawan* for Robert P. Baruch. Olin Stephens scored again in 1938 with the *Baruna,* a 72-foot yawl he designed for Henry C. Taylor. During this time, Stephens had produced another yawl, the *Stormy Weather,* which won the 1936 Transatlantic Race to Norway by a wide margin.

Alden and Hank Meneely were prowling around the Nevins yard at City Island, New York, one day, when, as Meneely recalls the incident:

We came upon a handsome hull hauled out and covered for the winter. John looked her over with care. He had a way of looking at a boat by taking positions a little away from her, then sighting along his hand in some manner

so that he could better understand the curves in the hull. He would study the boat from other angles until he could formulate the complete boat in his mind. After going through all this on this particular boat, he said to me, "In my opinion, a better design would be impossible to achieve." The boat turned out to be the *Stormy Weather.*

The duel between Alden and Stephens was brought into focus on the runs of the New York Yacht Club cruise. In 1936, Alden's *Mandoo II* showed up better than the *Stormy Weather,* but in 1937 and 1938, she ran neck and neck with the new Stephens boat, *Edlu II.* The Alden-designed *Tioga Too* dominated the division for cruising sloops and yawls on the 1939 squadron runs and also in the annual regatta of that year.

Alden designs continued to place in the money, but a new breed of ocean racer began to take over. The yacht type was replacing the type evolved from the fisherman in blue-water competition, and while the Alden operation continued to design hundreds of rugged and successful boats, some of which continued to win major ocean races, Alden boats no longer dominated ocean racing as they had in previous years.

Some top skippers turned to the newer winning designs, just as they once had turned to the *Malabars.* They turned to Olin Stephens perhaps more than any other. Stephens was another largely self-taught designer, although he studied for one year at M.I.T. As a very young man he had asked Alden for a job and had offered a design for a 6-meter as a sample of his work. Alden had little interest in meter boats designed to the International Rule, and he didn't hire Stephens. Somewhat later, after Stephens had sailed to Bermuda with Alden in the *Malabar IX* and also had raced with him in the Q boat *Hope,* John asked Olin to join his company, but by that time the young man was committed elsewhere.

Stephens said that what was happening in the 1930s was not new at all, but rather "a recognition of other traditions, a reversion to the Herreshoff type." Whereas Alden predicated his designs on a certain amount of inside ballast, Stephens adopted the idea of all-outside ballast. In contrast to an Alden hull, Stephens drew deeper sections with slacker bilges. He specified lighter construction and used steam-bent frames instead of sawn frames. He tried to plan cleaner decks and used the marconi rig.

Stephens's thinking was influenced partly by the fact that Robert N. Bavier won the 1924 Bermuda Race with the *Memory,* a Herreshoff-designed New York Forty that was rigged as a yawl. She was definitely of the yacht type, being fine-lined and deep. Two books that also helped shape Stephens's early ideas were *Yacht Cruising* and *Yacht Navigation and Voyaging,* written by a British yachtsman, Claud Worth. Worth believed in fine-lined but able vessels of a type that appealed to Stephens. Worth arrived at his models by giving the very deep, narrow English cutter less draft and more beam, but his *Tern III* and *Tern IV* were still considerably finer-lined than was a typical Alden schooner. Extensive racing in 6-meters was also an important influence on Stephens, and Olin has described the *Dorade* as an "overgrown 6-meter."

These were some of the influences that led Stephens in a new direction in design, but there were other factors that altered the balance toward the yacht-type ocean racer. While Alden survived the crash of 1929 quite handily, the Depression backwinded the sport of sailing. The Maine shipyards were no longer turning out Alden schooners at bargain prices. As the economy finally improved, Olin Stephens was the innovative designer, just as Alden had been after World War I. The *Dorade, Stormy Weather,* and *Edlu* caught the spotlight, and a new era in ocean racing got underway.

World War II brought other major changes to John G. Alden and Company. A neighboring design firm, Eldredge-McInnis, Inc., was awarded more large defense contracts than they were staffed to handle. Walter McInnis went to his friend John Alden and asked him to collaborate on the projects. Alden was not interested. He didn't like the type of craft that were to be built, and he resented government supervision. McInnis recalls a meeting with the military brass in Washington, which both he and John attended. While the vessels needed for the war effort were described,

A formal portrait of John Alden. (Courtesy Chester M. and Harriet Sawtelle)

Alden traced the lines of schooners on the tabletop with his forefinger.

McInnis, a persistent Scotsman, finally overcame Alden's prejudices, however, and the two formed a separate partnership for war work. To cope with this effort, the technical division at the Alden company had to be reorganized. Within a few months' time, the staff of two draftsmen was enlarged to 90 skilled engineers, designers, and others. Ethel Bacon handled this expansion program with remarkable skill and a minimum of traumas. Ethel was also responsible for financing the business through bank loans and through collections from the government and other creditors so that the greatly enlarged payroll could be met. Administratively, she ran the show, negotiating contracts with the government and dealing with investigative and regulatory agencies. Alden, as proprietary owner, had veto power over her decisions, but he never had to exercise it. His professional pride and reputation were at stake, but he had complete confidence in Ethel's business ability and was never embarrassed by her decisions.

During this war period, Dwight Simpson and Clifford Swaine supervised the technical staff and the production

John at the helm of Malabar XIII *during the 1946 Bermuda Race. (Courtesy Chester M. and Harriet Sawtelle)*

of designs and engineering data. Since many ships were built from each set of plans, there is no accurate estimate of the number of wartime vessels built to Alden designs. One source says 700. Another puts the value of these vessels at $300,000,000. In any case, working both on cost-plus and fixed-price contracts, the company made more money than it had in custom yachts. The various types of vessels designed for the Navy included a 183-foot salvage vessel, a 160-foot rescue tug, mine-sweepers, transports, and harbor tugs.

In addition to the designs for the U.S. government, the Alden office turned out plans for a 176-foot tug for the Soviet Union. Fifteen ships were built from this design. There was also considerable emphasis on designing commercial vessels during the war, including designs for tugs and draggers ranging in length from 45 feet to 150 feet.

The Korean War brought contracts from the U.S. Army Transportation Corps for three 222-foot self-propelled barges, one for dry cargo, one for liquid cargo, and one for refrigerated cargo. The Army also ordered 57 steel harbor tugs, all of them 45 feet long. This time Donald G. Parrot assembled a staff of 80 men, and Clifford Swaine and Ethel Bacon coordinated operations with the government. At about the same time, the U.S. Coast Guard ordered 18 patrol boats, all 95-footers, and once again the design office was carrying its maximum load.

During the late 1940s and early 1950s, John Alden's active interest in his business began to wane. A certain disenchantment probably started during World War II, when his office was dominated by government and commercial design work with few, if any, sailing vessels on the drawing boards. His executive staff assumed more and more responsibility, and, without very much to do, John became a figurehead.

There was no diminution, however, of his stature in the world of sailing. In the 1946 Bermuda Race, which was noteworthy only for the lack of wind, John placed fourth in Class B with his *Malabar XIII.* In 1947, he bought the *Abenaki,* a schooner he had designed in 1930. He modernized her rig to improve her rating according to the Cruising Club rule and finished second in Class C in the 1950 Bermuda Race.

Alden still had no fear of a breeze of wind. On the return trip from Bermuda in the *Abenaki,* as Bill Anderson recalls, "A strong front came through at the northerly edge of the Gulf Stream. At one point I had the watch and, carrying the fisherman staysail, we were taking deck loads of water. With the breeze freshening, I

John at the Morse yard in Thomaston, Maine, in 1955, just prior to his retirement. The occasion was the christening of Bill Anderson's ketch Windsong *(Alden design number 903). "The launching party was a great success," Anderson recalls. (Courtesy Chester M. and Harriet Sawtelle)*

went below and woke John, who always slept with sail bags banked around him. I said, 'John, it's freshening. May I hand the fisherman?' John rolled over and said, 'Call me when it moderates, and we'll get on some more sail.' "

Alden was 70 years old when he sailed his last race to the Onion Patch in 1954 in the *Minots Light,* a ketch he had designed for Clarence Warden in 1950. He fully expected to take charge of the boat, but he had trouble getting around the deck and the owner would not let him take the wheel. For the great ocean racing helmsman, this was a devastating experience.

A year later, Donald Parrot came to Bill Anderson, who had sailed with Alden and had owned Alden boats, and asked if Anderson would join him and a third man, Joseph Whitney, in purchasing the Alden Company. The three bought the business.

John retired, and he and his wife, Virginia, lived in Sakonnet in the summer, where John occasionally sailed one of the Sakonnet One-Designs he had designed. During the cold season, they lived in Winter Park, Florida.

At Winter Park, he died on March 3, 1962.

Part Two

---

100 Designs of John Alden
by Richard Henderson

5

The Malabars

As recently as the early 1700s, there was a sizable hook-shaped spit of land jutting eastward into the Atlantic off the end of Monomoy Point at the elbow of Cape Cod, Massachusetts. This spit gradually eroded away and became Bearse Shoal, but while still above water it was known as Cape Malabar. John Alden found the vanished spit on an old chart and apparently was taken with the mellifluous ring of the name. It was a part of local history yet sounded exotic (there is a Malabar Coast in India), and Alden felt the name would be a fitting one for a schooner he designed and had built for himself in 1921. This boat was the first of a series of schooners named *Malabar* that were destined to bring fame of legendary proportions to themselves and their designer.

In an article written for the October 1928 issue of *The Sportsman* magazine, Alden had some interesting comments about the beginning of the series:

> The first of my *Malabars* has the fisherman as the basis of her design. The present one [*Malabar IX*], together with many similar boats turned out by my office, though essentially intended for coastwise cruising, with the occasional ocean race in view, is a far cry from the first one.
>
> What then is the Malabar type? Why and how was it

developed? Let us first look at the true fisherman as exemplified in the Gloucesterman, which I have always admired and with a few of which I had something to do years ago. Simple in section, all her ballast inside, short ended, low sided for ease of handling dories, beamy to gain capacity, fast and able but never quite at her best until loaded, easy to build and therefore cheap — we find many qualities here desirable for the yachtsman.

> Let us also look at the *Lloyd W. Berry* — now on the Pacific Coast as *Zingara* — a sixty-foot schooner designed or rather modeled by Charles A. Morse of Friendship sloop fame, and built by C.A. Morse and Son at Thomaston, Maine . . . . She is a slightly modified fisherman and a fairly successful yacht.*

Everyone interested in boats has a dream ship of some kind, vague though he may be as to just what it should be. It was in just such a position that I found myself at the close of the War [World War I]. To complicate matters, my pocketbook was decidedly low. Nevertheless, I started on a hunt to acquire that dream ship.

Recalling the ease with which the *Lloyd W. Berry* handled and how well she sailed, my mind became fixed

---

* *The* Lloyd W. Berry *was influenced not only by the Gloucesterman but also by the round-bowed Friendship sloops that Morse modeled and built. She made a celebrated double crossing of the Atlantic in 1921 and 1922, weathering a severe winter gale on the notorious Bay of Biscay. At one point her all-amateur crew was forced to chop away her bulwarks with axes to clear her decks of ice.*

The Lloyd W. Berry, *a schooner that influenced the* Malabars, *at the C.A. Morse and Son yard. (Courtesy Roger Morse)*

Malabar I *anchored near the C.A. Morse and Son yard. Her white rail accentuates her high bow and sweeping sheer. Note the jib set in stops. (Courtesy Roger Morse)*

on the schooner rig and I wandered Down East to Morse's yard hoping to find some small fisherman that could be converted at small cost. My greeting was anything but encouraging. As Mr. Morse put it, he was "too busy to talk." He further volunteered the information that it would probably be cheaper to build than fix up an old boat. Disappointed by further endeavors to interest him, I gave up and walked off. I was half way up the hill when I was hailed to "come back here." I returned and Mr. Morse took me into his inner office to "thrash it out." The result was that I ordered a schooner from him, the 41½-foot-overall *Malabar I.* This had been far from my intentions, but, being the result, I hastened back to my office to draw the plans.

Alden had designed several rigs and interiors for Morse, beginning as early as 1912, and the two men came to a good understanding. The first five *Malabars* were built by Morse, mostly on a cost-plus basis without formal contracts. The usual arrangement was for the two men to discuss the plans, and after Morse agreed to build, Alden would say, "Let me know when you will need some money." Apparently these informal agreements worked well, although on later jobs Morse would quote a price for the hull, spars, and keel, and the rest of the work was done on a cost-plus basis.

The first three *Malabars* were quite similar in concept, even though the "Two" and the "Three" were just a bit sleeker and yachtier in appearance than the "One." Aside from the fisherman influence, there were several considerations that affected the design of those three early schooners. To begin with, Alden wanted a boat he could sail alone or with just a few friends, and this meant a simple, easily handled rig, a hull of fairly modest size, and accommodations laid out for a small amateur crew. Additionally, the designer insisted on an able boat that could be taken offshore shorthanded in safety. As he put it, "I wanted a cruising boat in which I could go anywhere along shore or off the coast, that would stay at sea in almost any weather, and at the same time, would not be too much to handle alone in case of necessity." Another consideration was stiffness. Before the first *Malabar,* Alden had owned an attractive, fast sloop named *Senta,* but she sailed on her ear, much to her owner's annoyance, so he was determined that his schooners would not be tender.

The original *Malabar* was an able-looking craft with short ends, a high bow, pronounced sheer, and a long curving keel, cut away forward but with considerable drag aft. She had two cabin trunks — primarily to allow extra-strong partners for the mainmast — and bulwarks to protect the crew and to prevent lines from washing overboard. The Alden records show her dimensions as

41 feet 3 inches length on deck, 31 feet 10¼ inches length on the waterline, and 11 feet 7⅛ inches beam.* Curiously, her draft is shown as 4 feet 6 inches in the records, but she actually drew about 6 feet 2 inches. Her design number was 155.

Each of the boat's two cabins had a pair of transoms, above which were folding pipe berths. There was also a fairly large fo'c's'le containing the head and another pipe berth. The only real drawback to the layout was a lack of standing headroom in the galley, which was located under the flush deck between cabin trunks. A good galley seat alleviated that problem. The forward cabin trunk was quite short to allow space for a dinghy on deck. No engine was installed, because the designer said he had "better use for the room."

The modern sailor doesn't often consider the gaff-rigged schooner handy for singlehanding, but the first *Malabar*'s bald-headed rig was really not difficult to handle. Although the mainsail was 523 square feet, Alden claimed it was "not too large for one man to hoist easily." Of course, the foresail and jib were much smaller, 284 and 156 square feet respectively, and all three sails were boomed and sheeted to travelers to make them self-tending. Lazyjacks, especially those for the jib, simplified lowering and furling sail. Alden put the foremast far forward because he liked a large, powerful foresail on a schooner yacht, which, unlike a commercial fisherman, does not have to spend long periods of time hove-to. He wrote that *Malabar* "handles perfectly under foresail alone, beating to windward under it in light weather," and he claimed too that she was well balanced and handled easily under mainsail and jib. The lack of running backstays simplified handling, although a pair for the mainmast might have been desirable as an extra precaution during heavy weather sailing. When the weather made it necessary to jog slowly, however, the boat behaved well and made little leeway under reefed foresail alone, and then there was no need for runners. Any forward pull of the foresail would be counteracted sufficiently by the spring stay, the shrouds, and the downward pull of the sheets.

Malabar was not as close-winded as *Senta,* but given the right sailing conditions she must have been fast

---

* With a very few exceptions, the dimensions given in this book are designed dimensions; changes in ballasting can alter a boat's draft and waterline length by several inches. Malabar I began with 3,156 pounds of outside ballast and a similar amount inside, but she found her best sailing trim with 8,650 pounds of inside ballast and a waterline length of 32 feet 6 inches.

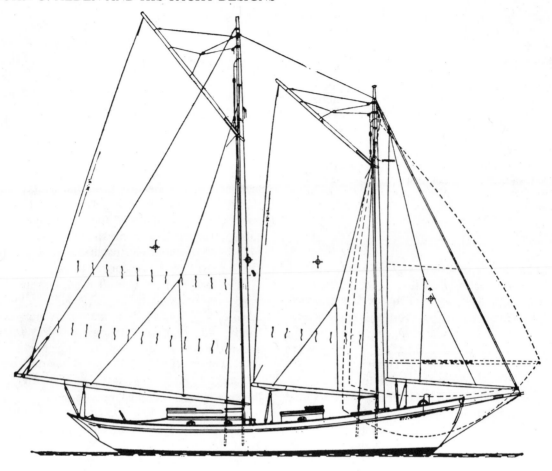

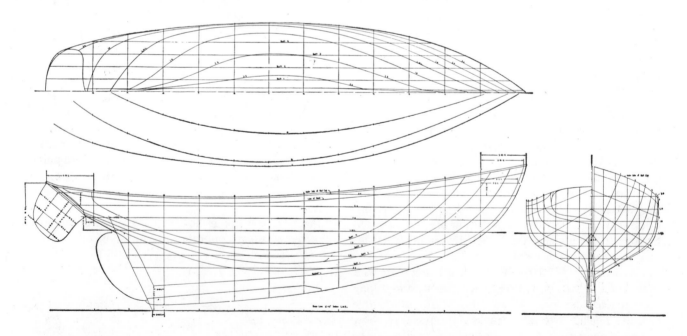

Although the long overhanging main boom and bowsprit of Malabar I *are not the safest features for singlehanding, the bald-headed, self-tending rig is a good one for a lone sailor. Dwight Simpson described the first* Malabar*'s lines as "a symphony of curves which delight the eye of a yachtsman."* (Yachting, *January 1962)*

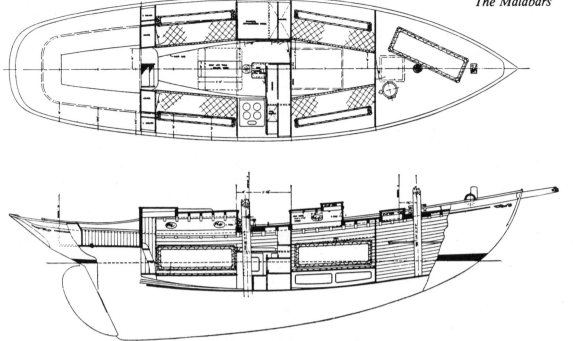

The first Malabar*'s cabin plan. Her two deck houses add to the degree of separation of her cabins. "When doing night sailing," Alden wrote, "it leaves the after cabin free for consulting charts, navigating, keeping the log, lighting one's pipe, etc., without disturbing the watch below who can occupy the forward cabin." (Yachting,* January 1962)

Looking at the first Malabar *under sail helps one understand why Alden called her (in 1934) the "most interesting" of the* Malabar*s. (Morris Rosenfeld photo)*

This photograph of Malabar I *shows a double-ended dory on deck. Somebody left the binnacle lid open. (Courtesy Mrs. John Robinson)*

enough; as *Damaris,* she was fourth in a fleet of 22 boats in the 1923 Bermuda Race. Alden achieved his primary design objectives, for she was certainly more comfortable and easier to handle than *Senta.* Despite the fact that she lived up to all that was expected of her, she was sold at the end of her first season. Thus began a routine for the following *Malabars.* During the 1920s, Alden built a new boat for himself almost every year. He would usually get an attractive offer for his old boat, and he seemed to thrive on planning dream ships, always feeling he could make minor improvements. As he put it, "A season's intimate living with one boat has shown me where to improve her or given me new lines to experiment with."

The second and third *Malabars* are actually only slight variations of the first. All three are similar in size and rig and alike in the concept of being cruisers that can be sailed singlehanded. *Malabars II* and *III* were built from the same lines, design number 162, and they are almost identical except in their accommodations and ballast. They both measure 41 feet 6 inches, by 32 feet, by 11 feet 3 inches, by 6 feet 2 inches. (For some unknown reason, however, the Alden records give *Malabar III* the same dimensions as the "One.")

The lines of all three schooners show fairly powerful hulls with fine entrances to cut through a chop and full quarters that give good bearing when heeled. The bilges are moderately slack but rather firm at the turn, especially in the Number 162 design. Minor differences between *Malabar I* and her immediate successors are that the "Two" and the "Three" had their bows drawn out a little and their sheers slightly flattened, but the greatest difference is that the later boats were given a single, long, unbroken cabin trunk.

The single cabin trunk allows more room and a more practical layout below. *Malabar II* has a sizable main cabin aft with two transoms and two quarter berths. Forward, there is an enclosed head with a hanging locker opposite, then the galley, and up in the bow, a couple of pipe berths. *Malabar III* has almost the same arrangement except that the port quarter berth has a bulkhead around it to make a small, private after stateroom. Like her predecessors, *Malabar III* had no engine, but she was provided with a shaft log and propeller aperture (closed in) in case a future owner wanted auxiliary power.

Alden sailed *Malabar II* from the C.A. Morse yard "up" to Boston in April 1922. Herb Stone was aboard for part of that maiden voyage, and he wrote in the July issue of *Yachting* magazine that the boat had surprising room below for her size. Referring to her ability in any weather, he said, "She was hove-to in a strong southeaster some 15 hours between Thomaston and Cape Ann, and under reefed foresail she fore reached slightly all night, making very little leeway, so that the next morning when the wind slacked off so that she could be put on her course again, she had made only some 5 miles leeway." *Malabar II* showed very well in her first long race, finishing third in the Brooklyn Challenge Cup in July 1922.

In 1955, the "Two" was given an entirely new hull, identical to the original and built on top of the original iron keel. In the April 1956 issue of *Yachting* magazine, Exton Guckes wrote that the rig, fittings, steering gear, binnacle, interior joinerwork — everything that "felt like *Malabar* when you laid your hand on it in the middle of the night" — was transferred to the new hull. *Malabar II*'s reconstruction was done for Guckes (who owned the schooner from 1938 to 1964) almost single-

handedly by Elmer Collemer, a Camden, Maine, crafts-
man who could swing an adze with old-school precision.
Interestingly, when Guckes went to Alden for the lines,
John warned him that "old Charlie Morse built
Malabar for me, but he did pretty much as he pleased
and you may find he made a few changes here and
there." Indeed, Morse's changes, it turned out, had included increased headroom and slight alterations to the
interior layout and the locations of fittings.

Soon after the "Two" was finished, Guckes took her
on a four-month Atlantic-circle cruise, making a double
ocean crossing between the first of April and the beginning of the peak hurricane season near the end of July.
The cruise was a great success, and the schooner proved
so easy to handle that she was never reefed. It was only
necessary to lower one or two sails in heavy weather and
the boat would stay well balanced. Cruising Club of
America historian John Parkinson, Jr., wrote that if
Guckes had made this voyage before blue-water cruises
became so numerous, he "would have received the Blue
Water Medal for 1956."

Malabar II at anchor, her mainsail keeping her head to wind.
(Courtesy John G. Alden, Inc.)

Malabar II looking pretty much as she did when Alden sailed her from the Morse yard on April 15, 1922. Her contract price was $1,800. The gallows frame aft is a nice feature when that long-boomed mainsail needs to be reefed. (Morris Rosenfeld photo)

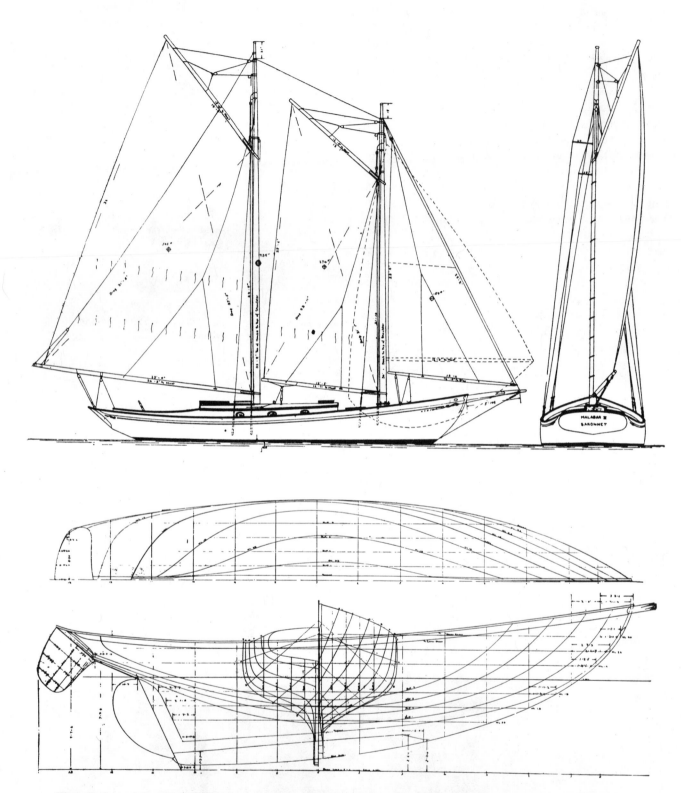

*The sail plans of the "Two" (shown here) and the "Three" are identical. With somewhat lighter hulls than the "One,"
Malabars II and III have a bit less canvas — 938 square feet. (Yachting, 1922) The "Two" and "Three" differ little
from the first Malabar in hull form. Their ends are a little longer, and they have slightly straighter sheer lines. The
"Three" has more of her ballast outside than the "Two." (The Rudder, May 1934)*

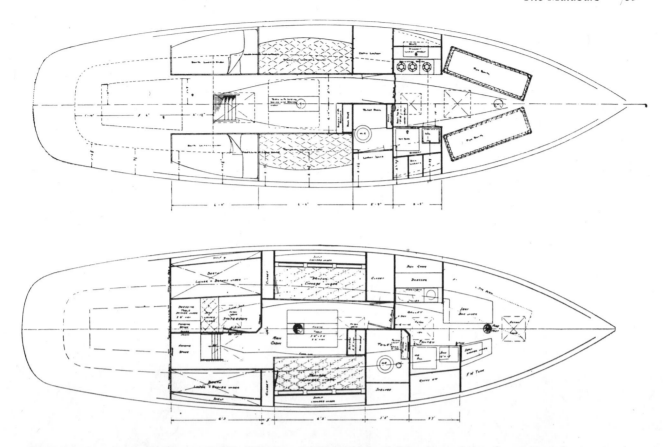

*With a single, unbroken cabin trunk, the "Two" and "Three" have full headroom below from companionway to galley. Note the small stateroom aft on the "Three." (*Yachting, *January 1922 and September 1922)*

Malabar III *reaching with her gollywobbler and making knots. (Edwin Levick photo. Courtesy Chester M. and Harriet Sawtelle)*

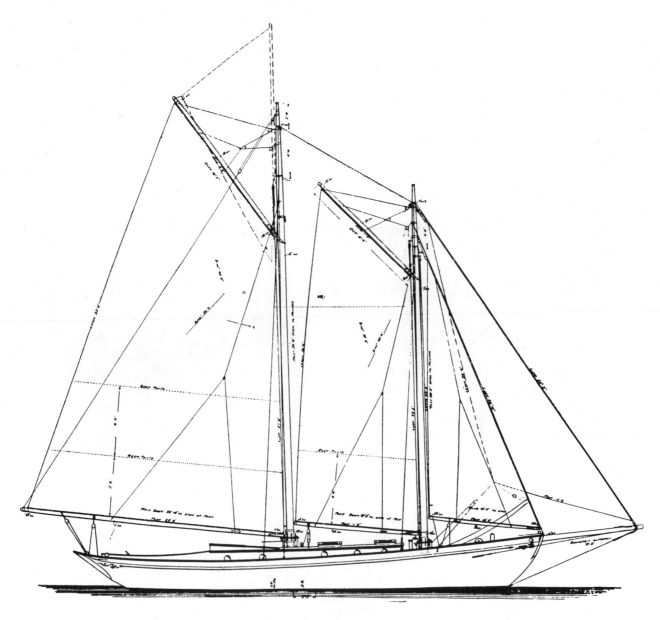

Malabar IV *and later schooners of the line were intended for some racing as well as cruising, so they have more sail. The* "Four" *was given 1,220 square feet.* (Yachting, *February 1923*)

Two additional sisters to *Malabars II* and *III* were built in 1922. One was ketch-rigged; the other, John Parkinson's schooner *Mary Ann,* finished fifth in the 1923 Bermuda Race.

The next major step in the evolution of this line of schooners came with *Malabar IV,* design number 205. She was based on quite a different concept, that of a boat that would be sailed with a crew, including a paid hand, and would be expected to compete seriously in ocean races.

John Alden lost his taste for singlehanding when he fell overboard while sailing alone across Massachusetts Bay in *Malabar III.* He went over the side up forward but somehow managed to catch hold of the boat near her main shrouds and haul himself back aboard. It was a close call. Although the designer made light of the experience by saying that his boat had turned around and picked him up, he reflected seriously on the incident and subsequently staged a number of man-overboard drills. It is interesting that when he deliberately repeated his fall over the side with crew aboard, he could never haul himself back aboard unassisted. This exercise demonstrated not only the power of the adrenalin gland but also at least one risk in singlehanding a boat of moderate freeboard in open waters. Then too, Alden often wanted to leave his boat in one port and meet her in another. These considerations convinced him it would be desirable to carry a paid hand.

Of course, the decision to have a professional living

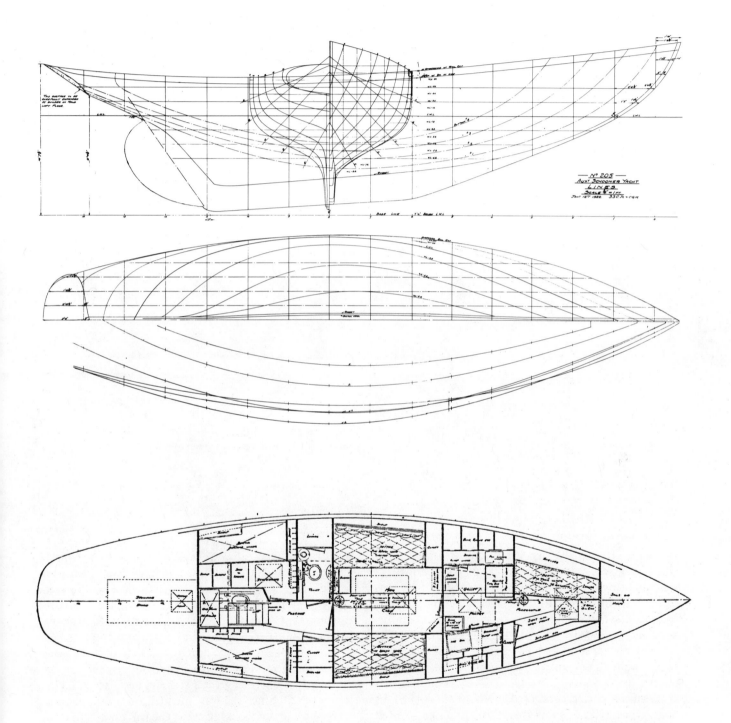

The lines of Malabar IV, *initialed by Sam Crocker and Charles MacGregor, are a bit finer than those of her predecessors, showing a narrower stern. (Courtesy John G. Alden, Inc.) Her cabin plan reflects the decision to have a paid hand live on board.* (Yachting, *June 1923)*

Malabar IV *anchored off the C.A. Morse and Son yard. (Courtesy John G. Alden, Inc.)*

A lee-quarter shot of Malabar IV *taken by Alden's associate John Robinson, Jr. That's Alden at the helm. (Courtesy Mrs. John Robinson)*

on board affected the size and layout of *Malabar IV.* She was given a length on deck of 47 feet with a waterline length of 35 feet 6 inches, a beam of 12 feet, and a draft of 6 feet 11 inches, according to the Alden records. She had complete quarters for the hand up forward and a good-size galley just abaft the fo'c's'le. The saloon with transoms and dining table was placed amidships, while the owner's stateroom, a head, and a quarter berth were aft.

Alden was always concerned about the stability of his boats, for he liked sailing reasonably level, and he felt strongly that his schooners performed better on their feet. Furthermore, he realized that it takes a lot of extra effort to sail a boat that is easily overburdened; conse-

quently, he was always experimenting with ballast changes. By and large, each succeeding *Malabar* seemed to have a greater percentage of her ballast on the keel and/or more total ballast and a higher ballast-displacement ratio. For instance, the first *Malabar,* in her best sailing trim, carried only about a third of her weight in ballast, but *Malabar IV* had a ballast-displacement ratio of approximately 49 percent.

Malabar IV needed greater stability because she had a lot more sail. Since she was intended for a fair amount of racing and carried a full crew, she was given an extra-long bowsprit, two headsails (she was the first *Malabar* to carry a forestaysail), and a main topsail. The area of her four lowers was 1,220 square feet. In addition, of course, she carried a fisherman staysail, gollywobbler, and spinnaker. All these sails made her somewhat of a workshop, but she handled easily and balanced well under main, foresail, and forestaysail.

This boat proved remarkably competitive, winning eight races in eight starts in 1923, her first season. One of these victories was an impressive win over a fleet of 22 boats in the first New London–Bermuda Race. Thus, *Malabar IV* became the first boat of that line to gain wide recognition, and she started her designer down the road to fame as an ocean racer. According to Clifford Swaine, the "Four" was always Alden's favorite *Malabar*.

Because of her success, a number of sailors called *Malabar IV* a racing machine and attributed her speed to light construction. This annoyed Alden, because he took pride in the fact that his boats had heavy scantlings. *Malabar IV* was no exception, although she did have bent oak frames, which need not be as heavy as sawn frames, and her ballast-displacement ratio indicates that she was comparatively lighter than her forerunners. Nevertheless, she was exceptionally strong, and she was no lightweight at 41,000 pounds final displacement. Her white oak keel was seven inches deep and 14 inches wide for most of its length. Her oak frames were 1⅞ by 2¾ inches, and they were set on 12-inch centers with a 2½ by 9 inch oak floor at every frame. Floors were through-bolted to the keel and to each frame. Longitudinal support was provided by a bilge stringer 1⅛ by 6 inches, a clamp of the same size, and a shelf 2⅞ by 4 inches. Planking was 1⅜-inch yellow pine. The deck was 1½-inch white pine. Deck beams of oak, 1⅞ by 2⅞ inches, were spaced on 12-inch centers. The hull was further reinforced with vertical and thwartships tie rods.

Only one sister was built. Originally named *Felisi* and now *Toddywax,* she participated in the 1982 Classic Yacht Regatta at Newport, Rhode Island, but shortly thereafter was stolen from her mooring.

The "Four" had such winning ways that few changes were made to *Malabar V.* Her ends were lengthened slightly and she was given a bit more freeboard for dryness, while a larger percentage of her ballast was assigned to the keel. (Cliff Swaine says that Alden figured he made a mistake drawing out the bow of the "Five" without sufficiently lengthening the stern.) Otherwise, the two schooners were much alike, even in their accommodations. There was little difference in rig, except that the "Five" was given slightly more sail area, but with a smaller topsail. A departure from Alden's previous thinking is evidenced by the fact that *Malabar*

V was the first of the series to be built with an engine, a Scripps F-4 driving a feathering propeller. This schooner's design number is 215. She measures 49 feet, by 36 feet 9 inches, by 12 feet, by 7 feet 3 inches. One sister ship was built for a Swedish owner.

Like her immediate predecessor, the "Five" did very well racing, winning eight out of eight starts in 1924, but her record is somewhat less impressive because she did not sail in the prestigious Bermuda Race that year.

Alden's longtime associate, Dwight Simpson, who had a hand in the designing of the *Malabar* schooners after the "Three" and wrote a series of articles about the *Malabars* for *The Rudder* in 1934, told an amusing story about the origin of *Malabar VI.* He wrote that he and Alden were sitting in the cabin of *Malabar V* with blueprints spread before them, planning the sixth schooner in the series, when the professional captain, who had been listening to the conversation, voiced his opinion that the "Five" was just about perfect and could not be improved. Alden explained that the new boat would be larger, faster, abler, and more comfortable. Captain Pendleton slowly but reluctantly agreed with each of the designer's points and then said, "Yes, she may be all you say, Mr. Alden, but by gorry, she won't be no better boat." Simpson wrote that, about a year later, after the new schooner had been built and well tried, he and Alden were pretty much in agreement with the captain.

Malabar VI, design number 248, was the first of the series to be built by a yard other than C.A. Morse and Son. She and the next four *Malabars* were built in the Boothbay (Maine) area, and all were constructed by Hodgdon Brothers except *Malabar VII,* which was built by Reed-Cook. Measuring 52 feet 3 inches, by 38 feet, by 12 feet, by 7 feet 4 inches, *Malabar VI* is no beamier than the "Five," but she has longer and finer ends. She was given a higher percentage of outside ballast and a slightly loftier rig with a bit more sail. This boat was not really campaigned, but she proved fast and did well in occasional races. Eight sisters were built. One, named *Black Goose* and owned by W. Findlay Downs, won Class B in the 1926 Bermuda Race.

Malabar VI was given more length than the "Five," primarily to make more room for accommodations, and her layout below as well as the break in the cabin trunk well abaft the mainmast is a departure from the previous *Malabars.* The trunk's break permits a deck-level companionway not far abaft amidships, leaving space for a sizable owner's stateroom aft. This aspect of the layout proved most successful, and it was used quite often on Alden boats. Not so successfully arranged was

Continued on page 49

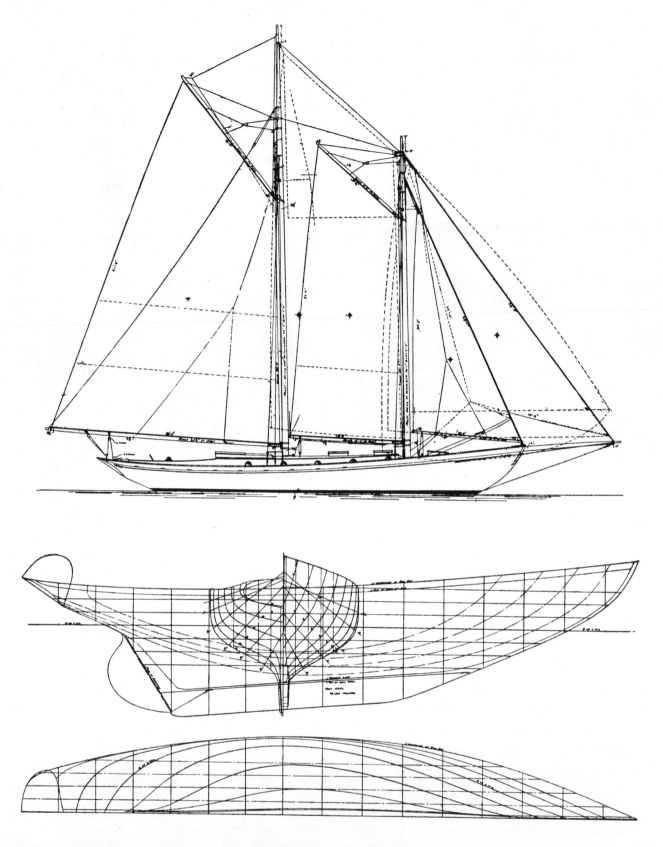

Like her immediate predecessor, Malabar V can carry a topsail and two headsails. Her 12,450 pounds of outside ballast — 3,450 pounds more than that of the "Four" — keeps her stiff under the 1,307 square feet of sail in her four lowers. (Yachting, February 1924) The lines of Malabar V *are similar to those of the "Four." "The only difference in the model of the two boats," Alden wrote the editors of* Yachting *magazine in 1923, "is that the moulds forward of amidships are each spaced two inches further apart, making the new boat about two feet longer overall and 18 inches longer on the waterline." (The Rudder, June 1934)*

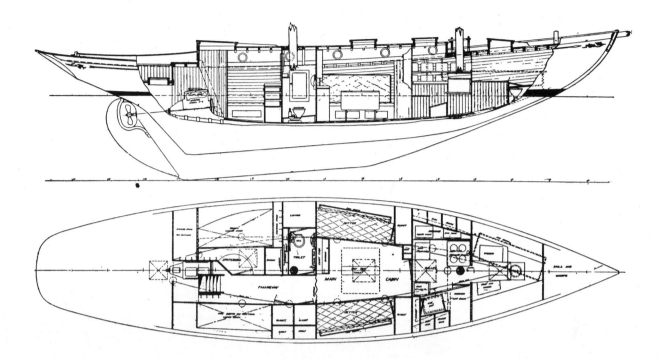

Malabar V's cabin plan is similar to the "Four's," but there is more locker space and a bigger main cabin, and the fo'c's'le is fitted with a pipe berth. For the first time, Alden installed an engine in a Malabar, *but he said he probably wouldn't use it. He claimed he simply wanted to demonstrate that the performance of his boat would not be hurt by the propeller.* (Yachting, February 1924)

Malabar V *climbs a sea. (Courtesy Mrs. John Robinson)*

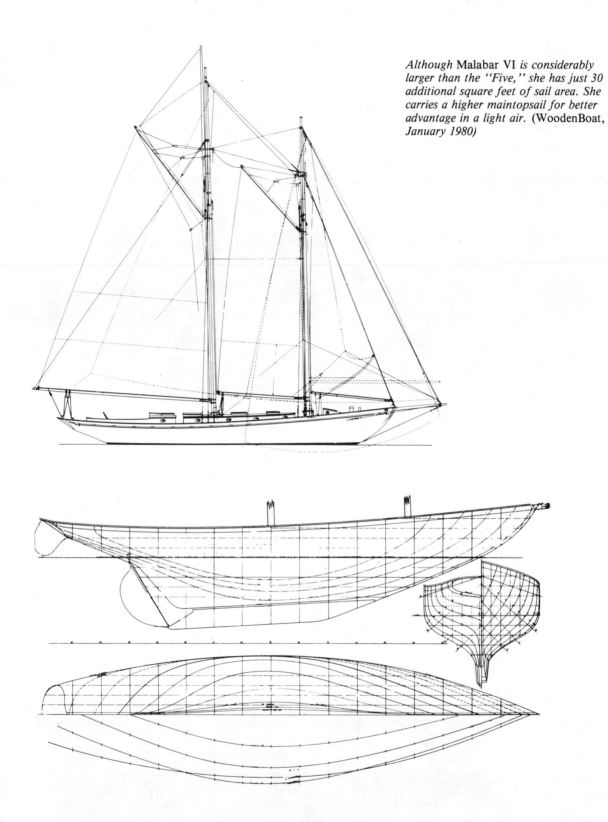

Although Malabar VI *is considerably larger than the "Five," she has just 30 additional square feet of sail area. She carries a higher maintopsail for better advantage in a light air.* (WoodenBoat, *January 1980)*

The lines of Malabar VI *show longer and finer ends than those of her forerunners. She has a harder bilge than the "Five" and still more of her ballast outside.* (WoodenBoat, *January 1980)*

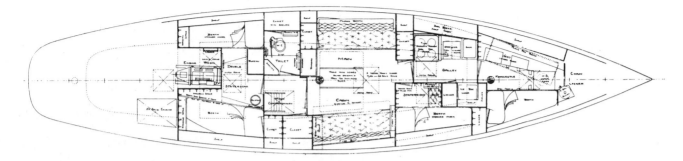

With two cabin trunks and her companionway closer to amidships, the "Six" has a large and private after stateroom. The small stateroom opposite the galley, however, was not successful. (Yachting, *February 1925*)

Malabar VI *sailing full and by carries both her foresail and golly. (Morris Rosenfeld photo. Courtesy Chester M. and Harriet Sawtelle)*

Right: *Looking forward on board* Malabar VI. *The port-side sliding hatch gives access to the engine room. (Courtesy John G. Alden, Inc.)* **Below left:** *The cockpit of* Malabar VI *lacks seats along the sides. (Edwin Levick photo. Courtesy John G. Alden, Inc.)* **Below right:** *John Alden perched on the windward coaming of* Malabar VI. *(Courtesy John G. Alden, Inc.)*

Top: Malabar VI *with a later rig. (Courtesy John G. Alden, Inc.)* **Bottom:** *A.L. Loomis's* Volante, *originally William McMillan's* Merry Widow, *a marconi-rigged sister to* Malabar VI. *(Courtesy John G. Alden, Inc.)*

the area forward of the saloon. The extra-small stateroom that was squeezed in alongside the galley not only stole room from the galley and fo'c's'le, but also proved cramped, hot, and stuffy. This forward stateroom was torn out before Alden sold the boat.

Recently, on a cold November afternoon in Newport, Rhode Island, I went aboard the third of the sisters to *Malabar VI*. She still has her original name, *Adventurer,* and little has been altered in rig, deck gear, and accommodations. I was impressed with her seamanlike appearance and the coziness of the main cabin, which was kept warm and dry with her Shipmate stove. *Adventurer* had just been bought by Mike Williams, who planned to take her to Florida for restoration.

Before moving on to the next boat in the series, I should mention another of the sisters to *Malabar VI,* one that hailed from my home waters on the Chesapeake. This boat, named *Merry Widow,* was owned by a great Alden fan, William McMillan.* He had a good racing record with *Merry Widow,* including a class third in the 1928 Bermuda Race and a class win in the 1927 Gibson Island Race, but he did still better with a later Alden schooner, *Water Gypsy,* which finished third in class and fleet and second in class and fleet, respectively, in the 1932 and 1934 Bermuda Races. The *Gypsy* was also first around the rock in the 1931 Fastnet Race.

In his series of articles about the *Malabars,* Dwight Simpson called *Malabar VII* "the black sheep of the family," and he wrote that Alden always considered her an unsuccessful boat. This is surprising, for she gave her designer his second fleet victory in the 1926 Bermuda Race. However, according to a 1926 *Yachting* article and the label on the lines drawing of the "Seven," her hull was designed for a knockabout-ketch rig. With little time for designing and building, Alden wanted a new *Malabar* for the 1926 race, and he chose this hull from available designs. Her good showing was attributed by Alden to luck, and he felt that the "Seven" was a very ordinary performer except when reaching with well-started sheets. Simpson wrote that she needed a deeper

* Bill McMillan is perhaps best known for putting up the McMillan Trophy, a prestigious prize awarded for a series of intercollegiate races still sailed annually at the U.S. Naval Academy.

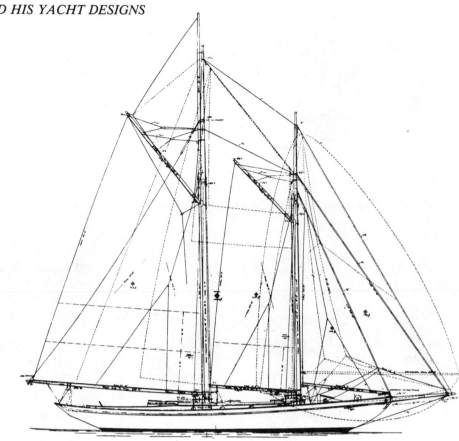

Malabar VII is lighter than the "Six," but she carries about 70 square feet more sail. For the first time in the Malabar series three headsails are carried. The jib topsail was not taxed under the CCA rule. (The Rudder, July 1934)

forefoot, more freeboard, and fuller lines forward to improve her performance and make her less wet. A lesser problem was that originally she had only a 10-horsepower engine, which proved far from adequate. Alden soon replaced it with a more powerful Scripps F-4.

Built to the lines of design number 280, *Malabar VII's* dimensions are 53 feet 9 inches, by 37 feet 11 inches, by 12 feet 5 inches, by 7 feet 3 inches. Her layout is basically like that of her predecessor, except that the newer boat was given an L-shaped cabin trunk aft (as opposed to a complete break in the trunk). This arrangement retained the forward position of the companionway while providing more headroom at the entrance to the after stateroom. Also, the forward galley and fo'c's'le were somewhat improved. Alden gave the "Seven" a triple-headsail rig, primarily because a jib topsail was not penalized in the Bermuda Race. This *Malabar* had six sisters, among which two with good racing records were *Fearless* and *Teal,* originally owned by A.T. Baker, Jr., and R. Graham Bigelow. *Teal* differed from the "Seven" in having a marconi main. Another sister, Demarest Lloyd's *Angelica,* was ketch-rigged, and she was raced hard and successfully in on-soundings events.

In the early 1930s *Malabar VII* went to Los Angeles, where she was bought by movie actor Dana Andrews and converted to a cutter. About 1940 she was given a yawl rig, and under the ownership of Charles Langlais she became a class champion at San Francisco. Kenneth M. Parsley of Delray Beach, Florida, owned her in the late 1970s, and he wrote me that he rebuilt the "Seven" extensively, replacing 39 ribs and giving her an entirely new interior.

Whether or not Alden was pleased with the "Seven," Parsley has nothing but praise for her performance, saying, "She pointed well within 30 degrees under sail, and I have had her over 10 knots." Parsley says she is extremely stiff, yet she is a great ghoster in light airs. Perhaps she is more comfortable with a yawl rig. On a coastal passage in 1976, *Malabar VII* encountered a white squall with winds in excess of 90 knots (as reported by the Coast Guard), and she behaved well, making seven knots under a 100-square-foot storm jib. She had been carrying a mizzen as well, but the strain was too great, and the mizzen step split.

Parsley donated the "Seven" to the Associated Marine Institutes in Florida, to be used for training youth in a variety of marine fields such as boat handling and repair.

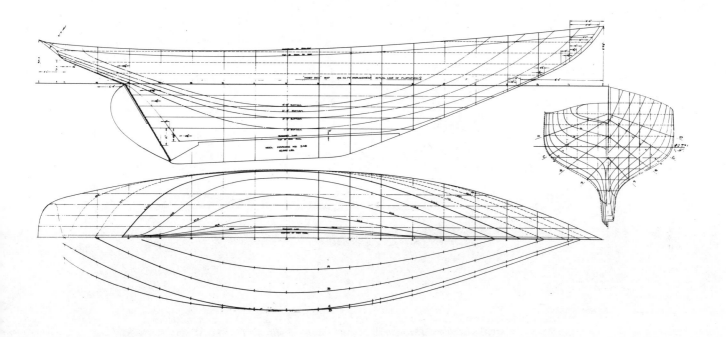

Malabar VII's *lines show a comparatively short keel with a prominent toe. Dwight Simpson claimed that she would have been improved with a deeper forefoot, fuller lines forward, and more freeboard. Clifford Swaine drew her lines, which are labeled "auxiliary knockabout ketch." (Courtesy John G. Alden, Inc.)*

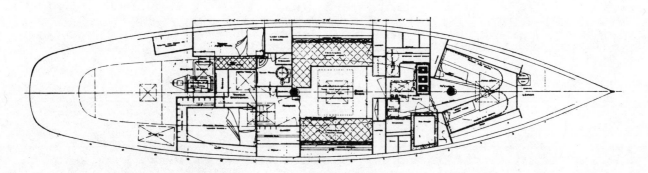

On Malabar VII, *Alden introduced a cabin trunk that was L-shaped at the after end, providing privacy and headroom to the after stateroom.* (The Rudder, *July 1934)*

Malabar VII *close-hauled, with a racing crew aboard. Alden felt she was an indifferent performer in windward work. (Morris Rosenfeld photo. Courtesy Chester M. and Harriet Sawtelle)*

Fearless, *a sister to* Malabar VII, *in a rail-down breeze. Her jib luff wants a bit of tightening. (Courtesy John G. Alden, Inc.)*

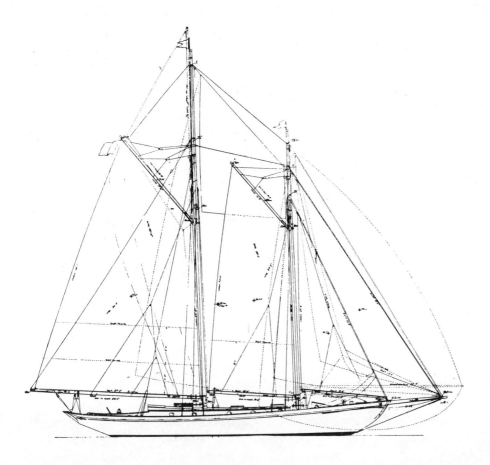

Malabar VIII has 60 square feet more canvas than her immediate predecessor, which is only three inches shorter in overall length. The lines of the "Eight" are quite similar to those of the "Seven," but she has more freeboard and almost no keel drag. (The Rudder, *July 1934*)

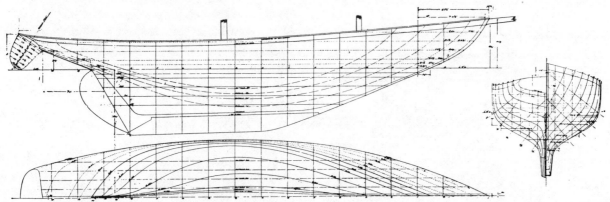

True to form, Alden had his eighth *Malabar,* design number 331, built in 1927, but he did not keep her the entire season. After winning the 270-mile Gibson Island Race (Cape May, New Jersey to Gibson Island) soon after the boat was built, the designer was offered a price for the "Eight" that he couldn't refuse; he sold her and spent the rest of the summer living on another Alden schooner, *Monomoy.*

In rig and hull form there are no great differences between *Malabars VII* and *VIII,* except that the latter was given double rather than triple headsails for easier handling when cruising, and she was made slightly larger, with dimensions of 54 feet, by 39 feet, by 12 feet 8¾ inches, by 7 feet 4 inches. The greatest change was made to the layout, for Alden returned to the after-companionway arrangement. This put the saloon aft and the owner's private stateroom amidships, while keeping the galley and crew's quarters forward. Such a plan makes it easier to go below from the cockpit, and it is a better arrangement for the navigator, but the owner's quarters are not as grand and the galley is quite a long way from the dining table.

Malabar VIII had one immediate sister, *La Goleta.* She was owned originally by Ralph St. L. Peverley, who later owned two Alden schooners named *Lelanta* (see Chapter 7).

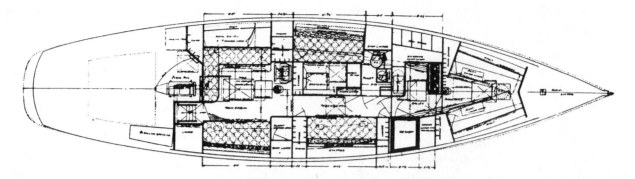

With Malabar VIII, *there is a return to the conventional after companionway, and the owner's stateroom is forward of the saloon. Alden said he did this "rather as an experiment." With the head between the stateroom and the galley, Alden felt that noises made by the cook "with his stove and pots and pans in the early morning" would not be a bother.* (The Rudder, *July 1934*)

Malabar VIII *showing a lovely, yacht-like profile at the Yale-Harvard Regatta, June 1927. (Edwin Levick photo. The Mariners' Museum, Newport News, Virginia)*

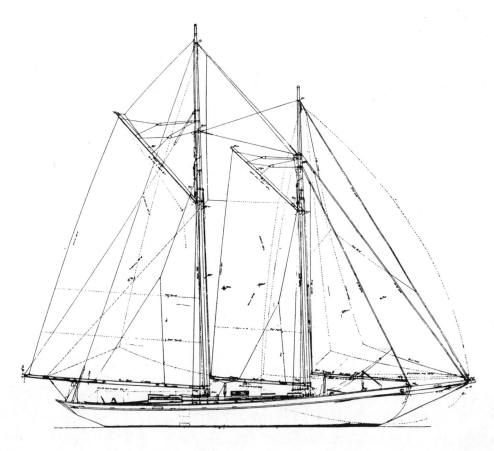

With 1,620 square feet of canvas, Malabar IX *has a lot more sail than any of her predecessors, but she is a much larger boat. In designing her, Alden took a slight step back toward the fisherman look. The fine entrance made her wet in head seas, but her generous beam made her stiff.* (The Rudder, *July 1934)*

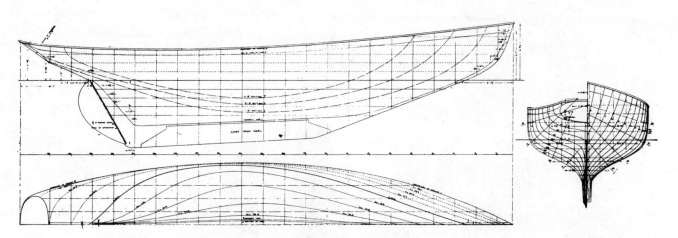

Malabar IX, design number 362, came out in 1928. She is the largest of the series in terms of designed waterline length, measuring 57 feet 11 inches, by 44 feet 3 inches, by 14 feet 2 inches, by 7 feet 9 inches. This schooner was given a sharper curve — almost a knuckle — in her stem profile. She also has more beam and a firmer bilge amidships, giving her greater power even though the bow is exceedingly fine. She was said to be a good sail carrier, but like the ''Seven,'' she proved somewhat wet in head seas. Her working sail area was 1,620 square feet, a significant increase over the earlier

Malabars (to go with her larger dimensions), although her mainsail was proportionally smaller.

The main reason for her larger size is that she was intended to carry two paid hands rather than one. Evidently, Alden had become spoiled by the professional cook carried on *Malabar VIII* (see Chapter 4), because the ''Nine'' was given adequate quarters for a cook as well as a captain forward of her midships saloon. Also, the L-shaped after end of the cabin trunk reappeared in order to move the companionway farther forward and allow a roomier, completely private state-

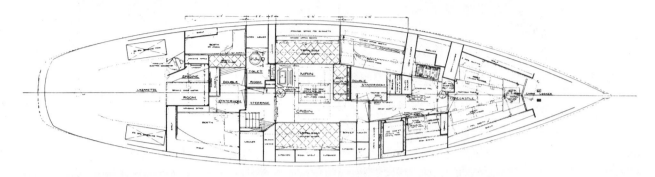

The "Nine" was conceived as a two-paid-hand boat, and this is reflected in her accommodations. Alden went back to the after-stateroom arrangement with an L-shaped trunk. (Yachting, September 1928)

The "Nine" close-hauled near the start of the 1928 Bermuda Race, with her jib topsail stopped and ready to break out. (Edwin Levick photo. The Mariners' Museum, Newport News, Virginia)

Left: *A deck view of* Malabar IX *showing interesting details such as the bulwarks and the sheeting arrangement for the staysail. (Courtesy Mrs. John Robinson)* **Below:** Malabar IX *being piloted into Bermuda after the 1928 race, with Alden on the left and young Olin Stephens on the right. (Courtesy Chester M. and Harriet Sawtelle)*

room aft. As in all the *Malabars,* Alden desired first and foremost a comfortable and able cruising boat.

Malabar IX took a class third and was fourth in fleet in the 1928 Bermuda Race, though she was beaten by *Teal,* a sister to *Malabar VII.* At any rate, *Malabar IX* was the first schooner of the series that Alden kept for more than one season.

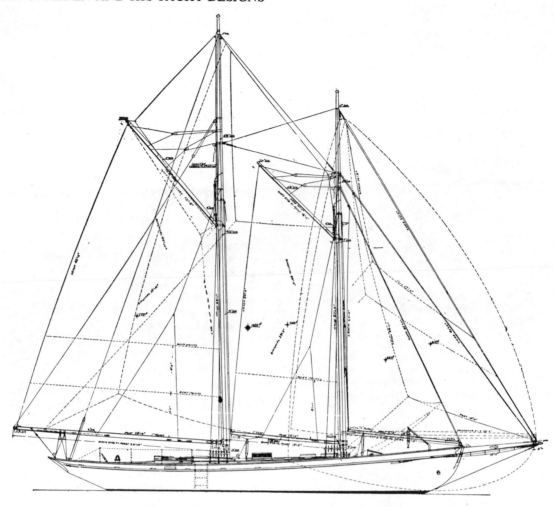

Throughout the schooner series, from Malabar I *through* X, *the dominant trend was a gradual increase in relative size of foresails and foretriangles.* Malabar X *has 17 square feet more sail area than the "Nine," but the sail plans of the two boats are identical otherwise.* (Yachting, *February, 1930)*

Dwight Simpson and a number of regular crew members such as Hank Meneely considered *Malabar X*, built in 1930, to be the finest schooner of the series. In a sense she is the culmination of the evolution of John Alden's schooners. This boat's design number is 453, and her measurements from the Alden records are 58 feet 3 inches, by 44 feet 2 inches, by 14 feet 2 inches, by 8 feet 1 inch. One sister was built. Although very close to the "Nine" in size and with a similar semi-knuckle bow, *Malabar X* has different lines. She is fuller in the ends, with a higher prismatic coefficient, and this gives her a more powerful hull with greater speed potential. Her sections amidships are rounder, which somewhat reduces the wetted surface while providing a very seakindly form. Her frames, unlike the "Nine's" and like the "Four's," were bent. Her ballast, about 44 percent of the designed displacement with more than two-thirds of it on the keel, seems just about ideal (consider-

ing the generous beam) as a compromise between easy motion and sail-carrying ability.

Below decks she almost duplicates the "Nine," but an extra head was added forward, and she was provided with a more powerful engine, a 40 h.p. Falcon driving a large propeller through a reduction gear.

In her rig and sail area, the "Ten" differs little from her immediate forerunner. Both schooners carry three headsails. It is worth noting that, beginning with the early *Malabars*, each boat had a comparatively smaller mainsail and larger foresail than the boat preceding. Writing of *Malabar VIII* in 1927, Alden said, "Unless I have a schooner that will sail well under forestaysail, foresail and whole mainsail, and besides this sail to windward under forestaysail and foresail, I do not want one. To my mind this is the reason for having a schooner, although I admit there are very few in existence that perform satisfactorily this way. I like to get

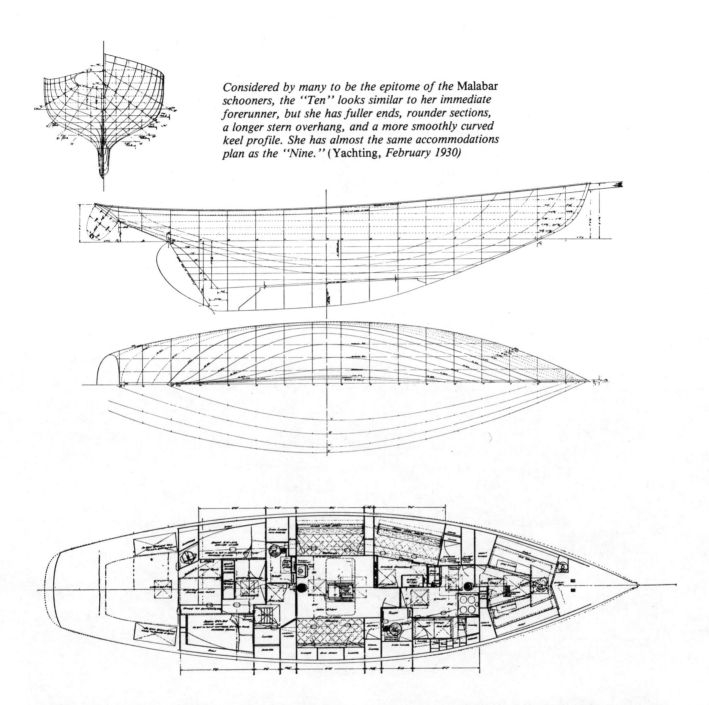

Considered by many to be the epitome of the Malabar *schooners, the "Ten" looks similar to her immediate forerunner, but she has fuller ends, rounder sections, a longer stern overhang, and a more smoothly curved keel profile. She has almost the same accommodations plan as the "Nine."* (Yachting, *February 1930*)

the jib off in bad weather before it is too late, and also believe a large foresail is most essential." It is also interesting that even though the staysail rig had been introduced about five years earlier, Alden retained the gaff rig for his own *Malabar* schooners. He particularly liked the power of a gaff foresail and apparently felt that this sail is almost as close-winded as a mainstaysail when it is fitted with a vang.

Alden kept *Malabar X* until 1933 (part of the time in co-ownership with Robert I. Gale), and her record is

replete with fine showings in top races. These include a class win over 27 competitors and a fleet second in the 1930 Bermuda Race, second in a class of 21 boats in the 1931 Cape May Race, and a fleet first in the 1932 Bermuda Race. Indeed, the "Ten's" early years were the pinnacle of Alden's designing and ocean racing career. The top three boats in Class A in the 1930 Bermuda Race were Alden designs, while the top four in fleet were Alden schooners in the 1932 race. The biennial race to the Onion Patch was especially important to

Malabar X *on the New York Yacht Club cruise of 1931. (Edwin Levick photo. The Mariners' Museum, Newport News, Virginia)*

Alden, because it was the most prestigious U.S. ocean racing event, and it was sponsored by the Cruising Club of America, of which the designer was a charter member.

The "Ten" was the end of the *Malabar* schooner line, for the next three boats of that name were yawl- or ketch-rigged. *Malabar XI,* built in 1937 by the Casey Boatbuilding Company of Fairhaven, Massachusetts, was modified slightly from design number 583, which came from the board of Carl Alberg. She is a near sister to *Dorothy Q* (the first 583) and *Sirocco* (see Chapter 7). *Malabar XI* measures 44 feet, by 30 feet 6 inches, by 10 feet 3 inches, by 6 feet.

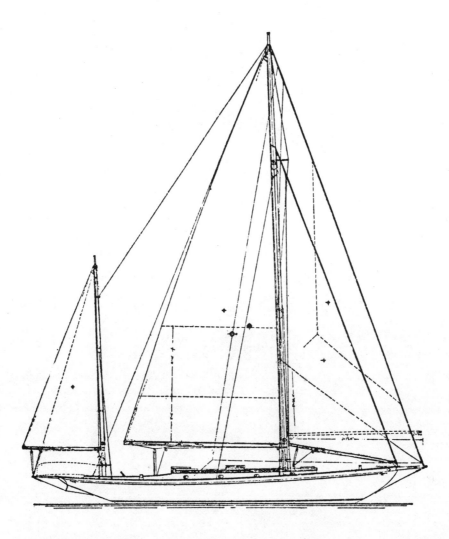

The "Eleven" stands in marked contrast to the previous Malabars. *Her mizzen, which contributes little to her 1,084 square feet of canvas, is primarily a balancing sail.* (The Rudder, *April 1937)*

She represents quite a drop in size from the last *Malabar* schooners, this being one reason why Alden decided on a yawl rig. The mainmast, with its masthead stay, can carry large headsails, yet on a boat of *Malabar XI*'s dimensions the sails are not an unmanageable size. The large self-tending forestaysail also enables the "Eleven" to be handled quite easily with a small crew. Another factor that probably influenced Alden in his rig switch is that schooners had become passé on the race courses, as yawls and single-stickers, almost always superior to windward, had become more competitive on a reach. This was due partly to the greater reaching efficiency of the parachute spinnaker as opposed to the old single-luff spinnaker, which could only be carried when the wind was far aft.

Although Alden was always concerned with simplifying the handling of his boats, he had no desire to take up singlehanding again. *Malabar XI* was given quarters for a paid hand, but they were in a very unusual location — in a tiny stateroom alongside the companionway, abaft the saloon.

Like *Sirocco, Malabar XI* turned out to be fast. Although she did not compete in the 1938 Bermuda Race, Alden did well with her in some lesser events, including the 1937 New London-to-Gibson Island Race, in which she finished second in Class B.

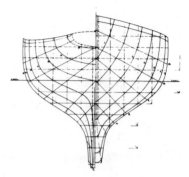

The lines shown here are those of Sirocco, *Number 583-B.* Malabar XI, *Number 583-E, is five inches longer on deck and four inches longer on the water, with the same beam and draft. She is considerably finer aft and fuller forward than the preceding* Malabars. *(Courtesy John G. Alden, Inc.)*

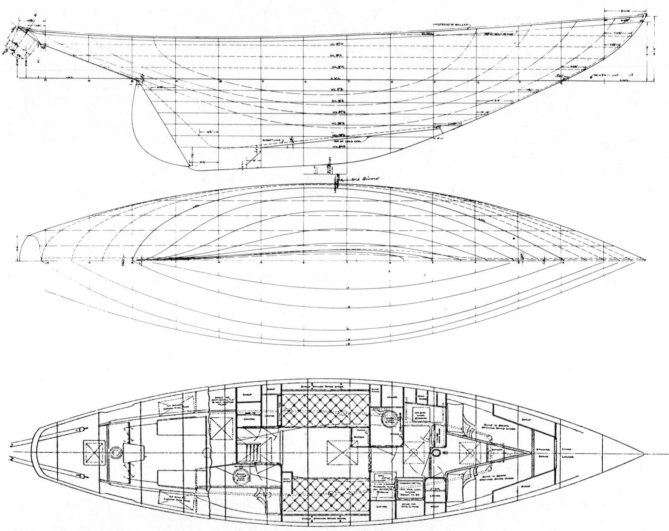

The cabin plan of Malabar XI *compromises privacy slightly by putting the paid hand's quarters aft. (* The Rudder, *April 1937)*

Malabar XI during the Gibson Island Race of 1937. She finished second in her class. Notice the jib tack downhaul for adjusting luff tension; it probably leads back to the cockpit. (Morris Rosenfeld photo)

An out-of-water look at Malabar XI. *Note the propeller installation. (Courtesy John G. Alden, Inc.)*

The twelfth *Malabar,* also an Alberg-drawn design (number 696), made her appearance in 1939. She is different from her predecessors in that she was given a ketch rig, and Alden claimed she was not intended for racing. Introducing her in *Rudder* magazine, he wrote that he wanted "an extremely stiff and comfortable 'ocean cruiser' (as distinguished from an 'ocean racer')." With dimensions of 46 feet 8 inches, by 34 feet 3 inches, by 12 feet, by 6 feet 9 inches, *Malabar XII* was, in her designer's opinion, "as large a hull as can be comfortably handled by a crew of one and one-half." In choosing the builder, Alden went back to C.A. Morse and Son (by then operating under the name Morse Boatbuilding Corporation) at Thomaston, Maine. Two sisters were built.

The ketch's layout is different from those of the preceding *Malabars,* for she is the first of the line to have a doghouse. This structure is raised considerably higher than the cabin trunk, and it has two fairly large windows per side. Its sole is high enough to allow ample room underneath for a 4-52 Gray engine. There are two transoms and what appears to be a folding chart table in the doghouse. Forward, at a slightly lower level, there is an enclosed head to starboard and a small but well-ventilated single stateroom to port. Then come the saloon, the galley, and a fo'c's'le with accommodations for a paid hand.

Alden had not completely lost his enthusiasm for schooners. Indeed, he returned to that rig when he bought *Abenaki* in 1947 (see Chapter 6), but he came to believe that the schooner rig was most suitable for boats larger than *Malabar XII.* He felt that the "Twelve" was the right size for a ketch rig, because, as he expressed it, "a ketch of this size can have less sail than a schooner of the same model [the *Malabar XII* carried 1,043 square feet in her jib, staysail, main, and mizzen] and yet be just as fast." (Apparently at this time Alden felt that the ketch rig was more efficient than the schooner considering all points of sailing.) He added: "The performance under staysail and mizzen is also taken into consideration, and the rig should balance properly under the three working sails." For smaller boats, Alden more often leaned toward the yawl or single-masted rig.

Alden must have been well satisfied with *Malabar XII,* for in 1941, when asked to recommend a design for long ocean passages, the "Twelve" was his choice. Interestingly, he suggested altering the design for the purpose by adding another foot of beam to make her more roomy and give her even greater initial stability. However, he saw no need to alter the marconi ketch rig.

Right after World War II, the yachtsman Carleton Mitchell bought *Malabar XII,* renamed her *Carib,* and cruised in her extensively in the West Indies and elsewhere. Although a very satisfactory boat for him in

Carib, *ex-*Malabar XII, *drives through a sea off the coast of Trinidad in 1947. (Carleton Mitchell photo)*

The "Twelve" is a further variation on the Malabar theme. Her mizzen is large enough to contribute some real drive on a reach. Carl Alberg, who drafted the lines of the last three Malabars, wrote in regard to the "Twelve," "John told me not to consider any rating, as he had no intention of racing her, but he did just the same." (Courtesy John G. Alden, Inc.)

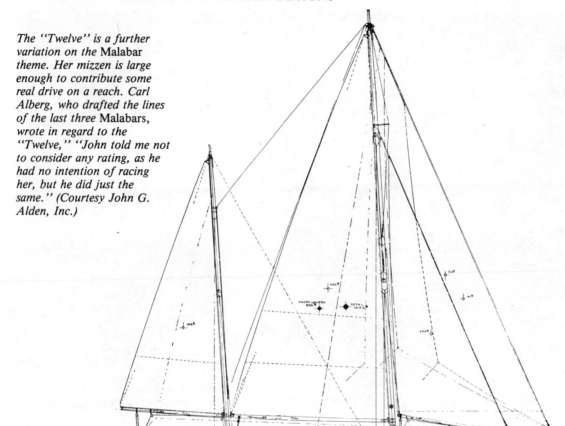

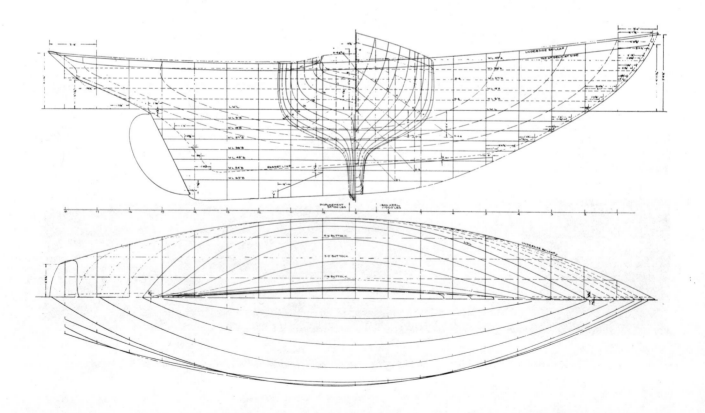

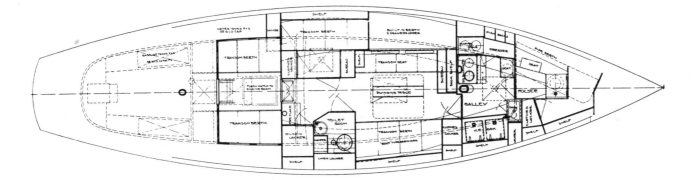

Malabar XII represents a different concept in cabin arrangements in that she has a doghouse, which is primarily a cockpit shelter and navigating or resting area for the deck watch , but can also be used for a guest stateroom. (The Rudder, May 1941)

most respects, she was a little too deep for such areas as the Bahamas and even the Chesapeake, and Mitchell wrote me that he "dragged bottom" quite often. Evidently, she contributed to his later thinking about cruising centerboarders, which eventually led to the development of the Sparkman and Stephens yawl *Finisterre.*

Renamed *Hope* after Mitchell sold her, *Malabar XII* cruised in the Bahamas until the early 1950s under the ownership of North Carolinian Will Irwin. She was then bought by John P. Lewis, renamed *Grenadier,* and taken to the Thousand Islands region of the St. Lawrence. Lewis gave her to the International Oceanographic Foundation of Miami, which in turn sold her to sailmaker Ted Hood of Marblehead. After extensive rebuilding by Hood, the ketch was again sold and taken south in the late fall. In a nor'east gale off the Carolina coast, she began taking on an alarming amount of water. Her crew of two were rescued by a naval vessel, which stove her in coming alongside. The abandoned ketch sank shortly thereafter.

The war interrupted the progression of *Malabars,* and the "Thirteen" did not appear until 1945. Built by Goudy and Stevens of East Boothbay, Maine, *Malabar XIII* has been called a "war baby" because she was put together when certain materials were hard to come by. Alden acquired an ancient New York Fifty, the *Andiamo,* to get the lead ballast, winches, turnbuckles, and even the skylights for use on the "Thirteen." (*Andiamo*'s previous owner was furious when he learned that his boat had been so used.) Like the preceding *Malabar,* she was ketch-rigged, and her mainsail came

from another Alden boat, George Ratsey's *Zaida.* The first of four boats built to design number 756 (from the board of Carl Alberg), *Malabar XIII* measures 53 feet 9 inches, by 40 feet 8 inches, by 14 feet 3 inches, by 7 feet 4 inches.

Alden's decision to give this boat a ketch rig may seem contradictory to his statement, made in connection with *Malabar XII,* that "the schooner rig might be better" on boats larger than the "Twelve." It should be kept in mind, however, that the latter was a pure cruiser, while *Malabar XIII* was intended for at least some racing. Her rig is a compromise between racing efficiency and easy handling by a small crew. The rigs of the "Twelve" and the "Thirteen" were basically alike, except that the latter was given a dolphin striker to improve the angle between bobstay and bowsprit, while the mizzenmast was given a boomkin and permanent backstay to take the strain of a large mizzen staysail.

Like the "Twelve," the "Thirteen" has a doghouse with two transom berths. Immediately forward of this is a double stateroom to starboard with a small single stateroom and enclosed head to port. The saloon, with three berths, is amidships; the galley, another head, and quarters for a paid hand are farther forward.

Alden didn't do as well racing this boat as he did with some earlier *Malabars,* but he sailed her to a respectable fifth in class in the light-weather 1946 Bermuda Race. The "Thirteen" had greater success in the 1948 Bermuda Race, when, under the ownership of Morgan Butler (but with Alden on board), she won her class and corrected to third in fleet. She finished second in the next year's Miami-Nassau Race under Butler, and she was first in the 1951 Transatlantic Race under the

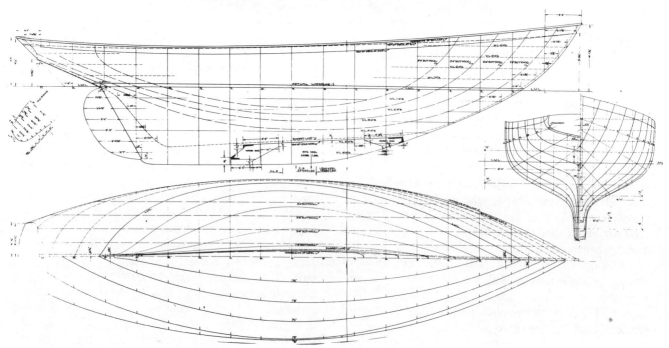

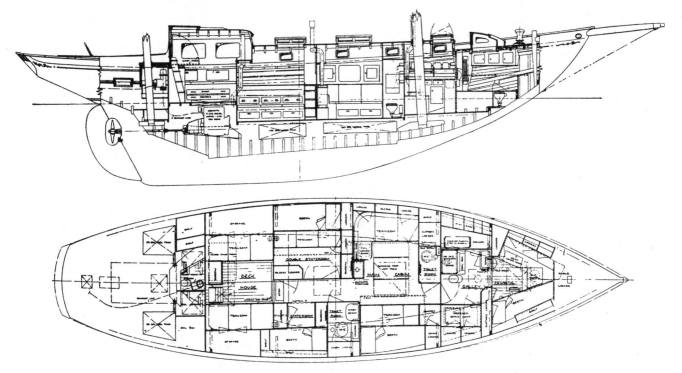

Opposite top: Malabar XIII's *sail plan has been improved over that of her predecessor. With the addition of a boomkin and permanent backstay, she can carry a large mizzen staysail efficiently in strong winds, and her headstay can be set up taut. (Courtesy John G. Alden, Inc.)* **Opposite bottom:** Malabar XIII *has a slightly fuller entrance than the "Twelve." The outside ballast was increased from 15,350 pounds to 20,386 pounds in 1946. Lead was hard to come by until the end of the war. (Courtesy John G. Alden, Inc.)* **Above:** Malabar XIII *has an accommodations plan similar to that of the "Twelve," but with her greater beam, she has room for another small stateroom forward of the deckhouse.* (Yachting, *December 1945)*

This lee-side shot of Malabar XIII *gives a clear view of her doghouse and a number of deck details. (Courtesy John G. Alden, Inc.)*

ownership of Kennon Jewett. She was not so fortunate, though probably as well sailed, in the 1951 Fastnet Race. In wind that was reportedly gusting to 60 knots, she lost first her jib topsail, and later, when a bronze turnbuckle failed, her mainmast. Relating the experience in *Count the Cats in Zanzibar,* Jim Crawford said, "I've never liked bronze turnbuckles since . . . ."

Chester Sawtelle, John Alden's son-in-law and dependable crew member, remembers the start of the 1946 Bermuda Race. John got away beautifully in the light air, and an hour later, with luck and skill in the fickle zephyrs, he had worked *Malabar XIII* to a position far ahead of the rest of the fleet. They were hailed by a Coast Guard cutter, the young crew of which apparently thought the "Thirteen" was a spectator blocking the race course. John was ordered to clear the area, the cutter refusing to believe that the "Thirteen" was racing. Alden held his course. The crew of the cutter grew more and more insistent and excited, the situation more tense. Grimly, John gripped the wheel, still holding his course. The cutter finally backed down.

I have a vivid recollection of *Malabar XIII* thundering past our 46-foot yawl in the Gulf Stream during the 1950 Bermuda Race. A moderate wind was just forward of the beam, and the ketch carried a large, high-cut reaching jib. She is a lovely-looking, able craft.

A Summary of the Malabars

	Design Number	Year Built	Dimensions	Designed Displacement (pounds)	Outside Ballast (pounds)*	Inside Ballast (pounds)*	Rig	Sail Area (square feet)	Builder	Sisters	Features
Malabar I	155	1921	41'3" x 31'10" x 11'7" x 6'2"	29,100	3,156	3,000 (designed) 8,650 (final)	bald-headed schooner	963	C.A. Morse & Son Thomaston, ME	none	2 deckhouses, 1 headsail
Malabar II	162-A	1922	41'6" x 32' x 11'3" x 6'2"	28,600	5,000	7,500 (final)	bald-headed schooner	938	C.A. Morse & Son Thomaston, ME	three, including Mary Ann	trunk cabin, 1 headsail
Malabar III	162-B	1922	41'6" x 32' x 11'3" x 6'2"	28,600		Total ballast similar to Malabar II, but higher percentage outside.	bald-headed schooner	938	C.A. Morse & Son Thomaston, ME	three, including Mary Ann	trunk cabin, 1 headsail
Malabar IV	205-A	1923	47' x 35'6" x 12' x 6'11"	37,200	9,000	11,000 (final)	topsail schooner	1,220	C.A. Morse & Son Thomaston, ME	Felisi (Toddywax)	trunk cabin, 2 headsails
Malabar V	215-A	1924	49' x 36'9" x 12' x 7'3"	38,540	12,450	6,000 (designed) 8,000 (final)	topsail schooner	1,307	C.A. Morse & Son Thomaston, ME	one	trunk cabin, 2 headsails
Malabar VI	248-A	1925	52'3" x 38' x 12' x 7'4"	46,250	15,240	6,000 (designed) 7,300 (final)	topsail schooner	1,337	Hodgdon Bros. East Boothbay, ME	eight, including Merry Widow, Black Goose, Adventurer	broken cabin trunk, 2 headsails
Malabar VII	280-A	1926	53'9" x 37'11" x 12'5" x 7'3"	43,300	15,000	8,250 (final)	topsail schooner	1,406	Reed-Cook Marine Construction Co. Boothbay Harbor, ME	six, including Teal, Fearless	L-shaped trunk, 3 headsails
Malabar VIII	331-A	1927	54' x 39' x 12'9" x 7'4"	48,000	15,000	5,000	topsail schooner	1,464	Hodgdon Bros. East Boothbay, ME	La Goleta	trunk cabin, 2 headsails
Malabar IX	362	1928	57'11" x 44'3" x 14'2" x 7'9"	53,000	16,000	7,500 (designed) 8,700 (final)	topsail schooner	1,620	Hodgdon Bros. East Boothbay, ME	none	L-shaped trunk, 3 headsails
Malabar X	453-A	1930	58'3" x 44'2" x 14'2" x 8'1"	61,700	21,000	6,100 (designed)	topsail schooner	1,637	Hodgdon Bros. East Boothbay, ME	one	L-shaped trunk, 3 headsails
Malabar XI	583-E	1937	44' x 30'6" x 10'3" x 6'	23,750**	10,080**	746**	yawl	1,084	Casey Boatbuilding Co. Fairhaven, MA	six, including Dorothy Q. Sirocco	trunk cabin, 2 headsails
Malabar XII	696-A	1939	46'8" x 34'3" x 12' x 6'9"	34,700	11,900	2,900	ketch	1,043	Morse Boatbuilding Co. Thomaston, ME	two	doghouse, 2 headsails
Malabar XIII	756-A	1945	53'9" x 40'8" x 14'3" x 7'4"	55,200	15,350 (designed) 20,386 (final)	n.a.	ketch	1,221	Goudy & Stevens East Boothbay, ME	three	doghouse, 2 headsails

*Ballast figures are in most cases approximate.
**Figures from *Sirocco*, Number 583-B.

The "Thirteen" is universally recognized as the last of the *Malabar* line, but it is a curious fact that the Alden records show a *Malabar XV,* design number 901A, built for the designer by Graves of Marblehead in 1955. She is a relatively small yawl, only 39 feet 2½ inches, by 26 feet, by 9 feet 9 inches, by 5 feet 9 inches, and Donald Parrot of the Alden firm remembers her design as that of a Coastwise Cruiser (design number 675) with drawn-out ends. Alden didn't keep her long (she went through two name changes before 1957). Indeed, his family and former shipmates do not remember his having sailed the boat. Alden never built a *Malabar XIV,* but Steven Pope, who was a draftsman in the Alden office, remembers drawing plans for a "Fourteen" with Fenwick Williams in 1947, "with John looking over our shoulders all the way." The design, Number 842 in the Alden records according to Pope, was a 47-foot-9-inch cruising ketch with a modest rig and doghouse in the tradition of *Malabars XII* and *XIII.*

In 1990 I received a letter from Richard Nichols of Gig Harbor, Washington, who owns the ketch *Cybele,* built to the 842 design. He wrote, "I like to think that possibly I have the missing *Malabar.*" Actually, Mr. Nichols owns 842-E, a sister to 842-A, the latter being the original design ordered by Alden for a boat that would have been named *Malabar XIV* had she been built. Donald Parrot informed Mr. Nichols that plans for 842-B went to Puerto Rico, C went to Brazil, and F were ordered from Holland (F plans are now in the hands of Mike Renitsky of San Diego). Records show that only one other sister was built, this being *Silverheels,* 842-D, which was built in Spain (see page 436).

After acquiring *Cybele* Mr. Nichols and his daughter spent three years completely rebuilding the ketch, and in the summer of 1989 he cruised her 4,000 miles in the waters of Alaska and British Columbia. He is delighted with the boat and said he is planning an extensive cruise in southern waters. His confidence in the boat must be reinforced by an early survey that stated, "She is capable of any ocean and any weather in the world."

To summarize the *Malabars,* the first three were small fisherman-type schooners intended for at least some singlehanded sailing. Number one was a particular favorite of Alden's, and many years after she was built, he said, "For practical purposes each *Malabar* was a definite improvement over its predecessor, but *Malabar I* with her short deckhouse and flush deck between the masts was the most interesting. Yachts were continually altering their course to have a look at her."

The "Four" was the beginning of the larger, slightly yachtier *Malabars,* intended for ocean racing and cruising with a paid hand. She too was a favorite of Alden's because of her all-around performance and unbeatable racing record. The designer once said that she had given him his greatest thrill when she won the 1923 Bermuda Race. The "Seven" also had a fleet win in the Bermuda Race, but Alden seemed to like her least of the *Malabars.*

The ninth and tenth boats of the series were considerably larger schooners, and they were conceived as two-hand boats (i.e., carrying two permanent professionals). The "Ten" seemed to be the popular favorite. She was an unusually comfortable and able cruiser yet had an outstanding racing record, which included a fleet win in the 1932 Bermuda Race.

The next three boats in the series were smaller, and they were entirely different in rig, one being a yawl and the other two, ketches. The "Thirteen" had a distinguished ocean racing record, and she is known as the last of the *Malabars.*

Many of the *Malabars* are still sailing, though, sadly, the first was reported lost on a reef in Tahiti, and the fourth, according to another report, sank in the Puerto Rican Trench, perhaps as a result of dry rot. The "Two" and the "Seven" are not the only *Malabars* that have been extensively rebuilt. Perhaps the most striking *Malabar* remains the "Ten," which is still schooner-rigged and in fine shape. Owned by William Lee Prior of Chicago, she visited the Chesapeake in 1982. The "Two" is kept in Bristol fashion, and in 1982, under the ownership of James Lobdell of Martha's Vineyard, she won an award as the best Alden schooner in the Classic Yacht Regatta at Newport, Rhode Island. Lobdell claims he knew the first season he had her that he would never want another boat. Several latter-day sisters to the "Two" are contemplated, including one by Roger Morse, grandson of C.A. Morse and boatbuilder in the family business for some 40 years. There remains great interest in all the *Malabars,* and well-informed sailors everywhere — even many of those from a more modern generation — seem to realize that the *Malabar* line is a permanent part of yachting history.

6

Early Sailing Cruisers*

John Alden once remarked that the smallest practical cruising boat is large enough to carry a dinghy on deck. While not every boat in this chapter qualifies as a cruising boat under this definition (in some cases the boom is simply too low to clear a tender stowed atop a cabin house), these boats are sailing cruisers in that they are large enough to venture offshore and to offer their crews reasonable, sometimes even luxurious comfort.

In the years before 1920, Alden did much of the drafting himself, but as his business expanded in the early 1920s he took on a number of talented assistants such as Clifford Swaine, Dwight Simpson, William McNary, Charles MacGregor, Fenwick Williams, Aage Nielsen, and Murray Peterson. With such a gifted group added to his already ensconced designer, Sam Crocker, Alden gave up drafting, but he made plenty of sketches to show his assistants what he wanted. He often used previous designs as points of departure, and Clifford Swaine writes that his usual procedure was to take the tracings of the good design that came nearest to what was needed and mark in the changes with a soft lead pencil. After many tries, he would put check marks on the result he wanted and turn the plan over to a draftsman to use in developing new working plans. Having

taken off the information needed, the draftsman would then spend several hours erasing the "improvements." Sam Crocker once said, "We should buy him a whitewash brush to use." The assistants often collaborated on the finished design, with one man drawing the lines, another the arrangement and construction plans, and perhaps still another the sail plan. Alden gave his designers ample freedom, but their creations had to look just right to him.

During this period Alden developed and refined the fisherman-influenced schooner yacht, the type for which he is so well known. At least among smaller yachts, this kind of boat was unusual in its particular combination of seaworthiness and speed, a characteristic shared with the American fishing schooners of the

---

* The boats in this chapter are early Alden designs, dating from 1911, not long after Alden opened his own office, until just before 1930. The division between the sailing cruisers in this chapter and later boats of the same type in the next chapter occurs near design number 400 (as shown in the Alden index). There is no particular reason for dividing the boats this way except that 1930 and 400 seem like nice round figures, and they are almost at the midpoint of the designer's career. Naturally, Alden's style changed over the years, but the change was gradual, with no sudden break in 1930.

early 1900s. An article in *The Rudder* (January 1903) described the superiority of the American fisherman as follows: "The fishing fleets of foreign countries all show types of vessels which are noted for their sea-worthiness, but as a rule they are slow sailers, and our country has been the first to develop a type of fisherman in which speed and seaworthiness are combined."

If I might be allowed a sweeping generality, one that has plenty of exceptions, I'd say that small yachts of those times were generally fully canvased, long-ended, low-freeboard, fast types designed for semiprotected waters (not many small racing craft went to sea then), or else they were relatively sluggish seagoers such as those designed by Colin Archer or Jack Hanna. However, there gradually developed an interest in dual-purpose yachts, those that could be taken to sea yet were fast enough for occasional racing. Yachtsmen were becoming interested in offshore sailing partly as a result of the exploits and writings of men such as Claud Worth, William Nutting, Harry Pidgeon, and especially Thomas F. Day, the colorful editor of *The Rudder*. At the same time, newly formed or revived offshore races such as the Bermuda, 'round Cape Cod, Transpac, and Mackinac races helped create a demand for boats that were both fast and able. The fisherman-type yachts developed by Alden (and to a somewhat lesser extent by William Hand, Starling Burgess, and a few others) seemed to fit the bill almost perfectly, for they were seaboats with a turn of speed. The success of these craft helped fuel a further demand for fast seagoers, and this brought the Alden firm plenty of business before the Depression years and beyond.

The 1903 *Rudder* article went on to cite certain designers such as Edward Burgess, Arthur Binney, George Stewart, Thomas McManus, and especially B.B. Crowninshield as the men largely responsible for producing the successful American fishermen of the early 20th century. Those vessels were inspirations for Alden, and of course, he was directly influenced by his former boss Crowninshield.

Needless to say, there were differences between the working schooners and the Alden fisherman-type yacht. The Alden schooner generally has more freeboard, especially amidships; it almost always carries more outside ballast; and it is shorter ended, particularly at the bow, than the yacht-influenced commercial fisherman. The working schooners had more depth of bilge, because considerable space just above the keel was needed for inside ballast and cargo.

Of course, the differences in function between a yacht and a workboat also suggested rig modifications to Alden. The yacht does not need a small foresail to facilitate spending lengthy periods hove-to; she does need power in her foresail and a fairly tall forward mast on which to hang racing sails, while her mainsail should be small enough for easy handling by a small crew. Alden was also concerned about the hazards of handing the jib from a bowsprit. As noted in the previous chapter, he thought it important to get the jib off early when the weather was threatening, and he therefore felt that a schooner should be well balanced with or without the jib.

Other sources of inspiration for Alden were the boats of Wilbur and Charles Morse. John admired the Morse-designed schooner, *Lloyd W. Berry,* and he also liked the looks of the Morse Friendship sloops. (Maritime historian Howard I. Chapelle, in his book *American Sailing Craft,* emphasized the close relationship, both in model and rig, between the Friendship sloop and the Gloucester schooner.)

If there were such a thing as a typical Alden boat of these years, it would most probably be a schooner with a relatively large gaff foresail set above a husky hull having generous freeboard (for her day), a graceful sheer, moderate overhangs, a rather short spoon bow, and a lovely oval transom with pronounced rake. She would also be inexpensively but well built and finished in a plain and simple manner. Her entrance would be sharp, her quarters powerful. She would not be particularly close-winded, but on a reach with her sheets eased, she would really come into her own. Above all, she would be seaworthy.

However, it would be a mistake to label John Alden as a designer of any particular type of yacht, even early in his career. He had an intuitive understanding of and appreciation for a boat that was well suited to her purpose, regardless of what that purpose was. The *Sea Fox,* the first boat he owned (see Chapter 3), was radically different from an "Alden schooner," yet years later he would still remember her as "the most remarkable small craft of her time (or almost any time)." As a perusal of the plans in this book will show, he could and did produce all kinds of yachts, from open daysailers, to racers intended for protected waters, to powerboats, to large, luxurious, and finely finished craft, in addition to the plain-finished, able, offshore cruising sailers for which he is so well known. I think his designs illustrate a degree of versatility that some readers may not have realized Alden possessed.

AN EARLY SLOOP

It seems appropriate to begin this chapter with an example of the fisherman type of hull with which John Alden was so often identified. The sloop shown here was designed in 1911, and she is listed as design number 15 in the Alden office index. Her dimensions are 48 feet 6 inches length on deck, by 38 feet length on the waterline, by 13 feet beam, by 6 feet 9 inches draft. She was designed for Charles A. Russell of New York City, who, to quote from *The Rudder* (March 1911), "desired an able, comfortable cruiser of the Gloucester fisherman type."

There were differences among the Gloucester fishermen of the early 1900s, and it can only be said that the type influenced this Alden boat in a general way. Some of her fisherman characteristics are the ample sheer and low freeboard aft, the generous depth at the garboards, and a rather long keel, in this case with a curving profile reminiscent of the "Indian Head" type of Gloucester schooner. The bow with its modest spoon is perhaps rather yachty in appearance (or at least like a yacht-influenced fisherman), but the stern, with its short counter and beautiful, raking, elliptical transom, is sug-

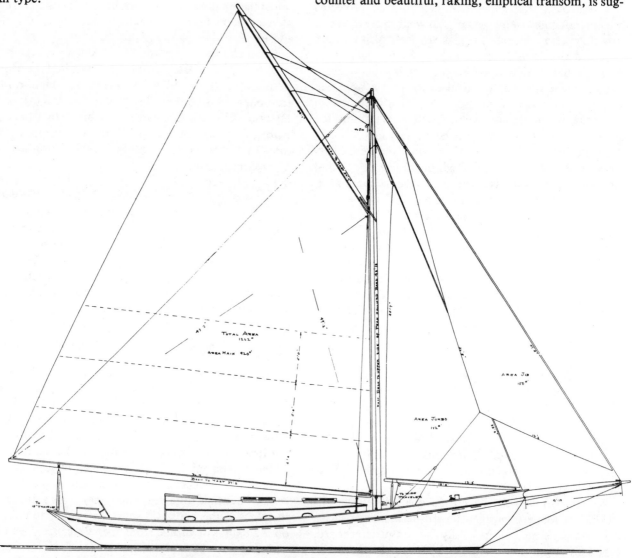

Above: *The 37-foot main boom on Charles Russell's sloop might seem awesome to a modern sailor, yet the end of the boom can be reached without too much difficulty when furling or reefing. (The Rudder,* March 1911) **Opposite top:** *Design number 15 has powerful lines with a high prismatic coefficient and firm bilges. (The Rudder,* March 1911) **Opposite bottom:** *With her sweeping sheer and the unbroken curve of her stem and keel, the Russell sloop has a lovely profile. The cabin sole has to be high to accommodate the large amount of inside iron ballast, but even so, there is 6-foot-2-inch headroom below. Her full ends and long cabin trunk give her enviable accommodations. (The Rudder,* March 1911)

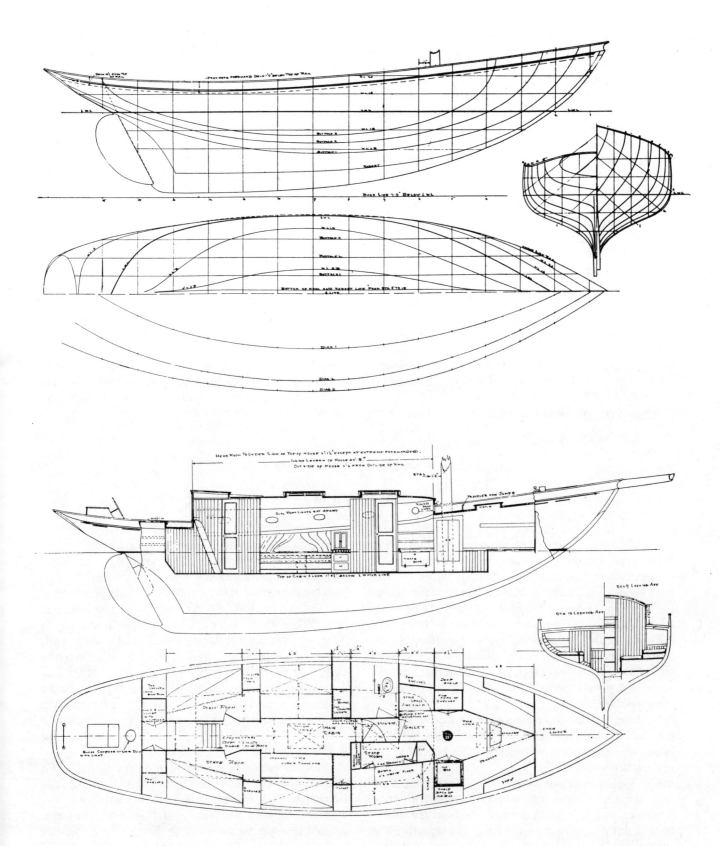

gestive of a pure fisherman. Howard Chapelle has written that this kind of transom with extreme tumblehome was probably first developed to keep the mainsheet from fouling, as might happen if there were square corners, but the shape of the transom is also pleasant to the eye. To a large extent its use was carried on for purely aesthetic reasons.

In true fisherman style, the sloop carries all of her ballast, six tons of iron, inside her bilge rather than on the keel. Many old-timers (Claud Worth among them) considered that inside ballast that was spread out longitudinally gave the boat an easy motion. Today it is generally recognized that spreading out the ballast increases the moment of inertia (the boat's resistance to turning about its transverse and longitudinal axes), but certainly the high position of inside ballast helps limit the increase while it shortens the righting arm. The net effect is to inhibit hobbyhorsing and jerky rolling. Of course, the relatively high center of gravity is not helpful to ultimate stability, but the boat's broad beam carried quite well forward and aft gives her good bearing at moderate angles of heel. All other things being equal, construction costs of an inside-ballast boat are significantly lower.

The gaff rig with double headsails provides plenty of sail area (1,202 square feet), yet keeps the center of effort low, which is also helpful to stability. This boat is about the largest Alden liked for a single-stick rig. The 920-square-foot mainsail is sizable, but once it is hoisted, the boat can be handled without much difficulty because there are no backstays, and the boomed forestaysail, which Alden usually called a jumbo, is self-tending.

The cabin plan was worked out by the owner. The three enclosed staterooms afford great privacy, but they must be a bit claustrophobic. With the forecastle and galley forward, the arrangement can accommodate a paid hand nicely. Two skylights on the cabin house admit light and air both to the passageway between the enclosed head and midships stateroom and to the main cabin farther aft. The cabin trunk is very long and quite high aft, which may detract somewhat from the boat's appearance, but it affords 6 feet 2 inches of headroom and a tremendous volume below.

The young designer seems to have fulfilled the owner's requirements admirably, for this fisherman-inspired sloop — with her heavy displacement, inside ballast, full, powerful lines, and generous accommodations — must have been comfortable both on deck and below.

A FAST YAWL

Soon after the aforedescribed sloop was designed, John Alden produced the plans for a very different type of sailing cruiser. This fast yawl, design number 19, was built for Philip Chase of Milton, Massachusetts. She differs from the earlier sloop in that she is finer lined, smarter, and — in almost any conditions — faster, but her hull is probably not as seakindly or comfortable for heavy weather offshore. Her measurements are 47 feet, by 30 feet 6 inches, by 12 feet, by 7 feet 6 inches, and she has 11,000 pounds of outside lead ballast for good sail-carrying ability.

With her cutaway forefoot and greatly raked rudder, the yawl has a short keel. Combined with her easy bilges, this gives her relatively low wetted surface. The underwater configuration is not unlike those of some fast cruisers turned out by the B.B. Crowninshield office. The keel is deep and salient for effective lateral resistance, and its shortness makes the boat responsive to her helm. Her ends are quite long, and the rather flat counter could slam in certain sea conditions. The deep draft makes the boat vulnerable to grounding when gunkhole cruising, but the rudder heel is well protected, for it is quite far above the bottom of the keel.

There is plenty of sail area for this easily driven hull, and the gaff-headed yawl rig keeps the center of effort low. When such a longitudinally spread-out rig is matched with a short-waterline hull and a short keel, balance is apt to be sensitive, and care must be taken to carry just the right combination of sails in order that there be neither lee nor excessive weather helm. With the mainmast cocked slightly forward for better balance, running backstays are provided to keep the forestays taut and to avoid the need to lead the shrouds very far abaft the mast.

Since the emphasis is on sailing performance, a few compromises had to be made in the cabin plan. The long overhangs limit the length for accommodations, and with the forward underbody so fine, even the main cabin's transom berths must be slanted in toward the boat's centerline at their forward ends. Nevertheless,

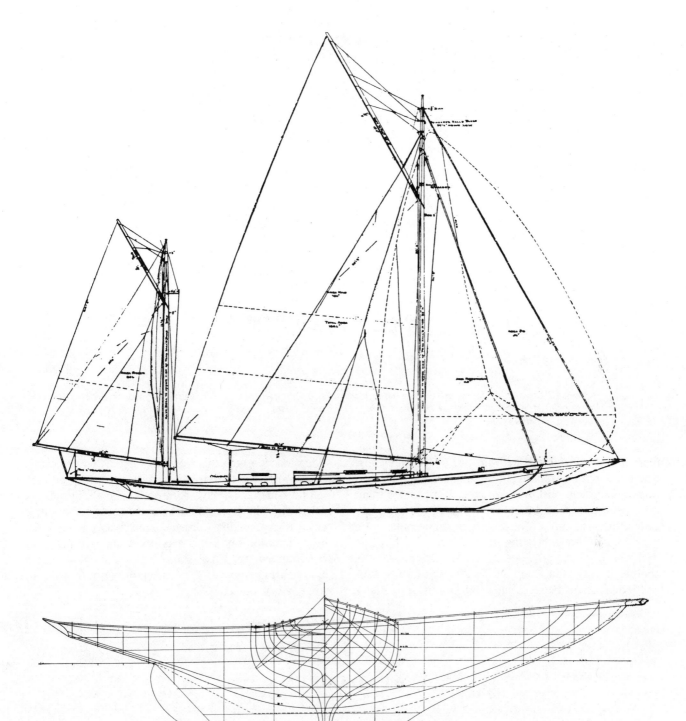

The longitudinally spread-out sail plan looks a bit incongruous with Number 19's short keel, but in a blow, lowering the jib and mizzen reduces and centralizes the canvas while retaining good balance. Although half-breadth lines are not shown, fine waterlines forward are suggested by the inward slant of the berths in the yawl's main cabin (next page). The toe on the keel allows a cutaway forefoot for maneuverability while retaining sufficient lateral plane for windward ability. (Yachting, April 1912)

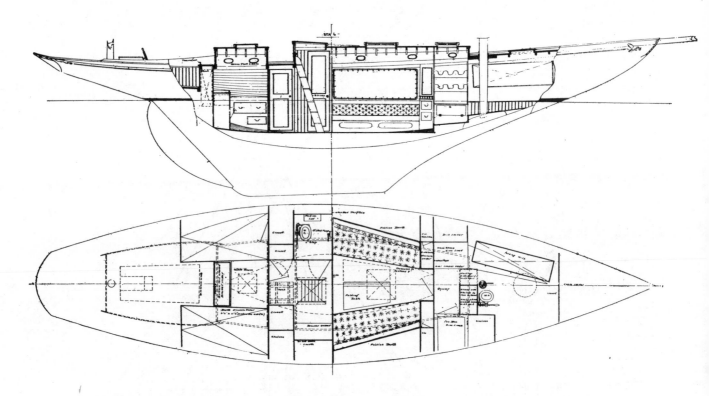

Number 19's two-cabin layout affords maximum privacy for the owner. Considerable emphasis on function is evident in the locations of the chart table, head, and oilskin locker, all near the companionway.
(Yachting, *April 1912)*

there is a comfortable stateroom just abaft amidships, where the motion is minimal; an ample head, a navigation area, and an oilskin locker amidships; a cozy main cabin with a large, folding table; a small but adequate galley forward; and a forecastle that can accommodate a paid hand. An interesting feature is the break in the deckhouse, which provides a central location for the companionway ladder and allows the use of a few full-width deckbeams between the cabin trunks. Years later

Alden incorporated this feature — modified somewhat with an off-center companionway — on *Malabar VI.*

John Alden must have been optimistic about the ease with which the boat could be driven, for he specified only a 10 h.p. auxiliary engine, which was located under the companionway steps. His optimism was probably well founded, for there seems little doubt that such a hull can be moved easily in reasonably smooth water by either sail or power.

WENDAMEEN

Design number 21 in the Alden office index is a handsome, rugged, cruising schooner. This vessel was built in 1912 by Adams Shipbuilding Company of East Boothbay, Maine, for Chester W. Bliss of Springfield, Massachusetts. Her dimensions are 67 feet, by 51 feet, by 17 feet, by 8 feet 9 inches, and she was given the name *Wendameen,* which means "to fish with hook and line" in the Delaware Indian tongue.

An article in *Yachting* (September 1912) stated that *Wendameen* was built on the lines of a pilot schooner, but the keel profile is very similar to that of the fisherman-inspired sloop discussed at the beginning of this chapter. It is true that the curving keel line may also be seen on a pilot boat, such as the *America* (not the famous schooner yacht *America*), designed by Thomas F. McManus, but McManus was primarily a designer of

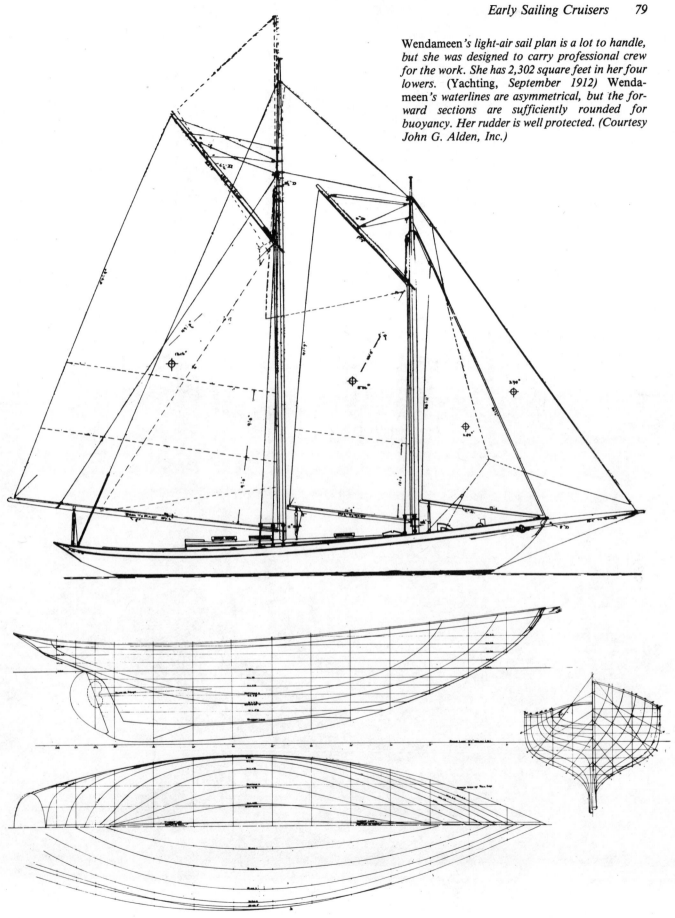

Wendameen's light-air sail plan is a lot to handle, but she was designed to carry professional crew for the work. She has 2,302 square feet in her four lowers. (Yachting, *September 1912*) Wendameen's waterlines are asymmetrical, but the forward sections are sufficiently rounded for buoyancy. Her rudder is well protected. (Courtesy John G. Alden, Inc.)

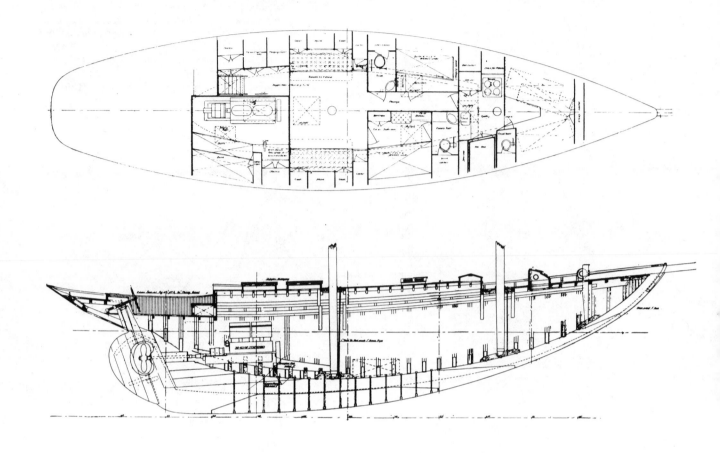

Opposite top: *Below decks* Wendameen *has quarters for a professional captain, an engineer, and a cook, and her main cabin seems almost big enough to accommodate a dance band and several couples. The cabin was finished in white and mahogany.* (Yachting, *September 1912)* **Center:** *The article in* Yachting *described* Wendameen*'s construction as "probably heavier than any other yacht of this size."* **Bottom:** *A deck view of* Wendameen *at anchor soon after she was acquired by Gerald Ford in 1933. (Courtesy Gerald W. Ford)*

fishing schooners. In the manner of many fishermen and pilot boats, *Wendameen* has a high bow and a sweeping sheer, which lowers the deck abaft amidships. However, her freeboard amidships is greater relative to her length than that of a typical fisherman, which needs to be low in order to facilitate bringing aboard dories or fishing gear.

Even a hasty glance at the construction plan suggests the strength and weight of *Wendameen*. Her timbers, frames, and deadwood appear massive for a yacht; her 32,000 pounds of ballast indicate that her displacement is considerable, since ballast-displacement ratios were generally modest (in the neighborhood of 33 percent) for such boats in those days. More than half the ballast was carried in the bilge, and this was said to give the boat an easy motion. Undoubtedly her heavy displacement, too, makes her a comfortable boat in rough water.

She is also comfortable in her accommodations, with a large saloon, well-ventilated staterooms, numerous lockers, three enclosed heads, a sizable galley forward, and a fo'c's'le that can sleep three paid hands. The nine-foot-long engine room houses a 65 h.p. Standard

engine, which the designer said could drive the boat at 10½ knots.

Wendameen's gaff-headed schooner rig allows fairly easy management under main, foresail, and jumbo in a breeze. She lacks power under this plan in light airs, but then her crew can set the main topsail, fisherman staysail, and jib. The writer who described *Wendameen* in *Yachting* was certainly impressed with her stiffness, for he wrote, "She can carry whole sail when everything else is seeking shelter."

In 1933 *Wendameen* was acquired by yacht broker Gerald W. Ford of City Island, New York. After keeping her in storage for a great many years, Ford has had her extensively rebuilt by the Minneford Yacht Yard. Restoration, which had cost in excess of $130,000 by 1983 and was not completed, included a new stem, keel timber, keel bolts, rudder, and about 80 percent of her frames and planking. The rig was changed in 1975 from schooner to jibheaded ketch, but Gerald Ford writes that he has never had *Wendameen* under sail. Let's hope that the old girl will sail again before long and that she still remembers how.

SOLITA

A sleek-looking yawl named *Solita,* design number 45, further illustrates Alden's early ability to turn out an able cruiser that is not an imitation of a Gloucester fisherman. In many respects, this yawl is similar to "The Ideal Two-Man Cruiser" Alden described for *Yachting* magazine readers in 1913 (see Chapter 3), although the *Yachting* boat might be a bit quicker in stays due to her slightly shorter, fully rockered keel.

With her straight shoe, *Solita* would be easier to haul on a marine railway, and in most conditions she's probably relatively faster with her more powerful main and her larger foretriangle. She was built in 1914 by Henry B. Nevins of City Island, New York, for Daniel Bacon, an experienced sailor who had shipped aboard the clipper *Hooghly* in his youth. According to Cruising Club historian John Parkinson, Jr., Bacon once sailed a cat-

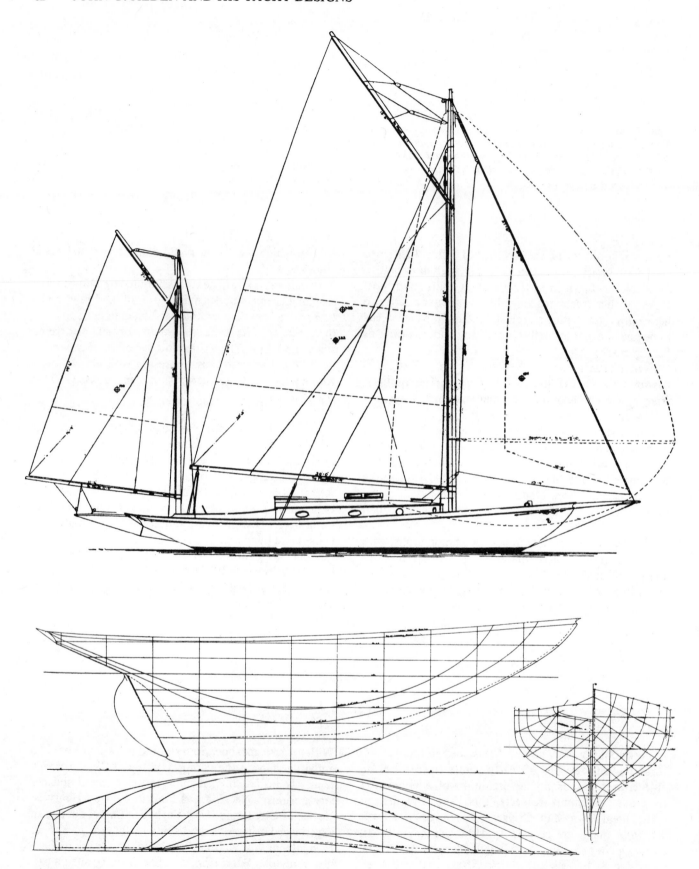

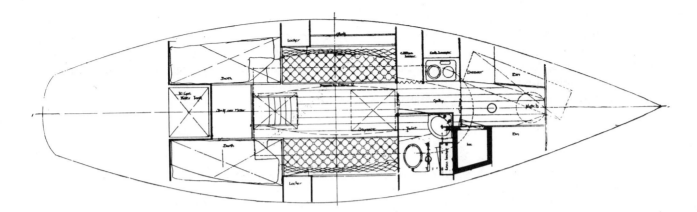

Opposite top: Solita*'s centers of effort are worked out so that she will balance well under main alone or jib and jigger. The plans show the old-fashioned single-luff spinnaker with its long pole.* (Yachting, *October 1913*) **Opposite bottom:** *The lines show* Solita*'s full afterbody. Her long keel encouraged helm steadiness and ability to heave-to.* (Yachting, *October 1913*) **Above:** Solita*'s cabin plan puts the galley forward, a common arrangement at that time even on small boats. The rounded forward end of the cabin trunk shunts aside any green water that may come over her low bow.* (Yachting, *October 1913*) **Left:** *Hauled out,* Solita *shows off her generous lateral plane and a new marconi rig with its elaborate rigging.* (Courtesy John G. Alden, Inc.)

boat from the Bahamas to Maine, and he won the Astor Cup in 1911 with his sloop *Avenger*. He specified that his new yawl should be an all-around coastwise cruiser that would have a good turn of speed and at the same time be able enough to take some bad weather offshore. *Solita*'s dimensions are 35 feet 6 inches, by 25 feet, by 10 feet 1 inch, by 5 feet 6 inches.

She is a handsome boat with attractive sheer, generous but not excessive overhangs, and a low cabin trunk that is nicely rounded forward. Her bilges are rather slack, but her waterline beam of 9 feet 6 inches gives her good form stability while the fullness at her garboards reduces wetted surface. With her moderately fine bow and ample keel, the boat must sail to windward well, despite her gaff rig. She carries 722 square feet of sail area, which is quite generous for her 25-foot waterline.

Solita has plenty of bunks: two quarter berths, two transoms in the main cabin, and a pipe berth forward. There is an adequate galley and a roomy enclosed head forward of the main cabin. Evidently, Bacon outgrew the accommodations, however, for about 10 years after this boat was built, he gave Alden the order for a larger, more comfortable cruiser named *Querida* (described in this chapter), thus becoming one of Alden's many repeat clients.

A CENTERBOARD SCHOONER

Design number 53, a schooner drawn in 1914 for Dr. Frank Baldwin of Peoria, Illinois, is in some respects more typical of a fisherman than anything presented so far in this chapter. She has the commonly seen curved stem without much overhang, the forefoot cut away to a point abaft the foremast, and then the usual long,

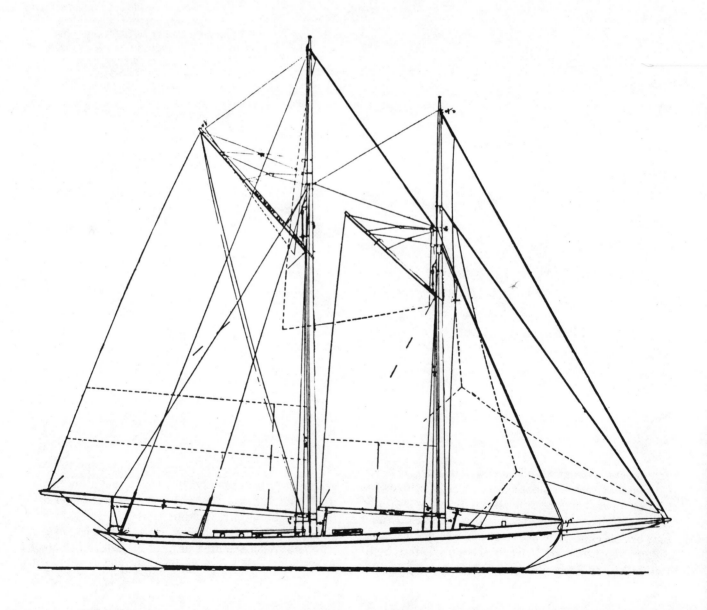

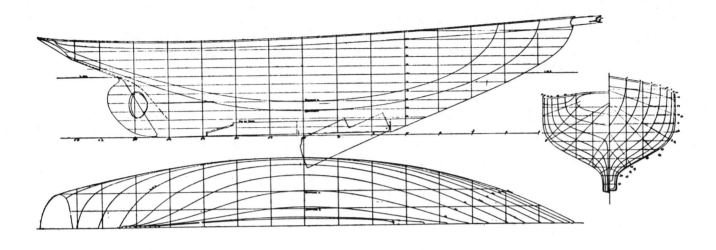

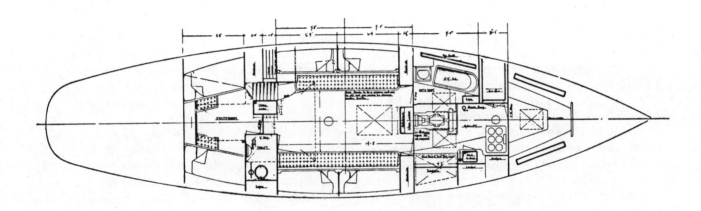

Opposite and above:
With her topsail, fisherman, and three headsails, design number 53 can crowd on a lot of sail in a light air. Beamy, shoal-draft centerboard schooners suffered a severe loss in popularity after the Mohawk — *a 140-footer with just six-foot draft and all inside ballast — capsized in 1876, causing the drowning deaths of five people. However, the type came back in a much healthier form. The lines of design number 53 show that good form stability over a broad range of heel angle can be provided by moderate draft and considerable outside ballast. Her saloon is over six feet wide between the transoms and nearly 14 feet long. Note the bath tub forward.* (Yachting, *December 1914*)

straight keel that facilitates hauling on a marine railway. Nevertheless, this schooner differs from typical fishermen in that she has less sheer and less molded depth, and her freeboard aft is relatively high. Also, she has much less drag to her keel, and, of course, a centerboard. Her measurements are 63 feet 8 inches, by 48 feet 4 inches, by 15 feet 10 inches, by 7 feet (board up).

With the help of 18,000 pounds of outside ballast, she carries 2,337 square feet of canvas in her four lowers. The long bowsprit is required not only for sail area but also for balance. The long keel tends to make the boat slow in stays, but undoubtedly she tracks well and can be hove-to easily. One might think the rather extreme

forward position of the centerboard would cause some weather helm when it is fully down, but this could be relieved by reefing the main in a fresh breeze.

This schooner might be called a flush-decker, although she has a small cabin trunk aft. The trunk is needed for full headroom in the owner's stateroom, the sole of which is a bit higher than that of the main cabin. In addition to an enclosed head nearly amidships, which is accessible both from the owner's stateroom and the main cabin, there is a large bathroom forward with a full-size tub. An unusual feature is that this bathroom can be converted to a stateroom by folding a pipe berth down over the tub. The main cabin is huge, and it has four pilot berths in addition to transoms. The galley and a space for crew's quarters are forward, with the engine located at the after end of the galley. A disadvantage of this arrangement is that the engine requires an exceedingly long propeller shaft.

This vessel is spacious and seakindly, well suited for offshore cruising; yet, with her seven-foot draft, she can enter almost any hole-in-the-wall big enough to offer her swinging room. It is not known whether she was ever built.

PRISCILLA ALDEN

An impressive vessel that gave Alden publicity early in his career is the large, three-masted schooner *Priscilla Alden,* design number 88, originally intended as a cargo carrier. Built by Frank C. Adams of East Boothbay, Maine, she was completed in 1919, not quite in time to meet the demand for tonnage that existed during World War I. Clifford Swaine writes that she was built on a cost-plus-23-percent basis. Her dimensions are 154 feet 6 inches, by 134 feet 4 inches, by 33 feet 4 inches, by 12 feet 6 inches, and her plans indicate that she could carry "700 tons dead weight."

It was mentioned in Chapter 3 that the three-master was christened by the owner's daughter, Priscilla Alden Dennett. Actually, there were 13 owners, and shares were divided into 64ths, with the designer himself owning four shares. Of course, the schooner's name was also that of the famous Pilgrim, who was an ancestor of the designer, which brings us full circle. In 1923, after commercial sail had become less profitable, the *Priscilla Alden* was converted to a yacht, and her name was changed to *Rocinante*. It was stated in E.J. Schoettle's book, *Sailing Craft,* that she embarked on a round-the-world cruise, but there was no indication of whether or not she completed the circumnavigation. She was sold to the Russian government in 1929.

The plans presented here are the original ones, so most of the hull's interior consists of cargo holds. Nevertheless, there are adequate accommodations in the forward and after deckhouses for the crew needed to handle the vessel. Aft, there are four staterooms, a large bathroom with tub, a saloon with transoms and table, and numerous lockers; the forward deckhouse contains the galley, a fo'c's'le, and housing for a large windlass, which would handle the ground tackle and other heavy gear.

The three-masted schooner rig was chosen, of course, to divide the sail area in such a way that the boat could be handled efficiently by a small crew. No one sail is exceedingly large, considering the size of the vessel, and the rig offers great versatility in achieving good balance in all kinds of weather. Furthermore, the main and foresail booms are convenient to the cargo hatches. A snug sail combination for heavy weather might be the mainsail, foresail, and jumbo.

Like most cargo schooners, *Priscilla Alden* has an exceptionally long, straight keel, which balances her longitudinally spread-out rig and holds her on a steady course. I would not care to sail her in restricted waters or attempt to beat off a lee shore in a blow, for she must be slow in stays with her lack of keel drag, her deep

Opposite: Priscilla Alden*'s rig allows a variety of sail combinations and keeps each sail a reasonable size. In the long term, squaresails cause less strain on the hulls of sailing cargo carriers, but Alden fitted this fore-and-after with vang tackles to hold the booms steady and to prevent flying jibes. (The Rudder,* January 1918) *The body plan shows a wall-sided hull with the accent on function, but the profile view shows how graceful something that is functional can be. (Courtesy John G. Alden, Inc.) It can be seen that most of the vessel's volume was to be used for cargo. With full holds, the low main deck might be frequently awash in heavy weather, but the quarterdeck is well raised for dryness and safety. (The Rudder,* January 1918)*

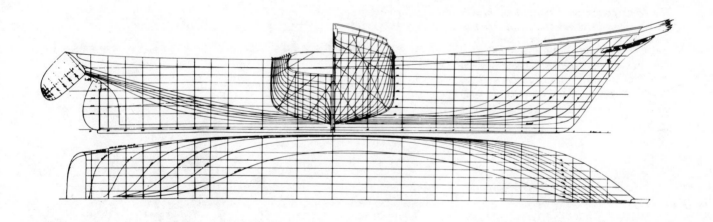

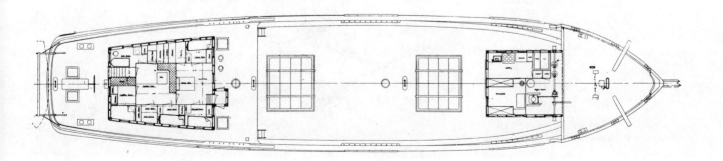

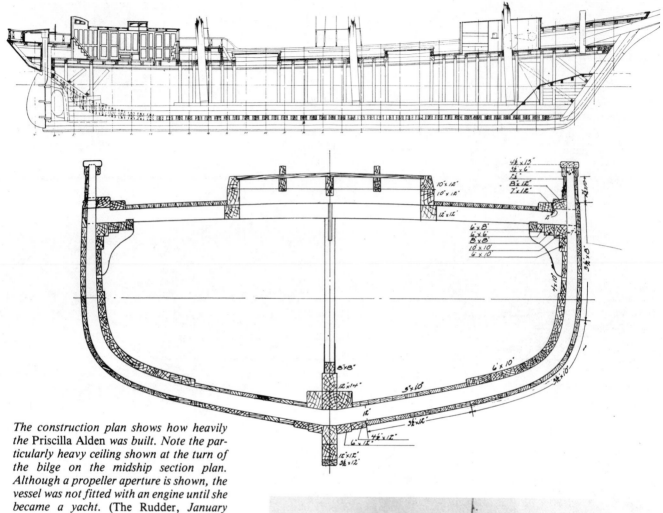

The construction plan shows how heavily the Priscilla Alden was built. Note the particularly heavy ceiling shown at the turn of the bilge on the midship section plan. Although a propeller aperture is shown, the vessel was not fitted with an engine until she became a yacht. (The Rudder, January 1918)

Priscilla Alden under whole sail. (Mystic Seaport Museum, Inc., Mystic, Connecticut)

forefoot, and her small rudder. Some sailing cargo-carriers have auxiliary power for the hard chance and for windless passages, but the Alden schooner had no engine until she was converted to a yacht in 1923. Originally, she probably used a yawl boat for auxiliary power in light airs.

The *Priscilla Alden*'s hull is rather boxy and slab-sided, almost barge-shaped, because of her purpose as a cargo carrier. Even so, Alden has managed to give her considerable shape with the raking transom, slight tumblehome, graceful sheer, and flaring clipper bow, accentuated by the pronounced steeve of the bowsprit, which has an outboard length of 48 feet. With the present energy shortage, commercial sail may be returning, and if so, there may still be a place for vessels with the same purpose as this three-master. Sailing cargo ships of the future probably will not at all resemble Alden's design. No doubt they'll be ugly by comparison.

A SLIM OFFSHORE KETCH

With design number 95, drawn for a man named Raymond in 1919, Alden showed some alternative thinking in regard to the ideal seagoer. This boat, a heavy ketch measuring 72 feet, by 52 feet, by 13 feet 6 inches, by 8 feet 3 inches, is narrow and has moderate sail area. Raymond wanted a large boat that could be handled easily

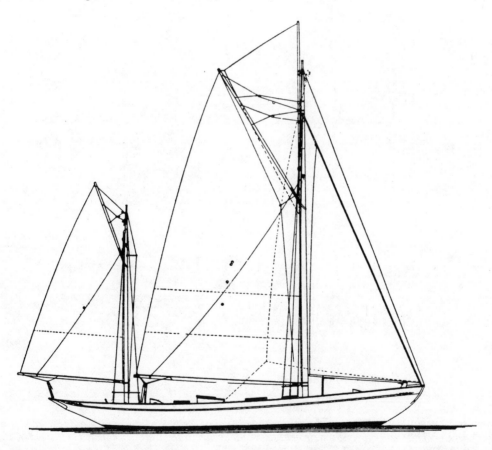

*A snug, inboard sail plan with just under 2,000 square feet of canvas in the three lowers makes the ketch easy and safe to handle. (*The Rudder, *June 1919)*

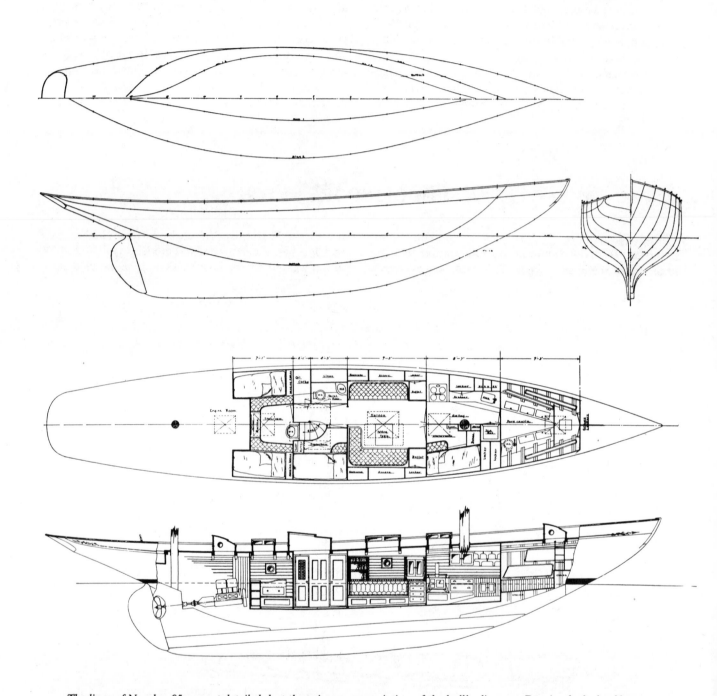

The lines of Number 95 are not detailed, but they give an appreciation of the hull's slimness. Despite the lack of beam, the quarters are powerful. The sheer line is quite straight from amidships to the bow. Although she is slender, this big ketch has ample accommodations for up to six people in the owner's party, plus a crew of three. (The Rudder, June 1919)

by a small crew, and the designer reasoned that a narrow hull could be easily driven and thus would need only a small, manageable rig.

At various periods during the history of yacht design, there has been considerable emphasis on beam as an important factor in hull resistance, and this notion has often been reflected in yacht rating rules. In more recent times, however, it has been found that the added stability afforded by reasonably broad beam will compensate for the added resistance to the extent that a beamy boat will often beat to windward in a fresh breeze better than her narrower counterpart. In a light breeze with a ground swell or in leftover seas after the breeze has died, the narrower boat will have the edge, provided she has enough sail to drive her through the seas.

The ketch in question should have enough sail to drive her through a slop in anything except the lightest airs, provided she carries her big Yankee jib and topsail. Obviously, those sails add to the difficulty of handling the boat, but she should be easy to manage in more breeze when only the working sails are needed, since the rig is inboard and the working jib is self-tending. The rather long counter obviates the need for a boomkin to

take the mizzen sheet, and this is a great help to the crew furling the mizzen in rough weather. Her heavy construction and her 20 tons of ballast, two-thirds of it outside, should make her less tender than she might otherwise be.

The narrow beam detracts from space below, but the ketch is large enough to accommodate comfortably the owner and his spouse plus guests and two or three paid hands. Although Raymond wanted a boat for short-handed sailing, it seems that he hedged his bet by specifying quarters for a fairly sizable crew. Aside from the owner's double stateroom aft, there are two guest staterooms, one abaft and one forward of the saloon. The galley is forward, just abaft the fo'c's'le, and there are two heads, one forward for the professional crew and the other in a room aft near the companionway and handy to the owner's cabin.

It would be interesting to know how well this boat might have fulfilled its intended purpose, but the Alden records do not reveal whether she was ever built. She does illustrate the flexibility of her designer in satisfying the requirements of a client.

NORSEMAN

Two designs after the previously described ketch, also in 1919, Alden turned out a design that was quite similar, but with a schooner rig and greater beam. The plans of this boat, named *Norseman,* show the initials S.S.C., Jr., which could only be those of Sam Crocker, one of the many Alden employees who would become well-known designers after leaving the firm. Perhaps Crocker also had a hand in the number 95 design, because the ketch and schooner are quite similar in their hull profiles and their arrangement below decks.

Norseman was designed for George B. Williams primarily for cruising in Labrador waters, and she was very strongly built by Frank C. Adams at East Boothbay, Maine. She measures 63 feet, by 47 feet, by 15 feet, by 8 feet. With her adequate freeboard, pronounced sheer, ample beam, short bow, long keel, and 15-inch bulwarks, the schooner seems a good boat for rugged northern waters. The only feature that might be a bit incongruous is the long overhanging stern, but it is well tucked up, and I doubt if many seas broke over it, although the counter might have taken a few slaps.

The rig is not very large for a vessel of such heavy displacement, but the lower sails are adequate for the fresh winds the boat was expected to encounter. The topsail and fisherman staysail put some extra area aloft, where it is needed in light weather. The shrouds are set far enough abaft their mast that there is no real need for running backstays. The trade-off for this arrangement is that the booms are somewhat restricted when the boat is running dead before it, but the gaffs can be allowed to swing broad off, thus putting most of the foresail and mainsail at right angles to the wind.

The cabin plan is like that of design number 95 except that *Norseman*'s engine is forward of rather than abaft the after stateroom and saloon. Another difference is that the schooner's wider beam allows an additional small stateroom adjacent to the engine, and this was used as quarters for a professional captain. The forward staterooms could become unbearably hot with the engine running if cruising in southern waters, but the heat was probably welcome off the coast of Labrador.

Norseman makes an interesting comparison with the

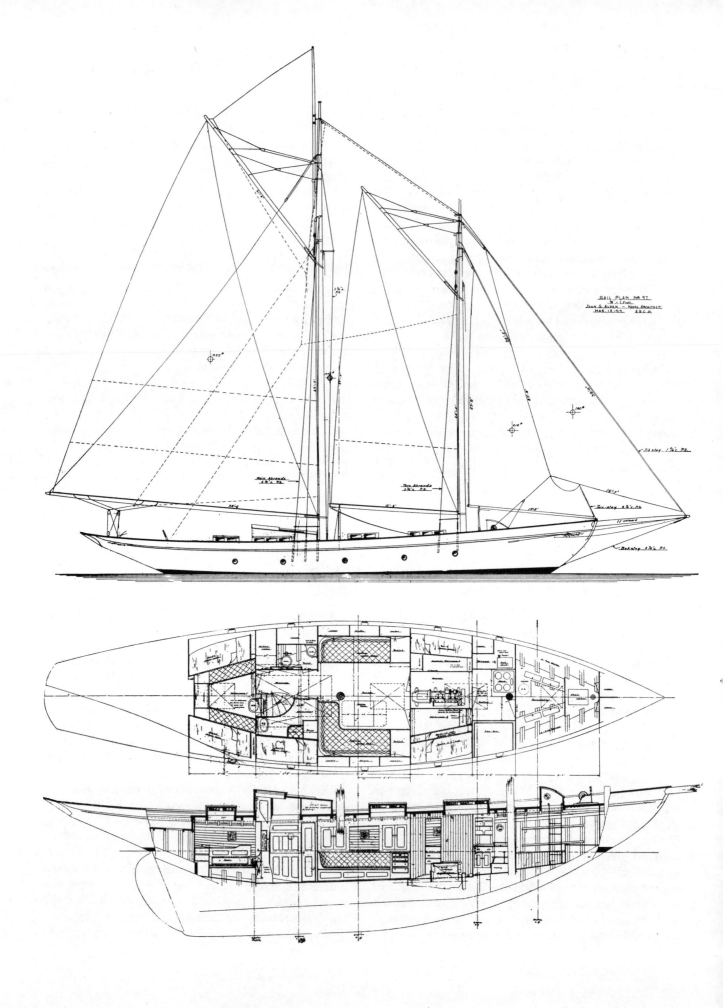

SAIL PLAN NO 97
JOHN G. ALDEN - NAVAL ARCHITECT
MAR. 13, 1919.

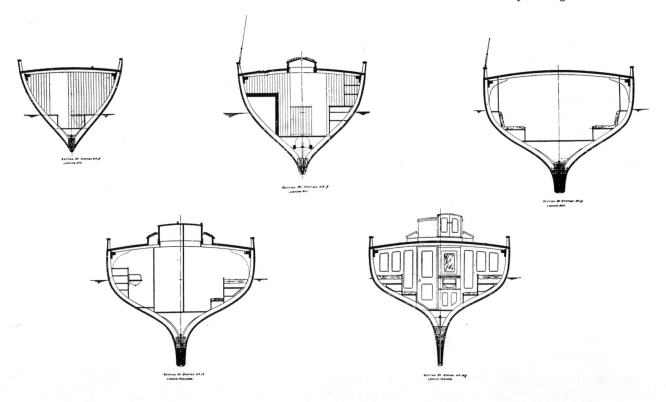

Opposite and above:
Designed for fresh winds and easy handling in heavy weather, Norseman's sail area is a modest 1790 square feet. Her accommodations offer privacy and utility. The curved stairway is an interesting detail. Norseman's sections show her sturdy bulwarks, broad decks, and spacious main cabin. (The Rudder, February 1920)

Norseman *spreading her wings. Her bow seems high, perhaps because of all the people aft. (Courtesy John G. Alden, Inc.)*

seagoing schooner *Wendameen,* built some eight years earlier. The boats are quite similar in hull form, rig, and construction, except for *Norseman's* longer counter and tucked-up transom. Perhaps the greatest difference between the two schooners is in their ballasting. *Wendameen* carried 14,000 pounds of iron outside and 18,000 pounds of lead in her bilge, whereas *Norseman* carried 10 tons of lead on her keel and only four tons of ballast inside. Evidently, Alden had concluded that his schooner yachts were sufficiently seakindly to allow greater use of outside ballast for greater sail-carrying ability.

THE CATBOAT FOAM

Since John Alden's home waters were cheek by jowl with Cape Cod it is not at all surprising that he designed a number of catboats. The one shown here, named *Foam,* is of the Cape Cod type. *Foam* was designed for S.K. Dimock and built in 1920 by G.W. Gardner of Swampscott, Massachusetts. Her design number is 104, and her measurements, although shown slightly smaller in the Alden records, turned out to be 21 feet, by 9 feet 6 inches, by 2 feet 3 inches.

The main advantages of a catboat are the ease of handling and making sail, the great roominess and initial stability afforded by enormous beam, and the shallow draft. Trade-offs for these features include some vulnerability to swamping or capsize (as compared with a deeper, keel boat with a small cockpit well); occasional steering difficulties, especially when running in a fresh breeze; occasional poor performance in head seas; lack of headroom; and not-infrequent problems with

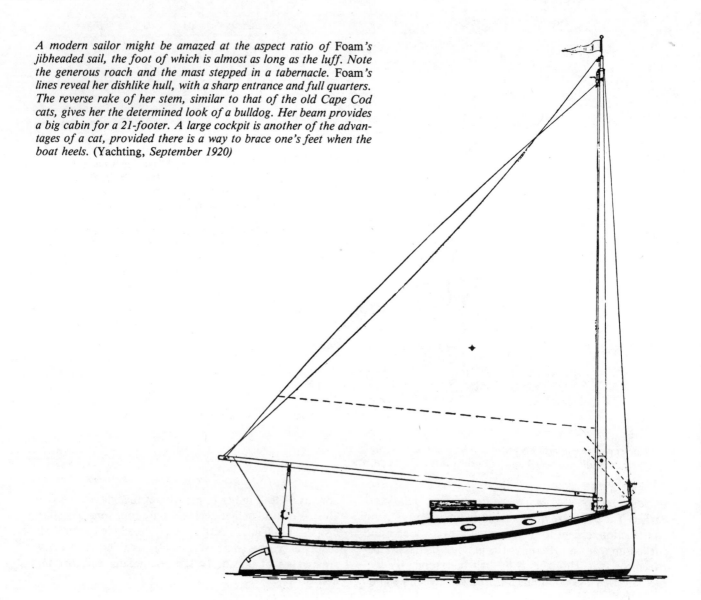

A modern sailor might be amazed at the aspect ratio of Foam's *jibheaded sail, the foot of which is almost as long as the luff. Note the generous roach and the mast stepped in a tabernacle.* Foam's *lines reveal her dishlike hull, with a sharp entrance and full quarters. The reverse rake of her stem, similar to that of the old Cape Cod cats, gives her the determined look of a bulldog. Her beam provides a big cabin for a 21-footer. A large cockpit is another of the advantages of a cat, provided there is a way to brace one's feet when the boat heels.* (Yachting, *September 1920)*

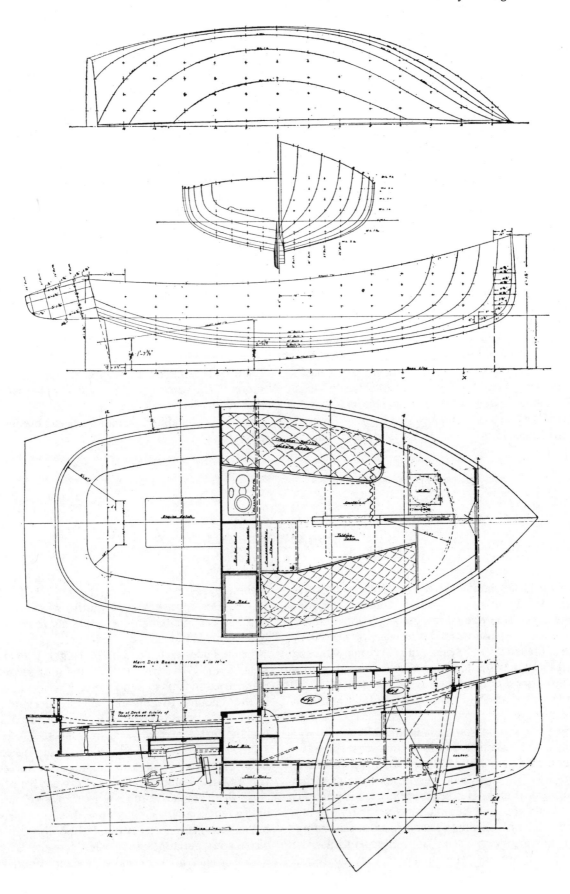

water in the shallow bilge. These remarks would generally apply to *Foam,* although she has a few special features that set her apart.

She has the typical hollow entrance that most cats need to ease their broad beam through a chop, but *Foam*'s waterlines are a little fuller forward; that is to say, they have a shoulder, which provides more buoyancy forward and should help prevent rooting when running in following seas. Her centerboard seems unusually far forward, and this might increase her weather helm. An old rule of thumb for this type of cat was that the forward lead of the center of effort relative to the center of lateral resistance should be one inch to every foot of waterline length, but *Foam*'s centers seem closer together. As every sailor knows, too much weather helm is "a real drag," yet a certain amount is a safeguard for capsizable boats, ensuring that during knockdowns (when the wind is forward of the beam) they will automatically round up.

Of course, the main difference between *Foam* and a typical Cape Cod cat has to do with her rig. The sail is not gaff-headed, yet it is not tall enough to be called a marconi sail. Leg-o'-mutton is probably the most suitable name for it. Another unusual feature is that the mast is hinged on a tabernacle so that it can be lowered. Howard Chapelle once wrote that many cats, built as

yachts, are given too much sail, and this is a major reason for their occasional wild behavior. *Foam* certainly doesn't have this problem, for, if anything, she is under-rigged, with a mere 230 square feet of sail area. In fact, she has only one row of reef points, whereas most cats have two, three, or even four rows. No doubt she is sluggish in light airs, but she has an auxiliary engine for those conditions.

The large cockpit looks comfortable indeed with seats all around, and it is sufficiently high above the waterline to be self-draining. Due to the broad beam and the fact that the centerboard is forward, the cabin is spacious for such a small boat. There are two comfortable berths, a heating-and-cooking stove with both wood and coal bins, and a sizable icebox. The centerboard trunk, together with a curtain, provides privacy for the head forward, and the trunk's after end supports drop leaves for a good-size table.

Chapelle has written: "For knocking around in sheltered waters and alongshore, for day sailing and week-end cruising, the cat is a splendid type. In fact, the Cape cat is suitable for any type of cruising, except offshore." The same could be said about *Foam,* except that with her small rig she could negotiate (with seamanlike handling) some fairly ambitious coastal passages.

∽

PRIMROSE IV

Another Alden schooner used extensively in northern waters was *Primrose IV,* design number 111. She became for a time one of the designer's most talked-about boats, because in 1927 she won for her young master, Frederick L. Ames, the Cruising Club of America's Blue Water Medal, which has been described as sailing's most coveted award.

Primrose IV was built in 1923 by Rufus Condon at Friendship, Maine, for Walter H. Huggins of Boston. She was the second, or "B" boat, built to the 111 design, which was created in 1920. In a sense she was a forerunner to the early *Malabars.* Like the *Malabars, Primrose IV* has a gradually curving keel profile with a fair amount of drag. Her beam at the deck is generous forward and aft, while her waterlines are fairly fine forward but full aft. Like the *Malabars,* she is quite short-ended, has a generous sheer, and in general, has the look of a fisherman. Her dimensions are 50 feet 2

inches, by 39 feet 11 inches, by 13 feet, by 7 feet 2 inches. Her construction is sturdy, with sawn frames and 1½-inch planking. She carries about eight tons of ballast, half inside and half outside.

While under the command of Huggins, *Primrose IV* sailed in the 1924 Bermuda Race and took second in her class. Then she was sold to Frederick Ames, who cruised in the schooner to Labrador a year later and in 1926 sailed her across to England for the Fastnet Race. She was the first American yacht to compete in this rugged event, and she did well, finishing second on corrected time. The heavy weather during that race forced many contestants, including the hard-driven British cutter *Jolie Brise,* to heave-to, but *Primrose IV* carried on under reduced canvas. Her crew discussed heaving-to, but as yachting reporter Alfred F. Loomis put it, "Their discussion outlasted the gale." Ames sailed the schooner back home by way of Iceland, Labrador, and

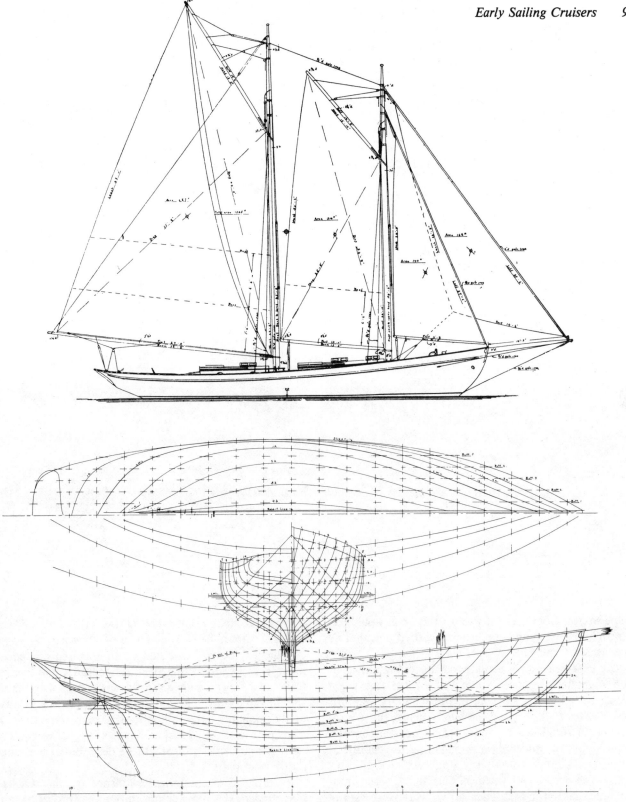

Without topsails or running backstays, Primrose IV's *rig is easy to handle. Her sail area is 1,305 square feet. The pronounced steeve to the bowsprit can keep the crew handing the jib from getting dunked. (*Yachting, *February 1920) The lines, drawn in December 1919, show a lot of similarity to the early* Malabars. *With about eight tons of ballast out of 48,200 pounds displacement,* Primrose IV *has a ballast-displacement ratio of about 33 percent, near that of* Malabar I. *The tracing was done by John Alden Crocker, Sam Crocker's brother. (Courtesy John G. Alden, Inc.)*

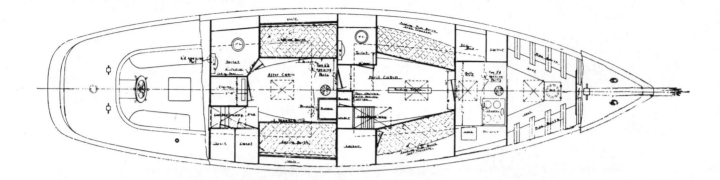

Above: *The layout below in* Primrose IV *is a good compromise between privacy and practicality. Since the companionways are to starboard, heaving-to on the starboard tack would be advisable.* (Yachting, *February 1920)* **Right:** *This schooner on a broad reach is either* Primrose IV *or her sister,* Black Arrow. *(Courtesy John G. Alden, Inc.)*

Cape Breton Island, and it was for this 58-day passage, carefully prepared and competently carried out, that he was awarded the Blue Water Medal.

The bald-headed rig permits easy handling, although one might be concerned about lack of sail area when racing in light airs. Of course, the schooner was not designed for typical round-the-buoys racing; she was intended for rough waters and strong winds. In contrast with some of Alden's later gaff-rigged schooners, *Primrose IV*'s foresail is fairly small, which facilitates lying-to in very heavy weather. During her worst mid-Atlantic gale, the schooner lay-to very successfully under reefed foresail and backed jumbo.

The arrangement below follows the typical plan used during the days of professional crew, when it was customary to place the galley between the fo'c's'le and the saloon. The owner's cabin aft has its own toilet room, and there is another at the after end of the saloon, with a head for the crew forward. A two-cylinder engine was installed in an enclosed compartment just forward of the cockpit. Separate cabin trunks have advantages and disadvantages, but they have special value for a schooner in that a flush deck in way of the mainmast allows substantial beams and strong mast partners. The companionways are off-center on the starboard side, so it might be desirable to heave-to on the starboard tack.

Yachting historian John Parkinson, Jr., has written that Frederick Ames was not only a fearless sailor but also a daring stunt flier whose life was cut short by an airplane accident. No doubt Ames's cruising exploits were considered daring too, but they were carried out with careful seamanship and in almost the safest boat that a yachtsman of that day could ask for.

A SMALL CENTERBOARD YAWL

In 1920, Alden produced an attractive 30-foot, centerboard yawl intended for singlehanded or shorthanded sailing. Her design number and name are unknown, and probably she was never built, but her plans show a very pretty boat, well suited for her purpose. She's 24 feet on the waterline, 9 feet 9 inches in extreme beam, and draws only 3 feet 8 inches with her board up. She could go almost anywhere, even venturing up the shallowest tidal creeks. It might not be prudent to take her on extended offshore voyages, for she may be lacking somewhat in reserve stability, and her freeboard is a bit low and her cockpit large. Nevertheless, she has some good seagoing features, including short ends, a bridge deck, high cockpit coamings, and small portholes.

The gaff rig provides ample sail area (554 square feet) yet keeps the center of effort low, and the sails should be managed easily by one person with the self-tending jib and all sheets leading close to the helm. In contrast

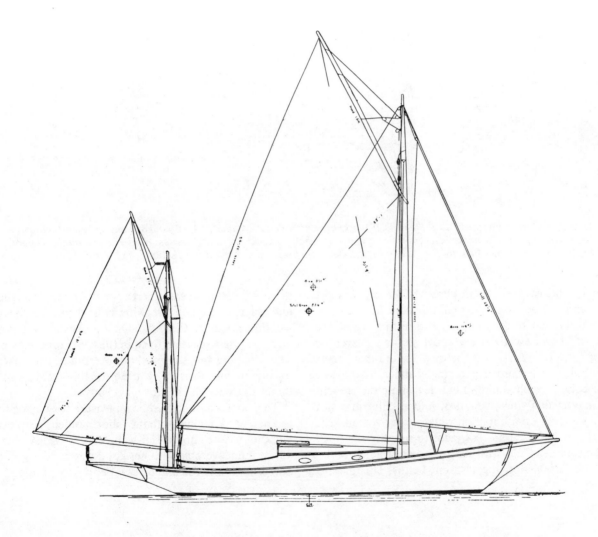

The sail plan of this centerboard yawl shows an easy rig to singlehand, but the lone sailor would have to be especially careful handing the mizzen. (Yachting, *February 1920)*

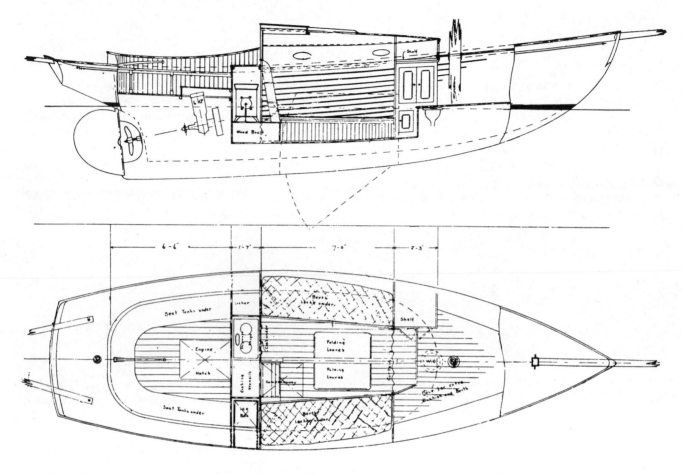

The cabin of the centerboard yawl looks particularly inviting for cool evenings, but you might want more ventilation on hot summer days. Her underwater profile shows a long, shallow keel. The nearly vertical rudder axis should make the rudder very efficient when the boat is not heeled. The one-lunger delivers 6 h.p. (Yachting, February 1920)

to many modern yawls, on this boat the centers of effort of jib and mizzen alone and mainsail alone lie in a nearly vertical line with the total center of effort. Thus, the boat will be nicely balanced under jib and mizzen or under main alone. Almost the only feature that seems undesirable, especially for a singlehander, is the low main boom, which could all but decapitate the crew in an inadvertent flying jibe. Also, a lone sailor may not relish standing on a boomkin when furling the mizzen, but at least that sail has lazyjacks to simplify the job.

The cabin is snug, with its coal stove, folding table, and comfortable-looking transom berths. Up forward

there is a head, an extra berth for the occasional guest, and plenty of room for stowing sails. A nice detail is the wood box beneath the stove. On a cool evening it would be exceedingly pleasant to sit in the cabin aft on the port side with your feet stretched out in front of the stove. If topside in cold weather, you'd probably want to sit on the bridge deck directly over the stove.

This boat would indeed be a pleasure for bay or river sailing or knocking about shorthanded, exploring gunkholes. She should sail well, hold a steady course, yet be maneuverable with her good-size rudder well aft. She'd be simple for one or two people to handle.

∽

SEAWARD

Not long after the little yawl was designed, Alden drafted plans for a large commercial trading schooner,

Number 115, named *Seaward*. She was built in 1920 by Frank C. Adams of East Boothbay, Maine, for the L.A.

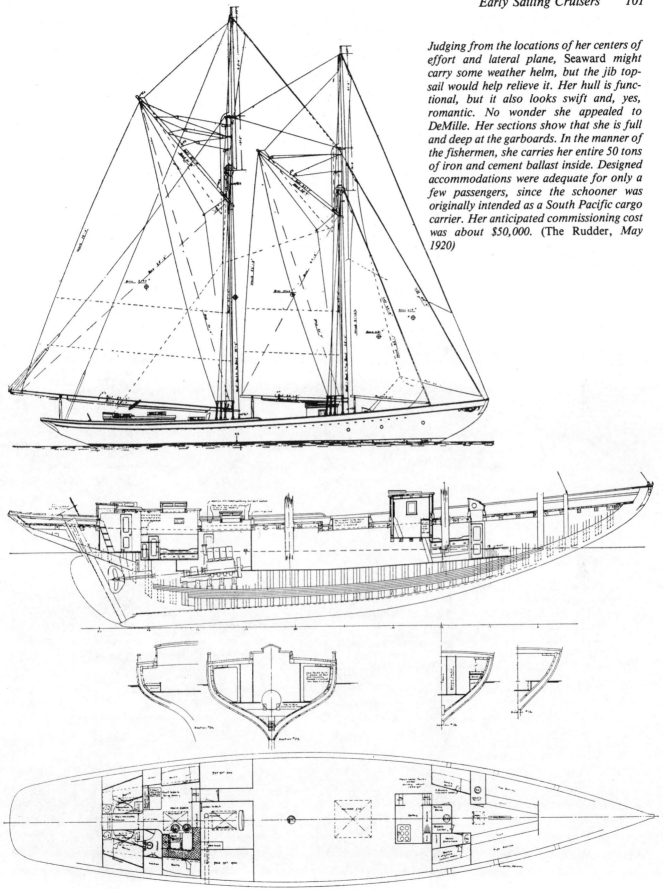

Judging from the locations of her centers of effort and lateral plane, Seaward *might carry some weather helm, but the jib topsail would help relieve it. Her hull is functional, but it also looks swift and, yes, romantic. No wonder she appealed to DeMille. Her sections show that she is full and deep at the garboards. In the manner of the fishermen, she carries her entire 50 tons of iron and cement ballast inside. Designed accommodations were adequate for only a few passengers, since the schooner was originally intended as a South Pacific cargo carrier. Her anticipated commissioning cost was about $50,000.* (The Rudder, *May 1920)*

Seaward *well heeled in a fresh breeze. Without her prominent sheer the schooner might have a hump-backed look in this view. (Courtesy Cecil B. DeMille Estate)*

Below in Seaward, *a well-lighted stateroom with a wide berth, a sink, and a functional simplicity underlying some Edwardian touches. (Courtesy Cecil B. DeMille Estate)*

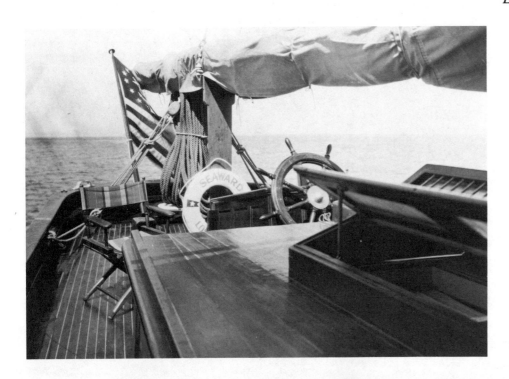

These two deck views show her sturdy bulwarks, broad decks, and large skylights. At her helm, you'd have a feeling of power at your fingertips. (Courtesy Cecil B. DeMille Estate)

A stern view of Seaward shows her boat boom and accommodation ladder and a huge ensign flying. (Courtesy Cecil B. DeMille Estate)

Norris Co. of San Francisco, for the purpose of carrying a few passengers and cargo in the South Pacific. In hull and rig, she bears a strong resemblance to the Gloucester knockabout schooners of that time or somewhat earlier. Her dimensions are 105 feet, by 82 feet, by 21 feet 8 inches, by 12 feet.

She proved a good sailer. The knockabout rig keeps the sails inboard, of course, and simplifies handling. One problem with many knockabout fishing schooners is that the lack of a bowsprit and the large mainsail with its long boom produce a strong weather helm. *Seaward,* with her shorter boom and fairly long forward overhang, would probably have reasonable balance, but it does appear that her total center of effort is slightly abaft her center of lateral resistance. She was fitted with a 65 h.p. Acme engine that could kick her along at 7 knots in light airs. Also, there is a Mianus deck engine for handling anchors and sails, thereby making a large crew unnecessary.

Most of the hull volume is devoted to cargo carrying, but there is limited space for passengers. In the after cabin house are two single staterooms, an enclosed head, and a saloon, which contains two berths, a chart table, and a U-shaped settee. The forward cabin contains the galley and houses the crew. A nice feature for

sailing in the tropics is the galley's caboose or deckhouse, which affords a lot of ventilation. Its elevation also simplifies carrying food aft on deck.

In 1942, *Seaward* became the property of the U.S. Navy, but earlier in her career she was owned by Cecil B. DeMille, the Hollywood movie producer, and she was used in several movies. DeMille's sea films are a cut above most in nautical detail. Perhaps *Seaward* contributed to the famous producer's knowledge of boats and helped make his films more accurate.

Imagining yourself at the helm of *Seaward,* you might almost believe you were on a Gloucester schooner racing home with a hold full of fish. She'd be close-hauled with the rail nearly down and occasional squirts of water shooting through the scuppers. Now and then a plume of spray would fly over the weather bow and rattle against the straining canvas as your vessel powered through the seas. The forward sails would be trimmed in rock hard, but the main would be eased off a bit to relieve her weather helm. You couldn't call the helm sensitive, but it would be responsive and steady. You'd have an awesome feeling of power at your fingertips. *Seaward* is that kind of vessel; she stimulates the imagination!

A KNOCKABOUT SCHOONER YACHT

A type similar to *Seaward* but on a much smaller scale is design number 151, a 40-foot knockabout schooner. Her waterline is only 27 feet long, while her beam and draft are 10 feet and 6 feet, respectively. She has a lot of overhang forward and aft, which eliminates the need for a bowsprit and boomkin. The bow is typical of certain

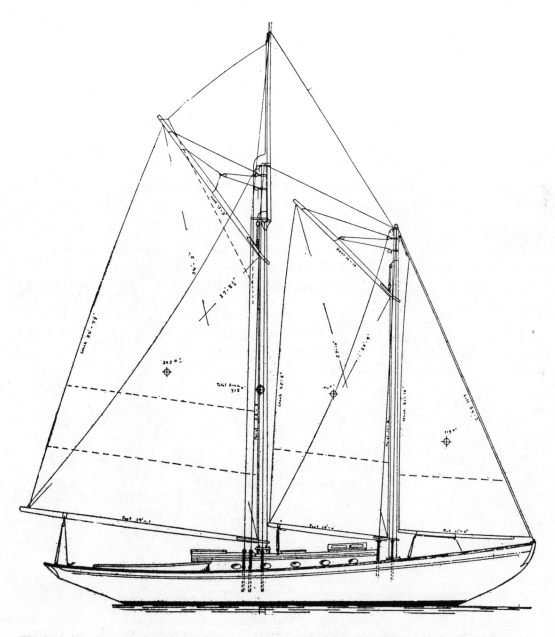

This little knockabout schooner shows fine character in her hull profile and rig. (Yachting, *May 1920*)

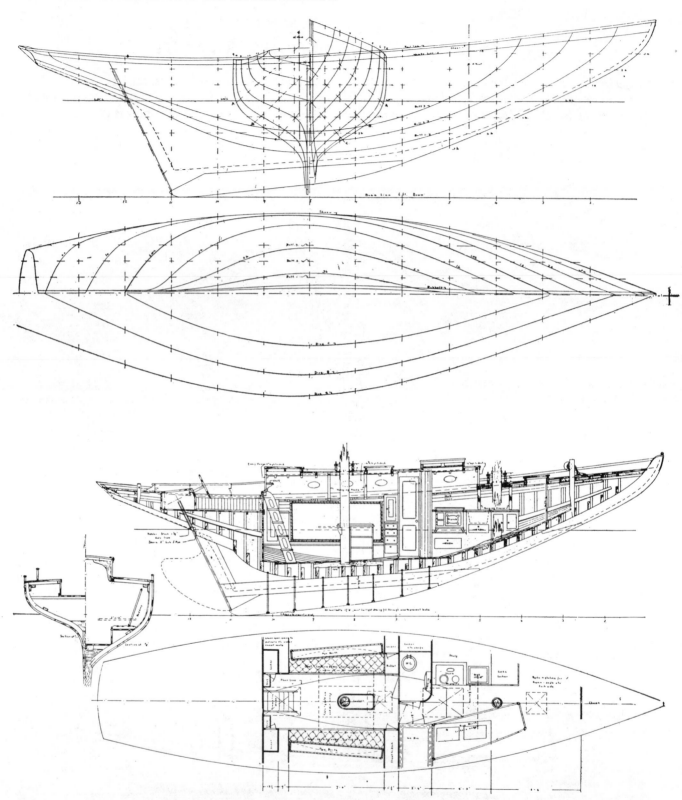

The lines of Number 151 show a deep-bodied hull, suggesting considerable displacement, but her wetted surface appears to be modest. She has a steep run, and the quarters are full; the entrance is sharp but not hollow. There is 7,000 pounds of iron ballast outside and 2,800 pounds of lead inside. The construction profile shows her heavy scantlings and the unusual proposed shape of her rudder. The length of the companionway ladder indicates the depth of her body. An interesting detail shown in the cabin plan and sections is the narrow transoms, which use the folding pipe berths as back rests. A drop-leaf table with locker beneath is built around the heel of the mainmast. (Yachting, May 1920)

Gloucester knockabout schooners, and I'm not sure that John Alden really admired the shape aesthetically, for he sometimes referred to it as a "snout."

Except for the topsail, the rig is easy to handle, with the lower sails nicely divided in area and self-tending when tacking. It is interesting to me to compare this boat with my own, a sloop-rigged Ohlson 38, which is roughly the same size in all dimensions except overall length. The schooner's lower sails alone have an area of 718 square feet, versus 570 square feet (100 percent foretriangle) for the Ohlson 38! Although the schooner is probably a good deal heavier than my boat, I would guess that there is not a lot of difference in wetted surface; therefore, the schooner should perform very well under her lowers alone in anything but the lightest breeze. The main topsail should be of real value in light air, because it gets some area up high where there is more breeze. The topsail moves the total center of effort farther aft, but this may not be bad, because many boats perform better with a fair amount of weather helm when sailing to windward in ghosting conditions.

Since the load waterline is short and the outside keel ballast and weight of rig are spread out longitudinally, it appears that the schooner would hobbyhorse, but the full waterlines aft help damp pitching. Also, the boat

carries 2,800 pounds of lead inside ballast, which, if concentrated amidships, should favorably affect the moment of inertia.

The rudder has an unusual squat shape, with its area carried low to clear the propeller immediately overhead. However, the shape is an efficient one for control under sail, since most of the blade is in relatively clear, less turbulent water. The trade-off for this arrangement is that the rudder will be less efficient under power than one with an aperture for a propeller, since steering control is improved when the prop wash can be directed against the blade. Final decisions of engine and propeller placement and rudder shape were to be made when the boat was built.

Accommodations are limited, but the boat was intended for singlehanded or shorthanded sailing. There are two transoms with pipe berths above in the main cabin, and another pipe berth forward. An enclosed head is amidships to port, and the galley is farther forward. Plans for the schooner were commissioned by three Boston yachtsmen who wanted three sister boats, but unfortunately not one of them was built. With their easily handled rig, many sail options, and seaworthiness, they would be the kind of boat for which any cruising sailor could develop an addiction.

SARACEN (KINKAJOU)

An Alden schooner built in 1924 attracted a good deal of attention after her adventures during a year's voyage around the North Atlantic were recounted in *Atlantic Circle,* a book by Leonard Outhwaite. This boat, built by J.F. James and Son in Essex, Massachusetts, from Alden's design number 210, was originally owned by William Whitman, Jr., who did some of the preliminary design work. Her original name was *Saracen,* but she became best known as the *Kinkajou* under Outhwaite's ownership.

This schooner is a sturdy, short-ended, long-keeled, modestly rigged type intended for the most rugged offshore use. She has high bulwarks and moderate sheer, with more freeboard amidships than a typical fisherman had. Her dimensions are 89 feet 6 inches, by 71 feet 5 inches, by 19 feet 7 inches, by 9 feet 6 inches, a size that allows palatial accommodations. Indeed, *Kinkajou* has no fewer than five enclosed heads, one with a full-size bathtub, and five staterooms, including three large doubles and two singles for the professional captain and the steward. In addition, there is a large engine room, a saloon, a forward galley, and a fo'c's'le that houses a

crew of three. The original owner drew up the basic arrangement; Samuel Crocker drafted the finished plans.

Kinkajou has a small rig (2,857 square feet), but she made some fast runs on her Atlantic circle, which went from New York to New York by way of England, Gibraltar, West Africa, and the West Indies. Her sails are quite easily handled, since the total area is well divided, the rig is entirely inboard, and there are no topsails. She was sometimes able to keep sailing in heavy weather when vessels with taller rigs might have been forced to heave-to. During a severe gale in the Bay of Biscay, for example, she kept sailing to improve her offing, but in this case it might have been better to jog along very slowly, for her fo'c's'le hatch was swept away and she took a lot of water below.

Despite a few anxious times, *Kinkajou* provided Outhwaite with a highly satisfactory vessel for his cruise. As he described her, "To our eyes she was beautiful; she looked her part — a ship that would take you there and back."

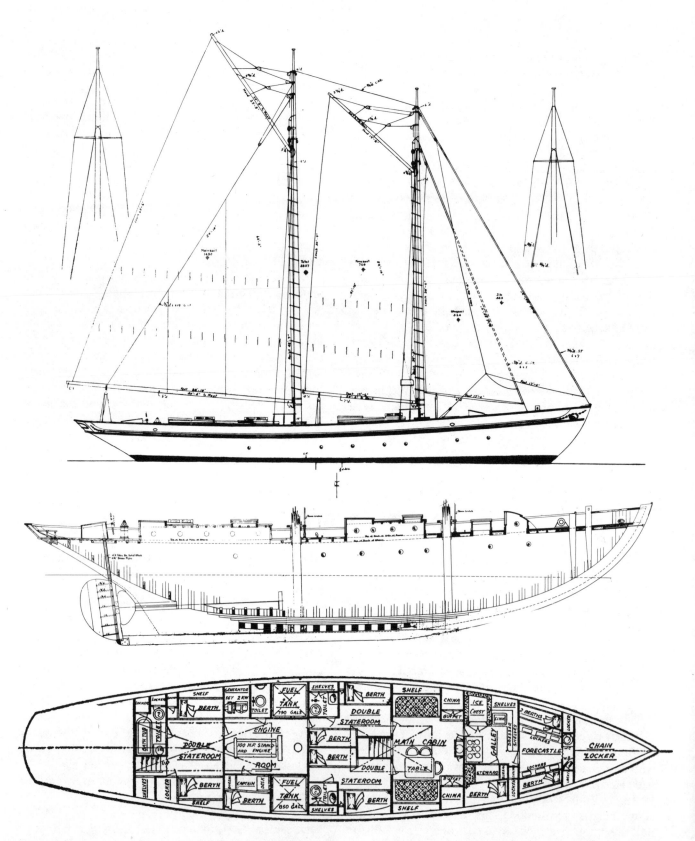

Saracen *certainly has a snug, seagoing rig. A good combination for heavy weather would be the jumbo and foresail. (Courtesy John G. Alden, Inc.) Drawn by Sam Crocker, her construction profile shows her deep underbody and shallow keel. (Courtesy John G. Alden, Inc.) With five heads and five staterooms, Saracen offers as much comfort and privacy as anyone could desire. (*Atlantic Circle *by Leonard Outhwaite)*

SVAAP

The Alden boat that is perhaps best known to offshore cruising sailors and well-read vicarious adventurers is the ketch *Svaap* ("dream" in Sanskrit), design number 224-B, which William Albert Robinson sailed around the world between mid-1928 and the end of 1931. With measurements of 32 feet 9 inches, by 27 feet 9 inches, by 9 feet 6 inches, by 5 feet 5 inches, she was the smallest boat to have made a circumnavigation at that time. Robinson wrote a lively account of the voyage in a book called *Ten Thousand Leagues Over the Sea* (with one edition entitled *Deep Water and Shoal*). This book ranks along with those of Joshua Slocum and John C. Voss as a classic in cruising literature.

From the initials on *Svaap*'s plans, it appears that Fenwick C. Williams and Samuel S. Crocker did the major work on her design. The plans indicate a stout, short-ended, soft-bilged and therefore seakindly hull with some flare forward and an inherent ability to heave-to. She had a deep enough forefoot, in fact, to ride reasonably well to a sea anchor off her bow; Robinson used this tactic for several days on his outward passage, while between Cape Hatteras and Bermuda, during a gale that he described much later as "one of the greatest storms I have ever seen." The hull is quite symmetrical and the keel is long, which suggests consistent balance and ability to self-steer, although Robinson seldom abandoned the helm for long periods. Doing this, he said, "is simply asking for trouble," and he felt that it was necessary to sacrifice some efficiency from the sails when rigged for self-steering.

The cabin plan shown here is the original one. Robinson sailed *Svaap* to the South Seas with this arrangement, but in Tahiti the after end of the boat was changed radically. The cockpit was torn out and a small after cabin put in its place, so that the skipper's Tahitian crew member could have his own quarters. Of course, this meant sacrificing the cockpit, and the helmsman had to perch on the after cabintop to steer. Although his legs would fit in a small footwell between the forward and after cabin trunks, the helmsman was somewhat vulnerable at times. Indeed, Etera, the crew, was washed overboard on one occasion and was saved only by his lifeline. There are no plans for the after cabin, but the forward one was not greatly modified from the original plan: the galley and an oilskin locker aft, two transoms in the saloon, and an enclosed head and pipe berth forward.

The Alden Company records show that three boats were built to the 224 design. The first, named *Eaglet,* was built on Long Island in 1925 for yachting writer Samuel Wetherill, an able offshore yachtsman who was a close friend of Alden's. The *Svaap* was built in the same year by Etherington in Shelburne, Nova Scotia, for a man named Sayle. Plans for the third boat went to Sydney, Australia, and they must have produced the boat now named *Nanook,* which was sailed around the world a number of years ago by Katie and Maurice Cloughley. The book *A World to the West* describes their adventures. According to Maurice Cloughley, *Nanook* is a slightly enlarged version of *Svaap,* because the builder had a timber for the keel that was slightly too long, and he didn't have the heart to cut it off.

The sail plan shown here is the original one, and it was not designed with a circumnavigation in mind. Robinson had the area cut down from 655 to about 560 square feet for his voyage, taking most of the area from the mizzen. I particularly like having a smaller mizzen for sailing in a blow and for heaving-to. Even with her generous forefoot, a boat like *Svaap* would need a scrap of sail aft to keep her bow up if riding to her sea anchor. However, Robinson did not always choose to lie to a drogue in heavy weather, and the Cloughleys never used one. Maurice has told me that they often preferred to lie ahull, and that tactic worked well for them. On some points of sailing, of course, the sails of a ketch rig can interfere with each other. Maurice said that his favorite sail combination to minimize blanketing and backwinding in moderate winds is the mizzen and a genoa jib.

After his circumnavigation, Robinson completely rerigged *Svaap* as a wishbone ketch. With a longer bowsprit and the space between the masts nicely filled with a boomed mizzen staysail and wishbone trysail, the boat's performance was decidedly improved, but the sail plan caused some added handling complications. Under this rig in 1933, Robinson sailed his *Svaap* to the Galapagos, but while there he suffered a ruptured appendix. He survived, but his ketch was left unattended while he was recovering. *Svaap* was confiscated by local authorities and then was plundered and wrecked. The sad story was told by Robinson in his book *A Voyage to the Galapagos.*

Clifford P. Swaine, John Alden's longtime associate, has written: "J.G.A. always said that this [*Svaap*] was a poor design for a world cruise, and it was not designed

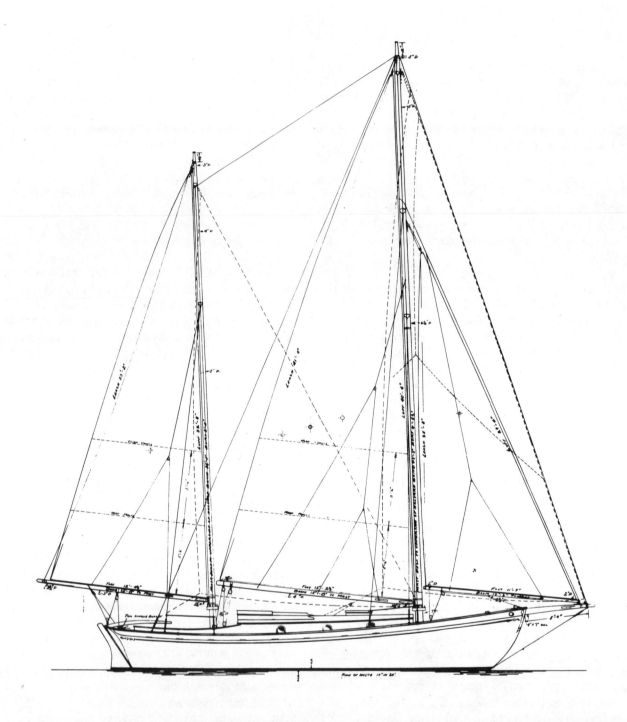

The original sail plan shows Svaap *with much taller masts than she had during her circumnavigation. Recent model-tank studies of capsizes, however, show that tophamper, if it is not excessive, increases the roll moment of inertia and thereby reduces the risk of rolling over in heavy seas. Svaap's lines show a well-balanced hull with short ends and with considerable lateral plane for course keeping and lateral resistance. Her midship section has a slow turn at the garboards, which not only provides strength but also allows headroom without a high cabin trunk. Her original cabin plan (shown here) was altered in the South Seas, when she acquired an after cabin and lost her cockpit. (Courtesy John G. Alden, Inc.)*

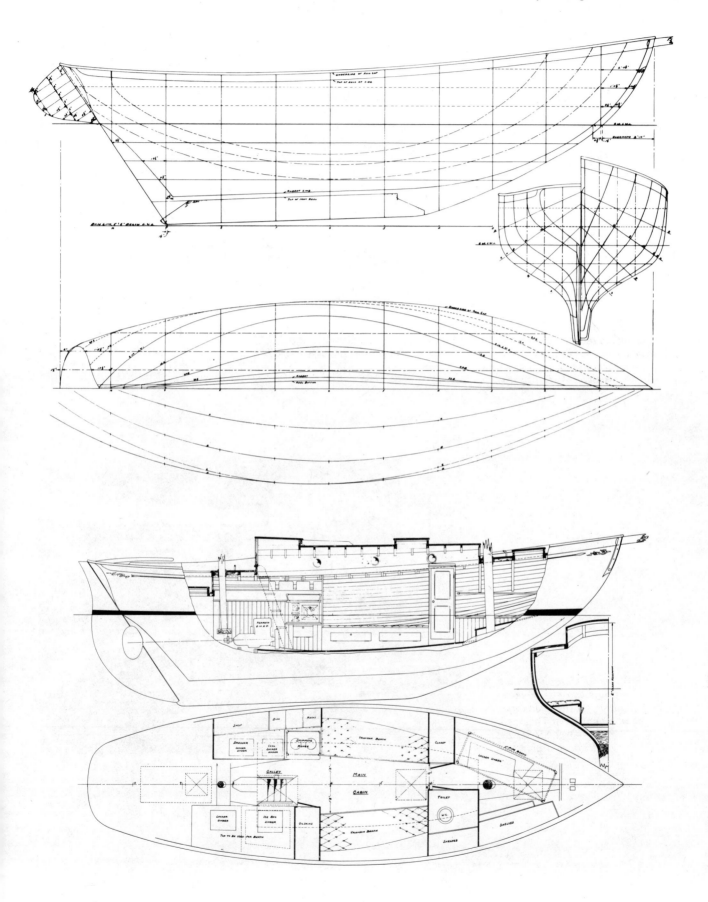

Svaap, *as seen from the* S.S. Slamat, *on the Indian Ocean during her circumnavigation.* (Ten Thousand Leagues Over the Sea *by William A. Robinson*)

William Robinson with his charts and his 200-book library in the main cabin of Svaap. (Ten Thousand Leagues Over the Sea *by William A. Robinson*)

Looking up at Svaap's *main trysail. The wishbone made her rig more complicated, but it allowed efficient shaping through camber adjustment with the outhaul.* Svaap's *windward ability was improved by this rig. (Courtesy William A. Robinson)*

as such." Indeed, she was not Robinson's ideal for a circumnavigation, but rather the best boat that he could find for his purpose for $1,000 in 1927. Nevertheless, *Svaap* seems like a nearly ideal boat for voyaging with a crew of two. Perhaps she could be a little larger or a little smarter under sail, but she is no slowpoke, for Robinson once pushed her to 190 miles per day, while *Nanook* (under the name *Safari Too*) once sailed 200 miles in a day. Some blue-water cruisers might prefer a low-maintenance fiberglass hull, and bowsprits are not

ideal for offshore work, but otherwise the 224 design seems nearly perfect for her task. Maurice Cloughley wrote: "When Katie and I bought *Nanook,* we believed her to be fairly close to our ideal of a solid, competent, seakindly long-distance cruising yacht suited for two people, and our years aboard her have fully justified that original faith." Robinson said about his *Svaap:* "If I can always accomplish successfully each small task in my life as *Svaap* accomplished each of hers, I shall have nothing to worry about."

QUERIDA

In 1925 Alden produced the plans for an interesting gaff-rigged sloop named *Querida*. With her partial raised deck and partial trunk cabin, she has a strange, hybrid look. Aesthetically it would perhaps be preferable if each set of ports were the same shape, instead of one set being round and the other oval.

Querida is unusual in more than looks, for her accommodations are also offbeat, and her draft is quite a bit shallower than that of a more usual offshore boat of her size. Her design, Number 240, was drawn for the same Daniel Bacon who had been the owner of the yawl *Solita,* which was discussed earlier. Bacon's new boat was a dramatic contrast to his earlier one. *Querida* was built by the Greenport Basin and Construction Com-

pany of Greenport, Long Island; her dimensions are 49 feet, by 38 feet 3 inches, by 14 feet, by 3 feet 9 inches. Her centerboard is undoubtedly needed for effective sailing to windward, since the keel is not deep enough for much lateral resistance.

The accommodations are unusual in that the port-side midships galley can be completely closed off from the saloon with a removable partition, and there are two heads opposite each other just forward of the galley and saloon. The owner's stateroom is just abaft the fo'c's'le. For privacy there is a bulkhead forward of the stateroom, and the crew's quarters in the fo'c's'le are entered through a booby hatch on the foredeck. The Scripps E-4 engine is mounted off center, and the shaft

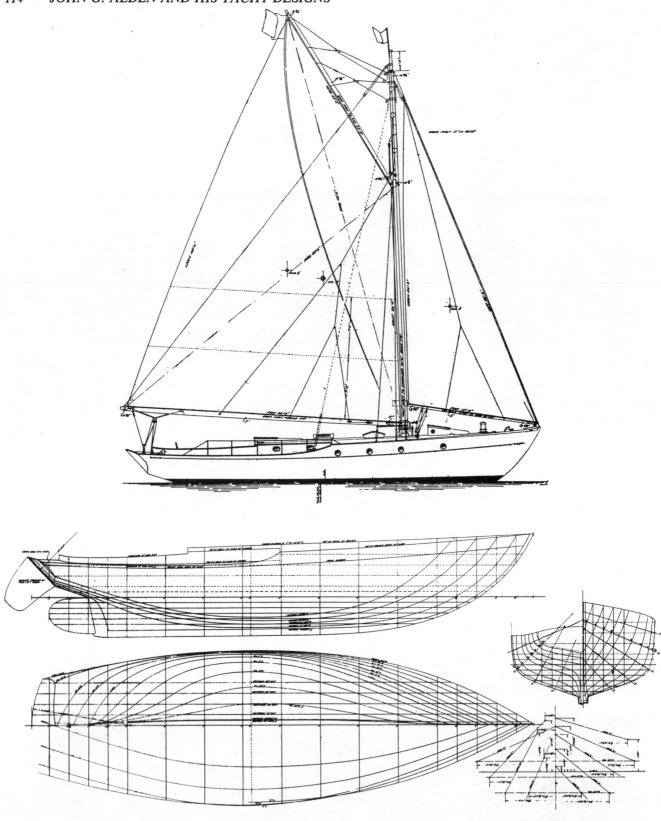

Querida's 1,171 square feet of sail consists of a huge mainsail and a small foretriangle. She should sail and balance reasonably well under main alone. Her hull is unusual in its shallow draft and lack of a salient keel. Her body depth accounts for most of her draft. (Yachting, *December 1927*)

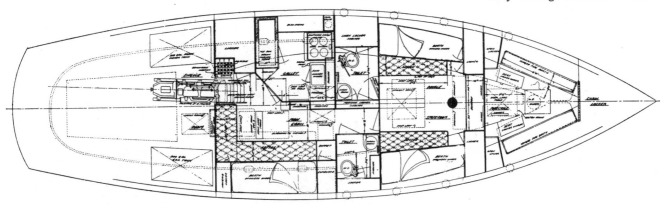

Above: *The offbeat accommodations accent privacy with little sacrifice to comfort. Note the closed-off port-side galley and the solid bulkhead abaft the fo'c's'le.* (Yachting, *December 1927*) **Below:** *It appears from this 1931 photo of* Querida *under sail that she has a longer boom and shorter gaff than shown in the sail plan. A bowsprit and pulpit have been added. (Edwin Levick photo. The Mariners' Museum, Newport News, Virginia)*

At the helm of Querida, *Commodore Bacon is a benevolent overseer of the Harlem and Larchmont Yacht Club Regatta in May 1930. (Edwin Levick photo. The Mariners' Museum, Newport News, Virginia)*

is angled slightly to counteract twist from propeller torque.

In 1930 Bacon was elected commodore of the Cruising Club of America, and *Querida* thus became that organization's flagship. John Parkinson, Jr., club historian, writes that Bacon, together with several marine biologists, once patrolled the New Jersey coastline in his sloop after a shark scare at one of the beaches. With her powerful auxiliary, she probably was well suited to this duty.

In 1947 *Querida* was bought by Claude B. Chiperfield, who put her back in top condition and renamed her *Rainbow*. The Chiperfields lived on the boat for a full year, sailing her from Maryland to Cuba and then to New York. Although not fast, the boat was easily handled, a competent sailer, and an exceptional course holder. Above all, she was sturdy and seaworthy, with an easy motion and comfortable accommodations. Remembering their year aboard, Elsie Chiperfield writes, "Of all the boats we had, I loved the *Rainbow* best. It was a happy year — no trouble and very comfortable." The Chiperfields sold the sloop in Florida in 1954.

If offered a choice between *Solita* and *Querida,* a young sailor might pick the yawl for her greater beauty and smarter performance, but an old-timer might very well choose *Querida* for her greater comfort and her ability to sneak into shallower anchorages.

LITTLE WARRIOR

Three designs after *Querida,* Alden produced the plans for a 30-foot sloop that has been called the first of the Malabar Juniors. Alden had been getting a lot of requests for designs similar to his schooners named *Malabar,* so it made sense to put out a smaller version of that type of hull with a single mast. It has been said that this boat, despite her different underwater profile, was also influenced by the Friendship sloop, an assertion

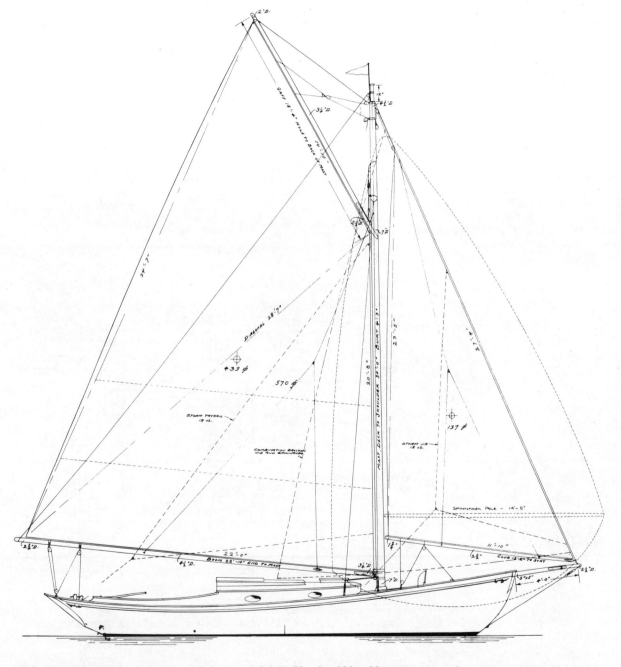

Little Warrior carried a little more sail than a stock 243. She should be able to carry on or heave-to nicely in a blow with her 12-ounce trysail and storm jib. (Courtesy John G. Alden, Inc.)

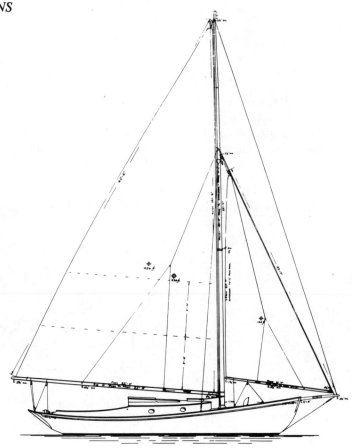

In March 1925, two months after Fenwick Williams drew Little Warrior*'s sail plan, Clifford Swaine and Dwight Simpson developed the sail plan for the jib-headed 243s. Compared to* Little Warrior*'s, this plan shows seven square feet less sail in the mainsail and 13 square feet less in the jib. Drawn by Dwight Simpson, the lines of Number 243 describe a hull that is a cross between an early* Malabar *and a round-bowed Friendship sloop. The long iron keel (3,405 pounds) affords good protection against grounding on a rocky bottom. Designed displacement was 12,190 pounds. The lines also show a later modification for one owner increasing the displacement by about a ton, raising the waterline, and flattening the counter near the transom. (Courtesy John G. Alden, Inc.)*

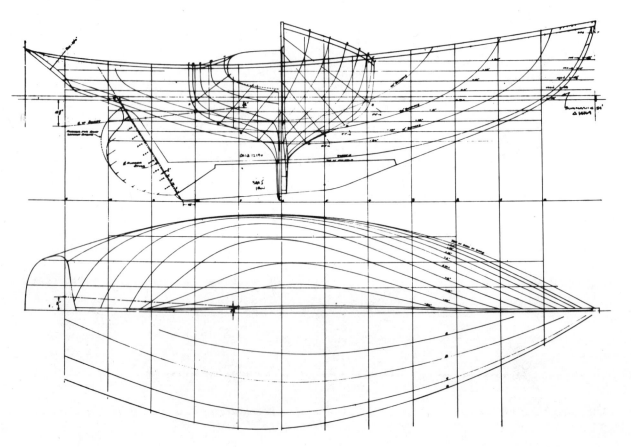

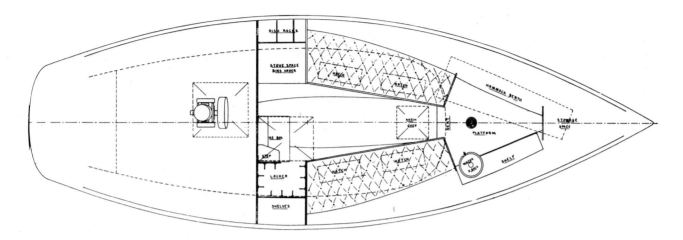

The 243 cannot accommodate more than a small crew, but she does not need more than one or two people to handle her. Note the five-gallon water can, complete with spigot, in the fo'c's'le. Even the shortest cruise would require additional water in portable containers. But for a bulkhead between the fo'c's'le and the main cabin, the 271 cabin plan is identical to this one. (Yachting, *December 1924)*

Little Warrior *in a whisper of a breeze shows her kinship to a round-bowed Friendship sloop. (Courtesy John G. Alden, Inc.)*

Number 243-D, with a tall sloop rig, is resting her wings. (Courtesy John G. Alden, Inc.)

Gamine, *Number 243-J, just prior to her launching in Vancouver in July 1925. Alden's brother Langford wanted a boat of the* Malabar *pedigree for his own use, and he settled on this one. She had berths for four in the main cabin. Langford raced her with gusto, and a better-than-25-knot blow became known locally as a* Gamine *breeze. Like other 243s, she was still sailing in the 1970s. (Courtesy Langford T. Alden)*

that seems plausible given the boat's springy sheer, high bow, flat floors, and powerful quarters, and the tumblehome in her transom. Although the typical Friendship sloop has a clipper bow, there are a few with spoon bows. This stock design (Number 243) was gaff-rigged with a marconi-rig option; it was not actually labeled Malabar Junior until a marconi-rigged version (Number 271) came out a year or so later. The first of the Number 243s was named *Little Warrior,* and she was designed for a well-known yachtsman, Dr. Alexander Forbes. Built in 1925 at Woolwich, Maine, by Blaisdell and Son, her dimensions were 29 feet 6 inches, by 23 feet 2 inches, by 9 feet 8 inches, by 4 feet 11 inches. Stock 243s, built by various Down East yards, were planked hull and deck with pine, and they were given minimal brightwork, a mere five-gallon water tank, and a one-cylinder Lathrop hand-cranked engine. They could be bought for about $1,800. Fenwick Williams, one of *Svaap's* designers, had a hand in the 243 design.

Little Warrior has a beamy hull, so, like a Friendship sloop, she must be well able to stand up to her sail in a breeze. With her fine bow and full stern, she might be expected to have some extra weather helm when well heeled, but this is alleviated by the cutback forefoot. There seems little doubt that she can slide through a chop or that she has a fairly easy motion, and a look at her lines indicates she ought to be able to claw off a lee shore in a gale. The lines plans show two different rudder shapes: the smaller one for use with auxiliary power

and the larger rudder being fitted when there is no engine.

The stock 243 cabin plan shows an icebox under the companionway, with a stove space to port and a hanging locker to starboard. There are two comfortable berths farther forward, and a head and "hammock berth" in the bow. The accommodations are fine for two people or a couple and child, but one might not want to go off for much longer than a weekend with more people than that.

Little Warrior's rig has 570 square feet of sail area, but later gaff-rigged 243s had only 553 square feet, while the jibheaded version carried 550 square feet. Both of these plans would be quite easy to singlehand with their small, self-tending jibs. It might be better, however, if the boom were on a pedestal rather than on the jibstay, since there is some wear with the latter arrangement. Also, it is difficult to tighten the jibstay without a turnbuckle, especially with a gaff-headed main, which prohibits the use of a permanent backstay. My father had a similar jibboom arrangement on his Alden yawl, and he complained to the designer that he could not set up the stay. John Alden wrote back: "It is not possible to use a turnbuckle on the jibstay and we have never used it on any of our boats. It interferes with the jibboom adjustment and also with the snaphooks on the jib, so I'm afraid a turnbuckle cannot be used. I would suggest taking off the jibstay and twisting it as much as possible, thereby shortening it somewhat. I should think this would do the trick." I don't know whether or not Dad tried that remedy.

Continued on page 127

The 271 sail plan — also used on 326-A, B, and C — has 572 square feet of working sail. Running backstays, which are not shown on the Number 243 sail plans, appear here. (Courtesy John G. Alden, Inc.) The 271 Malabar Junior is 30 feet, by 23 feet 3 inches, by 9 feet 8½ inches, by 5 feet ½ inch. The final revised profile is shown by the dashed lines. Charles MacGregor drew the lines in 1925 and Fenwick Williams drafted the revision in 1926. In its final form the iron keel weighed 4,800 pounds. The lines and dimensions of Number 326, which has a designed displacement of 12,683 pounds, are virtually identical to these. (Courtesy John G. Alden, Inc.)

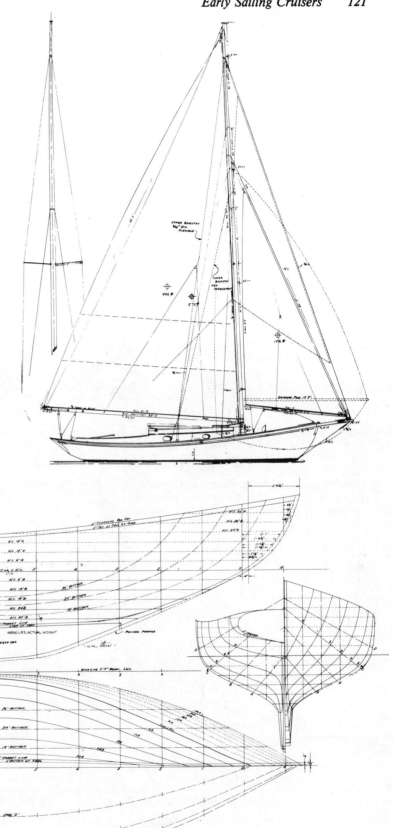

Above left: *Number 271-F shows her seakindly underwater form. (Courtesy John G. Alden, Inc.)* **Right:** *On January 10, 1927, Aage Nielsen completed a yawl rig (579 square feet) for Number 326-E,* Riptide. *(Courtesy* WoodenBoat *magazine)* **Above right:** Riptide *is shown here standing up well to her sail. (Courtesy John G. Alden, Inc.)*

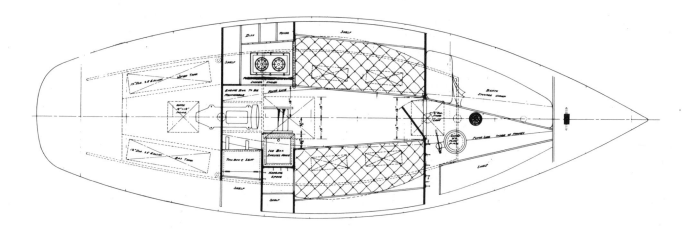

Above: *The standard Number 326 cabin plan shows, for the first time in the Malabar Junior series, a 25-gallon water tank aft. The one-lunger of the 243 and 271 has been superseded. (Courtesy* WoodenBoat *magazine)* **Below:** *On January 17, 1927, one month after Fenwick Williams signed the standard Number 326 cabin plan, William McNary finished this beautifully detailed alternate plan for Number 326-A. The quarter berths displaced the water tank to a new location under the raised sole forward of the mast. The head and galley are decidedly cramped. (Courtesy* WoodenBoat *magazine)*

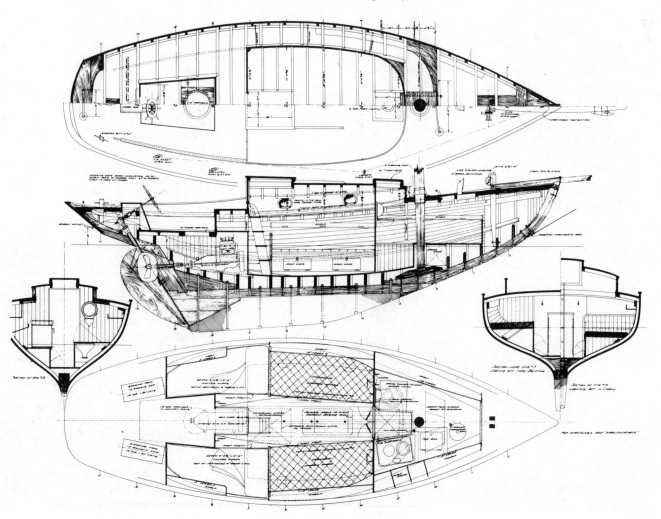

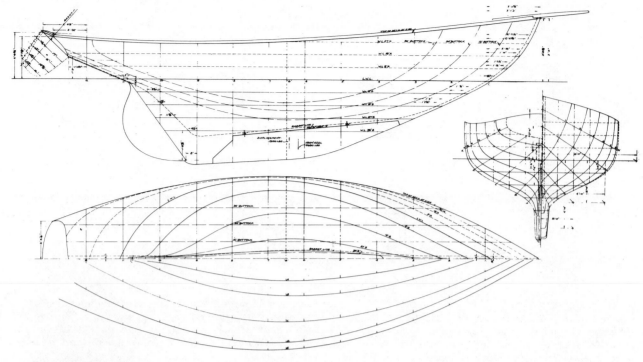

Drawn by Carl Alberg in 1935, the lines of Number 599, the fourth design in the Malabar Junior series, show a fuller entrance and a longer counter than her predecessors. Her dimensions are 30 feet 9 inches, by 23 feet, by 9 feet 8½ inches, by 5 feet, and her designed displacement is 13,100 pounds. Carl Alberg also drew Number 599's sail plan, which shows 535 square feet of sail with more of the total in the jib than on the 271-326 plan. (Courtesy John G. Alden, Inc.)

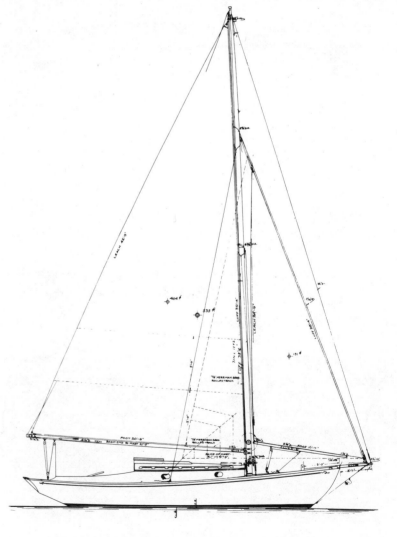

Entre Nous, *Number 599-G, under sail (left), and a close-up of her afterguard (above). (Courtesy John G. Alden, Inc.)*

Three 599s were rigged as yawls, including this boat, 599-F, originally named Debonair, *and another built for John Alden himself. (Courtesy John G. Alden, Inc.)*

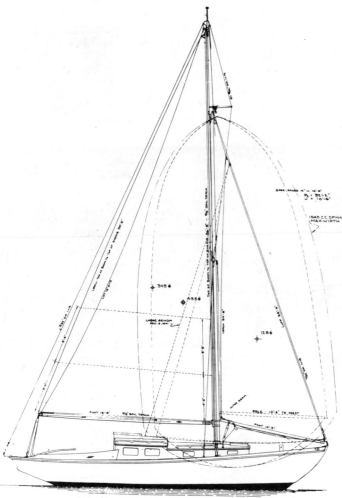

Below: *The last Malabar Junior, Number 762, has 480 square feet of sail, with 144 square feet in the jib.* (Your New Boat *by the Editors of* Yachting)

Above: *Number 691 has 433 square feet of sail — 100 square feet less than her immediate predecessor — but her designed displacement is only 10,360 pounds. She would be more easily driven under average sailing conditions. With dimensions of 31 feet 1 inch, by 22 feet 1 inch, by 8 feet 6½ inches, by 4 feet 8 inches, she is a little smaller than her successor, Number 762, but her lines and cabin layout are similar. Like Number 762, she has a doghouse, and her appearance is yachtier than that of the earlier Malabar Juniors.* (Courtesy John G. Alden, Inc.)

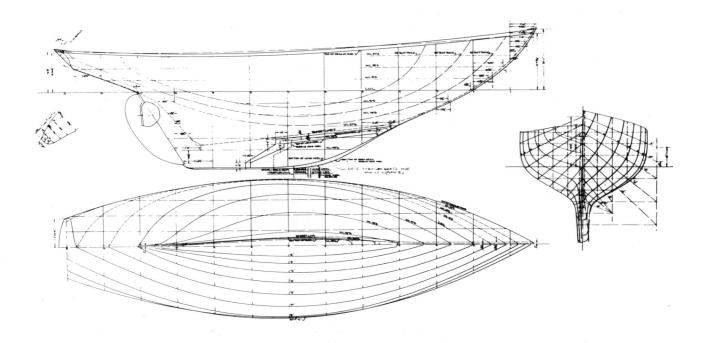

Carl Alberg completed the lines drawing for Number 762 in December 1944. The boat had 11,650 pounds designed displacement on dimensions of 32 feet 6 inches, by 22 feet 8 inches, by 8 feet 8 inches, by 4 feet 11 inches. The lead keel weighed 4,800 pounds. Three years later a modified profile was drafted — one inch deeper with a more prominent toe — to accommodate a change from lead to iron outside ballast. The waterlines are more symmetrical than those of the early Malabar Juniors. (Courtesy John G. Alden, Inc.) Number 762's cabin is roomier than those of the early Malabar Juniors. She has six-foot headroom in the main cabin and more than five feet forward. (Yachting, January 1946)

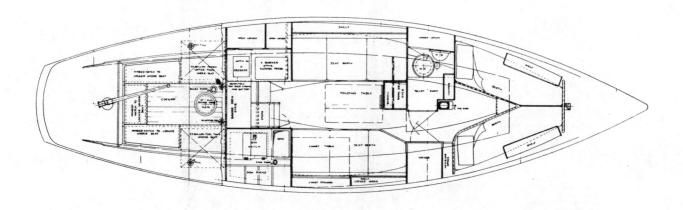

According to the Alden records, eight sisters to *Little Warrior* were built. This was far from the end of *Little Warrior*'s lineage, however, for the Malabar Juniors evolved through several later designs, as follows: Number 271 in 1926 (four sisters built); Number 326 in 1927 (five sisters built); Number 599 in 1936 (eight sisters built); Number 691 in 1939 (26 sisters built); and Number 762 in 1946 (16 sisters built). Drawings of all these designs are presented here. (Number 857, a 33½-foot sloop, is listed in the Alden records as a Malabar Jr., but no boats were built to this design.) The evolution of the Malabar Junior design in a sense encapsulates the evolution of small sailing-cruiser design over the same span of years — from a simple, inexpensive workboat type to a more expensive, yachtier type with longer ends, slacker bilges, and higher freeboard amidships. The later Malabar Juniors also have greater hull symmetry and hollower garboards. They are pretty little doghouse sloops, nimble under sail and with improved accommodations, and they proved popular; somehow, however, they don't have quite the character of their forerunner, *Little Warrior*.

GOLDEN HIND

Although it has been written that R.B. Forbes "invented" the staysail schooner rig in 1872, Starling Burgess is generally credited with introducing the rig to American yachtsmen in 1925. In that year the *Advance*, a staysail schooner of his design, attracted much attention after she arrived on the East Coast from Norway.

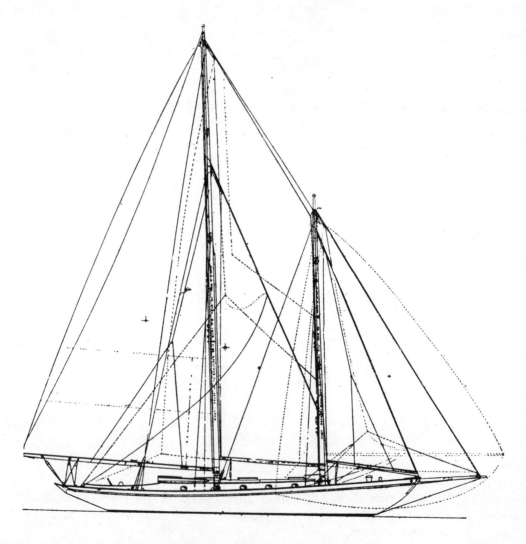

The lofty triangular-shaped staysail rig on Golden Hind *and the bold rake of her masts give her a jaunty romantic look.* (The Rudder, *May 1926*)

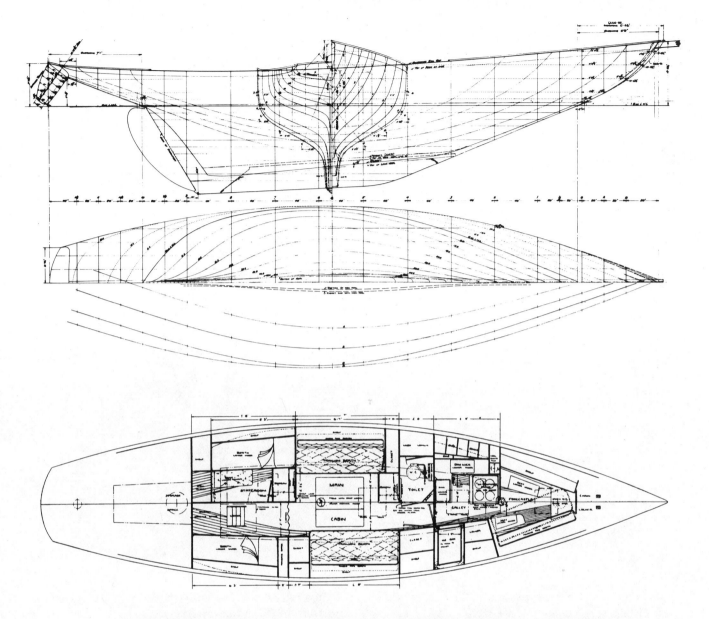

Golden Hind has a fine hull, but one with full quarters. Her profile is well cut away forward. Her designed displacement is 29,845 pounds, and her ballast-displacement ratio is 41 percent. (Courtesy John G. Alden, Inc.) Golden Hind's cabin lacks the space of the usual owner's stateroom, but it allows a companionway that is convenient to the cockpit and not far off center. The original owner had replicas of Sir Francis Drake's crest (a golden hind, or female deer) on all glassware and china. (The Rudder, May 1926)

Until that time it was customary to fill the gap between a schooner's masts with a gaff-headed foresail, but *Advance* was rigged with a boomed mainstaysail and a Queen staysail. The Queen was a sort of refined fisherman staysail (named after one carried by the schooner *Queen,* designed by Nathanael G. Herreshoff) that did not need to be lowered when changing tacks. There was even another small sail that could be set above the Queen with its luff on the foretopmast and its clew on the main topmast. The rig was close-winded and proved quite successful on closed race courses, and a number of other designers soon produced their own version of a staysail schooner. John Alden's first staysail schooner, I believe, was the lovely *Golden Hind* of 1926, design number 266.

Designed for Charles E. Goodwin, *Golden Hind* has long overhangs and a graceful sheer. She is double planked with mahogany, and her keel and stem are made from a single piece of oak that took her builder, the Dauntless Shipyard of Essex, Connecticut, two

Golden Hind *(then named* Marita*) with everything drawing at the start of the New London-Marblehead Race in 1936. (Courtesy Franklin M. Haines, Jr., and the American Yacht Club)*

weeks to find. She measures 46 feet 3 inches, by 33 feet, by 11 feet 3 inches, by 6 feet 6 inches.

Hank Meneely, Alden's longtime friend and associate, told me that John didn't care for the original form of the staysail-rigged schooner, partly because the mainstaysail is so small that it lacks power. On *Golden Hind,* Alden enlarged the mainstaysail by moving the base of its stay some distance up the foremast, with the top of the stay as far up on the mainmast as possible. This actually produces a quadrilateral sail, although the luff is not very long. The mainmast is much taller than the foremast, and the profile makes a striking appearance — that of a tall triangle with its apex quite far aft. One reason for this configuration is that rating rules of those times did not materially penalize the height of the mainmast. The sail plan shows in dotted lines a balloon main topmast staysail, usually called a gollywobbler. This sail greatly augments power on a

light-air reach. A few gollys have even been extended forward to fill in the foretriangle.

Below decks *Golden Hind* is laid out, starting aft, with a small stateroom to port and a quarter berth to starboard. Moving forward, there is a saloon with two transoms amidships, then a head and a galley, and a fo'c'sle with a pipe berth and head for a paid hand. An unusual detail is the curtain at the after end of the saloon. It is probably there not only for privacy, but also to keep drafts from the companionway from circulating forward into the sitting area. Also of interest is the particular way the backs of the transoms fold up to make upper berths in the saloon.

The schooner was not fitted with auxiliary power and so had plenty of stowage space abaft the companionway, where an engine would normally be located. The absence of an auxiliary indicates the faith of the designer and owner in the boat's ability to sail well in all conditions, and no doubt she fulfilled their expectations. However, power was added when she was sold to Franklin M. Haines in 1935.

Haines kept the schooner, which he renamed *Marita* (one of three Haines-owned Alden schooners of that name), until 1941, sailing her to a fleet first in the New London-Marblehead Race in 1936. In 1937-38, *Marita*'s foremast was heightened by six feet, her bowsprit was shortened, and her main boom was cropped and raised a foot on the hoist. Designed by Philip Rhodes, the alterations gave her a larger genoa and spinnaker with no change in rating.

Under new ownership and her original name, *Golden Hind* participated in the 1958 Bermuda Race. She was later sold to the West Coast. In the 1970s she sailed in the South Pacific, aging but still beautiful. Along with other Alden schooners, she took part in an Alden Day regatta at Tahiti in 1974. On April 12, 1983, she was one of 38 boats destroyed at Papeete, Tahiti, by Hurricane Zeena.

NICANOR (PINTA)

In his book, *Blue Water Vagabond,* Dennis Puleston called the Alden schooner *Nicanor* (later named *Pinta*) "a thoroughbred race horse — graceful, speedy — a creature of moods, and at times requiring very careful handling." *Nicanor* had some great moments of glory, but she also had her share of misadventures. Puleston

Nicanor's tall foremast allows substantial sails in the foretriangle and also a long vertical luff on the golly. Working sail area is 1,615 square feet. (Courtesy John G. Alden, Inc.)

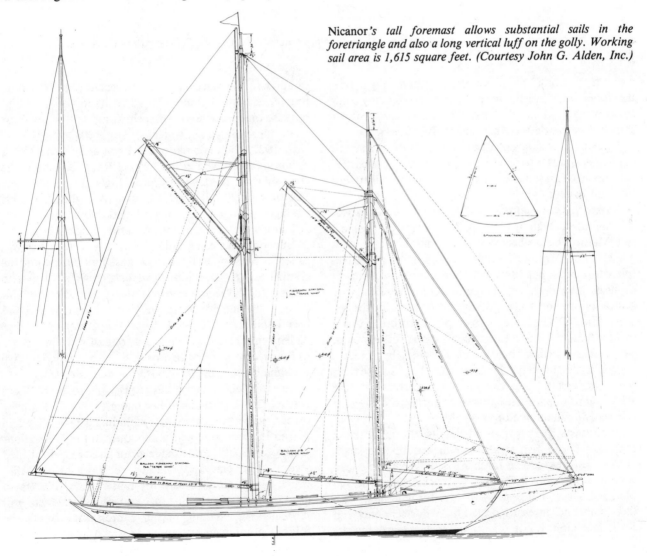

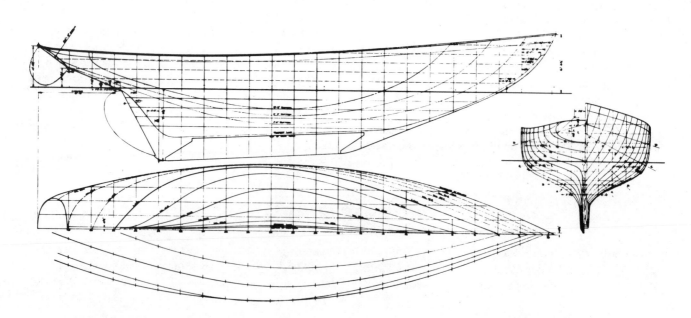

Nicanor's lines show a firm bilge, a fine forebody, and moderate overhangs. (Courtesy John G. Alden, Inc.)

wrote that at one time or another she had caught fire, was squeezed between two ships, and had so many collisions or groundings that she was called the "rubber ship." Her hardest chance probably came when she grounded on the sands of Cape Hatteras during a squall at night and was muscled up the foreshore by the battering surf. A Coast Guard cutter eventually pulled her off, and incredibly, she sustained little damage.

Nicanor, design number 267-B, was built for Alvan T. Simonds in 1926 by the C.A. Morse yard at Thomaston, Maine. She is a heavy, strongly built boat, but with graceful lines. Being fine forward, she can punch effectively through a head sea, although at some sacrifice to dryness. The decks might be wet at times, but her bulwarks provide a certain amount of security for the crew. The 267's lines were drawn by Clifford P. Swaine in July 1925; the hull measurements are 57 feet 3 inches, by 42 feet 5 inches, by 14 feet 2 inches, by 7 feet 8 inches. Unfortunately, the cabin plan has disappeared, but I understand she has sleeping quarters aft, the saloon amidships, galley forward, and a fo'c's'le that can accommodate one or two paid hands.

Both masts carry gaff-headed sails; the main has a topsail, while a fisherman staysail can fill the space above the foresail. The foremast is quite tall, so it can support a generous spinnaker or reaching jib. The sail plan also shows a huge gollywobbler for light airs. With these sails and an easily driven hull, this schooner can really move. She is not exceptional to windward, but she

can pick up her skirts and fly on a reach. In a freshening breeze, though, I'd be tempted to hand the jib early, because the long round bowsprit would not be the most secure perch in rough water.

In 1927, Simonds sailed *Nicanor* across the North Atlantic to compete in the Fastnet Race. She made the crossing from Boston to Bishop's Light, England, in the fast time of 20 days and 7 hours. (A highlight of this passage was an unplanned rendezvous near mid-Atlantic with a crew member's father who was crossing to Europe on a steamer.) The Fastnet Race that year was sailed in gale-force winds that caused all but two of the competitors to drop out. *Nicanor's* crew felt it best to retire after the schooner broke a gaff during a jibe. Until then, she had been doing very well in the race and had been handling the heavy weather competently. (Another Alden schooner, *La Goleta,* was one of only two boats to finish. She was first to cross the line but failed to save her time on the smaller British cutter, *Tally Ho.*)

The following year, *Nicanor* was sold to W.J. (Jack) Curtis, Jr., who changed her name to *Pinta.* The new owner, with a crew of experts including Linton Rigg and Alfred Loomis, entered the schooner in the Transatlantic Race to Spain. *Pinta* made a fast passage but finished second in her class to the larger, yet lower-rated, *Niña,* which was built expressly for that race. (*Niña* was a deep-draft yacht with an innovative, tall staysail schooner rig.) Sailing master Linton Rigg wrote the following commentary about the race in a letter to a

Nicanor *under sail — probably in 1927 — with her reaching jib and small fisherman set. (Courtesy Charles H. Vilas, Editor,* Cruising Club News)

friend: "I had selected a good crew, and when Paul Hammond commissioned Starling Burgess to design a boat to win that race, which was *Niña,* built at a cost of $75,000 (Jack Curtis had paid $10,000 for *Pinta*) we realized that our only chance to beat her was to drive like hell in any weather, which we did every minute day and night for twenty-three days. When we finally made our landfall on Spain, *Niña* was way down on the horizon *behind* us. We had beaten her across the ocean. One of our runs was 256 miles in twenty-four hours, on a 35-foot waterline boat. Then the wind died and came out dead ahead. The best an Alden schooner, gaff rigged, could make on the wind in that light going was six points, while *Niña* was doing four and a half. It almost broke our hearts to see *Niña* go by us to windward almost within sight of the finish."

Linton Rigg was mistaken about *Pinta*'s waterline length. It is just over 42 feet, but the day's run he mentioned is nothing to be sneezed at. Alf Loomis wrote in his book *Ocean Racing:* "We were jubilant that afternoon for we knew that we had set a mark for a 42-foot boat that might never be broken." As late as 1963 (and perhaps later) Loomis, who was usually well informed on such matters as sailing records, was still making the claim that *Pinta* had the longest day's run for a boat of her waterline length. I don't know whether or not he was right, but it is interesting that in 1971, the 42-foot-waterline ketch *Gipsy Moth V,* sailed by Francis Chichester, could do no better than 231½ miles in a day. Of course, she was sailed singlehanded, but she had excellent self-steering, a large, modern rig, and a relatively narrow, light, fin-keeled hull that was specifically designed to sail 4,000 miles in 20 days. *Gipsy Moth*'s performance was impressive, but her best day's run couldn't beat that of the heavy old *Pinta*.

TWILIGHT AND
THE 43-FOOT SCHOONERS

Although John Alden is probably best known for his fairly large ocean-racing schooners, he also turned out some smaller schooners that were popular in the 1920s. One semistock boat, at one time seen everywhere on the East Coast, was a comfortable cruising schooner measuring 43 feet on deck. This design, which usually had a marconi main and a gaff foresail, came in a keel model, design number 270, and then a centerboard version, Number 309. The former measures 32 feet 6 inches on the waterline and has a beam of 11 feet 6 inches with a draft of 6 feet 4 inches, while the centerboarder has a foot more beam and draws only 4 feet 2 inches. The Alden office records show that 16 of the keel boats and 17 of the centerboarders were built, but they were such a common sight for so many years that it seemed as though there were many more.

The first boat of the 270 series, named *Twilight,* was ordered by C.P. Cottrell, Jr., of Westerly, Rhode

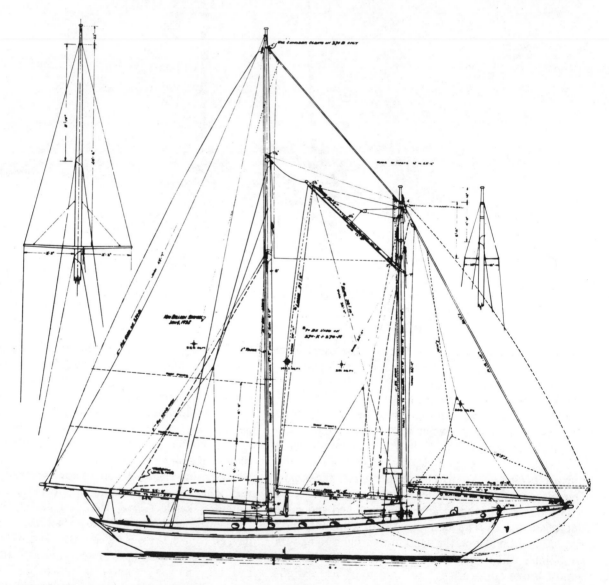

The handsome 270 schooner Twilight *and her generous marconi sail plan. Other 270s were gaff-rigged. Specifications called for standing rigging of galvanized steel. We had such rigging on our Alden yawl and didn't have to replace it for 30 years, a fact that indicates superior galvanizing in those days. (Courtesy John G. Alden, Inc.)*

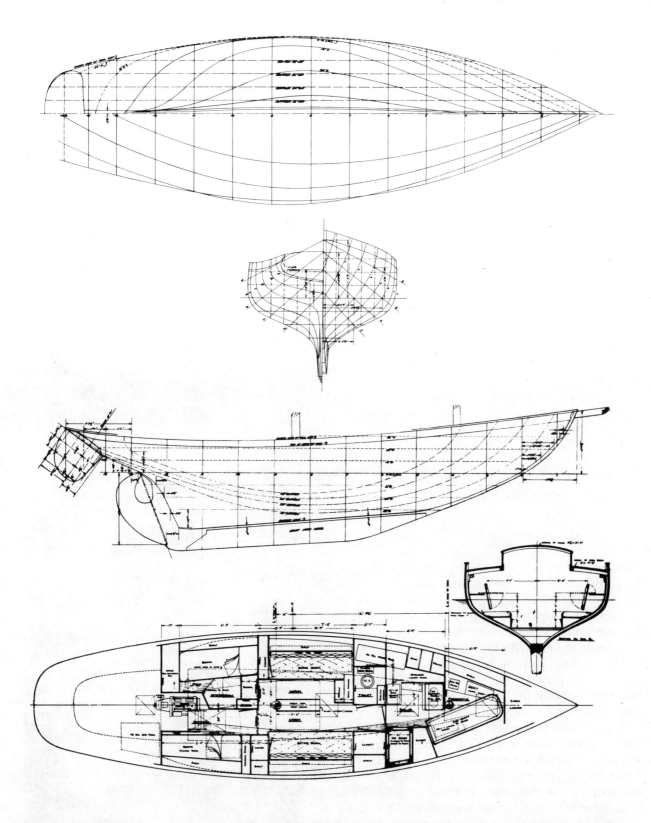

The lines of Number 270 — with sweeping sheer, spoon bow, raking oval transom, and powerful quarters — are vintage Alden. The standard Number 270 cabin is roomy and comfortable. The section shows the fold-up transom backs. (Courtesy John G. Alden, Inc.)

A sister of Twilight *showing her power. She could use a vang on her fore gaff. (Courtesy John G. Alden, Inc.)*

A dockside view of a 270 schooner showing her broad decks, her pin rail, and other details. (Courtesy Mrs. John Robinson)

Island, and she was built in 1926 by Harvey Gamage at South Bristol, Maine. She has what might be called a typical Alden look with her sweeping sheer, moderately low freeboard abaft amidships, spoon bow, raking oval transom, and low cabin trunk. Under the ownership of E.S. Bradford, Jr., and with Irving Johnson as skipper and navigator, *Twilight* participated in the rough-weather 1932 Bermuda Race, finishing fifth in Class B but correcting out to a respectable second in class behind the Olin Stephens yawl *Dorade.*

A few of the 270s had gaff-headed mainsails. All the boats had gaff foresails. For the first time in this book we see a sail plan that shows a vang on the foresail. This device, which, in effect, trims the upper half of the sail, is a great help in preventing excessive twist. With the vang properly set, the foresail becomes almost as close-winded as a mainstaysail but has more area. This sail plan, initialed by Clifford P. Swaine, includes 1,023 square feet of canvas in the four lowers.

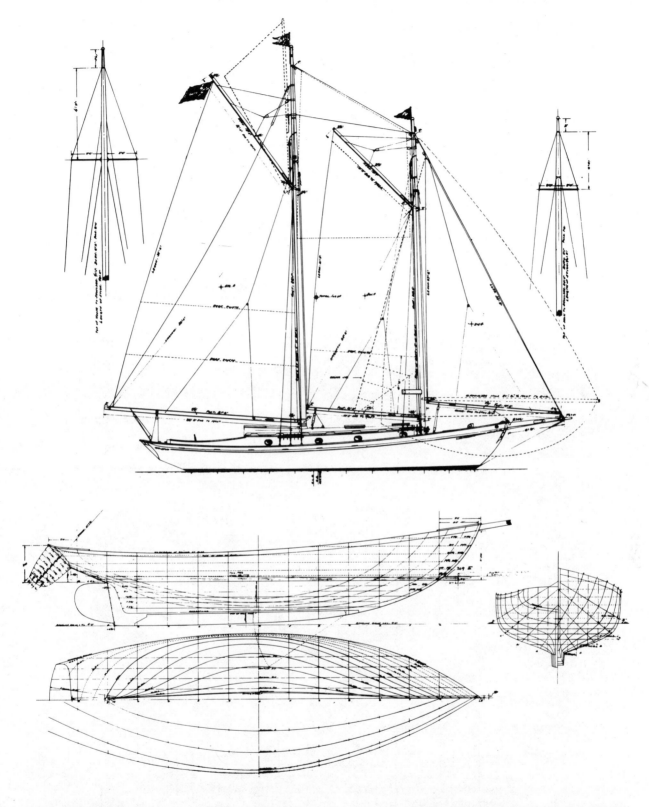

Like the 270s, the 309 schooners were designed with either a gaff or marconi main. The gaff-rig plan, drawn by Aage Nielsen, shows 1,208 square feet of working sail. (Courtesy John G. Alden, Inc.) Although the 270 and 309 look alike above water, their underbodies naturally differ. The 309 appears to have her center of lateral resistance farther forward, and this could give her more weather helm when heeled on a reach. Her designed displacement is 29,000 pounds. (Courtesy John G. Alden, Inc.)

Shallow-Draft Schooner
Alden Design No. 309
Ready for Delivery

~

43' o.a. x 33' w.l. x 12' 6" beam x 4' 2" draft
Able Offshore - Handy - Roomy

~

ONE OWNER WRITES:

This schooner has proved to be very able under all the conditions I have encountered. She sails at a small angle of heel, handles easily, and is dry. Incidentally, I do not carry a man. Much of my sailing is done with one other than myself for a crew, and I have had the boat out alone under sail in a whole sail breeze.

*Full Particulars
from*

JOHN G. ALDEN
Naval Architect
148 State Street   Boston, Mass.

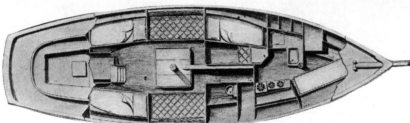

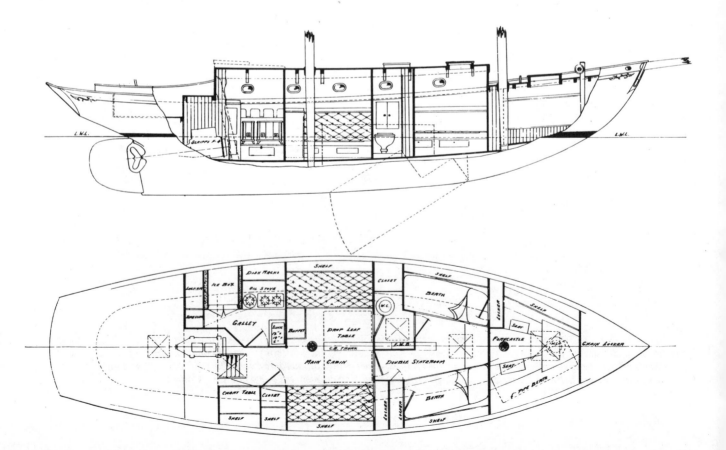

Opposite: *A choice of layouts could be had on the 43-foot centerboard schooners. One option was very close to the standard Number 270 cabin. One (shown here in a 1928 advertisement) offered a single stateroom forward of the main cabin. A third had the galley aft and a double stateroom forward. Note that even the after galley can be closed off with a door. The 309s were seven percent more expensive than the 270s because of their extra volume below. (Above:* Yachting, *October 1928. Below:* Yachting, *July 1926)*

The 309 Lanaki *showing her churchlike stiffness. The bowsprit pulpit is a great place for kids. (Courtesy John G. Alden, Inc.)*

Cliff Swaine also drew the accommodations plan, which is almost identical to that of the previously described *Golden Hind.* Even such details as the curtain at the after end of the main cabin and the fold-up transom backs are the same. The 270's hull is shorter than *Golden Hind*'s, but it is beamier and fuller in the ends, and there is about the same amount of room below.

In addition to *Twilight,* many of the later 270s were built by the Gamage yard, while all but one or two of the 309s were built across the Damariscotta River in East Boothbay at the Goudy and Stevens yard. These included *Black Squall* (309-C) and *Wogg Too* (309-F, originally *Pinafore*), both familiar members of the Cruising Club of America fleet. For 15 years, *Black Squall* was sailed out of Chatham, Massachusetts, by George A. Cutter, and she was his flagship when he was Cruising Club commodore in the late 1930s. *Wogg Too* was owned for many years by Ernest Ratsey of the Ratsey sailmaking family, and in 1945 she too became a Cruising Club flagship. Jim Stevens of Goudy and Stevens recalls the building of the 309s in the winters between 1926 and 1930. The yard would turn out several in a winter, launching one as soon as possible in order to make room for another. At one point the boats were building faster than Alden could sell them, and Goudy and Stevens wound up owning three of the boats themselves for a short time.

The 309s have the same above-water profile as the

Right: *In a reflective mood,* Nordlys *(309-L) is not getting the weather she likes, but she's handsome all the same. The schooner belonged to the grandfather of Jon Eaton, this book's editor. (Courtesy Franklin W. Eaton)* **Below:** Tibby Dunbar, *309-0, in surroundings that suggest her good ability to gunkhole. (Courtesy John G. Alden, Inc.)*

270s and nearly the same rig (again, with the option of gaff- or jibheaded main), but their greater beam affords more room for accommodations. There was a choice of an after galley or a forward galley, the former enabling a large double stateroom forward. The latter could be had with a double stateroom aft and a port-side single stateroom just abaft the galley, or with virtually the same layout as the Number 270. Any of these arrangements was comfortable, with good-size berths and a commodious main cabin.

Frank Eaton of Bangor, Maine, whose father owned Number 309-L in the 1940s (she was then named *Nordlys*), recalls that she was not a good light-air drifter, although a gollywobbler, which she did not have, would certainly have helped. She was most at home on a broad reach in a brisk breeze. For family cruising and shorthanded sailing, she was ideal. The forestaysail was self-tending; the leeward running backstays could of course be left set up for short tacks when she was strapped down for windward work. When reaching into an anchorage on a gentle breeze, a singlehander could leave the helm to hand a headsail, and the boat would hold her course until he returned.

Numbers 270 and 309 represent faithfully — in look

and feel and in such details as their sturdy bulwarks — an Alden sailing cruiser. Many cruising yachtsmen were attracted to the 43-footers because of their accommoda-tions, but these schooners are not just comfortable, they are handsome, quite easy to handle, and lively in the right conditions.

LA GALLEAS

If high priority is put on comfort, the plans of the ketch *La Galleas,* Number 296, deserve a careful study. This very sturdy vessel was based on the lines of a Baltic working ketch, of the type used not only for trading, but also for fishing and usually as a year-round home for the skipper and his family. Alden was introduced to the type by Aage Nielsen, who brought data and pic-tures of such boats from Denmark. John was much taken with the boats and agreed to build one on specula-tion. According to Clifford Swaine, the hull was built in the Israel Snow yard in Damariscotta, Maine, and it was launched and towed away after dark the night before the yard went bankrupt. She was taken to two other yards before being finished in 1927. Her measurements are 58 feet, by 49 feet 6 inches, by 16 feet 2 inches, by 6 feet.

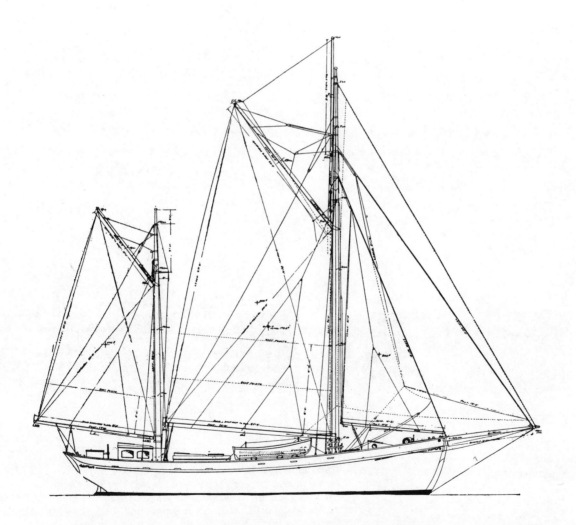

La Galleas *carried 1,728 square feet of sail in her four lowers.* (Yachting, *January 1928)*

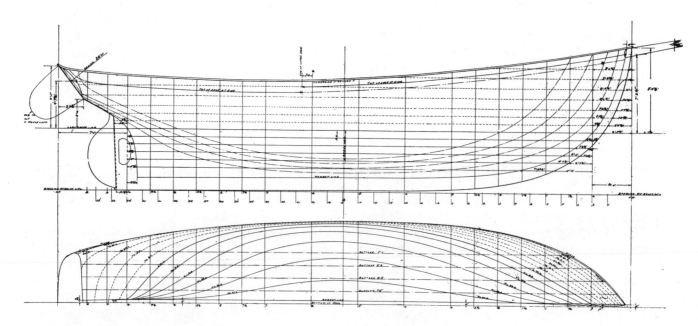

Based on the lines of a Baltic working ketch, the sturdy La Galleas *has a designed displacement of 89,250 pounds.* (Yachting, *January 1928)*

Two views of La Galleas *illustrating that despite her massiveness, she could walk along under sail. (Courtesy Mrs. John Robinson)*

Opposite: *The accommodations in* La Galleas, *shown here in a 1928 advertisement, are designed for seven to 10 people. This ad appeared in the same issue of* Yachting *magazine that featured the boat in its design section. Alden had built* La Galleas *on speculation, and he was at this point her designer, owner, broker, and no doubt insurer as well.* (Yachting, *January 1928)*

Auxiliary Keel Ketch

NO. 296 — FOR SALE — Auxiliary Keel Ketch. 58' x 49' 6 x 16' 2 x 6'. Modified design of Baltic Sea boats, with extraordinary accommodations yet good speed under canvas or power. Construction very heavy, with 1¾" yellow pine planking; finish, plain. 30 h.p. Lathrop gives speed of 6 to 7 m.p.h. An unusually comfortable boat, sure to take you there and bring you back in any weather.

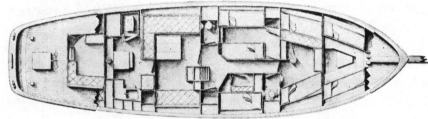

Brokerage Department

BASED on the belief that to buyer and seller alike the reliable yacht broker is of the utmost importance, this department has enjoyed a constantly increasing business for the past ten years. To establish a reputation as a dependable broker, a conservative policy in selling second-hand yachts is necessary.

Our policy, which has resulted in an increasing business every year since the war, *is* conservative. We endeavor

> To supply reliable information.
> To express our frank opinion of boats we know.
> To sell yachts suitable to the particular needs of our clients at prices fair to both seller and buyer.

Yacht Insurance

We insure many yachts of all types and sizes. We have insured more yachts of greater value every year since the establishment of this department. One yacht owner in every four insured by us during 1927 has had a claim for damage. No owner has ever criticized our settlement of a claim.

YACHT BROKER — NAVAL ARCHITECT — MARINE INSURANCE

JOHN G. ALDEN ⚓ 148 State Street, Boston·Mass.

With such dimensions, *La Galleas* had ample volume for accommodations for living on board. A semi-sunken deckhouse aft had a single berth and served as a chart room. Forward there was a galley; a large saloon; and sleeping quarters containing a single stateroom, two double staterooms, and two enclosed heads. The fo'c's'le had two berths and a head for the crew, and its entrance was through a booby hatch on the foredeck. A decided drawback of the after deckhouse is that there is no room for a cockpit.

The husky ketch was assuredly seakindly with her heavy displacement, short ends, and ample freeboard. Her great beam, 16 tons of inside ballast, and short,

gaff rig helped ensure that she would sail on her feet, while the long keel and symmetrical submerged water-lines helped keep her on a steady course. By no means could she be considered a smart sailer, but it was said that she sailed unexpectedly well, and her 30 h.p. Lathrop engine could drive her at seven m.p.h.

John Alden admitted that *La Galleas* was not at all fast. He said she was intended as a "seagoing auxiliary houseboat." Sad to say, the ketch was reported lost at sea in 1943. No details of her foundering are known; certainly, for a houseboat, she seemed unusually capable of handling bad weather offshore.

THUMBCAP

One doesn't often associate John Alden with double-enders, but he turned out some attractive boats of this type. The very next design after *La Galleas* was a

miniature — or, as the British say, "tabloid" — cruiser with a Norwegian type of stern. This boat, first named *Thumbcap*, has great character with her sharp stern and

In a boat of this size a gunter-type mainsail makes sense. The short mainmast can be unstepped easily for trailer-ing or storage, and, of course, it allows the boat to pass under low bridges. Thumbcap *has 236 square feet of sail. (Courtesy John G. Alden, Inc.)*

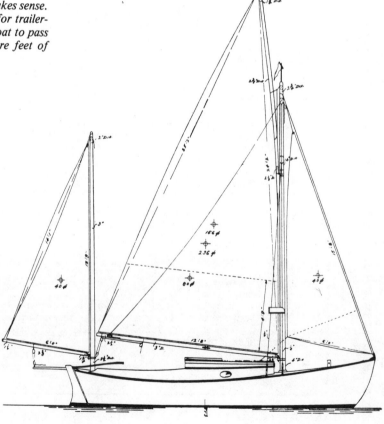

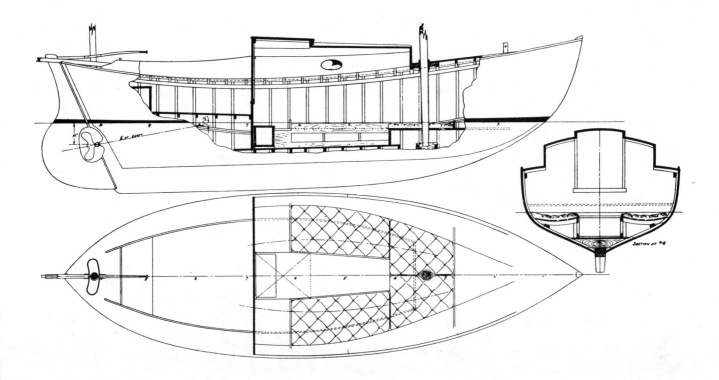

The profile plan and section show that Thumbcap *hasn't much of a salient keel, and she might need her engine to help her go to windward at times. One could hardly expect more in the way of accommodations in such a small boat, especially one heavily built of wood, since the frames and other structural members take away from the interior space.* (Yachting, *May 1928*)

Left: Thumbcap *slipping along nicely in a light breeze, despite towing a punt and a bit of rigging. (Courtesy Mrs. John Robinson)* **Right:** Thumbcap *demonstrates that a ketch as well as a schooner can be sailed wing-and-wing. (Courtesy Mrs. John Robinson)*

outboard rudder, pronounced sheer, small cabin trunk with one oval port per side, and her yawl rig. She was built in 1926 for Joseph Plumb of Geneva, New York, by Rice Brothers at Boothbay Harbor, Maine. Her diminutive measurements are 21 feet, by 18 feet 5 inches, by 6 feet 6 inches, by 2 feet 9 inches.

On such a small boat accommodations are minimal, but the cabin has two berths and sitting headroom, with space for a stove and ice chest aft. An uncommon feature is that the bunks are slightly concave in cross section to help prevent their occupants from being rolled out. The cockpit sole is sufficiently high above the waterline to allow self-bailing, at least when the boat is not heeled. A single-cylinder, four-cycle Gray engine is under the cockpit sole.

Ordinarily, it doesn't make sense to fit a very small boat with two masts, but in this case the rig seems to suit the hull, and of course it bestows versatility and ease of shortening sail. The center of effort of main alone is just a bit forward of the total center of effort, and the center of effort of mizzen and jib is just a little aft, so the boat should balance well under any of these sail combinations. The mizzen is jibheaded, but the main has a high-peaked gaff — almost a sliding gunter. This allows a tall sail while keeping the mast short, which the designer felt would obviate the need for backstays. I'd prefer a pair of runners to be used in a blow or to keep the mast from whipping in a chop.

Having the mizzenmast immediately forward of the rudderhead creates a problem when the steering is done with a tiller, and it is interesting to see the solution on *Thumbcap*. A short section of the tiller is cut out in way of the mast, and the forward part of the tiller is held to the after part with two U-shaped metal straps, one on each side, which enclose the mast. This restricts the swing of the tiller — but not seriously, unless the helmsman wants to "put on the brakes" when shooting for a mooring or when docking.

SACHEM

Alden's longtime associate Dwight Simpson once described the schooner *Sachem,* design number 333, as "John's racingest boat." Indeed, she looks the part, for it appears that this slender craft would cut through a head sea with barely a nod of her head.

Sachem was designed for a well-known repeat client, Rowe B. Metcalf of New York City, who owned five Alden boats. One of these was design number 283, a sturdy seagoing schooner, also named *Sachem,* which accompanied the expedition of Donald B. MacMillan to the Arctic in 1927. The antithesis of this Arctic schooner is her successor, the racing *Sachem,* which was built in 1927 by the Hodgdon Brothers yard at East Boothbay, Maine. She measures 65 feet 8½ inches, by 44 feet, by 12 feet 4 inches, by 8 feet 7 inches.

This sleek racer was designed to the Universal Rule, and her rated length of 37.7 feet enabled her to be plenty competitive: She won 10 races out of 16 starts during her first year. The major design work was done by Charles G. MacGregor, and Aage Nielsen had a hand in her lines. With her short load waterline, cutaway forefoot, raked rudder, and fairly slack bilges, she has minimal wetted surface. Although the long ends and low freeboard are not seagoing features, the low sides minimize windage, while the overhangs provide some reserve buoyancy and increase the sailing length as the boat heels. The waterlines are quite symmetrical, which indicates a well-balanced hull even at a considerable angle of heel.

For a narrow racing boat *Sachem* has comfortable accommodations. Her long, fine ends detract from cabin space forward and aft, but as a result the accommodations are concentrated near the middle of the boat, where the pitching motion is minimal. The narrow beam amidships is advantageous in heavy weather, for there is usually something for a crew member to grab, and he cannot be thrown a great distance. *Sachem* is large enough to have room for an owner's cabin aft, an adequate saloon, a guest or captain's stateroom opposite a sizable galley, and a fo'c's'le with three pipe berths. Several unusual features are the folding table in the fo'c's'le, the huge icebox forward, and a prominent skylight abaft the cabin trunk that supplies the owner's cabin with plenty of light and air. Originally *Sachem* had a 50 h.p. Kermath gasoline engine, but it was removed in 1936. Perhaps Metcalf felt his boat sailed so well that, when the original engine wore out, there was no need to replace it.

Considering how easily her hull can be driven, *Sachem* originally carried a tremendous cloud of sails.

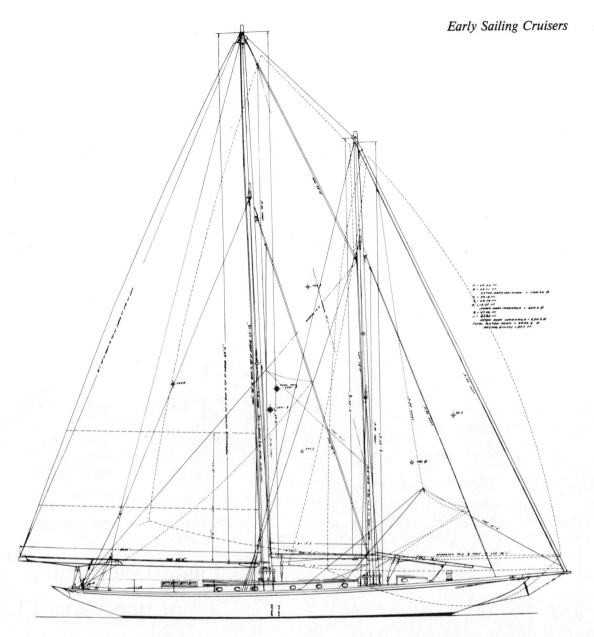

Sachem's sail plan is not only lofty but extensively spread out fore and aft. The narrow space between her masts gives her the look of a cutter when seen from a distance. (Courtesy John G. Alden, Inc.)

Her staysail schooner rig supported a whopping 2,461 square feet of canvas. Her unusually tall foremast allowed a large spinnaker and other headsails, especially since the base of the foretriangle was extended with a bowsprit. One might expect such a narrow boat to be a bit tender, and perhaps she was, for in 1936, as schooners grew less competitive on the race course, she was given a smaller sloop rig. I'm not sure that this change lowered the center of effort, but it did reduce the sail area by 556 square feet. Her speed was little affected, no doubt due partly to the removal of her propeller when the engine was taken out. At any rate, *Yachting* editor William H. Taylor wrote that "under both rigs she won many trophies in such top-flight events as the New York Yacht Club cruise runs and

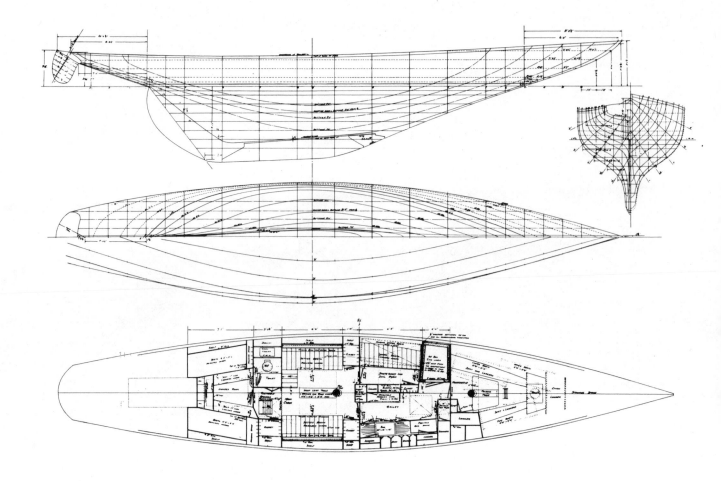

Fastest Schooner
of her size

FOR SALE — ALDEN NO. 333 — Fastest
schooner of her size. Winner of many prizes
including the majority of squadron runs of
New York Yacht Club, and Astor Cup. Fine
accommodations include two double staterooms. Sleeps four in main cabin. Large
galley, and engineroom. Raced with two
paid hands. The outstanding fast cruiser.
Designed by John G. Alden, built by Hodg-
son Bros. Bored for engine, since removed,
and equipped with fuel tanks. 65' 8" x 44'
x 12' 4" x 8' 7". In my opinion should be
logical winner of 1934 Bermuda Race.

John G. Alden

Naval
Architect

Yacht
Broker

131 STATE STREET, BOSTON, MASS.

Opposite: Sachem*'s sections and other lines describe a sleek, well-balanced hull with slack bilges and low wetted surface. Although she is fine lined and has no forefoot, the waterlines forward are full enough to prevent burying. (Courtesy John G. Alden, Inc.) For such a narrow racing boat with a waterline length of 44 feet, she has generous accommodations. (Courtesy John G. Alden, Inc.)* Sachem *was spectacular with her original staysail schooner rig. Alden's comment in this advertisement concerning* Sachem*'s chances in the 1934 Bermuda Race may have been an uncharacteristic overstatement, since she was not designed for offshore events. She never raced to the Onion Patch. (*Yachting, *February 1934)* **Below:** *Still a lovely sight was* Sachem *after her conversion to a sloop in 1936. The long spreaders may have prevented full exploitation of her weatherliness under genoa jib. (Edwin Levick photo. The Mariners' Museum, Newport News, Virginia)*

Sachem *with her yawl rig after 1955. A stemhead foretriangle might better balance her mizzen. (Courtesy John G. Alden, Inc.)*

races.'' Reportedly, she beat DeCoursey Fales' *Niña* with regularity.

Sachem's lead ballast was removed during World War II — as part of the war effort — and replaced with cement and iron. This change made her decidedly tender, and when George Devol bought her in 1955, he added five or six tons of lead to her keel. The added ballast alleviated but did not eliminate her tenderness.

Devol also gave *Sachem* a yawl rig to make her easier to handle. He did not campaign her extensively.

Sachem burned in a shipyard fire in the late 1950s, and Devol sold her rig to the owner of a New York Forty and her hull as scrap. Later she was towed to Eastport, Maine, and beached. It seems an untimely end for a fine yacht. Alden designed plenty of fast boats, but *Sachem* may have been the swiftest of them all.

A THREE-MASTED YACHT

One of the most impressive Alden designs, from the standpoint of beauty as well as size, is design number 347, a graceful three-masted schooner. Unlike the earlier three-master, *Priscilla Alden,* which was built to carry cargo, Number 347 was intended to be a yacht; thus, she has a much finer hull and luxurious accommodations. Her dimensions are 121 feet 2 inches, by 91 feet 6 inches, by 24 feet, by 12 feet 9 inches.

In her profile and the shape of her sections, her Gloucester-fisherman ancestry is discernible. (Her lines

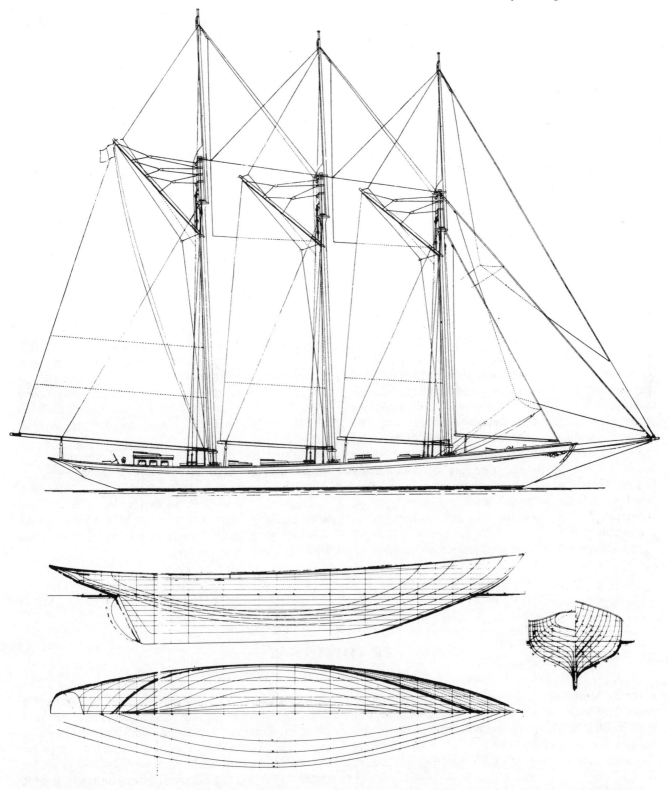

This schooner is about the largest embodiment of the Alden concept of a fisherman yacht, and she needs three masts to divide the rig. The mizzen, or spanker, is by far the largest sail, but it can be managed by a small crew. (Yachting, July 1927) Lines of the three-master show a hull form that is moderate in almost every respect. Someone — in all probability John Alden — doctored the lines with a soft lead pencil. (Courtesy John G. Alden, Inc.)

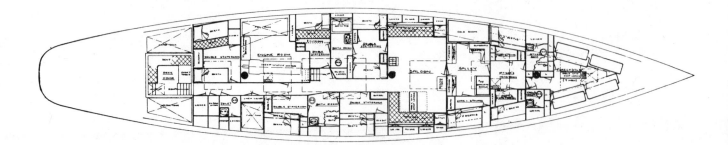

The layout below could nicely accommodate several families on a 'round-the-world cruise. (Yachting, *July 1927*)

plan, drawn by Clifford Swaine, appears to have been altered at some point by John Alden with his notorious soft lead pencil, possibly while rendering the verbalized concepts of a later, prospective client.) She seems fairly narrow, and it was intended that all ballast be carried inside, but stability is gained through the low rig and her large size (the larger the boat, the less proportional beam needed for a given amount of stability). In commenting on the rig, John Alden wrote: "The advantages of the three-masted rig for deep sea work are many. The area of the spanker is only about 60 percent of the mainsail of a two-master of the same hull design, and the weight of the boom and gaff are correspondingly lighter. There are, of course, many other advantages, and I would plan to have a small stationary gasoline engine on deck to hoist the sails and anchors, as all coasters do."

This schooner is able to accommodate a number of

guests in comfort, for there are no fewer than four double staterooms and three bathrooms abaft amidships. Farther forward is a huge saloon, a galley, and ample crew's quarters that even include an officers' mess. Alden wrote that a coasting schooner of this length is handled by five men for coastwise work and seven, including the cook, when offshore, and he saw no reason why his three-master should need more crew than that. There is a semisunken deckhouse aft and farther forward an engine room housing a 100 h.p. Winton diesel engine.

It is too bad that this vessel was never built. The Alden company records list John Alden as her owner, so probably she was to be built on speculation. Although the designer, throughout his career, had great success with building boats that had not been commissioned and then soon finding buyers, he may have lost his nerve with the large three-master.

TRADITION

A sturdy ocean racer once well known on the Chesapeake Bay is the Alden schooner *Tradition*. She was built in 1928 by Hodgdon Brothers in East Boothbay, Maine, for J. Rulon Miller, Jr., whom *Yachting* magazine called "the father of yachting at Gibson Island."

An ardent, competitive sailor, Jay Miller was also a man of decisive action. My father, who often sailed with Miller and greatly admired him, said that he carried an ax on board, and it was kept readily available for emergencies. On one reported occasion it was wielded

enthusiastically to all but amputate the bowsprit of a neighboring vessel that had dragged her anchor, drifting down on *Tradition* and fouling her rigging. After that experience, Dad always carried a hatchet mounted on the after end of the cabin house of his Alden yawl. He claimed that you can never tell when you might need it to cut a line or chop a bowsprit.

Dad sailed on *Tradition* in the 1928 Bermuda Race, and, although he was disappointed when the schooner finished in the middle of her class, he had a thoroughly enjoyable race and a memorable passage home. In the

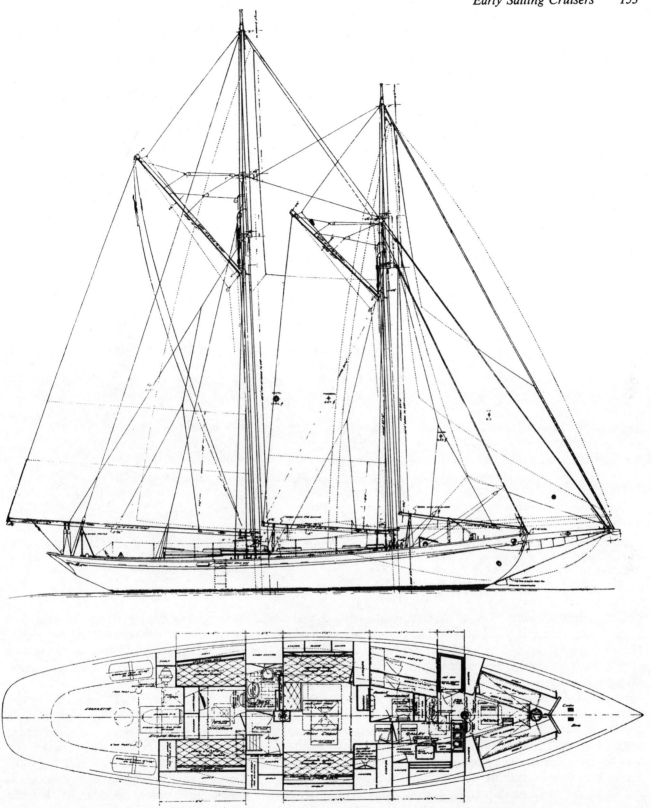

Tradition's sail plan illustrates a number of details often included in Alden plans. Notice, for example, the net under the bowsprit, leaders for the topsail sheets, the windward jib sheet led around the forestay, and even a swimming ladder over the side. As in many of Alden's offshore boats, Tradition's *cabin is well lighted and well ventilated, having a number of hatches and portholes, but the view from the cabin is obstructed by her bulwarks.* (The Rudder, *February, 1929)*

Tradition *with a following wind. The inscription is from Jay Miller to the author's father, who was her navigator in the 1928 Bermuda Race. (Courtesy William L. Henderson)*

Gulf Stream, homeward bound to the Chesapeake Bay, *Tradition* encountered a gale of wind and chaotic seas. Hove-to, she rode quite comfortably to her jumbo and reefed foresail, although most of the crew were seasick. Dad stood his watch with a brine-caked professional hand named Haskell, who really came to life when it began to blow. Captain Haskell told one story after another about shipwrecks and storms he had experienced, but Dad's favorite among Haskell's descriptions was his reference to the preparations for an elephant ride in Rangoon, Burma. He said, "When they brought her alongside, I looked aloft at her superstructure, and there sittin' on the fo'c's'le head was a little Hindu boy with a boathook."

Tradition is a seagoing schooner of the fisherman-yacht type, with an old-fashioned, fidded-topmast rig supporting 1,702 square feet of sail. The advantage of the fidded topmasts was thought to be that they can spread a lot of sail aloft in light weather, yet they can be struck if desired when going offshore or cruising in winter. An obvious disadvantage is that the rig requires complicated gear.

This schooner, design number 357, measures 59 feet 11 inches, by 45 feet 9 inches, by 14 feet 4 inches, by 8 feet 1 inch. The plans do not show the vessel under water, but a half model of her on the wall at the Gibson Island Club shows that her underbody is fisherman-like but with a shorter and more salient keel. Despite the schooner's rugged appearance, her entrance is quite fine. Alden must have expected plenty of water on deck at times, because in addition to nine rail scuppers per side there is a large spilling port on either side at the low point of the deck.

The cabin plan shows the owner's stateroom aft. On

Tradition *full and by, jib topsail ready to break out. (Courtesy John G. Alden, Inc.)*

opposite sides of the companionway are an enclosed head and an oilskin locker; forward, there is a large saloon, a double stateroom to port with the galley opposite, and finally the fo'c's'le with its own entrance through a booby hatch. There doesn't seem to be a separate navigator's area. An engine room way aft houses an F-4 Scripps gasoline auxiliary.

In 1930, Miller decided to build a larger, closer-winded, staysail-rigged Alden schooner (the *High Tide,* presented in Chapter 7), and *Tradition* was sold to Dr. Frank A. Calderone of New York. The doctor kept her

for many years, and she was used as a charter boat in the West Indies. Jay Miller's son, Robert Rulon Miller, told me that one of *Tradition*'s later owners lost his boat as well as his life in the 1970s, when the schooner foundered during a storm on a passage between St. Thomas and the Panama Canal. In recent times, Robert Miller has owned another *Tradition*. Although this boat is neither an Alden design nor a schooner (she is yawl-rigged), her name, at least, was inspired by the old schooner, and the original *Tradition* is remembered with great sentiment by the Miller family.

MOHAWK

Two designs after *Tradition,* Alden produced an equally lovely schooner named *Mohawk*. This boat was designed for Dudley F. Wolfe, who gained some notoriety not only through his ocean racing achievements with *Mohawk,* but also through his later ownership of the Frank Paine cutter, *Highland Light*. Built in 1928 by F.F. Pendleton in Wiscasset, Maine, *Mohawk* was double-planked mahogany with teak trim. Her dimensions vary slightly among the *Lloyd's Register,* the

Alden plans, and the Alden office list, but the dimensions shown on her plans are 60 feet 3½ inches, by 46 feet 2 inches, by 14 feet 5 inches, by 8 feet 9 inches.

With her rather small, tucked-up transom, generous counter, and relatively short, deep keel, *Mohawk* has a somewhat yachty appearance; yet she also has a fisherman look in the shape of her bow, the sheerline, the bulwarks, and her rig, to say nothing of the fact that she carried a couple of nested dories. She was a boat to

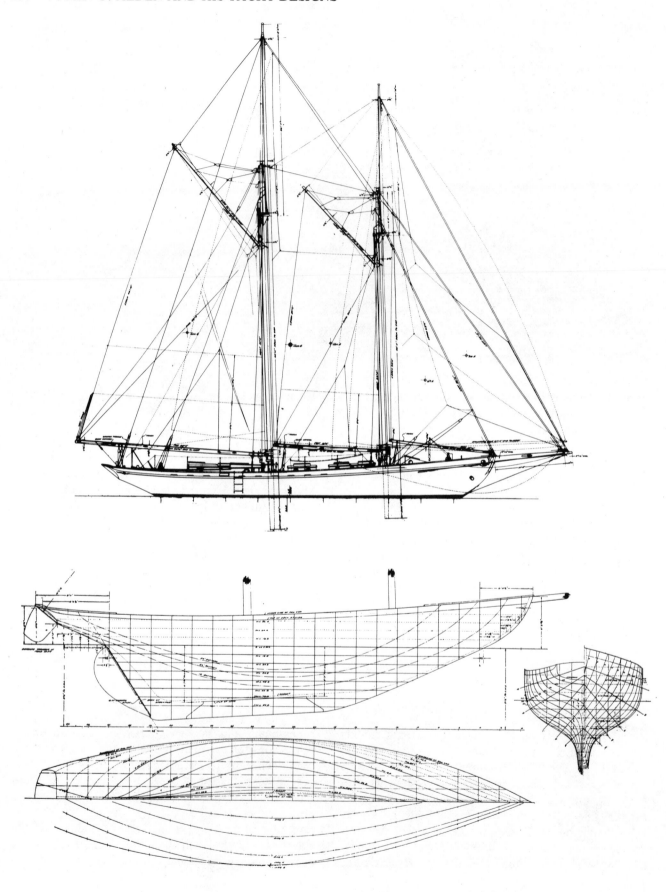

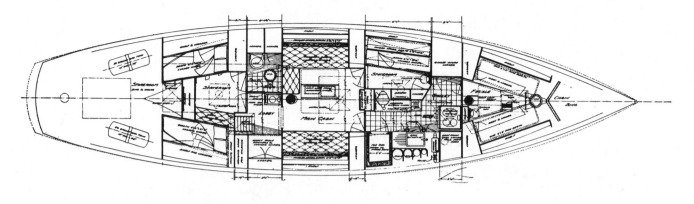

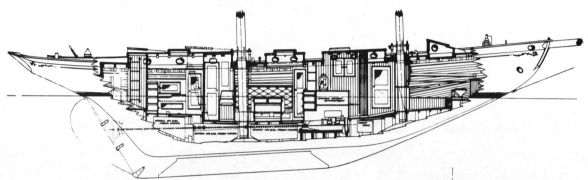

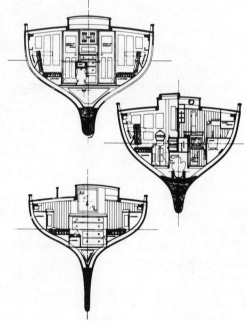

Mohawk *carries 1,607 square feet of sail in her four lowers. Her long spreaders result in generous topmast shroud angles. Perhaps in an effort to compensate for the shorter spinnaker poles of those times, sailmakers incorporated a lot of round in the foot of a spinnaker. (Courtesy John G. Alden, Inc.) The lines of* Mohawk *illustrate a fine, strong integration of hull and keel, a feature that is not at all characteristic of today's ocean racer. (Yachting,* April 1928) **Above and right:** *Drawn by Bill McNary,* Mohawk's *cabin, inboard profile, and sections plans reveal a number of interesting details. The chart table, oilskin locker, and heating stove arrayed around the foot of the companionway ladder and the large galley-store locker just abaft the fo'c's'le to port are among the features included with the comfort of a large offshore crew in mind. (Courtesy John G. Alden, Inc.)*

Mohawk in the 1928 Fastnet Race. She is boiling along on a broad reach with everything drawing, and there is for the moment nothing for her crew to do but gaze worriedly abeam at their closest competitor. (Beken and Son photo. Courtesy Clifford W. Wolfe)

gladden the hearts of the growing blue-water fraternity. She has a more symmetrical hull than many Alden boats, but her entrance is characteristically fine. Since her draft is eight inches deeper than that of *Tradition,* she might be the more weatherly of the two. Bill McNary and Cliff Swaine were responsible for her design.

According to the sail plans, *Mohawk* and *Tradition* have almost identical rigs, but yachting historian John Parkinson, Jr., who sailed on *Mohawk,* tells us that she carried a yardarm and squaresail. In addition, she had a raffee and a bonnet for the squaresail. Parkinson wrote: "The myriad of halyards, lifts, braces, and outhauls around the foremast formed a cat's cradle that took a smart man to find his way around on a dark night." Without the yardarm and headsails, the mainmast had relatively simple running rigging, but still there were

plenty of "strings" for the gaff mainsail, topsail, fisherman staysail, and gollywobbler, and this mast had two sets of running backstays.

As designed, *Mohawk* is also quite similar to *Tradition* down below, except that her engine is just forward of amidships between the galley and the port-side stateroom. This arrangement requires a long propeller shaft and detracts from space in the galley, but it keeps the owner's cabin quiet, allows a large storeroom aft, and places the engine's weight where it will be helpful to the yacht's trim and motion. A nice feature is the heating stove near the companionway, which can dry wet oilskins and provide some heat to both the owner's cabin and the saloon. Unlike *Tradition,* which has one continuous cabin trunk, *Mohawk* has three separate trunks; this arrangement provides extra deck strength, especially in way of the mainmast.

Mohawk as a ketch on the ways at Dion's Yacht Yard, Salem, Massachusetts, in the spring of 1945. (Courtesy Ralph H. Magoon)

Dudley Wolfe raced *Mohawk* across the Atlantic in the 1928 race to Spain. Although finishing behind her arch-rivals *Niña* and *Pinta,* she showed good bursts of speed, and in windward work early in the race she pulled ahead of *Pinta* and stayed close to *Niña* despite the latter's longer waterline and more modern rig. Later that year, *Mohawk* raced in the Fastnet and was again beaten by *Niña,* but she was the second boat of 13 starters to finish and took third overall on corrected time. (The *Jolie Brise,* introduced in Chapter 1, was second.) At one point in the race, when *Niña* had rounded Fastnet Rock and was beating back across the Irish Sea, she met the outward bound *Mohawk* driving before it. One of *Niña*'s crew members later said that the sight of *Mohawk* with all her kites flying worried them, but John Parkinson, who was aboard *Mohawk,* wrote that the sight of the closer-winded *Niña* "knifing to windward" spelled defeat to him. Alden wrote that *Niña* had a great advantage in her lighter construction, hollow

spars, and deeper ballast. Two years later, under A.T. Baker's ownership, *Mohawk* sailed in the Bermuda Race. She made a poor showing, yet in all her ocean races she proved an able, comfortable sea boat, fast in the right conditions.

Mohawk served in the Coast Guard's Offshore Patrol during World War II, but in 1944, after an honorable discharge, she was bought by Kenneth S. Magoon of Marblehead, whose Boston offices were for many years in the same building as those of the Alden firm. Magoon had Alden convert her from her short wartime rig to a marconi ketch rig, which, according to Magoon's son Ralph, improved her windward ability — especially with a good genoa set. Magoon used her as a family boat — for weekend and more extended cruising — and he removed two of her 10 berths to make room for a third head. She met her end in 1954 when she dragged onto the rocks at Marblehead during Hurricane Carol.

KELPIE

In the summer of 1928, my father, William L. Henderson, went to John Alden for a medium-size cruiser that he could race occasionally and use as a summer home at Gibson Island, Maryland. Alden suggested a stock yawl, design number 385, the first of which was then being built, and he offered one of these boats to Dad for an attractive price, provided two other buyers could be found. Dad persuaded two members of the Gibson Island Yacht Squadron, C. Ellis Ellicott and D.K. Este

Fisher, to join him in ordering one of the yawls, so three sister boats were built at the yard of N. Blaisdell and Sons at Woolwich, Maine, during the following fall and winter.

Soon after their launchings, the sisters sailed down the coast to New London, Connecticut, where they entered the New London-Gibson Island Race. After racing 475 miles in varied weather conditions, the yawls finished within 15 minutes of one another. My father's

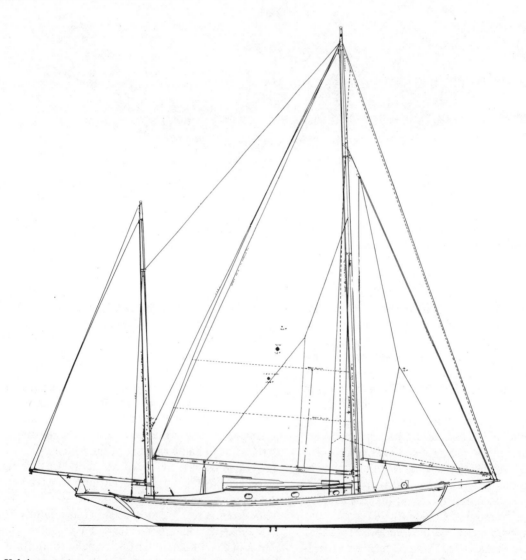

Kelpie *was given more sail area than her forerunner* Shag, *design number 358. Sail centers line up well vertically for good balance under the usual sail combinations.*

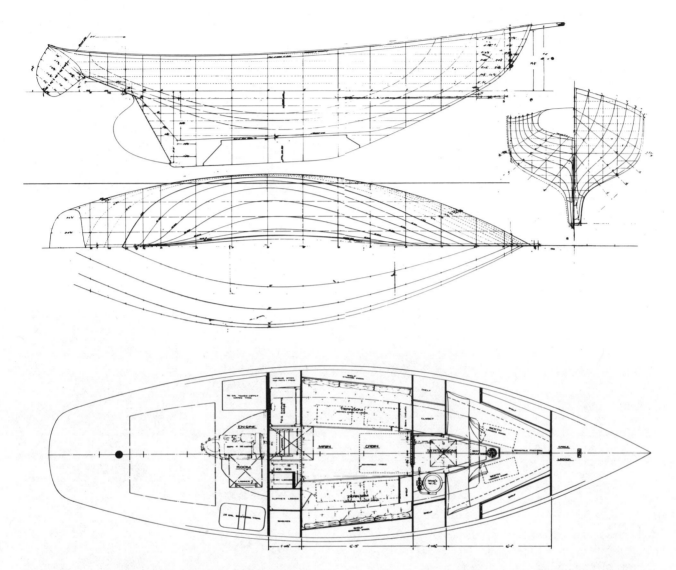

Kelpie was first, followed by Ellicott's *Merry Anne* and then Fisher's *Cynara*. There was a special rivalry between *Kelpie* and *Merry Anne*, because the latter was steered a good part of the time by Dad's older brother. The owners of all three yawls were proud to beat Alfred Loomis' cutter *Hotspur*.

During their early years, the three sisters, especially *Kelpie*, had good racing records on the Chesapeake Bay, but perhaps the greatest triumph for a boat of this design came when J.L. Williamson's yawl *Cynthia*, the first of the 385s, won the cruising division of the Chicago-Mackinac Race in 1930. Although these yawls do not excel at windward work, they are decidedly fast running in light winds and reaching in almost any conditions. In their day, at least, they were quite competitive in areas such as the Chesapeake, where there is plenty of reaching and running on point-to-point courses. Their

Aage Nielsen completed Kelpie's *lines drawing in May 1928. Her designed displacement is 16,552 pounds, with 6,560 pounds of iron on her keel. The sections reveal her moderately firm bilges. As with many Alden cruisers, the accommodations lost some space because the cabin was quite far forward, but this allowed a sizable engine room and a lazarette large enough for the author to crawl into when he was a boy.*

Kelpie *sailing past an anchored schooner off Gibson Island in the 1930s. The odd-looking middle porthole is a patented removable ventilator, which lets air through the porthole but keeps out rain or spray. (Courtesy William L. Henderson)*

fine bows can cut effectively through shallow-water chop, while their tall, generous rigs are well suited for regions of predominantly light winds.

Ten 385 yawls were built, all by Blaisdell and Sons except for one by C.A. Morse and Son at Thomaston, Maine. They were a development of two earlier designs, Numbers 303 and 358, both of which were drawn for the head of the Alden brokerage department, John Robinson, Jr. Robinson named both his boats *Shag,* and they were very similar in size, lines, and rig.

The 385s differ very little from the *Shags,* except that they have a larger rig, more ballast, and differently shaped portholes. Although the *Shags* were designed primarily by Clifford Swaine, Aage Nielsen had a major hand in the 385 design. All three designs share the same dimensions: 34 feet 4 inches, by 25 feet 5 inches, by 9 feet 9 inches, by 5 feet. They are distinctively Alden in looks, with their spoon bows, raking oval transoms, pronounced sheer, and somewhat wedge-shaped waterlines with considerable fullness aft.

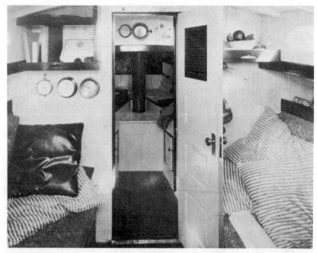

The cabin of a 385. The porthole in the forward end of the cabin trunk was a nice ventilation feature, for it was immediately abaft the mainmast, which blocked the spray.

A deck view of Kelpie *with the author's father at the helm during the New London-Gibson Island Race in 1929. The dinghy could not be carried flat on the cabintop because of the low main boom. (Courtesy William L. Henderson)*

The rig of the 385 is powerful, with 712 square feet of working sail area, yet it is easy to handle with no running backstays and a self-tending jib. The big drawback of the rig, for racing especially, is that a large masthead jib must be threaded through the narrow slot between the two forward stays when tacking or jibing. In a fresh wind, however, there is no great problem, because the working jib can be carried effectively to windward. We were able to race *Kelpie* for years with no sheet winches because of the working jib's efficiency in a good breeze. When beating in lighter winds with the large masthead jib, we'd use a pair of watch tackles for close trim.

Several details of the below-decks arrangement are less than perfect, for the dining table must be removed completely after meals, the head is not private with respect to the forward cabin, and there is no sink in the galley. However, there are four good-size bunks and plenty of lockers and stowage space, and the galley is aft, where it belongs on a boat of this size. Dad had a foredeck hatch installed on *Kelpie,* and this gave her excellent ventilation. A feature I recall with pleasure is the gravity-flow water tap in the galley, which did away with the necessity of using a hand pump.

Dad kept *Kelpie* for about 30 years, and he probably would have had her for another decade or so were it not for dry rot, weeping seams, and the fact that his son had some crazy notions about getting a boat that was a bit more up to date for racing.

THE 390 SERIES

A real Alden classic is design number 390, a 50-foot, knuckle-bow schooner with a pronounced sheerline. There were nine boats built to this design, six in the United States and three abroad. Most of the U.S. 390s were built by C.A. Morse and Son at Thomaston, Maine, in 1929 and 1930. John Alden himself ordered one of these schooners, originally named *Rogue,* but later better known under the name *Venturer.* Although he didn't keep her long, John bought a sister boat about 18 years later. This schooner, named *Abenaki,* is the boat Alden skippered at the age of 66 to a class second in the 1950 Bermuda Race.

Most sailors thought *Abenaki* was hopelessly out-dated for ocean racing when John bought her in 1947, and their opinion was reinforced when she finished at the tail end of the 1947 Newport-Annapolis Race. One of her crew, yachting journalist William Taylor, was scheduled to be the toastmaster at the awards banquet, but the banquet was over before *Abenaki* docked. This prompted some humorous comments, including one report that the Alden "schooner-rigged houseboat" was last seen drifting out of the entrance of Chesapeake Bay. Despite such remarks, Alden never lost confidence in the old design, and his triumph in the 1950 Bermuda Race must have given him great satisfaction.

The lines of the 390, drawn by Aage Nielsen, show

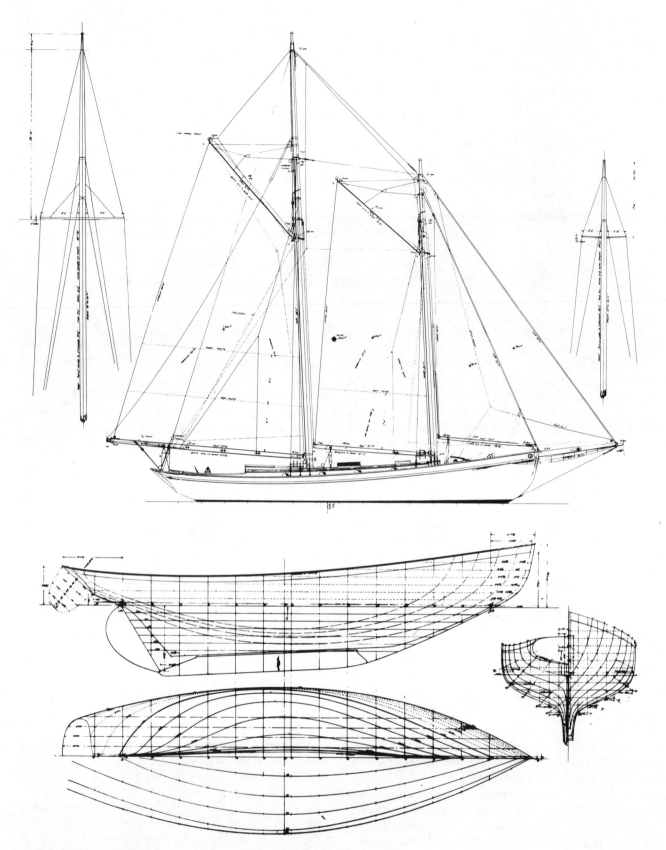

The standard 390 sail plan is a gaff-schooner rig with 1,309 square feet, including a large foresail. The 390's lines have many of the features of an Alden design of the period, but the extra beam and the degree of bow knuckle and sheer set her somewhat apart. The sections indicate great sail-carrying power. She carries 14,650 pounds of iron on her keel. (Courtesy John G. Alden, Inc.)

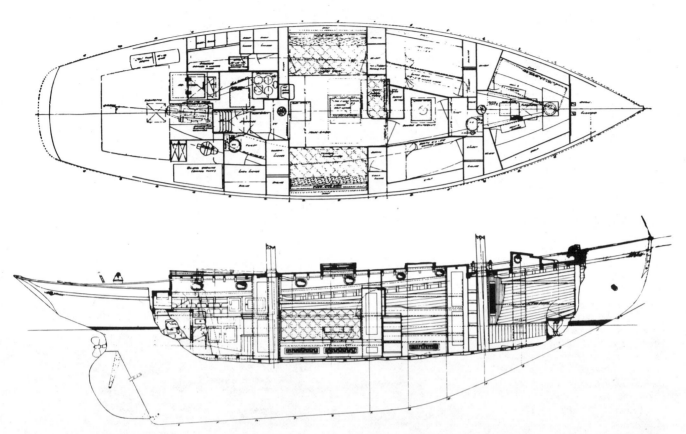

The standard 390 cabin plan has a comfortable sitting area in the saloon. There is a folding chart table just forward of the saloon table, folding upper berths above the saloon transoms, and another folding table in the fo'c's'le. Abenaki had a double stateroom aft and a forward galley. The inboard profile shows that the ceiling lacks wide seams between planks, but notice that there is a large open space above and ventilated lockers below to allow air to circulate between the skin and ceiling. (Courtesy John G. Alden, Inc.)

what might be considered a typical early Alden hull, except that it is beamier by about two feet than the normal Alden deep-keel schooner of that period. As with the Number 385 yawls and others, the hull is rather wedge-shaped, with full waterlines aft and a slightly hollow entrance. The bilges are firm and the keel moderately long. The long iron ballast not only affords good protection during a grounding but also gives the hull added longitudinal strength. The high bow, though it lessens visibility from the helm, helps keep water off the foredeck. Added freeboard forward is often needed on boats having fine bows without much flare, especially when the forward overhang is minimal. With its raking oval transom, the stern is particularly characteristic of Alden designs of that vintage. The dimensions of the first four 390s are 50 feet 1 inch, by 39 feet 10 inches, by 14 feet, by 7 feet 2 inches. *Zaida II* (390-E) is 51 feet 11 inches long on deck, and two boats of the series are 52 feet long, but the other dimensions were the same throughout the series.

The accommodations are somewhat unusual for a boat intended to carry a paid hand, the galley being aft and the owner's stateroom forward. This arrangement makes the galley inconvenient with respect to the fo'c's'le, but the after location minimizes motion, and there is some advantage in having the galley close to the cockpit. The plans show a saloon fireplace that apparently shares a stovepipe with the galley's Shipmate. There are two transom berths and two folding berths in the saloon. In rough weather, a fair amount of motion might be expected in the three-berth stateroom, but at least this cabin is quite private, since there is a solid bulkhead between it and the fo'c's'le, and it has its own head. There is another head and a convenient oilskin locker near the companionway. An engine room abaft the companionway houses a four-cylinder Red Wing gasoline engine, which is angled to place the propeller to port of the centerline. This offset may be useful to minimize lefthand torque, but if the prop were deeper, it would be well under water on the port tack. On a ketch-

For the 1950 Bermuda Race, Alden gave Abenaki *a tall marconi mainmast that could support a huge golly. "At that time,"* recalls Bill Anderson, who was mate and navigator in the race, *"the CCA rule did not count this sail as overlapping.*

"We started in a hard northwester that day in 1950, and the cook, asleep in his tuxedo in the fo'c's'le after a debutante party in Newport, was ordered to cook dinner. He was violently ill into the top-lifting icebox so John and I had to clean it out and cook the rest of the race. John had an iron stomach.

*"*Abenaki *was racing under a cruising rating. We got 90 miles to the westward, put the gollywobbler to her, and roared down to Kitchen Shoals . . . . Gifford Pinchot [in* Loki] *beat us on corrected time by 3 minutes 47 seconds for first place in Class C, but we became a very close crew, had a glorious time in Bermuda, and had a rough passage home. There are some yarns about that one, too . . . ." (Courtesy John G. Alden, Inc.)*

The first 390 Marneegil *(originally* Who II *and now* Tar Baby) *at anchor and showing to good advantage her pronounced sheer line and distinctive bow profile. (Courtesy John G. Alden, Inc.)*

Left: *A bow view of* Venturer *(390-C) on the ways reveals her considerable wetted surface. (Courtesy John G. Alden, Inc.)* **Below:** *The interior of George Ratsey's 390,* Zaida, *looking aft. She was built by C.A. Morse for a contract price of $4,800. The curtains allow either wide open spaciousness or privacy as desired. (Morris Rosenfeld photo. Courtesy Deborah Carmen)*

Abenaki, *the way John Alden had her rigged for the Bermuda Race in 1950. (Morris Rosenfeld photo. Courtesy Chester M. and Harriet Sawtelle)*

rigged version of this boat designed in 1938, the propeller was lowered by placing it in a rudder aperture on the centerline.

Originally, the 390s were gaff-rigged schooners, but at least one was later changed to a ketch, and George Ratsey's *Zaida II* was converted to a cutter in 1935. John Alden kept the schooner rig on *Abenaki*, but he altered her for the 1950 Bermuda Race by giving her a tall mainmast that carried a marconi mainsail and a tremendous gollywobbler. She was also fitted with a boomkin and permanent backstay to replace the runners.

George Ratsey (of the Ratsey sailmaking family) raced his *Zaida II* in on-soundings events. She did very well as both a schooner and a cutter, placing in the money with a regularity — according to William Taylor — "quite out of proportion to what you would have expected from glancing at her rather rotund lines." The aforementioned *Venturer* gained some notoriety under the ownership of Oswald Knauth, who cruised in his boat extensively. Mrs. Knauth published privately a

book containing logs of *Venturer*'s cruises in the West Indies. This schooner and other 390s proved their seaworthiness by serving in the rugged wintertime offshore patrols during World War II.

A November 1980 article in *Motor Boating & Sailing,* "Antique Boats," featured a 390 schooner named *Tar Baby* (390-A, originally *Who II*). Since her building, she has had only three owners; Carl Sherman bought her in 1973 and still owned her in 1982. Though he has refastened her with stainless steel, her oak frames and yellow pine planking are original. She was altered to a staysail schooner in the late 1960s. Besides *Tar Baby*, there is to my knowledge only one other 390 still sailing — *Voyager* (originally *Tyrone*), Number 390-B. In a *WoodenBoat* magazine article (March/April 1980), Peter Phillips described *Voyager*'s complete rebuilding in a Lunenburg, Nova Scotia, yard. The deck plan and accommodations have been altered, but her lines and rig are the same. Now entering her second half-century, she has made at least one transatlantic passage under

John Alden (middle) aboard Abenaki *in the 1951 New London-Marblehead Race, flanked by Ned Watson (right) and Ed Kittredge. Bill Anderson took the photograph. "We had a lively evening the night before the start," Anderson said, "and next morning we pushed the engine starting button and nothing happened. John, despite my protest, would not deign to ask a competitor for a tow to the starting line, and we missed the turn of the current at The Race. Undaunted, we went up inside, boiled through Woods Hole with a fair current, and finished fairly well in the fleet." (Courtesy Edward B. Watson, Jr.)*

Phillips' ownership, and more voyages are planned.

As for *Tar Baby*, Sherman is unequivocal in his praise, using phrases such as "absolutely well balanced," "easy sailing," and "magnificent creation." *Tar Baby* reportedly is insured for $150,000, and would-be buyers have offered more. She is kept immaculate and has won two Best of Fleet awards at the Mystic Seaport Antique and Classic Boat Rendezvous. This old design, Alden's "Schooner-rigged houseboat," is still very much appreciated.

In 1990 I received letters from Don Armitage of Auckland, New Zealand, saying that he bought the *Arcturus*, design number 390-F, at public auction. At the time of purchase she was in a deplorable condition with deteriorated deck, most of the ribs broken or rotted, and a lot of toredo worm damage to the planks and keel deadwood. Mr. Armitage and his partners were proceeding with a major rebuilding of the hull (including replacement of nearly half the planking and covering the hull exterior with ⅝-inch diagonal skins), deck replacement, and restoration of the interior to the original layout.

An Abstract of Title shows that the *Arcturus* was once owned by Beatrice A. Patton, wife of George S. Patton, and Mr. Armitage presumes that this ownership inspired the famous general (then a colonel) to order the larger schooner *When and If* from John Alden (see page 402). The Abstract of Title also shows that *Arcturus* was later owned by Oscar Kelly, who Mr. Armitage suspects was movie actor/dancer Gene Kelly.

Ira L. Foreman, the owner before Armitage, found *Arcturus* in a state of dereliction in Hawaii. He gutted her, shored up the hull's interior with dunnage, and then sailed her singlehandedly via various Pacific islands to New Zealand. About two years after her arrival there, Mr. Foreman was charged by the Customs Office a hefty import duty, which he was unable to pay. Hence the auction resulting in the old schooner's acquisition by *Arcturus* Partnership. Hopefully, her restoration will add many more years of life to this truly classic yacht.

7

Later Sailing Cruisers

In the early 1930s yacht designers were no less affected by the Depression than anyone else. Clifford Swaine recalls that on the day of the crash in October 1929, John Alden came into the drafting room repeatedly to announce that one client or another had canceled his design order, and work on the plans should be stopped. Still, Alden's firm was hit less hard than many others. He was at the height of his popularity in the early part of that decade, and his sawn-frame, plain-finished, Maine-built boats (sometimes framed with scraps left over from the planking of large fishing vessels) were relatively inexpensive. For all his apparent absent-mindedness, Alden could be a hard-nosed businessman, and he had Ethel Bacon — the shrewd, tough, office general — to make sure of it. Roger Morse recalls that John usually ordered only the hulls and rigs of the boats he had built on speculation by the C.A. Morse yard. He preferred to supply deck hardware, fittings, and engines himself, knowing he could get a better discount from the manufacturers. Morse also remembers that when the yard would wire Alden for, say, a $2,500 installment of a cost-plus contract on a boat then building, Alden might send $5,000 instead. His reason was simple: He wanted to be sure the yard had enough capital on hand to get whatever materials were needed without costly delays. When the stock market crashed, Alden had 16

schooners being built on speculation at various yards, but he had little trouble selling every one of them.

Although the top four boats in the 1932 Bermuda Race were Alden schooners, and their success prolonged the popularity of Alden designs in particular and the schooner rig in general, it was inevitable that finer-lined, generally faster yachts with higher-aspect-ratio rigs would gain favor for ocean racing. In the 1930 race to the Onion Patch, for instance, the top seven boats in Class A were schooners, but eight years later the top five finishers in A were yawls. Robert Bavier, with his marconi-rigged New York Forty, had started the trend when he won the Bermuda Race in 1924. Later Olin and Rod Stephens made a great impression on yachtsmen when they demonstrated that a close-winded "over-grown six meter" could easily handle a transoceanic passage. They proved it dramatically, sailing *Dorade* to an overwhelming victory in the 1931 Transatlantic Race to Plymouth, England.

Alden was often critical of the work of other designers (and, in fact, no less critical of his own work), but he came to admire the boats of Olin Stephens. In time, the Boston designer's own ocean racers became finer, with more cutaway profiles, longer ends, and tall, marconi yawl or sloop rigs, while many of his cruising boats were given marconi ketch rigs. Nevertheless, Alden always

The crew of the Morse yard, shown here about 1930, was one component of Alden's success. The blacksmith (front row, second from right) was in his 80s when this photograph was taken; at age 16 he helped build the Monitor *for the Union navy. The rigger (front row, second from left), who hired out to yards the length of the Maine coast, liked his drink, and young Roger Morse (far left, standing) once watched the man turn out a near-perfect wire splice while three sheets to the wind. The yard foreman could take a broadax to a 40-foot-long square timber of Oregon fir and have the first coat of varnish on the mast in four days. Working 10 hours a day, six days a week, this crew would receive John's orders in February after the New York Boat Show and have four or five boats ready for him that summer. (Courtesy Roger Morse)*

had a special sentiment for the husky schooner, a fact confirmed by his return to *Abenaki* (described in Chapter 6) in his later years.

Even though the introduction of the CCA rule, refinements in rig allowances, and the development of new sails such as the genoa jib and parachute spinnaker encouraged other rigs, Alden continued to admire the looks of the schooner, and he liked its reaching speed and the versatility of its sail plan. It is also probable that he recognized some inherently desirable steering characteristics that exist when a schooner hull is designed to match its rig. Perhaps the schooner's ability to track is being rediscovered, for in a technical paper on directional stability for the 1974 Chesapeake Sailing Yacht Symposium, Walter H. Scott, Jr., a designer of modern yachts, concluded: "For combined hull and rig directional stability both in course-holding and into-the-wind categories, the best type is probably the old-fashioned schooner, with the sail area and the hull area centered well aft."

Alden schooners have proven not only fast and well mannered, but also very comfortable. Thus, they are ideal for long voyages. John Parkinson, Jr., has written: "It is impressive how many Alden schooners have cruised successfully to the South Seas. Their able, seakindly hulls make them fine ships to live aboard for extended periods."

It is an interesting fact that early Alden schooners were by and large quite asymmetrical in hull form, with fine bows and full quarters, but in the years after 1930 they became more symmetrical. Although Alden recognized that an extremely fine bow can cause rooting and wetness, he liked fullness aft to give the boat some bearing when heeled, and as Carl Alberg has suggested to me, he felt that a schooner needs considerable buoyancy in her quarters to support her mainmast.

John gradually altered his thinking about the degree of asymmetry, however, for in 1934 he wrote in regard to the early *Malabars*: "If I were designing a boat for a similar purpose today I would probably not modify the lines to any great extent. I would fill their waterlines forward slightly, soften the quarters, and probably harden the bilge just forward of amidships to give her even a little more initial stability." Carl Alberg thinks that the introduction of the CCA rule of 1933 had a considerable influence in encouraging fuller bows, and it is true that some of Alden's top designers — such as Alberg and Fenwick Williams — preferred hulls with more balanced ends. Williams recently wrote me, "How I detested the fine forward, fat aft hull form."

Other influences, perhaps, were the successful, symmetrical-waterline boats (*Stormy Weather* was one) that were being turned out by competing design firms such as those of Philip Rhodes and Olin Stephens. It is even possible that the capsize at sea of William Nutting's ketch *Typhoon* had some effect on the trend toward more balanced-ended boats, for in the mid-1930s Uffa Fox, the popular designer-author, who had been aboard *Typhoon* when she rolled over, criticized the boat's fine bow and full stern, although he did not actually say the hull form was responsible for the capsize.

In more recent times there has been a trend the other way, in the direction of the hull forms originally favored by Alden. Carl Alberg now believes that after the appearance of the CCA rule he "overdid the fullness of the forepart," and his designs today have "a sharper waterline." Alden was always aware of the difficulty of choosing the perfect bow, for back in 1913 he wrote, "The problem is the eternal one, to eliminate the faults of the two extremes (fineness and fullness) and combine as much as possible their good points."

Regarding Alden's remark about hardening the bilge just forward of amidships to increase initial stability, it is interesting to note that some modern designers feel that only waterline beam and the vertical location of the center of gravity determine initial stability, while the shape of the bilge amidships has little if any effect on stiffness. Regardless, Alden boats nearly always have good form stability, and their bilges are rarely if ever hard enough to compromise seakindliness.

Needless to say, the Boston designer turned out many small seaboats with rigs other than the schooner. A number of yachtsmen in the 1930s, having been inspired by the likes of Howard Blackburn and William A. Robinson, were anxious to sail offshore. (Howard Blackburn was the fingerless singlehander who made two transatlantic crossings in fisherman-type sloops. He was honored by the Cruising Club of America in 1929.) Alden supplied them with some marvelously suitable boats. A favorite of mine is the ketch *Staghound,* which is described in this chapter. Not only is she handsome and a fine seaboat, but also she was fast enough to win the Transpacific Race twice.

Also in this chapter are several of the popular Alden stock designs, such as the Off Soundings and Coastwise Cruiser classes. These boats were particularly appropriate for the Depression and early post-Depression years, because they could be built cheaply, yet they were fast, reasonably able, and could be raced as one-designs.

For a good part of the 1930s, Alden's name dominated the references to designers in the *Lloyd's Register of American Yachts.* In the days before molded boats, at least, few if any designers supplied the American yachtsman with a greater number of successful sailing cruisers, particularly in terms of numbers built to the various designs.

∾

PURITAN

The large schooner *Puritan,* design number 435-B, is one of Alden's more magnificent yachts, combining size and beauty with strength, comfort, speed, and seakindliness. She does not have her center of lateral resistance as far aft as do some Alden schooners with deeper keel drag. Still, she is fairly cut away forward, and the keel extends aft to the waterline ending. Although she has a small centerboard, the lowering of which moves the center of lateral plane farther forward, the board was intended primarily for use when hard on the wind in a rough sea, and under other conditions it would seldom be lowered.

Puritan's keel was laid in November 1929 by the Electric Boat Company of New London, Connecticut, a builder of submarines for the U.S. Navy. She was launched in April 1931. The schooner's hull is steel,

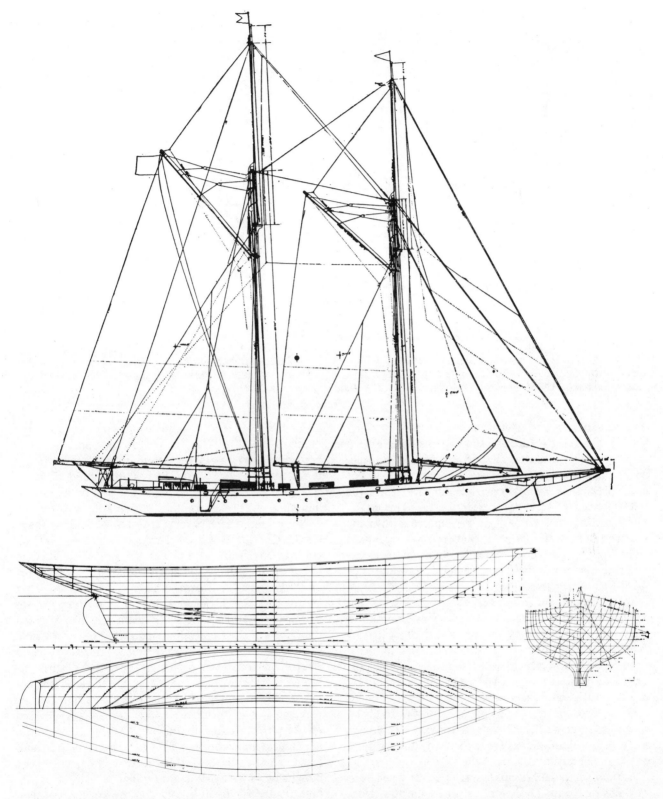

Puritan's sail plan features a relatively large foresail and small main, for easing the chore of handling her large rig. Still, with 4,297 square feet of working sail, her mainsail has 1,996 square feet. (The Rudder, February 1931) The lines of Puritan show a harmonious, well-balanced hull with firm bilges and smooth, flowing lines. The keel has a flat profile. Her draft increases to 14 feet 8 inches when the board is down. (Courtesy John G. Alden, Inc.)

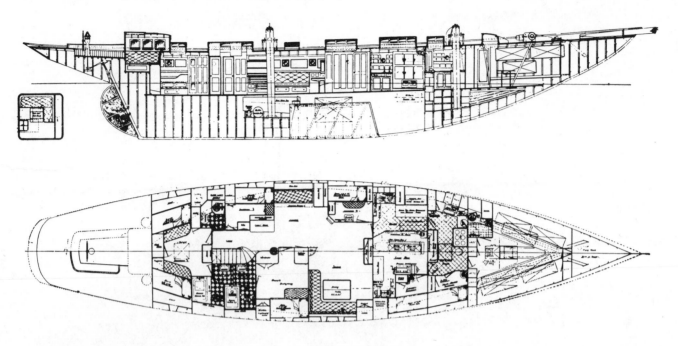

Puritan's inboard profile shows that her cabin sole is more than seven feet above the bottom of her keel, and the centerboard trunk does not intrude into the main saloon. When portholes are in the side, it is prudent to have them as high as possible. In her luxurious accommodations, a feeling of elegance and great spaciousness is achieved by keeping the number of longitudinal bulkheads amidships to a minimum. (The Rudder, *February 1931*)

with welded butts and riveted, lapped seams — the first such hull built by Electric Boat. Thus, she helped pioneer the construction method developed for deep-diving submarines, which have to withstand extremes of water pressure. *Puritan*'s generous dimensions are 102 feet 9 inches, by 74 feet 8 inches, by 22 feet 10 inches, by 9 feet with the centerboard up. Compared with many Alden schooners, she has a flatter sheer, more freeboard amidships, longer ends, a smaller transom, and less spoon to the bow. These features give her more of a yacht than a fisherman look.

She is certainly far from a fisherman below decks, for her accommodations can be described as sumptuous. There are six staterooms, the aftermost of which extends across the entire boat. The large dining saloon is amidships on the starboard side, and just aft on the port side is a spacious lounge. The galley has a six-burner stove, a refrigerator, and an adjoining pantry. I count four enclosed heads, including one for the fo'c's'le, which has seven berths. The engine room, which houses a 150 h.p. Winton diesel, is far forward; this location, of course, necessitates a very long shaft.

Puritan's teak decks provide a clean and generous working platform. One nice feature is the low deck-house just forward of the cockpit. It provides shade on sunny days and shelter in wet weather. The topmast schooner rig has a large foresail, so the total sail area is

divided fairly evenly. Despite this division, however, the mainsail is quite large, and with her topsails, triple headsails, heavy gaffs, and running backstays, *Puritan* is a workshop. Of course, she has accommodations for a large professional crew; when she was built, ease of handling was not always the consideration it is today.

According to Cliff Swaine, *Puritan* was taking shape on the drafting board on the day of the stock market crash when her intended owner, a Mr. Curtis, called up to cancel his order. Soon after, the contract was picked up by Edward M. Brown, a member of the New York Yacht Club, and his name appears in the Alden records as *Puritan*'s original owner. Evidently Brown also felt the effects of the Depression, and the schooner was sold to H.J. Bauer, a wealthy Californian. Bauer kept her in Bristol fashion, even protecting all parts of the varnished spars with canvas covers when the yacht was not under sail. As a boy of 17, actor-sailor-author Sterling Hayden was a member of the crew that delivered *Puritan* from the East to the West Coast. At one time in her career, the schooner was owned by Mariano Prado-Sosa, son of a president of Peru; sometime later she was bought by Floridian William Bolling, a restorer of vintage boats. He in turn sold *Puritan* to an Austrian, Oscar Schmidt, who had the boat extensively rebuilt in England.

During the summer of 1980 *Puritan* was brought to

Even when sailing under her lowers alone, Puritan *makes a magnificent sight. (Courtesy General Dynamics, Electric Boat Division)*

the United States, partly to attend the America's Cup races at Newport, Rhode Island. While in Newport, she entered the Classic Yacht Regatta and won her class. Her passage back to Europe in the fall was a stormy one, dramatically recounted in the *National Fisherman* (April 1981). During a gale in mid-Atlantic her mainmast went by the board, and after hanging up in the rigging, it thrashed around like a wild animal, pounding the deck and endangering the vessel and her crew. There was little the crew could do except watch helplessly and wait for the huge mast to fall. Eventually it did, after making a shambles of the boat. With forestaysail, jib, and engine, *Puritan* reached the Canary Islands. There

she was jury-rigged, and she subsequently made her way under sail and power to the Mediterranean, where she was refitted.

At the time of this writing her home port is the island of Jersey, in the Channel Islands, Great Britain. She attended the Wooden Boat Show in Newport, Rhode Island, in August 1982, and she was still in Newport when I went aboard her later that fall. She is in immaculate shape with her brass polished, decks scrubbed, and brightwork gleaming. A member of the professional crew, justifiably proud, asserted that there is no finer yacht afloat.

LELANTA

If old vessels could only talk, many would have some fascinating tales to tell. The Alden schooner *Lelanta* is one of those we wish could speak about her various adventures, especially those of the late 1970s when she served as a drug smuggler.

This schooner, Number 448, was designed in 1929 for Ralph St. L. Peverley, an American living near Liverpool, England. Measuring 65 feet 6 inches, by 46 feet 6 inches, by 14 feet 7 inches, by 8 feet 9 inches, *Lelanta*

was built of steel by G. de Vries Lentsch at Amsterdam, Holland. Although the schooner was built for the 1931 Fastnet Race, she was completed in time to participate in the 1930 Fastnet. Unfortunately, the untuned vessel encountered a heavy gale during the race, and along with four others out of the nine yachts competing, she withdrew. She did not enter the 1931 race.

Aage Nielsen had a major hand in *Lelanta*'s design, which illustrates the trend toward a more symmetrically

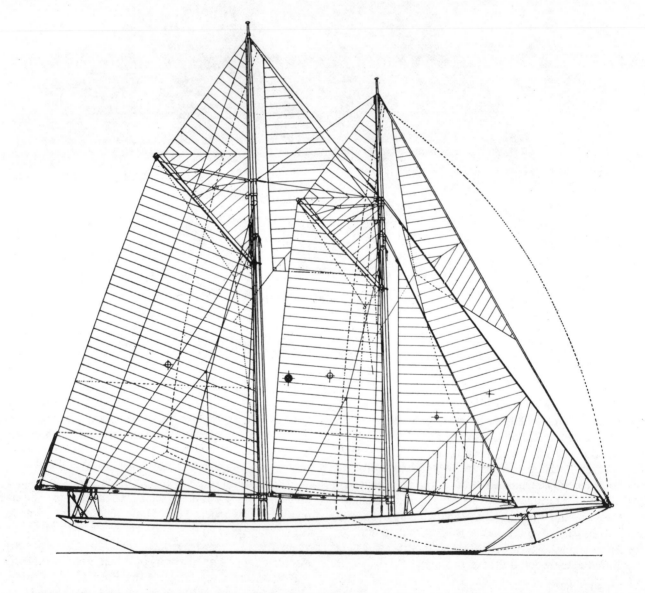

Writing about Lelanta*'s sail plan in 1937, Uffa Fox said "The [schooner's] combination of sails that can be set from calm to gale, is better than any other rig I know." (*Sail and Power *by Uffa Fox)*

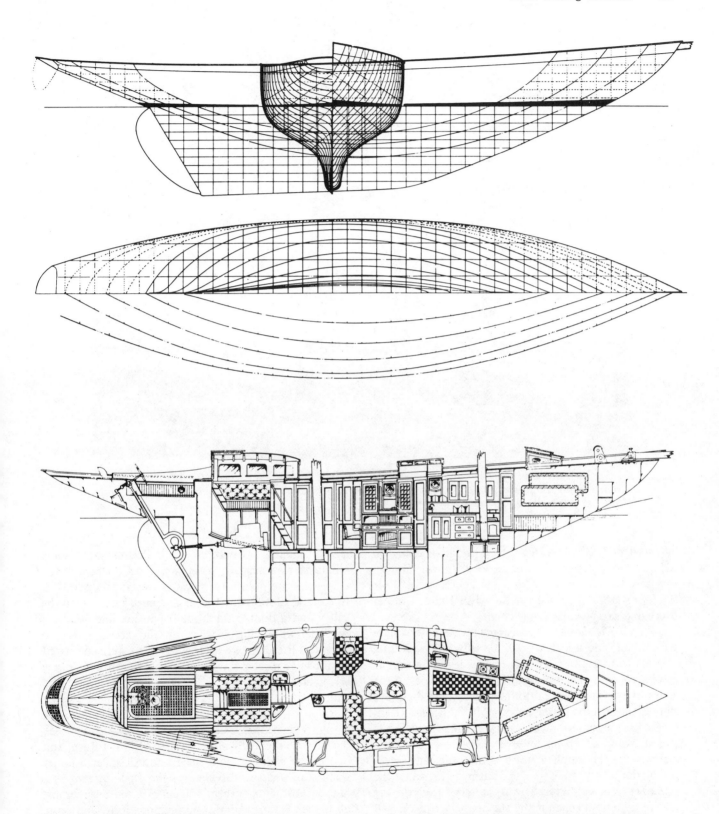

In comparison to many of Alden's earlier schooners, Lelanta *is fine aft and full forward, while her sheer line is much flatter.* (Sail and Power *by Uffa Fox) Her accommodations plans, redrawn for publication by Uffa Fox (as were her other plans presented here), show details such as the deckhouse grating, tile floors in the head and galley, and inviting bunks. (Courtesy Jan Iserbyt)*

Lelanta *in the Caribbean with all sails set. Let's hope the charter guests remembered to close their ports.* *(Bruce G. Lynn photo. Courtesy Jan Iserbyt)*

balanced hull. She is a deep-bodied boat, and her 40 tons of displacement gives her a lot of power and an easy motion in a seaway. With her conservative sheer she looks more like a yacht than a fisherman, and her overhangs are beautifully matched.

Originally, *Lelanta* was gaff-rigged with 1,790 square feet of sail, and the area could be enlarged by setting topsails from both masts. Her owner devised a unique system to hold the topsail luffs to their masts. Luff slides ran on jackstays up to the hounds and then into slotted tubes fixed to the spars aloft. This feature increased the aerodynamic efficiency of the topsails while still allowing them to be lowered to the deck. *Lelanta*'s rig was justly extolled as a handsome and well-proportioned one by Uffa Fox, but in 1973, when the schooner was modernized with stainless steel rigging and an aluminum mainmast, she was given a staysail rig.

During the first part of her life, *Lelanta*'s layout included a sunken deckhouse convenient to the cockpit,

then, forward, a pair of long double staterooms separated by a narrow passageway. Just forward of the port-side stateroom was the water closet, followed by a full-width saloon with a large L-shaped settee, then the galley and a double stateroom opposite, and finally a fo'c's'le with pipe berths for the crew. Later in *Lelanta*'s life, her two after staterooms were converted to one huge master stateroom with a queen-size double berth, and a berth was installed on either side of the saloon.

Ralph St. L. Peverley was an avid Alden fan. He formerly owned the Alden schooner *La Goleta,* which dueled with the *Tally Ho* in the 1927 Fastnet Race, and in 1938 he ordered from the Boston designer a larger version of *Lelanta*. Evidently, the first *Lelanta* was highly satisfactory except for her size, because almost all of her features of rig, accommodations, and basic hull form were incorporated into *Lelanta II*. St. L. Peverly sold the original *Lelanta* to an Englishman who in turn sold her soon after World War II to

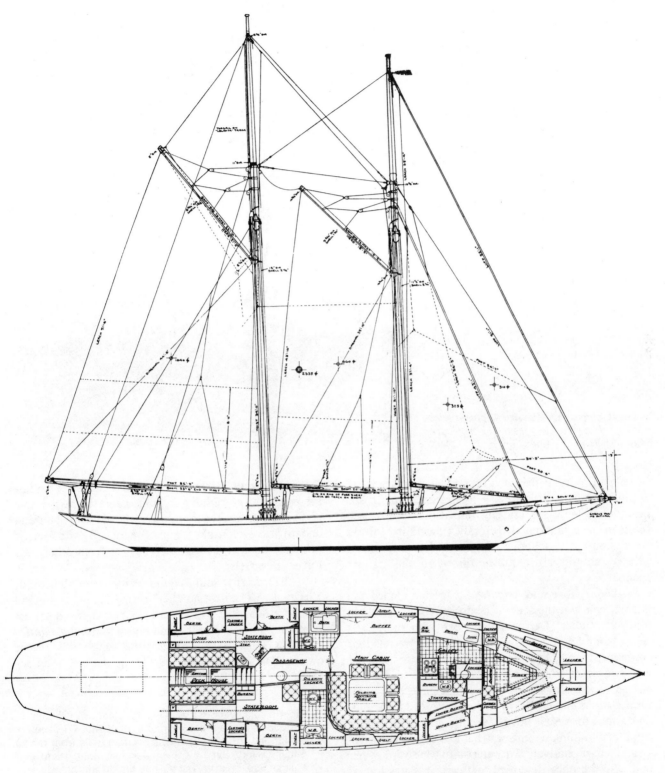

The sail plan of Lelanta II, *showing no deck structure, indicates that the rig is similar to her forerunner's except that there is no fore topsail. She carries 2,335 square feet of sail in her four lowers. Lelanta II's layout below is also similar to the first's, but of course, the larger schooner has more room everywhere, and there is an extra head amidships.* (Yachting, *March 1938)*

Lelanta II under sail. *The sizable boat on deck was lifted by tackles from the spreaders. (Courtesy John G. Alden, Inc.)*

Gwen-ael Bolore of Brittany, France, the manufacturer of cigarette papers. Bolore, a Renaissance man, used *Lelanta* not only for cruising but also as a research vessel in investigations of Brittany's dwindling lobster populations. The schooner also starred with Bolore's wife in an adventure movie filmed in the Canary Islands.

In 1966, Bolore sold *Lelanta* to a Belgian named Jan Iserbyt, who put the schooner into the charter trade in the West Indies. Iserbyt fell in love with the boat's dependability and her forgiving nature. He recalls that she was easy to sail (he once crossed the Atlantic in her with two other adults), fast enough to suit, and above all seaworthy. In a blow, he could leave her under foresail alone and lay below to the comfort of the cabin. She would forereach slowly, about four points off the wind, maintaining steerageway but keeping a drift wake — an area of relatively flat water — to windward of her hull. (Bolore once described to Iserbyt his method of shortening sail. He would hand the jib, then the foresail. If it breezed on more, he'd hand the mainsail and set the foresail again. Reefing was not easy in those

days.) Above all, Iserbyt remembers that despite her impressive array of running rigging, *Lelanta* was a simple boat, and this was the key to her dependability. Nothing aboard her ever broke or malfunctioned, and Iserbyt routinely booked last-minute charters from other, less fortunate vessels.

In 1972, Iserbyt sold *Lelanta* to Jonathan McLean of Virginia. McLean had her rerigged as a staysail schooner, installed a larger engine, and changed her accommodations. There is some mystery about *Lelanta*'s activities after 1978. One of the schooner's recent owners, Dr. Nicholas Iliff, wrote me the following account:

She was sold again to a person who planned to charter her, and soon after that she had a new GMC 471 diesel put in, and in 1978 she had new Ulmer sails from the Annapolis loft. Her most recent documentation was to a woman who lived in Miami, but the document, when mailed to her by the Coast Guard here [in Baltimore], was returned as undeliverable. She apparently at that point disappeared into the drug trade. It is not known how many trips she made before she was seized off the coast of Naples, Florida. According to the sheriff whom we spoke to, he was out fishing one night in his small runabout when he saw a boat flashing a light. He assumed it was in distress and he motored over with his police flasher on. The occupants of the boat jumped into several small boats and disappeared into the darkness. He stepped aboard her without trouble and found that she was stacked to the deck with marijuana, and it was estimated that she had 7 tons on board.

After her seizure, *Lelanta* was put up for auction by the sheriff's department, and Nick Iliff and his father, Dr. Charles Iliff, acquired her. With little time for thorough preparations and with a lot of defective equip-

ment on board, the Iliffs sailed *Lelanta* up to the Chesapeake Bay in eight days. There they spent about two years refurbishing their new prize, doing nearly all the work themselves. Nick wrote, "I put about 1,000 hours into her, sandblasting her, priming her with epoxy, and painting her with Imron. We installed an ice maker, a trash compactor, and rebuilt her interior, which had been stripped by the drug runners." The Iliffs cruised the Chesapeake, and in June 1981 they sailed the schooner to Bermuda. In December 1981, she was donated to the Landmark School for Dyslexic Children in Beverly, Massachusetts, but a year later she returned to private ownership.

HIGH TIDE

Near the end of the preceding chapter there was a discussion of J. Rulon Miller and his schooner *Tradition*. The replacement boat for *Tradition* was the larger staysail schooner *High Tide,* design number 456, built by M.M. Davis and Son at Solomons, Maryland, in 1931. Her designed dimensions were 70 feet 8 inches, by 50 feet, by 14 feet 3 inches, by 8 feet 6 inches. This schooner foundered during a gale in the fall of 1980. Then named *Mariah,* she opened up about 200 miles southeast of Cape May, and pumps could not keep up with her leaks. A couple of mechanical pumps failed, and three pumps dropped by the Coast Guard could not be reached. The crew were rescued.

High Tide continues the trend in Alden's schooners toward more symmetrical hulls. She sailed well to windward for a schooner, an ability due not just to her mainstaysail but also to her moderately deep draft and her 14 tons of outside ballast. Her staysail rig had a huge mainsail, and there was little space between her masts. Thus, in contrast with the previously discussed *Golden Hind, High Tide* had a small, high-aspect-ratio mainstaysail. It was a good sail for heaving-to or jogging along in a gale. The rather short foremast prohibited setting a large spinnaker, but her tremendous gollywobbler afforded awesome power on a reach. She was a fine light-air sailer.

No attempt was made to jam in a number of staterooms below decks, but there were ample berths for a racing crew. The owner's large double stateroom aft was private and had its own head. As one would expect

on a boat this size, the galley was forward of the saloon. There were quarters for paid hands to starboard and in the fo'c's'le.

In her maiden ocean race, from New London to Cape May, *High Tide* finished first but lost narrowly on corrected time to *Malabar X*. Miller died not long after, and *High Tide* was sold to Eugene E. DuPont. She raced in the 1933 New London-Gibson Island Race, and it seemed entirely fitting that she won the J. Rulon Miller Memorial Trophy for the best corrected time in the fleet. DuPont also entered her in the 1934 Bermuda Race, but she finished in the middle of her class in that event.

My wife, Sally, had the pleasure of sailing aboard *High Tide* (at the time named *Golden Eagle*) in the Caribbean in 1969, and she has vivid recollections of reaching up and down the Grenadines in the fresh trade winds. The schooner was fast, well balanced, and stiff but seakindly. The decks were broad and spacious. The boat's interior had by that time been converted for charter, and the accommodations were private but a bit chopped-up with small staterooms. Some of the original rigging, spliced by "Salty" Marks at Gibson Island when the boat was built, was still in good shape.

In 1973, the schooner, by then named *Mariah,* began a four-year circumnavigation. More than half a year was spent in Tahiti, and there owner Phineas Sprague, Jr., organized an "Alden Day" that was highlighted by a race with two other Alden schooners, the *Golden Hind* and the *Myan*. Despite her deep draft, *Mariah* proved a

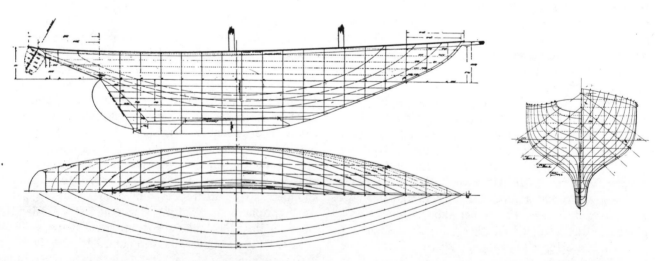

Although Alden didn't much like the rig, his staysail schooners were probably more weatherly than their gaff-rigged counterparts. High Tide carried 2,242 square feet of sail in her four lowers, with another 478 square feet in her upper staysail. Her hull is an excellent compromise between speed and seaworthiness. (The Rudder, August 1933)

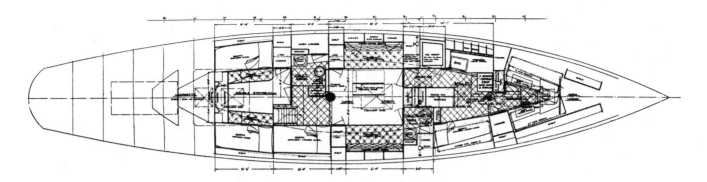

Above: High Tide*'s original cabin plan, shown here, was cut up by the addition of more staterooms — a change that befell a number of Alden schooners going into charter work — but was restored before she began her circumnavigation in the 1970s. (*The Rudder, *August 1933)* **Below:** *A lovely view of* High Tide *with all of her sails rhythmically curved in a fresh breeze. The 1936 New York Yacht Club cruise. (Edwin Levick photo. The Mariners' Museum, Newport News, Virginia)*

good boat for the world cruise, for she was able, comfortable, and capable of making fast passages. Before embarking on the cruise, Sprague restored the cabin plan to the original layout.

Sprague remembers a voyage down the East Coast in December 1973. *Mariah*'s planks and frames were still reasonably strong, but she broke several of each in a winter front off the Hudson Canyon. She fell 15 to 20 feet into a freak trough, tripping on her keel and careening under the weight of wind on her main and forestaysail. Because she was double planked, her crew never knew about the damage until they made port in Florida. But *Mariah*'s hardest chance came later, toward the end of the circumnavigation, when they encountered a gale in the Mediterranean. A short, steep sea built up rapidly, and they ran off before it trailing heavy warps. Despite their precautions and *Mariah*'s nicely raked counter, they were pooped, and Sprague was thrown forward from his helmsman's position, snapping off the wheel and the binnacle. He still has the wheel as a memento. Notwithstanding the age of most of *Mariah*'s planks and frames, she survived intact — an outcome attributed in part to the easy way she met the seas. Under jury rig they made port.

Mariah was easy to handle after Sprague shortened her main boom and rigged two permanent backstays (one as a backup to the other), and he made some passages with a crew of only two. The drill for shortening sail shorthanded in gradually increasing wind consisted of the following steps: Reef the main; hand the mainstaysail; double reef the main and reset the mainstaysail; hand the jib; lower the mainsail; and finally (this happened only once), hand the forestaysail, leaving the boat jogging under mainstaysail alone. *Mariah*'s circumnavigation was a success, leaving her crew with a host of varied memories, such as a race up Long Island Sound with the *Brilliant*, the two schooners shoulder to shoulder, mile after mile. That was near the end of her voyage; Sprague sold her two years later.

My father raced a few times on this schooner early in her career, and J. Rulon Miller gave him a cap with the name *High Tide* on its front. I'll never forget Dad wearing that hat after returning from a long, hard race. He was tired, unshaven, and discouraged after losing a close one. My sister took one look at him and said, "That hat may say High Tide, but to me it looks more like Mean Low Water."

LORD JIM

Lord Jim is a prominent name among Alden yachts, because no fewer than three well-known boats from the boards of the Alden company, designed for no fewer than three different owners, were named for the Joseph Conrad character. All three are introduced in this chapter. The first *Lord Jim*, design number 476, is a gaff-rigged schooner built in 1930 by M.M. Davis and Son at Solomons, Maryland, for Paul Nevin of New York and Bar Harbor, Maine. She measures 62 feet 8 inches, by 46 feet, by 15 feet, by 8 feet 7 inches, and she has 1,800 square feet of sail.

This boat was built the same year as John Alden's slightly smaller schooner *Malabar X,* and the accommodations of the two boats are quite similar. Aft, there is a double stateroom with a private head, and moving forward, one finds a large saloon, a small stateroom on the port side with enclosed head opposite, the galley, and a fo'c's'le with quarters for the paid hands. Almost the only difference in the basic arrangements of the two schooners is the chart table — certainly a desirable feature — near the companionway of *Lord Jim*.

Compared with *Malabar X, Lord Jim* has a more symmetrical hull with a finer stern. This helps provide a steady balance and perhaps a faster hull to windward, but she was not intended to be a contender in ocean racing. Designed for coastal cruising and offshore passages, she was given heavy scantlings and sawn frames (as opposed to *Malabar X*'s bent frames). An exceptionally able boat, she proved her seaworthiness during her first year while weathering a severe November gale off Cape Hatteras.

In June 1959, under the ownership and command of E. Ross Anderson, then commodore of the Boston Yacht Club, *Lord Jim* was the invited escort to Admiral Donald B. MacMillan's *Bowdoin* for that Arctic explorer's voyage from Boston to her "retirement" berth at Mystic Seaport. A Coast Guard cutter led the two schooners down the coast. Off Rhode Island they encountered thick fog, and the cutter's radar was malfunctioning. The schooners moved ahead cautiously, yet the Catumb Rocks appeared without warning under the *Bowdoin*'s lee bow. She narrowly escaped a grounding,

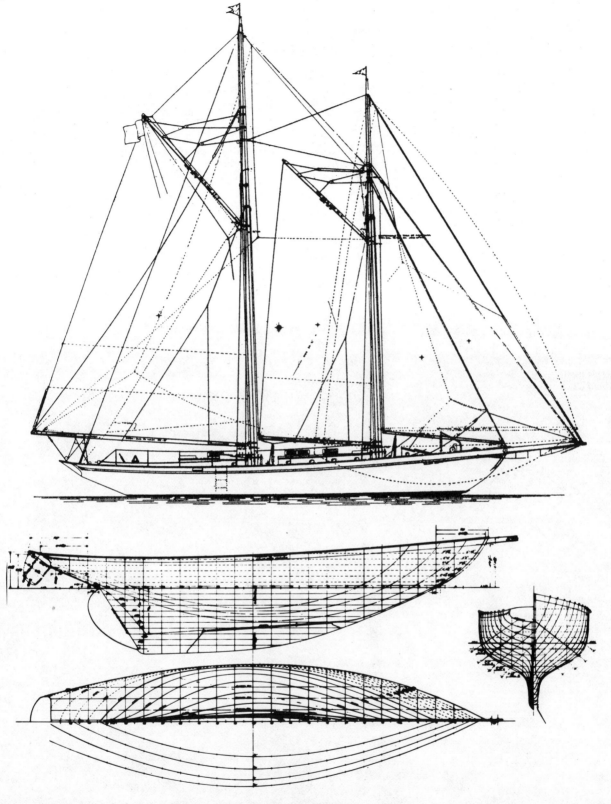

Lord Jim's sail plan is almost standard for an Alden gaff schooner, but it is on the small side considering her 77,800-pound displacement. (The Rudder, May 1931) As with *High Tide,* the lines of *Lord Jim* show a lot of symmetry, but there is a trifle more fullness in her quarters. She carries 12 tons of iron on her keel. (Courtesy John G. Alden, Inc.)

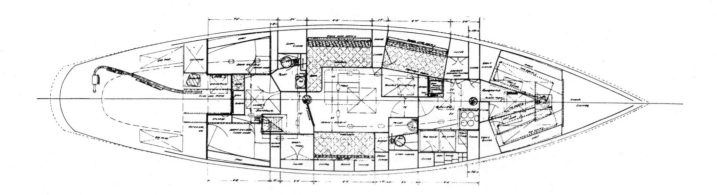

Above: *Unlike* High Tide, Lord Jim *has a forward cabin trunk, which detracts from deck space but raises the skylights and allows portholes on deck for more light and air in the saloon and galley.* (The Rudder, *May 1931)* **Below:** Lord Jim *leaving Padanarum Harbor and heading out into Buzzard's Bay on a made-in-heaven sailing afternoon in 1954, with E. Ross Anderson at the helm and Captain Oliveira on the afterdeck.* (Norman Fortier photo)

and her crew attempted without success to hail the *Lord Jim,* which was slightly behind them. The *Jim* was not so lucky. She struck and then held fast long enough for the heavy ground swell to pound her open against the rocks. Twenty minutes later she sank. The crew of seven were rescued, but of the ship, only the bell, the compass, and the flag were saved.

Like other Alden schooners, *Lord Jim* then began a second life, though the details are hazy. She was raised, and Mervin C. Briggs devoted four years of his own time to her rebuilding in a New Hampshire boatyard. Unable to complete the task, he sold her in 1964, and she was towed to another yard. In the 1970s she was sighted in Gloucester, equipped for longlining but with her rig unchanged. Fishing is hardly an ignominious occupation for a schooner, especially one whose ancestors were fishermen, and if John Alden had been living he might have appreciated *Lord Jim*'s circuitous return to her origins.

FREEDOM

The large schooner *Freedom* began life on the Great Lakes, but for many years she was owned by the U.S. Naval Academy. She helped teach the midshipmen how to avoid running aground and, when the lessons were

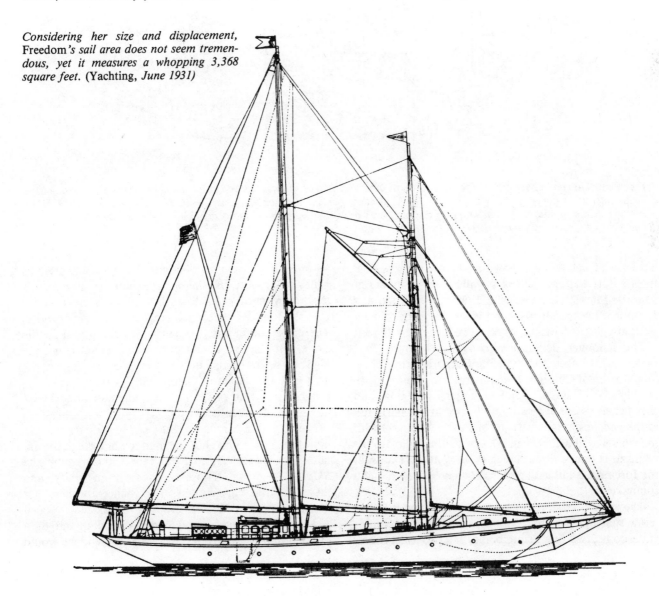

Considering her size and displacement, Freedom*'s sail area does not seem tremendous, yet it measures a whopping 3,368 square feet.* (Yachting, *June 1931*)

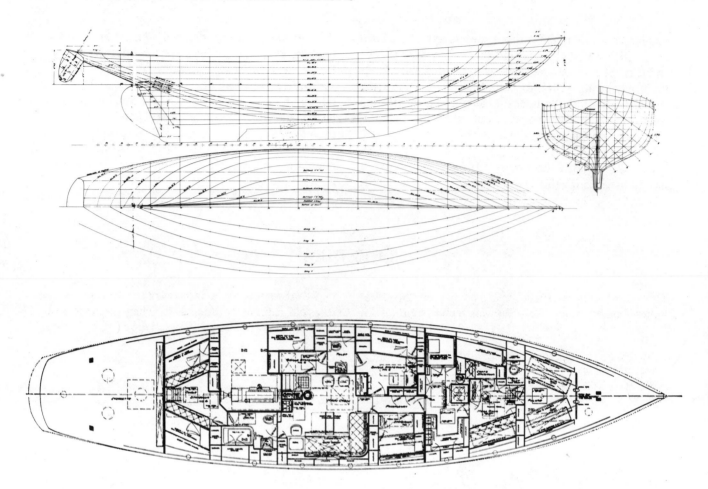

Freedom's lines are moderately full fore and aft. Her midbody is deep, but her garboards are pinched, thereby increasing the keel's lateral resistance. Draft was kept moderate to allow passage through the Erie Canal. Her displacement is 197,325 pounds. (Courtesy John G. Alden, Inc.) Freedom's well-appointed accommodations provide the greatest possible comfort and privacy. (Yachting, March 1931)*

not learned well enough, how to extricate a heavy boat from a soft bottom. Shoals are abundant around Annapolis, Maryland, home of the Naval Academy, and *Freedom* draws a full 10 feet of water. Her other dimensions are 88 feet 8 inches, by 66 feet 6 inches, by 20 feet.

This schooner, design number 492, was built in 1931 by the Great Lakes Boat Building Corporation for Sterling Morton of Chicago. Her construction is heavy, with double sawn frames, double mahogany planking, and with generous use of teak on deck. Her hull is fairly full at the ends, especially aft, and she has a long keel with the rudder well aft. As can be seen on the sail plan, the mainsail is marconi. Although there is no fore topsail, the foremast is tall enough to carry a large genoa and a spinnaker.

The vessel's large size, deep underbody, and full ends allow spacious accommodations, including two double staterooms, two single staterooms, and two toilet rooms

— one with a bathtub — abaft the large, thwartships galley. Forward of the galley there is a captain's stateroom, another enclosed head, crew's mess, and a fo'c's'le that can accommodate a crew of five or more. The main saloon has two berths, a writing desk, a tile stove, buffets, and fixed chairs. The deckhouse is quite high and might be ugly on a smaller boat, but it gives the boat a balanced look, being far forward, and it is suitably scaled for *Freedom*. Also, its small, arched windows are quite distinctive.

Freedom didn't race a great deal, being over the size limit for most events, but she used to compete in the annual Chesapeake fall windup race sponsored by the *Skipper* magazine. Those races are often windy, and they gave the big schooner the chance to show her awesome power. With a crew of 25 or more Naval Academy midshipmen and under the command of a bucko skipper like Frank ''Ski'' Siatkowski, she would

Left: *The interior of* Freedom*'s deckhouse. Notice the flag locker and handsome serpentine handrail at the companionway. (Edwin Levick photo. The Mariners' Museum, Newport News, Virginia)* **Below:** *A look at* Freedom*'s afterdeck and cockpit. (Edwin Levick photo. The Mariners' Museum, Newport News, Virginia)*

Freedom *under full sail on the New York Yacht Club cruise of 1931. (Edwin Levick photo. The Mariners' Museum, Newport News, Virginia)*

carry plenty of sail, and on at least one occasion she beat a splendid fleet of ocean racers, not only boat-for-boat but also on corrected time. I heard an account of a race between *Freedom* and the replica of the schooner *America*. According to the report, the Alden boat won handily, the *America* suffering from too many captains.

The last I heard of *Freedom,* she was still active as a sail-training vessel at the Harry Lundeberg school of the Seaman's International Union at Piney Point, Maryland.

THE CATBOAT MOLLY II

The Alden catboat presented here might have been included in Chapter 8, since a capsizable, non-self-righting boat with a huge cockpit could be considered an on-soundings boat, but the *Molly II* is a real cruiser. Her hull profile resembles that of the *Foam* (Chapter 6), but she is larger, relatively beamier, and much more

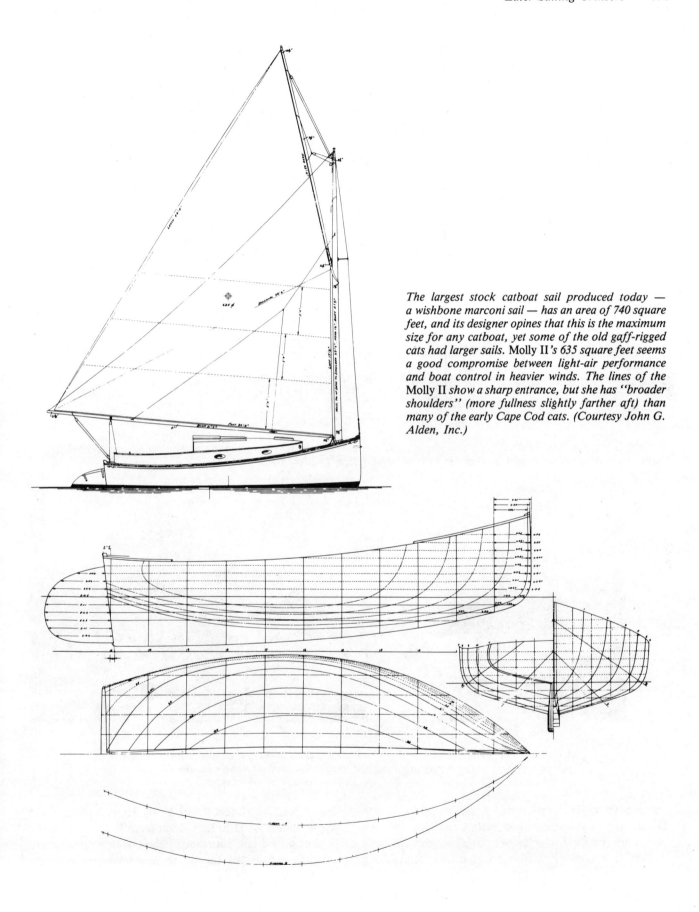

*The largest stock catboat sail produced today —
a wishbone marconi sail — has an area of 740 square
feet, and its designer opines that this is the maximum
size for any catboat, yet some of the old gaff-rigged
cats had larger sails. Molly II's 635 square feet seems
a good compromise between light-air performance
and boat control in heavier winds. The lines of the
Molly II show a sharp entrance, but she has "broader
shoulders" (more fullness slightly farther aft) than
many of the early Cape Cod cats. (Courtesy John G.
Alden, Inc.)*

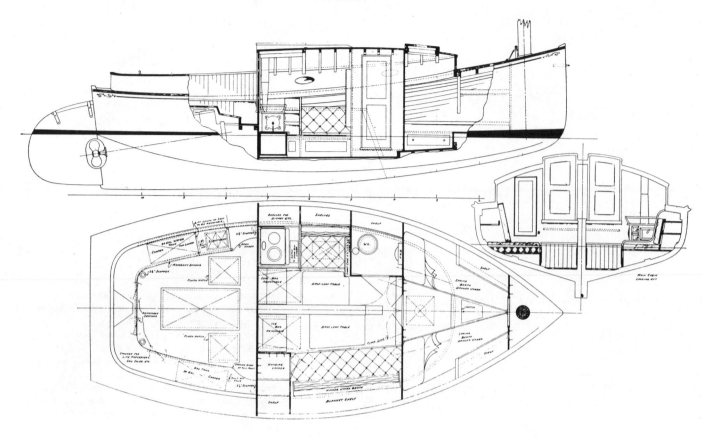

Molly II's *tremendous beam not only provides a lot of room below, but also it contributes to comfort underway by making the boat stiff and thus helping to keep her "on the level." (*The Rudder, *September 1931)*

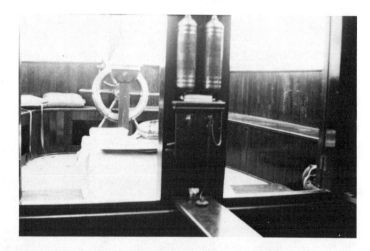

Molly II — *then named* Wah Wee II — *from astern, and the cockpit as seen from her cabin. Her engine box makes a dandy table in good weather. (Courtesy Robert Buffum)*

commodious. Her centerboard is farther aft, and she has the more typical rig of an early Cape Cod cat. She was built in 1931 by Reuben Bigelow for Kenneth Taylor of Woonsocket, Rhode Island. Her dimensions are 28 feet, by 12 feet 7 inches, by 3 feet 2 inches, and she is Number 503 in the Alden records.

Because of her enormous beam, which comes very close to being half the distance from stern to mast,

Molly II (later named *Wah Wee II*) has almost unbelievable room for a 28-footer with substantial framing. She has a sizable, private, double stateroom forward, an enclosed head, and a comfortable main cabin. Although the latter is divided by a prominent centerboard trunk, easy entrance and exit is provided by two companionways, one on either side of the trunk. The trunk is utilized as a support for the drop-leaf table. The head and the sizable coal stove (including wood bin) leave room only for a cozy seat on the port side, but there is a full-length berth and a hinged upper berth to starboard. One trouble with a wide cockpit is that there is no way to brace yourself when the boat heels, but this is no problem on *Molly II.* You can brace your legs against the engine box in the middle of the cockpit — not that this beamy cat would do a lot of heeling.

The hull appears to be heavy as well as fat, so a lot of sail area is needed to move the boat in light airs. She has 635 square feet of canvas, which should be ample in all but perhaps a whisper of a breeze. The high-peaked gaff rig is quite appropriate for this boat, as it not only gives a look of authenticity and gets the sail area up high, but also affords a quick means of reducing sail by scandalizing. The high peak, in combination with a fairly long boom, also minimizes twist. Incidentally, the simple reefing system used on the early Cape Cod cats, as described by historian Howard Chapelle, was not much different from present-day jiffy reefing, although the latter method is a bit simpler because modern boats have winches and much stronger sailcloth. *Molly II* needs little in the way of standing rigging, for her mast is short, thick at the deck, and well tapered, and it has plenty of bury. A short spreader for the forestay not only minimizes mast compression but also counteracts the forward thrust of the gaff.

Alden records show that *Molly II* was lost in a storm in 1945, but two sisters were built, one in 1933 and one in 1944.

GRENADIER

One of the sleekest seagoing yachts from the Alden board is the schooner *Grenadier,* design number 507. Her underwater profile is cut away forward, and her fairly long overhangs, together with her raked masts, give her a very dashing appearance. She looks fast and she proved so, but she also turned out to be an able seaboat. Her dimensions are 59 feet 10 inches, by 41 feet 8 inches, by 13 feet 8 inches, by 8 feet 2 inches.

Grenadier was built in 1931 by George Lawley and Son for Henry A. Morss, Jr., and his brothers Sherman and Wells. For 10 seasons the brothers cruised and raced their lovely schooner, often beating her designer in his fast *Malabar X.* The Morss schooner competed in three Bermuda races, finishing second overall to *Malabar X* in 1932 and third in her class of 23 boats in 1934. In 1933, *Grenadier* sailed across the Atlantic to compete in the Fastnet Race. She finished second in an uncharacteristically light-weather contest, losing only to *Dorade.* Another of this Alden schooner's racing achievements was winning the 138-mile Jeffrey's Ledge Race four times.

With her tall marconi mainsail, generous gaff foresail, and long bowsprit, *Grenadier* carries plenty of sail (1,900 square feet). The considerable rake in her mainmast allows an advantageous pulling angle for the running backstays, thus assuring that the jib and forestays can be set up taut. In 1929, Alden wrote my father that mast rake might improve windward performance, but he was not at all sure. Certainly this rake would be beneficial if it could prevent the headsail luffs from sagging off. In 1949, under the direction of Carl Alberg, *Grenadier* was converted to a knockabout ketch.

One feature that doesn't seem desirable for offshore work is the off-center companionway, but it allows a grand, well-ventilated private stateroom aft. The head compartment has two doors and may be entered from the stateroom or from the passageway leading to the saloon. Aside from the two berths in the stateroom, there are three berths in the saloon, a quarter berth, and two bunks for crew in the fo'c's'le. A large galley just abaft the fo'c's'le makes use of the vessel's entire width.

Like many other Alden schooners, *Grenadier* did rugged duty in the Coast Guard Offshore Patrol in World War II. John Magoon, whose brother Kenneth owned *Mohawk,* bought *Grenadier* after the War. She and *Mohawk* used to sail together out of Marblehead, pacing each other for miles. Magoon's son Ralph writes that "*Mohawk* . . . was a bit drier on the foredeck; when their rails were under, you knew you were moving!"

In the early 1950s *Grenadier* sailed under new ownership to the Mediterranean, and her previous American owners lost touch with her for over two decades. One of

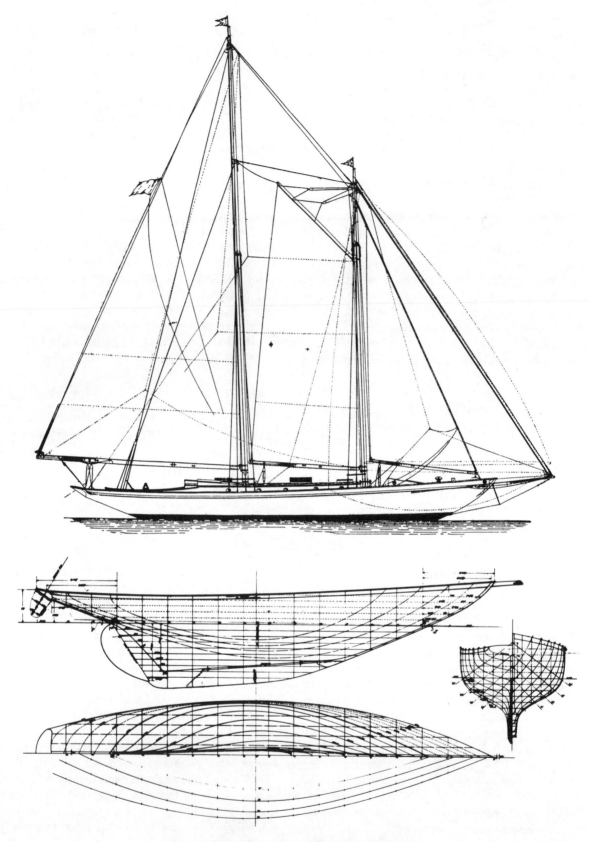

Grenadier carries plenty of sail. Notice her well-raked masts, the two fishermen staysails of different sizes, and the golly with a round foot and a sheet that trims to the end of the main boom. (The Rudder, *March 1932) Drawn by Aage Nielsen, Grenadier's lines show a fairly symmetrical hull with the turn of the bilge well rounded. Her designed displacement is 50,500 pounds, and she carries 11 tons of lead on her keel. (Courtesy John G. Alden, Inc.)*

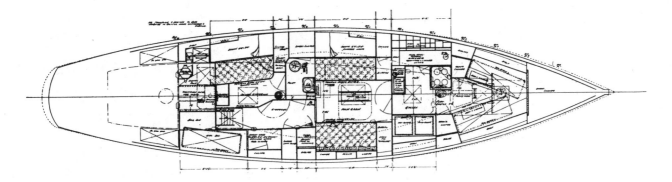

Above: *One feature of* Grenadier*'s accommodations admired by Ralph Magoon is her very long passageway, which permitted sail stopping while underway.* (The Rudder, *March 1932)* **Below:** *The Morss brothers and their crew coax the last fraction of a knot out of* Grenadier *in the 1931 New London-Cape May Race. (Edwin Levick photo. The Mariners' Museum, Newport News, Virginia)*

Her conversion to a knockabout ketch in 1949 detracted little from Grenadier's *appearance. (Courtesy John G. Alden, Inc.)*

the Morss brothers is sure he saw her — under the name *British Grenadier* — in a Florida boatyard in the mid-1970s. Ralph Magoon heard she was sailing out of Colombia in 1980.

Asked about her failings, Magoon's reply was brief: "None. Only people and nature can do in such a fine vessel."

§

COCK ROBIN

Two designs after *Grenadier,* Alden produced a boat with similar lines, but she was given a sloop rig. Number 509, named *Cock Robin,* was built in 1931 by the Dauntless Shipyard of Essex, Connecticut, for John P. Elton of Waterbury, Connecticut. With dimensions of 56 feet 5 inches, by 39 feet, by 12 feet 6 inches, by 7 feet 4 inches, she is quite large for a sloop rig, and the mainsail must have been a handful in a fresh breeze.

The original sail plan shows 1,314 square feet of working canvas (1,022 square feet in the mainsail), but the total area was later cut down to 1,230 square feet when the main boom was shortened to allow a permanent backstay. One troublesome aspect of *Cock Robin*'s rig is the narrow space between the forestay and the headstay, a feature that makes it difficult to come about when carrying a large jib. The sloop must be a good sail carrier, for she was built with 20,000 pounds of lead on

her keel, giving her a respectable ballast-displacement ratio of 43 percent. Judging from her easy bilges and the small amount of flare above her waterline amidships, she probably heels readily up to a point, then stiffens as the ballast does its work.

Elton may have found that mainsail too much to handle in comfort, for in 1938 he had the Alden office design a yawl rig for the boat, and she was converted before the 1939 season. She then carried 825 square feet of canvas in her main, 156 square feet in her mizzen, and 276 square feet in her staysail. Another 357 square feet was added when her Yankee was set.

Elton hired as his professional skipper a Captain Nielsen, who subsequently lived aboard *Cock Robin* for 20 years. Nielsen proved his worth during the hurricane of 1938 by staying aboard his command, battening, belaying, shifting anchors, and fending off until the

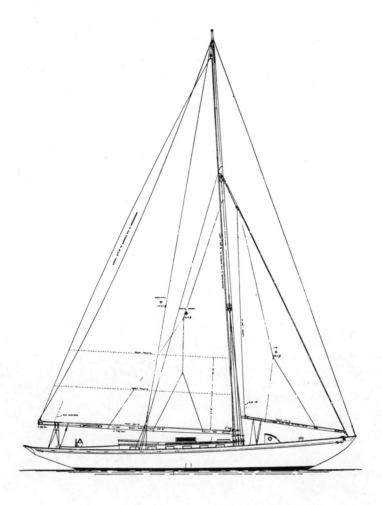

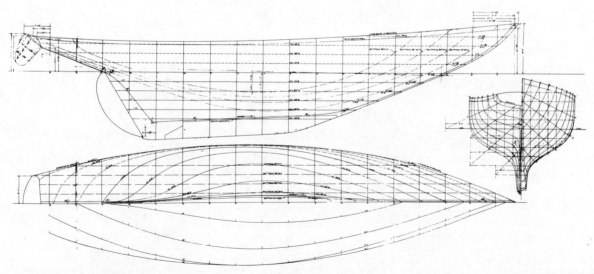

Cock Robin*'s original sail plan had over a thousand square feet in her mainsail. (Yachting, October 1932) The lines of* Cock Robin *are not unlike those of* Grenadier, *but her rudder is less raked and probably more efficient, if not quite as well protected. Her designed displacement is 46,275 pounds, with 19,850 pounds in her lead keel. (Courtesy John G. Alden, Inc.)*

Above: *The numerous square windows may not be as attractive as a lesser number of oval ports, but they provide plenty of light below. The comfortable fo'c's'le may have helped keep Captain Nielsen aboard for 20 years. (Yachting, October 1932)* **Below:** Cock Robin *sneaking along in a light breeze. The permanent backstay has been installed, but she is still using runners. (Edwin Levick photo. The Mariners' Museum, Newport News, Virginia)*

Mara (ex-Cock Robin) *rigged as a yawl under the ownership of Chester Bowles. (Courtesy John G. Alden, Inc.)*

blow was over. *Cock Robin* was the only boat in the Essex Harbor fleet that escaped unscathed.

In 1947, Chester Bowles bought *Cock Robin* from Elton and renamed her *Mara.* His plans to sail the boat to the West Indies with his family were scrapped when he was elected governor of Connecticut in 1948. Bowles went on to have a long and varied public career, including a stint as United States ambassador to India in 1963, but he cruised in *Mara* out of Essex Harbor whenever the opportunity presented itself. He got at least as far Down East as Eggemoggin Reach in Maine, where he scraped the Deer Isle bridge while passing beneath it and lost eight feet off the top of his mainmast.

In her accommodations as well as her hull form, *Cock Robin* resembles *Grenadier.* Almost the only big difference below decks is that *Cock Robin* was built with her 35 h.p. engine up forward in the galley. However, by the time Bowles sold the boat to the West Coast in 1957, her auxiliary was a 20 h.p. Gray gasoline engine, and it was located aft. This had the advantages of decreasing the length of the drive shaft and making the engine accessible from the cockpit, but it also had the decided disadvantage of doing away with the after stateroom, leaving the boat a little short on accommodations for her size.

Harold Dennis acquired *Cock Robin* in 1965, and, finding her in dire shape, he rebuilt her extensively.

Dennis installed a marine diesel in the original forward position, and the after stateroom reappeared. In limited racing, she proved competitive against much newer boats.

Between 1975 and 1980 *Cock Robin,* sporting a bow pulpit, sailed out of Santa Barbara as a commercially successful swordfisherman. Then, in 1980, she was purchased by Hastings Harcourt, who discovered that she was due another rebuild. Her planking was in good shape, but a number of ribs and floor timbers had to be replaced. Harcourt also gave her Hood sails and light, aluminum masts, and the reduced weight aloft enabled him to remove 1,800 pounds of lead from her keel ballast. The following season, *Cock Robin* won the King's Cup Race (Santa Barbara to King's Harbor, Los Angeles).

Woodson K. Woods bought the boat in 1981 and renamed her *Scottish Fantasy II.* In June 1982 he made a 14-day passage to Hawaii and cruised in the islands with two sons and three other crew. Woods calls her a stiff, well-balanced, unusually comfortable boat, a little wet at times but not badly so. She is an able performer on the wind and very fast off the wind. In a 50-knot blow in Hawaii, she roared along at 11½ knots under Yankee, staysail, and mizzen, leaving her crew with a memory that will never fade.

LADY RUTH AND ROUSTABOUT

Design number 521 is a seagoing tabloid cruising cutter, and, according to John Alden, she was adapted from a design by the British naval architect and editor of *Yachting Monthly,* Maurice Griffiths. She might have been inspired by the Itchen Ferry fishing boats, craft that worked coastal waters in the vicinity of the Isle of Wight and are handy and able little boats. Those who say she looks slow could be surprised, for she somewhat resembles Larry and Lin Pardey's *Seraffyn* (designed by Lyle Hess), which made some impressively fast passages considering her size.

Plans for the Alden cutter were published in *Yachting* (May 1932), and two boats of this design, *Lady Ruth* and *Roustabout,* were built in 1933. *Lady Ruth* was constructed by N. Philpott in Cleveland, Ohio, for Charles W. Taft, while *Roustabout* was built by the Harvey Gamage yard in South Bristol, Maine, for James G. Gibbs. The boats measure 26 feet 2 inches, by 23 feet 4 inches, by 8 feet 7 inches, by 4 feet 6 inches.

Husky and able looking, the tabloid design has an exceptionally long keel, which provides excellent tracking capabilities, although undoubtedly it makes the boat

A large sail plan is needed to push these husky boats through the water. Although the main boom is long, its end can be reached without undue fuss for reefing and furling. (Yachting, May 1932)

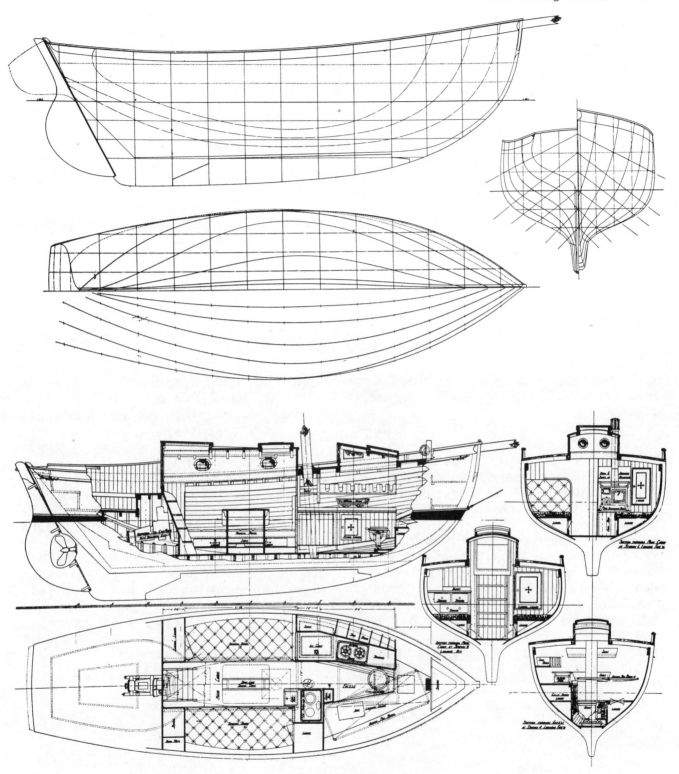

The hull is reminiscent of certain British craft such as the Itchen Ferry smacks and even, in some respects, the Vertue Class. Shared features are the snub bow, deep forefoot, steep sections aft, and semi-wineglass transom. The profile drawing shows a few details of the hefty construction. The great depth of hull allows 5 feet 8 inches of headroom under the cabin trunk. The head is about as private as one could expect it to be on a 26-foot boat, but note that it is below the waterline. (Yachting, *May 1932)*

Roustabout — *when named* Fogcutter — *had two roller-furling headsails and a boomkin for a permanent backstay. (Courtesy John G. Alden, Inc.)*

slow in stays. With her deep forefoot and small size, she might be able to lie-to in a gale with a sea anchor streamed from her bow.

These boats carry a lot of sail, 479 square feet, and they need it. The considerable mast rake, together with the fact that the chainplates for the lower shrouds are located well abaft the mast, obviates any real need for running backstays. The jib appears to be a roller-furling type, so the crew need not venture onto the bowsprit in rough weather.

The cabin trunk is extremely narrow, leaving unusually wide side decks for a boat of this size. Alden did this primarily for the sake of stowing a dinghy on the side deck. He was a great believer in carrying a tender on board in any size of cruising boat. Most cruising sailors prefer to carry their dinghy on the cabintop, but in those days the booms were so low that they barely cleared the hatches. The broad decks, of course, detract from the

headroom below. There is plenty of sitting headroom on the two wide berths in the main cabin, but it would probably be necessary to lean toward the centerline a bit when standing up or sitting down.

Another unusual feature for such a small boat by today's standards is the forward galley with booby hatch overhead. It is a very complete galley, however, and the hatch supplies good ventilation and some headroom. There are even two stoves, one burning liquid fuel for easy starting in warm weather, and the other, coal, for use in cold weather. One of Alden's talents was the ability to make a small boat's cabin cozy, as would be attested to by many an Alden boat owner who has been snugged down at anchor in a rattling autumn nor'wester or a chill, damp sou'easter.

All told, this boat would make an able and comfortable little packet for shorthanded cruising, and she'd attract attention wherever she might call.

∽

PILGRIM

A highly acclaimed cruising yacht of the mid-1930s was the Alden schooner *Pilgrim,* design number 529. Said to be a cross between a coaster and a fisherman of the late

1800s, she has a clipper bow, deep forefoot, long keel, and short, counter stern. Her high freeboard is characteristic of a coaster. She was built in 1932 by the

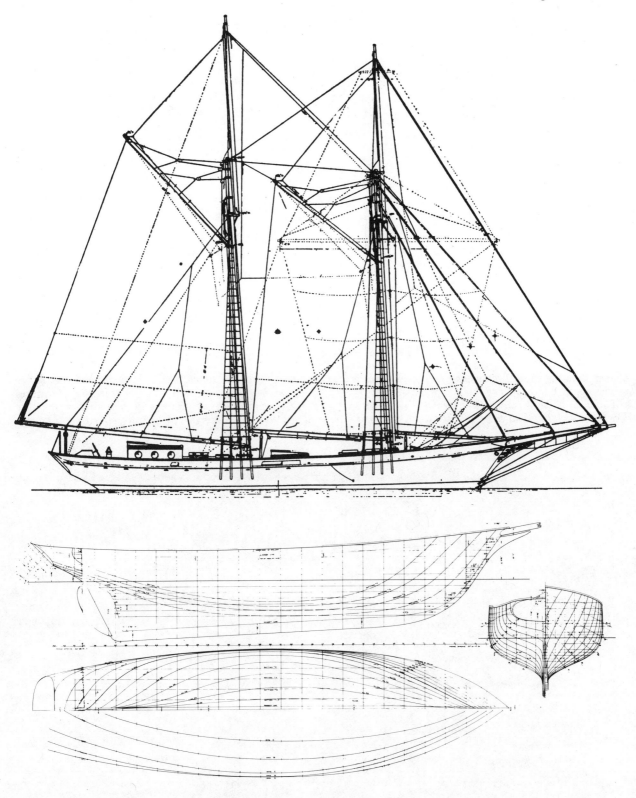

Pilgrim's versatile sail plan includes a squaresail and above it, a raffee (both shown in dotted lines). She can carry four headsails as well as two topsails and a fisherman staysail. (The Rudder, *March 1934) Drawn by Clifford Swaine,* Pilgrim's *lines show a run not quite as steep as one would expect for this type of vessel. The rudder is small. (Courtesy John G. Alden, Inc.)*

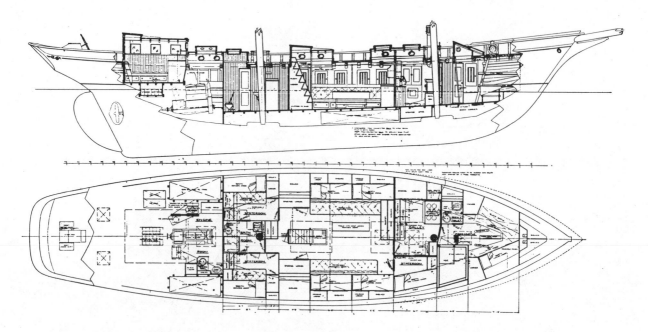

Above: *With her deep forefoot and long keel,* Pilgrim *looks her part. This plan shows her with square windows in her deckhouse, while her sail plan shows round portholes. Many views of her interior were seen in the television series* Adventures In Paradise. *(Courtesy John G. Alden, Inc.)* **Below:** *This photo of* Pilgrim *under sail shows that the round ports in the deckhouse won out, and they look just right. Note the squaresail brailed to the foremast. (Morris Rosenfeld photo)*

Reed-Cook Marine Construction Company of Boothbay Harbor, Maine, for Donald C. Starr of Boston. Her dimensions are 81 feet 2 inches, by 69 feet 9½ inches, by 20 feet 8 inches, by 10 feet 3 inches.

In 1934 *Pilgrim* completed a two-year, 40,000-mile circumnavigation, and an account of her voyage was published in the *National Geographic* magazine (August 1937). She went around the world by way of the Panama Canal and the Red Sea, stopping to visit remote South Sea islands uninhabited by white men. Horace W. (Hod) Fuller, a veteran sailor with whom I have corresponded, was aboard *Pilgrim* during her cruise, and one of his duties was tending to the balky engine, an 85 h.p. Winton diesel. On one occasion the engine's head blew off, and, reportedly, it missed Fuller's forehead by about an inch.

Pilgrim is not a racing machine, but she made some fast passages. It was thought that she held a record for the run of some 500 miles between Panama and Cocos Island, the same island where Captain John C. Voss had gone treasure hunting many years before.

The rig was planned with world cruising in mind, and it has a squaresail, which is effective for running before the trade winds. This sail sets on a permanent yard on the foremast, and one furls it by brailing it against the mast. There is also a raffee (a triangular sail set above the yard) and a variety of headsails, including a balloon jib for light-air sailing. Both masts carry gaff-headed sails and fidded topmasts. The mainmast is stepped well aft and is not much taller than the foremast, thus almost equally dividing the sail area to simplify handling.

The schooner has comfortable accommodations with two staterooms aft and a bathroom between, a saloon 18 feet long with plenty of seats and four pilot berths, and a large galley forward with such amenities as electric refrigeration. There is a captain's stateroom opposite the galley and a good-size fo'c's'le with bunks and an enclosed head for paid hands. Abaft the mainmast is a sunken deckhouse that contains two berths, lockers, and a chart table.

Pilgrim was later named *Tiki,* and she starred under that name as the beautiful interisland cargo schooner in the television series *Adventures in Paradise.* In 1976, when owned by the Seven Seas Sailing Club of New York, *Tiki* participated in Operation Sail, which commemorated the Bicentennial of the Declaration of Independence.

CASSIOPEIA (FIDDLER'S GREEN)

The Alden schooner *Cassiopeia,* design number 547, is perhaps best described as a small ship. She has very heavy construction, a roomy interior, a long keel with a deep forefoot, a clipper bow with carved billethead, high freeboard, generous bulwarks, a well-steeved bowsprit, ample deck space, and a foremast with fidded topmast, yardarm, and ratlines. Seemingly a much larger vessel than she really is, this schooner measures only 48 feet 4 inches, by 40 feet 1½ inches, by 14 feet, by 6 feet.

Designed in 1932 for Dr. Frederick R. Rogers of Boston, *Cassiopeia* was built the following year in the Kenneth McAlpin yard at Shelburne, Nova Scotia. To some extent she was modeled after a commercial coasting schooner, but she was intended as a go-anywhere cruiser that, as John Alden put it, "should be most livable on long trips at sea."

Her accommodations are amazingly complete and spacious for a 48-foot boat, thanks to the schooner's full, deep ends, high freeboard, and generous beam. Furthermore, she was intended to be manned entirely by amateur crew, so no quarters were needed for paid hands. What would ordinarily be a fo'c's'le on this type of vessel becomes in *Cassiopeia* the owner's private stateroom. Its location is not the best with regard to the boat's motion, but the heavy, deep hull is seakindly, so the motion was seldom violent.

Immediately abaft the stateroom is a large galley and an enclosed head with a bathtub. A homey saloon is amidships, and it has a transom, a large drop-leaf table, two berths, and, believe it or not, a piano. A large, sunken deckhouse is all the way aft, and this contains a settee, a berth, an oilskin locker, and a heating stove. The only lack is a proper chart table. A musician might worry about the piano being backed up against the stove even though there is a bulkhead between the two, but presumably the bulkhead is well insulated.

Cassiopeia's rig is an interesting combination of new

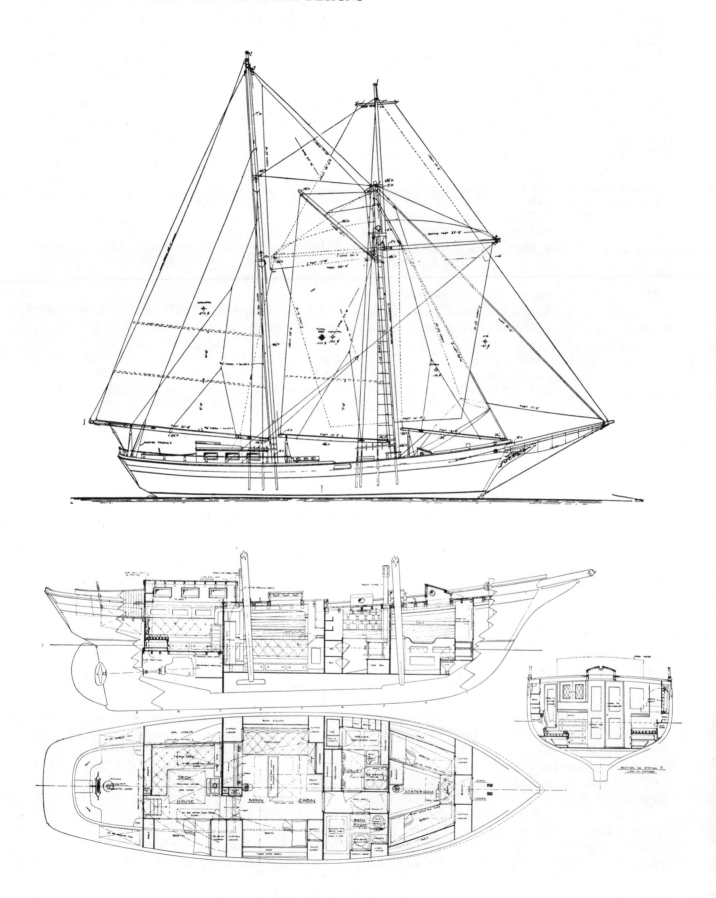

Opposite: *But for her mainsail,* Cassiopeia *looks almost like a miniature version of* Pilgrim. *There is a certain incongruity in the juxtaposition of the marconi main and the gaff-rigged foremast, with its fidded topmast, yardarm, squaresail, and ratlines. Her profile drawing lets us look at her unusually deep forefoot and long keel, with the rudder far aft. The section at station five (near amidships) shows firm bilges and a lot of waterline beam for high initial stability. With such accommodations — even to a piano — it's hard to believe this schooner is only 48 feet long on deck.* (Yachting, *November 1932)* **Below:** Fiddler's Green *(ex-*Cassiopeia*) grounded on the sands of Pawley's Island, South Carolina. Seas have been breaking over her windward side as evidenced by the water shooting through her leeward scuppers. (W.H. Burney photo. Courtesy Preston Kelly)*

and old elements. The old-fashioned squaresail and raffee are effective for trade-wind sailing, while the more modern marconi mainsail is easy to handle and helps give the boat some windward ability. With foresail and forestaysail only, she would have a reasonably well-balanced, inboard, and manageable sail plan for heavy-weather sailing. The sail area of the four lowers is 1,075 square feet.

In 1938, *Cassiopeia,* then named *Onward* and owned by General Sherwood A. Cheney, was badly damaged in the infamous New England hurricane. The schooner was then bought, repaired, and renamed *Fiddler's Green* by Dr. Edmund Kelly of Baltimore, Maryland. The doctor and a number of his close relatives sailed the boat so extensively that they became known locally as "the Cruising Kellys." Their prime cruising areas were Down East, Bermuda, the Bahamas, the West Indies, Panama, and the Galapagos Islands. One cruise begun in 1939 lasted 402 days and covered 16,000 miles.

During World War II, *Fiddler's Green* was taken over by the Coast Guard, painted gray inside and out (she had been white with a dark blue band just below the rail), and used for antisubmarine patrol. With the end of hostilities, the Kellys reclaimed the vessel and resumed cruising, but on a coastal passage in 1953 they suffered a serious nighttime grounding off Pawleys Island, South Carolina. One of the crew had placed a photographic light meter near the compass, and the

Number 547-B, Story II, *a sister to* Cassiopeia, *with a nice bone in her teeth. (Courtesy John G. Alden, Inc.)*

resulting deviation brought the vessel into shoal water. The Kellys could not free her, and they were forced to abandon her. Eventually, she was salvaged, but her voyaging days were over, and for many years thereafter she was used as a commercial barge — an ignominious ending for a great blue-water yacht.

∽

CARLES (FAIR TIDE)

One of Alden's smallest seagoing cruisers is the gaff-rigged sloop *Carles,* design number 562. Although she is quite similar to the tabloid cruisers *Lady Ruth* and *Roustabout, Carles* is even smaller. Another difference is that she has a shallower forefoot, giving her greater maneuverability and less wetted surface. Her measurements are 23 feet 4 inches, by 20 feet 9 inches, by 8 feet, by 3 feet 9 inches.

Carles was built in 1933 for Lester C. Leonard by Morton Johnson at Bay Head, New Jersey. She was ruggedly constructed with 1½-inch cedar planking on two-inch-square sawn oak frames, 14 inches on center. Her deck is one-inch teak. With her bold sheer, unob-

trusive cabin trunk with a single oval port per side, and raking transom with shapely outboard rudder, *Carles* is a handsome boat with a lot of character.

The cabin is snug and especially cozy with its Shipmate stove. One clever feature is the slightly elevated companionway. This allows full standing headroom beneath without the need of a high cabin trunk, which would detract from the boat's appearance. There are two bunks, one long and one short. This might seem like a "Mutt-and-Jeff" arrangement, but it is suitable for two crew members of unequal height, and the short bunk allows a combination locker-dresser forward of the stove. The head might be more private if it were

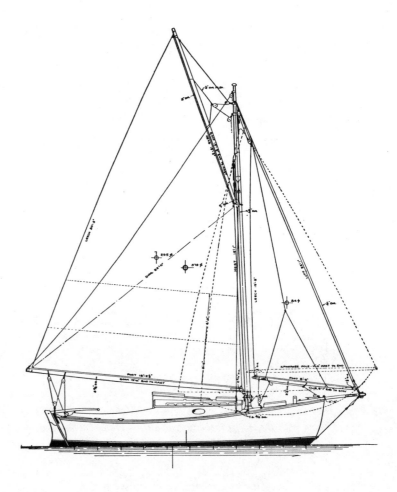

Carles's sail plan belies her light-air speed. Her mainsail is sizable, but it must push a heavy hull with considerable wetted surface. The jib's bar horse — unlike a modern, track traveler — will seldom stick, and it is nicely curved so that some tension is kept on the sheet when coming about. (Yachting, September 1933) Her designed displacement is 6,565 pounds, and with lead outside ballast she carries 2,300 pounds on her keel. Somebody — probably John Alden — sketched a later modification of the midship section in the body plan. (Courtesy John G. Alden, Inc.)

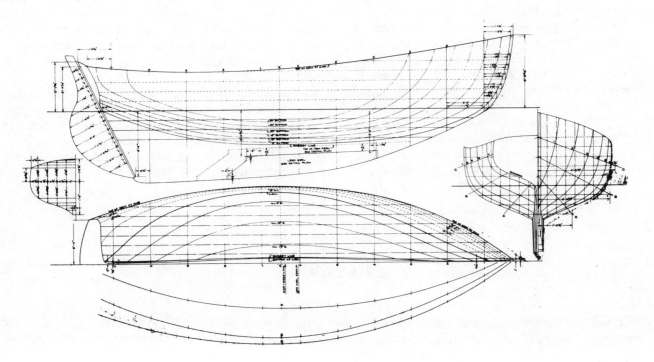

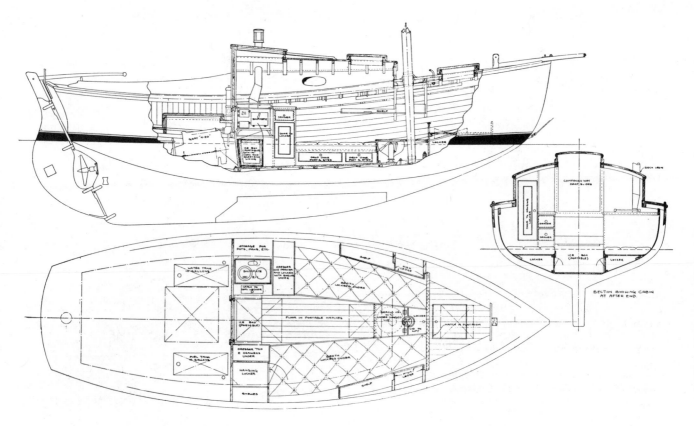

As with many of the older Alden craft, Carles *floats deeper than her plans indicate. A nice feature of the layout is the shelf for sail stowage forward with the hatch directly above it. William McNary drew all the plans. (Courtesy John G. Alden, Inc.)*

forward of the mast, but then it would be quite inaccessible, and its location abaft the mast allows a fine platform forward for bedding or sail stowage.

What is really unexpected about this boat is her sailing ability, which is quite out of proportion to her small size and heavy displacement. Now named *Fair Tide,* she is owned by Bartlett S. Dunbar, who raves about his sloop's performance. Although Bart admits that *Fair Tide* is a little wet at times, he says she is "stable, sturdy, and sails superbly." Despite her shallow draft, the sloop has enough lateral plane to prevent excessive leeway, and with her high-peaked gaff, which sags off very little, she sails to windward with a will. An ample

sail area of 380 square feet makes her a splendid ghoster in light airs. Bart said that on a Cruising Club of America run a few years ago, *Fair Tide* walked right away from a number of larger boats, much to the surprise of many. Of course, she is easy to handle with her self-tending jib and her simple rig, which needs no running backstays.

Fair Tide has been out of commission for the past few years, but Bart Dunbar and his wife, Kit, are planning to wood her, and they hope to put the sloop back into condition with their own time and labor. They are looking forward to the task, for they feel quite rightfully that their boat is a real classic.

FAYAWAY

A larger boat with a hull profile similar to that of the previously discussed tabloid cruisers is the ketch

Fayaway, design number 578. What really sets this boat apart from most Alden hulls, including the tabloids,

Fayaway has a relatively large mizzen and small mainsail. With her deep forefoot and moderate keel drag, she should be able to lie-to nicely under mizzen alone. The ketch's lines show a decidedly fine stern. This hull could move backward almost as well as it moves forward. Designed displacement is 23,300 pounds. (Yachting, *December 1934)*

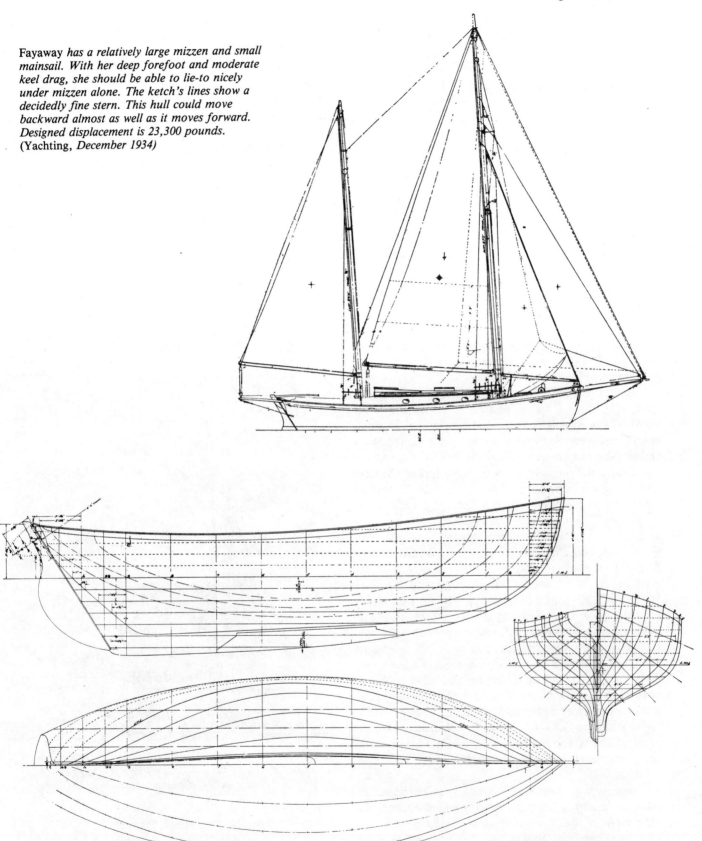

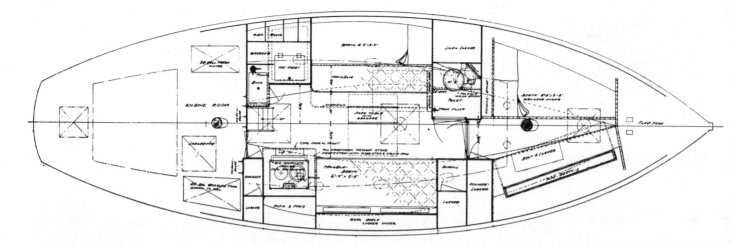

The arrangement below in Fayaway *is a flexible one, suitable for shorthanded sailing but easily converted for carrying guests.* (Yachting, *December 1934*)

however, is her pronounced fore-and-aft symmetry. Indeed, she is almost a double-ender with the tip of her stern sawn off.

This ketch was designed for Richard P. Drew of Sedgwick, Maine, who wanted a seaworthy boat capable of being singlehanded, but with enough room to carry several people in comfort on a cruise to the West Indies. She was built in 1934 at the Reed-Cook Marine Construction Company at Boothbay Harbor, Maine, and her dimensions are 35 feet 7 inches, by 31 feet 10 inches, by 11 feet 3 inches, by 5 feet.

Fayaway's symmetrical hull, together with her long keel and ketch rig, gives her unusual course-holding ability, an ideal characteristic for singlehanded sailing. A *Yachting* article in December 1934 reported that this boat can hold her course "indefinitely with the tiller lashed not only on all points of sailing but also under power." Like many seagoing double-enders, *Fayaway* has rather steep buttocks aft, and she probably draws a sizable quarter wave, but she has plenty of freeboard and some reserve buoyancy in her wineglass stern sections, characteristics that reduce the risk of being pooped in a following sea. Although the fine stern does not give her a lot of bearing at moderate angles of heel, the broad beam and fairly low ballast placement provide ample stability for her moderate rig. Her short ends, heavy displacement, and rounded sections make her seakindly.

There are only three fixed berths below, but when the sliding transom in the main cabin is pulled out and the pipe berth in the forward cabin is folded down, *Fayaway* can sleep five. With the pipe berth folded up, there is considerable room for sail stowage forward. The

This lee-side view of Fayaway *(then* Rusta II) *shows her close affinity to a double-ender. (Courtesy John G. Alden, Inc.)*

galley is aft, where it should be on a boat intended for singlehanding.

The divided sail plan allows flexibility, good balance, and handiness, and it keeps the center of effort low. The 685 square feet of sail area can be reduced quite easily, not only because the ketch rig keeps the individual sails small, but also because the jib can be roller-furled and the mizzen roller-reefed. Although most sailors today favor modern jiffy-reefing systems for reducing the mainsail's area, roller-reefing is still very handy for the mizzen on a ketch, because the roller gear and halyard can be reached from the cockpit.

Fayaway was owned in the 1950s by Charles I. Thompson of Southwest Harbor, Maine, who called her *Rusta II*. His widow remembers that she and her husband were beginning sailors, and they wanted a boat that was easy to handle. A friend recommended *Fayaway*, which was for sale at the time, and the ketch turned out to be ideally suited to the couple's needs. *Rusta II* was dependable, predictable, rugged, forgiving, and seakindly, though not fast (she was not intended to be). *Fayaway* is an excellent boat for offshore singlehanding, yet she is versatile enough for almost any other kind of cruising.

SIROCCO

In 1937, John Alden decided to switch rigs on his famous line of ocean racers named *Malabar*. Schooners were having difficulty competing with yawls and single-stickers on the average race course, primarily because they were not as close-winded and lacked the necessary mast height forward to carry large jibs and spinnakers. Then, too, the eleventh *Malabar* was smaller than her recent predecessors. With these considerations in mind, Alden gave *Malabar XI* a yawl rig.

The "Eleven" was a development of a successful yawl named *Dorothy Q.*, the first boat in the 583 design series. Under the name *Firebird* and the ownership of Alvin Cohan of Saugatuck Harbor, Connecticut, *Dorothy Q.* was still going strong in 1978. Indeed, she had an IOR rating at the time.

Number 583-B was the cutter *Sirocco*. Her hull was almost identical to that of *Dorothy Q.*, except that her bow was extended seven inches, making it a closer match to the considerable stern overhang. The cutter's dimensions were 43 feet 7 inches, by 30 feet 2 inches, by 10 feet 3 inches, by 6 feet, and her plans were drawn by Carl Alberg.

Sirocco was built in 1936 for Roger S. Robinson by the Quincy Adams Yacht Yard at Quincy, Massachusetts. She was well constructed, with an oak skeleton, double-planked mahogany skin, and teak decks. Although she lacked auxiliary power in her first year, she later had a Gray gasoline engine. *Sirocco* proved fast in local races, and she finished a respectable fourth in class

in the heavy-weather Bermuda Race of 1936. One of her sisters, *Estrella* (Number 583-F) was first in fleet in the 1939 Newport-Annapolis race under the ownership of E.S. Bradford, Jr., who had previously owned the 43-foot Alden schooner *Twilight*.

With her tall mast and moderately narrow beam, one might suspect *Sirocco* of being tender, but she had a respectable ballast-displacement ratio of slightly over 40 percent. Furthermore, the cabin trunk, freeboard, and keel ballast were quite low and the mast was hollow, all of which ensured a low center of gravity. The lofty masthead rig supported 1,028 square feet of sail area. Little wonder that *Sirocco* was such a good performer in light airs, yet she could also excel in heavy weather under her staysail and reefed main.

The cabin plan was somewhat unusual in that the berths were all quite far forward; however, this left considerable room aft for a large galley, a chart table, and lockers. The main cabin, mostly forward of amidships, had two transoms, one with a folding upper berth. There was an attractive bureau with overhead bookshelves alongside the mast, and forward of the mast was an enclosed head. Opposite that was a clothes locker and hanging space, and farther forward was a stateroom with two fixed berths.

This cutter had a very short life, for she was destroyed in the hurricane of 1938. At that time she was owned by Paul A. Sperry, the inventor of "Topsiders" boat shoes. It is a testimonial to the success of the 583 design

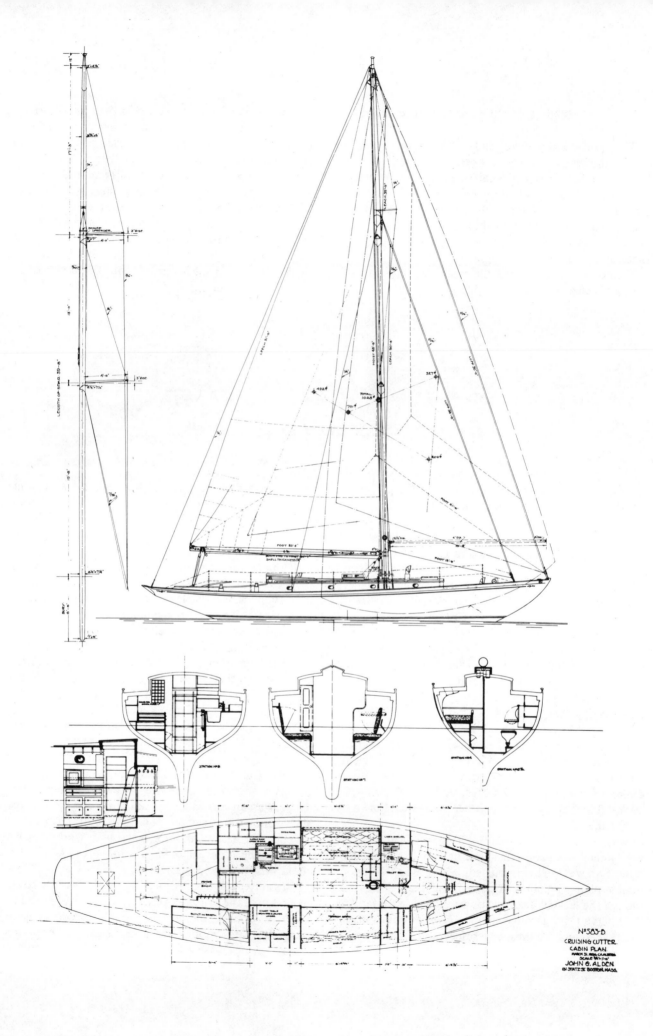

Nº 583-D.
CRUISING CUTTER.
CABIN PLAN.
JOHN G. ALDEN
131 STATE ST. BOSTON, MASS.

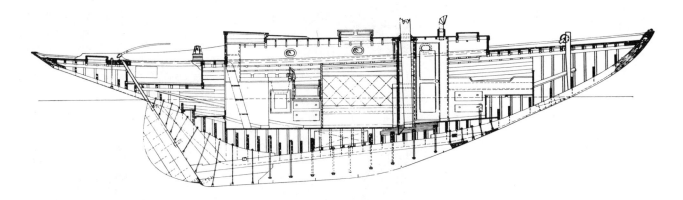

Sirocco was designated as a sloop in a 1936 Yachting *article, but she was called a cutter in the Alden records. An interesting feature is the miter-cut main, which became very popular in the late 1960s. Her profile and sections hint at the beauty of the boat, and her lines (shown on page 62) reinforce that impression. Her rudder looks efficient, with its area centered down low. It is a tremendous convenience to have a large chart table on a boat, and it is surprising how seldom this facility was found even on large yachts of the past. (Courtesy John G. Alden, Inc.)*

Sirocco sailing full and by with her miter-cut, loose-footed main. (Courtesy John G. Alden, Inc.)

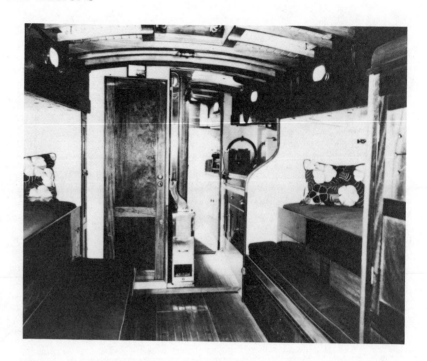

Below decks in the second Sirocco *(Number 583-H) looking forward. Sperry apparently requested a different layout in his second Siroc-co. (Courtesy John G. Alden, Inc.)*

that soon after the demise of *Sirocco,* Sperry ordered a sister boat. The new cutter was built in 1939 by Bjarne Aas in Norway, and she was also named *Sirocco*. She is the eighth and last of the 583s. Under the name *Contessa,* she has been reported gracing the harbor at Marblehead in recent years.

MERIDIAN (LORD JIM)

As mentioned earlier, there were three Alden boats named *Lord Jim*. The one discussed here is chronologically the second one, and she is probably the best known of the three. She started her career with the name *Meridian* and was subsequently called *Blue Water, Shoal Water, Genie* and *Shoal Water* again, before acquiring her present name, which has stayed with her for more than two decades. This boat, design number 614, is a 72-foot schooner commissioned by Milton Knight and his brother and built in 1936 by George Lawley and Son at Neponset, Massachusetts. Her other dimensions are 54 feet, by 16 feet 6 inches, by 10 feet.

Ruggedly built with double, sawn frames, heavy yellow-pine planking, a teak deck, and 33,000 pounds of ballast bolted to her keel, this schooner is a heavy-displacement offshore cruiser that, like the earlier *Lord Jim,* was never intended for keen racing. In fact, an article about her in *Yachting* (January 1936) said that

speed was a "secondary consideration." Nevertheless, her lines are sweet, and she has a well-balanced hull with easy sections and a keel only moderately long, which indicates that she is easily driven with sufficient sail.

Her layout below is well suited for comfortable living for the owner and a number of guests on lengthy blue-water cruises. There are three private, double state-rooms aft with two enclosed heads, one having a tub and shower. Forward of this area is a large saloon with a chart table and transoms that can be used for berths if necessary, and still farther forward is the galley with a four-burner Shipmate range and a huge icebox. One seldom-thought-of advantage of a forward galley in this size of boat is that the bilge underneath its sole is quite elevated (when the forefoot is not deep), and this creates there a large storage bin that is seldom subjected to bilge water. The fo'c's'le has three pipe berths and an enclosed head.

The schooner is essentially a flush-decker, but there

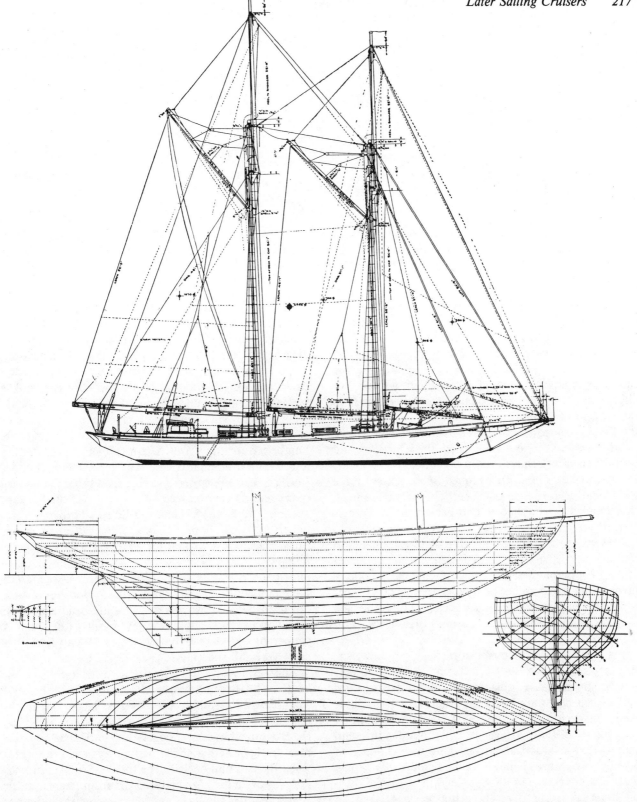

Meridian's original sail plan was less competitive than her later, greatly modified plan, but it is less disjointed, and it has a high aspect ratio for an old-fashioned rig. Meridian's hull is deep and well balanced. Notice the beautiful curve of her keel profile, and the way it harmonizes with the buttock lines forward. Her designed displacement is 117,000 pounds. (Yachting, January 1936)

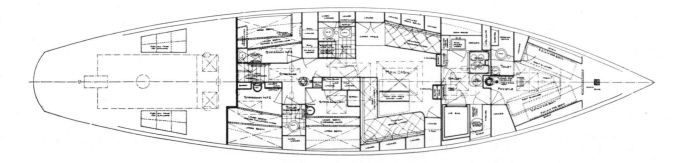

The accommodations include three private staterooms where the motion is minimal. An unusual detail is the angle made around the dining table by the transom and the seat. (Yachting, *January 1936)*

are two small trunks, one for the main companionway and another over the galley. Also, there is a fairly high deck shelter over the forward end of the cockpit. A booby hatch forward allows access to the fo'c's'le, while two tandem skylights nearly amidships supply the after accommodations with plenty of light and air.

This schooner, under the name *Blue Water,* served in the antisubmarine patrol during World War II. When the fighting ended, she was bought by Roscoe Prior of Boston (who at one time owned the *Querida*) and restored to yacht condition. Although not an avid racer, Prior entered his boat, then named *Shoal Water,* in the 1948 Marblehead-Halifax Race, and, despite being shorthanded, he finished second behind the L. Francis Herreshoff ketch *Ticonderoga.* The Alden schooner did not resume ocean racing until after she was donated to the New York State Maritime Academy, when she sailed in the 1954 Bermuda Race. About all that can be said in favor of her performance on this occasion is that she afforded valuable training for a student crew. In the next Bermuda Race, *Shoal Water* was disabled and forced to withdraw.

She was due some moments of racing glory, however, and they came when Boston yachtsman E. Ross Anderson bought her as a replacement for his earlier *Lord Jim,* which had sunk in Rhode Island waters in 1959. Anderson decided to campaign his new *Lord Jim* during the summer of 1961, so he consulted the Alden firm and sailmaker Ted Hood about rerigging the schooner to give her a fighting chance. Hood came up with a plan that took advantage of a loophole in the Cruising Club of America rating rule; the schooner was given an 86-foot aluminum foremast that carried no foresail but did support mammoth headsails, which extended back to the mainsail and filled in the space between the masts without penalty. *Lord Jim* originally had a gaff rig with

topsails and fidded topmasts, and her new rig left the mainmast unchanged. Thus, the boat had a look of incongruity, and her crew called the forward half of *Lord Jim* the 20th century and the after half the 19th century.

The new rig was not a complete panacea, for *Jim* still could not sail to windward very well and she took a beating in short round-the-buoys races, but she could make smoke when reaching and running. Her major triumph during the 1961 season was winning the Lambert Cup, top prize for a race more than 90 miles long over a triangular course. The 25-year-old schooner finished first on elapsed and corrected time. On one leg of the course she averaged 13¼ knots over the bottom, according to Don McNamara, who was *Lord Jim*'s tactician. In his book *White Sails, Black Clouds,* McNamara wrote of that leg as follows: ''In my years on boats, I have never heard, seen, or felt anything to match the passage of *Lord Jim* across Massachusetts Bay that night. She was a thundering avalanche crashing down on the purpling darkness. A mile and a half off the buoy we had caught and left *Legend* (the Class A winner of the 1958 Bermuda Race). A day later, her crew were still speechless.''

Another feat no less important to her crew was the boat-for-boat triumph over archrival *Niña* in the 1961 Marblehead-to-Halifax race. To a large extent the reason for rerigging *Lord Jim* was to compete against the Starling Burgess schooner, but until that 360-mile race to Nova Scotia, *Niña* had always been the victor when the two had dueled. The finish of the Halifax affair was dramatic. *Jim* had split off from the rest of the fleet soon after the start, and her position was unknown until she appeared with the suddenness of the *Flying Dutchman,* emerging from a bank of fog near the finish line. Sporting her huge spinnaker and a new drifter that measured 96 feet on the foot, she thundered across the

Lord Jim *sailing with three headsails before the forward half of her rig was modernized. (Courtesy John G. Alden, Inc.)*

line and got the gun for first to finish. *Niña* was close behind and actually beat *Lord Jim* on corrected time, but that mattered little to the crew of the Alden boat.

Anderson sold *Lord Jim* in 1966, and she became a charter boat in the West Indies. On her way south, she encountered a severe November gale that forced her to run off under bare poles, towing drags. The 60-knot gale on her bare rigging drove her an incredible 250 miles in 24 hours. It is not without evidence that I say her hull is easily driven with sufficient sail.

Lord Jim spent the next nine years in the West Indies, where she had some good times but also some bad, including a nearly fatal grounding on a coral reef in Antigua. Then, in 1975, in wretched shape, she was bought by Holger Kreuzhage, a photographer and television producer, who gradually restored her to mint condition. Kreuzhage still owns her, and he sails his beloved schooner to all parts of the world. She may even be the star of a television series one day. Like many old Alden yachts, *Lord Jim* has had more than one life.

MANDOO II (ROYONO)

D. Spencer Berger must have seen the handwriting on the wall, for in the mid-1930s, when he decided to replace his Alden schooner *Mandoo* with a larger and, he hoped, more competitive boat by the same designer,

he chose the yawl rig. Berger's yawl, which he named *Mandoo II,* was built in 1936 by the Herreshoff Manufacturing Company at Bristol, Rhode Island. Her design number is 623, and she measures 71 feet 3 inches,

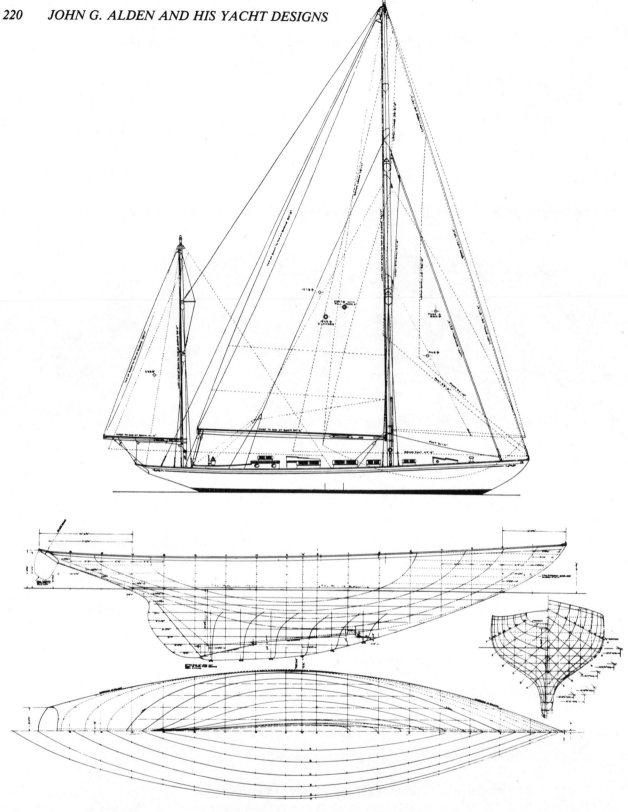

Mandoo II *has her mainmast quite far forward, which necessitates a long main boom and a short base for the foretriangle.* (Yachting, *June 1936) Her profile forward is strongly swept back. The deep rudder is nicely faired into the counter, and the long, overhanging stern makes a good sheeting base for the mizzen. Bill McNary drew these lines. (Courtesy John G. Alden, Inc.)*

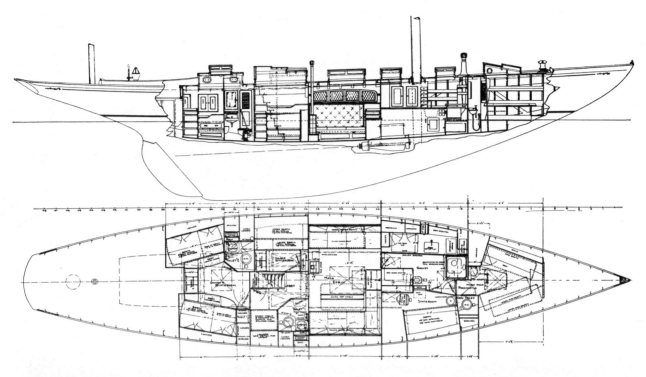

Above: *Although the companionway on* Mandoo II *is not very convenient to the cockpit, its placement permits private and comfortable quarters aft for the owner. The profile shows leaded-glass-door cabinets in the main cabin. (Yachting, June 1936)* **Below:** Mandoo II *is perched on the weather bow of a competitor with a long bowsprit. The occasion is the New York Yacht Club cruise of 1936, her first season. (Edwin Levick photo. The Mariners' Museum, Newport News, Virginia)*

Mandoo II, *as* Royono, *possibly being deck loaded for shipment to the Buenos Aires–Rio de Janeiro Race in 1962. (U.S. Naval Academy photo)*

by 50 feet 9 inches, by 15 feet 8 inches, by 9 feet. Construction was composite, with double mahogany planking over steel frames. Thirty-nine percent of her 88,750-pound displacement is in her lead keel ballast.

Originally, the boat was rigged as a masthead yawl with a sail area of 2,347 square feet. However, Alf Loomis, who raced to Bermuda on *Mandoo II* in 1938, wrote me, "As something to stow away in your memory, she raced that year as a cutter." Later she was converted back to her original rig, which, with its huge mainsail and relatively small mizzen and forestaysail, was typical of the large yawls of that vintage. She normally carried double headsails in heavy weather, but she could set a large, masthead genoa or a reaching jib in light or moderate weather.

The yawl is essentially a flush-decker, but the sweep of the decks is interrupted by two small cabin trunks, several skylights, and a booby hatch forward. The owner has a large stateroom with a private head aft, and there is a guest stateroom immediately forward, off the so-called lobby. Opposite that and convenient to the companionway ladder are another enclosed head and a chart table. The galley and a captain's stateroom opposite are just forward of the comfortable saloon. As one would expect, there are bunks and a head forward for the professional crew.

Mandoo II was forced to withdraw from her first Bermuda Race in 1936 when her stemhead casting failed, but in the 1938 race to the Onion Patch she finished a respectable fourth out of 19 in her class. Later she was sold to John B. Ford, who raced her very successfully on the Great Lakes. Under the name *Royono* she was first to finish in several Chicago-Mackinac races and corrected to fleet first in the 1947 event. The following year she tried the Bermuda Race again, ending up with a fleet second. After this she was donated to the U.S. Naval Academy at Annapolis, and the officers and midshipmen sailed her to a class third in the 1950 Bermuda Race. They did even better in the same race two years later, when they sailed *Royono* to a first in Class A on both elapsed and corrected times. Reportedly, John F. Kennedy was greatly taken with *Royono* when he saw her during a visit to the Naval Academy, and as president he cruised on her.

In recent years, this handsome yawl has been owned by Julius Elfenbein of Miami, Florida, and, in 1972, she became the property of Royono Yacht Charters of Miami and Kittery, Maine. Later she was sold again and fell into the hands of drug smugglers, and in 1975 she was intercepted by the Coast Guard in the Caribbean, loaded to her scuppers with marijuana. After her capture she was taken to Florida and put up for auction. Geoffrey Gibson and Mike Davis acquired the yawl for $25,000, which seemed like a bargain even though she had been gutted by the smugglers. With the help of

Davis and others, Gibson spent 2½ years returning the boat to mint condition. They plan to enter *Royono* in another Bermuda Race, "just to let her know how it feels again."

LORD JIM (ROMAHAJO II, GREETINGS)

Of the three Alden *Lord Jim*s, the smallest and most modern had the best racing record. She is a 39-foot stock cutter built in 1937 by James E. Graves, Inc., of

Marblehead, Massachusetts, for Ephraim Banning IV of Chicago. She is the fourth of seven boats built to design number 636. Measuring 28 feet 1 inch on the

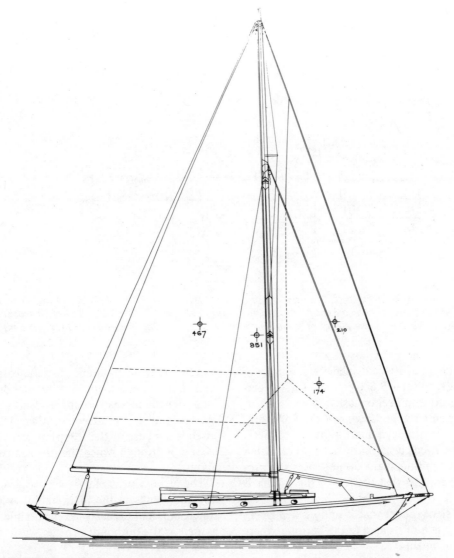

One of the main reasons for Lord Jim*'s success on the race course is the generosity of her sail plan. (Courtesy John G. Alden, Inc.)*

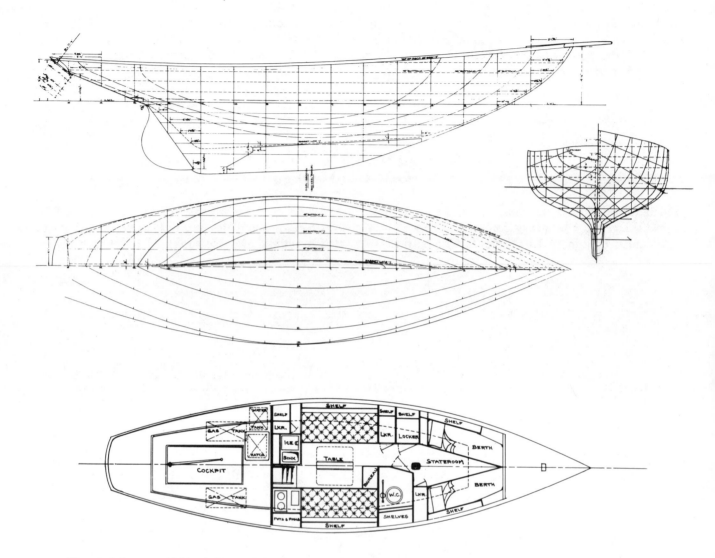

Her ample beam amidships helps Lord Jim *stand up to her large rig. The run aft is moderately flat, the quarters, fairly full. The accommodations are for the most part practical, although the stove looks a bit hard to reach. The forward berths are narrow, but they leave plenty of standing room in the stateroom. (Courtesy John G. Alden, Inc.)*

waterline, with a beam of 10 feet 5 inches and a draft of 5 feet 3 inches, she displaces 18,800 pounds, with 41 percent of her weight in iron keel ballast.

The lines of this cutter were drawn by Carl A. Alberg, and they show a beautiful, symmetrical hull with nicely balanced ends. She needs her healthy beam to carry her generous rig. Although the plans do not show the propeller location, it appears that the top of the rudder is cut away to clear an off-center wheel. This arrangement makes for an efficient rudder that is unbreached by an aperture and has much of its area at the bottom, where the water is less turbulent.

The rig supports 851 square feet of sail area, giving the boat plenty of power in light airs, yet she is easy to

handle when shorthanded, for she balances reasonably well under her main and self-tending forestaysail. Although there are running backstays, they are probably only needed in heavy weather. The short bowsprit extends the base of the foretriangle and affords a sufficient gap through which the jibs can pass when coming about.

The arrangement plan is very logical, with the galley aft, two bunks in the main cabin, two in the forward stateroom, and an enclosed head amidships. This plan, as well as the outboard profile, was drawn by Fenwick C. Williams.

Lord Jim built her racing reputation on the Great Lakes under the name *Romahajo II* and the ownership

Lord Jim, *as* Greetings, *with her spinnaker set. It appears that the base of the foretriangle has been extended with a longer bowsprit. (Mann photo. Courtesy Mrs. Winfield Tice)*

of Harvey C. Nedeau, and she added to it later under the ownership of Winfield Tice, when she was named *Greetings* (the Tices own a greeting-card company). As *Romahajo II* she was a consistent prize winner for years on Lake Michigan, but her greatest triumph came in

1961 when, as *Greetings,* she won the Mackinac Cup for the Chicago-Mackinac Race. The pretty cutter was competitive for much longer than she had a right to be. Mrs. Winfield Tice reported sighting the boat under sail in the Chicago area in 1982.

STAGHOUND

Another Alden race winner, though she certainly doesn't look the part, is the ketch *Staghound*. This boat appears to be an able offshore cruiser whose speed has been compromised to some extent for the sake of handiness and seakindliness, yet she won two consecutive

overall fleet awards in the 1953 and 1955 Transpacific races from Los Angeles to Honolulu. *Staghound* is design number 651, and her measurements are 39 feet 3 inches, by 31 feet 5 inches, by 10 feet 11 inches, by 5 feet 5 inches. She was built in 1937 for William C. Thum by

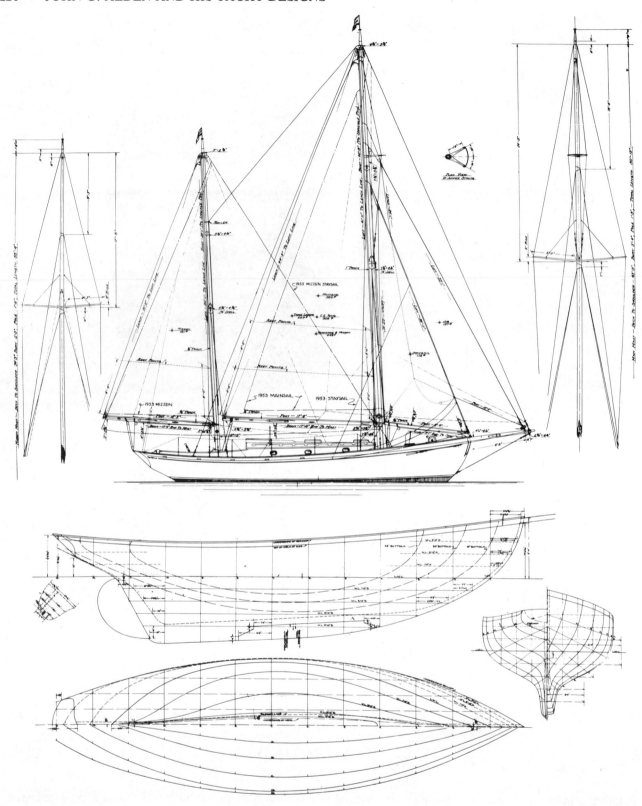

This sail plan shows Staghound*'s original rig and the 1953 modifications that reduced her rating and helped her win two Transpac races.* Staghound*'s hull form suggests directional stability, good balance at most angles of heel, and seakindliness. (Courtesy John G. Alden, Inc.)*

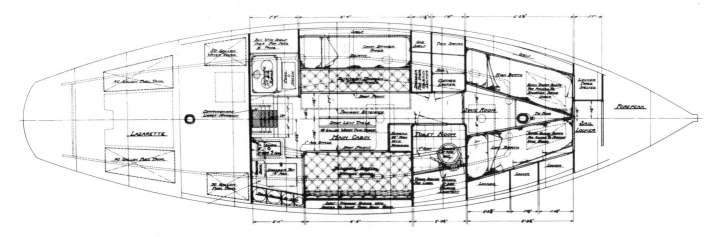

It's always a pleasure to study an accommodations drawing by Al Mason. That large bridge deck creates an unusually large engine room. (Courtesy John G. Alden, Inc.)

Staghound marching to windward under genoa and her original mainsail and mizzen. (Kent Hitchcock photo. Courtesy John G. Alden, Inc.)

Dittmar and Gardner at Newport Harbor, California. At the time of her Transpac triumphs, the ketch was owned and skippered by Ira P. Fulmore.

While on the subject of Alden boats winning the Transpac Race, I should mention the two schooners named *La Reine,* design numbers 304 and 498, both built for C.V. Watson. The earlier boat, under the name *Dolphin II* and the ownership of movie star Frank Morgan, won fleet first in the 1947 race, while the later

boat, then named *Constellation* and owned by Sally Blair Ames, won her class in the 1959 race.

One might expect a semiplaning, light-displacement boat with flattish bilges to be ideal for the downwind race to Honolulu, but the Alden winners don't remotely resemble such a type. *Staghound* is the antithesis of a blown-up dinghy. At 25,650 pounds, she is a heavy-displacement boat, with well-rounded bilges and a rather fine stern. Her lines were drawn by Carl A.

Showing her race-winning form off the wind, Staghound is carrying her small, low-rated mainsail, but it is compensated by the large mizzen and mizzen staysail. (Courtesy John G. Alden, Inc.)

Alberg, and he produced a symmetrical hull as compared with many earlier Alden designs. The long keel gives her the ability to track well, while the balanced ends help provide an easy helm at varying angles of heel.

Al Mason, who is noted for his meticulous draftsmanship, drew the cabin and sail plans of *Staghound*. In typical Mason fashion, the cabin plan shows such details as treads on the companionway ladder, plates in the galley locker, and, of course, buttons on the transom cushions. The boat is laid out with her galley aft; a main cabin with a fixed transom, a sliding transom, and a pilot berth amidships; the enclosed head and hanging lockers farther forward; and finally, a double stateroom. There is a coalburning Shipmate stove in the galley; a dresser opposite, which can be used as a chart table; a sail locker way forward; and numerous other lockers. About the only compromise is the placement of the foul-weather locker amidships rather than aft.

Despite a fairly low-aspect-ratio rig, *Staghound* can carry plenty of sail. Her original sail plan was heavily penalized under the CCA rule of the early 1950s, so before the Transpac wins, the rig was modified slightly to improve her rating. The mainsail was made shorter on the foot and luff, and the mizzen was made shorter on the luff. Evidently, both booms were raised. Two "secret weapons" were a huge mizzen staysail and a large, overlapping genoa staysail that was carried under a masthead jib.

The ketch's sail power was sufficient to drive her from Los Angeles to Honolulu in under 13 days at an average speed of 7.85 knots during the 1955 race. It is quite remarkable to have such race-winning speed in a heavy, seagoing cruiser of her waterline length.

THE OFF SOUNDINGS CLASSES

Off Soundings is the name given to several classes of medium-size Alden racing-cruisers. The first stock boat with this class name was design number 666, but only three of these craft were built. The first, a cutter named *Felicia III,* was built for Abner Morse by the Casey Boatbuilding Company at Fairhaven, Massachusetts, in 1938. Her dimensions are 41 feet 8 inches, by 28 feet 5 inches, by 10 feet 6 inches, by 5 feet 5 inches.

When she was five years old, *Felicia III* was bought for $5,500 by Melvin D. Southworth, who, along with

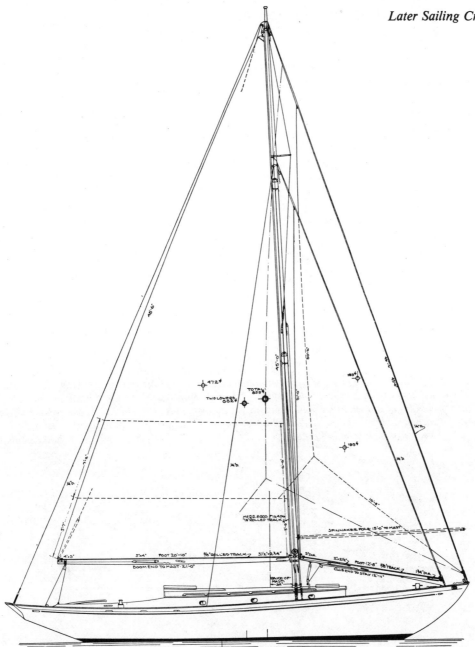

The sail plan of Number 666, the first Off Soundings design, shows considerable mast rake, which may help account for Felicia III*'s pronounced weather helm. She carries 858 square feet in her mainsail and two headsails. The mast rake was decreased four inches in the Number 689 sail plan, which was identical otherwise.* (Yachting, *December 1937*)

his brother, founded the Off Soundings Club, a sailing organization well known for its rating rule. Since by coincidence Southworth also owned the original Off Soundings boat, he became known as "Mr. Off Soundings." His daughter, Mrs. Edmund Kendrick, writes that their family raced the boat a lot in the spring and fall Off Soundings races, but they were never very successful against such hot boats as the New York 32s and the Owens cutters. Nevertheless, she describes *Felicia III*

as an able boat with a "lovely motion, always fun to sail." Although the accommodations were designed for a crew of four, the Southworths often cruised with five or six (sometimes including three generations). Mrs. Kendrick particularly liked the generous deck space; her mother appreciated the galley arrangement, which allowed her to sit down while preparing meals.

The sail plan of *Felicia III* shows considerable mast rake, which may have been a mistake, because the boat

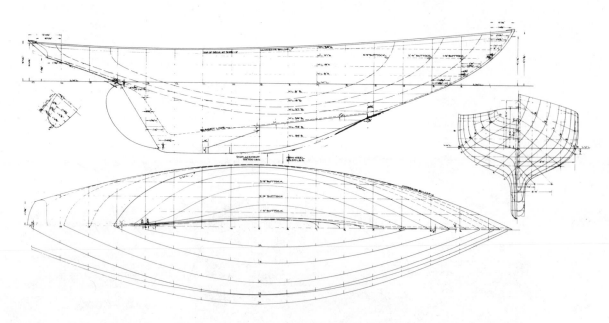

The lines of the Off Soundings boats were virtually unchanged throughout the series. After studying those of Number 704, shown here, it is easy to see why Felicia III *had a comfortable motion, although Carl Alberg now feels that the forebodies of some Alden boats designed in the early years of the CCA rule were a bit too full. Number 704's designed displacement is 22,700 pounds, and she carries 9,250 pounds of outside ballast. Her bilges are firm. The roughly sketched alternate keel profile is for iron ballast. (Courtesy John G. Alden, Inc.)*

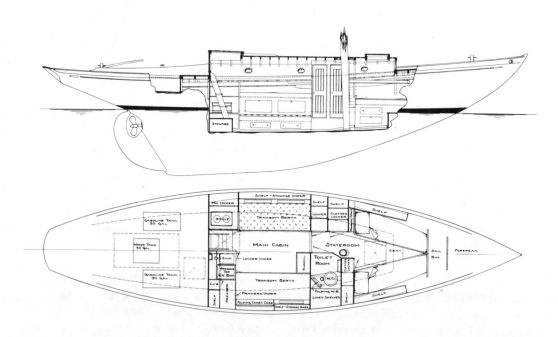

Ralph Winslow drew the cabin plan for Number 666 in November 1937, but for some reason, Al Mason redrew it less than two months later. Mason's drawing is shown here. With this cabin plan, Abner Morse used Felicia III *solely for daysailing out of Marblehead Harbor with a professional captain, but he told the Southworths, "You could even spend a night aboard." Like the other Off Soundings designs, Number 666 could also be had with the galley forward. (Courtesy John G. Alden, Inc.)*

Left: *An interior shot of* Madcap III, *a sister to* Felicia III, *showing the forward-galley layout. (Courtesy John G. Alden, Inc.)* **Below:** *The first Off Soundings boat* Felicia III *sailing close-hauled. Despite having a headstay, she needed jumpers to help control her limber fir mast. (Morris Rosenfeld photo. Courtesy Mayotta S. Kendrick)*

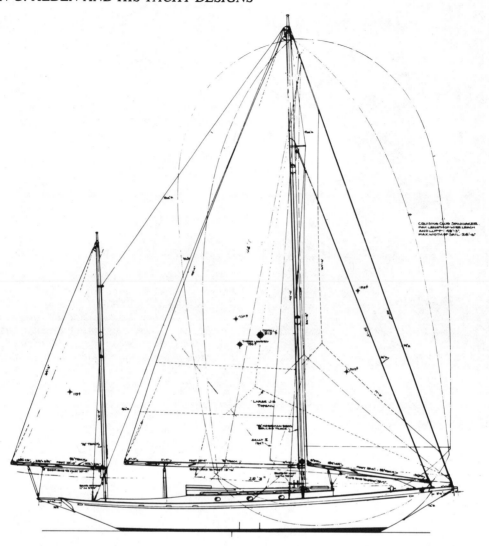

Number 672's yawl rig has 915 square feet of sail, 756 square feet in the three lowers. (Courtesy John G. Alden, Inc.)

had a strong weather helm. This was alleviated but not eliminated by shortening the main boom and setting the jib on the headstay. Another fault was some tenderness, due primarily to a heavy fir mast and the use of iron for keel ballast. No doubt a substantial heeling angle also contributed to the weather helm. The running backstays on slides were a nuisance but necessary for the fir mast with its tendency to whip. *Felicia III* was eventually sold to the West Coast, where she is still sailing.

The other Off Soundings boats are: Number 672, yawls with the same dimensions as 666; Number 689, cutters measuring 42 feet 2 inches, by 29 feet 2 inches, by 10 feet 6 inches, by 5 feet 10 inches; Number 690, yawls with the same lines and dimensions as 689; Number 704, measuring 42 feet 5 inches, by 29 feet 4½ inches, by 10 feet 7 inches, by 5 feet 11½ inches; and

Number 712, measuring 42 feet 2 inches, by 29 feet 3 inches, by 11 feet, by 6 feet. The later models have less mast rake and a short bowsprit to reduce the weather helm of the first Off Soundings design. Number 712's broad beam and additional keel ballast help her stand up to her tall rig. All the Off Soundings boats were designed primarily by Carl Alberg, although Al Mason had a hand in the earliest model. They have fairly symmetrical hulls with rather narrow, overhanging sterns, some fullness in the entrance, generous sheerlines, and firm bilges.

There are two different cabin arrangements for the Off Soundings: One is a conventional layout with an after galley, a main cabin with two berths, a forward stateroom, and an enclosed head between the two cabins; the other arrangement has an after stateroom,

Continued on page 236

Number 672-D, originally named Alice, *easing along in a light breeze. Boats of this vintage have their booms well raised, which simplifies carrying a dinghy on board. (Courtesy John G. Alden, Inc.)*

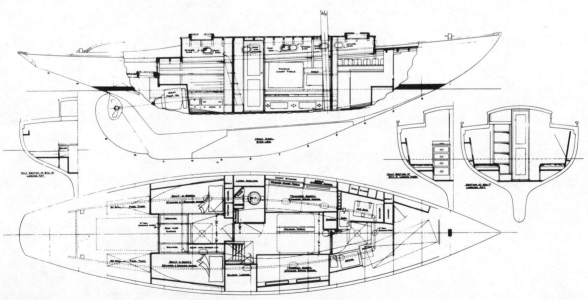

Fenwick Williams drew the forward-galley layout for Number 689 in November 1938. This plan was also used in Numbers 672-D, E, and F; its main compromise is that the companionway is quite far from the boat's centerline, making it vulnerable to flooding during a knockdown on the port tack. (Courtesy John G. Alden, Inc.)

Off Soundings Number 689-B, originally Joy Two. *Having the forestaysail set abaft the stem is helpful to changing tacks when a jib is hoisted. (Courtesy John G. Alden, Inc.)*

Number 690 is the yawl-rigged version of the 689. The short bowsprit increases the space between the forward stays. (Courtesy John G. Alden, Inc.)

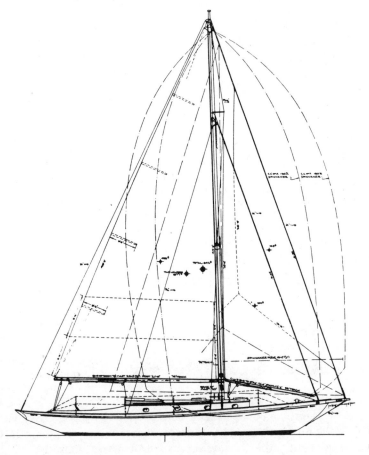

The sail plan of Number 704, the 1940 Off Soundings cutter, differs from the 666 and 689 plans in the addition of a short bowsprit to extend the foretriangle, just as had been done in the yawl-rigged 672 and 690. (The Rudder, June 1940) The last Off Soundings boat, Number 712, appeared in 1940, the same year as Number 704. She has more beam and about a thousand pounds more outside ballast to help her stand up to her sail. Her sail plan, however, is little altered from the Number 672 version. (Courtesy John G. Alden, Inc.)

Off Soundings 712-D, Panacea *(originally* Sandrala), *on the ways. This shot gives a clear view of her off-center companionway. (Courtesy John G. Alden, Inc.)*

the head near the companionway, a two-berth main cabin, a forward galley, and a small fo'c's'le with a pipe berth. The latter arrangement requires a slightly different deck layout, with the companionway relatively far forward and off center.

About 16 boats from the various Off Soundings classes were produced by the Casey yard in 1938 and 1939, and a couple more were built in California. All these boats are attractive and satisfying, but each model was a slight improvement over its predecessor. Like many of the smaller Alden cruising classes, they were reasonably priced, and thus could be enjoyed by many.

THE COASTWISE CRUISER

One of the most popular and successful classes in the medium-size range was the Alden Coastwise Cruiser, design number 675. This boat, called a cutter in the Alden office index, measures 36 feet 5 inches, by 25 feet 11 inches, by 9 feet 9 inches, by 5 feet 3 inches. The plans were drawn by Carl Alberg in 1937. About 10 years later, another, slightly larger Coastwise Cruiser, Number 779, was drawn by Philip L. Ross, but it was not as popular as its predecessor. Only six 779s were built, as opposed to 38 of the 675s.

Twenty-nine of the early Coastwise Cruisers were built by James E. Graves, Inc., of Marblehead, Massachusetts. They were put together with one-inch Philippine mahogany planking over white oak frames,

and all parts of their hulls were extensively treated with Cuprinol preservative to discourage rot. Fastenings were galvanized iron. The keel ballast was iron, weighing 6,600 pounds.

A pretty boat with generous sheer and moderate freeboard, the 675 Coastwise Cruiser has a long, narrow stern and a slightly shorter bow with considerable curvature. She has a low cabin trunk, but still there is six feet of headroom below. The accommodations include four fixed berths, two in the main cabin and two in a forward stateroom. The galley is aft, and there is an unusual folding chart table just forward of the stove. An enclosed head with a wash basin and a built-in clothes hamper is abaft the stateroom. One feature that seems

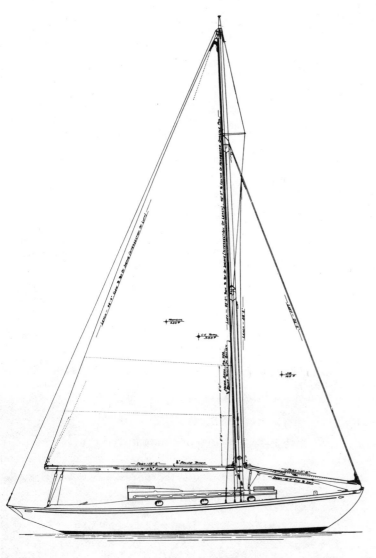

The original Coastwise Cruiser had a three-quarter rig that was almost the ultimate in simplicity. (Yachting, *April 1938*) Her lines reveal a fine stern and a continuously swept forefoot. Designed displacement was 17,500 pounds. (Courtesy John G. Alden, Inc.)

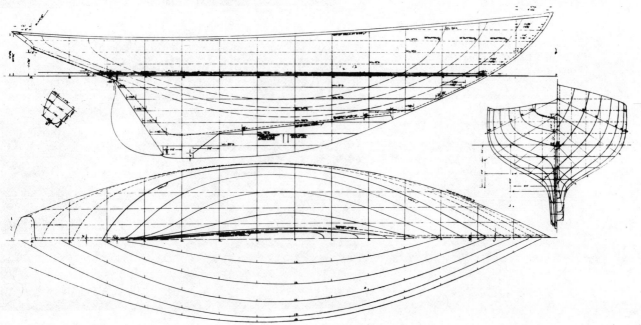

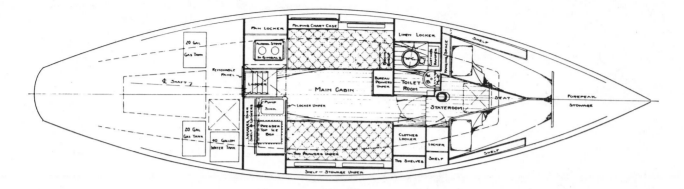

Number 675 has adequate accommodations for four. An interesting detail is the way the clothes-locker door can serve double duty and close off the forward stateroom. (Your New Boat *by the Editors of* Yachting)

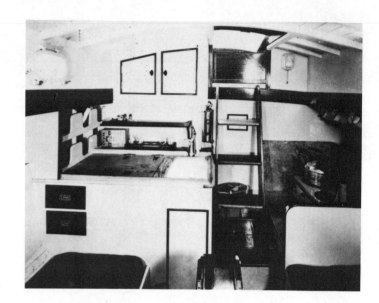

Looking aft in the cabin of a 675 Coastwise Cruiser. (Courtesy John G. Alden, Inc.)

Cocktail hour in the cockpit of a 675 Coastwise Cruiser. (Courtesy John G. Alden, Inc.)

A look at a 675 on the railway shows her well-rounded bilges. (Courtesy John G. Alden, Inc.)

A 675 building at the Graves yard. (Courtesy John G. Alden, Inc.)

Dawnell *(later* Charmalie *and* Big Chum*), the fourth 675, leans into it. (Courtesy John G. Alden, Inc.)*

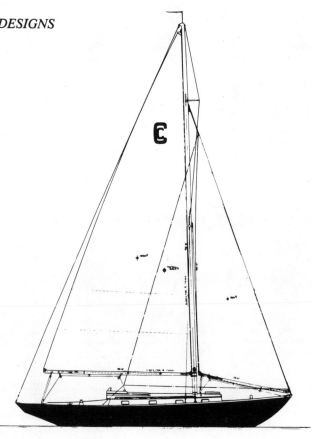

With her drawn-out bow, the 779 Coastwise Cruiser sloop is perhaps a bit prettier than the 675. She has 39 square feet more sail than her forerunner and a thousand pounds additional keel ballast to help her stand up to her sail. Numbers 779-E and F were yawls with even longer bows. The 779s were not quite as competitive and nowhere near as popular as the 675s. (Courtesy John G. Alden, Inc.)

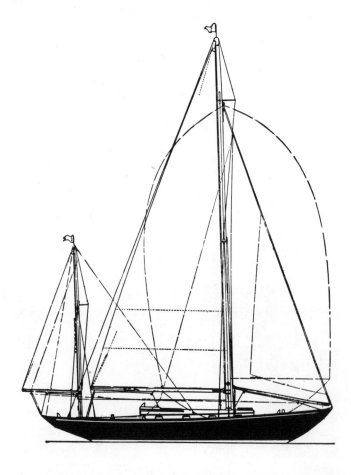

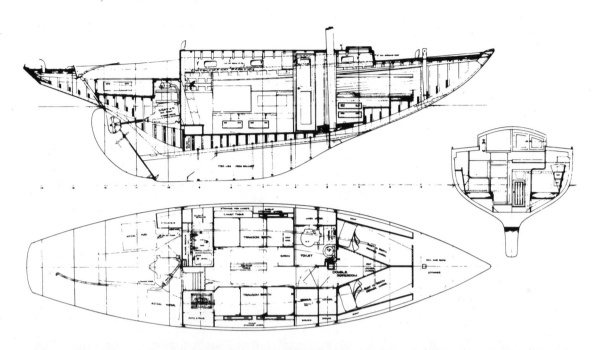

The cabin layout of Number 779 duplicates that of Number 675 in its essentials. The profile shows the suggestion of a keel toe, which the 675 does not have. (Courtesy John G. Alden, Inc.)

somewhat undesirable is the off-center 40-gallon water tank, which, when topped off, tends to give the boat a slight list; this is partly counteracted by the engine, which is mounted slightly off center on the opposite side.

Originally, the 675 design showed a fractional sloop rig with 585 square feet of sail area, but many of the boats were built with bowsprits and rigged as masthead cutters. Either rig is easy to handle by one person, since there are no running backstays, and the working jib on the sloop and the forestaysail on the cutter are self-tending. Also, this is a boat that can sail with reasonable ease and tolerable balance under her mainsail alone.

In 1938, a strict one-design class organization was formed, and eventually as many as 24 Coastwise

Cruisers were racing actively on Long Island Sound. The first of these boats, with sail number one, was the *Lucky Star,* owned by R.O.H. Hill. After she was wrecked in the hurricane of 1938, Hill rebuilt her, but in the process she was modified to the extent that she was not allowed back into the class. In order to continue racing, Hill sold this boat, bought a qualified sister, and transferred *Lucky Star*'s number to his new boat.

These craft not only raced as a class, but also had great success in handicap events. One of the boats, named *Fun* (originally *Sema*), won about 70 prizes racing under the ownership of Thomas H. Closs between 1939 and 1946. Tom has had a number of fine boats since then, but he still raves about the speed and versatility of his Coastwise Cruiser.

WHITE WINGS

Two designs after the Coastwise Cruiser, Alden produced a related but larger sloop, one of his loveliest single-masted creations. She was given the name *White Wings,* which befits her gracefulness. This sloop,

Number 677, was designed for Percy Grant of the Royal Canadian Yacht Club and built by J.J. Taylor and Sons, Ltd., in Toronto, Canada, in 1938. She was beautifully constructed, with mahogany planking over

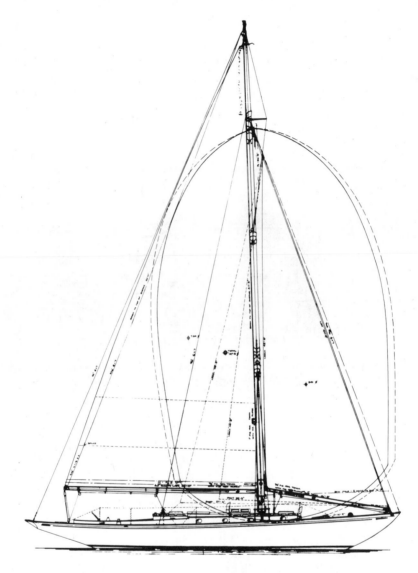

White Wings *carries enough sail up high for good speed in a light air. Her stick is 68 feet long. (Courtesy Robert K. Stryker)*

an oak skeleton and with laid teak decks. Her dimensions are 50 feet, by 33 feet 3 inches, by 11 feet 7½ inches, by 7 feet.

The lines for *White Wings,* like those for the Coastwise Cruiser, were drawn by Carl Alberg. There are marked similarities between the two designs, but *White Wings* has longer ends, while her underwater profile is slightly more cut away fore and aft. Her drawn-out bow enhances her appearance. The hulls of both designs are quite symmetrical, a characteristic that is conducive to good helm balance at various angles of heel. *White Wings* was built to the Royal Ocean Racing Club Rule; this may partially account for her slender stern, a form favored by the British rule.

The arrangement plan was drawn by Clifford P. Swaine, and it places the companionway off center and fairly far forward, allowing a large, private double stateroom aft. Convenient to the companionway are an enclosed head and the main cabin, which has a pilot berth, two transoms, a large drop-leaf table, and a cabinet with leaded-glass door. Up forward is the full thwartships galley, and the fo'c's'le has a pipe berth, another head, and a sail bin.

Clifford Swaine also drew the sail plan, and it is a generous one, containing 1,075 square feet of canvas. The foretriangle is fractional, and the 341-square-foot working jib is boomed and therefore self-tending. The plan also shows a 1964 rig modification that shortened

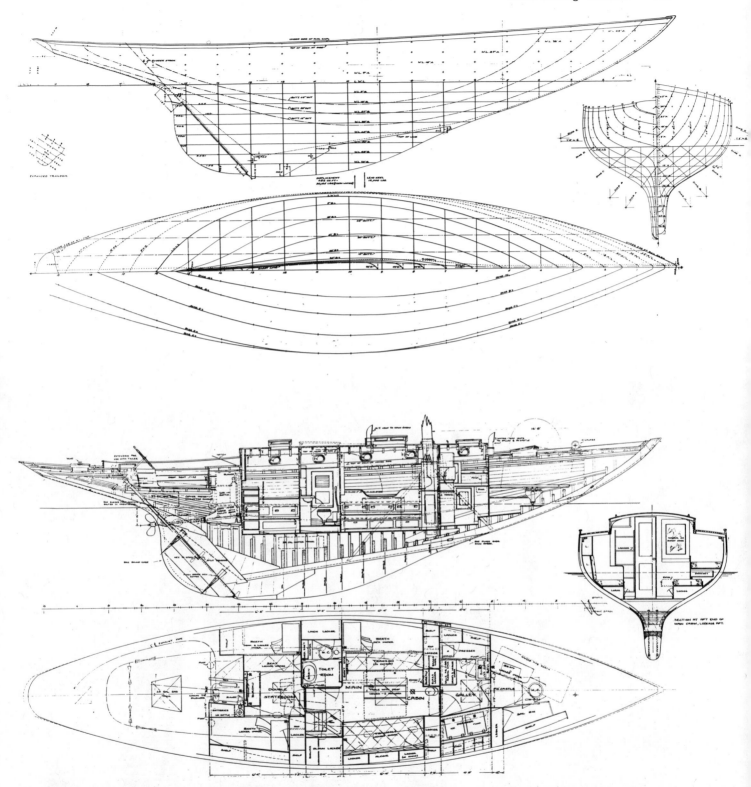

White Wings' lines reflect the influence of the RORC rule. She doesn't slow much when well heeled, probably because she picks up extra sailing length by submerging her long ends. Her designed displacement is 30,125 pounds, with 12,000 pounds of lead ballast outside. Drawn by Clifford Swaine in January 1938, White Wings' layout is quite suitable for Mr. Stryker's part-time crewed charter work. (Courtesy Robert K. Stryker)

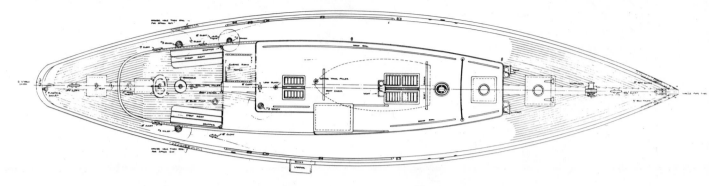

White Wings' *decks are clean and well planned. Her cockpit is roomy and versatile, with its drop seats. (Courtesy Robert K. Stryker)*

With her tall rig, White Wings *has plenty of reef points. (Courtesy Robert K. Stryker)*

A fine close-up lee-bow view of White Wings. *If the photographer were aft on a racing competitor of similar speed, this is about where he'd want to be for a safe leeward position, but the sound of that bow wash would make him nervous just the same. (Courtesy Robert K. Stryker)*

the mast, raised the main boom, and gave the boat a stemhead foretriangle, the base of which is longer by 17 inches, permitting a considerably larger spinnaker. The changes improved *White Wings'* rating. Her original rig was restored in 1977. The rigging includes diamond shrouds with struts and two sets of spreaders, all of which must cause a lot of windage, but no doubt the mast can be kept well tuned. Perhaps the permanent backstay should lead a bit farther aft, so that the boom would keep well clear of the stay during a sudden jibe. According to her present owner, the large rig causes the sloop to sail at a high angle of heel, but this doesn't seem to slow her in the least. She is at her best in either very light or heavy air.

White Wings was raced very successfully by Percy Grant and by his sons William and Robert on Lake Ontario. Her greatest achievement — no mean feat — was winning the 140-mile Freeman Cup Race three times. She took third in a Chicago-Mackinac Race and reportedly was the first Canadian yacht to win the coveted Lake Ontario Cup. The speedy sloop was kept by the Grant family until 1968, when she was sold to Peter Allen, who kept her at the Royal Canadian Yacht Club until 1977. At that time she was bought by Robert Stryker of Wayne, New Jersey, who now charters her part time from her home port at City Island, New York. Bob Stryker is rightfully proud of his classic yacht, and he keeps her in top shape.

TIOGA TOO

Among the numerous handsome Alden designs, one of the prettiest is the yawl *Tioga Too,* design number 687. She was designed for Alden's friend Harry E. Noyes, a resident of Marblehead and a New England-area Buick

distributor who could always locate a new car for John Alden to buy on short notice. Chet Sawtelle, Alden's son-in-law, recalls that John had a habit of watching sailboats instead of the road while driving alongside the

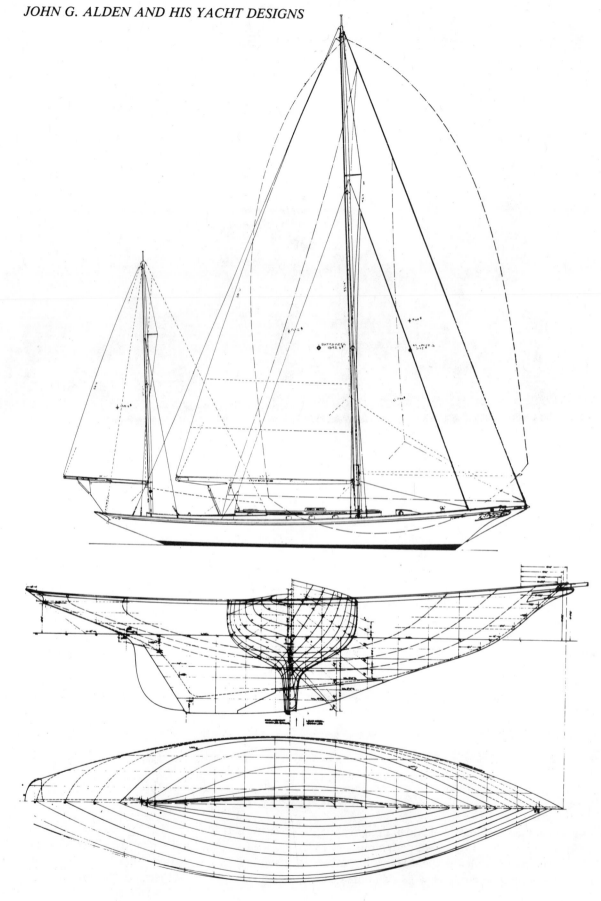

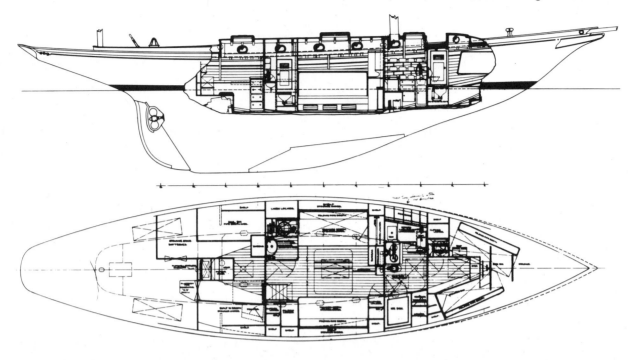

Opposite: Tioga Too*'s clipper bow with short bowsprit provides a sizable foretriangle. Note the size of her spinnaker. The short mizzenmast, however, allows only a tiny mizzen staysail. (*Yachting, *January 1939) She has fairly fine quarters. Her handsome bow lengthens the load waterline but allows the keel to be cut away forward. She has a rather modern rudder with most of its area deep, and it is nicely faired into the hull. Her designed displacement is 41,000 pounds, with a 15,000-pound lead keel. (Courtesy John G. Alden, Inc.)* **Above:** Tioga Too*'s layout is ideal for a couple who will have a paid hand or two. An interesting feature is the after ''sail room.'' (Courtesy John G. Alden, Inc.)*

Charles River on regatta days, and he used to rear-end the cars ahead of him with regularity. He wrecked four cars in one five-year span, and his family sometimes hoped he'd lose his driver's license before a serious accident occurred.

This yawl was third in a line of distinguished racing-cruisers named *Tioga* (an Indian word for "beautiful wife") and owned by the Noyes family. Although her clipper bow resembles that of the second *Tioga* (later the famous *Ticonderoga*), an L. Francis Herreshoff design, Alden wrote that *Tioga Too* was inspired by the fast little yawl *Sea Fox* (described in Chapter 3), which he had owned more than 30 years earlier when he was working as a draftsman in the office of B.B. Crowninshield. At Noyes's request, Carl Alberg drew the lines and other plans.

Tioga Too was built to the highest specifications by the Quincy Adams Yacht Yard in Quincy, Massachusetts, in 1939. She was double planked over white oak frames, and her fastenings were Everdur bronze screws. The decks were teak, while the cabin sole was teak inlaid with strips of holly. Her dimensions were 53 feet 6 inches, by 37 feet 6 inches, by 13 feet, by 7 feet 5 inches.

The beauty of this boat came primarily from her graceful sheerline, her low cabin trunk, and her long, well-balanced ends. The bow was particularly handsome with its clipper profile and decorated trailboards. Her outer planking was Honduras mahogany, which was originally finished bright.

The tall rig with considerable rake to the masts was also attractive, giving the boat a fast, dashing look. Her rated sail area was a generous 1,342 square feet, and this doesn't include her large, light sails. The masthead foretriangle was sizable, but it is curious that the big genoa shown on the plans does not have the longest possible luff. Perhaps the designer thought that a masthead sail would be more apt to foul the jumper struts when tacking.

Below decks *Tioga Too* was laid out like one of the aft-cabin Off Soundings boats, with the owner's stateroom aft, a head near the companionway (just abaft the main cabin), a forward galley, and a fo'c's'le. Almost the only difference between the two designs is that on *Tioga Too* everything was a bit larger, especially the fo'c's'le, which had a head and two pipe berths for paid hands. Most appealing is the fireplace in the main cabin.

This boat had an excellent racing record. Her finest

Right: Tioga Too *flying along on a spinnaker reach, but not disturbing the water overmuch. (Courtesy John G. Alden, Inc.)* **Below:** Tioga Too *on the New York Yacht Club cruise of 1939. (Edwin Levick photo. The Mariners' Museum, Newport News, Virginia)*

year was her first, 1939, when, with a teenage skipper and crew, she won 18 races in her 22 starts and was hailed as the outstanding boat of the season. Her victories included a first in the Boston Yacht Club Spring Cruising Race, three firsts on the Eastern Yacht Club Cruise, three firsts in the Edgartown Regatta, four firsts in the Marblehead Championship Series, and a first on the New York Yacht Club Cruise. She won the Halifax Race one year by 12 hours. She continued her winning ways under the name *Burma* when owned by Frank Bissell, who was the original owner of *Dorothy Q*. Among *Burma*'s triumphs was a Class A win in the 1949 Newport-Annapolis Race.

In 1954 she was bought by Paul C. Nicholson, Jr., of Providence, Rhode Island, who renamed her *Bellatrix*. Nicholson used her primarily for cruising, although he raced her in the Off Soundings events, in the 1962 Bermuda Race, and in the 1963 Annapolis-Newport Race. Aside from installing a 6-cylinder Gray gasoline engine (which gave her eight knots under power), a coffee grinder to handle the genoa sheets, and a new wooden mainmast, Nicholson made no major changes to the boat, and he was well pleased with her comfort and performance. He might have kept her indefinitely, but she was destroyed along with a number of other boats in February 1964, when two children accidentally started a blaze that consumed a storage shed in an East Greenwich, Rhode Island, boatyard.

DIRIGO II

Many Alden yachts have sailed around the world, but one of the best known is Number 693, the schooner *Dirigo II* (named after the square-rigger *Dirigo*, which sank in 1917). She has been publicized in a book, *Count the Cats in Zanzibar,* and at least five magazine articles, including two in *Yachting* (January and February 1960) that described the first half of her circumnavigation.

Measuring 60 feet 5 inches, by 45 feet 10 inches, by 15 feet 6 inches, by 7 feet 10 inches, *Dirigo II* was built in 1939 for Charles Van Sicklen of Northport, Michigan, by Goudy and Stevens of East Boothbay, Maine. Her construction is first rate, with bent oak frames, double Philippine mahogany planking, Everdur fastenings, and teak decks. Van Sicklen, who had made a passage around Cape Horn in Warwick Tompkins' ex-North Sea pilot schooner *Wander Bird,* had his Alden schooner specifically designed for a round-the-world cruise, but it was not until many years later, under the ownership of James W. Crawford, that *Dirigo II* made her circumnavigation.

Crawford, who was awarded the Cruising Club of America's Blue Water Medal in 1974 for his many voyages, including those in *Dirigo II,* began his circumnavigation in this schooner in 1959. Starting in Florida, her track went by way of Panama, the Galapagos, Tahiti, Samoa, Australia, the Cocos (Keeling) Islands, Rodrigues, the Cape of Good Hope, the West African coast, and St. Helena. She proved not only seaworthy but also fast, as evidenced by some exceptional runs, including one in the Pacific during which she sailed 1,067 miles in five days.

Dirigo II handles well. Crawford remembers bringing her up under sail to the quay at Raiatea. An old-timer in a straw hat said, "I haven't seen that done for 30 years." On one shorthanded passage from Honolulu to Santa Barbara, Crawford was able to do the morning sun lines without calling the watch below; the schooner would steer herself until he was done.

Dirigo II has a fisherman-type hull with generous sheer and a knuckle bow almost in the tradition of the Number 390 schooners, though she is not as beamy. She has fairly high bulwarks, which help keep sails and lines on board and afford some protection for the crew. A minor trade-off is that the bulwarks block the view somewhat through the cabin trunk portholes.

Her below-decks layout was influenced by that of the *Wander Bird.* There is a double stateroom aft; an enclosed head and a chart table near the companionway; a huge main cabin with a swinging table, a fireplace, long seats, and four pilot berths; a large galley running the width of the boat; and a fo'c's'le, which Crawford converted to a workshop.

She is gaff-rigged with fidded topmasts, and her masts are well raked. Her four lower sails provide an area of 1,564 square feet. Both masts have ratlines, which are needed (at least on the mainmast) for sail tending and are useful for conning the deep-draft vessel through reef-strewn waters. Crawford added lower backstays to stiffen the rig. One of her most effective

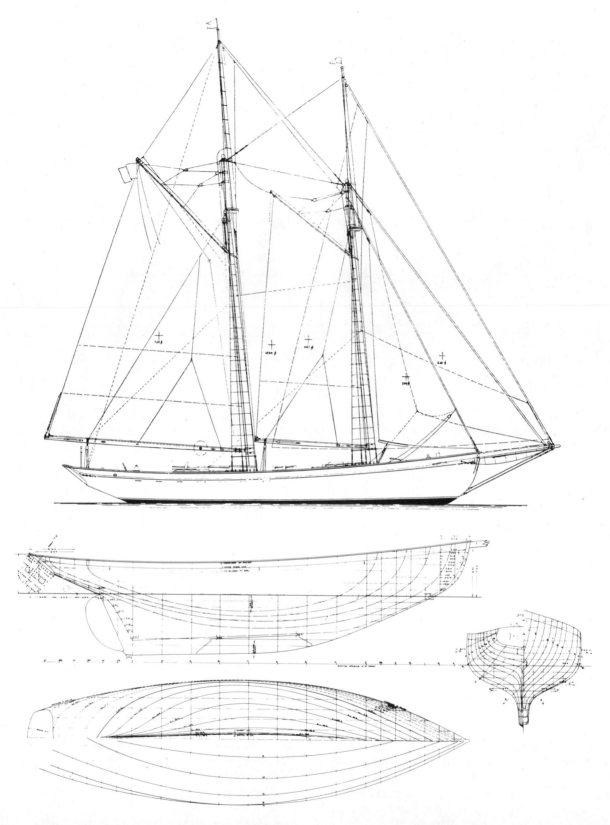

Jim Crawford called Dirigo II*'s rig "pure* Wander Bird.*" The only change he made for his 'round-the-world cruise was the addition of lower backstays. Of the schooner rig in general, he wrote, "It is a fine seagoing rig — very flexible in sail combinations."* Dirigo II, *in particular, "handled like a sailboat should. I used to say I could make her do the rumba — a youthful exaggeration." (*Yachting, *April 1939) Drawn by Cliff Swaine,* Dirigo II*'s lines are a partial throwback to fisherman ancestry. Her powerful quarters are balanced by some fullness in her entrance. (Courtesy John G. Alden, Inc.)*

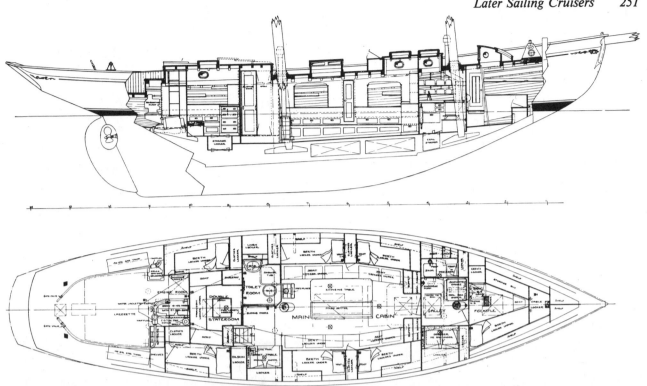

Above: *The rake of* Dirigo II*'s masts is apparent in her inboard profile plan. Crawford converted her fo'c's'le to a workshop.* (Yachting, *April 1939)* **Below:** *With her big golly pulling hard,* Dirigo II *finishes the Havana Race in 1953. She was second across the line, second in Class A, and first schooner to finish. (Florida State News Bureau photo. Courtesy James W. Crawford)*

Writing letters in Dirigo II*'s splendid main cabin in 1953 are Wilson Cross and yacht designer Frank Maclear. Note the numerous book shelves and the bunch of bananas hanging over the table. (James W. Crawford photo)*

Dirigo II *drying sails in Panama, 1953. (James W. Crawford photo)*

reaching sails, which contributed to many of her fast runs and even some very respectable finishes in a number of ocean races, is a sizable, high-clewed gollywobbler.

The seaworthiness of this schooner was demonstrated not only by her circumnavigation, but also by other experiences, such as one she had in 1955 when Crawford was sailing her to the Galapagos Islands from Acapulco, Mexico. She was caught in a Tehuantepec blow, which, as Crawford described it, "went from five knots to 75 knots in 40 seconds." The blow lasted for nearly a day and kicked up dangerously short, breaking seas. The schooner ran off under bare poles, and during the worst conditions, 50 fathoms of cable were towed astern and oil bags were put over the bow. She behaved well, and Crawford later wrote that *Dirigo II* was "the grandest seagoing vessel it has ever been my pleasure to command . . . ." At last report she was in Oregon, still going strong.

CAPT'N BILLY

In marked contrast to the kind of vessel one normally associates with Alden is design number 725, a skipjack yacht named *Capt'n Billy*. Designed for Harold C. McNulty in 1941, she was built at the Whitehaven Boat Yard, Maryland, on the shores of the Chesapeake Bay, home of the working skipjacks. *Capt'n Billy* measures 40 feet, by 35 feet 5 inches, by 12 feet 9½ inches, by 5 feet, and her displacement is a hefty 29,845 pounds.

Unlike working skipjacks, which are used primarily for oyster dredging, *Capt'n Billy* has a fairly deep keel without a centerboard, generous freeboard, and a long cabin trunk and sunken deckhouse. She is similar to the workboat, however, in her straight stem, graceful longhead beneath the bowsprit, long keel, outboard rudder, hard chines, and markedly raked mast. Indeed, photographs (too poor in quality to be reproduced here) and lightly traced lines on the plans both indicate that the longhead was extended farther forward on the finished boat, giving *Capt'n Billy* still more resemblance to a typical Chesapeake skipjack. Her flat bilges have a fair amount of deadrise, and in this respect her underbody resembles that of a Seabird yawl, which has proven to be a fine offshore boat. The underwater profile of *Capt'n Billy* is reminiscent of Slocum's *Spray,* and it would not be surprising if the Alden boat had some of the *Spray*'s ability to self-steer.

Capt'n Billy*'s original rig has the single raking mast of a skipjack, but her main boom is shorter and her jib has a boom rather than the club normally found on oyster dredgers. I count 17 scuppers in her rail. A crudely sketched line shows that the longhead was extended in building. (Courtesy John G. Alden, Inc.)*

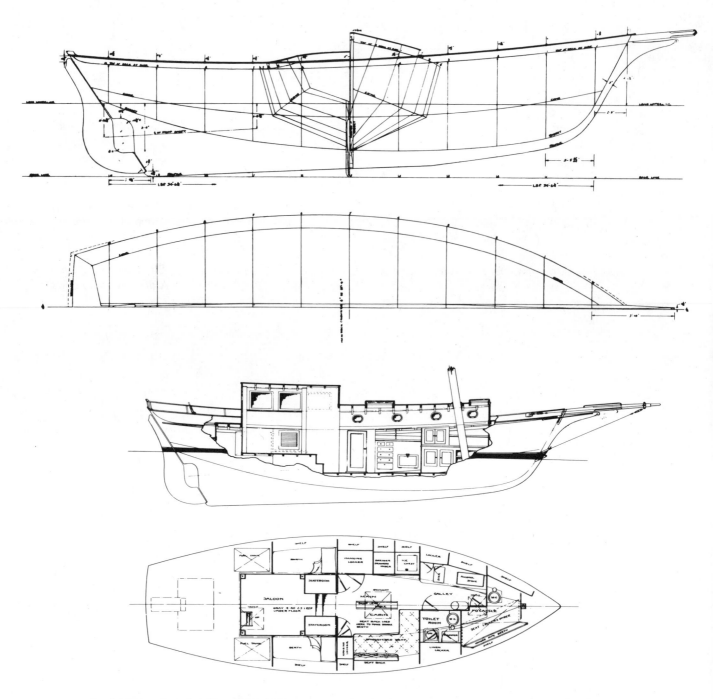

But for her outboard rudder, Capt'n Billy *suggests a cross between a* Seabird *(in her sections) and Slocum's* Spray *(in her profile). The layout below reflects many of the owner's ideas. They are refreshingly different but certainly would lack appeal for many experienced sailors. (Courtesy John G. Alden, Inc.)*

Plans of the skipjack yacht were drawn by W.B. Harris, and he gave her most unusual accommodations. The sunken deckhouse is labeled "saloon" on the cabin plan, and a small part of it is given up to walk-in spaces for two small staterooms on each side of the boat. Farther forward under the lower cabin trunk is the main cabin with an L-shaped settee to starboard and a large hanging locker and a galley to port. An enclosed head is forward of the settee, and there is a small fo'c's'le with a head and pipe berth for a paid hand. The sleeping arrangements might well suit those with a preference for privacy but would not appeal to anyone with claustrophobia. Photographs show that the cabin trunk was continued a short way abaft the deckhouse, probably during construction, but what this added to the accommodations remains a mystery. McNulty used *Capt'n*

Billy for coastwise cruising with his wife and often his grandsons, and he was always satisfied with the comfort of the accommodations.

The rig is easy to handle, and the 825 square feet of sail area has a relatively low center of effort. *Capt'n Billy* may not have the initial stability of a working skipjack with less deadrise, but compared with the normal, narrower-and-deeper, round-bottomed yacht, she must be quite stiff. Alden improved the efficiency of the skipjack rig by attaching the mainsail to the mast with slides on a track rather than with mast hoops. Also, the for-

ward end of the jibboom is attached to the bowsprit several feet abaft the tack, a feature that keeps the foot of the jib stretched out during a reach, yet allows the draft to change as the sheet is eased. *Capt'n Billy*'s mast broke in 1944, apparently due to dry rot, and McNulty decided to convert her to a ketch rig. He feels she handled even better after this change.

Capt'n Billy might be considered a hybrid boat, and her tall deckhouse with big, square windows doesn't enhance her appearance, yet she is functional and distinctive.

ℐ

THE 744 SERIES

Design number 744 is one of John Alden's most admired cruising hulls. Eric Hiscock, in his book *Voyaging Under Sail*, has written of the ketch *Rena* (Number 744-H): "I considered her to be one of the most beautiful yachts I had ever seen . . . . To me that clipper bow with its carved trailboards and upthrust bowsprit, the bold sheer, and the neatly tucked-up counter stern, are quite perfect in their sea-kindly grace and harmony." Carl Alberg drew the plans for this boat, and, as I've written before, there has never been an ugly boat from the board of this gifted designer.

Between 1944 and 1962, 11 of the 744s were built — one of them for an Egyptian prince. The individual boats are almost identical in hull and rig, but their accommodations and deck plans differ. At least one boat has a low, continuous trunk cabin, while others have cockpit shelters or doghouses of varying lengths. Several yards, including Baum's Yacht Yard in Kennebunkport, Maine, built these ketches, but *Rena* was built by her owner, R.R. Vancil, a retired naval officer. He and his wife not only worked on all phases of the construction, but also made the sails and many of the yacht's fittings. *Rena* has served as a home for the Vancils, and she has cruised offshore extensively. Her dimensions and those of the other 744s are 45 feet 6 inches, by 34 feet 8 inches, by 12 feet 7 inches, by 5 feet 10 inches.

The basic arrangement below decks consists of a central main cabin with two pilot berths and two extension transoms, a galley aft, and a large, enclosed head for-

ward. Most of these boats have a double stateroom way forward and a small single stateroom opposite the galley. Some models have another pair of berths and a folding chart table under the doghouse aft, but one or more of the 744s trade off this arrangement for a cockpit shelter that does not have an entrance into the cabin.

Tyler Burton, who owned 744-K, named *Timoneer* (originally *Sagaka*), is lavish in praising her. Although he admits she is a mite under-rigged for light-weather sailing, Tyler says she has a marvelously comfortable motion in a seaway and is unusually dry. Fine clipper bows can bury in certain conditions, but *Timoneer* and her sisters have considerable flare and freeboard forward, and this seems to afford ample reserve buoyancy. Tyler says that his boat never took water over her bow, nor, to his knowledge, was she ever pooped. Her long keel and relatively straight waterlines make her a good course-keeper, though naturally she does not have the maneuverability of a modern boat with a short keel.

The jibheaded ketch rig carries 974 square feet of working sail area. As mentioned, Tyler Burton found the rig a bit small for the light airs of the Chesapeake, but there is enough sail area for moderate breezes, and in light going the "iron jib" would normally be used on this kind of vessel. Given a decent breeze, *Timoneer* is a very competent performer running and reaching, while she sails close-hauled to an apparent wind angle of 40 degrees. The self-tending forestaysail is sizable, so the boat will handle easily in most conditions without her

The sail plans of the 744 ketches vary slightly with individual boats, but the working sail area averages around 1,000 square feet. (Above: Courtesy John G. Alden, Inc. Below: Yachting, *February 1944)*

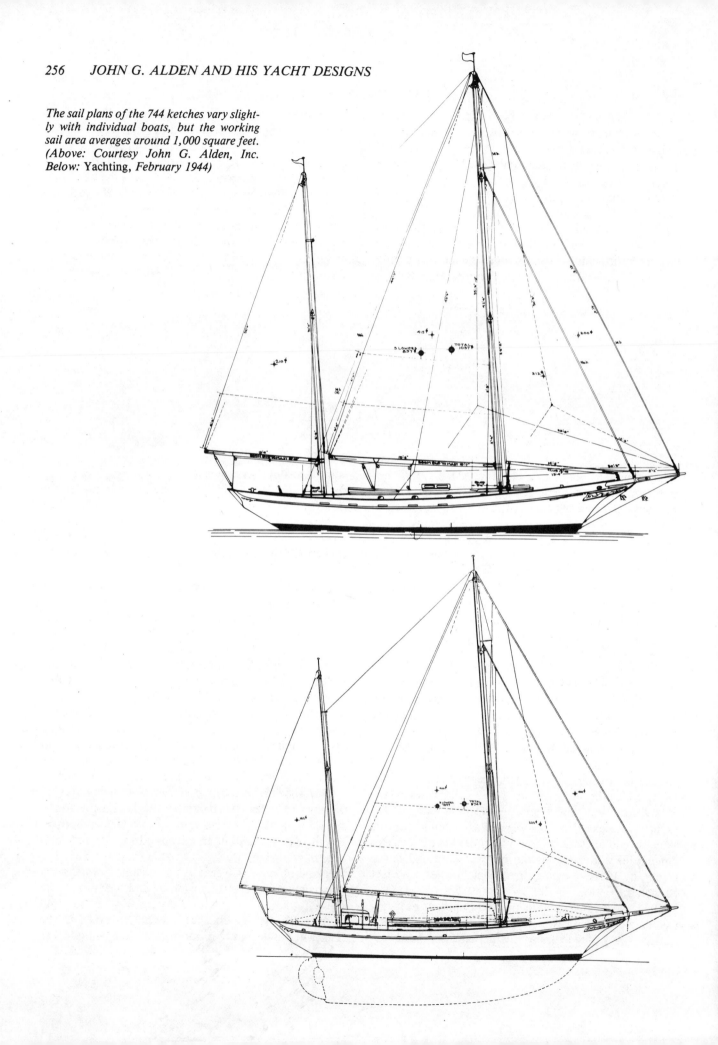

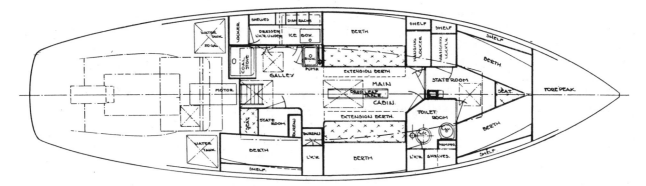

The Number 744 cabin plans also varied, depending primarily on the presence and location of a doghouse and the style of the cabin trunk. In the layout shown here, the doghouse serves solely as a cockpit shelter. (Yachting, *February 1944)*

Left: *The 744* Sagaka *(later* Timoneer) *making knots with a big masthead jib. (Courtesy John G. Alden, Inc.)* **Below:** *Two cockpit views of* Acadie, *Number 744-F, showing her handsome wheel and binnacle. The substantial bitts aft are a good feature. On some ketches the mizzenmast obstructs the companionway, but the problem is insignificant in this boat. (Courtesy John G. Alden, Inc.)*

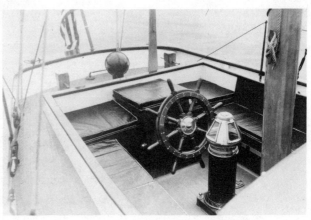

jib. She also balances well under mizzen and forestay-sail, but when so rigged in heavy weather at sea, it might be helpful to attach running backstays to the mast, opposite the forestay. With her prominent forefoot and her mizzen, this is the kind of boat that might lie to a drogue off the bow in a storm at sea, although some skippers would prefer to heave-to under storm sails or

perhaps run off under bare poles while towing drags.

The raking masts, bulwarks, and well-steeved bowsprit, together with the clipper bow, jaunty sheer, and shapely transom, make the 744 a distinguished-looking cruiser. As Eric Hiscock has written about *Rena,* the Alden firm "understands so well the need of a cruising yacht to possess some character."

HINCKLEY 28

Over the years, the Henry R. Hinckley Company of Southwest Harbor, Maine, has earned a solid reputation for producing first-class sailing yachts. The Hinckley

28, a stock Alden design, was far from the most popular class boat built by this yard (only six of them were produced), but she is certainly one of the prettiest. Further-

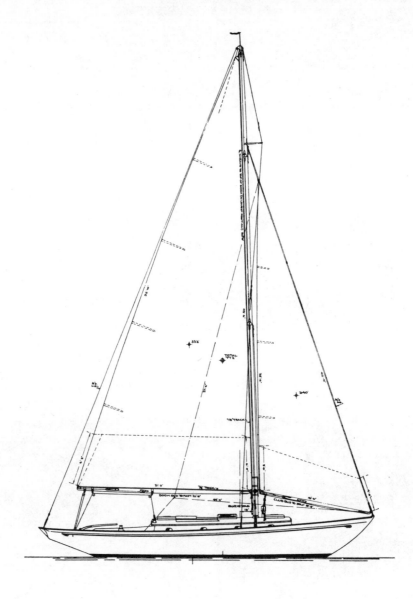

Opposite and above:
The Hinckley 28 could be had as a sloop (772 square feet) or yawl (787 square feet). The mizzen on the latter rig is small, and it seems to move the center of effort only slightly farther aft. (Courtesy John G. Alden, Inc.)

more, she is fast, comfortable, and able. Henry Hinckley kept Number 769-A, named *Jaan,* for his own use. This boat was built in 1945, and the others were built in 1946. Their measurements are 40 feet 9 inches, by 28 feet, by 10 feet, by 5 feet 9 inches.

The lines indicate an easily driven, well-balanced, and seakindly hull. The shape of the sections keeps the wetted surface low, while the moderate beam suggests slight initial tenderness until the 8,500 pounds of keel ballast gains enough leverage to overcome the heeling force. This characteristic has some advantages in that it eases strain on the rig, and in a long-ended boat like the Hinckley 28, moderate heel significantly increases the sailing length. Although a long counter is not always considered a good seagoing feature, the sections aft on this boat are slightly V'd to reduce any tendency to slam.

Hinckley gave the buyer a choice of two different cabin arrangements, one with the galley aft and the other with the galley forward. The latter plan is intended for a boat that carries a paid hand, and there is a pipe berth for him forward of the galley. This arrangement has a double stateroom aft, while the after-galley plan has the double stateroom forward. Both arrangements have an off-center midships companionway on top of the cabin trunk, providing privacy in the after-stateroom layout and a sequestered, curtained galley in the other arrangement. A cabintop companionway is a seaworthy detail, largely removing the hazard arising from the off-center location. The drawbacks of this arrangement are that the hatch needs a dodger for rain and spray, one has to climb onto the cabintop to enter or exit the cabin, and a very long companionway ladder is needed.

A recent trend in rigs for racing cruisers is the fractional sloop with a large, tall mainsail, and interestingly, this is similar to the Hinckley 28's rig. The basic difference between the earlier conception and the modern version is that the latter has a shorter, higher main boom and a bendy mast to flatten the main in a breeze.

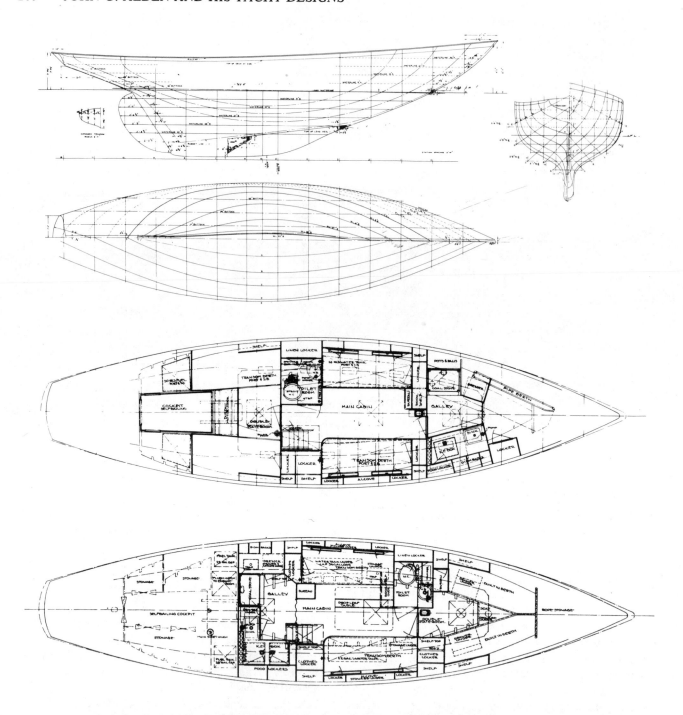

The lines show a long-ended hull with a full bow and slightly V'd sections aft. Designed displacement is 19,810 pounds, with 8,450 pounds of lead ballast outside. (Courtesy John G. Alden, Inc.) As with the rig, the buyer was offered a choice in cabin arrangements. (The Rudder, March 1946)

Although the Alden boat does not have this latter advantage to any degree with her relatively stiff wooden mast, the rig allows easy handling with the boomed self-tending jib, and no doubt she can sail reasonably well under her main alone. When it comes to reducing sail in a blow, the three-quarter rig has some advantages over a masthead plan. Reefing the main shortens sail significantly without sacrificing good balance. For racing in light air, however, the masthead rig has the great advan-

Number 769-E, originally named Vael, *slipping along with little fuss in a light breeze. This photo shows her considerable sheer. (Courtesy John G. Alden, Inc.)*

tage of larger, more powerful jibs and spinnakers.

Rigs, as well as other aspects of yacht design, go through cycles, with trends periodically returning in only slightly different forms. It would be most gratifying to see the return of hulls as graceful, well balanced, and shapely as those of the Hinckley 28s.

A SMALL DOUBLE-ENDER

John Alden did not turn out many double-enders, but he turned out some good ones. The canoe-stern sloop shown here is Number 798, designed in 1948 for John H. Read of Western Australia. Her dimensions are 28 feet 3 inches, by 22 feet, by 8 feet, by 4 feet.

This sloop is nearly a true double-ender in that her bow and stern are quite similar in both the half-breadth and profile views. She appears to be an able boat, with her long keel and fairly deep forefoot. These features indicate good course-holding ability but slowness in stays. Although her hull is symmetrical, the keel extends well forward, and it has no drag; the resultant profile indicates weather helm. Thus, it is not surprising that the center of effort leads the center of lateral resistance by a considerable amount. Such a lead without a bowsprit is brought about by stepping the mast quite far forward, and this necessitates a small jib.

There is 395 square feet of sail area, which is on the modest side for light-air regions and a boat that appears to be quite heavy. Nevertheless, the rig is a good one for shorthanded offshore sailing. Although the jib is not self-tending, it is easy to trim after tacking because of its

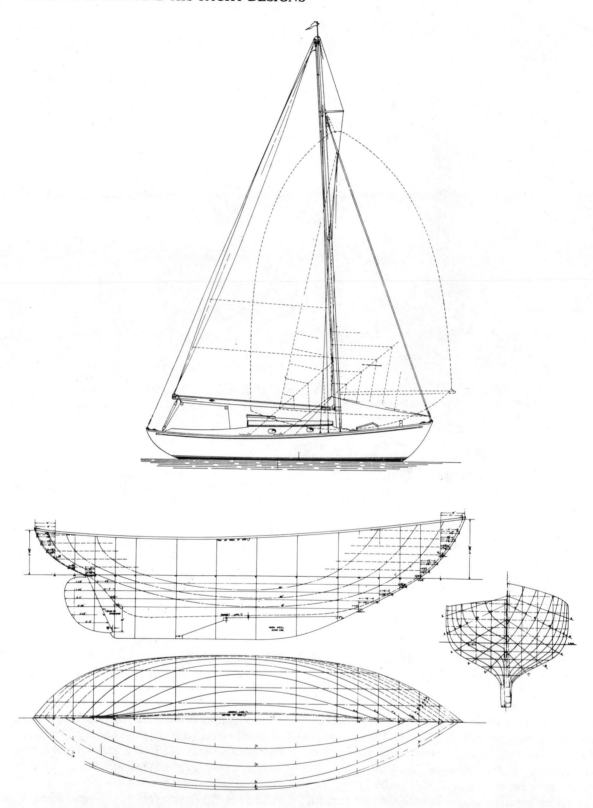

The double-ender's loose-footed jib requires tending when going about, but it affords a bit more power and perhaps a better angle of trim than a boomed jib. The main boom looks as though it just might strike the backstay during a flying jibe. (The Rudder, *November 1948) Her lines show that Number 798 is nearly a true double-ender. (Courtesy John G. Alden, Inc.)

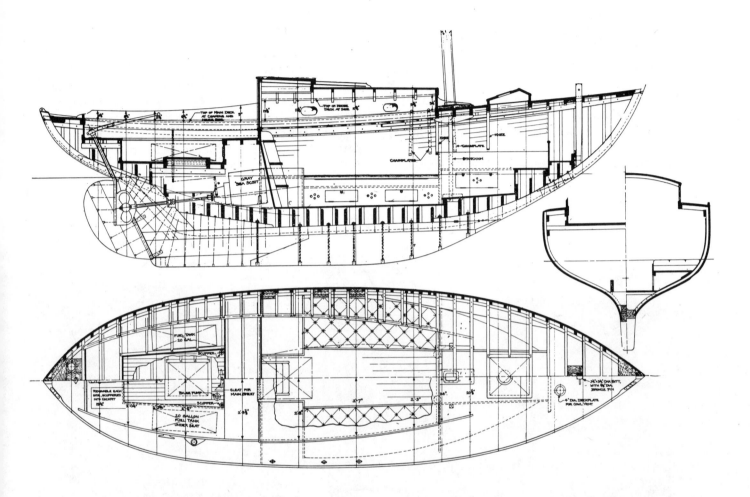

The profile plan shows Number 798's heavy scantlings. The keel is long for such a small boat. The cabin was designed for short cruises with two people, but for voyaging it would be better for a singlehander, since the space is small and there would always be a bunk to leeward. (The Rudder, *November 1948*)

size and the double-purchase sheets. The considerable mast rake not only adds to the boat's seamanlike looks, but also helps keep the boom from tripping on a reach in beam or quartering seas.

The deck plan could be that of a larger boat, since the cabin trunk is quite small and there is considerable deck space. The house sides have been extended forward to make a coaming around the mast, which is handy for stowing coiled halyards. Several features not always found on boats of this size are the bridge deck, the amply elevated cockpit well for good drainage, the miniature booby-type hatch on the foredeck, and the samson post forward.

The double-ender's heavy scantlings and small cabin trunk detract from room below, but still there is space for a galley aft, two comfortable bunks, and a large forepeak that could house a W.C. A stanchion accepts the thrust of the deck-stepped mast, and is less of an obstacle below than the heel of a mast would be.

With her able hull, sensible rig, ample auxiliary power supplied by a Gray Sea Scout engine, and her four-foot draft, this sloop could be taken anywhere in deep water or shoal. She would be easy to haul on any marine railway, and with her eight-foot beam she could even be trailered behind a powerful car. But no — this would be an ignominious way to move such a traditional little seagoer.

ELEUTHERA II

Design number 902, named *Eleuthera II,* is an example of John Alden's late thinking in moderately large, smart-sailing cruisers. This boat was built in 1954, the year before Alden retired. She was designed for Gustav H. Koven, of Green Village, New Jersey, who intended to use the boat for extensive cruising. Replacing a smaller Alden ketch of the same name, she has dimensions of 60 feet 5 inches, by 43 feet, by 14 feet 7 inches, by 7 feet 5 inches.

In hull shape, there is nothing radically different be-

tween *Eleuthera II* and Alden's earlier concepts of this type of boat. One minor difference is in the stem, which is straighter than the spoon bow characteristic of so many Alden boats of the 1920s and early 1930s. The gradual evolution toward straighter stems may have been influenced by the CCA rule, which based sailing length on the four-percent-waterline measurement. The main differences between *Eleuthera II* and earlier Alden craft, of course, are in the rig and accommodations. Concerning the former, the designer had eventually

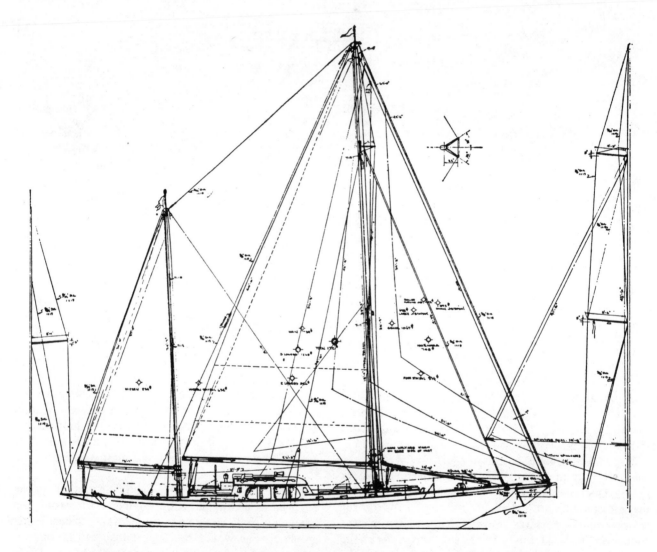

A low-aspect-ratio sail plan generally has to be spread out fore and aft to achieve sufficient area, but everything on Eleuthera II *except the roller-furling jib is inboard. The forestaysail is large enough (and the mizzen small enough) to preserve reasonable balance when the jib is furled. Note the numerous centers of effort shown on the plan.* (Yachting, *June 1955*)

Her companionway is high, and to use it one must mount the top of the after cabin trunk, but I doubt that much water went below when Eleuthera II *was pooped off Colombia. Her accommodations afford unusual privacy, and the deckhouse with its good light and view must be delightful.* (Yachting, *June 1955*)

changed his big-boat rig preference from schooner to yawl or ketch. He liked the yawl for racing because of its all-around performance and favorable rig allowance under the CCA rule (compared with sloops), but he felt that the ketch rig better divided the sail area for easier handling, with little sacrifice to reaching speed when cruising. Another factor favoring tall forward masts in the early 1950s was the introduction of Dacron sailcloth, which made it possible for large headsails to become highly efficient on all points of sailing.

Eleuthera II has a sail area of 1,721 square feet, yet the area of her mainsail is only 734 square feet. Twelve centers of effort are shown on the sail plan, and the fact that the centers of the main alone, two lowers, and three lowers all fall in a nearly vertical line indicates good balance under a variety of sail combinations. She can sail well without the jib in a fresh breeze and can be tacked easily with the self-tending forestaysail. Although runners on the mainmast must be tended, they are probably not needed in light-to-moderate winds, and the permanent backstay leading to the end of a boomkin obviates the need for mizzen runners. A roller-furling jib and huge mizzen staysail supply power in light airs.

In her accommodations, the ketch differs from

typical early Alden cruisers in that she has a prominent, large-windowed deckhouse nearly amidships, with the engine beneath and spacious cabins fore and aft. The owner's large stateroom is aft, while a double stateroom with galley opposite is forward. Still farther forward, there is an adequate fo'c's'le for two paid hands. Three heads serve both staterooms and the fo'c's'le. The main cabin, in the well-lighted and well-ventilated deckhouse, has two transoms, a large table, and a coalburning grate. Koven, an engineer, worked with the Alden firm in designing the arrangements, and he was inspired by the layout of the Alden-designed *Minots Light*.

Built of welded steel by Abeking and Rasmussen in Germany, *Eleuthera II* has a strong, heavy hull. About 30 percent of her 66,496-pound displacement is in iron keel ballast. Her decks are of teak, and she has mahogany trim.

Gustav Koven still owns *Eleuthera II,* and he has fulfilled his expectations of cruising her extensively. He and his family have crossed the Atlantic several times, and in the late 1950s they kept their boat in Europe, cruising between Germany and Lisbon in the summers and in the Mediterranean during the stormy winter months. Eventually the ketch was taken to the West Indies, and today she is based at Bequia Island in the northern Grenadines, where she is chartered part time.

Eleuthera II has been through two major storms. During a hurricane north of Bermuda she ran off under bare poles while towing heavy warps astern. This experience left her unscathed, but a later storm — a freak 90-knot blow off the mountainous coast of Colombia — seriously injured her crew. While running off (this time without towing drags), she was pooped by a 30-foot rogue wave. Koven, at the helm, was thrown forward with sufficient force to snap off the wheel and binnacle, exactly anticipating the later experience of Phineas Sprague aboard the *High Tide*. A guest was knocked unconscious and the professional captain was washed overboard. He saved himself by gripping the railcap with one hand, and Mrs. Koven helped him back aboard. Both the guest and the captain suffered broken ribs and punctured lungs. They were later attended to by two Air Force medics dropped from a helicopter. The ketch suffered a bent rudder stock and damaged mizzen step, but her hull was undamaged, and Koven believes the boat can take anything the sea can offer.

With her luxurious accommodations, seakindly but fast hull form, heavy weight, and easily manageable rig, this late design of John Alden's has proven a thoroughly satisfactory and comfortable boat for blue-water cruising. She is enough like his classic hulls to have a lot of beauty and character — but with the addition of many well-thought-out modern conveniences. The following tribute to Alden once appeared in *The Skipper* magazine: "The name of John G. Alden stamped on a yacht design merits the respect usually rated a diamond from Tiffany's." *Eleuthera II* is no contradiction to this statement.

8

Racing Classes and Daysailers

Because of his reputation as a creator of rugged cruisers and husky ocean racers, John Alden is not always recognized as a successful and prolific designer of small daysailers and fast one-design racers. In addition to producing catboats, knockabouts, sailing dories and tenders, and frostbite dinghies, he designed about 50 small one-design classes, both keel and centerboard. Thousands of these boats were built. Alden also produced a number of larger racing sloops — mostly R boats and some Qs — designed to the Universal Rule.

Widely acclaimed as an expert racing skipper who was a master at trimming the sails of an ocean-racing schooner, Alden didn't have quite the same success racing around the buoys in one-designs. Nevertheless, he was an avid small-boat racer, and many of his designs were prizewinners. The first and last boats he owned were small, open knockabouts. His active participation over the years in one-designs gave him a better understanding of the design requirements of small racers and daysailers, and helped to create superior boats.

CORINTHIAN ONE-DESIGN

The first one-design shown in the Alden records is a 15-foot-waterline sloop for the Corinthian Yacht Club of Marblehead, Massachusetts. Curiously, this boat was first numbered 20 in the Alden index, but then a specific boat of the same class, named *Dingbat,* was listed in the index as design number 31. These boats were built by the Stearns and McKay Company of Marblehead in 1912 and 1913. For daysailing racers, their construction was quite substantial, with $1\frac{1}{16}$-inch cedar planking over oak frames spaced on nine-inch centers. The boats are 25 feet long overall, with a beam of 6 feet 1 inch and a draft of 4 feet. New, they sold for about $550.

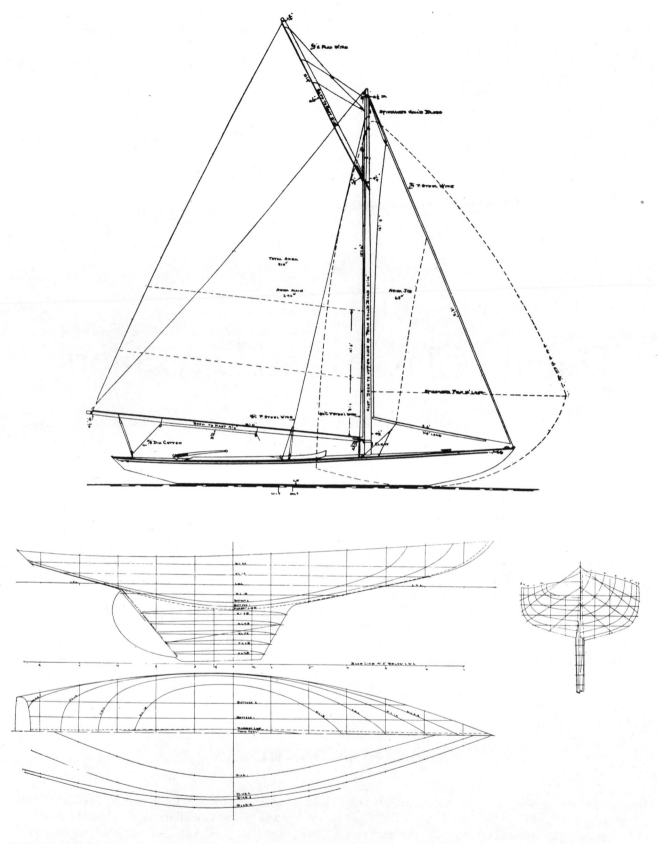

The sail plan of the Corinthian One-Design is spread out as much as possible. The jib leads serve either jib without adjustment. The lines show flat bilges — particularly aft — for a heavy keel boat. The sizable rudder with generous rake gives the boat good control when she is well heeled. Her least freeboard is just 16 inches. (Yachting, *March 1912*)

The Corinthian One-Design's hull is pleasing to the eye with its long, shapely ends and graceful sheerline. Although the boat's beam is modest, her 1,200 pounds of iron outside ballast is rather deep, and she has enough stability to compensate for her low freeboard. The wide, flat stern with straight buttocks gives the One-Design some bearing when heeled, inhibits hobby-horsing in a seaway, and encourages planing. The bow is full enough for reasonable buoyancy but sharp enough to cut through a chop. It might throw some spray but would not bury to any great degree. The coaming around the open cockpit is adequate to shed any water that comes over the bow.

The gaff sloop rig, with 310 square feet of sail area, provides a low center of effort. Running backstays must be used to keep the jibstay taut when beating and to hold the mast back when running or broad reaching. With the club on the working jib's foot, the lead position for the sheet need not be changed for the heavy-weather jib.

THE Q BOAT SHIRLEY

The first Q boat attributed to the Alden office was design number 41. This boat, named *Shirley,* was built in 1913 by the Pinaud Brothers in Sydney, Nova Scotia.

Her plans were drawn by John Pinaud, who was at that time associated with Alden. According to the Alden records, *Shirley* was built for "Sidney G. Dobson, et

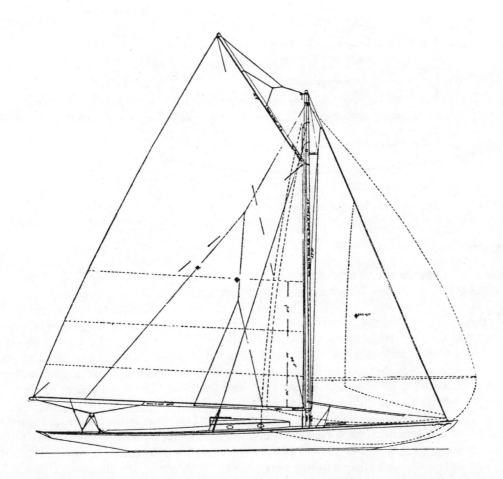

Shirley's sail plan is low and inboard, but ample to drive her splinterlike hull. (Yachting, *June 1913)*

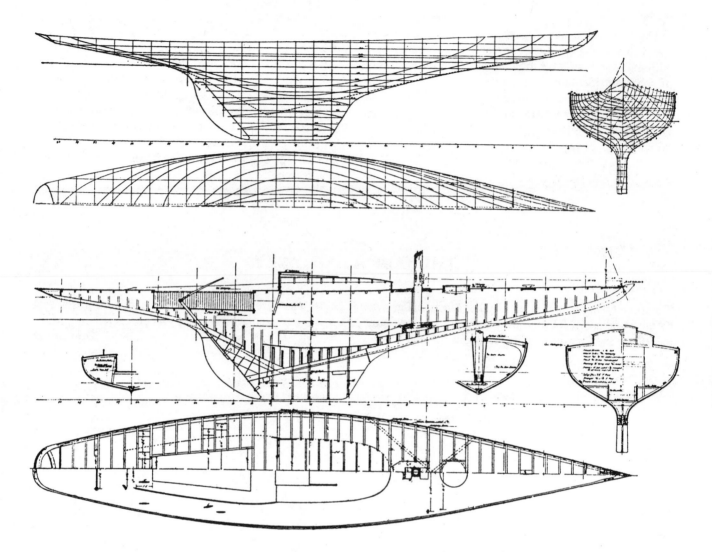

Shirley's hull has minimum wetted surface and a rapier bow. The overhang aft is almost unbelievable. She is well constructed, with closely spaced frames and deckbeams carried from toe rail to toe rail across the bridge deck to give her strength amidships. (Yachting, June 1913)

al.'' of the Royal Cape Breton Yacht Club. She measures 46 feet 4 inches, by 25 feet 11 inches, by 8 feet 10 inches, by 5 feet 10 inches.

The Universal Rule at the time *Shirley* was designed encouraged long, fine ends by a quarter-beam measurement (a measurement of buttock length taken at a distance of one-quarter of the beam from the centerline). Long ends give a boat a short measured length at rest, but a much longer sailing length when underway. Another effect of long ends is that wetted surface can be kept to a minimum in light airs, when the boat can be sailed upright and with crew weight fairly far forward. The upper waterlines forward are very sharp on *Shirley,* and some water probably comes over the bow in a chop, but the long overhang affords some

reserve buoyancy, while the cabin trunk and coamings help keep water out of the cockpit.

The cabin is little more than an enclosed cuddy, but there are a couple of bunks for overnighting and plenty of room for stowing sails. Despite the low freeboard, there is a self-draining cockpit well; however, it is very shallow and might give a feeling of insecurity to a crew member accustomed to a deeper cockpit.

A gaff rig often seems inappropriate for a boat with a short keel, but *Shirley*'s rig is inboard and the center of effort of her 930 square feet of sail is low. If a tall marconi rig were put on this boat, with her rudder so far forward, she might become as unsteady as a drunk on a dark night when she carries her spinnaker in a fresh breeze. The overlapping jib shown on the sail plan may seem advanced for the days before the advent of the genoa jib, but the lapper on *Shirley* seems to be a balloon jib that was commonly used sailing off the wind, often in conjunction with the single-luff spin-naker. It appears that the jumper stay leading down the forward side of the mast below the strut might foul the jib when tacking. A fairleader aloft would bring the stay closer to the mast, but the stay might be a welcome handhold for the foredeck crew in a seaway.

TWO EARLY CLASS R SLOOPS

Insofar as racing sloops are concerned, most of John Alden's efforts went into producing R boats, the Universal Rule class just under the rating measurement of 20 feet. He produced the lines of at least 25 different R boats between 1913 and 1928. He was an enthusiastic promoter of the class, which first flourished on the Great Lakes, and he helped introduce it to New England waters. The R class grew steadily until about 1930, then declined abruptly, perhaps partly as a result of the introduction of the International Rule. Evers Burtner, professor emeritus of the Massachusetts Institute of Technology and a noted designer-measurer, has even suggested that this decline in the early 1930s was due to "the fear or shock of Roosevelt's New Deal."

One of the first Alden R boats was a proposed design that appeared in the November 1913 issue of *Yachting*. This may have evolved into Number 55, the first of the class listed in the Alden records. Named *Banshee,* this boat was built in 1915 by Hodgdon Brothers of East Boothbay, Maine, for O.C. Schoenwerk, Jr., of Chicago. She measures 38 feet, by 23 feet 6 inches, by 8 feet, by 5 feet 4 inches. *Banshee* was an immediate success, winning the Chicago Championship her first year and cleaning up not only in her class but also in "mixed" events the following year.

Both *Banshee* and her forerunner, the *Yachting* R boat, which measures 40 feet, by 23 feet, by 8 feet 2 inches, by 5 feet 3 inches, are slim, low-freeboard boats with long, fine ends and low cabin trunks. The *Yachting* boat has her trunk rounded at the forward end, which is not a bad idea for a boat that is apt to take some green water over the bow in rough conditions. The keels of both boats are short, yet their leading edges are well sloped. *Banshee* has a sharper toe and some fairing at the top of her rudder. The boats have minimal accommodations, but there is about five feet of headroom below, and *Banshee,* at least, has two transom berths, with a thwartships pipe berth under the bridge deck.

Compared with many gaff sloops of that era, the rigs are fairly modest and well inboard, and this is helpful to sailhandling on fine-ended boats. It is interesting that even the racing boats of those times were fitted with lazyjacks. Although they cause a small amount of windage, they simplify lowering the mainsail, especially when the boat has no engine and cannot be held up to the wind longer than a moment. An interesting feature on the *Yachting* boat is the slightly curved jib club, which allows some round at the foot.

Many of the top yacht designers became involved with designing R boats, and keen rivalries developed, especially in the Marblehead area, where *Banshee*'s second owner, Caleb Loring, sailed her beginning in 1917. The competition between John Alden and L. Francis Herreshoff has been described as being as sticky as fresh varnish on a dank day. After World War I, the R boats were given tall, efficient, marconi rigs, and no doubt *Banshee* was rerigged at that time. (Later, in the mid-1920s, the restriction on mast bend was removed, and R boats began to carry sharp aft-directed curves in their spars.) The trend in R-boat development was toward greater length and displacement for the same beam and sail area, as designers discovered that 600 square feet or so of canvas could move a longer, heavier boat faster than a shorter, lighter one. *Banshee* has a longer waterline length than many of her contemporaries, and this probably contributed to her early success. Alden had his share of winning R boats, including not only *Banshee,* but also *Calypso, Ariel, Rogue* (sailed by yachtsman Charles F. Adams), *Vitesse,* and *Scorpion.* The "20-raters" disappeared completely from Marblehead waters at least 40 years ago, but there are still two of them sailing on the Chesapeake Bay.

These R boats have similar rigs, but Banshee *(below) has more sail area — 650 square feet as opposed to the other boat's 610 square feet. (Above:* Yachting, *November 1913. Below:* Yachting, *January 1917)*

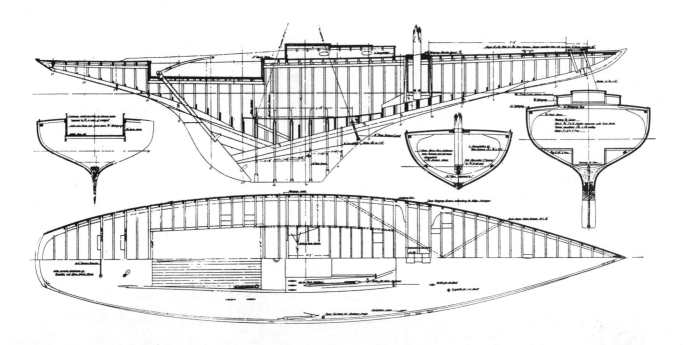

Banshee appears to be strongly built, with her knees and straps and the plentiful structural members in way of her mast. (Yachting, *January 1917)*

STAMFORD ONE-DESIGN

One of the prettiest classes of knockabouts designed by Alden is the Stamford One-Design, produced for the Stamford (Connecticut) Yacht Club in 1916. Their ends are shapely but not overlong, and they have a bit more freeboard than many racing sloops of that time. Their cabin trunks seem especially well proportioned. These boats were built to design number 67, and their dimensions turned out to be 26 feet 9 inches, by 19 feet, by 7 feet 3 inches, by 4 feet 3 inches.

Eleven boats were built by the Rice Brothers of East Boothbay, Maine, and each was sailed singlehanded to Stamford around Cape Cod in May, frequently a stormy month. They did indeed encounter some heavy weather and were blown some distance offshore, but all arrived safely at their destination. Despite not having self-bailing cockpit wells, the boats proved decidedly able.

Sizable, deep, and fitted with benches, the cockpit is quite comfortable, and the cabin is large enough for a couple of shelves for mattresses. The gaff sloop rig, carrying 342 square feet of sail, is conventional, but an off-beat feature for a racer is the club-footed jib on a traveler. Although it is common practice to rig a boomed jib's sheet to a traveler, the arrangement doesn't always work as well with a club-footed jib.

The records show that Alden designed only one S boat (boats rated under 17 feet by the Universal Rule), but he claimed that with minor modifications the Stamford One-Design could be made to fit into the S class. He predicted she would do well in that class. However, it seems that no more than a dozen Stamford One-Designs were built, and they were not an active racing class in the Yacht Racing Association of Long Island Sound. As with many of the small one-designs in those days, they were used exclusively for intraclub racing, and the class was not long lived.

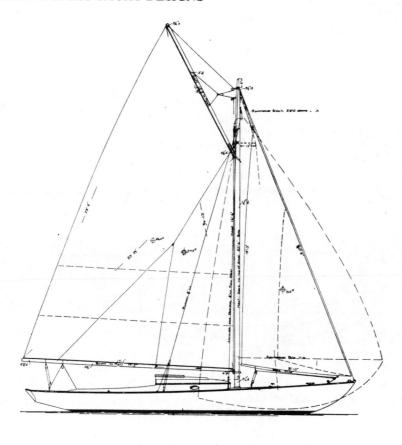

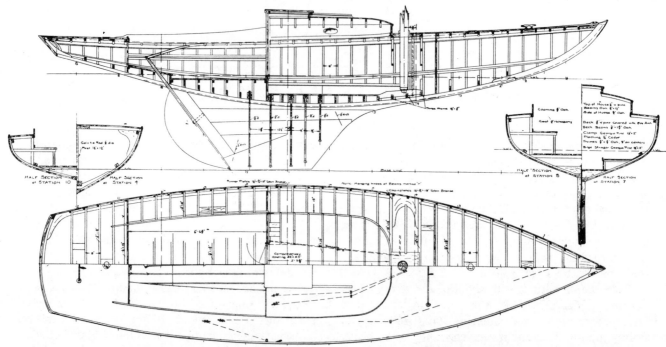

The Stamford One-Design is a most attractive boat with a moderate, easily manageable sail plan. Note the club-footed self-tending jib. The construction plans show us a pleasing profile with sensible overhangs. This boat's strength is increased by her bilge stringers. Her skeleton and house sides are of oak, and her hull is planked with cedar. There are watertight bulkheads forward and aft. She carries 1,500 pounds of outside ballast. (The Rudder, March 1919)

INDIAN HARBOR ONE-DESIGN
(ARROW CLASS)

Alden's next design after the Stamford One-Design was a class sloop for a club near Stamford, the Indian Harbor Yacht Club at Greenwich, Connecticut. Several designers submitted plans to an Indian Harbor selection committee, which included Clifford D. Mallory, later the founding father of the North American Yacht Racing Union. The Alden design was chosen, and it became known as the Indian Harbor Arrow class. Reportedly, the committee was influenced partly by the successful racing record of the R boat *Banshee*.

Compared with the Stamford One-Design, the Indian Harbor boat is somewhat larger, measuring 31 feet 10 inches, by 21 feet 10 inches, by 8 feet 1 inch, by 5 feet 3 inches. She does not seem quite as attractive, with her

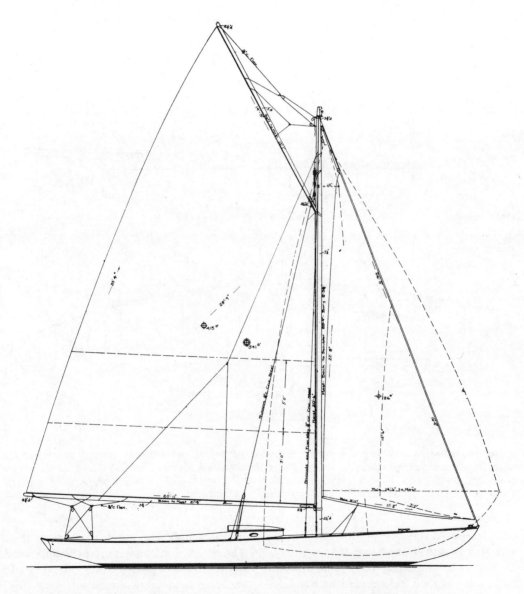

The Indian Harbor Arrows must have been fast in a light air. Notice that the storm jib cannot use the same sheet leads as those for the working jib. (The Rudder, February 1916)

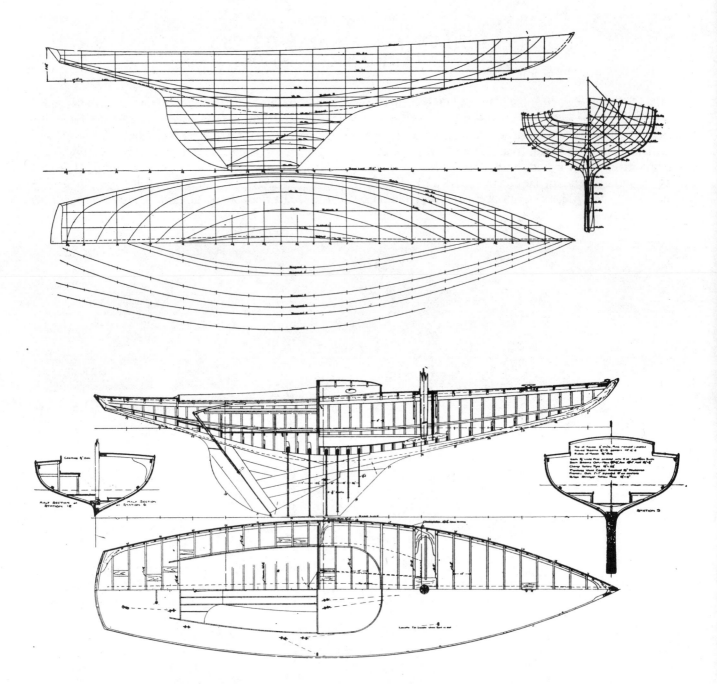

The Indian Harbor Arrow has a dishlike hull, but her garboards turn nicely into her keel, giving it strength and probably improving water flow around it. The boats were built of oak, cedar, and yellow pine. The rudder is raised slightly for protection during a grounding, and a nice feature in this boat and others of her type is that the ballast protects the entire bottom of the keel when it takes the ground. (The Rudder, February 1916)

relatively lower freeboard and disproportionately small cabin trunk, which is actually no more than a cuddy. Nevertheless, below the waterline, the Indian Harbor One-Design has some superior refinements such as lead (rather than iron) keel ballast, hollow garboards, and fairing at the head of the rudder. The lines show a well-

balanced hull with beautiful champagne-glass sections. The broad, flat counter gives the hull some bearing aft, but there might be some noisy slapping of waves under the stern in certain conditions.

The sail area of 541 square feet, with 415 square feet of it in the gaff-headed mainsail, is generous for this size

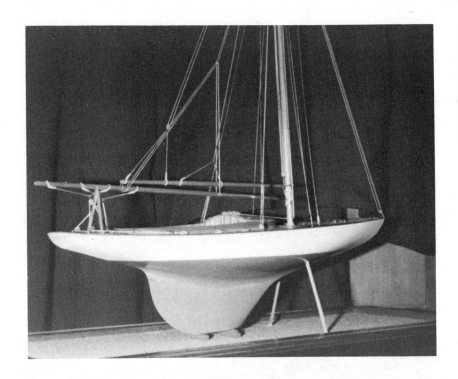

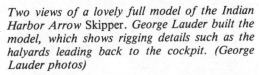
Two views of a lovely full model of the Indian Harbor Arrow Skipper. George Lauder built the model, which shows rigging details such as the halyards leading back to the cockpit. (George Lauder photos)

of boat. An interesting detail is the double-bridle arrangement on the boom for the mainsheet. (The strut just above the mainsail's throat is actually a shroud spreader shown as though it were viewed in the fore-and-aft direction.)

These sloops were built by the Narragansett Bay Yacht Yard in 1916. The Alden records indicate that only five boats were built, but George Lauder, a former

commodore of the Indian Harbor Yacht Club, recently wrote that he owned number 6, the boat originally owned by Clifford Mallory, and he thinks there were 10 boats in the club fleet. Although the Arrows were not one of Alden's most popular one-designs, Lauder describes them as "one of the nicest little boats I ever sailed. They were fast, able, and dry as any boat of that type could be." The class was short lived at Indian Harbor Yacht Club.

THE SAN FRANCISCO BIRD CLASS

One of the most talked-about one-designs from the Alden firm is design number 157, known as the Bird Class of San Francisco Bay. Number 157 was the result of a collaboration between Alden and F.C. Brewer, a naval architect from Sausalito, California, who did the

preliminary work on the design. The final plans were drawn by Sam Crocker of the Alden office in 1921, and the first boat was built for Brewer the following year, for a price of $1,800, by Herbert Madden of Sausalito. Originally called the San Francisco "S" boats, they

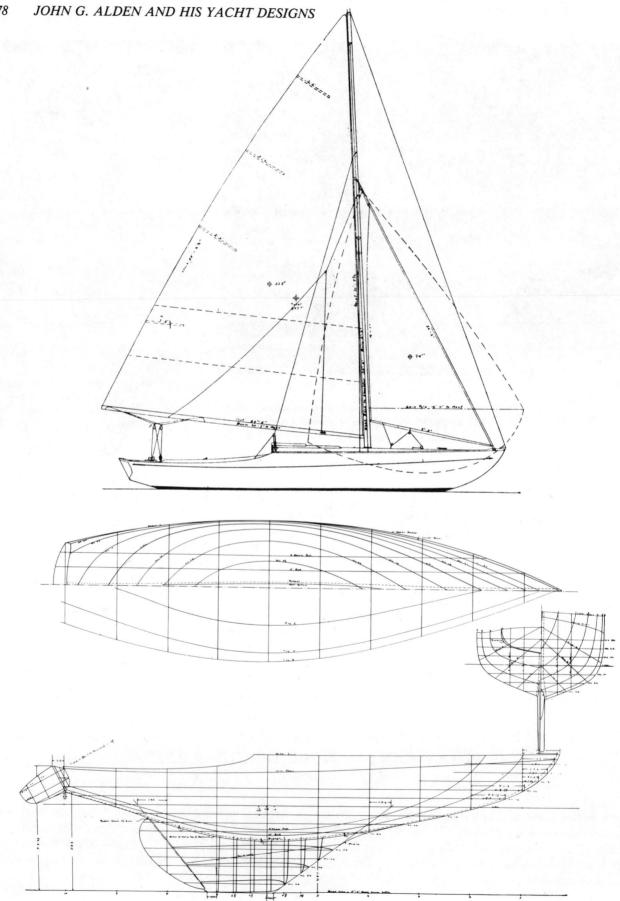

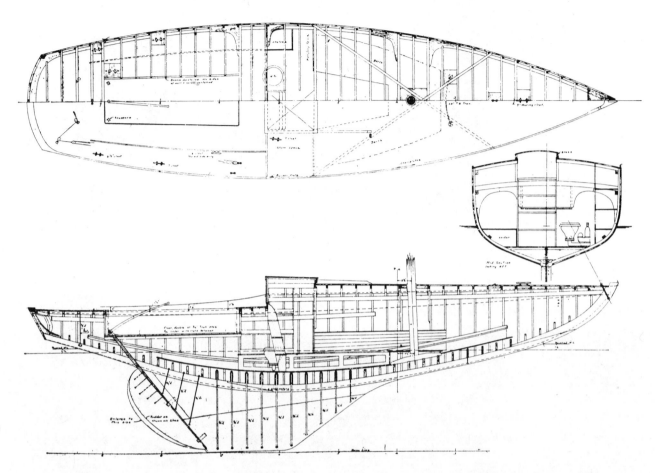

Opposite: *The Bird has a low-aspect-ratio sail plan with its center of effort well aft, which requires that her keel also be placed far aft. (Yachting, April 1922) Although not a beamy boat, the Bird is fairly wide at the waterline, and her full quarters and rounded forward sections help her initial stability. Stability at higher angles of heel is helped by her heavy lead keel. (Courtesy John G. Alden, Inc.)* **Above:** *Perhaps another reason for the Bird's excellence in heavy weather is her solid construction, including the substantial bracing around her cockpit, the full-width deck beams, the strapping, and the long bolts in the deadwood. (Yachting, April 1922)*

became known as the Bird Class when the early boats were given bird names. Their original dimensions were 29 feet 11 inches, by 22 feet, by 7 feet 8 inches, by 5 feet, but waterline length and draft increased after considerable ballast was added.

The fame of the Birds centers around their heavy-weather ability, which has become almost legendary. There is a plethora of tales about these boats carrying full sail in gales while other craft were seeking shelter under greatly reduced canvas. In fact, the Birds originally had no means of reefing, and they normally carry no storm sails. In breezy San Francisco Bay, this class has been a target for new, powerful designs. According to *Yachting* magazine (February 1969), for example, the successful, modern, California sloop

Lively Lady II was designed by Gary Mull to "beat a Bird to weather in a San Francisco Bay summer breeze." Whether or not she actually tangled with the Birds is not known, but she was fast enough to win many heavy-air contests, including the 1969 Miami-Nassau Race.

Since a Bird is not very beamy, one might wonder what gives her such sail-carrying power. Of course, the low-aspect-ratio rig with tiny headsail keeps the center of effort low, and she has plenty of bearing aft. But perhaps her most significant attribute is a ballast-displacement ratio of over 50 percent. At the same time, her modest beam, low-windage hull, and sharp entrance allow her to cut through a chop in a sometimes wet but always effective manner. The keel is quite thin and short

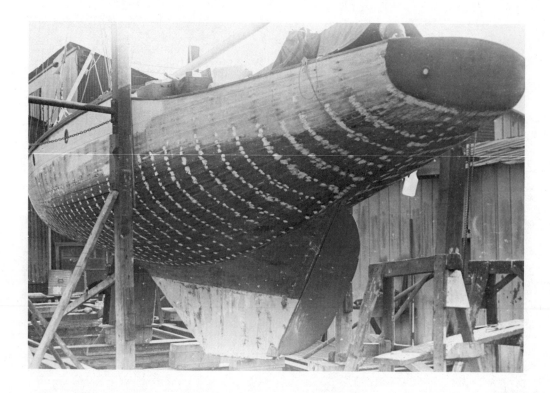

Above: *Howard Benedict's Bird* Mavis *undergoing a major refastening in 1969 at Oakland, Califor-nia. (Christopher Benedict photo)* **Below:** *A close-up 1972 photograph of* Curlew, *said to be the oldest surviving Bird, shows her wide jib traveler and the flattening reef eyelets for her mainsail. (Howard Benedict photo)*

to minimize head resistance and wetted surface, while the rudder is well raked, which enhances its effectiveness when the boat is heeled.

With 408 square feet of sail area in her short, jib-headed rig, the Bird has a long main boom, which necessitates running backstays. Still, the rig is quite easy to handle, since only one small jib is carried regardless of wind strength, and it is self-tending. The sail plan shows a spinnaker that is small and not powerful enough to severely bury the boat's fine bow. The forestay is attached to the stem fitting with a pelican hook, and it must be removed and carried back to the mast when the spinnaker is set. One must remember to set up the forestay again before rounding the leeward mark! There are no jumpers. Tall marconi rigs have been tried on the Birds, yet performance seems better, on San Francisco Bay at least, with the original rig.

Skylark in Mave Island Straits, Vallejo, California, in 1936. The lamp board indicates that she did some night sailing. (Courtney Benedict photo. Courtesy Howard Benedict)

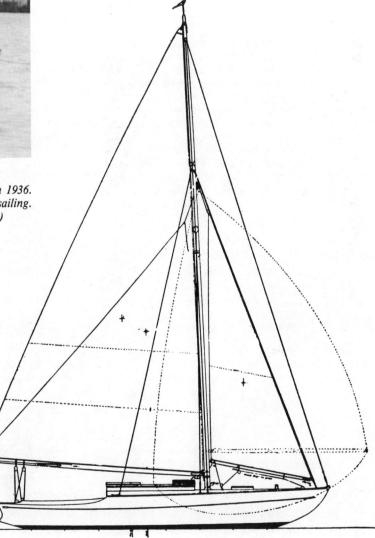

The 1931 Southern California Bird class, design number 516, has a taller rig and 70 square feet more sail area than the original Bird. (Yachting, July 1931)

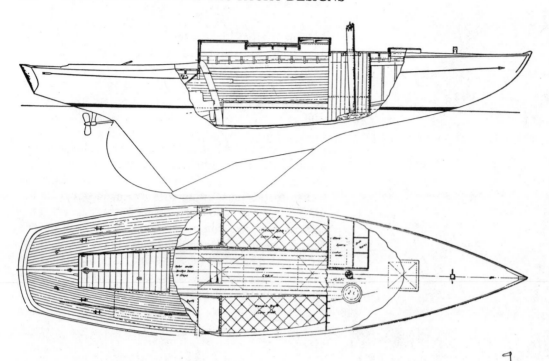

Above: *The inboard profile and accommodations plans of the Southern California Bird show her auxiliary engine and low cabin trunk. Accommodations have been improved by adding quarter berths and by moving the head forward and providing a privacy curtain.* (Yachting, *July 1931*) **Right:** *Designed in 1933, the 37-foot version of the Bird has a moderately long keel and wheel steering. She carries 625 square feet of sail. It was written in* Yachting *that she has "an ingenious arrangement of the runners, which makes it unnecessary to slack off the leeward runner when turning to windward."* (Yachting, *February 1933)*

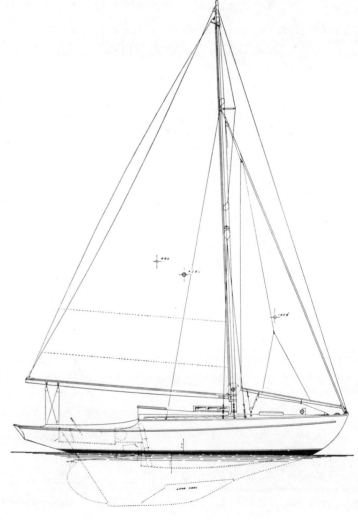

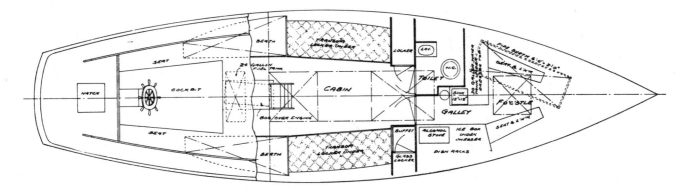

The accommodations plan of the enlarged Bird shows a spacious main cabin (with six-foot headroom), a forward galley, an enclosed head, and a fo'c's'le with pipe berth. (Yachting, February 1933)

Accommodations are minimal, and most often the cabin is used as a shelter and stowage area. Nevertheless, there are two bunks, a head alongside the companionway, and space for a stove. The raised deck improves sitting headroom below, but, more important, it raises the freeboard amidships, keeping the rail out of water at moderate angles of heel. A good feature is the coaming inboard of the rail, which provides not only a backrest but also a partial deterrent to water slopping into the cockpit well during a knockdown.

Two variations of the Birds were designed by Alden in the early 1930s, the first being a similar-size, "improved" one-design for the Los Angeles Yacht Club. This boat had an engine, two quarter berths, and a forward head with a curtain. She also had a taller rig and

about 465 square feet of sail area to cope with the lighter winds of Southern California. The second design based on the Birds is a 37-foot version designed for a San Francisco yachtsman. Her below-decks arrangement is similar to the Los Angeles model, except that the forward head is enclosed and there is a small galley opposite, as well as a fo'c's'le with a pipe berth. She has a moderate-aspect-ratio rig with a relatively larger percentage of the sail area in her jib.

The original Birds are now in danger of dying out, because they are not being replaced, but there were still 23 of these boats afloat in 1978. They are still admired, and they remain the standard for comparison whenever there is talk of sailing in a strong breeze.

ALDEN O BOATS

In terms of number of boats built, the most popular Alden one-design is the O class. Originally designed in 1921 for a group of yachtsmen at Marblehead, Massachusetts, the O boats were intended primarily as trainers for teenage sailors. Two other requirements, though, were that the boats could be built for a reasonable price (completely outfitted, they could be purchased for about $650) and that they be comfortable and safe enough for the parents of the teenagers to use, even in partly exposed waters. Curiously, the design is

numbered 188 in the Alden office index, but the original concept, referred to as the "Marblehead One-Design," was numbered 169.

Actually, there are two variations of the O boat: version number one, intended for moderate-weather localities, and number two, for use in areas with heavier winds. The former measures 18 feet 3 inches, by 15 feet 6 inches, by 6 feet 2 inches, and carries 450 pounds of inside ballast, while the other variation measures 18 feet 1 inch, by 15 feet 5 inches, by 6 feet 8 inches, and carries

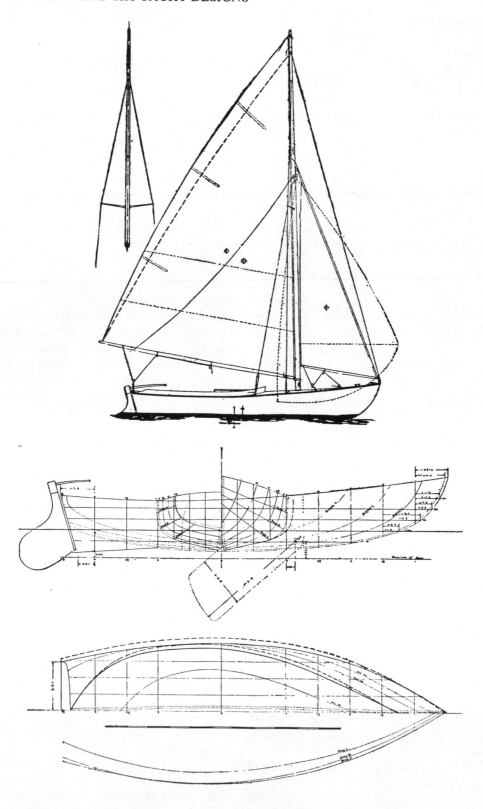

*In the sail plan of the Alden O boat, the dashed line running up the leech denotes the smaller main for heavy-wind localities. The attachment of the shrouds well below the top of the mast allows the use of short spreaders. The dashed lines in the lines drawing show the greater beam of the heavy-air model. (*Sailing Craft *edited by Edwin J. Schoettle)*

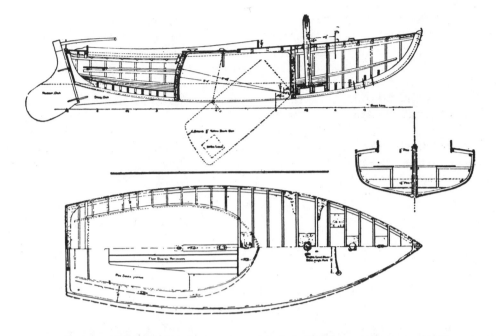

The construction plans are those of a solidly built little boat. Note her watertight compartment forward, the lead ballast on her centerboard, and her considerable deck space. (Sailing Craft, edited by Edwin J. Schoettle)

An O boat close-hauled and well heeled in a good breeze. The side decks are wide enough to sit on comfortably when the wind is fresh, and you can put your feet on the seats. (Courtesy John G. Alden, Inc.)

550 pounds of ballast. Version number one carries slightly more sail area than number two (200 square feet vs. 192 square feet), but at several yacht clubs the number two hull was fitted with number one's rig to make it a bit more lively.

The O boat is a centerboarder, because the type was slightly cheaper to build, easier to haul out and transport, and more usable in shallow-water areas. The number one version draws 11 inches with the board up, while the other is only a half inch deeper. For safety and comfort, the boat was given plenty of freeboard, a deep cockpit with coamings, and a watertight bulkhead forward, which prevents the ballast from sinking her in the event of a capsize. The sections are firm, and a pronounced sheer with high bow helps keep the boat dry.

The fractional sloop rig is basically the so-called three-stay type with a single pair of shrouds set slightly abaft the mast. This arrangement obviates the need for backstays except in a fresh breeze, and it allows the runners to lead quite far forward so that the boom will not be impeded by the leeward runner until it is almost broad off. The small jib is boomed and self-tending. A spinnaker and a genoa jib can be carried in light airs.

These boats were long ago abandoned as junior trainers at Marblehead, but they were successful in their day. In his youth, Richard Thayer of Marblehead trained in an O boat and went on to win the first Sears Cup championship in the early 1920s. Other young sailors graduated into the R and Q classes. The Marblehead fleet was about 30-strong in the latter part of the decade, and in 1927, Dwight Simpson wrote, "It is not a rare thing to find them with their young owners on a cruise, snug in some harbor with a tent over the boom . . . . And so far, with all this fleet, club racing, inter-club racing, and cruising through six seasons, we have heard of no casualties."

Then a minor disaster struck, when a fierce and sudden squall ripped through a Fourth of July regatta. Most of the fleet had rounded the windward mark and were running off before it, and all these boats capsized.

Because their watertight bulkheads had been removed, several boats sank under the weight of their ballast. All the crews were rescued, but Marblehead sailors feel that the resultant unfortunate and perhaps undeserved blot on the O boat's reputation for seaworthiness was responsible for the local decline of the fleet in the early 1930s.

Although O boats were sailed mostly in New England waters, they have been used (sometimes in a modified form) in other regions from Nova Scotia to Hawaii. It has been estimated that nearly 600 of these handy little sloops were built.

THE PEQUOT–BLACK ROCK ONE-DESIGN

In 1926, Alden designed a slightly larger variation of the O boat for use in California. This design became known as the Sun Class, and a keel development of the Sun, Number 293, was produced for the Pequot and Black

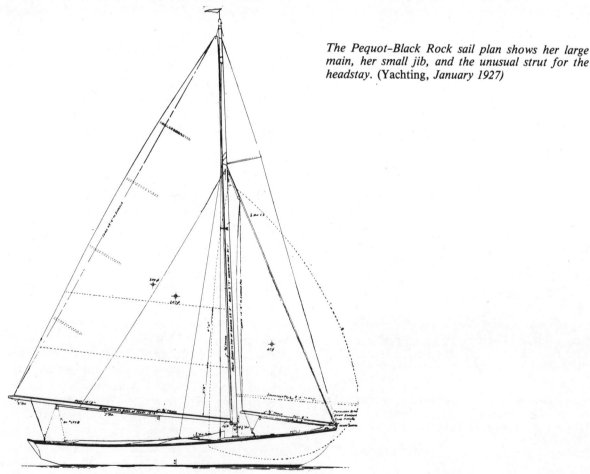

The Pequot–Black Rock sail plan shows her large main, her small jib, and the unusual strut for the headstay. (Yachting, January 1927)

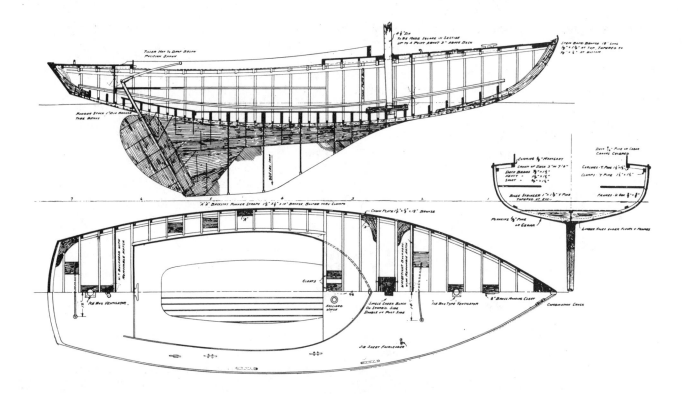

The deep fin keel carries 885 pounds of iron, which, along with the big rudder, exerts enough strain to give the keel bolts and floors plenty of work. (Yachting, *January 1927*)

This photo of a Pequot–Black Rock One-Design may have been taken soon after the boat went about, for the jib is not trimmed in. (Courtesy John G. Alden, Inc.)

Rock Yacht Clubs on Long Island Sound. The 293s were dubbed the Indian Class by their owners. However, coincidentally or not, several other Alden one-designs were also known locally as Indians, so it seems less confusing to refer to the 293 keel class as the Pequot–Black Rock Indians. The dimensions are 22 feet, by 16 feet 8 inches, by 6 feet 10½ inches, by 3 feet 10 inches.

Unlike O boats, the Pequot–Black Rocks have short counter sterns and curving, well-raked transoms in the manner of a larger yacht. Also, they have inboard rudders attached to their keels. With their ample beam and 885 pounds of keel ballast, the boats are bound to be stiff. They have generous freeboard and sheer; large, open cockpits with comfortable seats; and watertight bulkheads forward and aft.

The fractional sloop rig with 247 square feet of sail area is quite similar to an O boat's sail plan. An interesting and different feature is the long strut for the headstay. It increases the angle between the mast and stay very little, so its main purpose must be to counteract the pull of the jibstay. The tiny jib is self-tending; the curved traveler on the foredeck is a rather sophisticated feature shared by many small Alden boats. Four battens help control the leech of the mainsail, which has generous roach. The Pequot–Black Rock

Indian can probably sail reasonably well under her mainsail alone, since it has an area of 200 square feet, and the boat's keel is far enough aft to provide fairly good balance when the jib is lowered.

Despite their bulkheads, the Pequot–Black Rock Indians gained an unenviable reputation for sinking if they swamped. Possibly the bulkheads provided insufficient flotation. Possibly, as in the O boats, the bulkheads were removed or their watertight integrity was compromised. In any case, the Indian Class was discontinued at both the Pequot and Black Rock Yacht Clubs after four to six years.

THE NANTUCKET ONE-DESIGN
(INDIANS)

An Alden centerboard knockabout with an interesting underwater configuration is the Nantucket One-Design, Number 398. Designed for use not only on Nantucket Sound but also at Kennebunkport, Maine, Number 398 was a development of the earlier Number 135, called the Jamestown Class, and Number 148, the first Indian class. Indeed, the Nantucket boats were also called Indians. Number 148, in turn, was a refinement of the round-bottomed dory type of daysailer. The Nantucket One-Design was conceived by Buell P. Mills and other

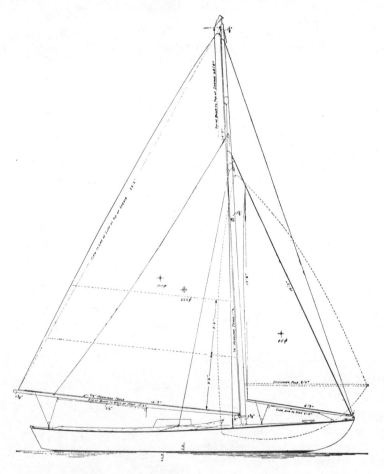

The original rig of the Nantucket One-Design was handy but for the running backstays, which, with their wire bridles, were difficult to operate. (Yachting, *January 1929*)

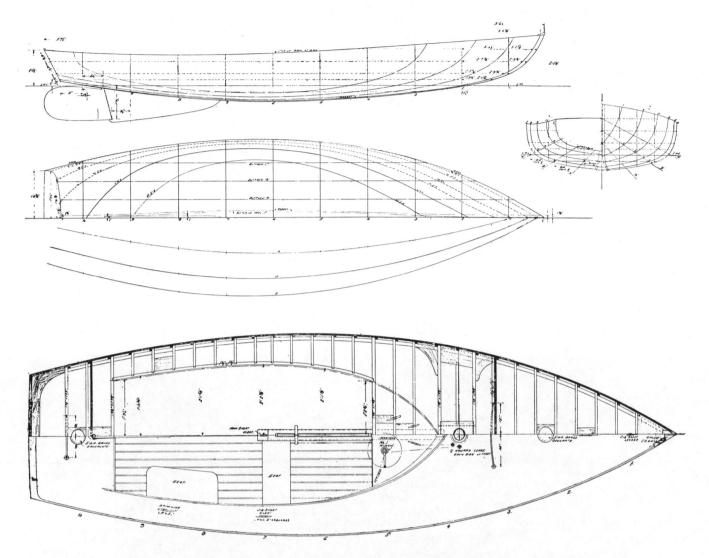

The Nantucket One-Design has unusually well-balanced lines for a boat with a skimming-dish hull. Her deck-and-cockpit plan shows an after seat that was later removed. For the first time in this chapter we see a winch with the deck hardware. (Yachting, *January 1929*)

members of the Nantucket Yacht Club. Mills, who was then rear commodore of the club, presented Alden with the basic requirements, and between them they worked out the specifications. Most of the boats were built by George L. Chaisson of Swampscott, Massachusetts, between 1929 and 1931. The boat measures 21 feet 2 inches, by 16 feet 2 inches, by 6 feet 5 inches, by 18 inches.

Atlantic City catboats and a few others notwithstanding, it seems somewhat strange to have an inboard rudder on such a shallow hull, which hasn't even the suggestion of a keel. Were it not for the rudder and skeg, the Nantucket One-Design could float on a dew drop, for her bottom is almost flat. The after appendages

seem to defeat the advantage of the extremely shallow hull, yet the Nantucket's rudder is not very deep, it won't easily ventilate at normal angles of heel, and it is better protected than an outboard type extending below the skeg, such as those seen on the O boats. Given her flat bottom, one might expect the Nantucket boat to do some pounding in a chop, but the round bilges and the moderately fine entrance should alleviate her slamming. Of course the boat is capsizable, but she has good form stability and carries 400 pounds of lead ballast inside. Watertight compartments make her unsinkable. The cockpit has a rather unusual seating arrangement for this size of boat, employing a midship thwart in conjunction with short fore-and-aft seats that can comfort-

A nice lee-bow view of a Nantucket Indian. (John McCalley photo. Courtesy Allen P. Mills)

ably accommodate only one person per side. Allen P. Mills, son of Buell Mills, tells me that the after seats were in the way and were soon removed. The thwart was retained as designed, however, partly because it braces the centerboard trunk.

The jibheaded sloop rig carries 222 square feet of sail area, and despite the running backstays, it is easy to handle with the small self-tending jib. The mast has a fair amount of rake, and this makes the mainsail hang well in light airs. It also moves the center of effort aft to

counteract any lee helm caused by the prominent skeg. The backstay runners, which consist merely of wires secured to the deck, were rather awkwardly arranged. The wire runners are still used, but the original system has been improved with the installation of modern fairleads and jam cleats for the lines that pull the stays forward and aft. The upper shrouds are quite far down from the masthead, thereby providing large shroud angles without the need for long spreaders.

When built, these knockabouts could be delivered at a

cost of less than $750. They proved quite popular, as evidenced by the fact that 22 boats were built for the Nantucket area alone. There are just four or five of these boats sailing today, two of them still in the hands of the original owners. It is unfortunate that the class has died out, for Allen Mills wrote: "The boats were very evenly matched and produced some wildly exciting racing all through the years."

THE Q BOAT HOPE

John Alden designed only five Q boats, but he was most interested in the class, and two of his five Qs, *Hope* and *Tartar,* were designed for his own use. *Hope,* the boat shown here, is design number 400. She was built by Hodgdon Brothers in East Boothbay, Maine, in 1929. Her dimensions are 50 feet 3 inches, by 31 feet 3 inches, by 8 feet 5 inches, by 7 feet.

The Universal Rule, to which the Q boats were de-

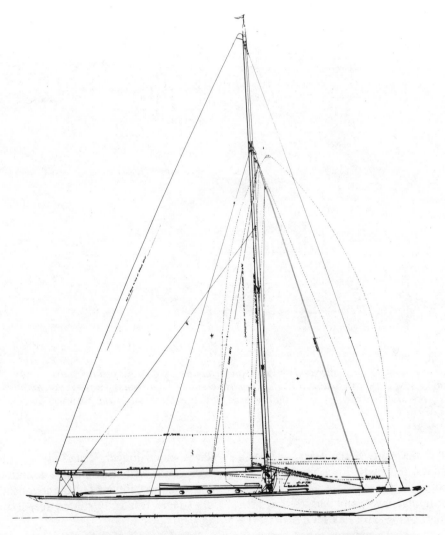

Hope *sports a sail plan with a large main and a club-footed jib of high aspect ratio. (Courtesy John G. Alden, Inc.)*

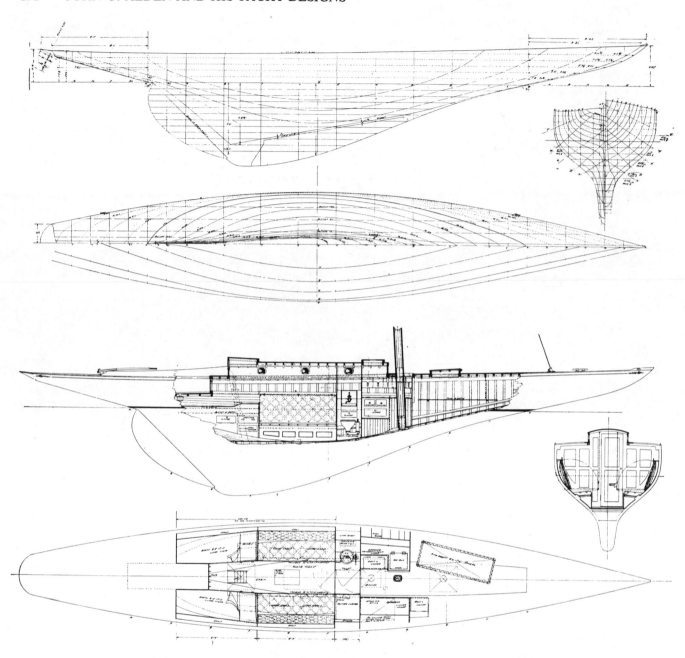

The lines of Hope *show her very slack bilge and almost U-shaped bow sections. According to one theory, the triangular profile is the best compromise between windward ability, maneuverability, and course keeping. Accommodations are not far from amidships, so the motion experienced by the sleepers and even the cook in the forward galley should not be bad.* (Yachting, *January 1930*)

signed, was slightly modified over the years, and, as a result of these changes, together with a gradual evolution of design theory, Qs (or "25-raters") of the late 1920s grew longer and narrower, and had less sail area than the original boats of the early 1900s. Of course, the newer boats also adopted the marconi rig. Compared with the Alden Q *Shirley, Hope* is slightly narrower, yet

she is much longer, especially on the waterline. Her high-aspect-ratio rig features a club-footed jib and a jibstay set well inboard of the stemhead. Her sail area of 893 square feet is 37 square feet less than that of the *Shirley.*

Hope's underwater profile is distinctively triangular, a configuration that has proved effective for outstand-

A lee-bow view of Hope *close-hauled and knifing to windward. The divergence of her course from that of the opposite-tack Q boat partly behind her jib shows how close-winded are these boats.* (Yachting, *January 1930)*

ing windward performance. Although it is widely recognized that high-aspect-ratio fin keels are most efficient for speed made good on light-displacement boats with canoe bodies, one school of thought contends that the triangular profile provides the most efficient shape for deep-bodied, heavy-displacement racers. It is probably true that *Hope*'s keel minimizes the energy-robbing, keel-tip vortex, and its short length, together with the boat's slack bilges, reduces the wetted surface. The bow sections and waterlines forward are fairly full, and the hull is quite symmetrical compared with *Shirley*'s. Thus, *Hope* should have a longer sailing length and perhaps better balance when heeled.

Despite her narrow beam, *Hope* has fairly comfortable accommodations. There is a long main cabin with two quarter berths and two folding berths, an enclosed head compartment, which can be extended across the boat with the use of doors, and a galley and pipe berth forward. The fold-up berths and the considerable fullness at the garboards give the boat a surprisingly wide cabin sole.

Although it took Alden about half a season to fine-tune *Hope,* he finally got her going, and she proved a very successful contender in the highly competitive Q class. She had a reputation in Marblehead as a heavy-weather boat, making her best showings under such conditions. In the late 1920s and early 1930s there were usually anywhere from eight to 13 Q boats entered in Marblehead races. Like the R boats, the class then went into a decline, but a few continued to race in a combined class with the 8-meters right up to the start of World War II.

MILADY

Although the popularity of the catboat had begun to decline after the mid-1920s, these craft were still in demand near the end of the decade. John Alden's design commissions included several daysailing cats. The one presented here is an attractive boat named *Milady,* which was built in 1929 for E.R. Willard by Reuben Bigelow's yard at Monument Beach, Massachusetts. Her design number is 427, and she measures 20 feet, by 18 feet 6 inches, by 9 feet, by 1 foot 8 inches.

Some of the cats of that period and earlier were quite outlandish, with boxy hulls, huge sails, and long overhanging booms, but not so *Milady*. She is gracefully curved and has a moderate, easily managed rig. Like most catboats, the Alden design has a sharp entrance so that the broad beam can be eased through a chop, yet there is plenty of flam in the bow sections and a nice sheer for reserve buoyancy forward. The forefoot is deep enough to provide a respectable bury for the mast but not so deep as to cause steering problems.

The cockpit is wide and comfortable with seats following the thwartship curve of the coaming. The broad beam allows moderately wide side decks, which

Milady *has a sensible rig with a reachable boom end. Cheek blocks at the base of the mast accept halyards led back to the cockpit, so there is no need to go forward on the small deck when hoisting or lowering sail. Drawn by Aage Nielsen, Milady's lines show average deadrise for the type, but in contrast to many of the old Cape Cod cats, the waterlines don't really sharpen forward until they close with the stem. There is no tumblehome even at the transom. (Courtesy John G. Alden, Inc.)*

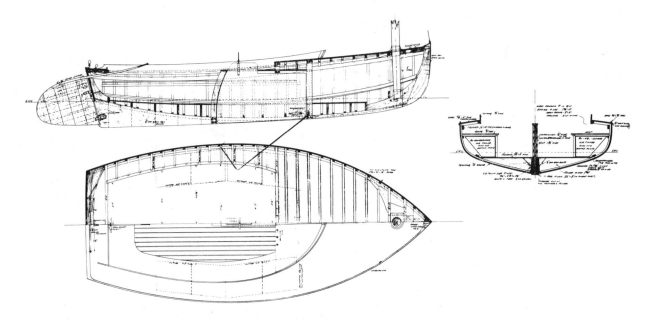

Milady has two 20-ounce-copper air tanks under either cockpit seat, so the thwartships bulkhead at the forward end of the centerboard trunk need not be watertight. Her centerboard trunk is open but high. (Courtesy John G. Alden, Inc.)

not only are convenient to step on but also offer safety by keeping water out of the cockpit when the boat is heeled in rough water. The centerboard supplies the lateral resistance needed for such a shoal-draft hull, and the board's trunk affords a foot brace for crew sitting amidships. The rudder is shapely, though if it were higher, the tiller could pass under a traveler rather than through a slot in the transom.

Milady's sail area of 298 square feet seems adequate for reasonable speed in light airs, yet not large enough to cause control problems in a breeze. Furthermore, there are three sets of reef points with which to shorten sail for any reasonable strength of wind. Some of the old catboats with long overhanging booms had to be brought alongside another boat or a dock to enable one

to reach the end of the boom when reefing, but this would not have to be done with *Milady*. On any cat, of course, having reefing gear always rigged would be a tremendous convenience. The rake in *Milady*'s mast obviates the need for setting the shrouds farther aft and elevates the end of the low boom when it is broad off. The forestay makes a very small angle with the mast, and it might be desirable to add a strut to alleviate compression.

Catboats have certain advantages with their roominess and simplicity, and in recent years they have been enjoying a revival. Modern catboat enthusiasts would do well to take a careful look at *Milady,* for she seems an eminently sensible design.

THE BERMUDA ONE-DESIGN

An unusually able and handsome knockabout from the Alden firm is Number 447, the Bermuda One-Design. The first boat of this class, named *Eleventh Hour,* was built in Bermuda in 1930 for Philip B. Smith. Her dimensions are 22 feet 4 inches, by 18 feet 3 inches, by 6 feet 9 inches, by 3 feet 6 inches.

With her long, salient keel; sweeping sheer; high, spoon bow; raked transom; and deep, outboard rudder

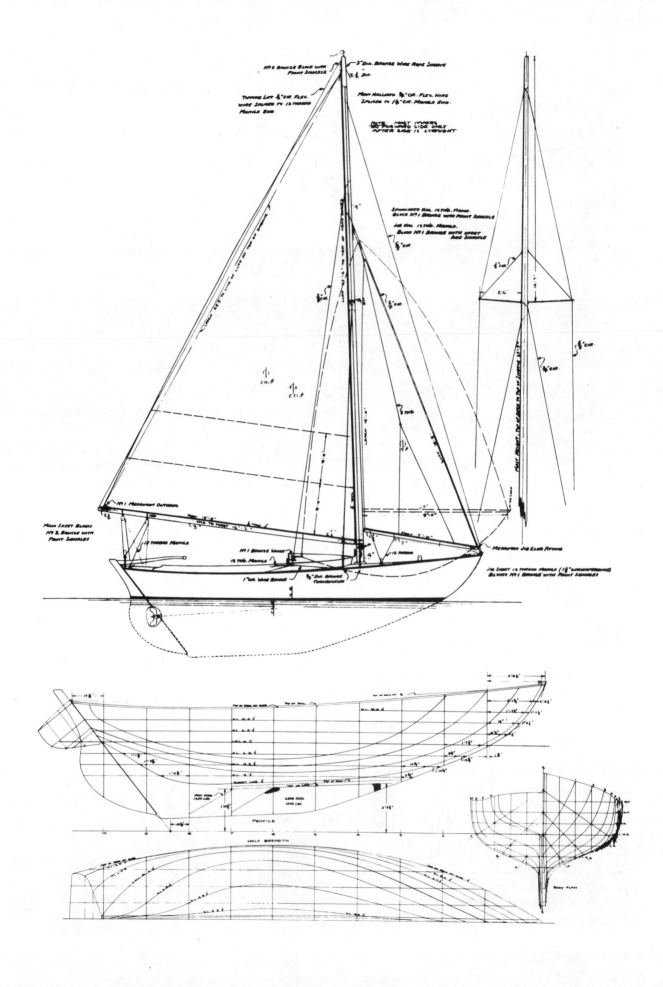

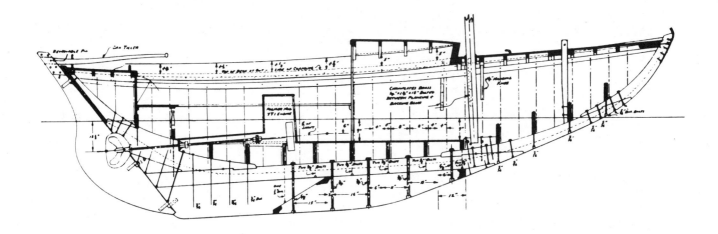

Opposite and above:

In Eleventh Hour*'s sail plan, after shrouds counteract the load on the forestay, but the backstays are necessary to keep the luff of the jib from sagging off in windward work. Her lines show a powerful, seagoing hull, but with a sharp bow to cut through a chop. Her inboard auxiliary, shown in the construction profile above, is a 2 h.p. Model YT 1 Palmer. (Courtesy John G. Alden, Inc.)*

having an aperture for a propeller, *Eleventh Hour*'s hull is similar to a scaled-down model of a larger, offshore cruiser. The knockabout's lines, drawn by Fenwick C. Williams, show a sharp entrance and full waterlines aft. Powerful quarters, flam in the forward sections, and the keel ballast ensure ample sail-carrying power. A choice is offered in the ballast, either 1,250 pounds of iron or 1,400 pounds of lead. It is amazing to see on the lines drawing how much larger the iron keel must be to provide less weight. The great difference in size is due partly to the fact that the keel is uniformly thin on both models.

The cockpit doesn't seem to be self-bailing, but it appears deep and comfortable, with full-length seats on each side. A cuddy helps keep solid water out of the cockpit and offers some shelter for the crew in bad weather. The inboard auxiliary, a 2 h.p. Palmer, is a convenient feature in this small open boat.

The fractional sloop rig supports 271 square feet of sail area, and it seems appropriate that *Eleventh Hour* should have a Bermudian (jibheaded) mainsail. As on the Nantucket Indians, wire bridles on the side decks accept the running backstays. Even though the mainsail is large and the jib is small, the latter is fitted with lazyjacks, while the former is not. This makes some sense, however, because the main can be handed fairly easily from the cockpit. Lazyjacks are effective on a boomed jib and they are a good feature for singlehanding, simplifying lowering sail when docking, mooring, or shortening down in a blow. An interesting note on the sail plan is the prominent instruction not to taper the after side of the mast. Perhaps the Alden firm had an unfortunate experience with a sparmaker who didn't understand the basic principles of fitting a sail to a marconi mast.

Eleventh Hour was still sailing in Bermuda in 1983.

∽

A FROSTBITE DINGHY

The "official" date accepted as the beginning of frostbite dinghy racing is January 2, 1932 (not New Year's Day, as is often proclaimed). It didn't take John Alden long to become involved with the sport, for that same year he started designing frostbiters, and the following year many of his dinghies were sailing the frigid courses on Long Island Sound. His boats were owned by some well-known sailors, such as Sam

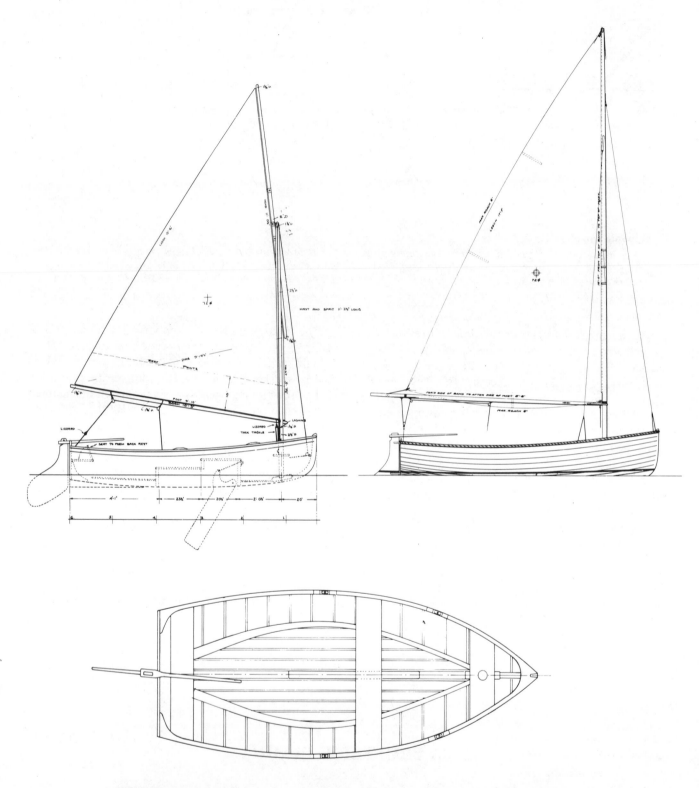

The Class A dinghy (left) *has a short mast and a yard, and the mainsail's foot is attached to* the boom. The Class X one-design (right) *has a two-piece pole mast and a loose-footed sail, which allows greater variation in camber. The Class A dinghy's breadth plan gives some indication of her sectional shape by the shape of the floor boards. She has well-rounded quarters without the fullness found in some planing dinghies. (Courtesy John G. Alden, Inc.)*

X dinghies in action. It appears that the foreground boat would be wise to tack immediately. (Morris Rosenfeld photo)

Wetherill, Drake Sparkman, and Hank Meneely. Alden even designed a boat for his own use, which he called *North Pole*.

The dinghy shown here is design number 559, a class A utility frostbiter. She was designed in 1933 for Alfred L. Loomis, Jr., who named her *Burp*. Her measurements are 11 feet 5½ inches, by 4 feet 9½ inches, by 19 inches.

Burp's plans, drawn by Clifford P. Swaine, show a roomy boat with slightly more beam than the average Alden boat of this type. Although the body plan is not shown, it appears that the sides have considerable flam. A high-aspect-ratio centerboard suggests efficiency to windward, and its short fore-and-aft length, together with the small skeg size, must allow the boat to "turn on a dime." The rudder appears to be effective, and its swept-back bottom allows it to lift rather than break or otherwise be damaged during a hard grounding. The boat can be rowed from two positions, making her ideal for use as a yacht tender. One desirable feature is the backrest that folds up from the after thwart.

Like other class A dinghies, *Burp* carries 72 square feet of sail area. Her rig appears to be a sliding gunter type, but there are no jaws for the yard or boom. A lizard and tackle hold the boom down and keep it reasonably stationary. A set of reef points is provided, not a bad idea for winter weather when the wind has extra weight and the waters are cold enough to cause rapid hypothermia in the event of a capsize.

On the subject of Alden dinghies, the Alden firm also developed a class X one-design from the class A utility dinghy, and the Fairfield Boat Works in Greenwich, Connecticut, owned by George Lauder, built 109 of these before World War II. The X has higher freeboard than the class A dinghies, with a modified centerboard and a more efficient rig. X dinghies competed with great success in class A events. Clinker built of white cedar, they could be purchased, with rig, for $325.

John Alden never did as well racing dinghies as he did with his large schooners. Dinghies didn't offer him the same opportunities for multi-slot sail trimming or for strategy based on a general weather system. Maybe Alden was too big to be really agile in a small boat, or perhaps he was just too cold. In one light-air race, a competitor accused him of sculling, but Alden replied, "I wasn't sculling; I was just shivering."

THE SAKONNET ONE-DESIGN

Alden probably got greater enjoyment from sailing his knockabouts than his dinghies, the former being considerably more able and comfortable. The Sakonnet One-Design was a particularly able knockabout, and Alden owned two boats of this class, one during his late sailing years. He designed this boat for the Sakonnet Yacht Club, where he learned to sail as a young boy. The class started as design number 662 in 1937. The

Alden records do not indicate that any boats were built to this design, but some longtime Little Compton (Rhode Island) residents believe that several were indeed built by the Herreshoff yard in Bristol, Rhode Island. If this is the case, many or most of the boats in this original fleet were destroyed by the hurricane of 1938, along with most of the rest of the small boats at Sakonnet. Alden then produced design number 694, to which

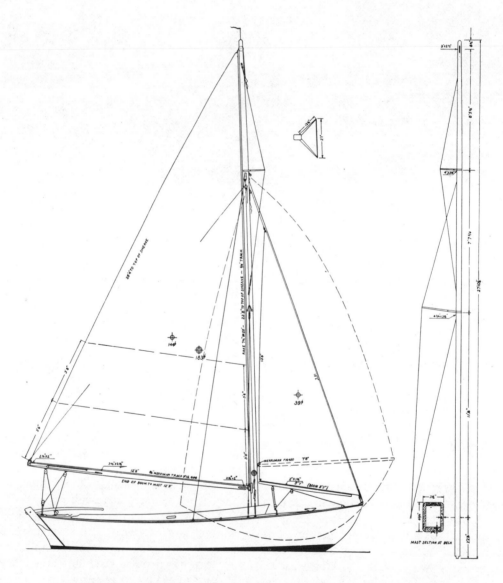

The Sakonnet One-Design has a tiny jib of only 39 square feet. After considerable experience sailing these boats, Alden came to believe that the foretriangle should be enlarged for the light airs frequently encountered around Sakonnet in the summer. (Yachting, May 1939)

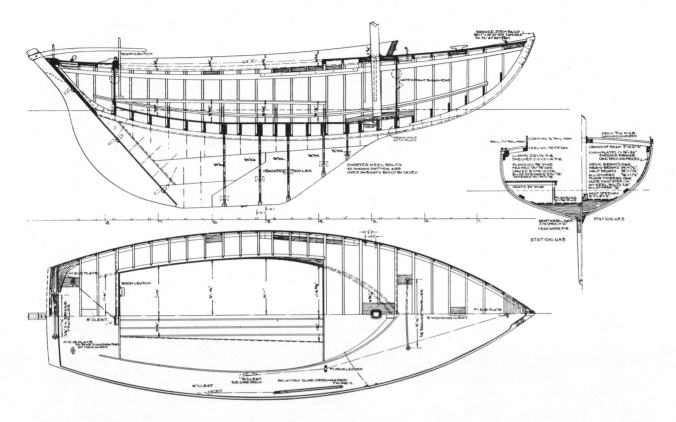

The Sakonnet One-Design's original construction plans. The profile shows the head locations of the alternate, shorter keel bolts used by the Casey yard. The half-section at station 5 shows a pretty tumblehome. (Yachting, May 1939)

the present-day Sakonnet One-Designs were built. The Casey Boatbuilding Company in Fairhaven, Massachusetts, built 10 of these in 1939. The dimensions are 18 feet 4 inches, by 14 feet 5 inches, by 6 feet 3 inches, by 3 feet 7 inches.

Though similar to the previously discussed Bermuda One-Design, the Sakonnet has a shorter but deeper keel. Both boats — with their heavy displacement, high freeboard, and modest sail area (for their weight) — trade off some speed for seaworthiness. The Sakonnet's forefoot is a little more cut away compared with the Bermuda boat, and, with her deep, outboard rudder unpunctured by a propeller aperture, the Sakonnet is undoubtedly more responsive to her helm. She doesn't have a cuddy, but the cockpit is deep and well protected with high coamings. The springy sheer and high topsides help keep water off the decks. Seven hundred pounds of keel ballast prevent capsizing, while watertight bulkheads forward and aft were meant to keep the boat from sinking if she should swamp.

The rigs of the Bermuda and Sakonnet classes are quite alike, both being fractional sloops. Number 694 was designed with a hollow, square-sectioned mast, but

for some reason the boats were fitted with solid masts, although the standing rigging was as designed. The backstays ran on tracks on the side decks, an arrangement that proved cumbersome and was modified in later boats. The sail area is 183 square feet, only 39 square feet of it in the self-tending jib.

John Alden took the last boat, Number 10, from the original Casey batch, and raced her through the 1939 season with success. An oft-repeated story concerning John's racing prowess appears to date back to this time. As the story goes, John was winning so many races that some of his competitors began to grumble, mostly in jest, that he had a "custom job." He put an end to this scuttlebutt by exchanging boats for the balance of the season with a skipper who'd been placing poorly. John went right on winning. When the season was over, Alden sold his boat in order to strengthen the class, and he then gave sailing lessons to the new owner and his daughter, now Elizabeth Dawson. Mrs. Dawson remembers that Alden taught them to sense boat speed by watching the form of the wake as it left the lee quarter.

The Dawson boat is the only one of the original Casey batch still in existence, having ridden out two hurricanes on the harbor bottom (her watertight bulkheads notwithstanding) and a third, Hurricane Carol, at her mooring. Meanwhile, the Palmer Scott yard built at least a half dozen new 694s for the Sakonnet fleet in 1947, and in 1948-49 Harry Towne built another three boats for the fleet at his Tiverton, Rhode Island, yard. Towne's boats were cedar planked (Mrs. Dawson's boat has mahogany planking) and had lighter scantlings than the original Casey boats, and the backstays were either permanently fixed or adjustable by levers. Alden bought one of Towne's boats, number 20, named her *Java* (an acronym developed from his name and that of his wife, Virginia), and sailed and raced her actively for several years. She was his last boat.

In 1954, Hurricane Carol decimated the Sakonnet fleet, leaving only two One-Designs intact. Harry Towne, who lost his Tiverton yard in the hurricane, bought the old Herreshoff yard and built 10 new Sakonnet One-Designs in the winter of 1954-55. Nine of those are still sailing. According to Noel Field, who has been active in the class, Towne returned to mahogany planking for these boats but decided against increasing the scantlings accordingly. When the planks swelled, they split the ribs at the turn of the bilge, and all the boats had to be sister-framed.

When the final boats were built, Alden apparently suggested a couple of possible rig changes, one of which was to step the mast farther aft, enabling a genoa jib to be carried in light air. However, even though the previous boats had been lost in Hurricane Carol, the sails, many of them new, had survived, and all suggested rig changes were vetoed.

Eight of the boats race actively today, with a possibility of one or two more in the future. Affectionately known as "Aldens," they are built for the

John Alden at the helm of his Java *as she "busts" into a wave. (Courtesy Chester M. and Harriet Sawtelle)*

wind and chop of their home waters, being heavy, stable, and admirably well balanced. The Towne boats have no watertight bulkheads; if they swamp, they sink. However, that hasn't happened since 1963.

ᔕ

U.S. ONE-DESIGN

The U.S. One-Design, a late, well-known Alden class, is much closer to a pure racing machine than a comfortable daysailing knockabout. About 30 of these craft were built in 1946 and 1947 by the Quincy Adams Yacht Yard at Quincy, Massachusetts. Construction was first class, with mahogany planking, bronze fastenings, and lead keel ballast weighing 3,600 pounds. Hull dimensions are 37 feet 9 inches, by 24 feet, by 7 feet, by 5 feet 3 inches.

Carl Alberg designed the boat, Number 757 in the Alden records, doing much of it while temporarily away from the Alden firm during World War II. The lines plans show a symmetrical, splinterlike hull with well-balanced ends. The sloop's short keel, together with her

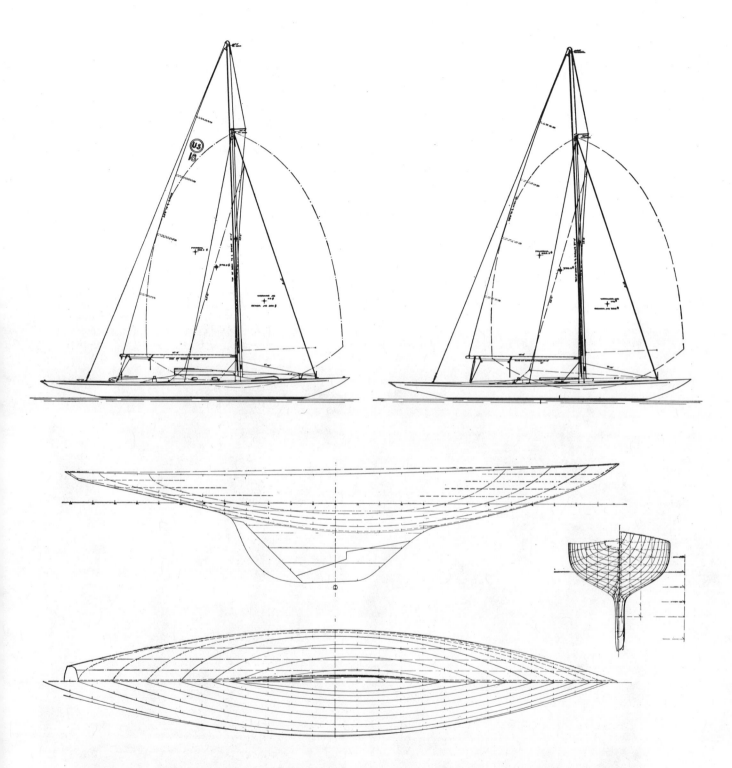

The sail plan of the U.S. One-Design is small but adequate. Note the spherically shaped parachute spinnaker, which has a larger girth than one designed for cruising-class racing. The lines show a hull that can be pushed through the water with a very minimum of effort, and one that will pick up sailing length at low angles of heel. (The Rudder, *February 1947*)

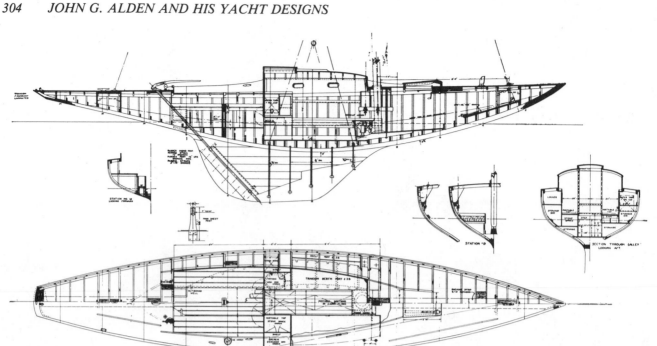

Construction plans of the U.S. One-Design (deckhouse model). An interesting feature is the jibstay adjustment system, which is operated below deck. (The Rudder, February 1947)

U.S. One-Designs showing off their beauty under sail. The main on U.S. number one is either a poorly cut sail, or it is receiving too much backwind from the genoa. (Courtesy John G. Alden, Inc.)

short load waterline, keep the wetted surface low, and, of course, the long overhangs increase her sailing length rapidly as she heels to a breeze. Except in the lightest airs, she ought to sail best at a substantial angle of heel. The rudder is as far forward as it could be and still provide good control on a heavy-air spinnaker run. The boat was available with or without a cabin trunk. The cabin model has two transom berths, a galley, and a head below, but even the trunkless model has a low cuddy with two sail-stowage shelves that can be used for bunks.

The sloop rig, with a sail area of 378.5 square feet, is small and well inboard. It is adequate for such an easily driven hull, especially when the genoa jib or parachute spinnaker is set. A headstay in lieu of the jumper stays would allow a larger genoa, although perhaps the thrust of the diamond struts is needed in addition to the pull of the runners to counteract the pull of the jibstay.

U.S. One-Designs were used mostly at Marblehead and Chicago, and they proved to be spirited performers for the most challenging kind of racing. There is still an active fleet at Marblehead, and Peter Dion, who owns one, writes without reservation that they are the prettiest boats in the harbor.

9

Powerboats and Motorsailers

Like many a true sailorman, John Alden felt that a sailing vessel was a lovely and responsive living creature with whom he could communicate when his hand was on the helm. Not so, however, with motorboats. They were inanimate, artificial objects driven by noisy, incomprehensible machinery. Nevertheless, he understood the hull behavior of most vessels, and he had associates who were competent, mechanical-minded engineers. Furthermore, he was a pragmatist and a businessman; thus he seldom turned down powerboat design commissions. The Alden firm produced some excellent and distinctive powerboats and motorsailers.

PIONEER

The first sizable motor yacht listed in the Alden records is a vessel similar in lines and general appearance to a miniature oceangoing tug. This boat, named *Pioneer,* is design number 37, and her plans were probably drawn in 1912. She measures 48 feet 6 inches, by 42 feet 3 inches, by 11 feet 6 inches, by 4 feet 4 inches. There is no record of her owner or builder.

Pioneer is an able, deep-bodied boat. She has a fine entrance, but there is considerable flare and high freeboard forward for dryness and reserve buoyancy. The full, overhanging fantail stern provides a reserve of buoyancy aft to help prevent squatting when that big gasoline engine is really throbbing. The long keel steadies her helm, yet reasonable steering response can be expected with the large propeller (appropriate for the slow-turning gasoline engines of the day) directly ahead of the balanced rudder.

The superstructure harmonizes with the hull and at

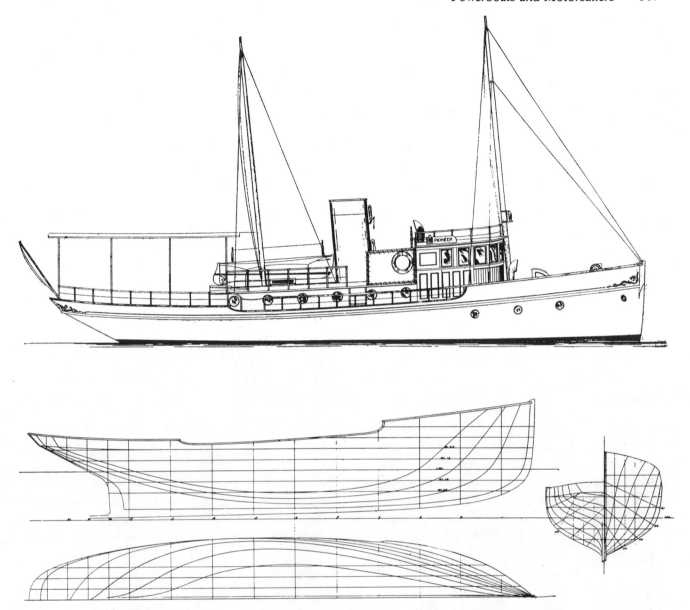

Pioneer is the kind of handsome vessel that many seamen would enjoy owning today. Her lines show distinctly her relationship to an oceangoing tug of that period. (Yachting, *January 1913*)

the same time offers a snug pilothouse, a well-elevated outside steering station on the bridge deck abaft the pilothouse, stowage space for a good-size tender, and a lounge deck aft with a cover for sun protection. Below decks, there is a saloon with two transoms aft, two staterooms, a galley and an enclosed head, the engine room under the pilothouse, and a fo'c's'le for a paid hand or two.

An article about this boat in the January 1913 issue of *Yachting* mentions the difficulty of reproducing a large vessel in greatly reduced form. One problem in *Pioneer*'s case is creating a pilothouse that is of practical

size yet is in scale with the rest of the boat. As the *Yachting* write-up put it, a full-size pilothouse would give the boat very much the appearance of "little Tommy masquerading in the 'gov'nor's' top hat." Alden solved this problem in a clever way by sinking the narrow sole of the pilothouse directly over the engine and gaining necessary headroom in the rest of the engine room under wide transoms on both sides of the pilothouse.

For a man who had little interest in powerboats, John Alden did a fine job with this early design. She was not designed to be a speed demon; rather, she has a seakind-

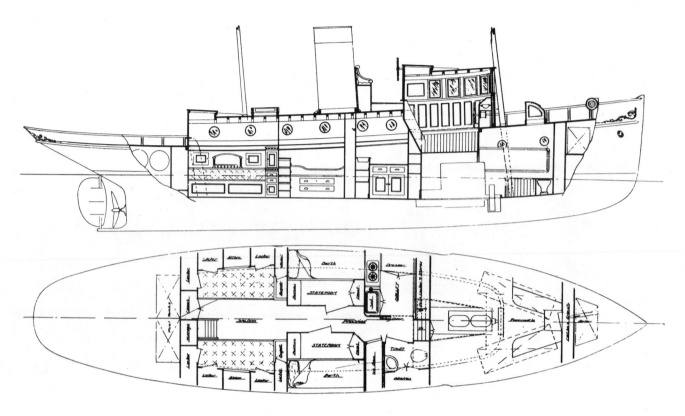

Pioneer's below-decks arrangement was designed with considerable emphasis on privacy. (Yachting, *January 1913*)

ly hull, and with more than four beams to her length, she should be easily driven at moderate speeds. She might occasionally get her decks wet from the low freeboard amidships, but canvas weather cloths on the side decks would help there. Altogether, she is a comfortable, able cruiser with plenty of character.

GROSBEAK

Perhaps a more typical early powerboat than *Pioneer* is the cabin runabout *Grosbeak,* Number 72 in the Alden records. Designed for Reginald C. Robbins of Boston for use at Northeast Harbor, Maine, *Grosbeak* was built to high standards in 1916 by Rice Brothers of East Boothbay, Maine. Her dimensions are 38 feet, by 37 feet 6 inches, by 8 feet 4 inches, by 2 feet 6 inches.

With her round bilges and fairly deep keel, which inhibits rolling, this boat has a seakindly hull. Her fine entrance lets her drive through a chop, while the flattish run aft allows her to climb onto a plane when pushed.

The semibalanced outboard rudder is well protected, and its extreme aft position helps it overcome the directional inertia of the very long keel.

The main cabin, with two transom berths and an enclosed head, is located aft, where the motion is minimal. There is a large, deep cockpit amidships, which, according to an article in *The Rudder* (October 1916), can hold "four armchairs." A removable canopy protects the cockpit. Although *Grosbeak* was intended primarily as a day boat, farther forward under a raised deck is another cabin, this one with a pipe berth, seats,

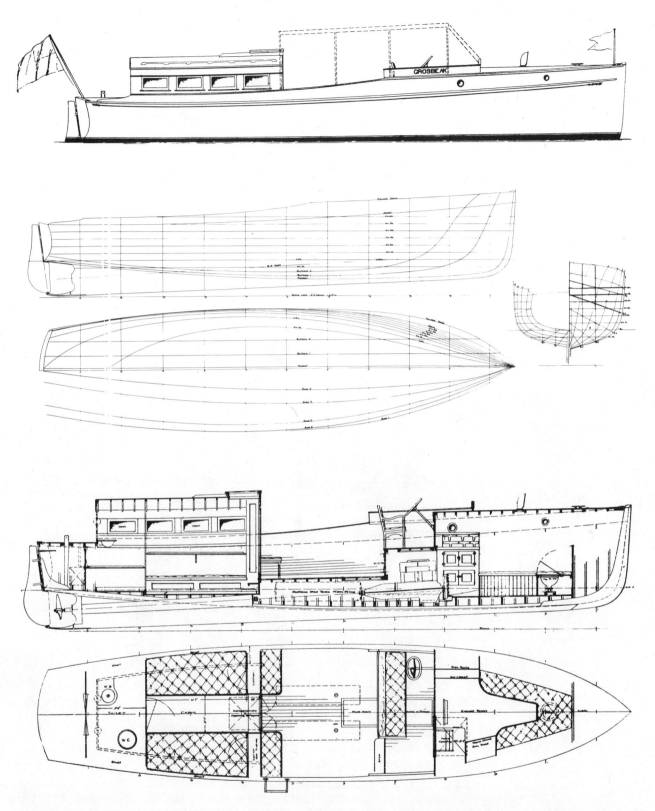

Grosbeak has an attractive profile. (The Rudder, October 1916) Despite her heavy displacement and round bilges, she could climb onto a plane given a powerful enough kick, and the way those after sections flatten toward the keel is one reason why. (Courtesy John G. Alden, Inc.) The galley is in the engine room, forward, along with some seats and a spare water closet. (The Rudder, October 1916)

and a small galley. The engine, a four-cylinder Van Blerck, is located under the raised helmsman's station at the forward end of the cockpit. It was Joe Van Blerck who designed the original engine for the Elco line of stock motorboats that first appeared in 1914. Alden may have lacked mechanical ability, but he was a shrewd judge of competence in any field.

Grosbeak is a powerboat of considerable displace-

ment, and her round bilges are not conducive to easy planing. However, she was clocked over a measured mile at Rockland, Maine, at 18½ m.p.h., a speed that came as a surprise to both the owner and the designer. With reasonable seakindliness and comfort, good fuel economy at low speeds, distinguished looks, and a pretty fair turn of speed, *Grosbeak* must have been a successful boat.

FAITH

In 1922, a large power cruiser named *Faith* was built to Alden's design number 114. This vessel may have been the first diesel-powered yacht. After a thorough study of power alternatives, the designer decided to install a newly developed, six-cylinder, 70 h.p. Mianus "heavy

oil" engine to give the heavy-displacement boat a speed of about 11 m.p.h., slightly less than her hull speed. *Faith*'s overall length is 77 feet 4 inches, and her beam and draft are 13 feet 8 inches and 6 feet, respectively. She was built by Charles Butson at Groton, Connec-

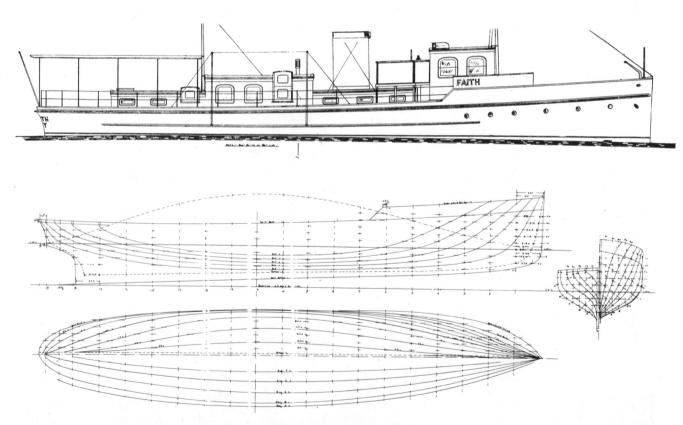

Faith has a low profile. With so little freeboard amidships, it is just as well the side companionways have sills that are well raised. (The Rudder, March 1921) Her bilges are slack for a powerboat. The interesting "destroyer" stern has little fullness down low, but its flare provides reserve buoyancy. (Courtesy John G. Alden, Inc.)

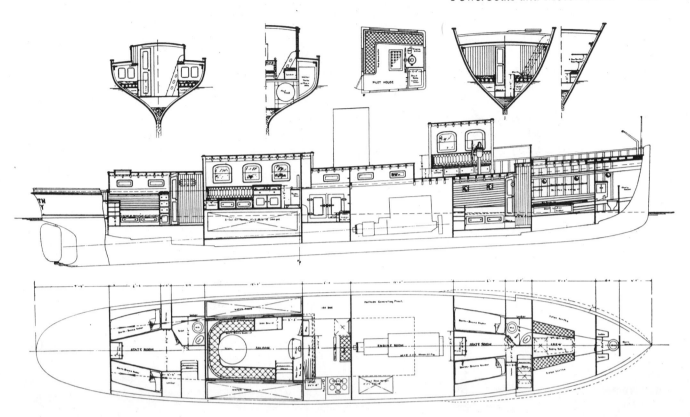

Above: *It is curious to see three companionways on the starboard side of* Faith *and none to port. Even the door to the pilothouse is on the starboard side. The inboard profile shows that her saloon is raised to provide a large space for tanks under the sole. Of course, raising the saloon also enhances the view through the windows. The sections show the companionway ladders and the way the slack bilges affect the accommodations.* (The Rudder, *March 1921*)

Left: *Were it not for the two people standing aft,* Faith *might be mistaken for a much larger vessel. (Courtesy Mrs. John Robinson)*

ticut, for Irving E. Raymond, a member of the New York Yacht Club.

Except for her stern, *Faith* has a hull shape that is similar to *Pioneer*'s. Both boats have plumb bows, fine entrances, deep hulls with considerable deadrise, and long keels. *Faith,* however, has a more symmetrical hull, while her stern is short and rounded. It was described in those times as a "modern destroyer stern." Even though there is almost no rake to any components

of the hull or superstructure (except for the break of the rail forward and the flagstaff aft), *Faith* has a sleek, racy look. This may be due to her low freeboard, narrow beam, and low, well-proportioned deckhouses and funnel.

Entrances to the accommodations are from the side decks. This arrangement is safe enough on a powerboat, but compared with companionways in the after ends of cabin trunks, side entrances are more subject to rain and spray. The cabin layout was planned largely by the owner. The owner's double stateroom and head are aft, with a raised saloon farther forward. This cabin has a large heating stove, a U-shaped settee, and, oddly enough, a round table that seems poorly matched to the settee. The galley is amidships at a lower level, while another stateroom, an enclosed head, and crew's quarters with head are up forward. The pilothouse has an L-shaped settee and a chart table in addition to the steering station. There is an outside helm just abaft the pilothouse.

Faith was no speed demon, but she must have afforded plenty of fun, comfort, and privacy. Eventually, she also proved practical as a utility workboat, for she was taken over and used extensively by the U.S. Army Engineers.

PANCHARA II

Panchara II, design number 249, is a noteworthy houseboat of the Roaring Twenties. Ruggedly built in 1925 by Britt Brothers at West Lynn, Massachusetts, she was first owned by Ledyard W. Sargent of the Sargent School (now a part of Boston University). Her keel is seven inches wide and nine inches deep at the forward end, thickening aft, and she has four-inch, sawn oak frames on two-foot centers, with double steam-bent frames between. The planking is 1¾-inch longleaf yellow pine, most of it in as good a condition in 1980 as when the boat was built. Although *Panchara II* is 52 feet 9 inches long overall, she has only one butt in each of her planks. Her other dimensions are 52 feet 1 inch, by 15 feet, by 3 feet 10 inches.

Her two E-4 Scripps engines give her a cruising speed of 9 or 10 knots and a top speed of 11 knots. The engine

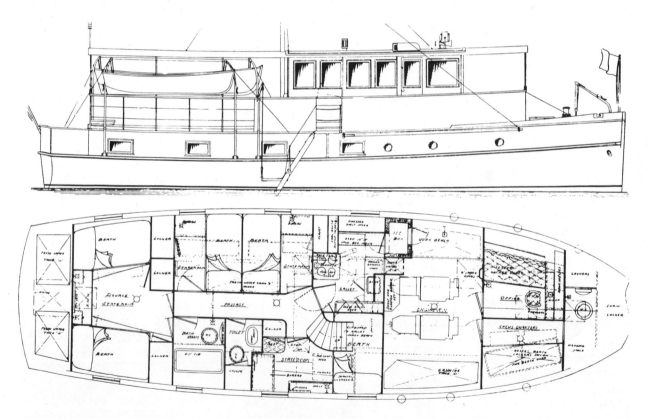

Although she is a houseboat, Panchara II's *hull profile is much like that of a cruiser. One can see plainly from the cabin plan, however, that she gives away nothing in the way of accommodations.* (The Rudder, *January 1926*)

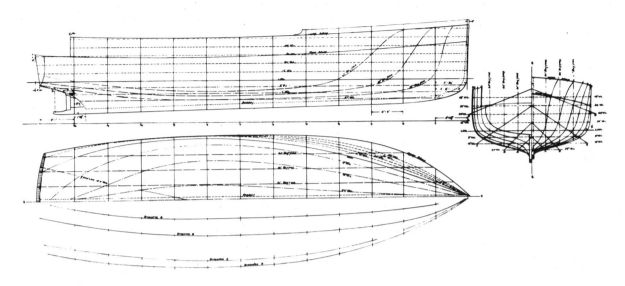

Above: *As might be expected,* Panchara II *has a voluminous hull with almost flat bilges. Her entrance is sharp, but there is considerable flare forward to help keep the decks dry. Dwight Simpson drew the lines in February 1925. (Courtesy John G. Alden, Inc.)* **Below:** *This photograph of* Panchara II *(then named* Highball II*) underway was taken circa 1950. She shows the changes aft made by Charles Bliven. (Courtesy Esther B. Schrot)*

These recent photographs show Panchara II*'s comfortable afterdeck enclosed with plastic curtains for cold or wet weather and her luxurious, houselike interior. One would have to be careful, of course, to secure all the loose furniture before taking the boat into rough water. (Courtesy F.E. Newbold, Jr.)*

room is forward to minimize its encroachment on the living quarters, and the weight is balanced by placing the water tanks way aft, although nothing could be done about the imposing, 30-foot propeller shafts.

In her accommodations, *Panchara II* rivals many a permanently grounded dwelling. "Downstairs" she has a double stateroom aft with extra-wide berths, three small double staterooms (one with a double berth), two enclosed heads (one with a bathtub), a large galley with a swinging door, a walk-in engine room, crew's quarters with a head, and even an office. There is a splendid saloon in the deckhouse with an electric dumbwaiter to deliver meals from the galley, and abaft that is a "back porch." Bunks in two of the small staterooms are cleverly arranged, upper and lower berths being placed at right angles to each other. This allows the person in the lower berth to sit upright with plenty of headroom, while at the same time permitting a lower-than-normal upper berth for easier access and more headroom there. The deckhouse paneling and stateroom doors are of Honduras mahogany.

The helm is in the forward end of the deckhouse, and a small "front porch" serves as a bridge deck and shades the helmsman's eyes. With the low side decks and the landing stage, boarding is an easy matter. Four davits aft service two good-size tenders, while an anchor

davit forward simplifies handling the ground tackle, which must be substantial for this size of vessel with her considerable windage.

During World War II, *Panchara II* was requisitioned by the Coast Guard and anchored in Lloyd's Harbor, New York, to be used for sick bay. She was bought after the war by Charles Bliven, who renamed her *Highball II* and kept her until his death in 1979. Bliven and his wife lived aboard the boat for many summers, making some changes in the accommodations to suit their purposes, and they cruised between New York and Florida and as far as the Bahamas. Bliven's only change to the boat's exterior appearance was to raise the sole of the small, after cockpit flush with the "back porch," creating a substantial after deck, and to extend the deckhouse and deckhouse roof aft accordingly. He also replaced the two Lathrop gasoline engines the Coast Guard had installed with two Ford Lehman 125 h.p. diesels. F.E. Newbold, Jr., of Washington, D.C., bought the boat in 1980 and had her extensively refurbished, and he thinks "she is now good for at least another 55 or 60 years." He had her hull covered with fiberglass by Allan Vaitses of Mattapoisett, Massachusetts.

It is seldom advisable to take any kind of houseboat on a passage in exposed waters, partly because its high, slab-sided, and often lightly constructed superstructure will not take much of a battering from seas, while the great amount of windage inhibits control and proper handling. *Panchara II,* however, is much more heavily built than most modern houseboats, and her two engines with twin screws give her good power and maneuverability. Furthermore, she has adequate beam for ample initial stability. Under the Blivens' ownership, she performed well in rough weather off the Jersey coast.

MILDRED IV

A most interesting little cruiser that was designed to be the ultimate in small powerboat seaworthiness is *Mildred IV,* design number 282. She was built in 1926 by Goudy and Stevens for Jere H. Wheelwright, Jr., of

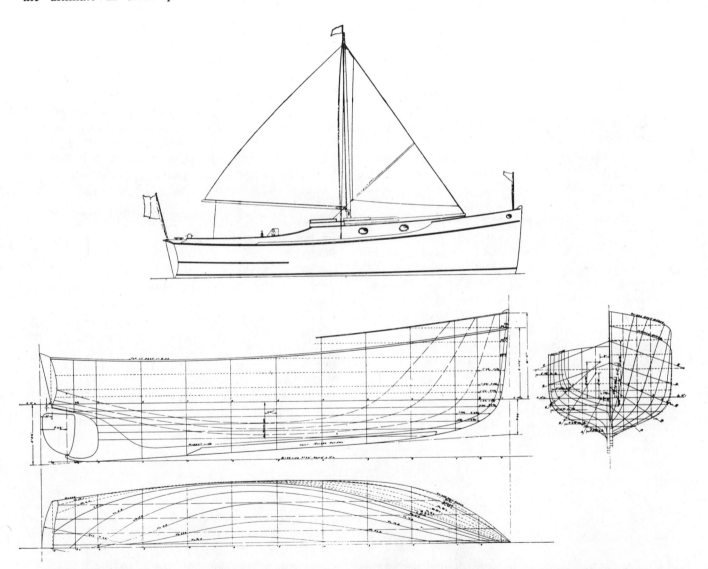

Mildred IV's profile is that of a seagoing boat. The sails' principal purpose is to steady her in beam seas. Her sharp entrance, high freeboard, and considerable flare forward, together with her moderate speed, make for a dry boat in head seas. If the waves were coming from astern you wouldn't have to worry much about being pooped. (Yachting, July 1927)

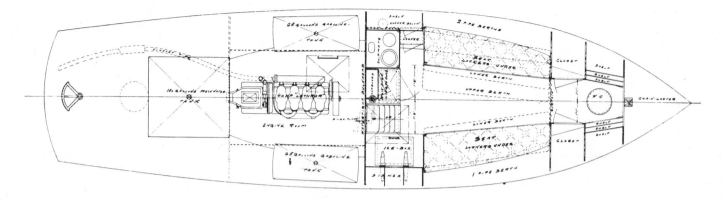

Mildred IV's cabin is adequate for two or three people. (Yachting, *July 1927*)

Princeton, New Jersey. Her dimensions are 34 feet, by 9 feet, by 4 feet.

Wheelwright wanted a boat that could handle any kind of weather during lengthy cruises along the coast of Maine, and he asked John Ives Sewall, a seaman friend, to contribute ideas. In an article for *Yachting* (July 1927), Sewall described himself as having no pretense to being a "hell-roarer or other species of daredevil seagoing scoundrel," so his thoughts, combined with Wheelwright's, produced the concept of a powerboat that was unusually conservative and able. This concept was presented to John Alden, who added some thoughts of his own and of course produced the finished plans.

Among *Mildred IV's* seagoing features are: plenty of freeboard; a high, flared bow; deep, powerful sections; a long keel with a heavy iron shoe; a self-bailing cockpit with large scuppers; and a small sloop rig for steadying purposes, lying-to, and emergency propulsion. Her outside ballast weighs 1,500 pounds, and she carries concrete in her bilges. With these features, she proved not only able, but dry and seakindly as well. Although her silhouette is that of a raised-decker, she in fact has a trunk cabin with a high toe rail forward. Wheelwright and Sewall rightfully thought this configuration safer than that of a raised-decker when it came to handling

ground tackle forward. Still more safety might be provided if the high rail were continued farther aft, but then it would block the view from the cabin ports and would make the boat look much too high-sided.

Mildred IV is powered by a reliable, heavy-duty, slow-turning Lathrop engine developing 40 horsepower. With a 26-inch by 22-inch propeller, she could cruise at eight knots in almost any weather. Flat out (with her engine turning 700 r.p.m.), she could do 9½ knots. A large engine room affords plenty of space to service the Lathrop, and her two 65-gallon fuel tanks give the boat a long cruising range. Her cabin is small but adequate for two or three people. There are two long seats with folding pipe berths over them, a galley aft, and a semiprivate head forward. Although the cockpit has no shelter, there would be some protection if the boom were raised enough to allow the installation of a folding dodger.

Many of the features of this boat were incorporated in Wheelwright's *Mildred V,* a larger, pilothouse version of the design, built by Goudy and Stevens in 1928. When *Mildred V* was being built, she was inspected by the crew of a Coast Guard patrol boat stationed nearby, and they expressed the wish that they be given similar kinds of vessels for their offshore work.

GYPSY

Gypsy, Number 355, is a large, impressive, Alden powerboat and one that attracted a lot of attention in New England waters. Designed around the strict re-

quirements of her owner, Robert F. Herrick of Boston, this yacht was built by George Lawley and Son at Neponset, Massachusetts, in 1928. Her hull is double

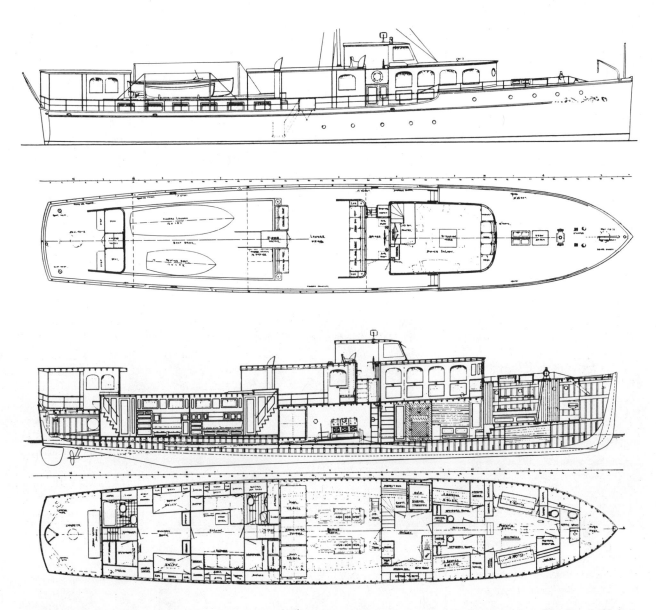

Gypsy's length becomes apparent when one realizes that the launch shown in her deck and outboard profile plans is 18 feet long. Where after staterooms are concerned, Gypsy *trades off quantity for quality. Clifford Swaine wrote: "Note only one stateroom for the owner — no guests." (The Rudder,* October 1928)

planked with mahogany for the outer layer, while the deckhouses and exterior trim are teak. Four steel bulkheads divide the boat into five watertight compartments, making her almost unsinkable. She measures 101 feet, by 99 feet 7 inches, by 18 feet, by 4 feet 9 inches.

Gypsy is versatile in the sense that she has a shallow hull, ample power, and twin screws, which provide good maneuverability. On the other hand, the accommodations are somewhat inflexible despite their large size, for they limit the number of guests that can be carried. Below decks there is a tremendous stateroom for the

owner aft; then a saloon that is convertible to guest quarters; the engine room, housing two 350 h.p. Winton gasoline engines; a sizable galley; and vast quarters for two paid officers and a crew of four up forward. The dining saloon is in the deckhouse above the galley. Two 816-gallon fuel tanks and a 720-gallon water tank provide a noise barrier between the engines and the after living quarters.

Like many power yachts of that era, *Gypsy* had well-sheltered decks. It seems that we are now rediscovering what was known in those times — that too much ex-

Gypsy accompanied the New York Yacht Club cruise of 1930, perhaps serving as committee boat. Here she rumbles past on her way to Mattapoisett from Newport. (Edwin Levick photo. The Mariners' Museum, Newport News, Virginia)

posure to the sun can be harmful to the skin. The deck shelter aft sticks up like a caboose, but otherwise the profile is handsome, and the overall silhouette is improved when the two tenders are stowed on the boat deck.

Robert Herrick must have been pleased with his yacht, for he kept her for many years. Exactly how she was used is not known, but she often served as the committee boat at important regattas. She was stationed in Norfolk as a floating office for the Navy brass during World War II, and the Navy cut a hole in her rosewood main-saloon bulkhead to accommodate radio equipment. After the war, *Gypsy* was acquired by William McRae, who made the repair of the bulkhead his first

priority. It took him over half a year to find an appropriate piece of rosewood.

McRae remembers that *Gypsy* at top speed was an imposing sight, with much of the forward half of her underbody out of water. He used to take pleasure in racing the Coast Guard at every opportunity.

Gypsy left McRae's ownership in 1951, and her history after 1955 is hazy. She was owned for a while by a Floridian, who replaced her Winton gasoline engines with Buda diesels, and McRae says that she subsequently served as floating quarters for a Brazilian multimillionaire who owned a fleet of shark-fishing boats in the Gulf of Mexico. A new owner discontinued *Gypsy*'s Coast Guard documentation in 1977.

ꝏ
MALLARD

The powerboats presented thus far have been round-bottomed boats, but the Alden firm also produced some fine V-bottomed craft. *Mallard,* Number 446, is an example. This boat, called a fast day cruiser in the Alden records, was designed for Josiah B. Chase primarily for commuting between Marblehead, Massachusetts, and Boston. Substantially constructed with double planking of Honduras mahogany, *Mallard* was built in 1930 by Britt Brothers at West Lynn, Massachusetts. Her

dimensions are 40 feet, by 39 feet 8½ inches, by 10 feet 3 inches, by 2 feet 9 inches.

William Hand, Alden's rival in the design of fisherman-type yachts and seagoing motorsailers, was a pioneer in V-bottomed powerboat design, and *Mallard* is similar to the kind of hard-chine boat he developed. Her deadrise is steep forward but flattens aft, and there is flare in her topsides forward with considerable tumblehome aft. (Uffa Fox was a proponent of gen-

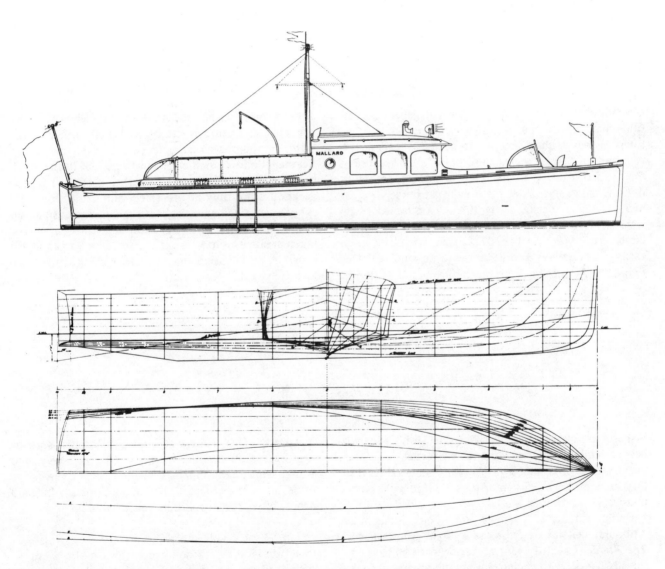

Mallard is a sporty-looking boat, with her low freeboard, flat sheer, fancy windows, and bow "rumble seats." (The Rudder, April 1930) With her hard chine and flat run aft, she has a planing hull. The tumblehome aft is aesthetically appealing. (Courtesy John G. Alden, Inc.)

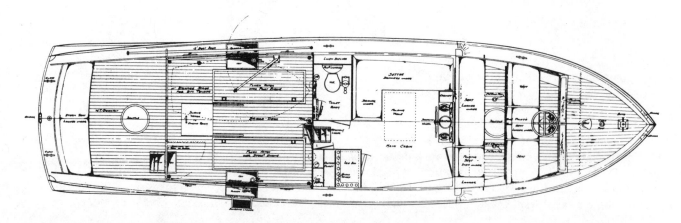

Mallard *has plenty of deck space but little in the way of accommodations, which were not needed for her intended service.*
(The Rudder, *April 1930*)

erous tumblehome near the transom, feeling that it mitigates air suction.) Charles MacGregor drew *Mallard*'s lines.

Shallow V-bottomed designs are not generally considered as able as similar craft with deeper, round bottoms. However, the former often have less tendency to roll, and, of course, they are normally faster because of their superior ability to climb up on a plane, an ability that increased steadily as the weight per horsepower of marine engines declined. By 1930, V-bottomed boats were achieving speeds previously reserved for much larger craft. *Mallard* has a hull that can plane quite easily, and her low profile causes little windage. Her twin 200 h.p. Sterling Petrels can push her at 32 m.p.h.

Because of her purpose as a commuter and day boat, *Mallard* has no berths, although there is an L-shaped settee in the deckhouse that can be used as a bunk. There is also an enclosed head and an icebox and bar. An unusual feature is the bow cockpit with its extra helm. In rough seas it might be a bit wet, but in fair weather it allows the helmsman to get out in the sun if he so desires. The canvas weather cloths abaft the deckhouse not only afford safety and protection from spray but also enhance the boat's appearance. An article in *The Rudder* (April 1930) stated that "the designer has taken great pains to turn out as good a looking model as possible, and it needs only a cursory glance to see that he achieved this goal."

HARD TACK

Fisherman-type schooner yachts aside, John Alden is best remembered by many old-timers for his successful motorsailers. Like those of William Hand, his rival in this area of yacht design, Alden's motorsailers emphasize seaworthiness.

Design number 577, named *Hard Tack,* looks able. Although she was described as a 50-50 motorsailer in *The Rudder* (August 1934), she appears to be closer to the 30-70 type, with engine power rather than sail as the principal means of propulsion. Designed for Horace B. Merwin, who previously owned the Alden schooner

Dauntless, Hard Tack was built by Bedell's Yard at Stratford, Connecticut, in 1934. She is heavy and strong, with 5,000 pounds of ballast, half of which is inside and half on the keel. Her dimensions are 42 feet 3 inches, by 39 feet, by 13 feet, by 4 feet 6 inches.

Hard Tack's sails are primarily for steadying purposes and for emergency propulsion in the event of engine failure, but they can also be used to save fuel when there is a fresh breeze from the right direction. The lead for the jibsheet is much farther forward than

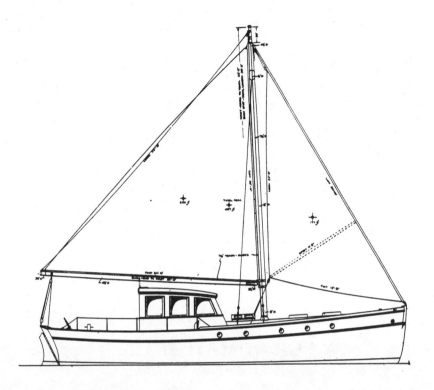

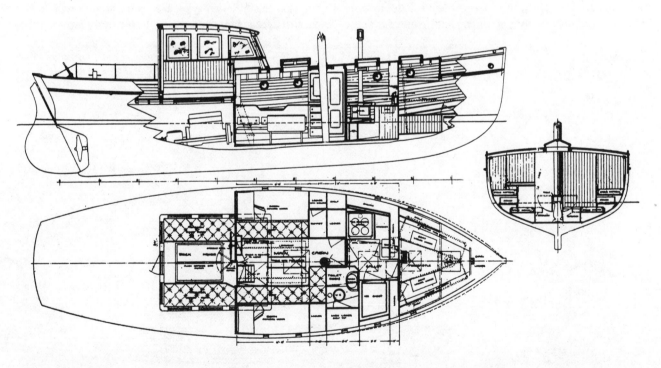

Hard Tack *appears to be the epitome of the husky motorsailer. The jib sprit prevented the foot from developing excessive camber due to the forward sheet leads. The after shrouds do away with the need for backstays but prevent the boom from going broad off. A pair of forward shrouds might have prevented her dismasting. At first glance* Hard Tack *does not seem to be tremendously spacious below decks, but she gains some not-so-apparent extra room with her raised deck. Her layout proved most comfortable for long periods of living aboard.* (The Rudder, *August 1934)*

usual, but it appears to be rigged that way to make the sail self-tending, for the plan indicates a sprit running from clew to headstay. Power is supplied by an 85 h.p., heavy-duty Lathrop engine.

The raised-deck cabin trunk must make *Hard Tack* seem very spacious below, although this is not so apparent from the cabin plan. There are two pilot berths in the main cabin, with a straight extension seat with buffet on one side and an L-shaped extension seat on the other side. The deckhouse has two transoms that can be used for sitting or sleeping, and the fo'c's'le has pipe berths for two hands if professionals are desired. A good-size galley and an enclosed head are between the main cabin and the fo'c's'le. The top of the deckhouse has an unusual crown and slope, and this alleviates the structure's boxy appearance.

Her first owner used *Hard Tack* mostly for fishing off Block Island, and during World War II she was used by the Coast Guard as a guard boat at the Cape Cod Canal, but under some owners she has been cruised extensively. Mrs. Richard W. Johnson, who with her husband cruised the boat for many years between Nova Scotia and the Bahamas, reports that *Hard Tack* was an exceptionally comfortable and able seaboat. Although the sails were used mostly to steady the boat, *Hard Tack* could really sail when the breeze piped up. On one occasion in a hard blow, she was dismasted when the jibstay turnbuckle failed. Despite nearly being struck by the mast as it fell aft, the Johnsons managed to get their boat safely back to port. A dismasting offshore can be devastating, but the problem of getting home is relatively small in a boat like *Hard Tack,* with her powerful and reliable engine, great range under power, and seaworthy hull.

A PAIR OF MOTORSAILER DESIGNS

In February 1937, both *Yachting* and *The Rudder* published plans of large Alden motorsailers. These vessels are similar in type, but there are enough significant differences to make an interesting comparison.

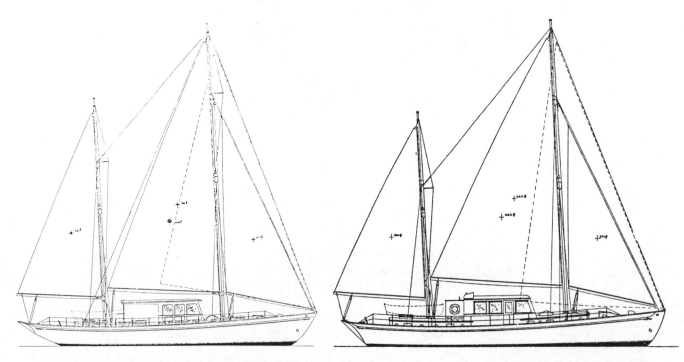

Of these two 1937 motorsailers, the 72-footer (left) has considerably more sail area (1,630 square feet versus 1,262 square feet), even though the two boats have similar waterline lengths. The 72-footer also has a higher-aspect-ratio rig, and her tall mizzen could support a substantial staysail. (Left: Yachting, February 1937. Right: The Rudder, February 1937)

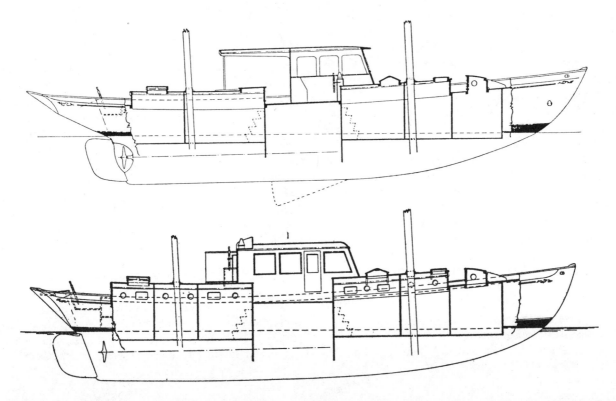

Above: *It is obvious that the 72-footer* (top) *will be the better sailer, particularly to windward with her centerboard.* (Top: Yachting, *February 1937. Bottom: The Rudder,* February 1937) **Below:** *The accommodations of the two motorsailers are similar but for the extra stateroom aft on the 72-footer* (top). *The deck-cabin plan of the 66-footer is shown.* (Top: Yachting, *February 1937. Bottom: The Rudder,* February 1937)

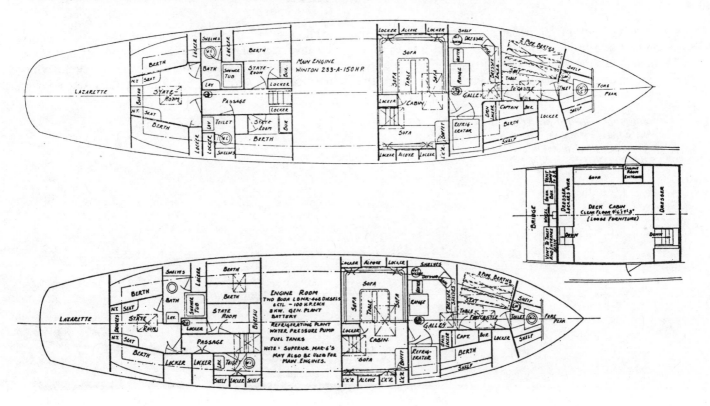

The Alden Company no longer has records for either vessel, but the *Rudder* design was drawn for either Albert Johnson or George Mixter, the author of *Primer of Navigation,* who previously owned the Alden schooner *Teragram.* This motorsailer's dimensions are 66 feet 3 inches, by 57 feet, by 16 feet, by 5 feet 9 inches. The *Yachting* boat is similar to a later design, Number 750, which the Alden records show was done for the late Arthur W. Herrington, a Chesapeake yachtsman who owned a series of motorsailers named *Ruwalla.* The *Yachting* design and Herrington's boat both measure 72 feet 1 inch, by 56 feet, by 16 feet 10 inches, by 7 feet 4 inches.

The *Rudder* and *Yachting* designs are quite similar in their rigs, deck plans, and accommodations. Both have moderate, ketch rigs; midships engines with prominent deckhouses above them; staterooms and two heads aft; and similar saloons, galleys, and fo'c's'les. Of course, the larger boat has more room, so she has three, rather than two, staterooms aft.

The main difference between the two vessels is that the larger one was designed to sail smartly, while the smaller has the emphasis placed on power. Related differences are that the smaller yacht is short-ended and has a longer keel than the *Yachting* design. Also, the latter has her helm in the deckhouse, whereas the former has her helm outside, just abaft the deckhouse. John Alden being the consummate sailorman, each boat has an additional helm aft for sailing in open waters.

Although the rigs of the two boats are similar, the larger motorsailer, with more of a sailboat hull, has a small centerboard for windward work (she draws only six feet with the board up) and a 150-horsepower engine for auxiliary power. The other vessel has no centerboard, and she is provided with two 100 h.p. Buda engines driving relatively exposed twin screws. One good feature of the *Yachting* boat's sail plan is that the mainmast has permanent backstays attached to quarter chainplates. On this boat, however, the reaching jib could foul the jumper struts when the boat goes about.

Both vessels are good, comfortable seaboats. Your preference for one or the other would depend on how soon you want to reach your destination, and whether you prefer sailing or powering while getting there.

GOSLING III

Although *Gosling III,* design number 654, has sails, she should be considered an offshore power cruiser rather than a motorsailer. Her sails are used primarily to prevent excessive rolling and for lying-to, although they could also be set in a fresh following wind for trolling, to save fuel, or to relieve the monotony of motoring. This boat was designed in 1938 for Geoffrey G. Whitney, and she was built by Willis J. Reid and Sons at

John Alden liked a powerboat with sails. Notice that Gosling III's *main boom is also used to lift the tender on and off the after cabintop.* (Yachting, *July 1938)*

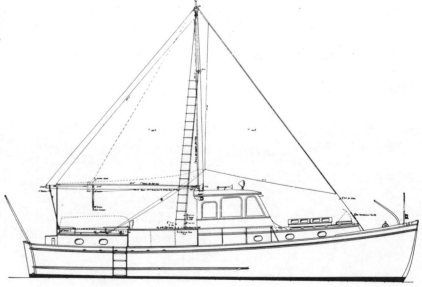

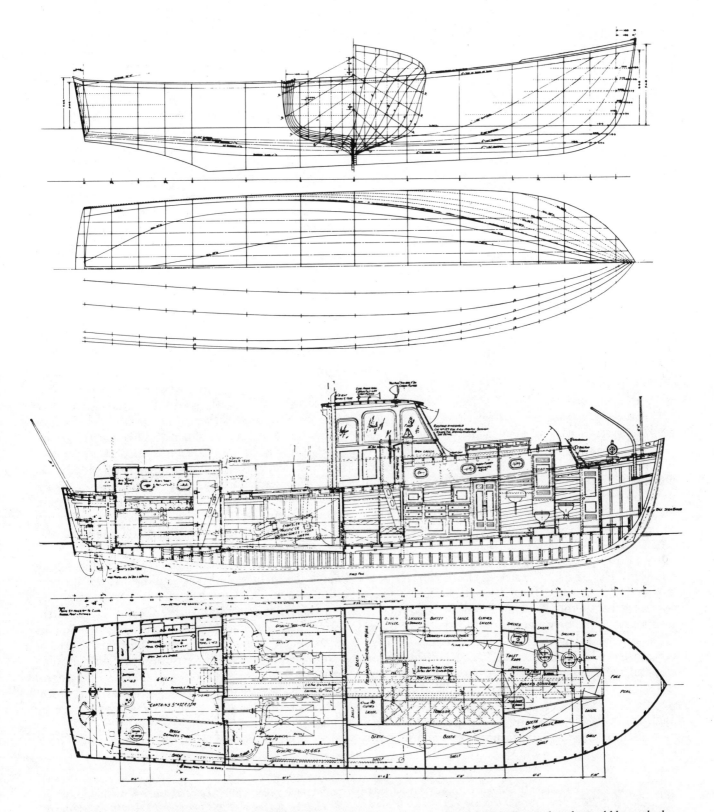

Gosling III *has a sharp entrance and a lot of flare forward. Her sections aft are flat, which indicates that she could be pushed onto a plane with relative ease. (Courtesy John G. Alden, Inc.) With her able hull, rugged construction, twin screws, reasonably shoal draft, and sailing rig,* Gosling III *is a versatile powerboat. Her accommodations provide privacy, but there are some trade-offs, including the distance of the galley from the dining area. (Yachting, July 1938)*

Winthrop, Massachusetts. Her dimensions are 50 feet 2 inches, by 47 feet 7 inches, by 13 feet, by 3 feet 9 inches. Fenwick Williams drew her lines.

She is a handsome boat with a pronounced, sweeping sheer and well-proportioned cabin trunks. The weather cloths amidships optically lower the considerable height of the pilothouse. Her layout is unusual in that the captain's stateroom and the galley are aft, while the owner's cabin is all the way forward. The saloon, just forward of and lower than the pilothouse, has three pilot berths (one being athwartships), a long L-shaped settee, and plenty of locker space. The engine room is amidships, and it houses twin, eight-cylinder Chryslers.

With her ample freeboard, high, flared bow, round bilges, and steadying canvas, *Gosling III* is a very able boat. Her Chryslers can push her up onto her flattish after sections for a fair turn of speed. In a lengthy blow at sea she might be hove-to comfortably with a storm trysail, which would tend to hold her bow up, especially since the keel is largely cut away at its after end. If it became necessary to run for shelter, a small headsail (in addition to drags astern, perhaps) would help prevent a broach. Her twin engines ensure that there is always a spare, and, of course, the twin screws provide excellent maneuverability.

The mast, with ratlines leading aloft, can be used for a lookout station, while the main boom is handy for bringing the dinghy aboard. (There is a permanently rigged tackle for just that purpose.) All in all, *Gosling III* is a sailor's powerboat.

MOBJACK

Another able powerboat, described by a former owner as "an excellent seaboat," is *Mobjack,* Alden design 678. She was designed for George Upton of Marblehead, Massachusetts, and built in the yard of George Gulliford at Saugus, Massachusetts, in 1938. Her construction is rugged, with oak skeleton and oak bottom planking. The topsides are planked with hard pine. The decks are teak and the cabin trunks are of Philippine mahogany. She measures 60 feet 7 inches, by 58 feet, by 14 feet 6 inches, by 4 feet 3 inches.

Like most of the previously discussed powerboats, *Mobjack* has a heavy-displacement, round-bottomed hull form. Her single, on-center screw is well protected by a keel that runs all the way aft, and she has a large, semibalanced, outboard rudder, which helps make steering easy. The bow sections don't have much flare for a powerboat, but her freeboard is high, particularly beneath the raised deck forward, and the boat is not very fast, so she is probably dry. With her round bottom and shallow keel, *Mobjack* can do some rolling in rough water unless a steadying sail or "flopper stoppers" are used. The original plans show a short, web-construction mast used mostly to support an antenna and lift the tender, but later it was replaced with a much taller mast that carried 742 square feet of sail. Former owner Edward B. (Ned) Freeman writes that he used "the steadying sail to advantage crossing places like the Tongue of the Ocean and the Gulf Stream." *Mobjack* has a narrow stern and balanced hull in comparison with many, less seaworthy powerboats, and she could probably be run off without fear of broaching when making for port in heavy weather. There is always the possibility of being pooped, but the after cockpit is small and the after companionway well elevated.

It doesn't appear that living aboard this boat would impose the slightest hardship, and this is confirmed by Ned Freeman, who lived aboard her (when she was named *Snow Goose*) most of the time for six or seven years. There is a large cabin for the owner and a double stateroom aft, a saloon in the sunken deckhouse, and a large galley with crew's quarters forward. Some unusual features are three companionways, the small stateroom in the fo'c's'le, and the tremendous engine room, which Freeman recalls as having almost nine feet of headroom.

The original power plant was a huge, 120 h.p.

Opposite: Mobjack*'s outboard profile plan shows a distinctive powerboat with a fine offshore capability. (*Yachting, *June 1938) Her lines show a deep body and a shallow keel of great length. Despite her high freeboard forward, she should "keep her head" in beam seas because of her deep forefoot and sharp entrance. (Courtesy John G. Alden, Inc.)* Mobjack*'s inboard-profile plan gives us a hint of how ruggedly she was constructed. Looking at her accommodations, it is not hard to see why Ned Freeman could live comfortably aboard her for so many years. The large owner's cabin is particularly attractive with its fireplace, desk, and private companionway. (*Yachting, *January 1938)*

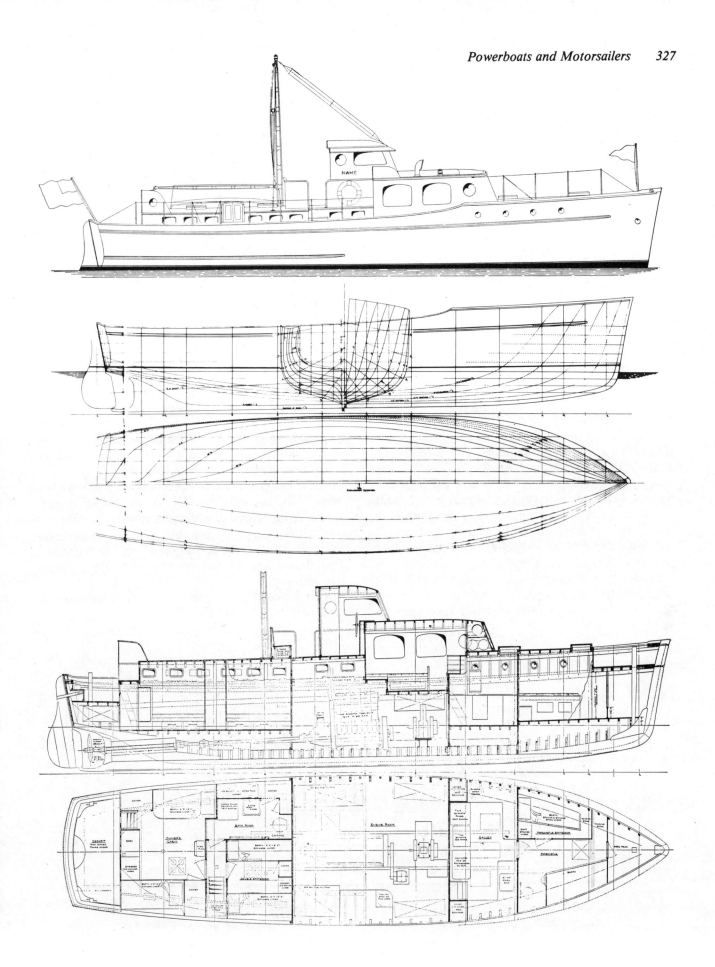

Cooper-Bessemer diesel, but later it was replaced by a satisfactory GM-671. Under the ownership of Bromo-Quinine magnate James Grove, *Mobjack* (then named *Jubilee*) was given an additional two-cylinder GM engine, which drove a port-side, off-center feathering prop to counteract the torque of the main engine when docking and also to provide standby auxiliary power.

At one time *Mobjack,* under the name of *Exact,* was owned by Burr Bartram of Greenwich, Connecticut, and, according to Freeman, she was lovingly called "Bartram's diesel Goliath." One can only hope that this classic seagoing cruiser will never meet her David.

YUMA PEARL

A more modern and sporty-looking boat than most of the previously presented Alden powerboats is design number 794, *Yuma Pearl.* She was built in 1947 by August Nelson at Portland, Oregon, for Frank Russo of Vancouver, Washington. Her dimensions are 45 feet 2 inches, by 43 feet 9 inches, by 12 feet, by 3 feet 7 inches. Clifford Swaine drew her lines.

Despite her nearly vertical ends, *Yuma Pearl* has a streamlined look, reflecting post-World-War-II styling. She is a fairly fast boat, yet she is a round-bottomed, reasonably seaworthy type. Her bottom is sufficiently flat aft to allow planing when pushed, but the stern is not so wide as to cause difficulty steering at cruising speeds in following seas. Although the entrance is quite fine, there is considerable flare up high to help keep the decks dry. Power was originally supplied by twin Hall-Scott Invaders, which reportedly could drive the boat at 22 m.p.h. top speed. Her recent owner, Ray E. McGowan, writes that she now has Chrysler Majestic engines, which afford great fuel economy and a 700-mile cruising range turning over at 1,600 to 1,800 r.p.m. and driving her at eight knots.

The boat has a large, sunken deckhouse, which accommodates a galley and dinette abaft a thwartships bulkhead and a transom berth and a steering station forward. All the way aft there is a cockpit, and ahead of this, a large stateroom with enclosed head. Forward of the deckhouse is another stateroom, this one with a double berth and an enclosed head with shower. August Nelson did a superb job of building and finishing the boat, and McGowan writes, "All hull and cabin carpentry has been done to perfection by skilled personnel. You should see, to admire, the fine joints evident throughout."

Now named *Wana, Yuma Pearl* is still going strong in the Pacific Northwest.

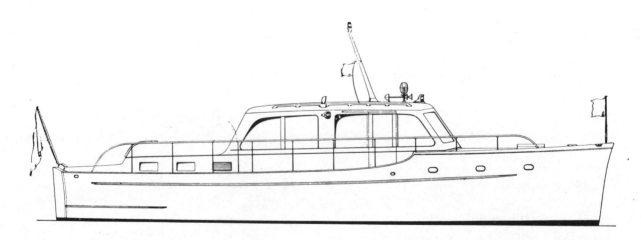

Yuma Pearl's profile gives her an attractive and functional look. (Courtesy John G. Alden, Inc.)

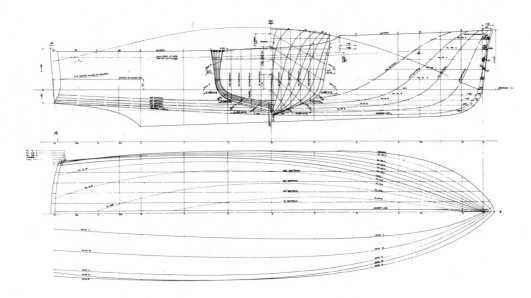

Clifford Swaine put the finishing touches on Yuma Pearl*'s lines on May 31, 1946. Her designed displacement is 32,320 pounds. (Courtesy John G. Alden, Inc.)*

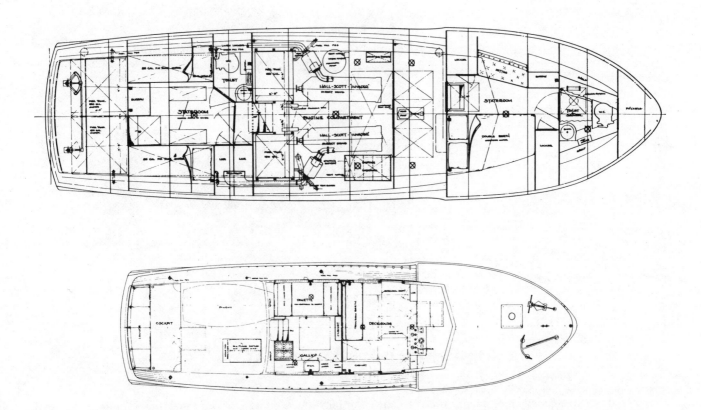

Yuma Pearl*'s accommodations offer an outstanding combination of room and privacy. A novel feature is her large deckhouse with sizable windows. When asked about the comfort of her layout, the present owner wrote, "This boat is one in a million." (Courtesy John G. Alden, Inc.)*

Wana *(ex-*Yuma Pearl*) coming and going. (Courtesy Ray E. McGowan)*

ᔭ

A SEAGOING MOTORSAILER

The rugged, double-ended, motorsailer presented here seems to be the last word in seakeeping ability. This vessel was a proposal developed from a smaller motorsailer, Number 752, designed for C.V. Watson in 1944 but never built. (Watson had previously owned two Alden schooners, both named *La Reine.* As previously mentioned, the first of these, under the name *Dolphin II* when owned by actor Frank Morgan, won the 1947

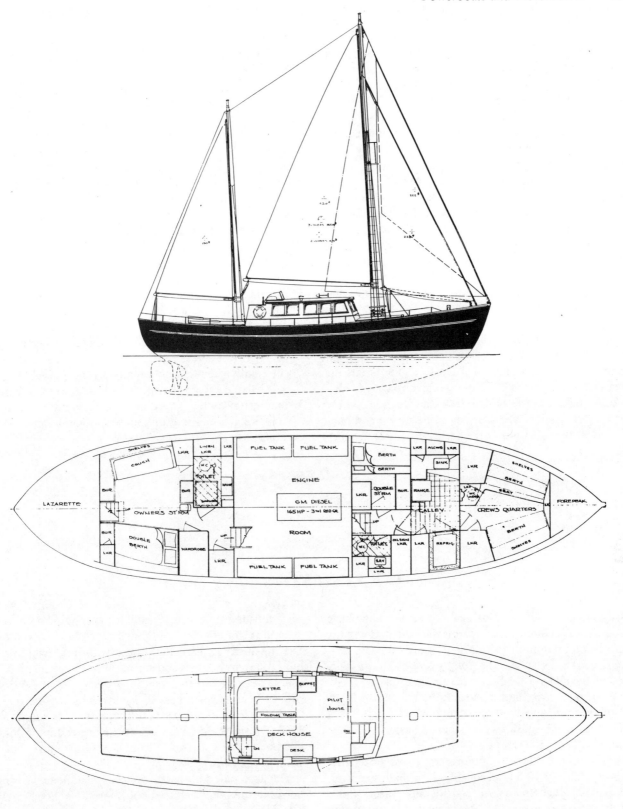

This motorsailer looks as if she could take almost anything the sea can dish out. The rig is well balanced, easy to handle, and entirely inboard. The accommodations plans show not only comfortable and private quarters, but also a cavernous engine room. (The Rudder, *August 1938)*

Transpac Race, and the second, as *Constellation,* won her class in the 1959 Transpac Race.) This motorsailer bears a resemblance to the sardine carriers still seen in New England fishing ports. Her overall length is 60 feet, her beam is 15 feet 3 inches, and her draft is 6 feet 6 inches.

The qualities that make her seaworthy are immediately apparent in the plans: the short ends; the high freeboard; the rugged construction; the long, deep, well-ballasted keel; and the short, well-balanced rig. Then, too, many seamen feel that the full, pointed stern is the best type for heavy weather offshore, although there are arguments to the contrary. Her 165 h.p. GM diesel driving a large, well-protected screw provides reliable mechanical propulsion, while her four fuel tanks add to her seakeeping ability.

At least one feature, however, detracts somewhat from this vessel's seaworthiness — the side-opening doors to the deckhouse. These entrances could be vulnerable on a sailboat when she is knocked down during heavy weather. The side doors could be sealed in bad conditions, but then the only access to and from the decks would be through the after companionway, which is quite far from the bridge deck and helm. It would seem more prudent and convenient to have a companionway at the after end of the deckhouse, near the out-side helm and reasonably close to the boat's centerline.

The owner's stateroom aft affords a lot of room and privacy (provided the weather permits use of the side doors). The large deckhouse has an inside steering station in addition to the commodious sitting and dining area with its L-shaped settee. Farther forward are a small double stateroom and a galley, with crew's quarters in the fo'c's'le. There are two enclosed heads, one just forward of the deckhouse and another (with a shower) in the owner's cabin. One drawback of the layout is the wide separation of the galley from the dining area.

The smallness of the rig (858 square feet in the three lowers) puts this vessel close to the 50-50 category of motorsailers. Still, she should be able to sail fairly well in a good breeze, with her generous lateral plane and her well-balanced, masthead sail plan. It makes a good deal of sense to shape an offshore motorsailer out of a rugged, heavy, double-ended hull. Since this kind of vessel could never be considered a smart, responsive sailer, why not give her plenty of engine power and a rig for use only when there is a really decent breeze? Add a large, reliable engine or two, and one is assured of being able to get away from a lee shore in a real blow and also of reaching a destination on schedule in reasonable weather.

ROLLING STONE IV

Design number 908, a 43½-foot motorsailer, may have been the last design produced by the Alden Company before John retired in 1955. The first of two boats issuing from this design was the *Rolling Stone IV,* originally owned by Donald C. Stone of Newark, New Jersey. Built of oak, teak, and mahogany by the Morse Boatbuilding Company of Thomaston, Maine, she has a waterline length of 38 feet 6 inches, a beam of 13 feet, and a draft of 5 feet.

Like most of Alden's motorsailers, *Rolling Stone IV* is a real seagoer with a reasonably deep, ballasted keel, short ends, high freeboard, considerable sheer, and a fairly short rig. Her single GM diesel drives a protected propeller (originally three-bladed but now five-bladed) just ahead of a balanced rudder (which is also well protected), giving her a cruising speed of 8½ knots. Her fuel consumption is 2¼ gallons per hour with the generator running, and her cruising range is 1,000 miles. She has a rather high deckhouse with large windows, but Stone carried plywood storm shutters for emergency use in heavy weather offshore. *Rolling Stone IV* first proved her seaworthiness by successfully weathering a Gulf Stream gale on her way home from Bermuda in 1956. On the West Coast, under the ownership of John G. Bacon, she passed through several more gales without incident.

The accommodations drawings are detailed, showing books in the bookshelf and bottles in the liquor locker. The owner has a large, double stateroom aft, where there is also a spacious enclosed head with shower. The deckhouse contains a seat, a transom, and an inside steering station. The outside helm abaft the deckhouse

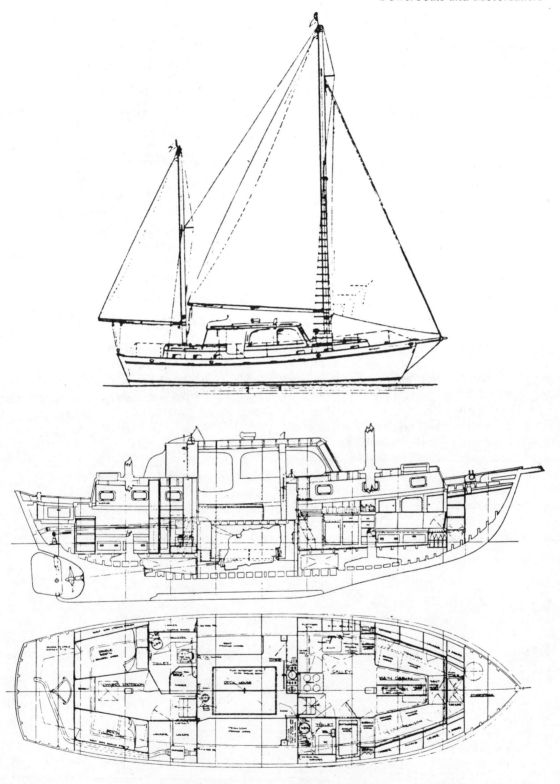

Rolling Stone IV, *the last boat designed by John G. Alden, Inc., before Alden's retirement, is an aesthetically pleasing, seago-ing boat of considerable versatility. Depending on conditions, her rig can be used for lying-to under storm trysail, heaving-to, trolling, conning from aloft, or sailing. The layout provides luxurious quarters for the owner and easily convertible accom-modations for guests. Two attractive features are the well-lighted deckhouse with a view and the spacious, convenient galley.* (The Skipper, *September 1955*)

A recent photograph of Rolling Stone IV, *now called* Sea Shell, *under full sail and power in California waters. (Courtesy John G. Bacon)*

is well suited for fair weather use and for better visibility when under sail. The forward cabin contains an L-shaped galley, another enclosed head, and transom berths on either side of a drop-leaf table.

Although *Rolling Stone IV* does not pretend to be a smart sailer, and her fractional ketch rig divides the sail plan into small, individual areas, the total sail area is a respectable 759 square feet, and at least once she was clocked at nine knots under sail alone. The size of the individual sails and the well-balanced plan make the boat easy to handle, while the reasonably deep keel gives her the ability to make progress to windward. She is equipped with wooden "ratlines" on the shrouds;

Donald Stone confessed that they chafed the mainsail, but he covered the offending parts with baggywrinkle, which only added to the boat's able appearance.

Rolling Stone's present owner, retired Navy captain Bob Wolf, lives aboard her in San Diego and cruises locally. The boat is in excellent shape.

Perhaps it would have been more fitting if John Alden's last design had been a fishing-type schooner yacht with a glorious cloud of canvas and, at most, a small auxiliary engine, but the 908 design has some sail, and she is a bona fide seagoer. She was not a bad note on which to end his distinguished career.

Album

To keep the size of this book within reason, there had to be a limit to the number of Alden designs treated in detail in the foregoing text. Establishing that limit was a difficult and somewhat arbitrary process because of the large number of accessible plans and photographs of Alden designs. It seemed a pity that other important or interesting designs could not be included, at least in abbreviated form; thus, the idea of this album evolved. Presented here in chronological order are more than 100 additional yachts designed before John Alden's retirement. Further, there are some 600 other good Alden designs that appear neither in the text nor the album. You have to stop somewhere. Basic information on all Alden yacht designs is available in the Appendix.

Captions in the album give the boats' original names, but later names are also given when they are known.

The 25-foot-waterline, clipper-bowed, topmast sloop *Aimee*, designed by Alden for Channing Williams in 1905. Alden was working for Crowninshield at the time, but *Aimee* was an independent design commission. Listed as design number 8 in the Alden office index, she was built by Wilbur Morse in 1906. She was probably influenced by the yawl *Sea Fox* (Chapter 3) that Alden owned about that time and greatly admired. Williams intended to keep the boat in commission right through the New England winter. *(The Rudder, January 1906)*

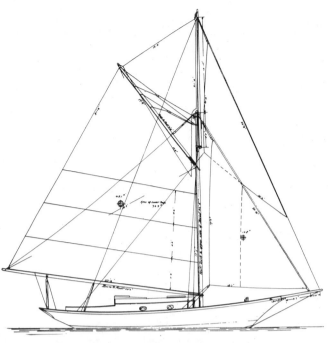

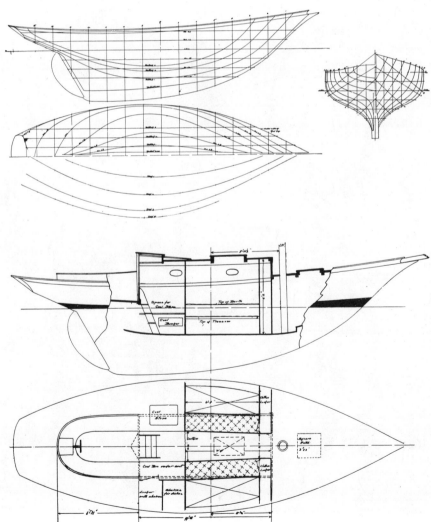

The 43-foot sloop *Discovery*, design number 13, turned out by Alden in 1909. She is a fisherman-type yacht with two cabin trunks and a private stateroom aft. *(Lo Yacht* by Carlo Sciarrelli)

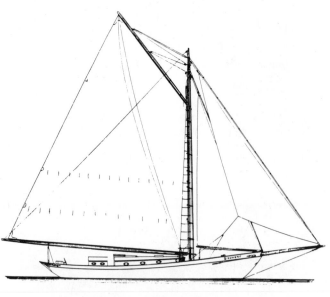

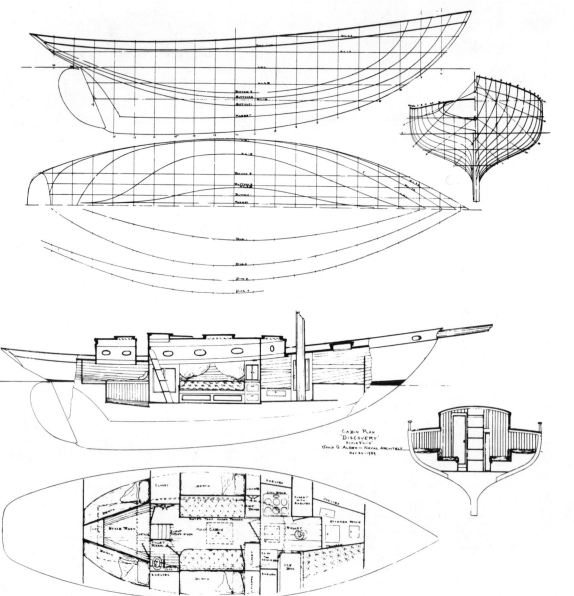

338

A 27-foot-waterline ketch, probably design number 14, built at Sandusky, Ohio, circa 1911 for Captain Richard McKean. She was used as a part-time home and for commercial fishing on Lake Superior. Total sail area is 656 square feet, with 226 square feet in the mizzen. *(The Rudder,* 1911)

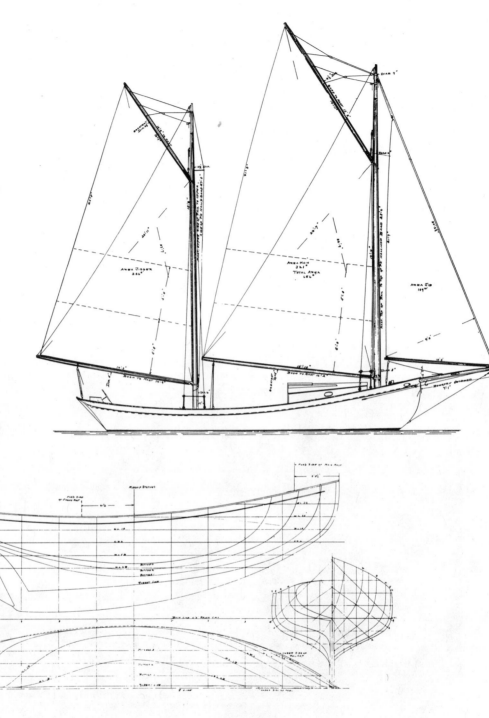

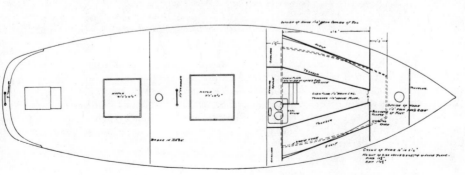

Alden designed the 63-foot schooner *Volante* for Charles Cobb of Marblehead, and Adams Shipbuilding Company of East Boothbay, Maine, built her in 1916. She was planked mahogany, and the joinerwork for her solid mahogany interior was done by a Boston cabinetmaker and shipped to Boothbay. These photographs, taken not long after her building, speak for themselves. She was the culmination of Charles Cobb's dreams, but he was only able to sail her a few short years, and she was sold to the Great Lakes in 1919. She was still sailing on the Lakes at last report in 1970. Mr. Cobb's granddaughter contributed these photographs. Her son works in the Alden office today. (Nathaniel Stebbins photos. Courtesy Lydia C. Perkins)

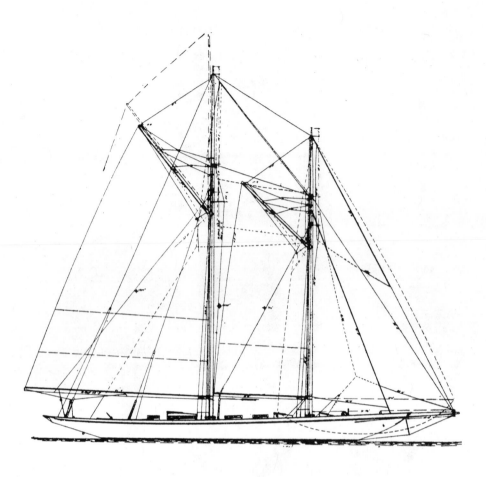

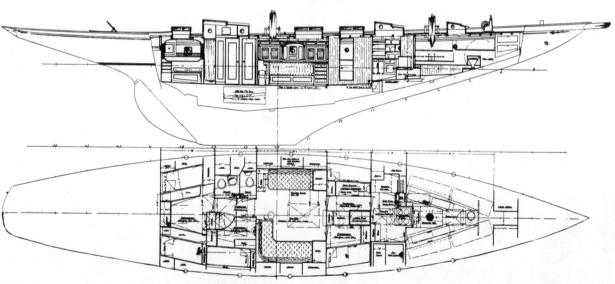

The 83-foot schooner *Serena* (originally *Amorilla),* design number 70, was built for Demarest Lloyd of Boston by George Lawley and Son in 1916. The photograph shows her with a staysail rig, sailing on San Francisco Bay in the 1970s. She was a frequent winner in the West Coast classic yacht regattas before being sold back to the East Coast in 1982. *(The Rudder,* March 1918. Diane Beeston photo)

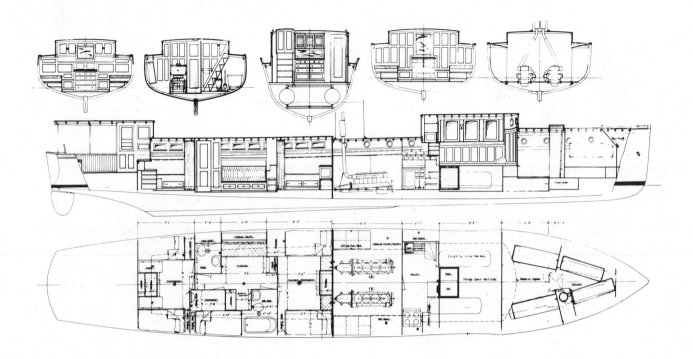

Design number 79 was the 80-foot-10-inch power cruiser *Polly,* built for William T. Rich of Newton, Massachusetts, by F.F. Pendleton in 1917. Shoal draft without undue sacrifice to seaworthiness was a design requirement. She had two 150 h.p. gasoline engines, which gave her a cruising speed of 15 m.p.h. (Courtesy John G. Alden, Inc.)

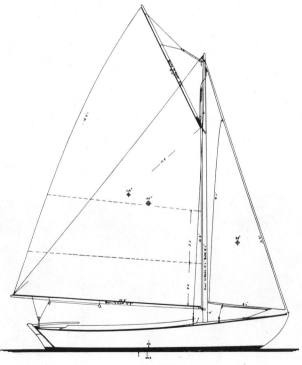

Here and opposite:
Number 83, the Biddeford Pool One-Design, was designed for W.A. Dupee and others and built by W.B. Calderwood in 1917. The sloops carry 197 square feet of sail and 900 pounds of ballast, and they have watertight compartments for flotation at either end. *(The Rudder,* December 1917)

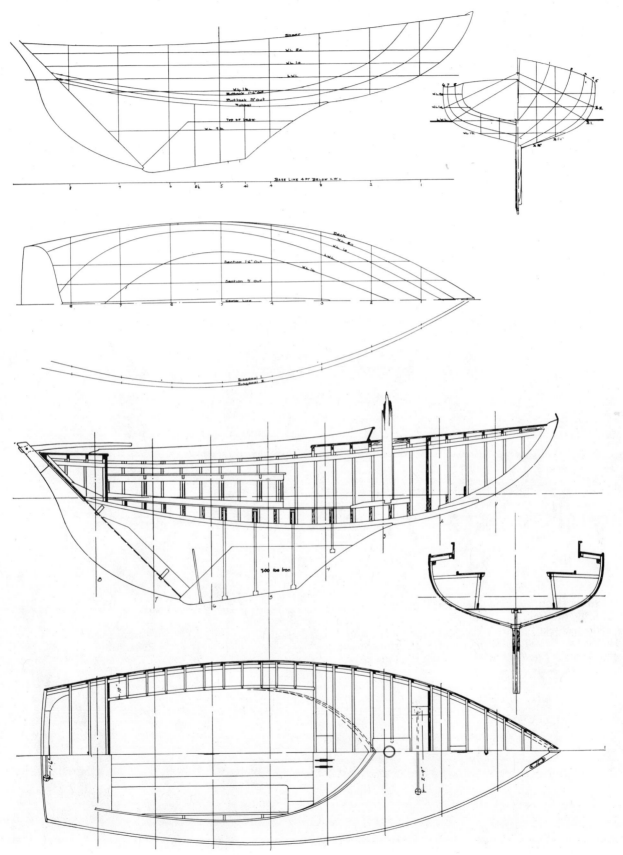

345

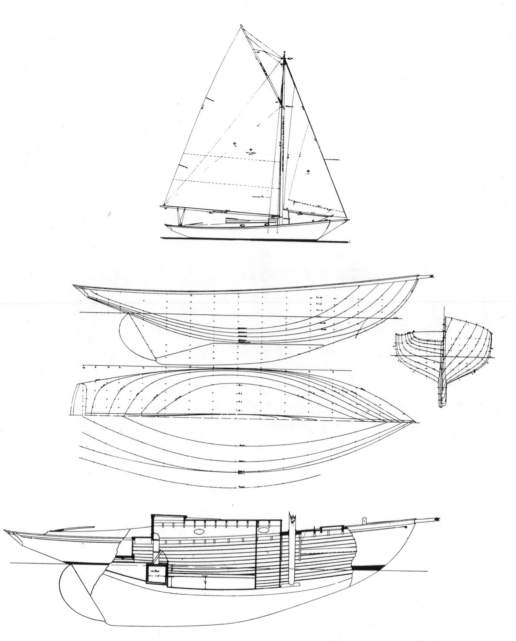

The 29-foot sloop *Vigilance* (later yawl-rigged), design
number 89, was built for H.C. Cushing of New York City
by William E. Haff in 1918. The photograph was taken
when she was owned by Harold C. McNulty, who praises her
sailing ability. *(The Rudder,* March 1918. Photo courtesy
Harold C. McNulty)

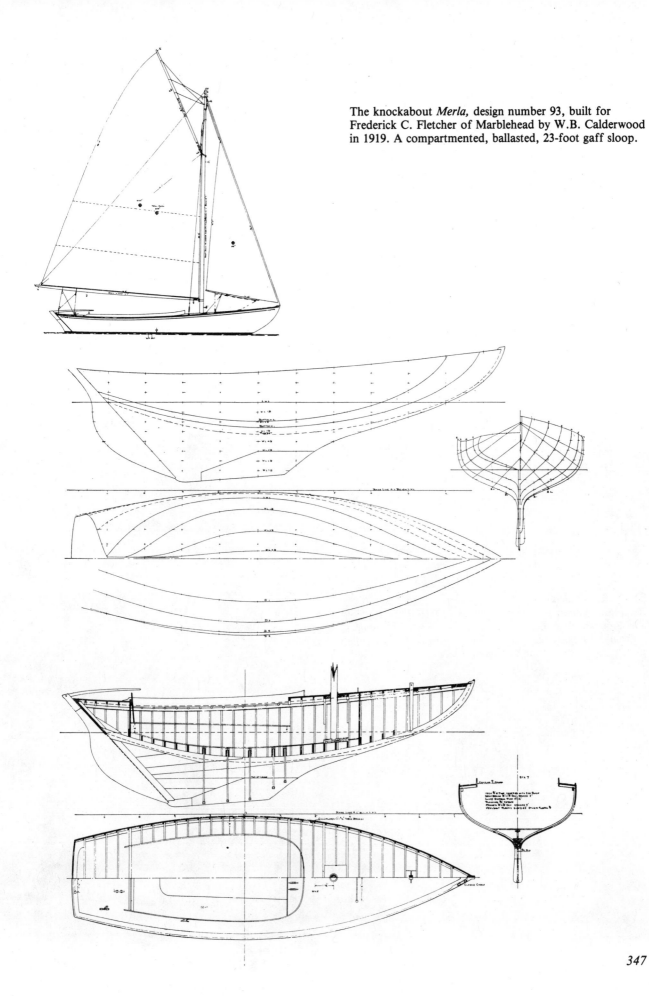

The knockabout *Merla,* design number 93, built for
Frederick C. Fletcher of Marblehead by W.B. Calderwood
in 1919. A compartmented, ballasted, 23-foot gaff sloop.

The Jamestown Class, Number 135, designed for the Conanicut Yacht Club. These are 21-foot marconi-rigged centerboard sloops with 214 square feet of sail and 1,000 pounds of ballast, forerunners of the Nantucket Indians (Chapter 8). They were built by George L. Chaisson and William Chamberlain for $915 each. *(Yachting,* March 1921)

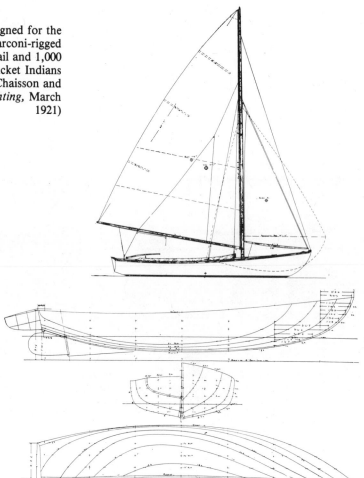

The 31-foot-8-inch sloop *Welwyn,* design number 141, lying to her mooring in a quiet harbor. Built in 1920 for a Dr. Hallock, the sloop was described by her present owner, Ed Coogan, as "strong, fast, capable, kindly, and comfortable — hard to match!" (Courtesy John G. Alden, Inc.)

348

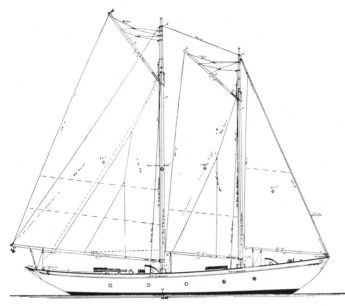

Originally a knockabout fisherman-type schooner, the 60-foot *Sunbeam* (design number 146) was built for Stephen D. Baker of New York by the Reed-Cook Marine Construction Company in 1922. Later named *Sinbad,* she saw extensive duty in the antisubmarine patrol during World War II. The photograph shows her with a bone in her teeth, driven by a new rig having a marconi main and a bowsprit. *(Motor Boat,* November 10, 1923. Photo courtesy John G. Alden, Inc.)

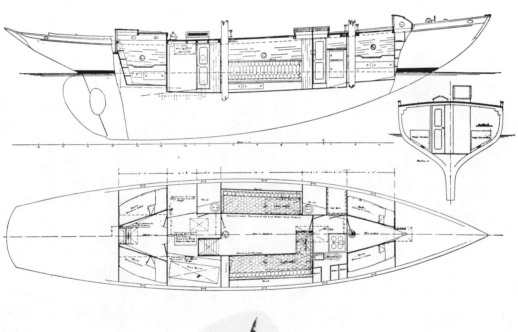

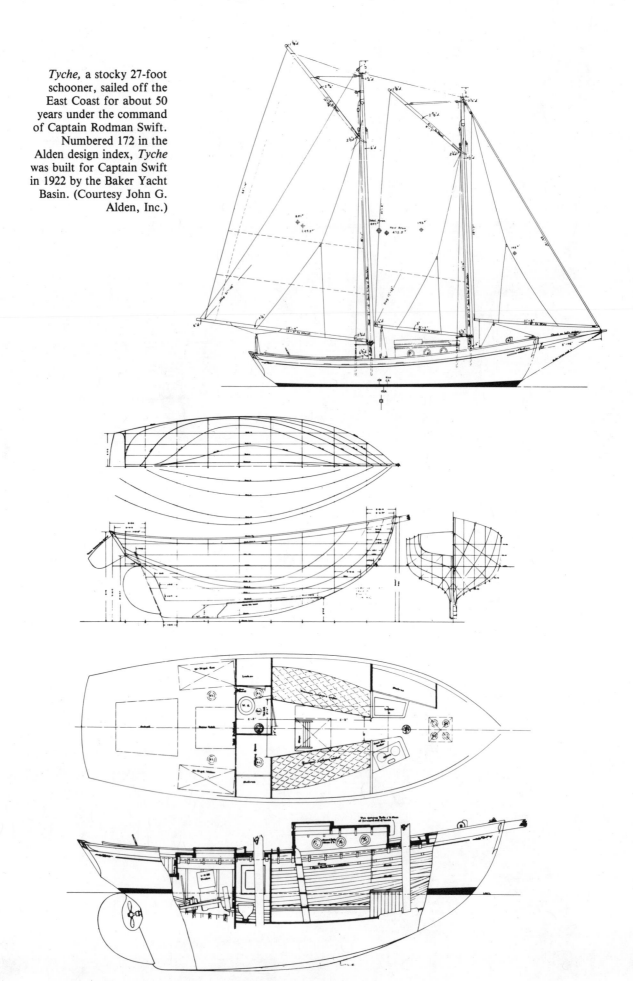

Tyche, a stocky 27-foot schooner, sailed off the East Coast for about 50 years under the command of Captain Rodman Swift. Numbered 172 in the Alden design index, *Tyche* was built for Captain Swift in 1922 by the Baker Yacht Basin. (Courtesy John G. Alden, Inc.)

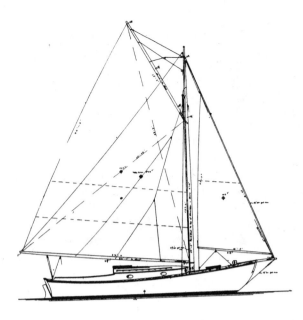

Design number 186 was the 25-foot-9-inch-waterline centerboard sloop *Shere Khan,* built by the Baker Yacht Basin. Douglas Richmond received her as a college graduation present from his mother in 1922, and he cruised the boat extensively for 23 years. After she was lost in the hurricane of 1954, Alan Vaitses built a raised-deck replica for Richmond using what was left of *Shere Khan,* including her iron keel. The replica, named *Amy D.,* was sailed by Richmond until he reached an advanced age. In 1976 he wrote, "After a total of 54 years in essentially the same boat . . . I have never wished for another." *(The Rudder,* August 1921)

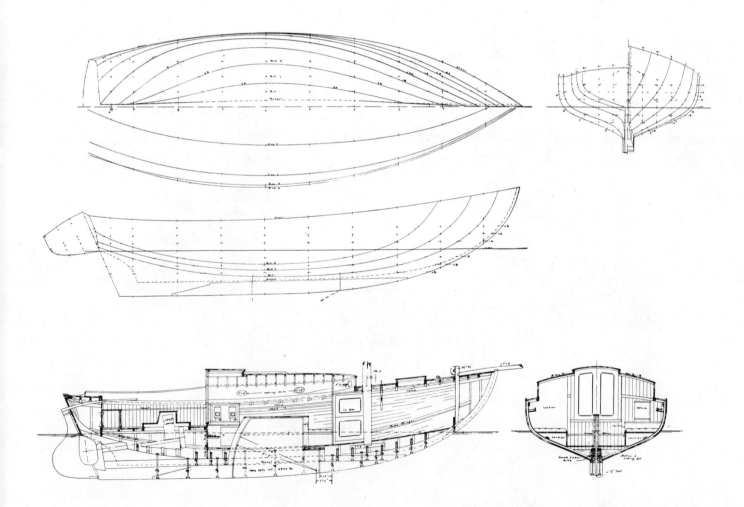

White Squall, later *Amberjack,* is a 42-foot
gaff-rigged schooner. Number 207-D, she
was built for Ralph L. Colton of
Philadelphia by C.A. Morse and Son in
1924. Edward Yeomans bought her in 1953,
gave her a main topmast, and kept her 25
years. "She won the so-called Great
Schooner Race in Gloucester three times,"
Yeomans wrote, "and after each of those
races we met the champion of the Canadian
schooner fleet either in Lunenburg or
Gloucester. Each time we lost, but we did
win in one of their local races — which included the same competitors, among others
— on corrected time. I was pretty proud of
her, considering that she was a 50-year-old
boat at the time." (Courtesy John G. Alden,
Inc.)

Two 55½-foot schooners were built to design number
226 in 1924 by the Rice Brothers of East Boothbay,
Maine. The first (shown here) was *Blue Water,* owned
first by Melville R. Smith of New York City and later
by J. Rulon Miller. She carries 1,491 square feet of
sail in her four lowers. The second, originally named
Beacon Rock and later *Bagheera,* was built for
Marion Eppley of Newport, Rhode Island. *(Yachting,*
August 1924)

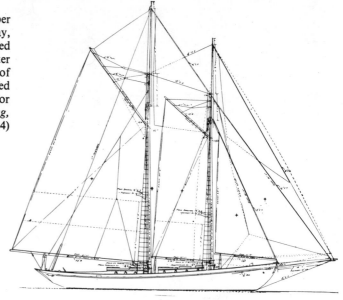

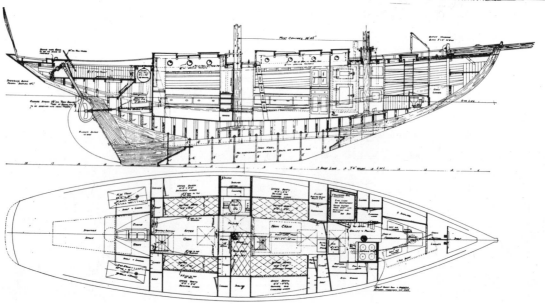

Poseidon II (originally *Privateer,* later *Sayanara),* a 42-foot-9-inch schooner built to design number 236. This design was a forerunner to the Alden 43s (Chapter 6). (Courtesy John G. Alden, Inc.)

The 31-foot-10-inch yawl *Escape,* design number 238, was originally a sloop named *Wildcat.* She has a saucy sheer and a cockpit that will seat several adults comfortably. (Courtesy John G. Alden, Inc.)

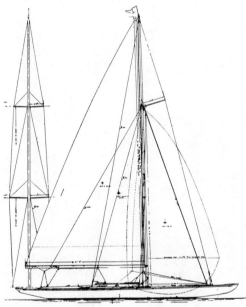

This R class sloop of 1925 (no design number) was 39 feet 6 inches, by 25 feet, by 6 feet 6 inches, by 5 feet 9 inches. The fullness in her entrance reduced her quarter-beam penalty. Her sail area of 585 square feet was balanced by 7,500 pounds of outside ballast. *(Yachting,* November 1925)

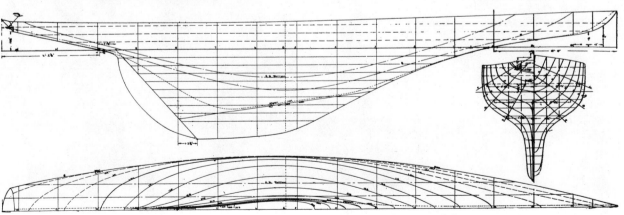

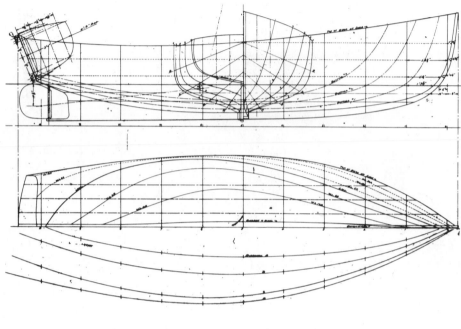

Design number 241, a 27-footer named *Peto,* is a "fishing launch" in the Alden records, and the pair of fighting chairs in the large cockpit indicate that she is a sport fisherman. She might also be called a small motorsailer with her sloop rig and centerboard. Dwight Simpson and Fenwick Williams collaborated on her plans. (Courtesy John G. Alden, Inc.)

Design number 253-A is the schooner *Heart's Desire,* a 43-footer built for A.S. Neilson of Marblehead, Massachusetts. Planked in yellow pine and heavily framed, she was delivered at a cost of $5,200 from her builder, T.H. Soule of South Freeport, Maine. Inspired by the fishing schooner *Lottie S. Haskins, Heart's Desire* was a forerunner of the Alden 43s and has the same cabin plan as a 270. Both she and a sister, *Venus* (originally *Picaroon),* have been much loved, much cared for, and familiar to many. Here, under the name *Athena* and the ownership of Peter and Norma Stanford, she sails in New York Harbor, 1967. More recently, new owners have rebuilt her completely. (Courtesy Norma Stanford)

354

An R class sloop, either *Alarm* (design number 262), owned by Clifford D. Mallory and Hamilton Hitt, or Dr. H.E. Potter's *Calypso* (Number 261). Both boats were built in Germany by Abeking and Rasmussen in 1925. (Courtesy Mrs. John Robinson)

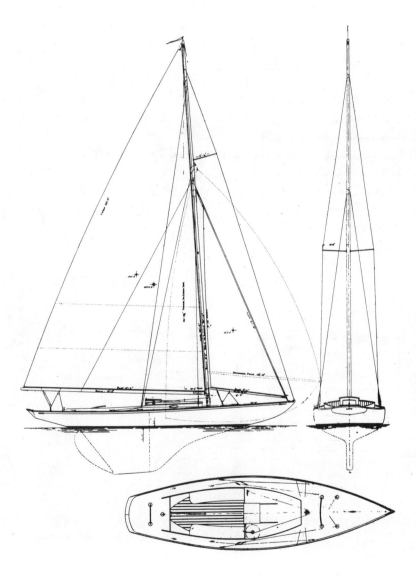

Number 278 is the Triangle One-Design. Eight were built for Marblehead in 1925, and another five were built the following year. Displacement of the 18½-foot-waterline sloop is 5,017 pounds, with 2,500 pounds of lead outside ballast and 407 square feet of sail. A few are still around. Julian D. Fischer found one on Lake Champlain in 1975, resurrected her, and sails her out of Little Harbor, New Hampshire. In 1978 he wrote that she was wet but stiff, and fast in any conditions. "We have sailed . . . in drifting matches in August and in 35 m.p.h. northwesters in October with equal success." (*Yachting,* March 1926)

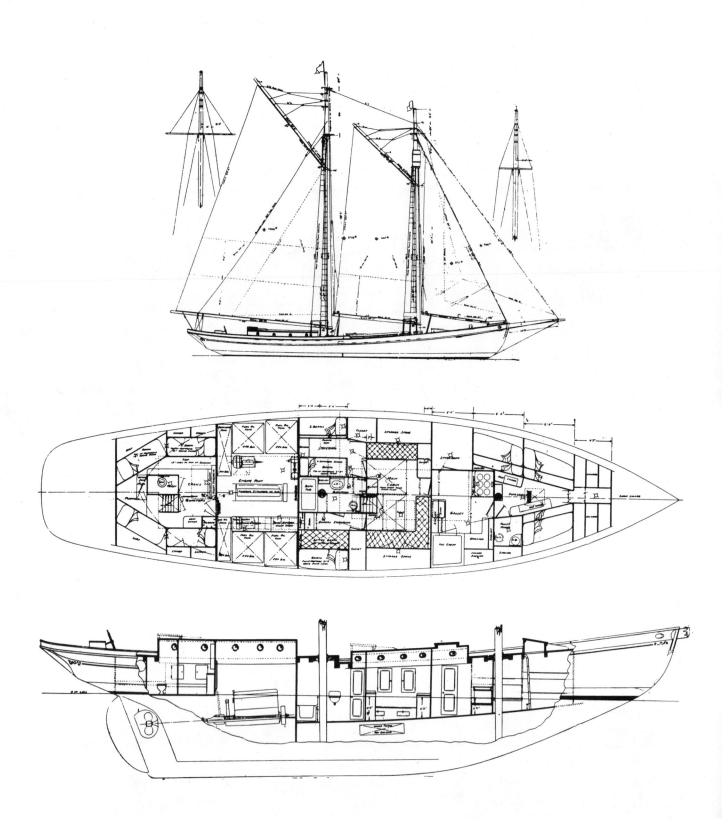

Sachem III, design number 283, a rugged 79-foot schooner, accompanied Donald B. MacMillan's schooner *Bowdoin* on an Arctic expedition in 1926. She was designed for Rowe B. Metcalf and built by C.A. Morse and Son in 1926. Metcalf's next *Sachem* (Number 333) was a very different boat. *(Yachting,* October 1926)

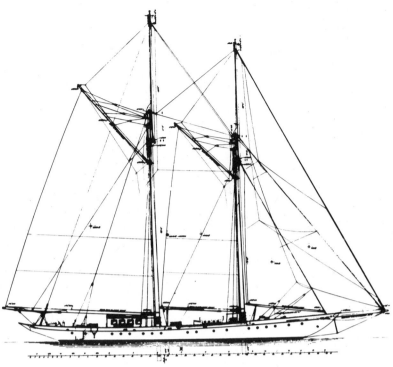

The 126-foot schooner *Starling*, design number 284. The book would not have been complete without her. She was built of steel in 1926 for George F. Tyler of Philadelphia. Note the *grand* piano in her saloon! The photograph was taken at Rice Brothers in East Boothbay, Maine, while she was building. William McNary drew the sail plan, which shows 6,219 square feet in the lowers. The mainsail, which sets on a 60-foot boom, has 3,153 square feet. (Courtesy John G. Alden, Inc. Photo courtesy Mrs. John Robinson)

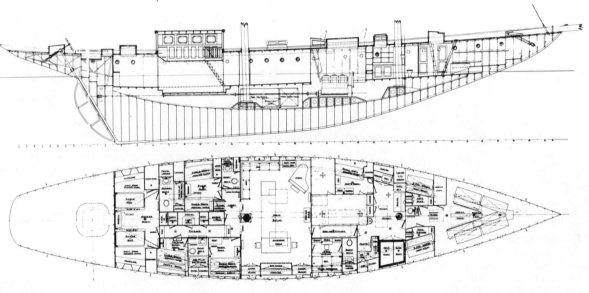

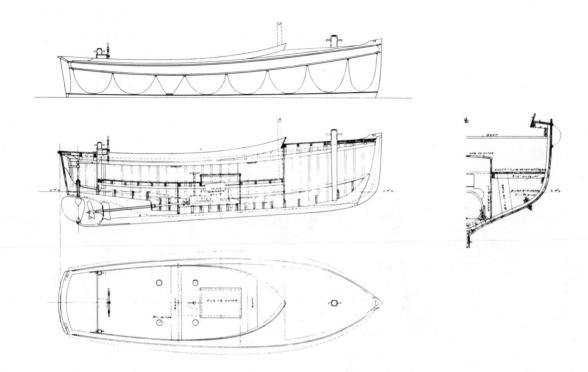

These plans for a 30-foot motor lifeboat, Number 302, were drawn by Aage Nielsen. She was built for the Marblehead Humane Society by Israel Snow in 1926. (Courtesy John G. Alden, Inc.)

Here and opposite:
John Robinson's first *Shag,* Number 303, was a forerunner to the second *Shag* (Number 358) and the Number 385 yawls (Chapter 6). Both *Shags* differ from the 385s in that they have shorter keels and slightly firmer bilges. Clifford Swaine and Fenwick Williams drew the plans for Number 303, which was built by C.A. Morse and Son in 1926. A member of the Cruising Club of America from its first year (1922), Robinson was an avid cruiser as well as an enthusiastic observer of boats and coastal fisheries, and his carefully compiled and cross-referenced scrapbooks were a valuable source of photos for this book. (Courtesy John G. Alden, Inc. Photos courtesy Mrs. John Robinson)

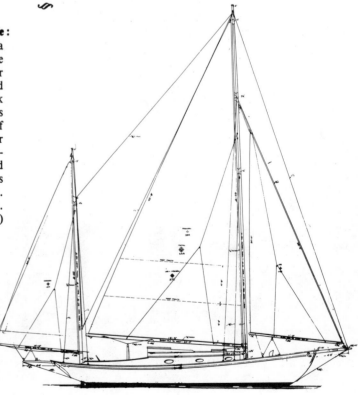

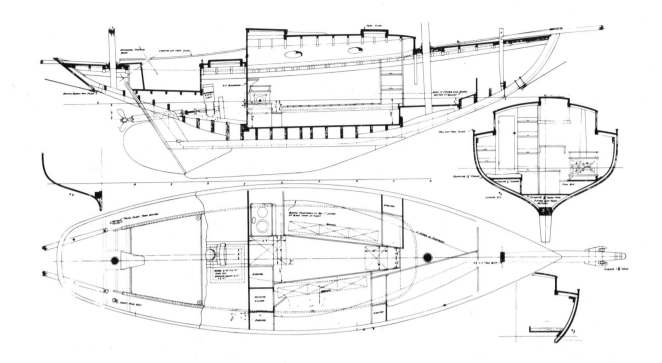

The 39-foot-7-inch R class sloop *Vitesse,* Number 305, built for William P. Barrows of Rochester, New York, by Lawley in 1926. She won the International George Cup in 1927 racing against the best American and Canadian Rs on Lake Erie. (Courtesy John G. Alden, Inc.)

The 307 ketches were close relatives of the *Svaap.* Three out of these four 33-foot-9-inch seagoing craft were built by C.A. Morse and Son in 1927. The second, named *Iron Duke* (originally *Topsie),* sailed for several years under the ownership of Richard McSherry in the author's home waters at Gibson Island, Maryland. (Courtesy John G. Alden, Inc.)

Valkyrie (originally *Arbella)* close-hauled with a big Yankee and a genoa staysail. This striking 73½-foot ketch, Number 308, was built for Robert Saltonstall of Boston by Lawley in 1927. She was abandoned at sea in 1954. (Courtesy John G. Alden, Inc.)

Number 316 was a flat-bottomed sailing skiff designed in 1926 for Youth's Companion and the Brooks Boat Company. She has a beam of 4½ feet and carries 108 square feet of sail. (Courtesy John G. Alden, Inc.)

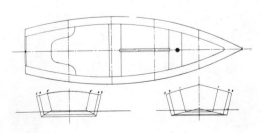

Number 323 was *Truant* (originally *Rowdy),* a 44-foot-4-inch boat with an interesting hybrid rig. She was built for Frederick Meyer by Nunes Brothers of Sausalito, California, in 1927. The Alden records call her a yawl but a later owner, Dr. W.T. Mooney, calls her a ketch. (Courtesy John G. Alden, Inc.)

∾

Susan Ann (originally *Hajada),* Number 327-A, was built for F.G. Towle by Harvey Gamage in 1927. Now named *Sara L.,* she cruises the Chesapeake. Bill McMillan's *Jolly Roger,* which burned in her first season when a paid hand poured gasoline into the kerosene stove, was a sister. (She was later restored.) These 43-foot schooners are a development of the 270 design. (Courtesy John G. Alden, Inc.)

362

Tyehee, design number 335, is a handsome 36-foot-4-inch fisherman-type schooner. Built in 1927 by Harvey Gamage as a day-sailer for W.H. Stuart, Jr., she was owned at one time by Alexander Moffat, who cruised her extensively and (with other owners over the years) added to her accommodations. Her lines and sail plan, both drawn by Aage Nielsen, show 697 square feet of canvas, 18,600 pounds designed displacement, and 6,600 pounds of outside ballast. The topmast was added in 1965 and the second jib in 1969 (to correct a weather helm), yet she is in essence unchanged, a schooner worthy of admiration. William Wertenbaker, her present owner, calls her "spirited, as they say of horses, but well behaved . . . . She tacks in 100 degrees in fair weather, making 6 knots upwind if the sea is fairly flat, and nothing at all in 4-foot waves. Off wind she cranks up to 8 knots pretty readily." A good sea boat, she once rode out a hurricane-force storm off Cape Hatteras. Wertenbaker enters her in schooner races with consistent success. (Courtesy John G. Alden, Inc. Photos courtesy William Wertenbaker)

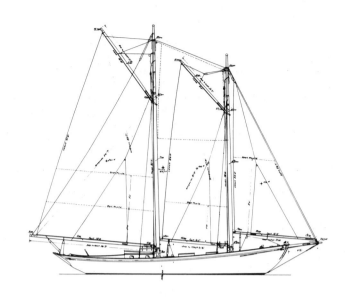

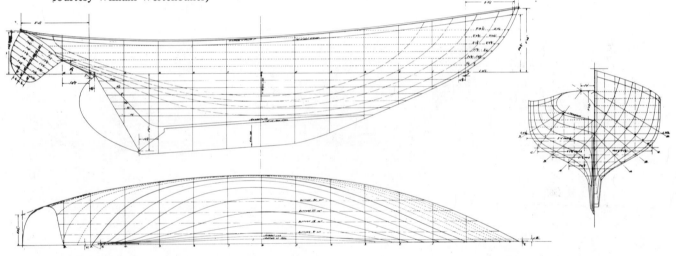

Hispaniola (now *Ulysses),* Number 353, is a hefty centerboard schooner designed for David B. Bannerman for cruising the shoal waters of Great South Bay. She was built by
Frank M. Weeks of Patchogue, Long Island, in 1928. She
has had 14 owners, and the most recent one, U.E. Gallanos,
described her as a seakindly boat that "sails beautifully with
a heavy feel." *(Yachting,* May 1929)

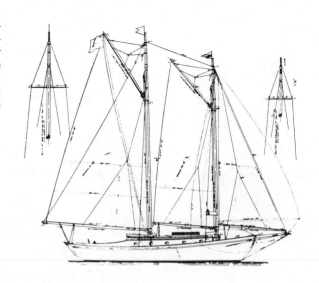

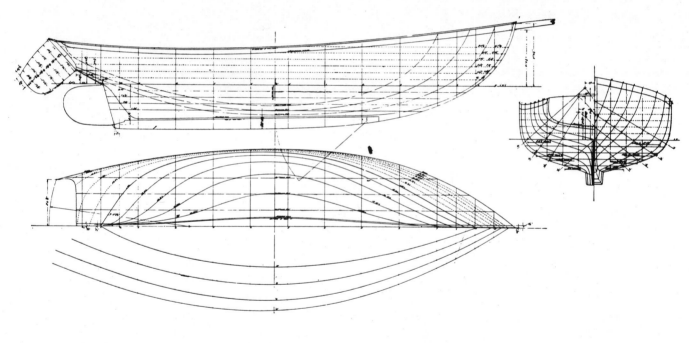

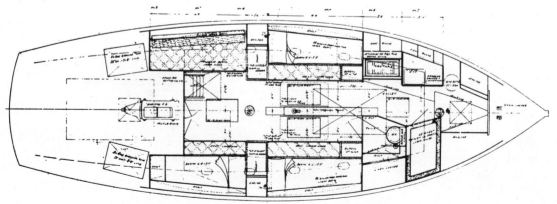

John Robinson's second *Shag,* Number 358. Robinson replaced his first *Shag* (according to Fenwick Williams) primarily because he wanted a Lawley-built boat. She was completed in 1928. A later owner, Mrs. H. Graham Pope, wrote that *Shag* was known as a "John Harvey boat," a laudation reserved for boats built under the careful supervision of Harvey, who was head of the Lawley small-boat shop. Except for her rudder and four inches of additional length, she is virtually identical to the first *Shag,* and both boats are forerunners of the 385 yawls (Chapter 6). (Courtesy John G. Alden, Inc. and Mrs. John Robinson)

Number 367 was a 54-foot-9-inch auxiliary sailing cruiser, the keel design of which, in typical Alden fashion, was borrowed from Number 248 *(Malabar VI* and her sisters). The first seven 367s were ketches, but the last one, shown here, was the yawl *Sea Witch.* Her yawl rig made her faster than her sisters. *(The Rudder,* April 1932)

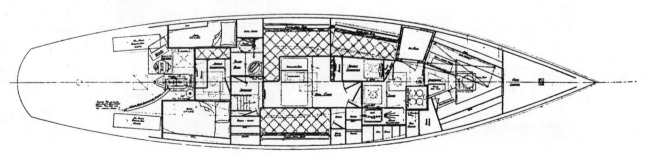

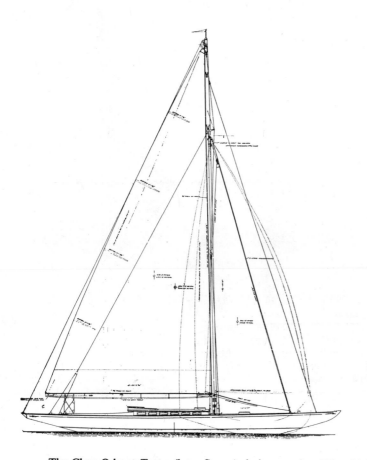

The Class Q boat *Tartar* (later *Scapa),* design number 370, which Alden designed for his own use in 1928. The designer had only moderate success racing her, and according to Carl Alberg she was not as fast as *Nor'easter IV,* which Alden designed two years earlier. The 50-foot-4-inch *Tartar* sank in a hurricane in 1960. *(Yachting,* November 1928. Photo courtesy John G. Alden, Inc.)

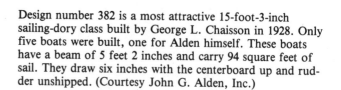

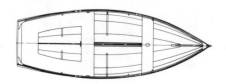

Design number 382 is a most attractive 15-foot-3-inch sailing-dory class built by George L. Chaisson in 1928. Only five boats were built, one for Alden himself. These boats have a beam of 5 feet 2 inches and carry 94 square feet of sail. They draw six inches with the centerboard up and rudder unshipped. (Courtesy John G. Alden, Inc.)

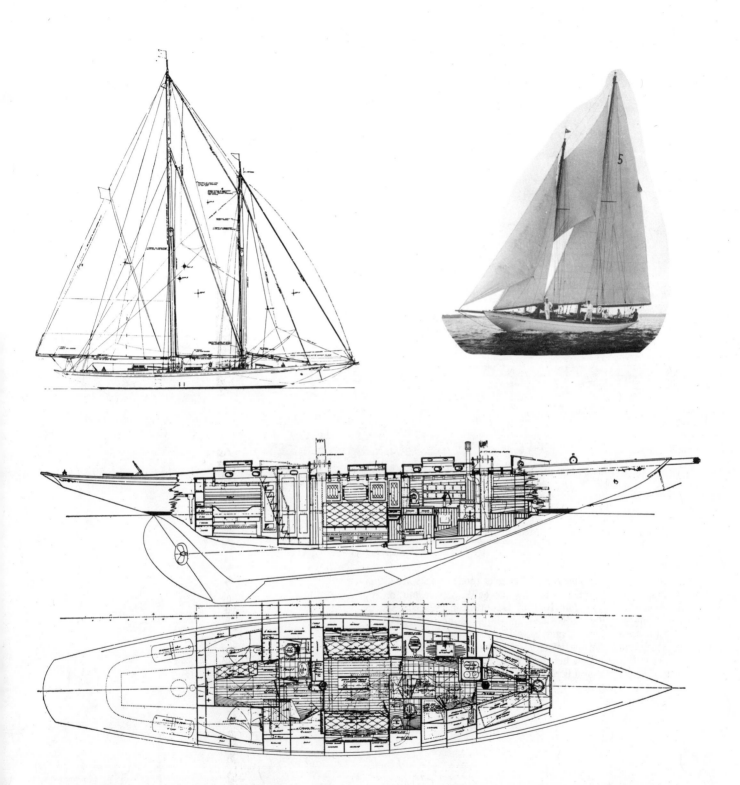

Number 394 was the sleek 60-foot staysail schooner *Minikoe V,* built for C.D. Alexander by Fred Pendleton in 1929. She had double mahogany planking, teak decks, hollow spars, and 1,960 square feet of sail. *(Yachting,* December 1928. Photo courtesy John G. Alden, Inc.

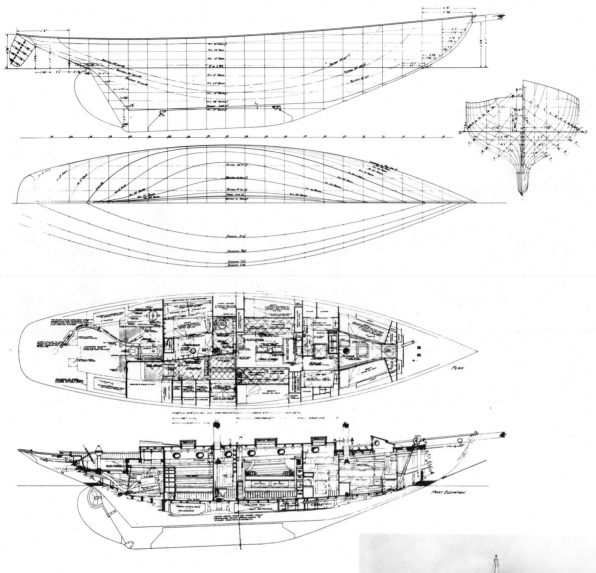

Number 397 was *Teragram* (Margaret spelled backward), the 58-foot-5-inch schooner owned by George W. Mixter, author of the *Primer of Navigation*. Built by Dauntless in 1929, she sailed in a number of Bermuda Races, finishing second in her class in 1930 and fourth in 1932 and 1936. Her designed displacement is 61,400 pounds, with a ballast-displacement ratio of 37 percent.

Aage Nielsen drew her lines, Bill McNary, her accommodations. The photograph is recent. (Courtesy John G. Alden, Inc. Ralph J. Naranjo photo)

Number 406 was a pretty 21-foot double-ended knockabout. Five sisters were built. (Courtesy John G. Alden and Mrs. John Robinson)

∽

Varuna, design number 411, was an 80-foot schooner built for Dr. J. Remsen Bishop by Fred Pendleton in 1929. She sank in 1930, and her wreck was bought by Benjamin C. Smith of the Standard Motor Construction Co. Smith must have restored the schooner, because a later name — *Parca de Oro III* — is listed for her. (Courtesy Deborah Carmen)

Three 58-foot schooners were built to design number 440. The top photograph shows Number 440-B, originally owned by Charles T. Russell and named *Pitzi*. The aerial photograph is of *Marita,* 440-C, with her spinnaker and golly pulling hard, and the cockpit view shows *Marita*'s crew, including two later commodores of the American Yacht Club, at the start of the 1931 New London-Cape May Race. Built for Franklin M. Haines by Harvey Gamage in 1930, *Marita*'s later names include *Ibis* and *Zambeze*. The third sister, originally *Penzance,* sails on the West Coast under the name *White Cloud II. (Marita*'s photos courtesy Franklin M. Haines, Jr., and the American Yacht Club. *Pitzi* photo courtesy John G. Alden, Inc.)

370

The 93-foot-7-inch schooner *Kestrel II* (later *Countess),* Number 444, was built for Guy P. Gannett in 1930. She was truly elegant below decks, as befit the head of the Gannett publishing empire. (Courtesy Deborah Carmen)

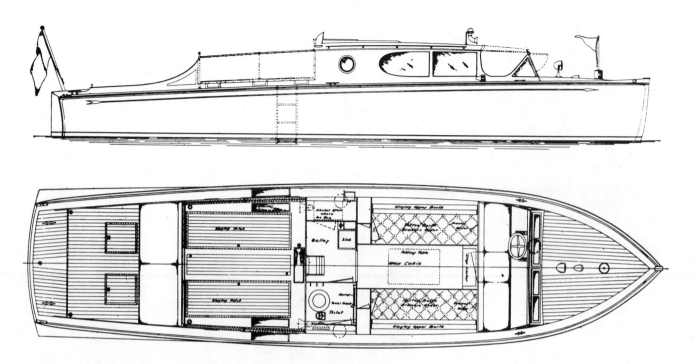

Cathalene, Number 479, was a 38-foot, round-bottomed commuter boat built for Cornelius Crane by Goudy and Stevens in 1930. She had two Sterling Petrel gasoline engines and double mahogany planking, the inner skin being laid diagonally, and she was capable of 26 knots on long runs and 33 knots wide open. Crane used her for frequent trips between Ipswich, Massachusetts, and Newport, Rhode Island. *(Yachting,* November 1930)

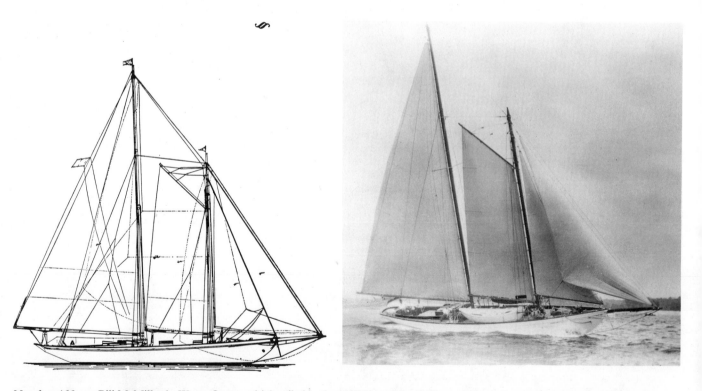

Number 466 was Bill McMillan's *Water Gypsy,* which sailed in the 1931 Transatlantic Race and was first around the rock in the 1931 Fastnet. She was third in class and fleet in the 1932 Bermuda Race and second in class and fleet in 1934. Built by Hodgdon Brothers in 1931, the 59-foot schooner was lost in the hurricane of 1938. Aage Nielsen drew her plans. (Courtesy John G. Alden, Inc.)

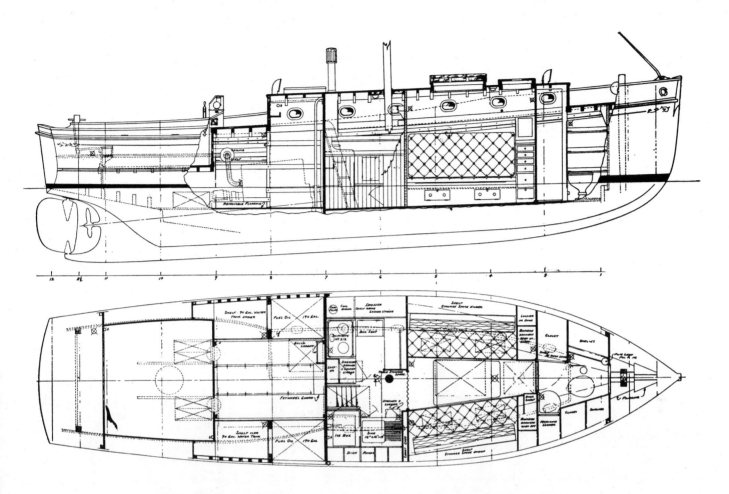

The husky, diesel-powered 38-foot cruiser *Stowaway,* design number 483, was influenced by *Mildred IV* (Chapter 9). Her owner said that Alden himself "fussed over her lines." She was heavily built by the Gamage yard (under the close supervision of Dwight Simpson) for Holcombe J. Brown. *(Yachting,* February 1933. Photo courtesy Mrs. John Robinson)

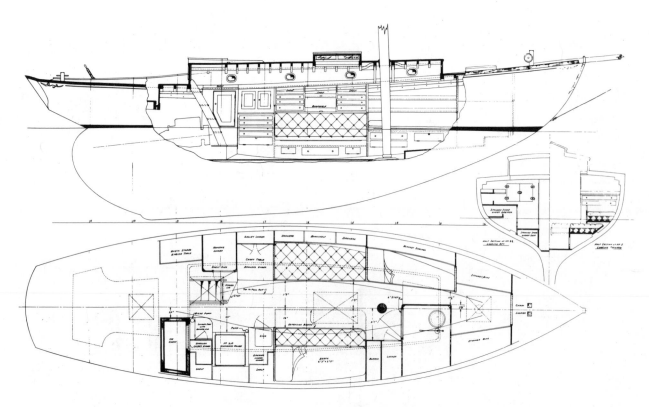

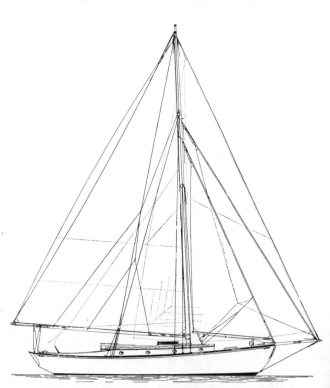

Number 485 was *Mandalay,* a 38½-foot cutter designed for marine artist Frank Vining Smith. The accommodations plans were drawn by Fenwick Williams. (Courtesy John G. Alden, Inc.)

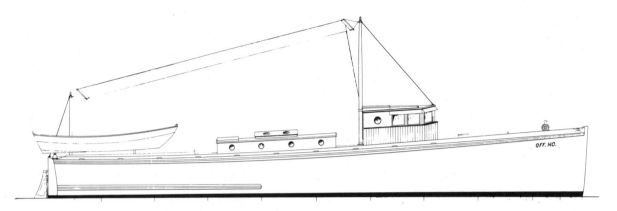

Design number 487, a fast 55-foot powerboat named *Viola,* is called a "Special Boat" in the Alden index. She was built by Dauntless Shipyard in 1930 and has a huge Sterling Viking eight-cylinder engine producing 565 h.p. at 1,200 r.p.m. She may have been a rumrunner. (Courtesy John G. Alden, Inc.)

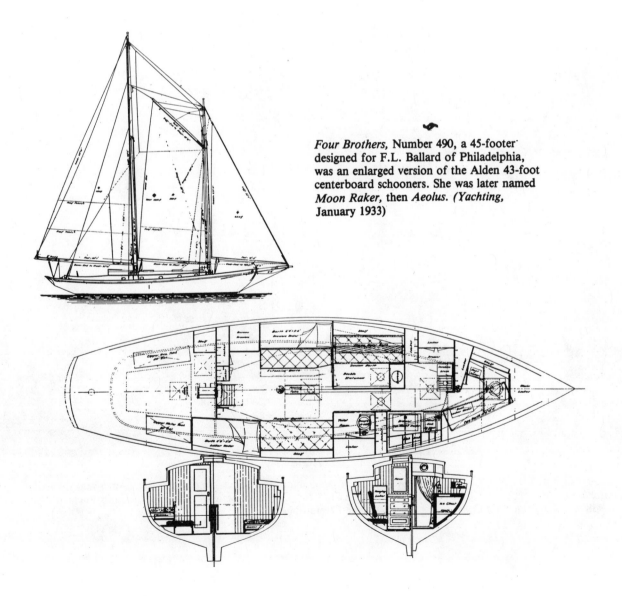

Four Brothers, Number 490, a 45-footer designed for F.L. Ballard of Philadelphia, was an enlarged version of the Alden 43-foot centerboard schooners. She was later named *Moon Raker,* then *Aeolus. (Yachting,* January 1933)

Number 498 was C.V. Watson's second *La Reine,* which later, under the ownership of Sally Blair Ames and the name *Constellation,* won her class in the 1959 Transpac Race. The 75-foot-9-inch schooner, built by Hodgdon Brothers in 1932, was still sailing on the West Coast at last report. (Diane Beeston photo)

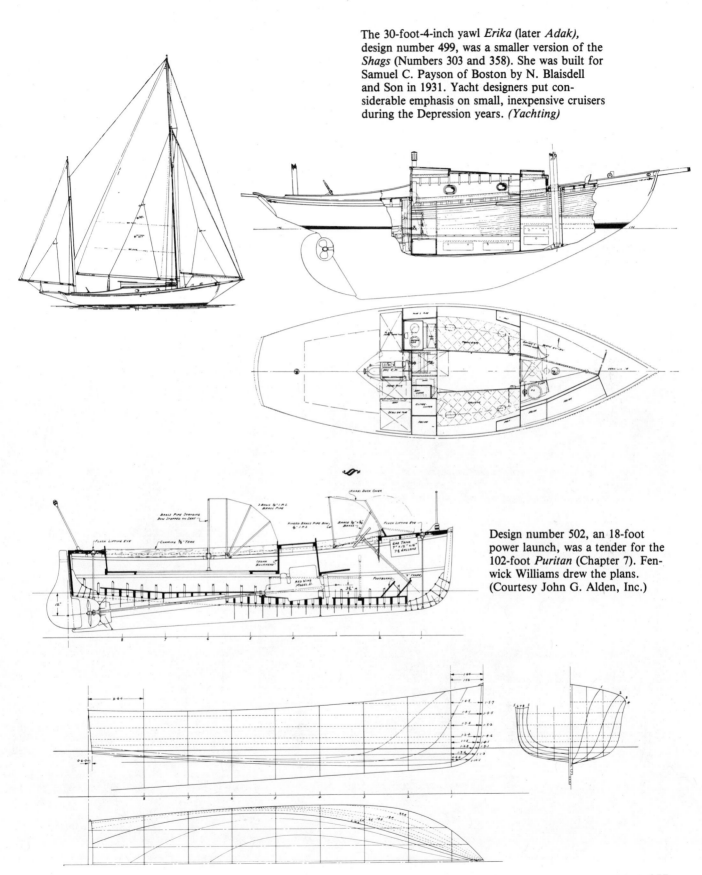

The 30-foot-4-inch yawl *Erika* (later *Adak*), design number 499, was a smaller version of the *Shags* (Numbers 303 and 358). She was built for Samuel C. Payson of Boston by N. Blaisdell and Son in 1931. Yacht designers put considerable emphasis on small, inexpensive cruisers during the Depression years. *(Yachting)*

Design number 502, an 18-foot power launch, was a tender for the 102-foot *Puritan* (Chapter 7). Fenwick Williams drew the plans. (Courtesy John G. Alden, Inc.)

Number 506 was a 32-foot cutter designed with an emphasis on easy handling for a small crew. Two sisters were built by C.A. Morse and Son in 1932. *Bantam* (cabin and sail plans) was first owned by A.S. ("Sandy") Neilson. The photograph is of her sister *Saree* (originally *Sweet Honey*). *(Yachting.* Photo courtesy John G. Alden, Inc.)

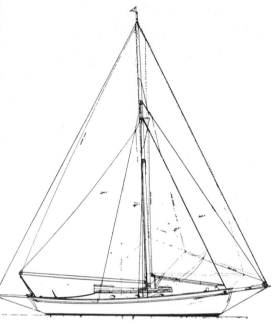

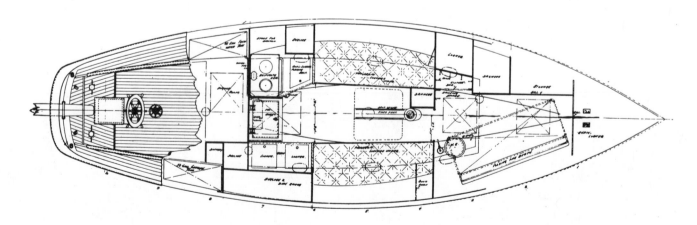

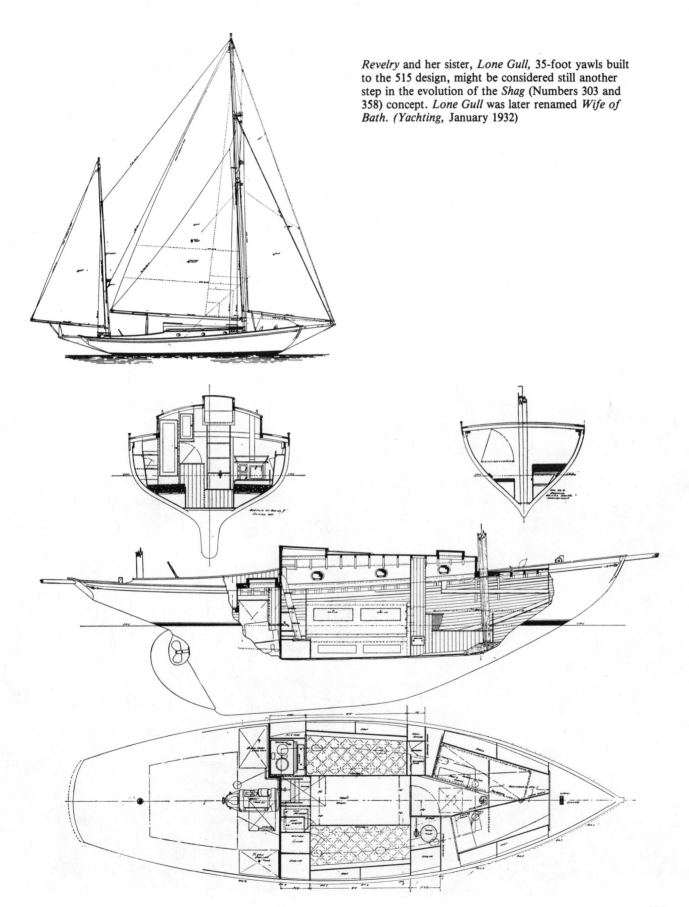

Revelry and her sister, *Lone Gull,* 35-foot yawls built to the 515 design, might be considered still another step in the evolution of the *Shag* (Numbers 303 and 358) concept. *Lone Gull* was later renamed *Wife of Bath. (Yachting,* January 1932)

This unnumbered 1933 design was drawn for a contest the Cruising Club of America sponsored while developing a new rating rule. Alden's 72-foot yawl, which took second prize, was the only design by a "name" designer to be selected. The results of this contest contributed to the establishment of a "base boat," the standard of wholesomeness from which a designer could not deviate to any great extent without incurring a severe penalty. The yawl's other dimensions are 55 feet load waterline, 18 feet beam, and 10½ feet draft, and her sail area is 2,680 square feet. *(Yachting,* September 1933)

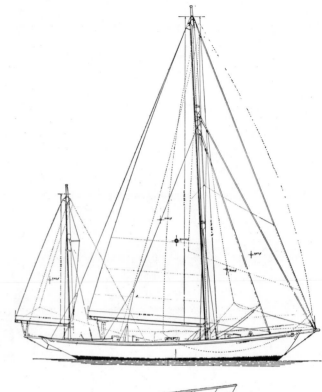

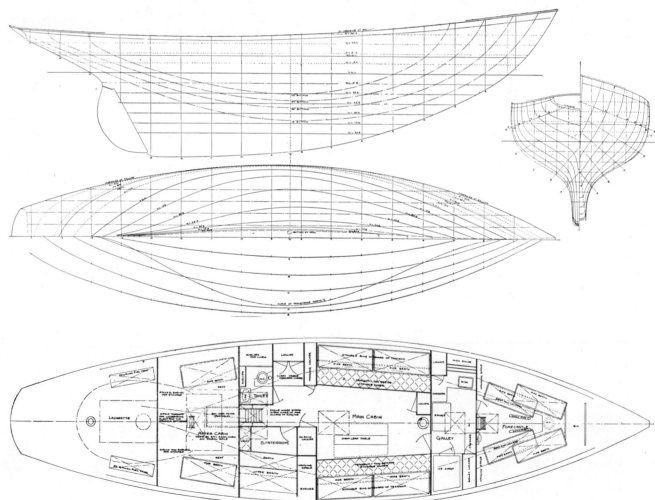

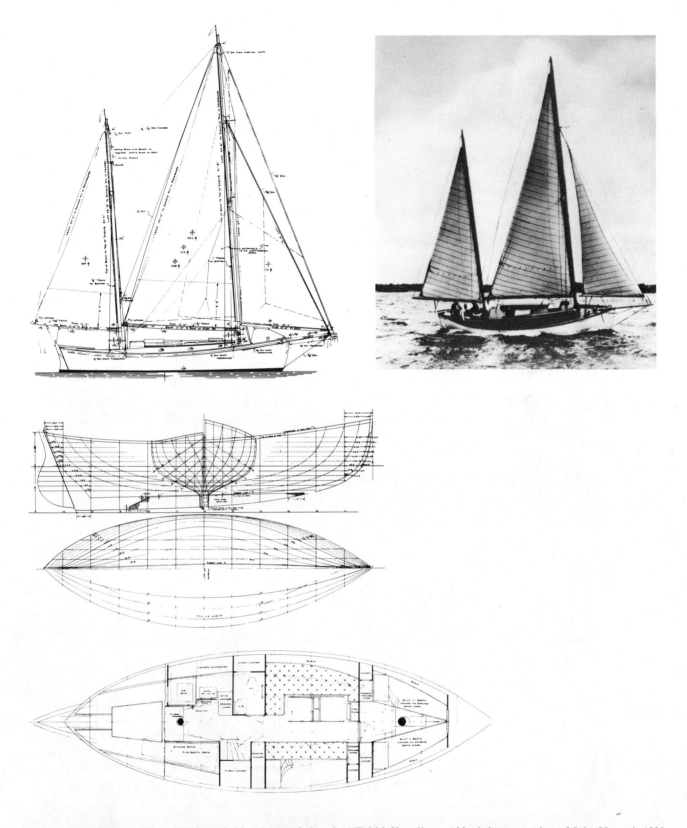

Design number 522, a 35-foot double-ended ketch recorded as the "Tahiti Class," was Alden's interpretation of John Hanna's 1923 *Tahiti* design (originally known as the *Orca* design). Alden's version is undoubtedly the better sailer, for she has a taller, more efficient rig and a little more draft than Hanna's *Tahiti* or larger *Carol* model. The prototype of Number 522 was designed for Henry T. Meneely, but she was never built. The first of the class was *Beluga* (most recently *Rena),* shown in the photograph above. Fenwick Williams drew the plans. (Courtesy John G. Alden, Inc.)

Number 525-B was *Vagabond,* a 52-foot schooner with a generous bowsprit. She was built in 1932 for S. Howard Martin of Boston by George Lawley. (Courtesy John G. Alden, Inc.)

The centerboard schooner *Janelburn,* Number 528, was a 66-footer built for Mrs. R.M. Roloson of Cotuit, Massachusetts, by Goudy and Stevens in 1932. Later names include *Rip Tide, Regal Lady,* and *Charmian II.* (Courtesy John G. Alden, Inc.)

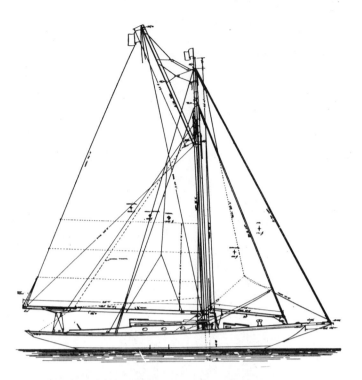

Number 531 was a low-freeboard 45-foot sloop. With her cabin trunk rounded forward and her gaff rig, she looked as though she had been designed in an earlier time. Originally named *Lark,* she was built for Ralph E. Forbes of Boston by F.D. Lawley in 1932. Somebody (John Alden?) doctored the lines drawing. The Forbes family, owners of the Elizabeth Islands, daysailed *Lark* in Buzzards Bay and Vineyard Sound for many years. She was recently completely rebuilt by her present owner, Eric Little of Woods Hole. *(The Rudder,* September 1932, and courtesy John G. Alden, Inc.)

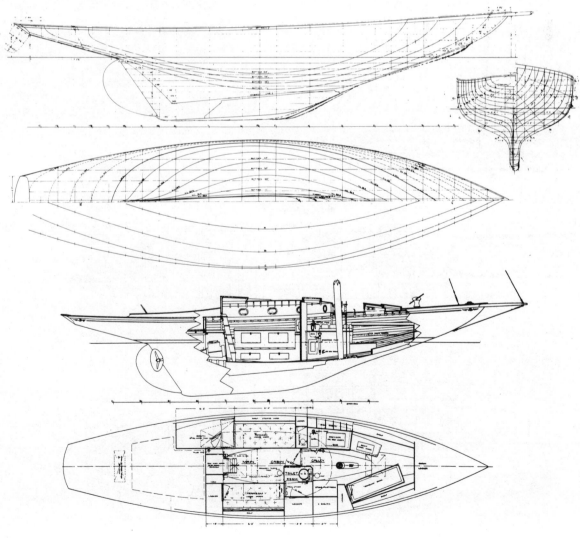

D. Spencer Berger's first *Mandoo* was a 62-foot schooner (design number 534), built in 1932 by George Lawley. She crossed the Atlantic after the 1934 Bermuda Race, in which she finished a respectable sixth in Class A. *(Yachting,* April 1932. Photo courtesy John G. Alden, Inc.)

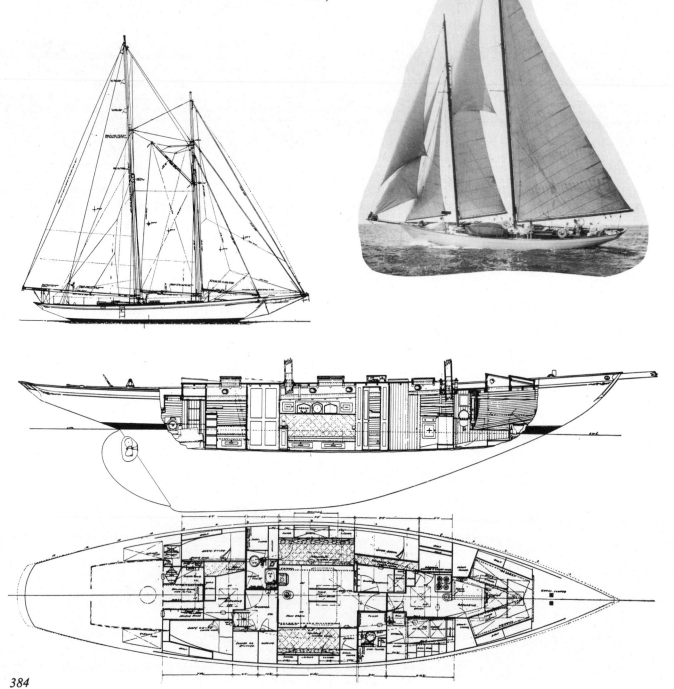

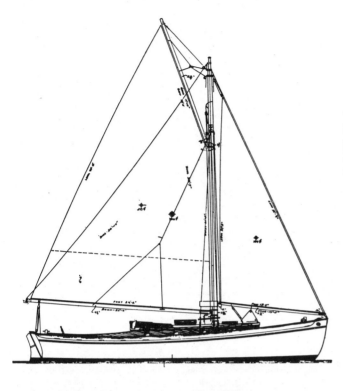

The 40-foot motorsailer *Conquest,* Number 558, was
built by C.A. Morse and Son in 1933 for C.A. Sawyer,
then vice commodore of the Boston Yacht Club. She was
later called *Captain Caution,* an appropriate name for a
safe, conservative boat. *(Yachting)*

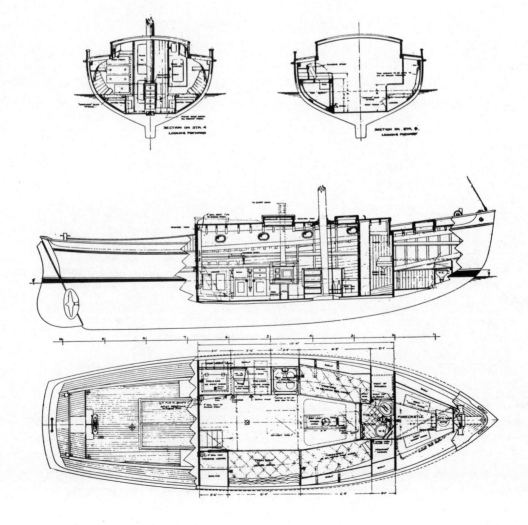

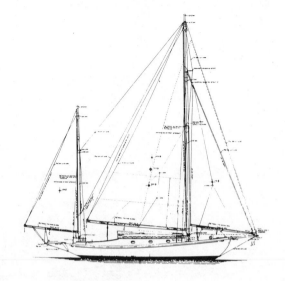

Number 573 was a beamy 35-foot-4-inch centerboard yawl named *Quest* (later *Monk),* one of several small, seaworthy, shallow-draft yawls developed by Alden. The plans show an interesting folding berth in the main cabin. *(The Rudder,* December 1934)

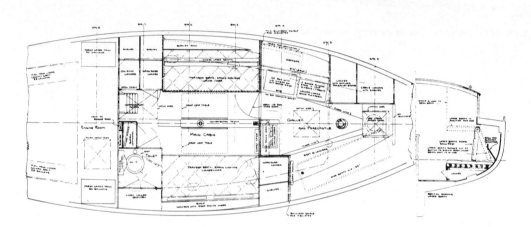

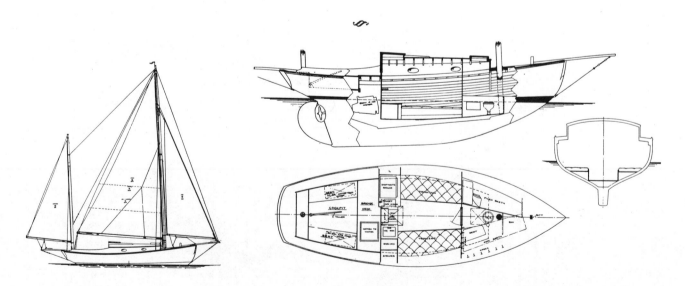

The 28-foot-5-inch yawl *Little Gull* (design number 574) is an attractive pocket cruiser. She was built for John Killam Murphy by Harvey Gamage in 1934. *(Yachting,* March 1934)

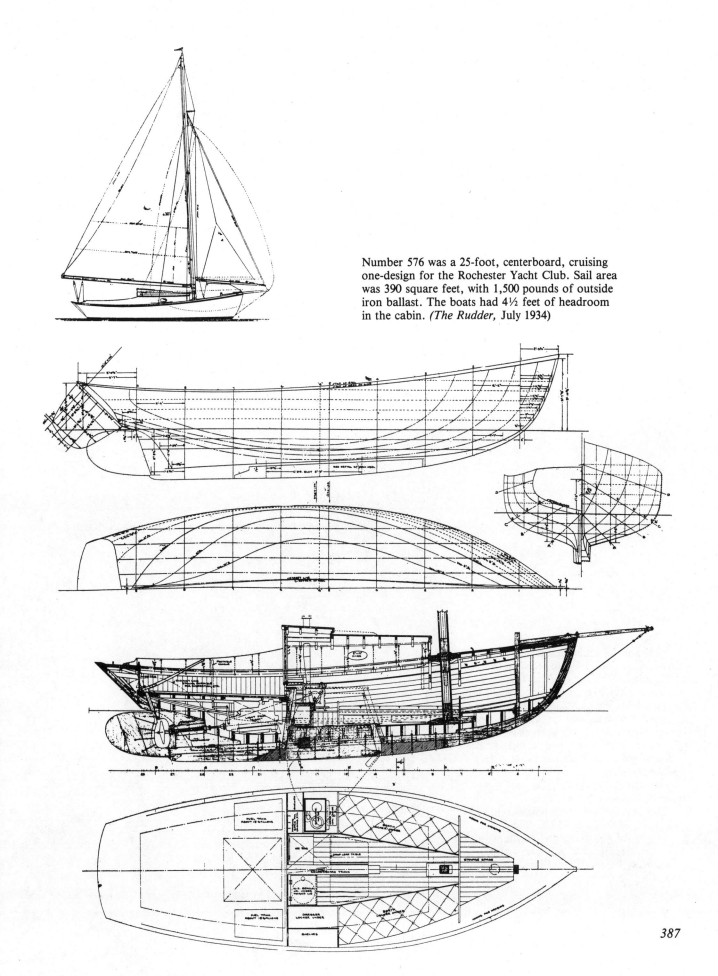

Number 576 was a 25-foot, centerboard, cruising one-design for the Rochester Yacht Club. Sail area was 390 square feet, with 1,500 pounds of outside iron ballast. The boats had 4½ feet of headroom in the cabin. *(The Rudder,* July 1934)

Tamora (later, *Tide Over,* then *Heart's Desire),* Number 579, is a 34-foot, high-freeboard motorsailer built in 1934 for John M. Butler by Willis J. Reid. (Courtesy John G. Alden, Inc.)

The 47-foot schooner *Discovery III,* Number 581, was built for R.W. Everest of Plainfield, New Jersey. The third yacht designed for Everest by Alden, she is a modification of *Malabar IV.* A sister named *Dart* was built for A. Sosnovsky of Riga, Latvia. The boats have 1,148 square feet of sail, hollow spars, and double planking (mahogany over cedar) on white-oak frames. As *Vela,* under the ownership of Reynolds Miller, and more recently, Reynolds's son David, *Discovery III* has made her home port Boothbay Harbor, Maine, since 1940. Rock solid, she has yet to require rebuilding or refastening. (Alden Stickney photo. Courtesy Reynolds and Eleanor Miller)

Number 593, the 36-foot-4-inch centerboard yawl
Rowena (later *Seagreg)*. (Courtesy John G. Alden, Inc.)

$\wp$

Here and on the next page:

Number 598, a 32-foot-9-inch cutter, was the first of two
Alden Traveler classes (the second being Number 875). The
first of the series, *Wind Whistle,* was built for R.D.
McMillan by the Morse Boatbuilding Corporation in 1935.
A recent owner of *Traveller* (Number 598-B), Carl Berg,
writes that his boat is "beautiful to look at and to sail."
The Morse yard went on to build eight of the boats between
April and the end of October that year. Carl Alberg drew
the sail plan, which shows 644 square feet of sail. Designed
displacement is 17,725 pounds, with 5,450 pounds of outside
iron ballast. Fenwick Williams drew the cabin plans. The
photographs show *Traveller* (above) and *Bounty,* 598-B
(below). (Courtesy John G. Alden, Inc.)

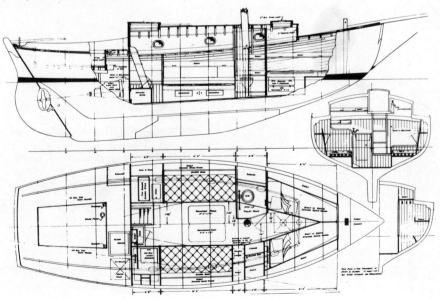

One of Alden's more successful racers was *Rubaiyat,* a 43-foot-2-inch cutter (Number 605) built for Nathaniel Rubinkam by George Lawley in 1935. She won the Chicago-Mackinac Race in 1936 and 1937. She was later converted to a yawl. (Courtesy John G. Alden, Inc.)

ꝯ

Brenda (later *Brindaban),* Number 610, is a 44½-footer with a small, inboard rig. Called a "fast cruising yawl" in the Alden records, she was built by the Herreshoff Manufacturing Company in 1935 for Charles A. Goodwin, who wanted a fast boat that was easy to handle. Her beam is just eight feet on a 30-foot waterline, and she carries 746 square feet of sail. *(Yachting,* February 1936)

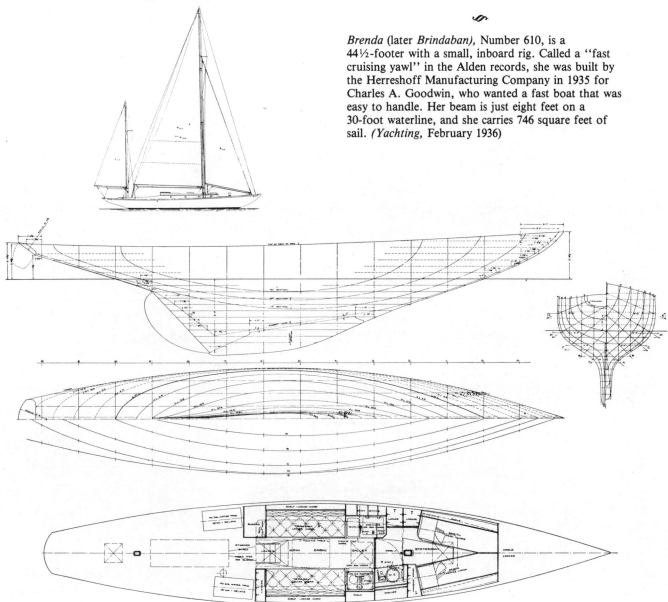

Number 616 was a 35-foot-10½-inch cutter with 752 square feet of sail and 7,800 pounds of outside iron ballast on a designed displacement of 18,800 pounds. Carl Alberg drew the plans. The sail plan shows a long lead of the center of effort over the center of lateral resistance. Twelve sisters were built, seven of them by the Morse Boatbuilding Corporation. (Courtesy John G. Alden, Inc.)

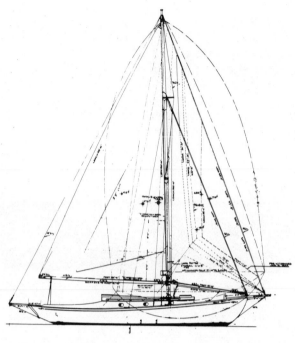

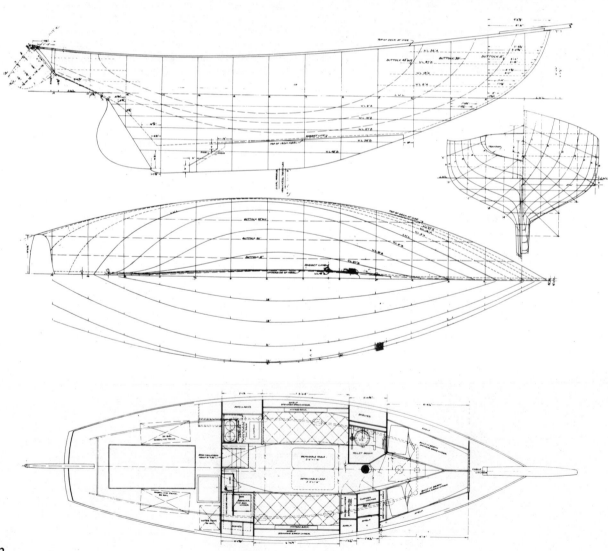

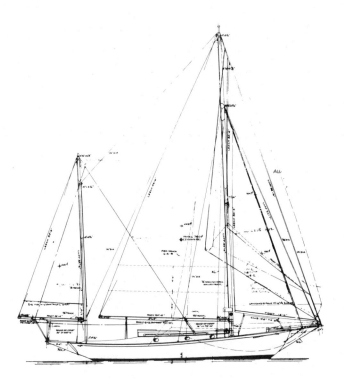

Number 618 was a yawl with the same lines and cabin plan as Number 616. She carries 760 square feet of sail in her three lowers. Ten sisters were built, most of them by James E. Graves, Inc., and the Casey Boatbuilding Corporation. Shown in the photograph is *Jinx,* Number 618-H. (Courtesy John G. Alden, Inc.)

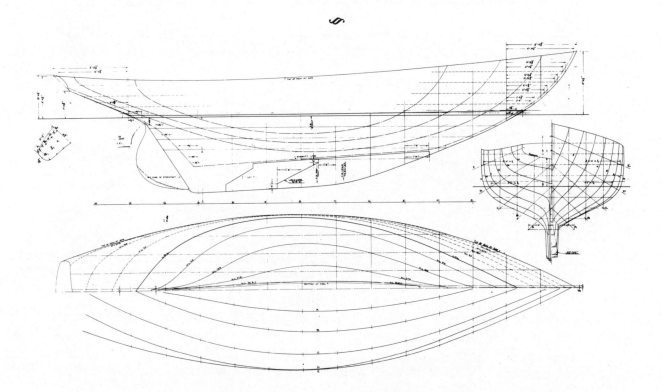

Number 619 has the same sail plan as Number 618 and the same cabin plan as Numbers 616 and 618, but her ends are longer (although her designed displacement is the same). Cliff Swaine drew her lines. The crudely sketched alternate rudder profile was the one actually used. Three to five sisters were built. (Courtesy John G. Alden, Inc.)

Number 622 was a design for a 32-foot-waterline sloop submitted to the New York Yacht Club as a replacement for the old New York Thirties, but it was beaten out by a Sparkman and Stephens submission, which became the New York 32. The Alden 32-footer has been compared with *Dorothy Q.* (see *Sirocco,* Chapter 7), and the lines, drawn by Carl Alberg, are quite similar, but the 622 has a more triangular profile. She carries 961 square feet of sail and displaces 24,760 pounds, with 44 percent of it in her lead keel. (Courtesy John G. Alden, Inc.)

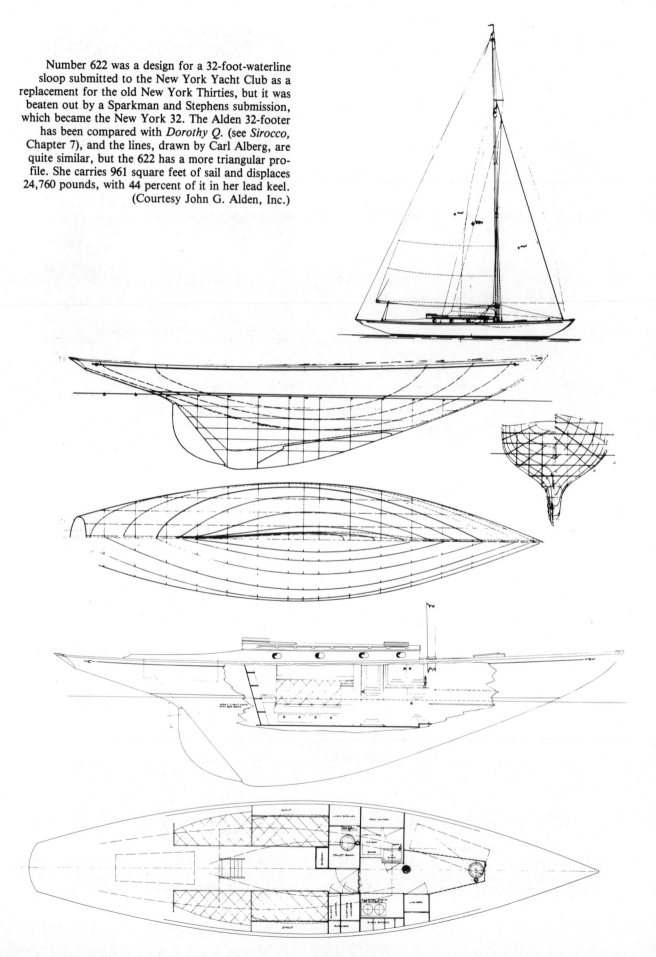

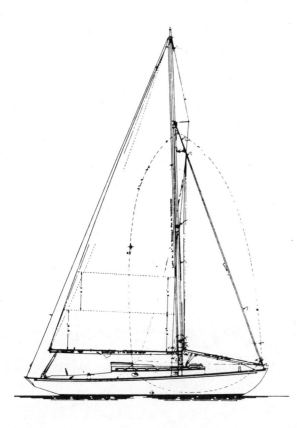

Elliot White, Number 628, was a keel-centerboarder drawing less than three feet. A pretty 34-foot sloop, she was designed for Dr. C. Malcolm Gilman for use on Barnegat Bay, and built by Mantoloking Boat and Engine Company in 1936. Later names have included *Tranquilla* and *Sandpiper. (Your New Boat* by the Editors of *Yachting)*

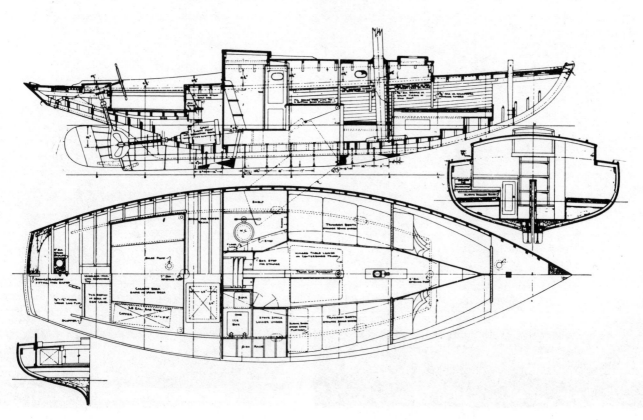

Gitana, Number 630, was originally a 39-foot-9-inch sloop (below right) with a raised deck. Below left is a photograph developed from a negative on which Alden sketched a mizzen and a mizzen staysail, probably while discussing *Gitana*'s proposed yawl rig with her owner. The photograph at right shows how the yawl rig actually appeared. Sisters were built in the Isle of Wight and Martinique. (Courtesy John G. Alden, Inc.)

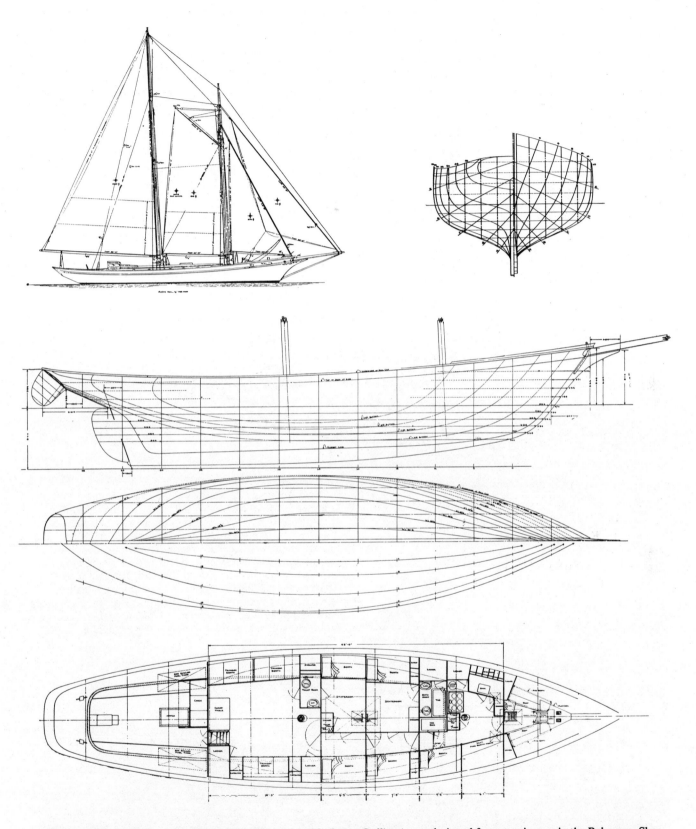

Number 635, the 84-foot clipper-bowed schooner *Merida* (later, *Gulliver),* was designed for extensive use in the Bahamas. She was built for Robert C. Rathbone by Symonette Shipyards, Inc., at Nassau in 1938. Her draft was kept light for the shallow Bahamian waters, and her ballast was all inside. Her sail plan shows 3,000 square feet in the four lowers. *(The Rudder,* July 1937)

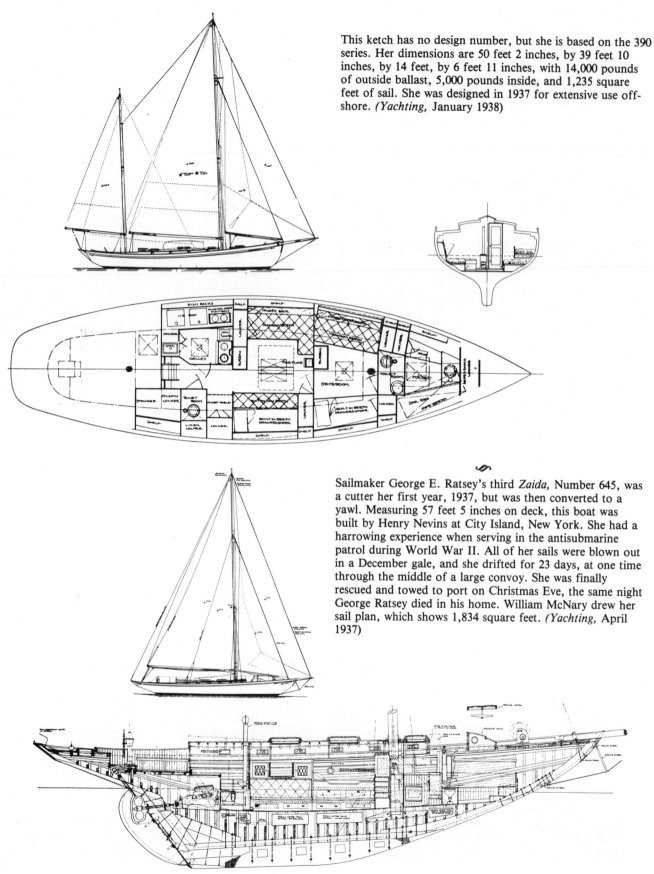

This ketch has no design number, but she is based on the 390 series. Her dimensions are 50 feet 2 inches, by 39 feet 10 inches, by 14 feet, by 6 feet 11 inches, with 14,000 pounds of outside ballast, 5,000 pounds inside, and 1,235 square feet of sail. She was designed in 1937 for extensive use offshore. *(Yachting,* January 1938)

Sailmaker George E. Ratsey's third *Zaida,* Number 645, was a cutter her first year, 1937, but was then converted to a yawl. Measuring 57 feet 5 inches on deck, this boat was built by Henry Nevins at City Island, New York. She had a harrowing experience when serving in the antisubmarine patrol during World War II. All of her sails were blown out in a December gale, and she drifted for 23 days, at one time through the middle of a large convoy. She was finally rescued and towed to port on Christmas Eve, the same night George Ratsey died in his home. William McNary drew her sail plan, which shows 1,834 square feet. *(Yachting,* April 1937)

Four boats — three yawls and a schooner — were built on the lines of design number 647. Drawn by Cliff Swaine, the lines show a balanced hull (62 feet 8 inches long on deck) which, according to Virginia C. Jones, a recent owner of *Foam* (Number 647-A), is virtually self-steering. Swaine also drew the yawl sail plan, which has 1,697 square feet of sail in the four lowers. Shown here is the cabin plan of *Fish Hawk,* Number 647-B, owned by the Saltonstall family of Massachusetts and for years a familiar sight along the Maine coast. *Foam*'s first owner, Donald D. Dodge, kept her for many years in her own cove with her own dock and storage shed at the Dodge estate near Rockport, Maine. She went through a period of neglect in the early 1970s, but more recently, she was restored at a cost of $100,000. The third yawl-rigged sister was *Saedk,* built with the other two by Goudy and Stevens. The schooner-rigged *Magic* (photograph) was built by F.F. Pendleton. (Courtesy John G. Alden, Inc.)

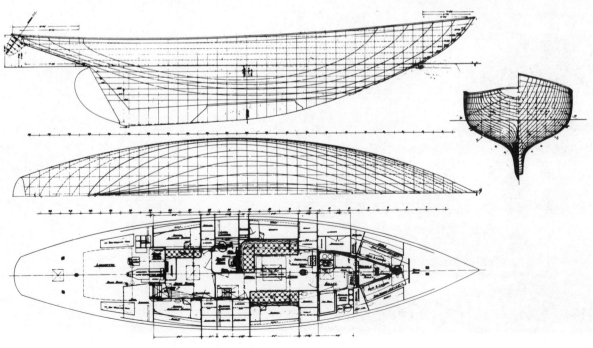

399

Number 648 was *Sonata,* a 49-foot cutter built by F.F. Pendleton in 1937 for Robert R. Williams of Detroit. This Alberg design had her draft limited to 6 feet 3 inches for cruising in shoal waters. Her designed displacement is 31,300 pounds, with 12,100 pounds of lead outside ballast and 1,335 square feet of sail. (Courtesy John G. Alden, Inc.)

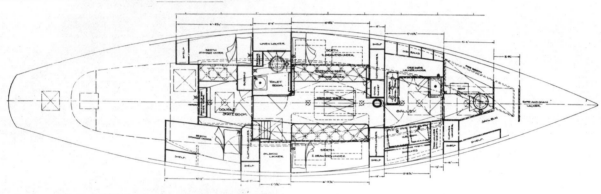

Design number 653 was the 48-foot yawl *Dauntless II,* built for Rufus C. Cushman by the Quincy Adams Yacht Yard in 1937. (Courtesy John G. Alden, Inc.)

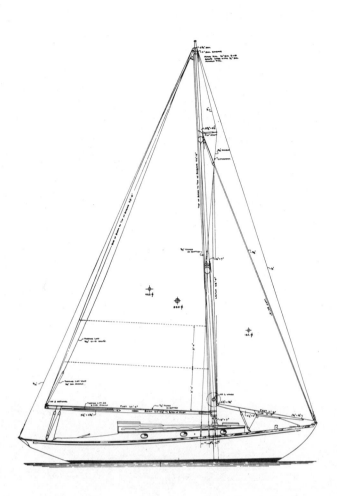

The photograph shows *Sir Tom* (later *Topaz),* one of 10 boats
built to design number 655. She carries 585 square feet of sail,
with some 6,000 pounds of ballast on her keel. A sister named
Banshee spent many years at Gibson Island, Maryland. These
35-foot-10-inch sloops were forerunners of the highly successful Coastwise Cruiser, Number 675. *(Yachting,* July 1937.
Photograph courtesy John G. Alden, Inc.)

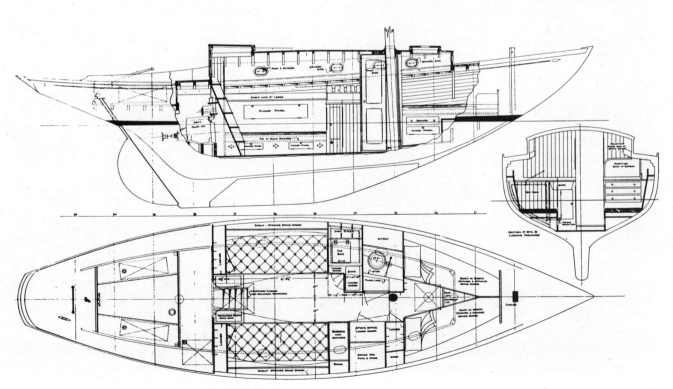

Number 669 was a 63-foot-5-inch schooner built by F.F. Pendleton in 1938 for George S. Patton, at that time a U.S. Army colonel. Patton planned to sail her around the world someday, and casting a wary eye toward Europe and his own uncertain destiny, he named his boat *When and If*. He once wrote Clifford Swaine that he had been twice passed over for promotion to brigadier general by President Roosevelt, with whom Patton shared a mutual dislike. He said that if, as anticipated, he were passed over a third time, he would resign from the army and cruise in his new boat around Cape Horn to the West Coast and Catalina Island, which his family once owned.

According to Swaine, who drew *When and If*'s lines, they share a close affinity with Number 667, the schooner *Kadiac*. *When and If* has 24,800 pounds of lead outside ballast on 84,640 pounds designed displacement, and she carries 1,771 square feet of sail in her four lowers. Barely visible in the sail plan is the squaresail on her foremast. The doghouse has ample navigating space and a berth. Her hull is double planked, with cedar inside and mahogany outside.

In a 1938 letter, Patton told Swaine the United States would soon fight Germany, but Russia would be the eventual enemy. The general served the Allied forces well in World War II, and the bold tactics and dogged determination of "Old Blood-and-Guts" became legendary. He survived the war but was killed in a traffic accident in Europe in 1945. *When and If* passed from his wife, Beatrice Ayer Patton, to Frederick Ayer, to Frederick Ayer, Jr., while her home port remained Manchester Harbor, Massachusetts. In 1972 she was donated to the Landmark School for Dyslexic Children, Beverly, Massachusetts, which built a semester-at-sea program around her. The school maintains her in good shape, calls her "a magnificent sailer," and has no intention of selling her. (Courtesy John G. Alden, Inc. Photo courtesy Landmark School)

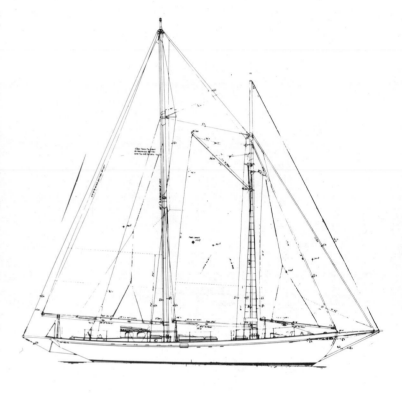

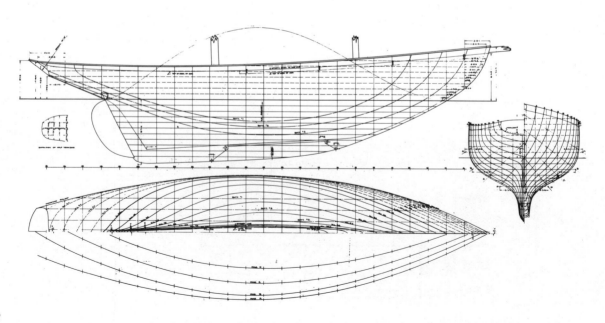

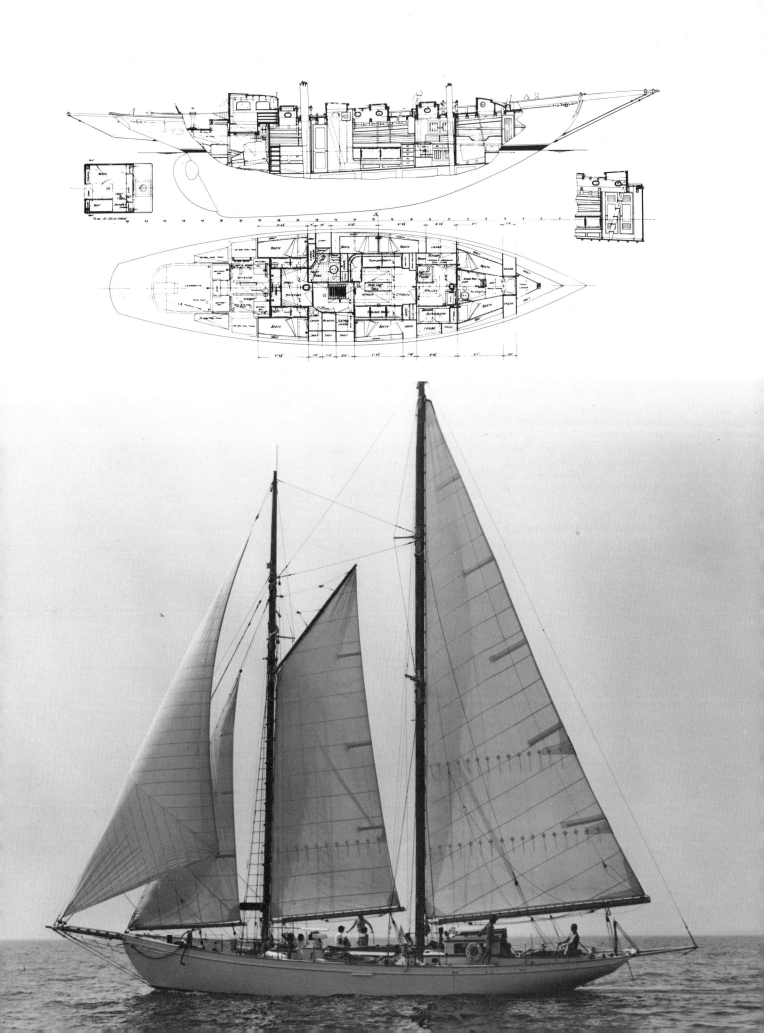

John B. Ford's second *Royono* (later, *Estrellita),* a 51½-foot yawl (Number 673), in a ghoster. (Courtesy John G. Alden, Inc.)

✌

Design number 682 was a twin-screw 32-foot powerboat named *Quill,* built by Palmer Scott in 1938 for Walbridge S. Taft of New York. Taft used her as a tender for his International One-Design sloop, *Feather. Quill*'s top speed was 22 m.p.h. *(Your New Boat* by the Editors of *Yachting)*

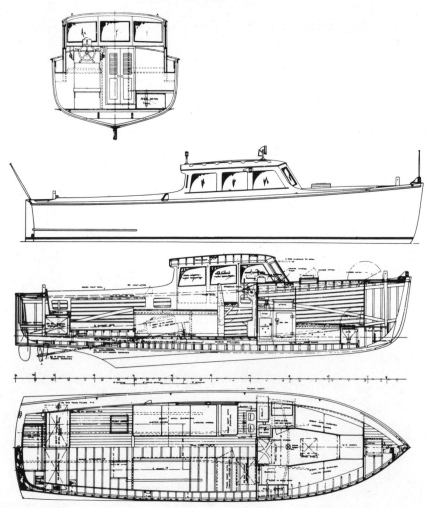

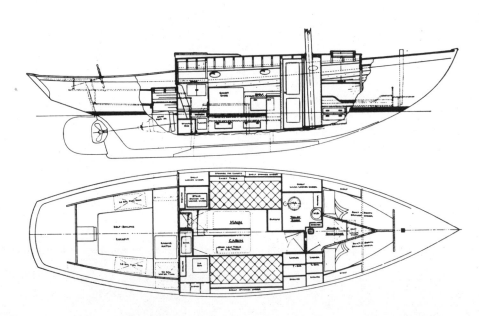

Raised-deck cruisers are not often as handsome as the Explorer Class, Number 699. The 37-foot-5-inch sloop is also a practical and versatile boat because of her handy rig, shoal draft, roomy cabin, and the lowered foredeck with its substantial toe rail. There were six sisters. The first of these sloops, *Norsquam* (later, *Kookaburra*), was built for Clifford Roberts by Morton Johnson in 1939. *(Your New Boat* by the Editors of *Yachting)*

Rose, design number 700, was a 65-foot yawl built by the Quincy Adams Yacht Yard in 1940 for George Peabody Gardner, who wrote *Hard a' Lee, Ready About,* and other books. *Rose*, which Gardner called his "dreamboat," ran aground on a sandbar off Cape Cod Light during the same December 1942 gale that disabled George Ratsey's *Zaida III. Rose*, like *Zaida III*, was serving in the offshore patrol at the time. Her crew were rescued by Rod Stephens in an amphibious DUKW, which he helped develop for troop landings in World War II, but *Rose* came off the bar and disappeared. She was last sighted a month later, 350 miles northeast of Bermuda. (Courtesy John G. Alden, Inc.)

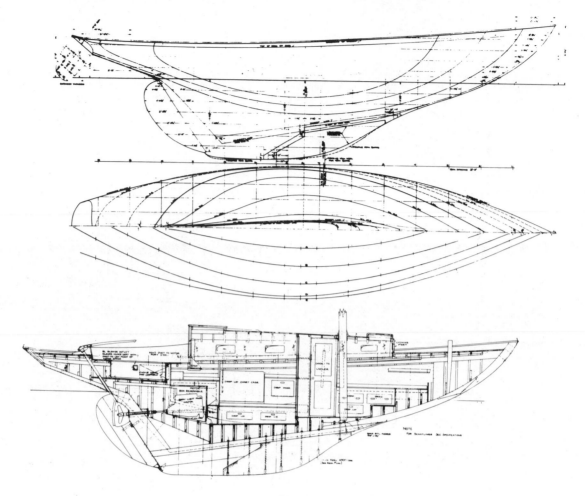

Number 709, a Clifford Swaine design, was the first version of the Barnacle Class. Designed displacement was 12,340 pounds, with some 4,800 pounds of outside ballast. The first of these 34-foot sloops (photograph) was named *Leveche,* and she was built by Bristol Yachtbuilding Company in 1940 for Helen C. Taylor. A friend of the author owned 709-D, *Grayling II.* Eight sisters were built. The more popular version of the Barnacle was design number 792, which was introduced in 1946. (Courtesy John G. Alden, Inc.)

The 45½-foot *Duchess* (originally *Merriel),* design number 711, is an attractive centerboard cutter with a deck shelter. She was built for Paul Jones by George Lawley in 1940. (Courtesy John G. Alden, Inc.)

∽

The 61-foot *Irondequoit II,* design number 713, was built by George Lawley in 1940 for Thomas H. Shepard. She was later named *Esbro VI.* (Courtesy John G. Alden, Inc.)

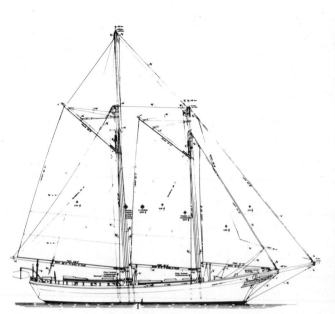

Keewatin is a 55½-foot coaster-type schooner in the tradition of *Cassiopeia (Fiddler's Green)*. She was built to design number 716 by Newfoundland Shipyards in 1947 for Donald G. Parrot, who took over the reins of the Alden company after John retired. In the Foreword to this book, Parrot recalls Alden roughing out the lines with a dull pencil and giving them to Carl Alberg to develop. Fenwick Williams drew the sail and accommodations plans. (Courtesy John G. Alden, Inc.)

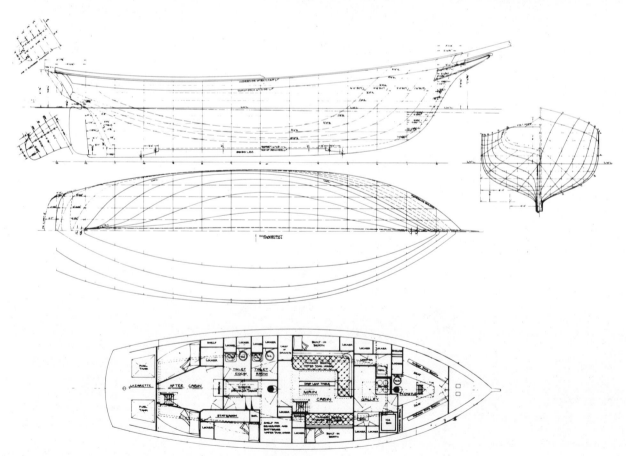

Revision II, design number 719-B, the sister of the 39-foot-10-inch yawl *Salmagal.* She was built for Robert W. Scott by Paul Molich of Hundested, Denmark, in 1956. (Courtesy John G. Alden, Inc.)

Design number 761 was the first version of the Hinckley 21, 28½-foot sloops produced by Henry R. Hinckley, Inc., in 1946. Attractive round-bilged cruisers drawn by Carl Alberg, they sold for $6,000. Designed displacement was 9,030 pounds, with 3,150 pounds of lead outside ballast and 391 square feet of sail. Twenty-one sisters were built. The photograph shows 761-K, *Noremac.* The 1948 version of the Hinckley 21 is design number 839. (Courtesy John G. Alden, Inc.)

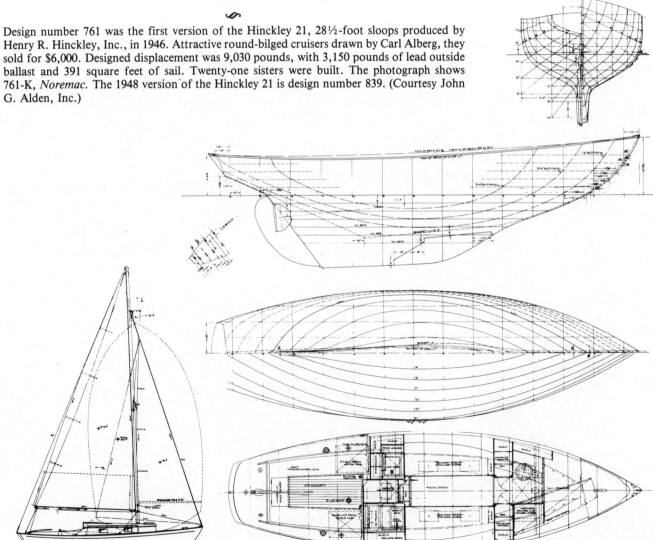

Golden Fleece Two was near hull speed when these photographs were taken, judging from her quarter wave. This 47-foot-4-inch ketch, design number 768, was built for Charles E. Dearnley of Philadelphia by Hubert Johnson. (Courtesy John G. Alden, Inc.)

The 35-foot sloop *Swift*, Number 778-B. This handsome sister to William Barrows' *Queen* was built by Hodgdon Brothers in 1946 for Earle Chapman. She was reported wrecked on a reef in Lake Erie in 1956. (Courtesy John G. Alden, Inc.)

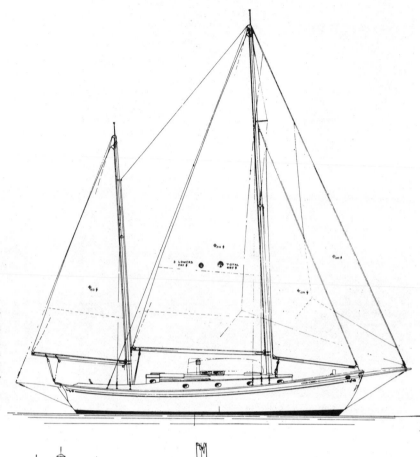

This husky 38-foot-2-inch ketch, Number 784, designed for Norman C. Nourse of Los Angeles, has an unusual cabin layout, with the galley amidships and the main cabin forward. Sail area in the three lowers is 595 square feet, and she has 8,700 pounds of outside ballast and 1,500 to 2,000 pounds inside. *(The Rudder, July 1946)*

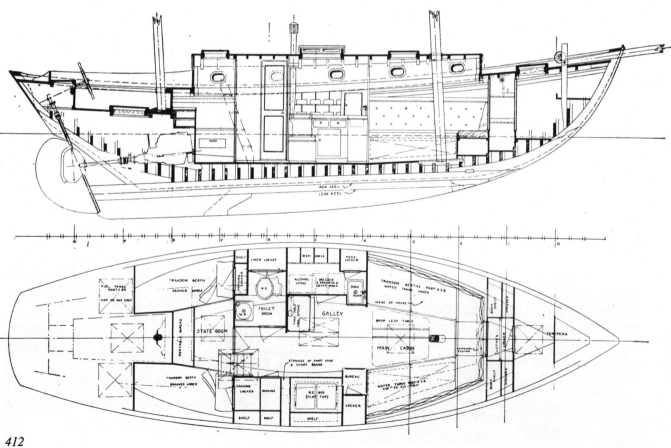

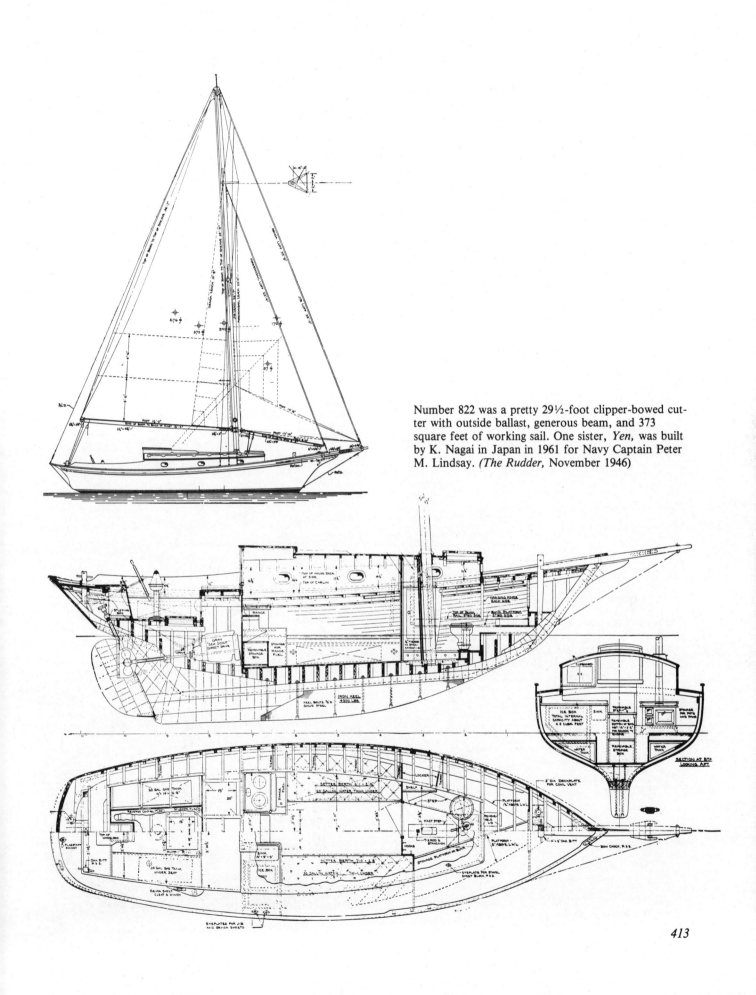

Number 822 was a pretty 29½-foot clipper-bowed cutter with outside ballast, generous beam, and 373 square feet of working sail. One sister, *Yen,* was built by K. Nagai in Japan in 1961 for Navy Captain Peter M. Lindsay. *(The Rudder,* November 1946)

413

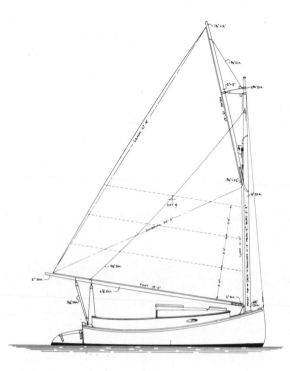

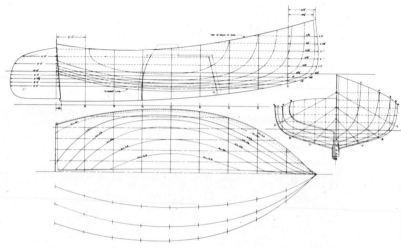

Number 838 was an 18-foot catboat designed by Fenwick Williams. Sail area was 257 square feet. The first of 15 sisters was *Tabby,* built in 1947 for John K. Murphy. (Courtesy John G. Alden, Inc.)

Here and opposite top:
Number 851 is an example of Alden's late work. She is a 53½-foot ketch with a tall, inboard rig (1,002 square feet) and a well-swept forefoot. She was designed for A.B. Homer, but there is no record of her building. *(The Rudder,* April 1950)

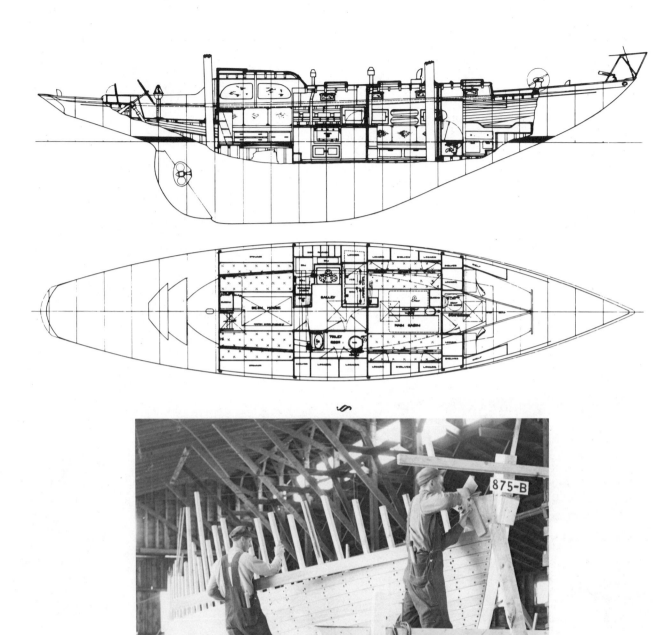

Design number 875 is the Traveler Class, 33½-footers available with either a trunk cabin or a raised deck. The first of seven or eight sisters was *Encore,* built by Morse Boatbuilding for A.D. Chesterton in 1950. *Sea Girl,* 875-B, is shown under construction at the Morse yard. (Courtesy Roger Morse)

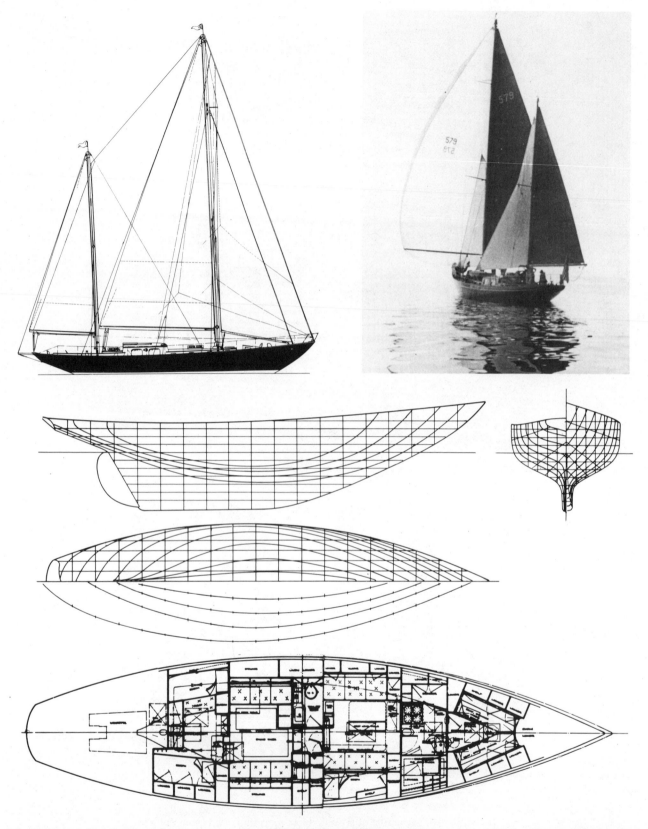

The 58-foot steel ketch *Minots Light* (design number 879) was built by Abeking and Rasmussen in 1951 for Clarence Warden, Jr., of Philadelphia. She was later owned by Arthur Beiser, author of *The Proper Yacht,* who called his boat "close to being the perfect cruising yacht." J.W. Darrin drew her lines, which show a designed displacement of 58,250 pounds, with 19,050 pounds of iron outside ballast. Final displacement was 64,000 pounds, and her sail area is 1,518 square feet. *(The Proper Yacht* by Arthur Beiser)

Norumbega (shown under sail) was the first of the 1951 Seagoer Class. Six to eight sisters — 45-foot ketches, cutters, or yawls — were built to this design, Number 880. The photograph above shows a proud owner of a Seagoer flanked by the builders, Roger Morse (left) and Wilbur Morse (right). A later Seagoer Class, Number 894, was a development of Number 880, which in turn was developed from Number 877. (Courtesy Roger Morse)

Appendix

John Alden's Yacht Design Index

The following is a complete list of Alden yachts, beginning with the first boats John designed at night while working for B.B. Crowninshield, and ending with his retirement in 1955. Each yacht is listed by its company design number; entries include boat type, original name, dimensions, original owner, name and location of builder, building completion year (or, if not built, year of design), and the original names and years of building of known sister boats. If a design appears elsewhere in this book in either a chapter or the Album, the appropriate reference is given at the end of the entry. The Alden company assigned design numbers in chronological sequence; design numbers missing from this appendix were assigned to commercial or military designs.

To reproduce faithfully the Alden office index, the same boat-type descriptions have been used here.

7   Yawl (lug mizzen), 27'9" x 18' x 7'10" x 4'6".

8   Clipper-bowed topmast sloop *Aimee,* 33'6" x 25' x 5'6", for Channing Williams of Boston, MA. Built by Wilbur A. Morse, Friendship, ME, 1906. (Album) (Another Number 8 was a small, open sailing tender, but its number was probably changed to 26.)

9   Yawl, 27'7" x 18' x 7'6" x 4'6".

11   Cruising yawl, 42'3" x 22' x 12'6" x 6'8".

13   Keel sloop *Discovery,* 43' x 34' x 12' x 6'. (Album)

14   Ketch, 32' x 27' x 9'9" x 4'5", for Capt. Richard McKean. Built at Sandusky, OH, about 1911. (Album)

15   Sloop, 48'6" x 38' x 13' x 6'9", for Charles A. Russell of New York, NY, 1911. (Chapter 6)

16   Ketch, 54' x 40' x 12' x 8', for Hannan.

19   Yawl, 47' x 30'6" x 12' x 7'6", for Philip Chase of Milton, MA, 1912. (Chapter 6)

20   One-design class, 15' LWL, for Corinthian Y.C., Marblehead, MA. (Chapter 8)

21   Auxiliary schooner *Wendameen,* 67' x 51' x 17' x 8'8", for Chester W. Bliss of Springfield, MA. Built by Adams Shipbuilding, East Boothbay, ME, 1912. (Chapter 6)

22   Powerboat (gillnetter).

23   Tender, 12'.

24   Tender, 13'.

25   Powerboat (gillnetter), 59' x 13' x 9'. Designed 1912.

26   Sailing tender, 11'6". (Probably originally numbered 8.)

27   Dory, 15'.

28   Power tender, 28'.

29   Launch, 27'.

31   Corinthian One-Design *Dingbat* (development of Number 20), 15' LWL, for Edwin Moller, et al, of the Corinthian Y.C., Marblehead, MA. Built by Stearns & McKay, Marblehead, MA, 1913. (Chapter 8)

34   Auxiliary sloop *White Cap,* 30' x 21'3" x 8'6" x 4'5", for B.D. Barton of Boston, MA, 1916.

36   Auxiliary ketch *Outlaw,* 41'6" x 28'10" x 10'6" x 6'. Designed 1912. (Chapter 3, Ideal Two-Man Cruiser)

37   Deep-sea motor yacht *Pioneer,* 48'6" x 42'3" x 11'6" x 4'4". Probably designed 1912. (Chapter 9)

38   Catboat, 18' x 14'9" x 8' x 1'6", for Johnson.

40   Auxiliary schooner *Nikkao,* 57' x 42' x 14'8" x 7'10", for C.C. Wilder. Built by Irving Reed, Boothbay, ME, 1913.

41   Class Q sloop *Shirley,* 46'4" x 25'11" x 8'10" x 5'10", for Sidney G. Dobson, et al, of the Royal Cape Breton Y.C., Sydney, Nova Scotia. Built by Pinaud Bros., Sydney, Nova Scotia, 1913. (Chapter 8)

43   Schooner, 77' x 59'.

43-B   Centerboard yawl, 38' x 27' x 11'6" x 2'6".

44   Tunnel-stern, flat-bottomed launch, 14' x 4'6" x 4".

45   Yawl *Solita,* 35'6" x 25' x 10'1" x 5'6", for Daniel Bacon of Oyster Bay, Long Island, NY. Built by Henry B. Nevins, City Island, NY, 1914. (Chapter 6)

46   Sloop *Bonnie Jean,* 40'2" x 26' x 10' x 4'5", for Charles W. Hood of Danversport, MA. Built by George Lawley & Son Corp., Neponset, MA, 1914.

47   Auxiliary ketch *Bonita IV,* 45' x 34' x 12' x 6'6", for F.C. Grant. Built by Adams Shipbuilding Co., East Boothbay, ME, 1914.

48   Runabout, 20'.

49   Runabout, 20' (same as Number 48).

51   Counter-stern cruiser, 62' x 58'3" x 12'6" x 5'5", for Fred A. Walton.

51-B   Yacht tender, 12'6".

52   Schooner, 60' x 46' x 14' x 8'3". Not built.

53   Keel-centerboard schooner, 63'8" x 48'4" x 15'10" x 7', for Dr. F.W. Baldwin of Peoria, IL. Designed 1914. (Chapter 6)

54   Runabout *Lapwing,* 30' x 5'9" x 2', for A.P. Homer. Built by Camden Iron Works, Camden, ME, 1916.

55   Class R sloop *Banshee,* 38' x 23'6" x 8' x 5'4", for O.C. Schoenwerk, Jr., of Chicago, IL. Built by Hodgdon Bros., East Boothbay, ME, 1915. (Chapter 8)

57   Auxiliary schooner *Jeanette,* 72' x 50' x 16' x 9'6", for George B. Williams of Farmington, CT. Built by Hodgdon Bros., East Boothbay, ME, 1915.

58   Auxiliary yawl *Cygnet,* 41'6" x 29' x 10'6" x 6', for George Crompton. Built by F.F. Pendleton, Wiscasset, ME, 1915. One sister built: *Outlaw* (1916).

59   Launch, for A.P. Homer.

60   Knockabout, 38' x 30' x 10'6" x 5'3", for A.P. Brayton.

60-B   Commercial schooner, 124' x 110' x 24'6" x 11'6", for F.S. Grubey.

61   Auxiliary yawl *Nahma,* 43'4" x 30'11" x 11' x 6'4", for J. Frank Duryea of Springfield, MA. Built by George Lawley & Son Corp., Neponset, MA, 1916.

62   Auxiliary yawl *Dawn,* 48'6" x 37'6" x 12' x 7'4½", for Franklin Farrell, Jr., of New Haven, CT. Built by Adams Shipbuilding Co., East Boothbay, ME, 1916.

63   Motor yacht, 102' LOA. Not built.

64   Power cruiser *Islander,* 50'10" x 50' x 11'10" x 3'5", for J.B. Osborn of Boston, MA. Built by F.S. Nock, Inc., East Greenwich, RI, 1916.

65   Knockabout, 27' x 19'10" x 7'6" x 3'9", for Charles Power.

66   Auxiliary schooner *Volante,* 63' x 44'6" x 14'6" x 8'10", for Charles K. Cobb of Marblehead, MA. Built by Adams Shipbuilding Co., East Boothbay, ME, 1916. (Album)

67   Stamford One-Design knockabout, 26'9" x 19' x 7'3" x 4'3", for Stamford Y.C., Stamford, CT. Eleven boats built, by Rice Bros., East Boothbay, ME, 1916. (Chapter 8)

68   Indian Harbor One-Design (Arrow Class), 31'10" x 21'10" x 8'1" x 5'3", for Indian Harbor Y.C., Greenwich, CT. At least five boats built, by Narragansett Bay Yacht Yard, Riverside, RI, 1916. (Chapter 8)

69   Runabout, 18' x 17'6" x 4'7", for E.E. Conway, 1916.

70   Schooner *Amorilla,* 83' x 56' x 16' x 10'3" x 9'4", for Demarest Lloyd of Boston, MA. Built by George Lawley & Son Corp., Neponset, MA, 1916. (Album)

71   Launch, 16' x 15'7" x 4'3", for E.E. Conway, 1916.

72   Cabin runabout *Grosbeak,* 38' x 37'6" x 8'4" x 2'6", for Reginald C. Robbins of Boston, MA. Built by Rice Bros., East Boothbay, ME, 1916. (Chapter 9)

73   Class R sloop *Pam,* 37' x 24'2" x 7'8" x 5'6", for H.A. Parsons of Cleveland, OH. Built by W.B. Calderwood, Manchester, MA, 1916.

74   Schooner, 95'6" x 69'9" x 20' x 11'4", 1919.

75   Class R sloop *Rogue,* 37'7" x 25'2" x 5'9", for Charles F. Adams of Boston, MA. Built by W.B. Calderwood, Manchester, MA, 1917.

76   Class R sloop *Sari,* 38' x 29' x 5'9", for Samuel Dauchy of Chicago, IL. Built by W.B. Calderwood, Manchester, MA, 1917.

77   Power cruiser. Designed 1917. Not built.

78   Power cruiser *Entante,* 40'10" x 12' x 3', for O.G.

Schoenwerk, 1917.

79 Power cruiser *Polly,* 80'10" x 79'4" x 14' x 3'10", for William T. Rich of Newton, MA. Built by F.F. Pendleton, Wiscasset, ME, 1917. (Album)

80 Auxiliary yawl, 53' x 37' x 11' x 6'7", for Allen S. Weeks, 1917.

81 Power cruiser *Machantam III,* 33' x 32' x 9'6" x 2'7", for Dr. Samuel Crowell of Boston, MA. Built by Howard H. Linnell, Boston, MA, 1917.

82 Power cruiser, 120', for Raymond.

83 Biddeford Pool One-Design, 18'1" x 14'3" x 6'2" x 3'7", for W.A. Dupee and others. Built by W.B. Calderwood, Manchester, MA, 1917. (Album)

84 Clipper-bowed schooner, 110' x 98' x 26'4" x 12'6", for William G. Raoul of New York, NY. Built by F.S. Nock, Inc., East Greenwich, RI, 1918.

85 Auxiliary ketch, 45' x 36' x 11'8" x 5'10", for W.I. Bowditch of Ludlow, MA. Built by Hodgdon Bros., East Boothbay, ME, 1917.

86 Class R sloop *Yank,* 38'4" x 25'2" x 7'3" x 5'7", for Ogden S. McClurg. Built by W.B. Calderwood, Manchester, MA, 1917.

87 Patrol boat, 135'5" x 133'7" x 19'1½" x 6'4". Not built.

88 Three-masted schooner *Priscilla Alden,* 154'6" x 134'4" x 33'4" x 12'6", for Dennett. Built by Frank C. Adams, East Boothbay, ME, 1919. (Chapter 6)

89 Knockabout *Vigilance,* 29' x 21' x 8' x 4', for H.C. Cushing of New York, NY. Built by William E. Haff, New Rochelle, NY, 1918. (Album)

90 Schooner, 56' x 41' x 12'2" x 7'3", for C.W. Allison.

91 Powerboat, 42', for F.W. Baldwin.

92 Canoe yawl.

93 Knockabout *Merla,* 23' x 18'1" x 7' x 4', for Frederick C. Fletcher of Marblehead, MA. Built by W.B. Calderwood, Manchester, MA, 1919. (Album)

94 Yawl, 21' LWL.

95 Ketch, 72' x 52' x 13'6" x 8'3", for Raymond. Designed 1919. (Chapter 6)

97 Auxiliary schooner *Norseman,* 63' x 47' x 15' x 8', for George B. Williams of Farmington, CT. Built by Frank C. Adams, East Boothbay, ME, 1920. (Chapter 6)

98 Ketch, 38' LWL, for Raymond.

99 Knockabout *Azor Cole,* 35' x 10' x 2'9", for C.M. Merrill of Newton Center, MA. Built by W.B. Calderwood, Manchester, MA, 1919.

100 Ketch, for C.H.W. Foster of Boston, MA.

101 Cruising Class R sloop, for Elliot Milldram.

102 Houseboat, for Shaw.

103 Three-masted schooner, for Raymond. Designed 1919. Not built.

104 Auxiliary catboat *Foam,* 21' x 9'6" x 2'3", for S.K. Dimock of Hartford, CT. Built by G.W. Gardner, Swampscott, MA, 1920. (Chapter 6)

105 Power cruiser, for Webber.

106 Power cruiser, for Davol.

107 Sakonnet One-Design.

108 Power cruiser, for Sturtevant.

109 Freighter, for Bridgeport Co.

109-B Sailing tender, 11'6", for Dupee.

111 Auxiliary schooner, 50'2" x 39'11" x 13' x 7'2", for Gilbert D. Maxwell. Built by F.F. Pendleton, Wiscasset, Me, 1920. One sister built: *Primrose IV* (1923). (Chapter 6)

112 Three-masted schooner, 139', for Howell.

113 Power cruiser *Pitpen,* 40' x 39'3" x 9'6" x 3', for M.J. Mullen, 1920.

114 Power cruiser *Faith,* 77'4" x 13'8" x 6', for Irving E. Raymond of Stamford, CT. Built by Charles Butson, Groton, CT, 1922. (Chapter 9)

115 Knockabout trading schooner *Seaward,* 105' x 82' x 21'8" x 12', for L.A. Norris Co. of San Francisco, CA. Built by Frank C. Adams, East Boothbay, ME, 1920. (Chapter 6)

116 Knockabout, 35'6" x 31'10" x 11' x 2'9", for F. Farrell, 1920.

117 Knockabout, 26'10" x 18'10" x 7'2½" x 4'3", for C.A. Gamble, 1920.

118 Knockabout schooner, 41' x 29' x 10'4" x 6', for Edward Reynolds, 1920.

119 Class R sloop *Alastor,* 35'2" x 25' x 7'10" x 5'8½", for F.C. Paine of Boston, MA. Built by George Lawley & Son Corp., Neponset, MA, 1920.

120 Power cruiser *Sunbeam,* 40' x 38'8" x 10'3" x 3'6", for H.E. Sawtelle of Winthrop, MA, 1920.

121 Auxiliary yawl, 39'10" x 31'10" x 11'9" x 6', for D.D. Henwood, 1920.

122 Centerboard knockabout, 19'6" x 16'3" x 7' x 2', for A.P. Hemmenway. Built by W.B. Calderwood, Manchester, MA.

123 Auxiliary knockabout schooner, 87', for Smith.

124 Sailing tender, 14', for Norman White, Jr., 1921.

125 Schooner, 32'3" x 24'6" x 9' x 5', for G.W. Ford, NY, 1921.

126 Auxiliary yawl *Dolphin,* 39'10" x 31'10" x 11'9" x 6', for C.E. Eveleth, Sargentville, ME. Built by F.H. Harding, Sargentville, ME, 1921.

127 Schooner *Rusalka,* 47'5" x 36'10" x 12'6" x 6'6", for E.G. Taylor. Built by F.F. Pendleton, Wiscasset, ME, 1921.

128 Auxiliary knockabout, 30' x 21'7" x 8'6" x 3'6", for Drummond, 1921.

129 Schooner, 40', for Stewart.

130 Marconi sloop, 61'2" x 42'8" x 14' x 8', for J.W. Bird, 1921.

131 One-design class skiff, 13', for Manchester Y.C., Manchester, MA, 1921.

132 Seine boat, 45' x 37' x 12' x 3'6", for Myreck.

133 Power cruiser, 42', for D.L. Pickman of Boston, MA. Not built.

134 Power cruiser, 32', for Parker W. Whittemore of Boston, MA. Not built.

135 One-design centerboard knockabout (Jamestown Class), 20'9", for the Conanicut Y.C., Jamestown, RI. Built by George L. Chaisson, Swampscott, MA, and William Chamberlain, Marblehead, MA, 1921 to 1926. (Album)

136 Auxiliary sloop *Thelma,* 40' x 34' x 12' x 6', for Jesse Willey, New Bedford, MA. Built by D.N. Waddell, Rockport, MA, 1921.

137 Sailing dory, 21' x 6'2" x 1'6", for Sewall of Puerto Rico. Built by G.W. Gardner of Swampscott, MA.

138 Auxiliary schooner *Ellida,* 62' x 48' x 15'7" x 8', for Dr. Austin Riggs of Stockbridge, MA. Built by C.A. Morse & Son, Thomaston, ME, 1922. One sister built (1922).

138-C Auxiliary schooner *Dolly Pentreath* (similar to Number 138 but lengthened to 71' LOA), for Capt. P.W. Phillips, Penang, Malaysia.

139 Auxiliary centerboard yawl *Hermita,* 47'3½" x 36'10¼" x 13' x 5'2", for George M. Angier of Marion, MA. Built by F.F. Pendleton, Wiscasset, ME, 1921.

140 Power cruiser, 38'10" x 10'¾" x 3', for D.C. Roberts of Marblehead, MA. Built by Britt Bros., West

Lynn, MA, 1921.

141 Auxiliary sloop *Welwyn,* 31′8″ x 25′9″ x 9′9″ x 3′, for Hallock, 1920. (Album)

142 Power cruiser *Katherine,* 56′6″ x 12′5″ x 5′9″ x 3′6″, for H.R. Dalton of Boston, MA. Built by F.F. Pendleton, Wiscasset, ME, 1921.

143 Auxiliary schooner *Abaco,* 45′4″ x 33′ x 11′8″ x 6′6″, for Robert L. Saltonstall of Boston, MA. Built by W.B. Calderwood, Manchester, MA, 1920.

144 Class R sloop *Opechee,* 35′3″ x 25′ x 7′6″ x 5′8½″, for W.C. Morrison of Brookline, MA. Built by James E. Graves, Marblehead, MA, 1921.

145 Auxiliary schooner *Mistral II,* 64′8″ x 47′3″ x 14′6″ x 8′3″, for E.P. Simpson of Australia. Built by Ford, Berry's Bay, Australia, 1921.

146 Auxiliary schooner *Sunbeam,* 60′ x 43′6″ x 13′5″ x 8′, for Stephen D. Baker. Built by Reed-Cook Marine Construction Co., Boothbay Harbor, ME, 1922. (Album)

147 One-design knockabout (Padanaram Class), 15′10″ LOA, for J.W. Stedman, Carl O. Foster, and Lydia E. Knowles. Built by George Lawson, Neponset, MA, 1921.

148 One-design sailing dory (Indian Class), 21′2″ x 6′3″, for various owners. Built by William Chamberlain and by Reed, 1921 to 1930. (Used at Scituate, Winthrop, South Boston, Hull, Squantum, Sakonnet, and Fenwick yacht clubs.)

149 Cruising Class R sloop, for Goodwin.

150 Raised-deck cruiser *Passaic,* 32′ x 8′6″ x 2′10″, for Calderwood. Built by W.B. Calderwood, 1921. (Same lines as Number 134.)

151 Knockabout schooner, 40′ x 27′ x 10′ x 6′, for three yachtsmen of Boston, MA. Designed 1920. Not built. (Chapter 6)

152 Sailing-dory tender, 13′, for Robert Saltonstall, 1921.

153 Tender, 10′6″, for Donohan, 1921.

155 Schooner *Malabar I,* 41′3″ x 31′10¼″ x 11′7⅛″ x 6′2″, for John G. Alden. Built by C.A. Morse & Son, Thomaston, ME, 1921. (Chapter 5)

156 Schooner, 51′, for Odin Roberts.

157 San Francisco S or Bird Class, 29′11″ x 22′ x 7′8″ x 5′, for F.C. Brewer of Sausalito, CA. Built by Herbert Madden, Sausalito, CA, 1922. Twenty-six boats built. (Chapter 8)

159 Power cruiser *Nomoko,* 42′4″ x 40′ x 9′5¼″ x 2′, for D.R. Sortwell. Built by F.F. Pendleton, Wiscasset, ME, 1921.

160 Class R sloop *Goblin,* 34′6″ x 24′ x 7′7¼″ x 3′, for T.B. Van Dorn. Built by T.B. Van Dorn, 1922.

161 Powerboat, 48′ x 46′2″ x 11′ x 4′6″, for F. Bent.

162 Schooner *Malabar II,* 41′6″ x 32′ x 11′3″ x 6′2″, for John G. Alden. Built by C.A. Morse & Son, Thomaston, ME, 1922. Three sisters built, including *Malabar III* (1922) and *Mary Ann* (1922). (Chapter 5)

163 Proposed one-design class, for King.

164 Knockabout, 32′3½″ x 21′11″ x 7′9½″ x 5′3″, for Mrs. Keith McCloud. Built by W.B. Calderwood, Manchester, MA, 1922.

166 Auxiliary schooner *Michabo,* 92′ x 85′ x 21′6″ x 10′6″, for William M. Butler of Boston, MA. Built by C.A. Morse & Son, Thomaston, ME, 1922. (Hull designed by Morse, sail plan and interior by Alden.)

167 Auxiliary schooner *Diana,* 44′11″ x 35′ x 12′1½″ x 4′10″, for Yandell Henderson. Built by F.F. Pendleton, Wiscasset, ME, 1922.

168 Class R sloop *Frances,* 38′ x 27′6″ x 8′2″ x 6′, for San Francisco Y.C. Syndicate (Demming), San Francisco, CA. Built by George W. Kneass, San Francisco, CA, 1922.

169 Marblehead One-Design class (forerunner to Number 188), 18′3″ x 15′6″ x 6′2″ x 1′, for J.G. Gray, 1921. (Chapter 8)

170 Point Judith One-Design class, 23′ x 15′11″ x 7′ x 4′1″, for Doherty. Built by J.G. Wyman, New Haven, CT, 1922. (Only one boat built.)

171 Sloop (English), 26′ LOA. (Profile and deck lines taken off original boat.)

172 Schooner *Tyche,* 27′1″ x 22′1″ x 9′ x 3′1¼″, for Rodman Swift of Hingham, MA. Built by Baker Yacht Basin, Quincy, MA, 1922. One sister built: *Mary* (1929). (Album)

173 Powerboat *Duck,* 50′ x 45′ x 10′10″ x 3′6″, for L. H. Dyer. Built by J.R. Greenwood, Wilson's Beach, New Brunswick, 1922.

174 Knockabout, 35′ LOA, for A. Chupin. Not built.

175 Schooner, 53′ LOA, for Watson.

176 Launch (for *Michabo,* Number 166), 17′6″ x 5′6″ x 9″, for William M. Butler. Built by G.W. Gardner, Swampscott, MA, 1922.

177 Schooner *Alca,* 44′11″ x 35′ x 12′1½″ x 4′, for J.W. Stedman of Newark, NJ. Built by F.F. Pendleton, Wiscasset, ME, 1922.

178 Schooner, 111′ x 88′ x 22′6″ x 13′, for Hannan of New York, NY. Not built.

179 V-bottomed tender, 12′, for Dupee.

180 Six-meter class sloop *Syce,* 32′8″ x 21′6″ x 6′3″, for Stamford Y.C., Stamford, CT. Built by George Lawley & Son Corp., Neponset, MA, 1922.

181 Schooner, 85′ LOA, for Robert A. Vihlen of Milwaukee, WI, 1922.

182 Schooner, 55′, for Frank B. Draper of New York, NY, 1922.

184 Schooner, 64′6″ x 44′4½″ x 15′ x 6′, for Horace Binney.

186 Sloop *Shere Khan,* 31′8″ x 25′9″ x 9′9″ x 3′, for W.D. Richmond of Brookline, MA. Built by Baker Yacht Basin, Quincy, MA, 1923. Three sisters built, including: *Lucy H.* (1923) and *Amy D.* (1956). (Album)

187 Class R sloop *Angela,* 34′11″ x 24′3″ x 7′ x 5′5″, for Silsby M. Spalding of Los Angeles, CA. Built by Wilmington Boat Works, Wilmington, CA, 1922.

188 O class one-design, 18′3″ x 15′6″ x 6′2″ (moderate-weather version) and 18′1″ x 15′5″ x 6′8″ (heavy-weather version), for various owners. Nearly 600 built by various builders. (Chapter 8)

189 Schooner *Discovery,* 45′6″ x 35′6″ x 11′11″ x 6′9″, for William P. Barrows of Rochester, NY. Built by C.A. Morse & Son, Thomaston, ME, 1923.

190 Class R sloop *Lillian E.,* 34′9″ x 24′7½″ x 7′2½″ x 5′7″, for R.A. Wright of Toronto, Ontario. Built by James Andrews, Oakville, Ontario, 1923.

191 Auxiliary gaff schooner *Anonta,* 45′6″ x 35′6″ x 11′11″ x 6′9″, for Joseph W. Crowell of Newton, MA. Built by F.F. Pendleton, Wiscasset, ME, 1923.

192 Bar Harbor One-Design class, 28′6″ x 21′5″ x 8′ x 4′10″, 1923.

193 Six-meter class sloop, 31′6″ x 22′10″ x 6′8″ x 4′11¾″, for Finland, 1923.

194 Auxiliary schooner *Mary Rose,* 62′2″ x 42′8″ x 14′ x 8′, for Harold Brooks. Built by Robert Jacobs, City Island, NY, 1923.

195 Auxiliary schooner, 75′ x 58′ x 18′ x 9′6″, for Joseph Pulitzer of NY. Built by F.F. Pendleton, Wiscasset, ME, 1924.

196 Auxiliary schooner, for A.N. Peck of New York, NY. Not built.

200 Class R sloop *Hilda,* 34′6″ x 24′9″ x 7′3″ x 5′8″, for C.H.W. Foster of Boston, MA. Built by George Lawley & Son Corp., Neponset, MA, 1923.

201 Power cruiser *Esmonda,* 62′ x 61′4″ x 13′ x 3′8″, for Clarence Whitman of New York, NY. Built by Herreshoff Manufacturing Co., Bristol, RI, 1923.

202 Yawl *Laura,* 47′ x 37′ x 13′ x 5′2″, for Arthur N. Peck of New York, NY. Built by George Lawley & Son Corp., Neponset, MA, 1923. (Used lines of Number 139.)

203 Class R sloop *Katia,* 36′6″ x 24′9″ x 7′2½″ x 5′8″, for Samuel Dauchy of Chicago, IL. Built by Hodgdon Bros., East Boothbay, ME, 1923.

204 Power cruiser *Kinkora,* 43′ x 10′ x 3′, for Carroll S. Tyson, Jr., of Philadelphia, PA. Built by F.F. Pendleton, Wiscasset, ME, 1923.

205 Auxiliary schooner *Malabar IV,* 47′ x 35′6″ x 12′ x 6′11″, for John G. Alden. Built by C.A. Morse & Son, Thomaston, ME, 1923. One sister built: *Felisi* (1924). (Chapter 5)

206 Schooner *Radiant,* 48′7″ x 37′ x 12′ x 7′, for R.E. Traiser of Boston, MA. Built by Baker Yacht Basin, Quincy, MA, 1923.

207 Schooner *Harlequin,* 42′ x 32′3″ x 11′3″ x 6′2″, for George B. Knowles of New Bedford, MA. Built by C.A. Morse & Son, Thomaston, ME, 1923. Four sisters built: *Fairmaid* (1923); *Williwaw* (1923); *White Squall* (1924); and *Anna A* (1924). (Album)

208 Auxiliary knockabout *Witega,* 30′10″ x 23′ x 9′8″ x 3′9″, for P.Y. de Normandy of Wings Neck, MA. Built by Reuben Bigelow, Monument Beach, MA, 1923.

210 Auxiliary schooner *Saracen,* 89′6″ x 71′5″ x 19′7″ x 9′6″, for William Whitman, Jr., of Marblehead, MA. Built by J.F. James & Son, Essex, MA, 1924. (Chapter 6)

211 Auxiliary schooner, 54′ LOA, for J.W. Hayworth.

212 Auxiliary ketch *Alice,* 51′10″ x 42′ x 13′7″ x 3′6″, for Henry Howard of Newport, RI. Built by A.C. Brown & Sons, Staten Island, NY, 1924. (One sister, for A. C. White of Trinidad. Lines by Ralph M. Munroe.)

212-B Auxiliary schooner *Sea Drift,* 84′3″ x 62′ x 20′ x 10′3″, for C.S. Somerville of England. Built by Livingston & Cooper, Hull, England, 1924.

213 Auxiliary schooner *Yvonne,* 50′11″ x 37′6″ x 12′4″ x 7′, for Duncan S. Ellsworth, Southampton, NY. Built by C.A. Morse & Son, Thomaston, ME, 1924. One sister built: *Elizabeth* (1924).

214 Auxiliary knockabout schooner, 62′ x 53′4″, for Fred Kip. Designed 1923. Not built.

215 Auxiliary schooner *Malabar V,* 49′ x 36′9″ x 12′ x 7′3″, for John G. Alden. Built by C.A. Morse & Son, Thomaston, ME, 1924. One sister built. (Chapter 5)

216 Auxiliary schooner *Sea Love,* 62′ LOA, for J.W. Bird. Built by Robert Jacob, City Island, NY. (Cabin of Number 194 used.)

217 Auxiliary schooner *Namoa,* 43′9″ x 33′3″ x 11′4″ x 6′2″, for W.H. Dixon of Westport, CT. Built by F.F. Pendleton, Wiscasset, ME, 1924.

218 Auxiliary schooner *Chauve Souris,* 68′8½″ x 49′6″ x 15′6″ x 8′10½″, for Humphrey Birge of Buffalo, NY. Built by Cumberland Shipbuilding Co., Portland, ME, 1924.

219 Auxiliary schooner *Panchara,* 42′4″ x 32′3″ x 11′2″

x 6′2″, for L.W. Sargent of Cambridge, MA. Built by C.A. Morse & Son, Thomaston, ME, 1924. One sister built: *Hilda* (1924).

220 Auxiliary ketch, 50′ x 38′ x 12′ x 7′, for H.H. Sayers, 1924.

221 Knockabout, 22′ LWL, for Manchester Y.C., Manchester, MA. Designed 1925. (Plans not completed.)

222 Sloop, 36′1″ x 28′3″ x 11′ x 5′7½″, for William P. Barrows of Rochester, NY.

223 Auxiliary marconi yawl *Amrita,* 40′10″ x 28′ x 10′ x 5′7″, for R.L. Saltonstall of Boston, MA. Built by F.S. Nock, Inc., East Greenwich, RI, 1924.

224 Auxiliary ketch *Eaglet,* 32′9″ x 27′9″ x 9′6″ x 5′5″, for Samuel Wetherill of New York, NY. Built by W.J. Deed, Huntington, L.I., NY, 1925. Two sisters built, including: *Svaap* (1925). (Chapter 6)

225-B Auxiliary schooner *Roberta,* 54′6″ x 42′6″ x 14′2″ x 7′6″, for Robert S. Cooper of Kenosha, WI. (Original Number 225, not built, designed for Dr. Frank Baldwin.) Built by Burger Boat Co., Manitowoc, WI, 1926.

226 Auxiliary schooner *Blue Water,* 55′6″ x 42′1″ x 14′2″ x 7′6″, for Melville R. Smith of New York, NY. Built by Rice Bros., East Boothbay, ME, 1924. One sister built: *Beacon Rock* (1924). (Album)

227 Auxiliary schooner *Voyager,* 36′3″ x 28′6″ x 10′1″ x 5′9″, for W.B. Lockwood of Cambridge, MA. Built by C.A. Morse & Son, Thomaston, ME, 1924. One sister built: *Nirvana II* (1925).

228 Power tender, 15′ x 4′7″ x 11″, for William Whitman. Built by G.W. Gardner, Swampscott, MA, 1923. One sister built (1926).

229 Auxiliary centerboard yawl *Tautog,* 50′ x 39′2″ x 13′7″ x 4′11½″, for Winchester Bennett of New Haven, CT. Built by Dauntless Shipyard, Inc., Essex, CT, 1924. One sister built: *Gesine* (1926).

230 One-design knockabout (Thousand Islands Class), 15′ LOA x 6′ beam. Built by George L. Chaisson, Swampscott, MA, 1924.

231 Auxiliary yawl, 34′ x 24′ x 9′ x 5′6″, for Prof. F.J. Moore of M.I.T., Cambridge, MA, 1925.

232 Utility launch *Starfish,* 26′ x 7′ x 2′2″, for Robert Saltonstall of Boston, MA. Built by George L. Chaisson, Swampscott, MA, 1924.

233 Cabin cruiser, 32′11″ x 31′11″ x 10′ x 2′5″, for T.S. Ross of Boston, MA, 1925.

234 Auxiliary sloop *Westerly,* 30′9″ x 27′ x 9′6″ x 4′, for Samuel L. Fox of Torresdale, PA. Built by Reuben Bigelow, Monument Beach, MA, 1925.

235 Auxiliary schooner *Sachem II,* 59′3″ x 42′6″ x 13′6″ x 8′2″, for Rowe B. Metcalf of New York, NY. Built by F.F. Pendleton, Wiscasset, ME, 1925.

236 Auxiliary schooner *Seguin,* 42′9″ x 32′9″ x 11′3″ x 6′4″, for Dr. S.W. Merrill of Long Island City, NY. Built by Kenneth McAlpin, Shelburne, Nova Scotia, 1925. Five sisters built: *Sagamore* (1925); *Privateer* (1925); *Allana* (1925); *Aurora III* (1926); and *Sauk* (1926?). (Album)

237 Auxiliary marconi yawl *Fidelity,* 40′6″ x 28′3″ x 10′ x 5′7½″, for H.M. Adams of West Barrington, RI. Built by Miller, 1925.

238 Auxiliary sloop *Wildcat,* 31′10″ x 25′ x 10′2″ x 5′2½″, for J.A. Will of Boston, MA. Built by J. Brown, Vinalhaven, ME, 1925. (Album)

239 Class Q sloop *Nor'Easter III,* 49′11″ x 32′3″ x 8′2½″ x 6′10½″, for Grafton Smith of Boston, MA. Built by Hodgdon Bros., East Boothbay, ME, 1925.

240 Auxiliary centerboard sloop *Querida,* 49′ x 38′3″ x

14′ x 3′9″, for Daniel Bacon of New York, NY. Built by Greenport Basin & Construction Co., NY, 1925. (Chapter 6)

241 Centerboard, sloop-rigged fishing launch *Peto,* 27′ x 24′4″ x 8′6″ x 2′4″, for R.L. Agassiz, Nassau, Bahama Is. Built by R.J. Symonette, Nassau, Bahama Is., 1925. (Album)

242 Centerboard yawl *Pieces of Eight,* 32′6″ x 25′11″ x 10′8″ x 3′, for Paul Reese of St. Petersburg, FL. Built by Riverheights Boat Yard, Tampa, FL, 1925. One sister (1925).

243-A Auxiliary sloop *Little Warrior* (the first Malabar Junior), 29′6″ x 23′2″ x 9′8″ x 4′11″, for Dr. Alexander Forbes of Milton, MA. Built by N. Blaisdell & Son, Woolwich, ME, 1925. Eight sisters built: *Lady* (1925); *Kappi* (1925); *Molly-O* (1925); *Actaea* (1925); *Wamawa* (1925); *Lascar* (1925); *Dolphin* (1926); and *Gamine* (1925). (Chapter 6)

244 Auxiliary ketch *Polly II,* 50′11″ x 37′6″ x 12′4″ x 7′, for E.A. Randall of Portland, ME. Built by C.A. Morse & Son, Thomaston, ME, 1925. One sister built: *Matinicus* (1925).

245 Class R sloop, 39′6″ x 25′3″ x 6′10½″ x 5′9¼″, for William P. Barrows of Rochester, NY. Designed 1924. Not built.

245-B Class R sloop *Safara,* 38′6″ x 25′3″ x 6′10½″ x 5′9¼″, for William P. Barrows of Rochester, NY. Built by George Lawley & Son Corp., Neponset, MA, 1925.

246 Auxiliary motor fisherman, 35′ x 33′ x 12′ x 4′4″, for E.G. Faile of White Plains, NY, 1925. One to three sisters, one built in 1933.

247 Power cruiser *Radiant,* 74′ x 14′4″ x 4′, for Clifford R. Hendrix of Larchmont, NY. Built by Luders Marine Construction Co., Stamford, CT, 1926.

248 Auxiliary schooner *Malabar VI,* 52′3″ x 38′ x 12′ x 7′4″, for John G. Alden. Built by Hodgdon Bros., East Boothbay, ME, 1925. Eight sisters built: *Troubador* (1925); *Adventurer* (1925); *Mystic* (1925); *Heather* (1925); *Madrigal* (1926); *Yankee Girl* (1926); *Merry Widow* (1927); and *Sheepscot* (1928). (Chapter 5)

249 Power houseboat *Panchara II,* 52′9″ x 52′1″ x 15′ x 3′10″, for Ledyard W. Sargent of Wayland, MA. Built by Britt Bros., West Lynn, MA, 1925. (Chapter 9)

250 One-design centerboard knockabout (Duxbury Ducks), 18′ x 15′1″ x 6′4″ x 7″, for Duxbury Y.C., Duxbury, MA. Built by C.H. Chaisson, Swampscott, MA, 1925-28. (Also used at Plymouth Y.C.)

251 18′–rater, for Clifford D. Mallory of New York, NY. Designed 1925. Not built.

252 Auxiliary schooner *Jolly Roger,* 60′3″ x 45′5″ x 15′2″ x 8′, for Dr. Merriman. Designed 1925. Not built.

253 Auxiliary gaff schooner *Heart's Desire,* 43′2″ x 32′6″ x 11′6½″ x 6′4″, for A.S. Neilson of Marblehead, MA. Built by T.H. Soule, South Freeport, ME, 1925. One or two sisters built, including: *Picaroon* (1925). (Album)

254 Class S sloop *Nassau,* 31′4″ x 21′ x 6′9″ x 5′1¼″, for John P. Wilson of Chicago, IL. Built by Herreshoff Manufacturing Co., Bristol, RI, 1925.

255 Auxiliary gaff schooner *Harlequin,* 50′11″ x 37′6″ x 13′8″ x 6′4″, for George B. Knowles of New Bedford, MA. Designed 1925. Not built.

256 Auxiliary centerboard sloop, 43′3″ x 29′ x 11′3″ x 3′6″, for W.S. Whitehead. Designed 1925. Not built.

257 Auxiliary centerboard sloop, 45′ x 30′3″ x 12′6″ x

3′, for Harry Horner of Newark, NJ. Designed 1925. Not built.

258 Auxiliary schooner, 64′ x 42′ x 13′4″ x 8′3″, for Hayworth. Designed 1925. Not built.

259 Fast cabin cruiser, 40′ x 39′ x 10′6″ x 3′2″, for Sprague. Not built.

260 Class R marconi sloop *Doress,* 39′7¾″ x 25′6″ x 6′7½″ x 5′7⅜″, for Robert Law, Jr., of New York, NY. Built by George Lawley & Son Corp., Neponset, MA, 1925.

261 Class R marconi sloop *Calypso,* 39′7¾″ x 25′6″ x 6′7½″ x 5′7⅜″, for Dr. Hollis E. Potter of Chicago, IL. Built by Abeking & Rasmussen, Bremen, Germany, 1925. (Album)

262 Class R marconi sloop *Alarm,* 39′7¾″ x 25′4⅞″ x 6′7½″ x 5′7⅜″, for Clifford D. Mallory and Hamilton Hitt. Built by Abeking & Rasmussen, Bremen, Germany, 1925.

263 Class R marconi sloop *Barbara,* 40′ x 24′7″ x 7′ x 5′8″, for Clifford D. Mallory of New York, NY. Built by Abeking & Rasmussen, Bremen, Germany, 1926.

264 Auxiliary gaff schooner *Hardi Baiou,* 79′8″ x 60′ x 18′ x 10′, for Dr. Henry Lloyd of Brookline, MA. Built by F.F. Pendleton, Wiscasset, ME, 1926.

265 Open launch, 18′ x 5′ x 1′7¼″, stock design for Kermath Manufacturing Co., 1925.

266 Auxiliary marconi schooner *Golden Hind,* 46′3″ x 33′ x 11′3″ x 6′6″, for Charles E. Goodwin. Built by Dauntless Shipyard, Essex, CT, 1926. One sister built: *Schoodic* (1926). (Chapter 6)

267 Auxiliary gaff schooner *Trade Wind,* 57′3″ x 42′5″ x 14′2″ x 7′8″, for Henry B. Anderson of New York, NY. Built by C.A. Morse & Son, Thomaston, ME, 1926. One sister built: *Nicanor* (1926). (Chapter 6)

268 One-design keel knockabouts (Charles River Basin Class), 15′ x 12′6″ x 5′6″. Built by George L. Chaisson, Swampscott, MA, George F. Lawson, Boston, MA, and Sam H. Brown, 1926. (Eleven boats built.)

269 Auxiliary yawl *Adhara,* 34′6″ x 24′ x 9′4½″ x 5′6″, for Philip Rheinlander. Built by Williams & Manchester, Newport, RI, 1926.

270-A Auxiliary marconi schooner *Twilight* (first of the keel-version Alden 43s), 43′ x 32′6″ x 11′6″ x 6′4″, for C.P. Cottrell, Jr., of Westerly, RI. Built by Harvey F. Gamage, South Bristol, ME, 1926. Fifteen sisters built, including: *Katinka* (1926); *Half Moon* (1926); *Hilaria* (1926); *Melodie* (1926); *Sea Lady* (1926); *Dolphin* (1926); *Seabreeze* (1926); *Discovery II* (1926); *Lion's Whelp* (1927); *Ethel-May* (1927); *Vagabond* (1927); *Ptarmigan* (1930); and *Spindrift* (1930). (Chapter 6)

271-A Malabar Junior marconi sloop *Tinker* (development of Number 243), 30′ x 23′3″ x 9′8½″ x 4′10¾″, for Melville Haskell of Tucson, AZ. Built by N. Blaisdell & Son, Woolwich, ME, 1926. Four sisters built: *Wamawa* (1926); *Beezie* (1926); *Alnxark* (1926); and *Saginaw* (1926). (Chapter 6)

272 Auxiliary centerboard marconi yawl *Chinook,* 36′3″ x 28′ x 11′11″ x 4′, for Russell Hammons of Portland, ME. Built by Britt Bros., West Lynn, MA, 1926.

273-B Auxiliary schooner *Curlew,* 65′3″ x 46′4″ x 14′8″ x 8′4¼″, for Charles L. Andrews of New York, NY. (Original Number 273, not built, designed for George B. Gibbons of New York, NY.) Built by F.F.

Pendleton, Wiscasset, ME, 1926.

274 Auxiliary marconi ketch *Danai,* 37′3″ x 28′6″ x 10′6″ x 5′10″, for Hans Faviele of New York, NY. Built by Kenneth McAlpin, Shelburne, Nova Scotia, 1926. Six sisters built: *Wanderlure II* (1926); *Seaward* (1926); *Nonnette* (1926); *Nor'wester* (1926); *Quack Quack* (1926); and *Southern Cross* (1926).

275-B Auxiliary centerboard marconi schooner *Delight* (with squaresail), 45′3″ x 35′3″ x 13′6″ x 4′, for L.W. Fogg. (Original Number 275, not built, designed for Houston Wall of Tampa, FL.) Built by Henry Stowman Co., Dorchester, NJ, 1926.

276 Auxiliary three-masted schooner, 162′8″ x 130′ x 29′6″ x 15′, for George F. Tyler of Philadelphia, PA. Not built.

277 Power cruiser, 71′4″ x 14′2″ x 4′, for Arthur N. Peck of New York, NY. Not built.

278 Triangle One-Design sloop (Marblehead Class and Jamestown Class), 28′6″ x 18′6″ x 7′7″ x 4′9″. Built by J.E. Graves, Marblehead, MA. Eight boats built, 1926; five boats, 1927. (Album)

279 One-design centerboard schooner, 65′ x 44′6″ x 15′4″ x 5′6″, for Clifford D. Mallory of New York, NY. Not built.

280 Auxiliary gaff (main topsail) schooner *Malabar VII,* 53′9″ x 37′11″ x 12′5″ x 7′3″, for John G. Alden. Built by Reed-Cook Marine Construction Co., Boothbay Harbor, ME, 1926. Six sisters built: *Angelica* (1926); *Teal* (1926); *Verona II* (1926); *Fearless* (1927); *Sea Dream* (1927); and *Moby Dick* (1927). (Chapter 5)

281 Class Q sloop *Nor'easter IV,* 49′8½″ x 31′7″ x 8′6″ x 6′8½″, for Grafton Smith of Boston, MA. Built by George Lawley & Son Corp., Neponset, MA, 1926.

282 Power cruiser *Mildred IV,* 34′ x 9′ x 4′, for Jere H. Wheelwright of Princeton, NJ. Built by Goudy & Stevens, East Boothbay, ME, 1926. (Chapter 9)

283 Auxiliary schooner *Sachem III,* 79′3″ x 64′7″ x 20′ x 10′, for R.B. Metcalf of New York, NY, for an Arctic expedition. Built by C.A. Morse & Son, Thomaston, ME, 1926. (Album)

284 Auxiliary gaff schooner *Starling,* 126′6″ x 94′8″ x 26′ x 14′6″, for George F. Tyler of Philadelphia, PA. Built of steel by Rice Bros., East Boothbay, ME, 1926. (Album)

285 Auxiliary marconi ketch *Aloha,* 55′ x 38′10″ x 13′ x 6′, for F.B. Drake of San Francisco, CA. Built by Lester Stone, Oakland, CA, 1926. One sister built: *Noname* (1926).

286 V-bottomed runabout, 26′ x 6′1″ x 2′3″, for Metropolitan District Commission, 1926.

287 Auxiliary ketch, 71′9″ x 50′6″ x 17′ x 9′, for H.S. Layman. Not built.

288 Fast auxiliary schooner, 60′ x 40′ x 12′. Not built.

289 Commuter runabout, 29′ x 7′ x 2′1″, for A.E. Whitney, 1926.

290 Auxiliary ketch *Canonchet,* 53′9″ x 37′11″ x 12′5″ x 6′5″, for L.M. Brooks. Built by Portland Yacht Yard, Portland, CT, 1926.

291 Power cruiser *Muskeeta,* 68′6″ x 13′6″ x 3′8″, for Howard Whitney, Glen Cove, NY. Built by Hodgdon Bros., East Boothbay, ME, 1926.

292 Raised-deck power cruiser *Felicia,* 47′ x 46′1″ x 11′6″ x 3′5″, for Abner Morse of Brookline, MA. Built by Luders, Stamford, CT, 1926.

293 One-design centerboard sloop (Sun Class), 22′ x 16′8″ x 6′10½″ x 1′9½″. Built in San Diego, CA, 1926.

293-B One-design keel version of Number 293 (Pequot-Black

293-C Rock Indian Class), 22′ x 16′8″ x 6′10½″ x 3′10″, for Sachem's Head, Pequot, and Black Rock yacht clubs. Built by Portland Yacht Yard, Portland, CT, 1927. (Chapter 8)

294 Open launch, 24′6″ x 7′6″ x 2′, for William P. Barrows of Rochester, NY, 1926.

295 Double-ended centerboard sailing lifeboat, 16′6″ x 14′7″ x 5′6″ x 10″, for Ledyard W. Sargent of Wayland, MA. Built by G.W. Gardner, Swampscott, MA, 1926.

296 Auxiliary ketch *La Galleas,* 58′ x 49′6″ x 16′2″ x 6′, for John G. Alden. Built by Israel Snow, Rockland, ME, 1927. (Chapter 6)

297 Double-ended auxiliary yawl *Thumbcap,* 21′ x 18′5″ x 6′6″ x 2′9″, for Joseph Plumb of Geneva, NY. Built by Rice Bros., East Boothbay, ME, 1926. (Chapter 6)

298 Auxiliary gaff yawl, 34′ x 26′ x 10′ x 5′6″, for E.P. Rowland. Not built.

299 Auxiliary topsail schooner, 69′ x 49′6″ x 16′8″ x 8′8½″, for H.K. McHarg, Jr. Not built.

300 Sedan yacht tender *Bob Cat,* 23′6½″ x 22′10½″ x 6′ x 1′8¾″, for George F. Tyler of Philadelphia, PA. Built by Samuel Brown, Marblehead, MA, 1926.

301 Crew's launch, 22′ x 6′6″ x 1′8″, for George F. Tyler of Philadelphia, PA. Built by Goudy & Stevens, East Boothbay, ME, 1926.

302 Motor lifeboat, 30′ x 29′ x 8′ x 2′8″, for Marblehead Humane Society, Marblehead, MA. Built by Israel Snow, Rockland, ME, 1926. (Album)

303-A Marconi yawl *Shag,* 34′ x 25′5″ x 9′8½″ x 4′11½″, for John Robinson, Jr., of Salem, MA. Built by C.A. Morse & Son of Thomaston, ME, 1926. Six sisters built: *Cadenza* (1927); *Primrose V* (1927); *Betsinda* (1928); *Four Bros.* (1928); *Naumset* (1928); and *Sea Lure II* (1928). (Album)

304 Auxiliary gaff schooner *La Reine* (main topsail), 69′9″ x 49′6″ x 16′8″ x 8′8½″, for Carlisle V. Watson of Lowell, MA. Built by Hodgdon Bros., East Boothbay, ME, 1927.

305 Class R sloop *Vitesse,* 39′7″ x 26′ x 7′ x 5′9″, for William P. Barrows of Rochester, NY. Built by George Lawley & Son Corp., Neponset, MA, 1926. (Album)

306 Auxiliary gaff schooner *Monhegan* (main topsail), 57′6½″ x 42′8″ x 14′2″ x 7′8″, for George Crompton of Worcester, MA. Built by C.A. Morse & Son, Thomaston, ME, 1927. One sister built: *Monomoy* (1927).

307 Auxiliary gaff ketch *Joloma,* 33′8½″ x 29′7″ x 9′9½″ x 4′6″, for Alfred W. Olds of Windsor, CT. Built by C.A. Morse & Son, Thomaston, ME, 1927. Three sisters built: *Topsie* (1927); *Lode Star* (1927); and *Papoose* (1928). (Album)

308 Auxiliary marconi ketch *Arbella,* 73′6″ x 51′ x 16′6″ x 9′, for Robert Saltonstall of Boston, MA. Built by George Lawley & Son Corp., Neponset, MA, 1927. (Album)

309-A Auxiliary gaff schooner *Sartartia* (first of the centerboard-version Alden 43s), 43′ x 33′3″ x 12′6″ x 4′2″, for Benjamin Clayton. Built by Goudy & Stevens, 1927. Sixteen sisters built, including: *Bimesa* (1927); *Black Squall* (1928); *Blue Sea* (1928); *Gamecock* (1928); *Altair* (1928); *Nooya* (1928); *Niliraga* (1928); *Bald Eagle* (1929); *Beatrice B* (1929); *Evanthia III* (1929); *Emma Jean* (1930); *Pinafore*

310 Auxiliary gaff schooner *Clotho,* 70′6″ x 50′2″ x 16′8″ x 8′8½″, for Henry B. Anderson. Built by George Lawley & Son Corp., Neponset, MA, 1927.

311 Diesel-auxiliary gaff ketch *Istar,* 89′ x 67′ x 20′ x 9′6″, for Harry S. Leyman. Built by George Lawley & Son Corp., Neponset, MA, 1927.

312 Auxiliary gaff schooner (main topsail), 47′3″ x 35′6″ x 12′8″ x 7′2″, for John G. Alden. Designed 1926. Not built.

314 Auxiliary centerboard ketch *Hobomok,* 46′3″ x 35′11″ x 13′6″ x 4′, for Paul Whitin. Built by Harvey F. Gamage, South Bristol, ME, 1927.

315 Auxiliary schooner, 73′2″ x 55′3″ x 17′2″ x 9′8″. Designed 1926. Not built.

316 One-design centerboard sailing skiff (Youth's Companion), 15′ x 4′6″. Designed 1926. (Album)

317 Auxiliary gaff schooner (steel hull), 97′6″ x 69′3″ x 20′ x 11′8″, for H.G.S. Noble. Not built.

318 Class R sloop *Lady Pat,* 37′9″ x 24′6″ x 6′8¼″ x 5′7″, for Ronald M. Maitland. Built in Vancouver, British Columbia, 1927.

319 Auxiliary marconi ketch, 37′8″ x 28′8″ x 10′6″ x 5′10″, for John G. Alden. Not built.

321 Auxiliary centerboard yawl, 30′ x 23′9″ x 10′ x 3′. Not built.

322 Auxiliary centerboard ketch *Spindrift,* 49′4″ x 36′6″ x 12′9″ x 6′8″, for Orrin G. Wood. Built by Hodgdon Bros., East Boothbay, ME, 1927.

323 Auxiliary yawl *Rowdy,* 44′4″ x 33′3″ x 12′ x 5′9″, for Frederick Meyer. Built by Nunes Bros., Sausalito, CA, 1927. (Album)

324 Auxiliary topsail schooner, 85′7½″ x 65′ x 19′6″ x 8′9″, for Robert Herrick of Boston, MA. Not built.

325 Marconi sloop (Pirate Class and Cub Class), 18′2″ x 14′5½″ x 6′2″ x 3′8″, for Indian Harbor Y.C., among others. One built for Carlyle Pope by N. Blaisdell & Son, Woolwich, ME, 1927. At least 11 built.

326-A Malabar Junior auxiliary sloop *Tarolinta* (development of Number 271), 30′ x 23′3″ x 9′8½″ x 5′½″, for Amory S. Carhart. Built by George Lawley & Son Corp., Neponset, MA, 1927. Four sisters built: *Martin Pring* (1927); *Genesee* (1927); *Brinda II* (1927); and *Gurkha* (1927). (Chapter 6)

327 Auxiliary marconi schooner *Hajada,* 43′1″ x 32′6″ x 11′6″ x 6′4″, for F.G. Towle. Built by Harvey F. Gamage, South Bristol, ME, 1927. One sister built: *Jolly Roger* (1927). (Album)

328 Auxiliary schooner *Pandora,* 46′1″ x 39′10″ x 11′3″ x 5′, for R.L. Ireland, Jr. Built by Wesley Mahan, 1927.

329 V-bottomed double-cockpit runabout *Sea Urchin,* 25′10″ x 6′1″ x 2′3¼″, for Walter L. Hill of Scranton, PA. Built by James W. Black, 1927.

330 Cabin day cruiser *Rosamond III,* 32′ x 7′6″ x 2′7″, for Emil G. Schmidt. Built by Britt Bros., West Lynn, MA, 1927.

331 Auxiliary gaff schooner *Malabar VIII,* 54′ x 39′ x 12′8¾″ x 7′4″, for John G. Alden. Built by Hodgdon Bros., East Boothbay, ME, 1927. One sister built: *La Goleta* (1927). (Chapter 5)

332 Auxiliary centerboard marconi ketch *Nippekontu,* 42′ x 32′8″ x 12′ x 3′11″, for Robert D. Russell. Built by Reuben Bigelow, Monument Beach, MA, 1927.

333 Auxiliary marconi schooner *Sachem,* 65′8½″ x 44′ x 12′4″ x 8′7″, for Rowe B. Metcalf. Built by

Hodgdon Bros., East Boothbay, ME, 1927. (Chapter 6)

334 Raised-deck centerboard sloop *Windward,* 31′9″ x 18′6″ x 7′6″ x 3′6″ for Paul Burke. Built by Simmons, 1927.

335 Auxiliary schooner *Tyehee,* 36′4″ x 27′4″ x 9′9″ x 5′9″, for W.H. Stuart, Jr. Built by Harvey F. Gamage, South Bristol, ME, 1927. One sister may have been built. (Album)

336 Open launch, 17′6″ x 5′7″ x 1′6″, for Henry Morss. Built by Samuel Brown, Marblehead, MA, 1927.

337 Centerboard marconi sloop, 25′ x 20′7″ x 7′6″ x 15″, for Harold I. Sewall. Built in Puerto Rico, 1927.

339 Open launch, 21′ x 6′8″ x 1′10″, for Eastern Y.C., Marblehead, MA. Built by George L. Chaisson, Swampscott, MA, 1927.

340 Rowing tender, 12′ x 4′2″, for R.L. Ireland. Built by Wesley Mahan, 1927.

341 Auxiliary fast marconi ketch, 63′3″ x 42′ x 10′9″ x 8′4¼″, for Demarest Lloyd. Not built.

342 Class R sloop *Scorpion,* 39′10″ x 26′3″ x 6′6″ x 5′5½″, for William C. Warren, Jr., of Buffalo, NY. Built by George Lawley & Son Corp., Neponset, MA, 1927.

343 Auxiliary knockabout marconi sloop, 32′11″ x 22′11″ x 8′11″ x 5′, for John G. Alden. Designed 1926. Not built.

344 Auxiliary marconi schooner *Marita,* 45′ x 32′10″ x 11′6″ x 6′7″, for Franklin M. Haines. Built by Harvey F. Gamage, South Bristol, ME, 1927. Two sisters built: *Madoc* (1928) and *Aleda* (1928).

345 Coupe tender, 22′ x 6′ x 1′8″, for George F. Tyler of Philadelphia, PA. Built by Goudy & Stevens, East Boothbay, ME, 1927.

346 Centerboard sailing dinghy, 14′ x 12′8″ x 5′10″ x 8½″, for William B. Lloyd. Built by Samuel Brown, Marblehead, MA, 1927. One sister built (1931).

347 Auxiliary three-masted schooner, 121′2″ x 91′6″ x 24′ x 12′9″, for John G. Alden. Designed 1927. Not built. (Chapter 6)

348 Auxiliary schooner *Cacouna,* 61′ x 45′9″ x 15′ x 8′2″, for F.Y.T. Dawson. Built in England, 1927.

350 Auxiliary schooner *Hardi Biaou* (steel), 110′6″ x 84′5″ x 24′4″ x 13′, for Dr. Henry Lloyd. Built by George Lawley & Son Corp., Neponset, MA, 1928.

351 Auxiliary ketch, 62′ x 47′ x 15′4″ x 8′11″, for Serge Geibel. Built in France, 1928.

352 Auxiliary marconi ketch, 38′8″ x 28′10″ x 10′9″ x 5′10″, for O.C. Schoenwerk of Chicago, IL. Not built.

353 Centerboard gaff schooner *Hispaniola,* 37′4″ x 30′ x 12′ x 3′6″, for David B. Bannerman. Built by Weeks Boat Yard, 1928. One sister built: *Droon* (1930). (Album)

354 Powerboat *Annona,* 38′9″ x 38′ x 11′ x 3′, for Stanley Forbes. Built by Britt Bros., West Lynn, MA, 1927.

355 Twin-screw power cruiser *Gypsy,* 101′ x 99′7″ x 18′ x 4′9″, for Robert F. Herrick of Boston, MA. Built by George Lawley & Son Corp., Neponset, MA, 1928. (Chapter 9)

356 Auxiliary centerboard schooner (marconi main) *Sartartia,* 58′11″ x 45′6½″ x 16′5″ x 4′5″, for Benjamin Clayton. Built by Goudy & Stevens, East Boothbay, ME, l928. One sister built: *Mayan* (1946).

357 Auxiliary schooner *Tradition,* 59′11″ x 45′9″ x 14′4″ x 8′1″, for J. Rulon Miller, Jr., of Baltimore, MD. Built by Hodgdon Bros., East Boothbay, ME, 1928.

358 Auxiliary yawl *Shag*, 34'4" x 25'4½" x 9'8½" x 5', for John Robinson, Jr., of Salem, MA. Built by George Lawley & Son Corp., Neponset, MA, 1928. (Album)

359 Auxiliary gaff schooner *Mohawk*, 60'3½" x 46'2" x 14'5" x 8'9", for Dudley F. Wolfe. Built by F.F. Pendleton, Wiscasset, ME, 1928. (Chapter 6)

360 Twin-screw diesel power cruiser *Penguin*, 70' x 68'4" x 15'3" x 4'9", for Dr. Austen F. Riggs. Built by C.A. Morse & Son, Thomaston, ME, 1928.

362 Auxiliary schooner *Malabar IX,* 57'11" x 44'3" x 14'2" x 7'9", for John G. Alden. Built by Hodgdon Bros., East Boothbay, ME, 1928. (Chapter 5)

363 Cabin cruiser *Pow Wow*, 38' x 37'6" x 9'6" x 2'6", for F.S. Sawyer. Built by Staples, Johnson, 1928.

364 Twin-screw power cruiser *Mildred V*, 53' x 51'5" x 13' x 5', for Jere Wheelwright, Jr., of Princeton, NJ. Built by Goudy & Stevens, East Boothbay, ME, 1928.

365 Auxiliary schooner *Camilla* (similar to Number 306), 57'8" x 43'2" x 14'2" x 7'9", for Bayard Warren. Built by Reed-Cook Marine Construction Co., East Boothbay, ME, 1928.

366 Auxiliary schooner *Kinkajou* (steel), 50'3½" x 36' x 12'2" x 6'11", for B.E. Ruys, Holland. Built by G. de Vries Lentsch, Amsterdam, Holland, 1928.

367 Auxiliary marconi knockabout ketch *Vagabond*, 54'9⅜" x 37'11" x 12'5" x 7'3", for Clarence G. White. Built by Reed-Cook Marine Construction Co., East Boothbay, ME, 1928. Seven sisters built: *Spindrift* (1928); *Dreamer* (1929); *Surprise* (1929); *Joan* (1929); *Blazing Star* (1930); *Jessica* (1930); and *Sea Witch* (1930). (Album)

368 Auxiliary centerboard schooner *Stella*, 47'5" x 35'9" x 12'9" x 4'6", for John Sherman Hoyt. Built by Franklin G. Post, 1928.

369 Auxiliary schooner *Windigo*, 49'3" x 36' x 11'11" x 7', for Matthew P. Whittall. Built by Harvey F. Gamage, South Bristol, ME, 1928.

370 Class Q sloop *Tartar*, 50'4" x 32' x 8'4" x 6'10", for John G. Alden. Built by George Lawley & Son Corp., Neponset, MA, 1928. (Album)

372 Raised-deck sloop, 30' x 22' x 7'8" x 5'3", for Langford T. Alden. Designed 1928. Not built.

373 Raised-deck power cruiser *Clivea*, 45' x 44'2" x 11'1" x 3'8", for Col. Beardmore. Built by Gidley Boat Co., 1928.

374 Class R sloop, 40'4" x 26'8" x 6'10" x 6', for William P. Barrows. Not built.

375 Auxiliary ketch *Keok*, 55' x 38'10" x 13'1¾" x 6'7½", for Dr. John Dane. Built by Goudy & Stevens, East Boothbay, ME, 1928. (Used Number 285 sail and construction plans.)

376 Power cruiser *Maravel* (auxiliary sails), 74'8" x 66'9" x 16'6" x 6'3", for Dr. Wilfred Grenfell. Built by C.A. Morse & Son, Thomaston, ME, 1928.

377 Auxiliary topsail schooner *Nedrah*, 59'9½" x 48'3" x 15'6" x 8', for Ross Harden. Built by Dauntless Shipyard, Inc., Essex, CT, 1928.

378 Power cruiser *Tortoise,* 35' x 34' x 9' x 2'10", for Melville Haskell. Built by Wesley Mahan, 1928.

379 Class R sloop *Shadow*, 40'9" x 26'8" x 6'9"x 6', for William P. Barrows. Built by George Lawley & Son Corp., Neponset, MA, 1928.

380 Sailing dory, 15'6" x 4'5¼", for Dr. Austen F. Riggs. Built by George L. Chaisson, Swampscott, MA, 1928.

381 Auxiliary keel-centerboard gaff yawl *Wanderer II*, 32'4" x 25'11" x 10'8" x 3'6", for W.K. Dunbar. Built by Morton Johnson, Bay Head, NJ, 1928.

382 Newport sailing dory, 15'3" x 5'½" x 6", for John G. Alden. Built by George L. Chaisson, Swampscott, MA, 1928. Five boats built. (Album)

383 Auxiliary topsail schooner, 80'5" x 63'9" x 18'½" x 10'8". Not built.

384 Auxiliary sloop, 21' x 18'7" x 6'6" x 3'9". Not built.

385 Auxiliary yawl *Cynthia*, 34'4" x 25'5" x 9'9" x 5', for J.L. Williamson. Built by N. Blaisdell & Son, Woolwich, ME, 1928. Nine sisters built: *Kelpie* (1929); *Merry Ann* (1929); *Cynara* (1929); *Thyrza* (1929); *Lorelei* (1929); *Ginjack* (1929); *Sea Pacer* (1929); *Dolphin* (1929); and *Molly* (1930). (Chapter 6)

386 Auxiliary keel-centerboard clipper-bowed gaff yawl *Northern Light*, 38'11" x 30'8" x 12' x 3'6", for Richard T. Crane, Jr., and Florence Crane. Built by Hodgdon Bros., East Boothbay, ME, l928.

387 Fast cabin cruiser *Blue Bill*, 34' x 33'2" x 9'3" x 2'6", for Gerald D. Boardman. Built by Walter A. Cross, 1928. One sister built: *Sou'Wester* (1928).

388 Outboard motor tender, 12' x 4'6", for George Crompton.

389 Cabin cruiser *Oumiak*, 37'10" x 37'1" x 11' x 2'6", for Rowe B. Metcalf. Built by Franklin G. Post, 1928.

390 Auxiliary schooner *Who II*, 50'1" x 39'10" x 14' x 7'2", for George C. Gordon, Jr. Built by C.A. Morse & Son, Thomaston, ME, 1928. Eight sisters built: *Tyrone* (1929); *Rogue* (1930); *Abenaki* (1930); *Zaida II* (1930); *Arcturus* (1930); *Pavana* (1932); *Snow White* (1931); and *Heron* (1932).

391 Yacht tender, 8' x 3'3", for John G. Alden. Built by George L. Chaisson, Swampscott, MA, 1929.

392 Auxiliary cruising centerboard ketch *Four Winds*, 47'1" x 35'10½" x 13'6½" x 3'8", for Frank J. Mather, Jr. Built by Harvey F. Gamage, South Bristol, ME, 1929. One sister built: *Sunshine* (1929).

393 Auxiliary cruising schooner, 59'6" x 43'2" x 14'2" x 7'9". Not built.

394 Auxiliary marconi schooner *Menikoe V*, 60'6" x 40' x 13' x 8'3", for C.D. Alexander. Built by F.F. Pendleton, Wiscasset, ME, 1929. (Album)

395 Diesel auxiliary schooner, 75'9" x 54' x 17'9" x 8'9", for Hart S. Weaver. Built by Lester Stone, Oakland, CA, 1929.

396 Power cruiser *Margin*, 43'1" x 42'7" x 10'5" x 2'9", for A.F. Porter. Built by Goudy & Stevens, East Boothbay, ME, 1928. One sister built in South America (1928).

397 Auxiliary schooner *Teragram*, 58'5" x 43'2" x 14'2" x 7'10", for George W. Mixter. Built by Dauntless Shipyard, Inc., Essex, CT, 1929. (Album)

398 One-design knockabout (Nantucket Class and Kennebunkport Class, development of Numbers 135 and 148), 21'2"x 16'2" x 6'5" x 1'6". Built by George L. Chaisson, Swampscott, MA, 1929-31. Thirty-nine boats built. (Chapter 8)

399 Auxiliary yawl *Marianette II*, 40'3" x 29'8" x 10'9" x 6'5", for Roger D. Hale. Built by Harvey F. Gamage, South Bristol, ME, 1929.

400 Class Q sloop *Hope*, 50'3" x 31'3" x 8'5" x 7', for John G. Alden. Built by Hodgdon Bros., East Boothbay, ME, 1929. (Chapter 8)

401 Auxiliary cruising yawl *Gringo*, 38'7" x 28'9" x 10'8" x 5'9", for Harold Amory. Built by Harvey F.

Gamage, South Bristol, ME, 1929. One sister built: *Eliza* (1929).

402 Fast cabin runabout *Snapper III*, 32' x 31'4" x 7'6" x 2'7", for Eleanor Saltonstall. Built by Britt Bros., West Lynn, MA, 1929.

403 Fast raised-deck cabin cruiser *Alibi*, 34' x 33'2" x 9'3" x 2'7", for George P. Metcalf. Built by Britt Bros., West Lynn, MA, 1929. Four sisters built: *Tarpon* (1929); *Shawna III* (1929); *Sou' Wester* (1929); and *Arion* (1929).

404 Auxiliary schooner, 96'½" x 71'10¼" x 20'8" x 10'9", for Cotton Wachtmann. Built in Europe, 1929.

405 Auxiliary ketch *Narwhal*, 35'8" x 30' x 10' x 5'3", for John G. Alden. Built by Britt Bros., West Lynn, MA, 1929. One sister built: *Maya* (1929).

406 Double-ended knockabout, 21' x 18'7" x 7' x 3', for J.H. Jewett, Jr. Built by Ah King, Hong Kong, 1929. Four sisters built, including: *Alibi* (1929); *Black Duck* (1929); and *Viking* (1929). (Album)

407 Class Q sloop, for John G. Alden. Not built.

408 Centerboard schooner *Sartartia*, 84'8" x 64' x 21' x 6', for Benjamin Clayton. Built by Goudy & Stevens, East Boothbay, ME, 1929.

409 Power cruiser *Lophius*, 55'5" x 54'10" x 12' x 3', for William Proctor. Built by Camden Yacht Yard, Camden, ME, 1929.

410 Motor ketch *Nadiranga*, 43' x 36'1" x 12' x 3'10", for P.W. Wadsworth. Built by Harvey F. Gamage, South Bristol, ME, 1929.

411 Auxiliary cruising schooner *Varuna*, 80' x 61'6" x 18'9" x 10'2", for Dr. J. Remsen Bishop. Built by F. F. Pendleton, Wiscasset, ME, 1929. (Album)

412 Auxiliary schooner *Queen Tyi*, 78'5" x 61'9" x 18'4" x 10'2", for Arthur Crisp. Built by C.A. Morse & Son, Thomaston, ME, 1929.

413 Auxiliary schooner *Bimesa*, 84'2½" x 65' x 20' x 7', for W.W. Knight. Built by Reed-Cook Marine Construction Co., Boothbay Harbor, ME, 1929.

414 Auxiliary schooner *Boekanier* (steel), 64'8" x 44'9¼" x 14'7" x 7'6", for W. Ruys. Built by G. de Vries Lentsch, Amsterdam, Holland, 1929.

415 Auxiliary sloop *Nancy Baker*, 50'2" x 32' x 10'6" x 6'5", for Robert H. McCurdy. Built by George Lawley & Son Corp., Neponset, MA, 1929.

416 Diesel auxiliary schooner *Two Brothers*, 54'9" x 40' x 14'3" x 7'2", for Walter W. Duffett. Built by Harvey F. Gamage, South Bristol, ME, 1929. One sister built: *Saracen* (1930).

417 Rowing tender, 11' x 4', for John G. Alden. Built by Joseph T. Davidson, 1929.

418 Power tender, 15' x 5', for Arthur Crisp. Built by William Chamberlain, Marblehead, MA, 1929. Seven sisters built.

419 Power cruiser *Sally B*, 37'10" x 37' x 11' x 2'10", for James M. Beale. Built by Britt Bros., West Lynn, MA, 1929.

420 Auxiliary sloop, 30'7" x 23'1½" x 9'8½" x 5'. Not built.

421 Tabloid cruiser *Curlew* (like Number 406 but with transom stern), 21'2" x 18'7" x 7' x 3'3", for Albert T. Gould. Built by C.A. Morse & Son, Thomaston, ME, 1929.

422 Auxiliary racing and cruising ketch *Karenita*, 74'7" x 48'9" x 14'11" x 9'6", for Demarest Lloyd. Built by George Lawley & Son Corp., Neponset, MA, 1929.

423 One-design knockabout (Pilot Class), 16'6" x 11' x 5'9" x 2'11", for Rockport, MA and Jamestown, RI. Built by Charles A. Anderson, Wareham, MA, and William Chamberlain, Marblehead, MA, 1929-30.

424 V-bottomed raised-deck cruising sloop *Nancy and Anstiss*, 26'3" x 22'6" x 9'6" x 2'6", for Dana. Built by William Chamberlain, Marblehead, MA, 1929.

425 Auxiliary cruiser *Clovelly*, 55'6" x 47'7" x 14' x 4'6", for Charles Tifft. Built by Franklin G. Post, 1929.

426 Auxiliary ketch *Gamecock*, 29'11" x 23'9" x 8'9" x 4'3", for William B. Allen. Built by Britt Bros., West Lynn, MA, 1929.

427 Catboat *Milady*, 20' x 18'6" x 9' x 1'8", for E.R. Willard. Built by Reuben Bigelow, Monument Beach, MA, 1929. (Chapter 8)

428 Auxiliary schooner, 93'6" x 70'9" x 23' x 11'6", for Charles T. Stork. Not built.

429 Knockabout sloop *Leebird*, 17' x 14'8" x 5'10" x 2'11½", for Walter W. Duffett. Built by James E. Graves, Marblehead, MA, 1929. One sister built: *Oriole* (1929).

430 Auxiliary sloop, 31'6" x 27'6" x 9'6" x 4'6", for Benjamin C. Tilghman. Designed 1929. Not built. Plans purchased by Felix Lake of Attleboro, MA. Sloop *Faith* built by Harvey F. Gamage, South Bristol, ME, 1932. One sister may have been built.

431 Auxiliary schooner *Dreamer*, 40' x 31'6" x 11'6" x 5'11", for C. R. Hinchman. Built by Goudy & Stevens, East Boothbay, ME, 1930. One sister built.

432 Motorsailer *Bonnie Dundee II*, 48' x 43'5" x 13'6" x 5', for Clifford D. Mallory. Built by Britt Bros., West Lynn, MA, 1930.

433 Auxiliary keel sloop *Ulysses* (modification of Number 172), 27'2" x 22'4" x 9' x 4'6". Designed in 1929. Not built.

435 Auxiliary schooner *Puritan* (steel), 101' x 74'6" x 22'9" x 9', for S.P. Curtis. Later converted to #435-B, 102'9" x 74'8" x 22'10" x 9', for Edward W. Brown. Built by Electric Boat Co., New London, CT, 1931. (Chapter 7)

436 Centerboard sloop, 25' x 22' x 9'6" x 3'. Designed 1929. Not built.

437 Cruising sloop, 27' x 19' x 7'8" x 3'8". Designed 1929. Not built.

438 Power tender, 13' x 4'7", for Charles Tifft. Built by Franklin G. Post, 1929. One sister built (1930).

439 Raised-deck yawl, 34'7½" x 25'7½" x 9'10" x 5'2". Not built.

440 Auxiliary schooner *Penzance*, 58'3½" x 41'4" x 13'8" x 7'6", for F.J. Frost. Built by Harvey F. Gamage, South Bristol, ME, 1930. Two sisters built: *Pitzi* (1930) and *Marita* (1930). (Album)

441 Auxiliary keel-centerboard yawl *Trident*, 55'8" x 38'6" x 12'10" x 5'6", for Alger Shelden. Built by Herman Lund, Erie, PA, 1930.

442 Auxiliary centerboard yawl *Onward II*, 34'6" x 27'2" x 11'7" x 3'1½", for Phillips N. Case. Built by Harvey W. McFarland, 1930.

443 Raised-deck power cruiser *Marazul*, 38' x 32'8" x 10' x 3', started for J.A. Cook of Florida and finished for Albert W. Johnston of New York. Built by Britt Bros., West Lynn, MA, 1930.

444 Auxiliary cruising schooner *Kestrel II*, 93'7" x 70' x 19'6" x 11' for Guy P. Gannett. Built by F.F. Pendleton, Wiscasset, ME, 1930. (Album)

445-A Auxiliary cruising schooner *Hathor II*, 84' x 64' x 18' x 10'2", for Sidney A. Beggs. Built by Hodgdon Bros., East Boothbay, ME, 1930.

446   Fast day cruiser *Mallard*, 40′ x 32′8½″ x 10′3″ x 2′9″, for Josiah B. Chase. Built by Britt Bros., West Lynn, MA, 1930. (Chapter 9)

447   Bermuda One-Design, keel knockabout *Eleventh Hour*, 22′4″ x 18′3″ x 6′9″ x 3′6″, for Philip B. Smith. Built in Bermuda, 1930. At least three sisters built. (Chapter 8)

448   Auxiliary schooner *Lelanta* (steel), 65′ x 46′ x 14′7″ x 8′9″, for Ralph St. L. Peverley. Built by G. de Vries Lentsch, Amsterdam, Holland, 1930. (Chapter 7)

449   Auxiliary schooner *Mattakeeset*, 52′8″ x 41′5″ x 14′3″ x 5′6″, for Dr. George C. Sears. Built by C.A. Morse & Son, Thomaston, ME, 1930.

450   Raised-deck cabin cruiser (lines are those of Number 443 revised), 38′ x 10′, for John G. Alden. Not built.

451   V-bottomed fast day cruiser, 39′6″ x 9′10″, for Gerald Boardman. Not built.

452   Auxiliary schooner *Skylark*, 68′ x 49′ x 15′ x 8′8″, for Marshall J. Dodge. Built by Dauntless Shipyard, Inc., Essex, CT, 1930.

453   Auxiliary cruising schooner *Malabar X*, 58′3″ x 44′2″ x 14′2″ x 8′1″, for John G. Alden. Built by Hodgdon Bros., East Boothbay, ME, 1930. One sister built. (Chapter 5)

454   Auxiliary schooner, 53′10½″ x 42′ x 14′3″ x 7′3″, for William H. Dixon. Not built.

455   Auxiliary ketch *Saquish*, 37′2″ x 30′ x 10′3″x 5′2″, for E.M. Farnsworth, Jr. Built by Harvey F. Gamage, South Bristol, ME, 1930.

456   Auxiliary schooner *High Tide*, 70′8″ x 50′ x 14′3″ x 8′6″, for J. Rulon Miller, Jr. Built by M.M. Davis & Son, Solomons, MD, 1931. (Chapter 7)

457   Auxiliary cruising schooner *Camilla*, 70′3″ x 54′4″ x 16′9″ x 9′2″, for Bayard Warren. Built by George Lawley & Son Corp., Neponset, MA, 1930.

458   Auxiliary cruising schooner *Dauntless*, 61′ x 43′3″ x 13′4″ x 8′3″, for Horace B. Merwin. Built by Dauntless Shipyard, Inc., Essex, CT, 1930.

459   Auxiliary marconi yawl *Petrel*, 35′9″ x 26′2½″ x 9′9½″ x 5′2″, for John H. Harwood. Built by N. Blaisdell & Son, Woolwich, ME, 1930. Four sisters built: *Hostess II* (1930); *Emma* (1930); *Delight* (1931); and *Moonbi* (1936).

460   Auxiliary schooner, for Arthur Crisp. Not built.

461   Raised-deck cruiser (standard type), for Dr. Traub. Not built.

462   Cabin cruiser *Mariner*, 25′11″ x 25′3½″ x 7′1½″ x 2′8″, for Orrin Wood. Built by S.F. McFarland, 1930.

463   North Haven dinghy, 14′, 1929.

464   Auxiliary cruising schooner *Alpha*, 64′10½″ x 45′9″ x 15′ x 8′, for A.P. Armour. Built by Greenport Basin & Construction Co., 1930.

465   Eight-meter class sloop, 49′7″ x 30′3″ x 7′11½″ x 6′3″, for William P. Barrows of Rochester, NY. Designed 1930. Not built.

466   Auxiliary schooner *Water Gypsy*, 59′1″ x 43′2″ x 13′9″ x 8′, for William McMillan of Princeton, NJ. Built by Hodgdon Bros., East Boothbay, ME, 1931. (Album)

467   Auxiliary centerboard ketch *Beatrice B*, 52′8″ x 41′5″ x 14′3″ x 5′, for Dr. Fritz B. Talbot. Built by Reed-Cook Marine Construction Co., Boothbay Harbor, ME, 1930.

468   Auxiliary schooner, 43′7″ x 32′3″ x 11′9″ x 6′4½″, for Dr. Oskar Mustelin. Built in Finland.

469   Auxiliary fisherman schooner *Pegasus*, 80′5″ x 63′9″ x 18′ x 10′8″, for Frederick M. Lee. Built by J. F. James, 1930.

470-B   Auxiliary cutter *Aries*, 45′ x 35′ x 12′ x 7′6″, for L.M. Brooks. Built by Dauntless Shipyard, Inc., Essex, CT, 1931.

471   Diesel sailer *Ungava*, 58′6″ x 50′6″ x 13′6″ x 5′, for Albert W. Johnston of New York. Built by Britt Bros., West Lynn, MA, 1930.

472   Power cruiser, 29′ x 28′2½″ x 9′6¼″ x 2′9″. Not built.

474   Knockabout *Akawi*, 32′ x 25′6″ x 9′ x 4′6″, for P.Y. De Normandie. Built by James E. Graves, Marblehead, MA, 1930.

475-B   Auxiliary sloop *Lady Ann*, 36′3″ x 28′ x 11′ x 3′6″, for George F. Hunt. (Original Number 475, not built, designed for George H. Patterson.) Built by Morton Johnson, Bay Head, NJ, 1935. One sister built: *Sirius II*, 1936.

476   Auxiliary cruising schooner *Lord Jim*, 62′8″ x 46′ x 15′ x 8′7″, for Paul Nevin of New York, NY. Built by M.M. Davis & Son, Solomons, MD, 1930. (Chapter 7)

477   Launch, 25′6″ x 7′, for Eastern Y.C., Marblehead, MA.

478   Auxiliary cruising yawl *Faith* (Number 367 hull with changed sheer), 54′10″ x 37′11″ x 12′5″ x 7′3″, for Walter W. Duffett. Built by F.F. Pendleton, Wiscasset, ME, 1930.

479   Twin-screw cabin runabout *Cathalene*, 38′ x 9′ x 2′8″, for Cornelius Crane. Built by Goudy & Stevens, East Boothbay, ME, 1930. (Album)

480   Auxiliary schooner, 37′9″ x 29′6″ x 10′6″ x 5′7½″, for Joe Will. Designed 1930. Not built.

481   Launch (tender for Number 457, *Camilla*), 14′6″ x 4′9″, for Bayard Warren. Built by William Chamberlain, Marblehead, MA, 1930.

482   Cabin launch *Yolande*, 30′ x 8′2″, for P.S. Keeler. Built by Kenny & Kenny, 1930. One sister built: *Polly C. II* (1930).

483   Diesel power cruiser *Stowaway*, 38′ x 36′8″ x 10′1″ x 4′3″, for Holcombe J. Brown. Built by Harvey F. Gamage, South Bristol, ME, 1930. (Album)

485   Auxiliary cutter *Mandalay*, 38′6″ x 30′11″ x 10′8″ x 6′, for Frank Vining Smith. Built by Casey Boat-building Co., Inc., Fairhaven, MA, 1931. (Album)

487   Special powerboat *Viola*, 55′ x 54′5¾″ x 11′4½″ x 3′4½″. Built by Dauntless Shipyard, Inc., Essex, CT, 1930. One sister built (1930). (Album)

489   Rowing tender, 15′ x 4′6″, for Cotton Wachtmann. Built in Estonia, 1930.

490   Auxiliary centerboard schooner *Four Brothers*, 45′ x 33′11″ x 12′6″ x 4′3″, for F.L. Ballard of Philadelphia, PA. Built by Goudy & Stevens, East Boothbay, ME, 1931. (Album)

492   Auxiliary cruising schooner *Freedom*, 88′2″ x 66′6″ x 19′8″ x 10′, for Sterling Morton of Chicago, IL. Built by Great Lakes Boat Building Corp., 1931. (Chapter 7)

493   One-design knockabout, 24′6″ x 15′ x 7′ x 3′10″, for Rockport Y.C. Built by James E. Graves, Marblehead, MA, 1931. Four boats built.

494   Power cruiser *Mary III*, 28′11″ x 27′9″ x 9′8″ x 2′10″, for W. Chandler Bowditch. Built by George L. Chaisson, Swampscott, MA, 1931. At least one sister built: *Maskie* (1934).

496   Auxiliary centerboard yawl, 37′9″ x 29′ x 11′7″ x 3′6″. Designed 1930. Not built.

497   Auxiliary schooner *Alouette*, 37′3″ x 28′6″ x 10′6″

x 5'10", for J. William Duggan of Boston, MA. Built by Willis J. Reid, Winthrop, MA, 1931. One sister built: *Kenetta* (1936).

498 Auxiliary cruising schooner *La Reine*, 75'9" x 59' x 18'2" x 10'3", for Carlisle V. Watson of Lowell, MA. Built by Hodgdon Bros., East Boothbay, ME, 1932. (Album)

499 Auxiliary yawl *Erica*, 30'4" x 23'4" x 9'8" x 5'2", for Samuel C. Payson of Boston, MA. Built by N. Blaisdell & Son, Woolwich, ME, 1931. One sister built: *Corma II* (1932). (Album)

500 Auxiliary schooner (steel), 164'2" x 125'10" x 33' x 16'6", for Floyd L. Carlisle of New York, NY. Designed 1930. Not built.

501 Cabin cruiser, 45' x 44' x 12' x 3'6", for C.A. Sawyer, Jr., of Boston, MA. Designed 1930. Not built.

502 Yacht tender (for Number 435, *Puritan*), 18' x 5'1", for Edward W. Brown of New York, NY. Built by William Chamberlain, Marblehead, MA, 1931. (Album)

503 Auxiliary catboat *Molly II*, 28' x 12'7" x 3'2", for Kenneth Taylor of Woonsocket, RI. Built by Reuben Bigelow, Monument Beach, MA, 1931. Two sisters built, including: *Sharon L* (1933). (Chapter 7)

504 Auxiliary cutter, 28'4" x 25'10" x 10' x 3'5½", for John G. Alden. Designed 1930. Not built.

505 Auxiliary cruising yawl *Two Brothers*, 42' x 32'4" x 11'7" x 6', for Stephen Wheatland of Bangor, ME. Built by Willis J. Reid, Winthrop, MA, 1931.

506 Auxiliary marconi cutter *Bantam*, 32' x 25'9" x 8'10" x 4'9", for A.S. Neilson of Boston, MA. Built by C.A. Morse & Son, Thomaston, ME, 1931. One sister built: *Sweet Honey* (1932). (Album)

507 Auxiliary schooner *Grenadier*, 59'10" x 41'8" x 13'8" x 8'2", for Sherman, Wells, and Henry A. Morss. Built by George Lawley & Son Corp., Neponset, MA, 1931. (Chapter 7)

508 Cabin power launch *Dolphin*, 29' x 28' x 8'6" x 3', for J. Malcolm Forbes of Boston, MA. Built by Britt Bros., West Lynn, MA, 1931.

509 Auxiliary marconi sloop *Cock Robin*, 56'5" x 39' x 12'6" x 7'3", for John P. Elton of Waterbury, CT. Built by Dauntless Shipyard, Inc., Essex, CT, 1931. (Chapter 7)

510 Auxiliary marconi yawl *Black Friar*, 37'6" x 27'6" x 10'3" x 5'9", for Edward P. Jastram of Providence, RI. Built by Goudy & Stevens, East Boothbay, ME, 1931. Two sisters built: *Chicadee* (1931) and *Sea Gypsy* (1932).

511 Shoal-draft launch, 18' x 5' x 7", for Olmstead Bros., Brookline, MA (built for Indian River Assoc.). Built by Goudy and Stevens, East Boothbay, ME, 1931.

512 One-design sailing dinghy, 14' x 5'6" x 3', production boat for Old Town Canoe Co., Old Town, ME. Built by Old Town Canoe Co., 1931.

513 Raised-deck ketch, 40'4" x 32'9" x 10'6" x 6'6", for Issac Harter, Jr., of New York, NY. Built in Nova Scotia, 1932.

514 Auxiliary ketch *Katharine III*, 43' x 31'6" x 12' x 6'5", for William H. Gibbs of New York, NY. Built by C.A. Morse & Son, Thomaston, ME, 1931.

515 Auxiliary yawl *Revelry*, 35'1" x 25'4" x 10'2" x 5'5", for Reginald Johnson of Boston, MA. Built by N. Blaisdell & Son, Woolwich, ME, 1931. One sister built: *Lone Gull* (1931). (Album)

516 Raised-deck sloop ("improved" Bird Class, development of Number 157), 30' x 22' x 7'8" x 5'2", for

Los Angeles Y.C., Los Angeles, CA (F. C. Brewer). Built by Harbor Boat Building Co., Wilmington, CA, 1931. (Chapter 8)

517 One-design sloop (Navigator Class), 21' x 15' x 6'4" x 2'6", for Edgartown Y.C., Edgartown, MA. Built by Reuben Bigelow, Monument Beach, MA, 1931. Two boats built.

518 Centerboard knockabout, 22' x 16'9" x 7'9" x 2'6", for a client of Burger Boat Co., Manitowoc, WI. Designed 1931.

519 Stock schooner, 48' x 36'3" x 13'2" x 6'8", for John G. Alden. Designed 1931. Not built.

520 Auxiliary schooner, 71'10" x 54'9" x 16'8" x 9'3", for George Mixter of New York, NY. Designed 1931. Not built.

521 Auxiliary cruising cutter *Lady Ruth*, 26'2" x 23'4" x 8'7" x 4'6", for Charles W. Taft of Cleveland, OH. Built by N. Philpott, Cleveland, OH, 1933. One sister built: *Roustabout* (1933). (Chapter 7)

522-A Tahiti Class, double-ended cruising ketch *Beluga*, 35' x 32'4" x 11'2½" x 4'2½", for Walter Ott. (Original Number 522, not built, designed for Henry T. Meneely of Troy, NY.) Built by J. Scott McBurney & Co. Four sisters with deeper draft built: *Chinook* (1936); *Linnea*; *Loiterer*; and *Pandora* (1937). (Album)

523 Auxiliary ketch *Tinic*, 37' x 29'10½" x 10'2" x 5'3", for John G. Alden. Built by C.A. Morse & Son, Thomaston, ME, 1932.

524 Shoal-draft cabin cruiser, 45' x 44'3" x 12' x 2', for Rowe B. Metcalf of New York, NY. Designed 1931.

525-B Auxiliary cruising schooner *Vagabond*, 51'11" x 39'10" x 14' x 7'2", for S. Howard Martin of Boston, MA. (Original Number 525, not built, designed for C.H. Cuno of Meriden, CT.) Built by George Lawley & Son Corp., Neponset, MA, 1932. (Album)

526 Auxiliary schooner, 45'6" x 33'3" x 12'2" x 6'7½", for Jere Wheelwright of New York, NY. Designed in 1932.

527 Auxiliary centerboard schooner *Goblin*, 43' x 33'3" x 12'6" x 4'5", for J.T. Van Dorn of Cleveland, OH. Built by W.E. Hathaway, Port Clinton, OH, 1932.

528 Auxiliary centerboard schooner *Janelburn*, 66'3" x 52'9" x 17' x 4'6", for Mrs. R.M. Roloson of Cotuit, MA. Built by Goudy & Stevens, East Boothbay, ME, 1932. (Album)

529 Auxiliary seagoing schooner *Pilgrim*, 85' x 81'2" x 69'9½" x 20'8" x 10'3", for Donald C. Starr of Boston, MA. Built by Reed-Cook Marine Construction Co., Boothbay Harbor, ME, 1932. (Chapter 7)

530-B Auxiliary gaff sloop, 26'8¼" x 21'5¾" x 8'6" x 4'8", for Dr. A.G. Holmes of Miami, FL. (Original Number 530, not built, designed for H.W. Shugg, Jr., of Boston, MA.) Built by John D. Fitch, Miami, FL, 1934.

531 Auxiliary gaff sloop *Lark*, 44'4" x 29'6" x 10'9" x 5'5", for Ralph E. Forbes of Boston, MA. Built by F. D. Lawley, Inc., Quincy, MA, 1932. (Album)

532 Auxiliary ketch *Werdna*, 46' x 35'10" x 13'3" x 4'6", for Charles D. Jencks of Pawtucket, RI. Built by Albert Lemos, Riverside, RI, 1932.

533 One-design knockabouts, 18'3" x 6'10½" x 1'6", for Chase Mellon and others of Small Point, ME. Designed 1932. Not built.

534 Auxiliary marconi schooner *Mandoo*, 62' x 44'3" x 14'8" x 8'3", for D. Spencer Berger of New Haven,

CT. Built by George Lawley & Son Corp., Neponset, MA, 1932. (Album)

535 Power tender (for Number 528, *Janelburn),* 12' x 4'5" x 1'½", for Mrs. R.M. Roloson of Cotuit, MA. Built by N. Blaisdell & Son, Woolwich, ME, 1932.

536 Centerboard cabin knockabout, 25' x 20'6" x 8'4" x 2'6", for William P. Barrows. Designed 1932. Not built.

537 Auxiliary cutter, 37'3" x 30' x 10'9" x 5'3½", for Maumus Claverie of New Orleans, LA. Built by Zane Carter, LA, 1932.

538 Stock centerboard sharpie, 15' LOA, for Boston Liquidating & Appraising Co., Boston, MA. Built by Amasa Pratt Co., Lowell, MA, 1932.

539 Stock outboard launch, 15' LOA, for Boston Liquidating & Appraising Co., Boston, MA. Built by Amasa Pratt Co., Lowell, MA, 1932.

540 Sailing tender, 11'6" LOA, for Old Town Canoe Co., Old Town, ME. Built by Old Town Canoe Co., 1932.

541 Sailing dinghy, 11'6" LOA, for Portland Y.C. Designed 1932. Not built.

542 Centerboard catboat, 12' LOA, Built by George L. Chaisson, Swampscott, MA, 1932. Several sisters built.

543 Auxiliary knockabout, 31'1½" x 23'3½" x 9'4½" x 5'1", for John G. Alden. Designed 1932. Not built.

544 Sailing canoe, 17' x 16'4½" x 3'4" x 4", for Old Town Canoe Co., Old Town, Me. Built by Old Town Canoe Co., 1932.

545 Dinghy, 10' x 4', for Old Town Canoe Co., Old Town, ME. Built by Old Town Canoe Co., 1932.

546 Auxiliary sloop, 21'2" x 18'6" x 8' x 3'7", for Franc John Gardner of Chicago, IL, 1933. At least five sisters built, including: *Safari* (1936) and *Sea Biscuit* (1938).

547 Auxiliary schooner *Cassiopeia,* 48'4" x 40'1½" x 14' x 6', for Dr. Frederick R. Rogers of Boston, MA. Built by Kenneth McAlpin, Shelburne, Nova Scotia, 1933. Two to four sisters built, including: *Story II* (1937) (Chapter 7)

548 One-design sailing skiff, 10' x 3'9", for Leland J. Clark of Bellevue, WA. Built by N.J. Blanchard, Seattle, WA, 1933.

549 Auxiliary schooner (marconi main), 60' x 42'11" x 13'4" x 8'4", for Morgan H. Stedman of New Haven, CT. Designed 1932. Not built.

550 Auxiliary marconi ketch *Great Circle,* 33'8" x 29'8" x 10'4" x 4'6", for George H. Gibson of New York, NY. Built by Mark C. L'Hommedian, Browns River, Sayville, Long Island, NY, 1933. Five sisters built.

551 Class A frostbite sailing dinghy, 11'5½" x 11'3½" x 4'9" x 8", for Ernest G. Post, 1932.

552 Class A V-bottomed frostbite sailing dinghy *Ouch,* 11'5½" x 4'10", for Henry T. Meneely and others, 1933.

553 Centerboard yawl *Patrician II,* 46' x 36' x 13'3" x 4'6½", for Parker Converse.

554 Auxiliary staysail ketch *Svaap,* 50' x 45'9" x 17'6" x 6'6", for William A. Robinson, 1933.

555 Flat-bottomed frostbite dinghy, 11'5½" x 4'6", for Claflin.

556 Arc-bottomed sailing skiff, 11'5½" x 4'6", for Elger Shelden.

557 Class B frostbite dinghy *North Pole,* 11'5¾" x 4'7½" x 19", for John G. Alden. Built by Patrick O'Connell, Neponset, MA, 1933.

558 Motorsailer *Conquest,* 40' x 36'6" x 11'6" x 4', for C.A. Sawyer, Jr., of Boston, MA. Built by C.A.

Morse & Son, Thomaston, ME, 1933. (Album)

559 Class A utility frostbite dinghy *Burp,* 11'5½" x 4'9½" x 19", for Alfred L. Loomis, Jr. Built by Patrick O'Connell, Neponset, MA, 1933 (Chapter 8)

560 Class B frostbite dinghy *Bobby,* 11'6" x 4'10" x 1'8", for Clifford D. Mallory of New York, NY. Built by Patrick O'Connell, Neponset, MA, 1933.

561 Class A utility dinghy, 11'5½" x 4'8" x 19", for Charles Belkush, Henry T. Meneely, Samuel Wetherill, Drake Sparkman, and others. Built by Patrick O'Connell, Neponset, MA, 1933.

562 Auxiliary sloop *Carles,* 23'4" x 20'9" x 8' x 3'9", for Lester C. Leonard of Red Bank, NJ. Built by Morton Johnson, Bay Head, NJ, 1933. (Chapter 7)

563 Auxiliary centerboard yawl, 34'4" x 27'4" x 11'6" x 3', for Raul Couzier of Rosario, Argentina. Designed 1933.

564 Auxiliary centerboard yawl, 36'8" x 28' x 10'9" x 4', for J.L. Williamson.

565 Auxiliary cutter, 32'2" x 28'3" x 10'3" x 4'6", for W.W. Claflin, Jr.

566 Class B dinghy *Zenith,* 11'5¾" x 4'7½", for John G. Alden. Built by Patrick O'Connell, Neponset, MA, 1933.

566-B Class B dinghy *Dovekie* (alteration of Number 566), for George B. Mackay. Built by Patrick O'Connell, Neponset, MA, 1933.

567 Auxiliary yawl, 36'11½" x 29'10" x 10'4" x 5'4½", for Alger S. Johnson.

568 Class B dinghy *Arcturus,* 11'5¼" x 4'7½", for Alfred L. Loomis, Jr. Built by Patrick O'Connell, Neponset, MA, 1933.

569 Cabin launch *Sachem,* 22' x 6'9½" x 1'5", for Rowe B. Metcalf of New York, NY. Built by Harvey F. Gamage, East Boothbay, ME.

570 Class B dinghy *Cognac,* 11'5¾" x 4'7", for Alfred L. Loomis, Jr. Built by Patrick O'Connell, 1933.

571 Utility launch, 48'6" x 43'2" x 11'6" x 4', for Farm and Trade School, Boston, MA. Built by F.F. Pendleton, Wiscasset, ME, 1934.

572 Auxiliary ketch, 35'7" x 31'10" x 11'2" x 5', for P. Pedersen of Hayward, CA. One sister built (1946).

573 Auxiliary centerboard yawl *Quest,* 35'4" x 27'4" x 11'6" x 3'10", for Martin J. Quigley. Built by Casey Boatbuilding Co., Inc., Fairhaven, MA, 1934. One sister built: *Picaro* (1934). (Album)

574 Auxiliary centerboard yawl *Little Gull,* 28'5" x 23'4" x 9'8" x 4'7", for John K. Murphy. Built by Harvey F. Gamage, South Bristol, ME, 1934. (Album)

575 Sloop-rigged motorsailer *Shrimper,* 40'4½" x 36'6" x 11'6" x 4'3", for T.B.Van Dorn. Built by Eau Gallie Boat Basin, Eau Gallie, FL, 1934.

575-B Twin-screw power cruiser *Blue Peter,* 38'5" x 34' x 11'6" x 4'4", for A.B. Jacobsen of Babylon, NY. Built by Carl Hoffer, Long Island, NY, 1941.

576 Keel-centerboard sloop *Forecastle,* 25' x 20'6" x 8'4" x 2'7", for John H. Castle. Built by Rochester Boat Works, Rochester, NY, 1934. Four sisters built, including: *Four Bells* (1934); *Naiad* (1934); and *Spoondrift* (1934). (Album)

577 Motorsailer *Hard Tack* ("Block Island type"), 42'3" x 39'10" x 13' x 4'6", for Horace B. Merwin. Built by Bedell's Yard, Stratford, CT, 1934. One sister may have been built. (Chapter 9)

578 Auxiliary ketch *Fayaway,* 35'7" x 31'10" x 11'3" x 5', for Richard P.Drew of Sedgwick, ME. Built by Reed-Cook Marine Construction Co., Boothbay Harbor, ME, 1934. One or two sisters may have been

built. (Chapter 7)

579 Motorsailer *Tamora,* 34′ x 31′10″ x 11′1″ x 3′9½″, for John M. Butler. Built by Willis J. Reid, Winthrop, MA, 1934. (Album)

580 Sailing dinghy *Mae West,* 9′11¾″ x 4′5½″, stock boat built by Skaneateles Boat & Canoe Co., Skaneateles, NY, 1934.

581 Auxiliary schooner *Discovery III,* 47′ x 35′9″ x 12′ x 6′6″, for R.W. Everest. Built by Hodgdon Bros., East Boothbay, ME, 1934. One sister built: *Dart.* (Album)

582 Auxiliary schooner *Onward III,* 60′8″ x 45′ x 14′9″ x 7′10½″, for Phillips N. Case. Built by Goudy & Stevens, East Boothbay, ME, 1934.

583 Auxiliary yawl *Dorothy Q,* 43′ x 30′ x 10′3″ x 6′, for Frank Bissell. Built by Quincy Adams Yacht Yard, Quincy, MA, 1934.

583-B Auxiliary cutter *Sirocco* (sister to Number 583 but with bow extended 7″), for Roger S. Robinson. Built by Quincy Adams Yacht Yard, Quincy, MA, 1936. Six sisters built: *Aleria* (1937); *Lone Gull II* (1937); *Malabar XI* (1937); *Estrella* (1937); *Blue Sea IV* (1937); and *Sirocco* (1939).(Chapters 5 and 7)

584 Power cruiser *Bay Queen,* 28′ x 27′1″ x 9′8″ x 3′6″, for Frederick Mason. Built by Harvey F. Gamage, South Bristol, ME, 1934.

585 V-bottomed sloop, 10′ x 4′5″, for Franklin M. Haines and others. Built by Franklin G. Post, 1934-1935. Eleven boats built.

586 Auxiliary schooner, 43′1″ x 32′11½″ x 11′7″ x 6′1″, for Rev. James W. England, Jr., of St. Davids, PA.

587 Auxiliary centerboard ketch *Gurnet,* 50′1″ x 36′4″ x 13′3″ x 5′2½″, for E.M. Farnsworth, Jr., of Brookline, MA. Built by Casey Boatbuilding Co., Inc., Fairhaven, MA, 1935.

588 Sloop-rigged motorsailer *Blue Peter,* 35′1″ x 32′10″ x 11′1″ x 4′1″, for S. Eliot Guild, Boston, MA. Built by Willis J. Reid, Winthrop, MA, 1934-1935. Two sisters built: *Pompano* (1935) and *Arual* (1939).

589 Twin-screw power cruiser *Griguet,* 38′ x 36′5″ x 11′ x 3′6″, for Henry Warren. Built by Simms Bros., 1935. Two sisters built (1944 and 1947).

590-A Auxiliary schooner, 70′ x 52′ x 17′ x 9′, for J. Burton Miller of San Pedro, CA. Built 1945. (Original Number 590, not built, designed for Milton Knight et al.)

591 Auxiliary ketch, 78′6″ x 56′3″ x 17′6″ x 9′, for Frederick Ford.

592 Auxiliary yawl, 67′1″ x 48′ x 15′2″ x 8′10½″, for Sterling Morton.

593 Auxiliary centerboard yawl *Rowena,* 36′4″ x 27′4″ x 11′5″ x 3′10″, for Stephen Bowen. Built by Casey Boatbuilding Co., Inc., Fairhaven, MA, 1935. One sister built: *Mari-Mari* (1958). (Album)

594 Fishing schooner, 127′2″ x 108′ x 27′4″ x 14′, for M. Agassiz (for model purposes only). Designed 1935.

595 Twin-screw power cruiser *Gerda,* 47′1″ x 44′7″ x 13′ x 4′, for Matthew T. Mellon. Built by Goudy & Stevens, East Boothbay, ME, 1935.

596 Knockabout, 16′ x 13′9″ x 6′6″ x 10″, for Seth V. Freeman. Built by Patrick O'Connell, Neponset, MA, 1935.

597 Motorsailer *Acadie,* 35′3″ x 32′ x 11′1″ x 4′2″, for W. Scott Libbey. Built by Harvey F. Gamage, South Bristol, ME, 1935.

598-A Traveler Class, auxiliary cutter *Wind Whistle,* 32′9″ x 28′6″ x 10′10″ x 5′10″, for R.D. McMullan. Built by Morse Boatbuilding Corp., Thomaston, ME, 1935. Nine sisters built, including: *Traveller* (1935); *South Wind* (1935); *Bounty* (1935); *Billy Bones* (1935); *San Blaque* (1935); *Toccata* (1935); *Almare* (1935); and *Tusitala* (1940). (Album)

599-A Malabar Junior auxiliary sloop *Revelry* (development of Number 326), 30′6″ x 23′ x 9′9″ x 5′, for Philip G. Hoffman. Built by Harvey F. Gamage, South Bristol, ME, 1936. Eight sisters built, including: *Negus; Kassy B.* (1936); *Fawn* (1936); *Musketeer* (1936); *Debonair* (1937); *Entre Nous* (1936); and *Cutty Sark II* (1937). (Chapter 6)

600 Auxiliary ketch, 35′8″ x 31′ x 11′7″ x 5′, for E.G. Bevis of Portland, OR. Two sister built: *Wind Song* (1936) and *Islander* (1936).

601 Motorsailer sloop *Parthenia,* 32′6½″ x 28′10″ x 10′10½″ x 4′3½″, for Parker Converse. Built by James E. Graves, Inc., Marblehead, MA, 1935. Eight sisters built, including: *Saidah* (1935); *Moby Dick* (1935); *Cockaigne* (1935); *Polaris* (1935); *Puffin* (1936); *Physalia* (1937); *Marival II* (1936?).

602 Auxiliary yawl *Winsome Too,* 64′1″ x 47′4″ x 14′5″ x 8′, for Harkness Edwards. Built by F.F. Pendleton, Wiscasset, ME, 1935.

603 Motorsailer *Nutmeg,* 36′3″ x 33′ x 11′1″ x 4′2″, for Dr. Raynham Townshend. Built by West Mystic Shipyard, Mystic, CT, 1935.

604 Day cabin cruiser *Arbella,* 34′11″ x 33′4″ x 9′ x 2′9″, for Robert Saltonstall. Built by Quincy Adams Yacht Yard, Quincy, MA, 1935.

605 Auxiliary cutter *Rubaiyat,* 43′2″ x 30′4″ x 10′8″ x 6′, for Nathaniel Rubinkam. Built by George Lawley & Son Corp., Neponset, MA, 1935. (Album)

606 Auxiliary ketch *Seaway,* 37′ x 30′ x 10′2″ x 5′5″, for Edmund Hayes of Portland, OR. Built by August Nelson, Portland, OR, 1936.

607 Knockabout centerboard sloop, 18′3″ x 15′4½″ x 6′6″, a stock boat for Moulton Boat Co. Two built in 1935; eight built in 1936.

608 Motor tender (for Number 602, *Winsome Too*), 12′ x 4′4″, for Harkness Edwards. Built by Goudy & Stevens, East Boothbay, ME, 1935.

609 Auxiliary knockabout sloop *Highland Fling,* 24′9″ x 16′3″ x 7′ x 3′6″, for M.W. Bowden. Built by Patrick O'Connell, Neponset, MA, 1935.

610 Fast cruising yawl *Brenda,* 44′6″ x 30′ x 8′ x 6′, for Charles A. Goodwin. Built by Herreshoff Manufacturing Co., Bristol, RI, 1935. (Album)

611 Auxiliary schooner, 72′3″ x 54′2″ x 16′6″ x 10′, for John Archbold.

612 Auxiliary fisherman-type schooner, 130′10″ x 103′3″ x 25′3″ x 13′6″, 243 tons displacement, for John Hays Hammond, Jr. Built by J. Ernst & Son, Mahone Bay, Nova Scotia.

613 Auxiliary cutter *Anacapa,* 43′3″ x 31′9″ x 12′ x 6′5″, for Robert S. Cooper. Built by Fellows & Stewart, Terminal Island, CA. One sister built: *Westerner.*

614 Auxiliary schooner *Meridian,* 72′ x 54′ x 16′6″ x 10′, for Milton Knight, et al. Built by George Lawley & Son, Neponset, MA, 1936. (Chapter 7)

615 Canoe-stern ketch, 50′7″ x 42′ x 12′8″ x 6′8″, for F.B. Clapp. Not built.

616-A Auxiliary cutter *Seguin II,* 35′10½″ x 27′10½″ x 10′5″ x 5′3″, for D.R. Stoneleigh. Built by Morse Boatbuilding Corp., Thomaston, ME, 1936. Eleven sisters built, including: *Bo'sun Bird* (1936); *Spartel* (1936); *Kittiwake* (1936); *Padda* (1936); *Suwarro* (1936); *Cygnet* (1936); *Pronto* (1936); *Navigo* (1937);

Ruth S (1937); *Sunda* (1939). (Album)

617   Motorsailer ketch *Gee Jay*, 42'3" x 39'8" x 13' x 4'7", for J.H.W. Whitcomb. Built by Harvey F. Gamage, South Bristol, ME, 1936.

618-A   Auxiliary yawl *Juno* (same lines and dimensions as Number 616), for Elizabeth Trott. Built by James E. Graves, Inc., Marblehead, MA, 1936. Nine sisters built: *Koloa* (1936); *Bally Trim* (1936); *Briny Breeze* (1936); *Stowaway* (1936); *Tradewind* (1936); *Volya* (1936); *Jinx* (1936); and *Red Bird* (1944). (Album)

619-A   Auxiliary yawl *Adventure*, 36'11" x 27'10½" x 10'5" x 5'3" (development of Numbers 616 and 618), for Logan McMenemy. Built by Peterson Boat Works, Sturgeon Bay, WI, 1936. Two to four sisters built, including: *Mary Ann* (1937) and *Mollie* (1940). (Album)

620   Auxiliary yawl *Capella*, 56'6" x 40'3" x 13'3" x 8', for James W. Hubbell. Built by Quincy Adams Yacht Yard, Quincy, MA.

621   Launch, 19' x 5'6" x 1'3", for Mrs. H.R. Pyne of Far Hills, NJ. Built by Goudy & Stevens, East Boothbay, ME, 1936.

622   One-design sloop, 46'6" x 32' x 10'6" x 6'9½", for New York Y.C. (Album)

623   Auxiliary yawl *Mandoo II*, 71'3" x 50'9" x 15'8" x 9', for D. Spencer Berger. Built by the Herreshoff Manufacturing Co., Bristol, RI, 1936. (Chapter 7)

624   Penn Yan 16-footer (sail plan of Number 596).

625   Auxiliary raised-deck sloop *Ho-Hum*, 28'2" x 21'4" x 8'6½" x 4'8", for William C. Wolf. Built by Milton Point Boat Yard, 1936. One sister built: *Heyday II* (1937).

627   Launch *Kaymere*, 19', for M.L. Gordon. Built by Minett Shields, Ltd., Bracebridge, Ontario, 1936.

628   Auxiliary shoal-draft sloop *Elliot White*, 34' x 24'10" x 10'8" x 2'9", for Dr. C. Malcolm Gilman. Built by Mantaloking Boat & Engine Co., 1936. One or two sisters built (1948? and 1949?). (Album)

629   Auxiliary cruising cutter *Gay Head*, 46'5" x 33' x 11'4" x 6'6", for J. Frederic Bohmfalk. Built by F.F. Pendleton, Wiscasset, ME, 1936.

630   Raised-deck sloop *Gitana*, 39'9" x 27'10" x 10'7" x 5'11", for R.S. Danforth. Built by Nunes Bros., Sausalito, CA, 1936. Two sisters built, including: *Hinerangi* (1938). (Album)

631   Auxiliary cutter *Moosebec*, 33'11" x 27'1" x 9'7" x 5'3", for A.S. Neilson. Built by Simms Bros., 1937.

633   Sport fisherman *Cudacatcher*, 59'4" x 55' x 13'6" x 3'4", for Rowe B. Metcalf of New York, N.Y. One sister built (1947).

634   Auxiliary centerboard yawl *Nandeyara*, 45'8" x 35'9" x 13' x 4'3", for Raul Couzier of Sante Fe, Argentina. Built by Aslillero Baader, Argentina.

635   Auxiliary clipper-bowed schooner *Merida*, 84' x 68'9" x 19'7" x 8'7", for Robert C. Rathbone. Built by Symonette Shipyards, Inc., Nassau, Bahama Is., 1938. (Album)

636-A   Auxiliary sloop *Stormy Petrel* (stock boat), 39'4" x 28'1" x 10'5" x 5'3", for William H. Hart. Built by James E. Graves, Inc., Marblehead, MA, 1937. Six sisters built: *Edythe II* (1937); *Helen S* (1937); *Lord Jim* (1937); *Nimbus* (1937); *Iseult* (1937); *Amitie* (1937). (Chapter 7)

637   Dinghy, 12', for D. Spencer Berger. Built by Fairfield Boat Works, 1936.

638   Auxiliary yawl *Evening Star*, 54'3" x 39'10" x 14' x 7'4", for Frederick Ford. Built by Herreshoff Manufacturing Co., Bristol, RI, 1937.

639-A   Auxiliary yawl *Royono* (stock boat), 38' x 27'10½" x 10'5" x 5'3", for J.B. Ford, Jr. Built by Casey Boatbuilding Co., Inc., Fairhaven, MA, 1937. Six sisters built: *Cynthia II* (1937); *Nerissa* (1937); *Parthian* (1937); *Kwoneshe* (1937); *Zephyr* (1938); and *Grenadier* (1938).

640   Auxiliary cutter *Matey*, 33'8" x 24'6" x 9'9" x 5', for Robert T. Nye. Built by Bristol Yachtbuilding Co., South Bristol, ME, 1937. Two sisters built: *Chuckle* (1937) and *Eslyn* (1937).

641   Auxiliary schooner *Lelanta II*, 74' x 54' x 16'8" x 9'6", for Ralph St. L. Peverley, England. Built by Abeking & Rasmussen, Bremen, Germany, 1937. (Chapter 7)

642   Auxiliary sloop *Scoter*, 29' x 22' x 9'7½" x 4', for H.W. Buhler. Built by Bristol Yachtbuilding Co., South Bristol, ME, 1937.

644   Cutter, for John Archbold.

645   Auxiliary cutter *Zaida III*, 57'5" x 41' x 14'1" x 7'8", for George E. Ratsey. Built by Henry B. Nevins, Inc., City Island, NY, 1937. (Album)

646   Auxiliary ketch *Dovekie*, 45'6" x 32' x 11'5½" x 5'11½", for Winchester Bennett. Built by West Haven Shipbuilding, 1937.

647   Auxiliary yawl *Foam*, 62'8" x 45' x 14'9" x 7'11", for Donald D. Dodge. Built by Goudy and Stevens, East Boothbay, ME, 1937. Three sisters built: *Fish Hawk* (1937); *Saedk* (1937); and *Magic* (1937). (Album)

648   Auxiliary cutter *Sonata*, 49' x 34'6" x 12' x 6'3", for Robert R. Williams. Built by F.F. Pendleton, Wiscasset, ME, 1937. (Album)

649   Auxiliary centerboard yawl *Avelinda*, 48'3" x 36' x 13'7½" x 5', for Thomas D. Cabot. Built by Bristol Yachtbuilding Co., South Bristol, ME, 1937.

650   Auxiliary cutter *Halcyone*, 47'4" x 33' x 11'8" x 6'7", for William G. Burt. Built by Quincy Adams Yacht Yard, Quincy, MA, 1937.

651   Auxiliary ketch *Staghound*, 39'3" x 31'5" x 10'11" x 5'5", for William C. Thum. Built by Dittmar & Gardner, Newport Harbor, CA, 1937. (Chapter 7)

652   Yawl, 36'6" x 27'8" x 9'7" x 5'3", for Donald C. Starr. Not built.

653   Auxiliary yawl *Dauntless II*, 48' x 33' x 11'8" x 6'7", for Rufus C. Cushman. Built by Quincy Adams Yacht Yard, Quincy, MA, 1937. (Album)

654   Power cruiser *Gosling III*, 50'2" x 47'7" x 13' x 3'9", for Geoffrey G. Whitney. Built by Willis J. Reid, Winthrop, MA, 1938. (Chapter 9)

655-A   Auxiliary sloop *Leilani*, 35'10" x 24'8" x 9'9" x 5', for Marion B. Willis. Built by Bristol Yachtbuilding Co., South Bristol, ME, 1937. Nine sisters built: *Karin* (1937); *Sanibel* (1938); *Alibubu* (1938); *Armorel* (1938); *Banshee* (1938); *Norjan* (1938); *Sir Tom* (1939); *Holiday* (1940); *Carolyn* (1940). (Album)

656   Auxiliary schooner *Athlon IV*, 45' x 33' x 11'8" x 6'4", for Harry H. Walker. Built by Fred J. Dion, Salem, MA, 1938.

657   Diesel power cruiser, 48' x 42'9" x 12'6" x 5', for H.J. Brown.

660   Auxiliary ketch *Sabine II* (development of Number 651), 39'6" x 31'5" x 10'10" x 5'5", for R.M. Hafer. Built by August Nelson, Portland, OR, 1941. One sister built (1945).

661   Auxiliary cutter, 40'7" x 28' x 10'6" x 5'5", for Charles Vincent of Australia.

662   Sakonnet One-Design (forerunner to Number 694),

21′3″ x 16′6″ x 6′10″ x 3′3″, for Sakonnet Y.C., Sakonnet, RI, 1937.

663 Auxiliary sloop *Elf*, 40′10″ x 28′ x 10′1″ x 4′11″, for J.T. Van Dorn. Built by J.T. Van Dorn, 1938.

665 Auxiliary yawl (intended stock design), 39′11″ x 28′3″ x 10′6″ x 5′5″.

666-A Off Soundings auxiliary cutter *Felicia III*, 41′8″ x 28′5″ x 10′6″ x 5′5″, for Abner Morse. Built by Casey Boatbuilding Co., Inc., Fairhaven, MA, 1938. Two sisters built, including: *Madcap III* (1938). (Chapter 7)

667 Auxiliary schooner *Kadiac*, 64′2″ x 46′ x 15′ x 8′8″, for A.F. Brigham. Built by Kenneth McAlpin & Son, Shelburne, Nova Scotia, 1938.

668 Power cruiser *Passing Jack*, 87′6″ x 82′ x 14′3″ x 4′, for A.T. Levy. Built at Eleuthera, Bahamas.

669 Auxiliary schooner *When and If* (similar to Number 667), 63′5″ x 47′3″ x 15′1″ x 8′6″, for Col. George S. Patton, Jr. Built by F.F. Pendleton, Wiscasset, ME, 1938. (Album)

670 Auxiliary cutter *Naushon*, 47′3″ x 33′ x 11′10″ x 6′7″, for Philip G. Woodward. Built by Casey Boatbuilding Co., Inc., Fairhaven, MA, 1938.

671 Auxiliary Ketch, 47′6″ x 34′1″ x 11′6″ x 6′4″.

672-A Off Soundings yawl *Miss Jean* (same dimensions as Number 666), for W.S. Finlay, Jr. Built by Casey Boatbuilding Co., Fairhaven, MA, 1938. Five sisters built: *Departure* (1938); *Sally II* (1938); *Alice* (1938); *Zodiac* (1938); and *Marlyn* (1938). (Chapter 7)

673 Auxiliary yawl *Royono II*, 51′6″ x 34′6″ x 12′2″ x 7′, for John B. Ford, Jr. Built by Pouliot Boat Works, Inc., 1938. (Album)

674 Twin-screw motorsailer *Trade Wind*, 62′ x 55′11″ x 16′ x 5′9″, for W. L. Gilmore. Built by Robert Jacob, Inc., 1938.

675-A Coastwise Cruiser auxiliary cutter *Lucky Star*, 36′5″ x 25′11″ x 9′9″ x 5′3″, for R.O.H. Hill. Built by James E. Graves, Inc., Marblehead, MA, 1938. Thirty-seven sisters built, including: *Temptress* (1938); *Sequest* (1938); *Dawnell* 1938); *Vigilance II* (1938); *Sema* (1938); *Coquina* (1938); *Flying Cloud* (1938); *South Wind* (1938); *Pluggy Ann; Valiant* (1938); *Chaperon* (1938); *Marrob II* (1939); *Austral* (1939); *Suzon* (1939); *Lucky Star* (1939); *Natanis* (1939); *Wendigo* (1939); *Ibid* (1939); *Whisper* (1939); *Folly* (1940); *Cricket II* (1940); *Infanta* (1940); *Free Lance* (1940); *Wave Wing* (1940); *Patricia* (1940); *Mary* (1940); *Hannah* (1941); *Elbert* (1941); *Asgard* (1940); *Rainbow* (1945); *Pamlin* (1947); and *Primavera* (1946). (Chapter 7)

676 Auxiliary cutter *Freedom*, 47′7″ x 34′2″ x 11′ x 7′, for William P. Barrows. Built by Herreshoff Manufacturing Co., Bristol, RI, 1938.

677 Auxiliary sloop *White Wings*, 50′ x 33′3″ x 11′7½″ x 7′, for Percy Grant. Built by J.J. Taylor, Toronto, 1938. (Chapter 7)

678 Power cruiser *Mobjack*, 60′7″ x 58′ x 14′6″ x 4′3″, for George Upton of Marblehead, MA. Built by George Gulliford, Saugus, MA, 1938. (Chapter 9)

679 Auxiliary sloop *Sterex*, 23′ x 18′6″ x 7′2″ x 3′10″, for Dr. R. Smithwick. Built by Mandon Bates, 1938. Two sisters built, including: *Jekell* (1953).

680 Auxiliary cutter *Avenir*, 44′6″ x 29′6″ x 10′8″ x 5′8″, for George E. McQuesten. Built by James E. Graves, Inc., Marblehead, MA, 1938.

681 Sailing dinghy, 14′.

682 Twin-screw powerboat *Quill*, 32′ x 8′9″ x 2′6″, for Walbridge S. Taft. Built by Palmer Scott Co., New Bedford, MA, 1938. (Album)

683 Auxiliary ketch, 56′4″ x 45′ x 16′4″ x 7′4½″, for Zimmerman. Designed 1938.

684 Auxiliary cutter *Crusader*, 42′2″ x 29′2″ x 10′6″ x 5′10″, for M.S. Hirsch, Jr., of Los Angeles, CA. Built by J.M. Fernandez, CA, 1939.

685 Fishing launch *Early Light*, 21′9″ x 7′9″ x 2′, for R.W. Orrell. Built by Leonard Boat Works, Daytona Beach, FL, 1939. One sister may have been built.

686 Lifeboat (sail and power), 17′ x 5′, for John Hays Hammond.

687 Auxiliary yawl *Tioga Too*, 53′6″ x 37′6″ x 13′ x 7′5″, for Harry E. Noyes, Marblehead, MA. Built by Quincy Adams Yacht Yard, Quincy, MA, 1939. (Chapter 7)

688 Fishing cruiser *Sea Otter*, 47′5″ x 44′7″ x 12′6″ x 3′6″, for H.W. Cannon, Jr. Built by Quincy Adams Yacht Yard, Quincy, MA, 1939.

689-A Off Soundings cutter *Sequest* (development of Number 672), 42′2″ x 29′2″ x 10′6″ x 5′10″, for Irvin G. Ammen. Built by Casey Boatbuilding Co., Inc., Fairhaven, MA, 1939. One sister built: *Joy Two* (1939). (Chapter 7)

690-A Off Soundings yawl *Quita* (same lines and dimensions as Number 689), for George Woodward, Jr. Built by Casey Boatbuilding Co., Inc., Fairhaven, MA. Five sisters built: *Windfall* (1939); *Mary L* (1939); *Nerissa* (1939); *Skylark II* (1939); and *Morning Star* (1939). (Chapter 7)

691-A Malabar Junior auxiliary sloop *Nern* (development of Number 599), 31′ x 22′1″ x 8′6″ x 4′8″, for Donald Newhall. Built by Bristol Yachtbuilding Co., South Bristol, ME, 1939. Twenty-six sisters built, including: *Wench* (1939); *Aura* (1939); *Timaru* (1939); *Frolic* (1939); *Tusker* (1939); *Nimrod II* (1939); *Flub Dub V* (1939); *Juniata* (1939); *Little Dipper* (1939); *Mischief* (1939); *Tide Over* (1939); *Boojum III* (1939); *Voodoo* (1939); *Kristen* (1939); *Stardust* (1939); *Fantasy; South Wind* (1939); *Morning Light* (1940); *Regret* (1940); *Nautilis* (1940); *Marimil* (started 1942, completed 1953); *Nausica* (1950); and *Truant* (1946). (Chapter 6)

693 Auxiliary schooner *Dirigo II*, 60′5″ x 45′10″ x 15′6″ x 7′10″, for Charles Van Sicklen of Northport, MI. Built by Goudy and Stevens, East Boothbay, ME, 1939. (Chapter 7)

694 Sakonnet One-Design sloop (development of Number 662), 18′4″ x 14′5″ x 6′3″ x 3′7″, for Sakonnet Y.C., Sakonnet, RI. Built by Casey Boatbuilding Co., Inc., Fairhaven, MA, 1939. More than 24 sisters built. (Chapter 8)

695 30-square-meter sloop *Taaroa*, 42′2″ x 28′ x 7′ x 5′, for E.B. Dane, Jr. Built by Britt Bros., West Lynn, MA, 1939.

696 Auxiliary ketch *Malabar XII*, 46′8″ x 34′3″ x 12′ x 6′9″, for John G. Alden. Built by Morse Boatbuilding Co., Thomaston, ME, 1939. Two sisters built, including: *Madelon* (1953). (Chapter 5)

697 Schooner *Alvee*, 86′10″ x 68′5″ x 20′ x 8′10″, for A.R. Roberts. Built by Sachau Marine Construction Co., Toronto, Ontario, 1940.

698 Auxiliary cutter *Primrose VI*, 40′2″ x 28′1″ x 10′5″ x 5′3″, for Walter H. Huggins. Built by Rufus Condon, Friendship, ME, 1939.

699-A Explorer Class, auxiliary centerboard sloop *Norsquam*, 37′5″ x 26′9″ x 10′11″ x 3′8″, for Clifford Roberts. Built by Morton Johnson, Bay Head, NJ, 1939. Five sisters built: *Hi-Ho* (1940); *Kaintuck*

(1953); *Sirena II* (1940); *Arrowhead* (1946); and *Alfredem* (1945). (Album)

700   Auxiliary yawl *Rose*, 65′6″ x 45′ x 14′10″ x 8′6″, for George P. Gardner. Built by Quincy Adams Yacht Yard, Quincy, MA, 1940. (Album)

701   Sloop, 23′ x 15′6″ x 6′6″ x 3′6″, for Donald McClure of Rockford, IL. Not built.

702   Motorsailer *Last Buccaneer*, 52′6″ x 45′ x 12′8″ x 5′, for L.A. Ferguson. Built by Palmer Johnson, Sturgeon Bay, WI, 1940.

703   Auxiliary cutter *Seiglinde*, 32′ x 22′6″ x 8′4″ x 5′2″, for Leeds Mitchell. Built by F.M. Nimphius, South Milwaukee, WI, 1939. Five sisters built: *Rapscallion* (1940); *Brunnhilde* (1940); *Nimphius* (1940); *Matelot* (1941); and *Vanitie* (1941).

704   Off Soundings cutter (development of Number 690), 42′5″ x 29′4½″ x 10′7″ x 5′11½″. (Chapter 7)

705   Sail and power dinghy, 14′. Designed 1939.

706   Powerboat, 65′, for A.T. Levy.

707   Motorsailer, 70′ x 57′9″ x 18′ x 7′6″. Designed 1939.

708   Yawl, 45′ x 32′ x 11′1″ x 6′8″.

709-A Barnacle Class, auxiliary cutter *Leveche*, 33′11″ x 23′4″ x 8′5″ x 5′4″, for Helen C. Taylor of Farmington, CT. Built by Bristol Yachtbuilding Co., South Bristol, ME, 1940. Seven sisters built, including: *Elise* (1940); *Limpet* (1941); *Sulin II* (1941); *Escape* (1940); and *Marimil* (1948). (Album)

710   Centerboard yawl, 43′11″ x 31′2″ x 11′6″ x 4′5″.

711   Auxiliary centerboard cutter *Merriel*, 45′6″ x 34′2″ x 11′8″ x 4′3″, for Paul Jones. Built by George Lawley & Son Corp., Neponset, MA, 1940. (Album)

712-A Off Soundings yawl *Miriam* (development of Number 690), 42′2″ x 29′3″ x 11′ x 6′, for P.R. Tappan. Built by Goudy & Stevens, East Boothbay, ME, 1940. Four sisters built: *Maggie Fury* (1940); *Verano* (1940); *Sandrala* (1940); *Snow Goose* (1946). (Chapter 7)

713   Auxiliary sloop *Irondequoit II*, 61′ x 43′ x 15′ x 8′6″, for Thomas H. Shepard. Built by George Lawley & Son Corp., Neponset, MA, 1940. (Album)

714   Auxiliary sloop *Sea Waif*, 25′ x 20′ x 8′6″ x 4′, for Dr. Graham Pope. Built by Moudon Bates, 1940.

716   Topsail schooner, 55′6″ x 48′3″ x 16′ x 6′5″, for Ford. One or two sisters built, including: *Keewatin* (1947). (Album)

718   Auxiliary ketch *Mike*, 44′ x 32′6″ x 12′ x 6′3″, for George M. Jones, Jr. Built by M.M. Davis & Son, Solomons, MD, 1941. One sister built: *Pussy Willow* (1941).

719   Auxiliary yawl *Salmagal*, 39′10″ x 29′6″ x 10′4″ x 6′2″, for A.B. Homer of Bethlehem, PA. Built by Mt. Desert Yacht Yard, Mt. Desert, ME. One sister built: *Revision II* (1956). (Album)

720   Auxiliary sloop, 23′5″ x 17′3″ x 7′8″ x 4′, for Franklin Remington of Nassau, Bahama Is. One sister may have been built.

721   Sport fisherman *Relaxer III*, 47′ x 45′8″ x 12′6″ x 3′6″, for F.E. Schluter. Built by Casey Boatbuilding Co., Inc., Fairhaven, MA, 1941.

722   Motorsailer *Little Tramp*, 48′ x 44′6″ x 13′6″ x 5′, for Alan S. Browne. Built by W.C. Dickerson, Whitehaven Boat Yard, Whitehaven, MD, 1941. Two sisters built, including: *Deep Water II*.

725   Skipjack yacht *Capt'n Billy*, 40′ x 35′5″ x 12′9½″ x 5′, for Harold C. McNulty. Built by Whitehaven Boat Yard, Whitehaven, MD, 1941. (Chapter 7)

733   West Indies schooner, for Coordinator of Inter-American Affairs.

744-A Clipper-bowed ketch, 45′6″ x 34′8″ x 12′7″ x 5′10″, for Arthur F. Luce of Brockton, MA. Designed 1944. As many as 10 sisters built, including: *Acadie* (1946); *Rena* (1962); *Windward Star* (1962); and *Sàgaka* (1962). (Chapter 7)

746   One-design sloop *Mistress*, 21′3″ x 15′ x 6′4″ x 3′8″, for J. Warren Pfeifer. Designed 1944.

747   Cutter, 41′6″ x 36′6″ x 12′ x 4′10″, for Admiral W.L. Goldsmith of Liverpool, England. Designed 1944.

750   Motorsailer (steel), 72′1″ x 56′ x 16′10″ x 7′4″, for Arthur Herrington of Indianapolis, IN, 1944.

752   Motorsailer, 54′6″ x 48′7″ x 14′6″ x 6′10″, for Carlisle V. Watson. Designed 1944. Not built. (Chapter 9)

753   Powerboat (steel), 25′11″ x 9′ x 2′4″, for Churchward & Co. Designed 1944.

756   Auxiliary ketch *Malabar XIII*, 53′9″ x 40′8″ x 14′3″ x 7′4″, for John G. Alden. Built by Goudy & Stevens, East Boothbay, ME, 1945. Three sisters built. (Chapter 5)

757   U.S. One-Design sloop, 37′9″ x 24′ x 7′ x 5′3″. Thirty sisters built by Quincy Adams Yacht Yard, Quincy, MA: *Iris* (1946); *Leenane* (1946); *Nancy III* (1946); *Marianne* (1946); *Loafer* (1946); *Evanthia* (1946); *Wind* (1946); *Jackanapes* (1946); *Sea Saga* (1946); *Goose* (1946); *Gemarda* (1946); *Jennifer* (1946); *Hoo-Doo* (1946); *Dilemma* (1946); *Miramar* (1946); *Hi-Ho* (1946); *Kutty's Ark* (1946); *Iris* (1946); *Lovilla* (1946); *Sonata* (1946); *Trey* (1946); *Sliver* (1946); *Harmony* (1947); *Tinker Too* (1947); *Chimaera* (1947); *Susan Two* (1947); *Merandol* (1947); *Grenadier* (1947); *Blue Lady* (1947); and *Adonde* (1947). (Chapter 8)

758   Pram dinghy, 7′11″, for Hagerty, Inc., Cohasset, MA, 1944.

759   Auxiliary cruising ketch, 39′6″ x 30′ x 11′ x 5′10″, for Richard B. Hovey of Boston, MA. Designed 1944.

761   Hinckley 21, auxiliary sloop, 28′6 ¼″ x 21′ x 8′ x 4′7″. Twenty sisters built by Henry R. Hinckley, Inc., Southwest Harbor, ME: *No Name* (1946); *Margaret Ann* (1946); *Sayles* (1946); *Halo* (1946); *Barbara F.* (1946); *Stardust II* (1946); *Cyndy* (1946); *Christie* (1946); *Diamiph* (1946); *Noremac* (1946); *Jan* (1946); *Polaris* (1946); *Showgirl* (1946); *Alert*; *Wee Lyn* (1946); *Naiad* (1946); *Wintap* (1946); *Holiday* (1946); *Sea Fever II* (1946); and *Welcome* (1946). (Album)

762-A Malabar Junior sloop *Khorasan* (development of Number 691), 32′6″ x 22′8″ x 8′8″ x 4′11″. Built by R. B. Williams, Pleasure Craft Boat Builders, Tacoma, WA, 1946. Sixteen sisters built, including: *Jaunty* (1946); *Caprice* (1946); *Euphoria*; *Scotch Mist* (1950); *Nixie* (1948); *Judy C III* (1949); *Pobo Moto* (1950); *Coquette* (1951); *Cimba* (1957); *Interlude* (1959); *Brujest* (1957); *Oasis* (1959); *Koala*; and *Sea Lotus* (1963). (Chapter 6)

763   Auxiliary ketch, 48′ x 38′4″ x 13′ x 7′, for George Cochrane of New York, NY. Designed 1945. Not built.

766   Auxiliary cutter *Gaffer*, 46′ x 35′11″ x 12′6″ x 4′8″, for Frank H. Wheaton, Jr., of Millville, NJ. Built by Stowman Shipyard, Dorchester, NJ, 1945.

767   Wheeler 48, auxiliary sloop, 48′ x 35′ x 12′6″ x 4′7″, intended stock boat for Wheeler Shipbuilding Corp., Whitestone, Long Island, NY. Designed 1946. Not built.

768   Ketch *Golden Fleece Two*, 47′4″ x 35′ x 12′6″ x 4′7″, for Charles E. Dearnley of Philadelphia, PA. Built

by Hubert Johnson, Bay Head, NJ, 1947. (Album)

769 Hinckley 28, auxiliary sloop, 40'9" x 28' x 10' x 5'9". Five sisters built by Henry R. Hinckley, Inc., Southwest Harbor, ME: *Jaan* (1945); *Rubia* (1946); *Kimmie* (1946); *Tandria* (1946); and *Vael* (1946). (Chapter 7)

772 Ketch *Flo*, 46' x 36'2" x 14' x 6'6", for Ian McKenzie of Cristobal, Canal Zone. Built 1951.

776 Centerboard yawl *Heloise*, 49' x 36'6" x 12'6" x 4'7", for Paul R. Tappan of Mansfield, OH. Built by Wirth Munroe, Nassau, Bahamas Is., 1949.

777 Auxiliary ketch *Surazo*, 46'8" x 34'3¼" x 12'8" x 6'9", for G. de Giorgio of Chile. Designed 1947. Three to four sisters built, including: *Sikrid* (1947); *Ocean Cruiser* (1947-1955); and *Tondelayo* (1948).

778 Auxiliary sloop *Queene*, 35'1" x 24'4" x 8'10" x 5'6", for William P. Barrows of Rochester, NY. Built by Hodgdon Bros., East Boothbay, ME, 1946. Two sisters built: *Swift* (1946) and *Solano* (1949). (Album)

779 Coastwise Cruiser, sloop *Widgeon* (development of Number 675), 37' x 26' x 9'9" x 5'9", for Harold R. Robinson of Portland, ME. Built by James E. Graves, Inc., Marblehead, MA, 1948. Five sisters built: *Comanche* (1950); *Cygnet* (1950); *Zara* (1953); *Corinthia III* (1953); and *Nancy West* (1954). (Chapter 7)

781-A Auxiliary yawl *Flying Swan*, 37'5" x 27'8" x 10'7" x 4'11", for H.J. Hagemeister of Green Bay, WI. (Original Number 781, not built, designed for Richard C. Borden of Newark, NJ.) Built by Palmer Johnson, Sturgeon Bay, WI, 1946. Four or five sisters built, including: *Windsong* (1946) and *Corisande* (1949).

782 Auxiliary yawl, 63'5" x 47'3" x 15'1" x 8'6", for Capt. Duncan Lawrie, England. Designed 1946.

783 Dinghy, 10', for H.A. Anthony, Benten Harbor, MI.

784 Auxiliary ketch, 38'2" x 32'4" x 11'2" x 5', for Norman C. Nourse of Los Angeles, CA. Designed 1946. (Album)

785 Powerboat, 49'6" x 48' x 12'9" x 3'8". Designed 1946. Not built.

786 Power cruiser *Wallaby*, 49'10" x 48' x 12'9" x 3'10", for Phillip C. Barney of Hartford, CT. Built by Mystic Shipyard, Mystic, CT, 1947.

787-B Auxiliary cutter *Foxen*, 39'4" x 28'10" x 10'10" x 5'7", for Leonard H. Brown, Jr., of San Mateo, CA. (Original Number 787, not built, designed for Charles T. Cuno of Meriden, CT.) Built by W.F. Stone & Son, Alameda, CA, 1957.

788-B Auxiliary ketch *Halmar*, 42'10" x 34'4" x 12'6" x 5'6", for Harold P. Churchill of South Weymouth, MA. (Original Number 788, not built, designed for Frederick T. Moses of Providence, RI.) Built by Harold P. Churchill, 1949.

789 Auxiliary ketch, 43' x 32' x 12' x 4'6", for V.W. Knauth. Not built.

790 Motorsailer, 54'6" x 48'7" x 14'10" x 7'6", for Alberto Samuel of Brazil. Designed 1946.

791 Auxiliary ketch, 106' x 80' x 23'8" x 9', for Benjamin Clayton of Pasadena, CA. Designed 1946.

792-A Barnacle Class, auxiliary sloop *Aldebaran* (development of Number 709), 33'11" x 23'4" x 8'7" x 5'4", for James H. Beal of Pittsburg, PA. Built by Adams & Hayden, Stonington Deer Isle Yacht Basin, Stonington, ME, 1946. Twenty-seven sisters built: *Sky* (1946); *Margaret*; *Sou Markee*; *Cindy II*; *Gannet* (1947); *Wanderer* (1947); *Picaro II* (1947); *Wing-*

Ding (1947); *Four-oh* (1947); *Septar* (1947); *Sonata*; *Herring Gull* (1947); *Sandra* (1947); *Jessica* (1947); *Quinta* (1947); *Aurora* (1947); *Gay Girl* (1947); *Parmachene Belle* (1947); *Tangeo* (1947); *Malamani* (1947); *Tiger Lily* (1947); *Edith R.* (1947); *Windigo* (1948); *Bamay* (1947); *Cantuta* (1947); *Liaro* (1947); and *Djinn* (1947).

794 Power cruiser *Yuma Pearl*, 45'2" x 43'9" x 12' x 3'7", for Frank Russo of Vancouver, WA. Built by August Nelson, Portland, OR, 1947. (Chapter 9)

795 Power cruiser, 38' x 35'10" x 11'5" x 3', for Truscott Boat & Dock Co. of St. Joseph, MI.

796 Auxiliary ketch, 46'8" x 34'3" x 12'8" x 6'9", for Lt. Col. R.F. Bellack, 1946.

797 Auxiliary sloop, 46'2" x 32' x 11' x 6'8", for Gardner Gamwell of Seattle, WA.

798 Auxiliary double-ended sloop, 28'3" x 22' x 8' x 4', for John H. Read of Mt. Lawley, West Australia. Designed 1948. One sister may have been built. (Chapter 7)

799 Power cruiser, 42'4" x 40' x 12'3" x 3'3", for Truscott Boat & Dock Co. of St. Joseph, MI. Built by Truscott Boat & Dock Co.

801 Adventurer Class, auxiliary yawl (development of Number 712), 42'2" x 29'3" x 11' x 5'11½".

802-A Adventurer Class, auxiliary cutter *Anfitrite* (same dimensions as Number 801), for Manuel A. Famagalli of Lima, Peru. Built 1947.

803 Discoverer Class, ketch (development of Number 784), 38'2" x 32'4" x 11'2" x 5'. One built by Morgancraft Boat Co., Gardena, CA, 1950.

804 Corsair Class, sloop (development of Number 675), 36'5" x 25'11½" x 9'9" x 5'3¼".

804-A Corsair Class, yawl (same dimensions as Number 804), for S.G. Blankinship. Designed 1947. Two sisters built: *Tern* (1955) and *Zoroya* (1958).

805 Pathfinder Class, centerboard sloop (development of Number 699), 37'4" x 26'8" x 10'10" x 3'8".

806-A Rambler Class, sloop (development of Number 691), 31'4" x 22'1" x 8'6" x 4'8", for Jose E. Ceballero of Ponce, Puerto Rico. Designed 1948.

807 Playmate Class, sloop (development of Number 694), 18'5" x 14'6" x 6'2½" x 3'7".

808 Pastime Class, sloop (development of Number 746), 21'3" x 15' x 6'5" x 3'8".

809 Pal Class, centerboard sloop (development of Number 607), 18'3" x 15'4½" x 6'6" x 11'¼".

810 Motorsailer (development of Number 601), 32'10".

811 Little Gull Class (development of Number 574), 28'5".

812 Auxiliary sloop, 25'2" x 20'3" x 8' x 4'2".

821 Auxiliary cruising sloop, 28'6" x 21' x 8' x 4'7", for Norman D. Adams of Houston, TX. Designed 1946.

822 Auxiliary cruising sloop, 29'6" x 23'1" x 9' x 4'6", for R.B. Hovey. Designed 1946. Two sisters built: *Yen* (1961) and *Crony*. (Album)

823 Auxiliary cruising ketch, 57'1" x 41' x 14'2" x 7'3", for Robert W. Conrad, U.S.N., of San Juan, Puerto Rico. Designed 1946. Three or four sisters built, including: *Wraith of Odin* (1951); *Algue* (1951); and *Square Head II* (1951).

824 Auxiliary sloop *Ulalume*, 40'9" x 28' x 10' x 5'9", for M.G. George of Santa Cruz, CA. Built by W.F. Stone & Son, Alameda, CA.

825 Yawl, 40'1" x 29'1" x 10'10½" x 4'4".

826 Powerboat, 25'11" x 24'9" x 8'7" x 2'2½", for Lloyd Brace. Built by Norman Wood, Belfast, ME, 1947. One sister may have been built.

827 Yawl, 62'10" x 44' x 14' x 8'9", for James A. Farrell.

828 Auxiliary centerboard yawl *Nandeyara III*, 36'7" x 25'6" x 11' x 3'10", for Raul Couzier of Rosario, Argentina. Built by Marcos Rudi, Santa Fe, Argentina, 1951. Two sisters built: *Spray* (1955) and *Shenandoah* (1963).

829 Power fishing launch, 32'1" x 30' x 8'7½" x 2'10", for Russell D. Bell. Three sisters built, including: *Espadarte* (1952).

830 One-design raised-deck sloop, 31'11" x 23'2" x 7'8" x 5'2", for William G. Whipple of Mercer Island, WA. Designed 1946.

831 Ketch, 50' x 40'8" x 14' x 6', for MacFadden.

832 Ketch, 47'9" x 35'2" x 13'3" x 7', for Paul Wing.

833 Ketch, 40'1" x 29'2" x 10'10½" x 5'3", for Ten Eyck.

834 Motorsailer *Briny Breeze III*, 43'6" x 35'3" x 12' x 5'3", for Maurie Frank of the Yale Club, New York, NY. Built by Hodgdon Bros., East Boothbay, ME, 1948.

835 Yawl *Criterion*, 60'10" x 43'6" x 14'10" x 6', for C.H. Cuno. Built by Mystic Shipyard, Inc., Mystic, CT.

836 Yawl, 54'1" x 35'6" x 12' x 7'1½", for A.B. Homer.

837 Ketch *Chiriqui*, 60'10" x 45' x 13'11" x 7'7½", for Tucker McClure of Los Angeles, CA. Built by Tucker McClure, Inc., Balboa, Canal Zone, 1949.

838-A Catboat *Tabby*, 18'1" x 17'6½" x 8'7" x 2', for John K. Murphy, 1947. Fourteen sisters built, including: *Catmarie* (1957); *Tattoo* (1950); *Marston Tabby* (1952); *Marsh Nymph II* (1953); *Little Bess* (1954); *Mudhen* (1952); *Figaro*; and *Kitty Small* (1952). (Album)

839-A Hinckey 21, auxiliary sloop *Showgirl* (development of Number 761), 29'2½" x 21'1" x 8' x 4'7", for A.E. Frazer of Stonington, CT. Built by Henry R. Hinckley Co., Southwest Harbor, ME, 1948. Five sisters built, including: *No Mame*; *Sprite* (1949); *Kit* (1949); and *Velsheda* (1950).

840 Auxiliary ketch, 46'9" x 36'6" x 14' x 6'6", for H.R. Peacock of Costa Mesa, CA, 1947. One sister may have been built.

841 Auxiliary centerboard ketch, 60'5" x 44'5" x 15' x 5', for F.C. Jones of Passaic, NJ.

842-A Auxiliary ketch, 47'9" x 36'6" x 14' x 6'6", for John G. Alden. Designed 1947. Two to five sisters built, including: *Silverheels* and *Cybele* (1971).

843 Powerboat *Jay Maid*, 25'10½" x 24'7½" x 8'6½" x 2'1", for Harold P. Johnson of Belmont, MA. Built by Harold P. Johnson, 1947. One sister may have been built.

844 Auxiliary centerboard ketch *Quail*, 68'2" x 52'8" x 18' x 5'9", for B.O. Cone of Crawford Mfg. Co., Inc., Richmond, VA. Built by Goudy & Stevens, East Boothbay, ME, 1947.

845 Auxiliary schooner, 43'1" x 32'7" x 11'6" x 6'4", for Donald B. Frost of Rockport, MA.

846 Auxiliary centerboard yawl, 46'4" x 32'3" x 12'10" x 4'6½".

847 Scout Class, auxiliary sloop, 28'3" x 20'5" x 8' x 4'2".

848 Barnacle Class, auxiliary sloop (development of Number 792), 34'6" x 23'4" x 9' x 5'4".

849 Motorsailer, 28'3" x 23'4" x 10'6" x 3'6".

851 Auxiliary ketch, 53'7" x 35'6" x 12' x 7'1½", for A.B. Homer. (Album)

852 Yacht tender, 13' x 12'7" x 5'3" x 1'5", for W.A. Parker. Built by Quincy Adams Yacht Yard, Quincy, MA.

853 Knockabout ketch *Suzelle*, 59'9" x 42'8" x 14'3½"

x 7'4", for Harold W. McGregor of Adelaide, Australia. Built 1951.

855 Dinghy, 12'3½" x 4'8".

856 Ketch *Sandpiper*, 33'3" x 24' x 8' x 4'6", for M.H. Haskell of Maysville, CA. Built by Charles Olsheski, Seattle, WA.

857 Malabar Junior, auxiliary sloop (development of Number 762), 33'6" x 22'8" x 9' x 5'.

858 Auxiliary centerboard yawl *Mareva*, 49'2" x 37'1" x 13'7" x 5'1", for Don C. McRae of Miami, FL. Built by Don C. McRae, 1951.

859 Little Tramp Class, motorsailer, 30'10" x 23'6" x 10'6" x 4'. Ten to 12 sisters built, including: *Cara* (1952); *Barbara West VIII* (1956); *Zwerver* (1956); *Days Off* (1956); and *Joluma*.

860 Centerboard yawl, 35' x 24'6" x 10'8" x 4'.

861 Auxiliary yawl *Nirvana*, 65' x 45'1" x 14'3" x 8'4", for Harry G. Haskell of Wilmington, DE. Built by Henry R. Hinckley & Co., Southwest Harbor, ME, 1950. One sister built: *Valhalla* (1949).

862 Auxiliary yawl *Rarotonga*, 39' x 26' x 9'9" x 5'9", for William Dwinell Nansen of Webster Groves, MO. Built by Campbell Boat Works, Holland, MI, 1952.

863-B Auxiliary yawl *Salmagal II*, 54'1" x 35'6" x 12' x 7'1½". for Arthur B. Homer of Bethlehem, PA. Built by Abeking & Rasmussen, Bremen, Germany, 1950.

864 Auxiliary cutter (intended stock design), 30'3" x 24'7" x 9'6" x 4'6". Not built.

868 Auxiliary ketch *Eleuthera*, 48'2" x 35'2" x 13'3" x 7', for Gustav H. Koven of Jersey City, NJ. Built by Abeking & Rasmussen, Bremen, Germany, 1951.

869 Motorsailer *White Hart*, 48' x 41'7" x 14'6" x 7', for A.J. Reeves of Walnut Creek, CA. Built by Royal Bodden, Georgetown, Grand Cayman Is., British West Indies, 1950.

870 Auxiliary centerboard sloop *Juno*, 24' x 22'5" x 10'4" x 2'8", for Frederick Mason of Barrington, RI. Built 1950.

871 Motorsailer *Escape II*, 40'5¾" x 33'9½" x 11'6" x 5'4", for Russell E. Craig of Newport Beach, CA. Built 1954. Two sisters built: *Natalie II* (1956) and *Wailana* (1956).

872 Auxiliary daysailing sloop *Clara Brown*, 34'4" x 22'5" x 7' x 4'1", for W.R. Christopherson of Burlington, VT. Built by Goudy & Stevens, East Boothbay, ME, 1950.

873 Alden 33, auxiliary sloop *Carissima III*, 33'3" x 22'8" x 9'1½" x 5', for Henry P. Chaplin of Windsor, VT. Built by Harvey F. Gamage, South Bristol, ME, 1950. One sister built: *Wedgebill III* (1950).

875-A Traveler Class, auxiliary cutter *Encore* (development of Number 598), 33'6" x 28'6" x 10'10" x 5', for A.D. Chesterton of Everett, MA. Built by Morse Boatbuilding Co., Thomaston, ME, 1950. Six or seven sisters built, including: *Sea Girl* (1950); *Bali Hai* (1950); *Sea Cloud II* (1950); *Puffin* (1950); *Tusitala* (1956); and *Nanuk II* (1962). (Album)

876 Powerboat, 30'3" x 29' x 10'2" x 2'8", for Kenneth Knight, Jr., Newburyport, MA. Built by Kenneth Knight, Jr. Two sisters may have been built.

877 Auxiliary ketch (forerunner to Number 880), 42' x 32' x 11'4" x 5'1", for H.T. Hemphill of Oakland, CA.

878 Courier Class, motorsailer, 42' LOA. Not built.

879 Auxiliary ketch *Minots Light*, 58'1" x 41'2" x 14'3" x 7'5", for Clarence Warden, Jr., of Philadelphia, PA. Built by Abeking & Rasmussen, Bremen, Ger-

many, 1951. (Album)

880-A Seagoer Class, auxiliary ketch *Norumbega* (development of Number 877), 45' x 32'6" x 11'4" x 5'3", for Henry S. Noble of New York, NY. Built by Morse Boatbuilding Co., Thomaston, ME, 1951. Five to seven sisters built, including: *Silver Dawn* (1957); *February* (1951); *Sea Chief* (1951); *Lodestar* (1952); and *Polly* (1953). (Album)

881 Wayfarer Class, auxiliary sloop, 35' LOA. Not built.

882 Auxiliary sloop *Alibubu IV*, 44'7" x 32'9" x 11'8" x 5'5", for Jack Aron of New York, NY. Built by Abeking & Rasmussen, Bremen, Germany, 1951.

885 Traveler Class, auxiliary sloop (development of Number 875), 39'4½" x 28'5½" x 10'10" x 5'. Not built.

888 Twin-screw diesel power cruiser, 61'6" x 54' x 16'2" x 6'8", for Ray Van Clief of Charlottesville, VA. Not built.

889 Auxiliary yawl *Enchanta* (steel), 66'2" x 46' x 14'10" x 9', for Richard Stiegler of Bronxville, NY. Built by Abeking & Rasmussen, Bremen, Germany, 1953.

890 Auxiliary ketch, 45'6" x 32' x 12'10 ½" x 5'2", for John G. Alden. Not built.

891 Auxiliary ketch, 47'3" x 33'1" x 12'1" x 5'5", for John G. Alden. Not built.

894-A Seagoer Class, auxiliary ketch *Margaretta* (development of Number 880), 44'11" x 32' x 11'4" x 5'3", for Leonard Dyer of Winter Park, FL. Built by Morse Boatbuilding Co., Thomaston, ME, 1953. Three sisters built: *Cygnet II* (1954); *Kialoa* (1954);

and *Santelmo*.

895 Power cruiser *Chiloe IV*, 65' x 61' x 14'6" x 3'9", for John H. Eden, Jr., of Inverness, FL. Built by John H. Eden, Jr., Trident Boat Works, St. Petersburg, FL.

901 Auxiliary yawl *Malabar XV*, 39'2½" x 26' x 9'9" x 5'9", for John G. Alden. Built by James E. Graves, Inc., Marblehead, MA, 1955.

902 Auxiliary ketch *Eleuthera II* (steel), 60'5" x 43' x 14'7" x 7'5", for Gustav H. Koven of Green Village, NJ. Built by Abeking & Rasmussen, Bremen, Germany, 1954. (Chapter 7)

903 Auxiliary ketch *Windsong*, 49'11" x 40' x 13'11" x 6'6", for William G. Anderson of Sherborn, MA. Built by Morse Boatbuilding Co., Thomaston, ME, 1955.

904 Motorsailer ketch *Sunquest*, 46'1½" x 39'9" x 13' x 4'6", for Donald K. Ross. Built by Lymington Slipway, England, 1954. One sister built: *Sun-Quest* (1959).

906 Round-bottomed sailing dinghy, 8'½" x 7'8" x 4'1¾" x 6", for Roger E. Avery of Oyster Bay, NY.

907 Auxiliary ketch *Abigail*, 39' x 30'2" x 11'½" x 5'6", for Richard Chapin of Newtown, CT. Built by Seth Persson, Old Saybrook, CT, 1955. Three to five sisters built, including: *Karmatan II* and *Horizon*.

908 Motorsailer *Rolling Stone IV*, 43'6" x 38'6" x 13' x 5', for Donald C. Stone of Newark, NJ. Built by Morse Boatbuilding Co., Thomaston, ME, 1955. One sister built: *Santa Claus II* (1959). (Chapter 9)

Index

445